D0939892

PRINCIPLES OF HTML, XHTML AND XML

THE WEB T...

DON GOSSELIN

COURSE TECHNOLOGY
CENGAGE Learning

Australia • Brazil • Japan • Korea • Mexico • Singapore • Spain • United Kingdom • United States

Marie Lee: Executive Editor

Acquisitions Editor: Brandi Shailer

Senior Product Manager: Alyssa Pratt

Development Editor: Dan Seiter

Editorial Assistant: Jacqueline Lacaire

Production Service: Integra

Content Project Manager: Lisa Weidenfeld

Art Director: Faith Brosnan

Text Designer: Shawn Girsberger

Cover Designer: Cabbage Design Company

Cover image: © CSA Images

Copyeditor: Michael Beckett

Proofreader: Suzanne Huizenga

Indexer: Rich Carlson

Marketing Manager: Shanna Shelton

Compositor: Integra

For product information and technology assistance, contact us at
Cengage Learning Customer & Sales Support, 1-800-354-9706

For permission to use material from this text or product,
submit all requests online at **cengage.com/permissions**
Further permissions questions can be emailed to
permissionrequest@cengage.com

Library of Congress Control Number: 2010936687

ISBN-13: 978-0-538-47461-0
ISBN-10: 0-538-47461-0

Course Technology
20 Channel Center Street
Boston, MA 02210
USA

Some of the product names and company names used in this book have been used for identification purposes only and may be trademarks or registered trademarks of their respective manufacturers and sellers.

Any fictional data related to persons or companies or URLs used throughout this book is intended for instructional purposes only. At the time this book was printed, any such data was fictional and not belonging to any real persons or companies.

Course Technology, a part of Cengage Learning, reserves the right to revise this publication and make changes from time to time in its content without notice.

The programs in this book are for instructional purposes only. They have been tested with care, but are not guaranteed for any particular intent beyond educational purposes. The author and the publisher do not offer any warranties or representations, nor do they accept any liabilities with respect to the programs.

Cengage Learning is a leading provider of customized learning solutions with office locations around the globe, including Singapore, the United Kingdom, Australia, Mexico, Brazil, and Japan. Locate your local office at:
www.cengage.com/global

Cengage Learning products are represented in Canada by
Nelson Education, Ltd.

To learn more about Course Technology, visit
www.cengage.com/coursetechnology

To learn more about Cengage Learning, visit **www.cengage.com**

Purchase any of our products at your local college store or at our preferred online store: **www.cengagebrain.com**

Printed in the United States of America
1 2 3 4 5 6 7 14 13 12 11 10

*I dedicate this book to my entire family
for loving—and standing by—each other
during our darkest hours.*

Brief Contents

iv

v

Contents

CHAPTER 3 Cascading Style Sheets **120**

CHAPTER 4 Adding Images and Text **185**

CHAPTER 5 Using Tables and Lists **238**

CHAPTER 13   Introduction to the Document Object Model (DOM) **690**

CHAPTER 14   Creating Dynamic HTML (DHTML) **737**

APPENDIX E   Updating Web Pages with AJAX **849**

Preface

HTML is one of the most widely used technologies on the Internet because it is the key ingredient for building most types of Web pages. *Principles of HTML, XHTML, and DHTML* provides an introduction to authoring Web pages with HTML. If you are a beginning Web page author, this book introduces you to the basics of building structured Web pages with HTML. You will learn why HTML was developed and the skills you need for building basic Web pages. You will also learn to format and design Web pages using Cascading Style Sheets (CSS), how to add text and images to Web pages, how to create tables, lists, and forms, and how to incorporate multimedia and executable content into a Web page.

In addition to HTML, you will study JavaScript, which is a client-side scripting language that allows Web page authors to develop interactive Web sites. Although JavaScript is considered a programming language, it is also a critical part of Web page design and authoring because JavaScript "lives" within a Web page's HTML elements. The language is relatively easy to learn, allowing non-programmers to quickly incorporate JavaScript functionality into a Web page. In fact, because it is used extensively on countless sites on the World Wide Web, JavaScript is arguably the most widely used programming language in the world.

Principles of HTML, XHTML, and DHTML teaches Web page development with JavaScript for students with little or no programming experience. This book covers the basics of JavaScript, along with advanced topics that include form validation, Dynamic HTML (DHTML), and the Document Object Model (DOM).

The book assumes no prior knowledge of HTML, JavaScript, or any technologies. Each chapter provides clear, nontechnical explanations of important concepts and techniques. The focus, however, is on learning by doing as students complete typical Web authoring tasks, such as adding tables to Web pages. After you complete this course, you will be able to use HTML and JavaScript to build professional-quality, dynamic Web sites.

The Approach

This book introduces a variety of techniques, focusing on what you need to know to start authoring Web pages. In each chapter, you learn techniques that help you create Web pages or build important Web page components such as tables and forms. The step-by-step tasks are guided activities that reinforce the skills you learn in the chapter and build on your learning experience by providing additional ways to apply your knowledge in new situations. In addition to step-by-step tasks, each chapter includes objectives, short quizzes, comprehension checks, and reinforcement exercises that highlight major concepts and let you practice the techniques you learn. At the end of each chapter, you will also complete Discovery Projects that let you use the skills you learned to author a Web page on your own.

Overview of This Book

The examples and exercises in this book will help you achieve the following objectives:

- Understand the history and basics of Web page authoring.

- Format your Web pages with CSS.

- Link and publish basic Web pages.

- Add text and images to your Web pages.

- Organize information with tables and lists.

- Interact with visitors to your Web pages using forms.

- Incorporate multimedia elements into your Web pages.

- Work with JavaScript variables and data types and learn how to use the operations that can be performed on them.

- Add functions, events, arrays, and control structures to your JavaScript programs.

- Write JavaScript code that controls the Web browser through the browser object model.

- Use JavaScript to make sure data was entered properly into form fields and to perform other types of preprocessing before form data is sent to a server.

- Add animation and interactivity to your Web pages using the Document Object Model (DOM) and Dynamic HTML (DHTML).

Principles of HTML, XHTML, and DHTML presents 14 chapters that cover specific aspects of Web page development.

- **Chapter 1** summarizes the history of HTML and the World Wide Web and explains the basic building blocks of authoring Web pages with HTML.

- **Chapter 2** discusses how to add basic document structure to your Web pages and how to publish your Web pages.

- **Chapter 3** discusses how to format your Web pages using CSS.

- **Chapter 4** teaches you how to add text and images to your Web pages.

- **Chapter 5** discusses how to organize the data on your Web pages using tables and lists.

- **Chapter 6** introduces how to use forms to gather information from visitors to your Web site.

- **Chapter 7** explains how to add multimedia elements to your Web pages.

- **Chapter 8** introduces the basics of the JavaScript programming language.

- **Chapter 9** covers functions, data types, and how to build expressions.

- **Chapter 10** introduces how to store data in arrays and explains structured logic using control structures and statements.

- **Chapter 11** teaches you how to use JavaScript to manipulate the Web browser using the `Window`, `History`, `Location`, `Navigator`, and `Screen` objects.

- **Chapter 12** explains how to use JavaScript to make sure that data is entered properly into form fields, and how to perform other types of preprocessing before form data is sent to a server.

- **Chapters 13** and **14** teach you how to add animation and interactivity to your Web pages using the Document Object Model (DOM) and Dynamic HTML (DHTML).

Features

Principles of HTML, XHTML, and DHTML is a superior textbook because it also includes the following features:

CHAPTER OBJECTIVES: Each chapter begins with a list of the important concepts presented in the chapter. This list provides students with a quick reference to a chapter's contents as well as a useful study aid.

FIGURES AND TABLES: Screen shots allow students to check their work against the desired output. Tables consolidate important material for easy reference.

CODE EXAMPLES: Plentiful code examples throughout each chapter are presented in an easy-to-read font, with keywords highlighted in color.

NEW TERMS: New terms are shown in boldface to draw the reader's attention to new material.

 HELP: These margin notes provide more information about the task the student is performing.

 POINTER: These useful asides, located in the margin, provide practical advice and proven strategies for the concept being discussed. They also contain cross-references to other sections in the book or to related Web sites.

 FACT: These margin elements provide additional helpful information on specific techniques and concepts.

 CAREFUL: These cautionary notes point out troublesome issues related to a particular technique or concept.

SHORT QUIZZES: Several short quizzes are included in each chapter to help ensure that students understand the major points introduced in the chapter.

SUMMING UP: These brief overviews revisit the ideas covered in each chapter, providing students with a helpful study guide.

COMPREHENSION CHECK: At the end of each chapter, a set of 20 review questions reinforce the main ideas introduced in the chapter. These questions help students determine whether they have mastered the concepts presented in the chapter.

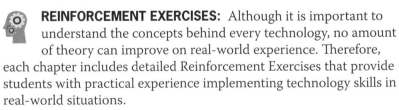 **REINFORCEMENT EXERCISES:** Although it is important to understand the concepts behind every technology, no amount of theory can improve on real-world experience. Therefore, each chapter includes detailed Reinforcement Exercises that provide students with practical experience implementing technology skills in real-world situations.

DISCOVERY PROJECTS: The end-of-chapter projects are designed to help students apply their learning to business situations, much like those a professional Web developer would encounter. The projects give students the opportunity to independently synthesize and evaluate information, examine potential solutions, and make recommendations, similar to an actual programming situation.

Instructor Resources

The following supplemental materials are available when this book is used in a classroom setting. All of the instructor resources available with this book are provided to the instructor on a single CD. Most resources are also available for download at *login.cengage.com*.

ELECTRONIC INSTRUCTOR'S MANUAL. The Instructor's Manual that accompanies this textbook includes additional instructional material to assist in class preparation, including items such as Sample Syllabi, Chapter Outlines, Technical Notes, Lecture Notes, Quick Quizzes, Teaching Tips, Discussion Topics, and Additional Case Projects.

EXAMVIEW®. This textbook is accompanied by ExamView, a powerful testing software package that allows instructors to create and administer printed, computer (LAN-based), and Internet exams. ExamView includes hundreds of questions that correspond to the topics covered in this text, enabling students to generate detailed study guides that include page references for further review. The computer-based and Internet testing components allow students to take exams at their computers, and save the instructor time by grading each exam automatically.

POWERPOINT PRESENTATIONS. This book comes with Microsoft PowerPoint slides for each chapter. These slides are included as a teaching aid for classroom presentation, to make available to students on the network for chapter review, or to be printed for classroom distribution. Instructors can add their own slides for additional topics they introduce to the class.

DATA FILES. Files that contain all of the data necessary for the Reinforcement Exercises and Discovery Projects are provided through the Companion Web site at *login.cengage.com*, and at *www.cengagebrain.com*. The files are also available on the Instructor Resources CD.

SOLUTION FILES. Solutions to end-of-chapter exercises and projects are provided on the Instructor Resources CD, and may also be found at *login.cengage.com*. The solutions are password protected.

DISTANCE LEARNING. Course Technology is proud to present online test banks in WebCT and Blackboard to provide the most complete and dynamic learning experience possible. Instructors are encouraged to make the most of the course, both online and offline. For more information on how to access your online test bank, contact your local Course Technology sales representative.

Read This Before You Begin

The following information will help you as you prepare to use this textbook.

To the User of the Data Files

To complete the steps and projects in this book, you will need data files that have been created specifically for this book. To access these data files, please visit *www.cengagebrain.com*. At the *CengageBrain.com* home page, search for the ISBN of your title (from the back cover of your book) using the search box at the top of the page. This will take you to the product page where these resources can be found. Note that you can use a computer in your school lab or your own computer to complete the steps and exercises in this book. To use your own computer, you will need the following:

- **A Web browser.** You can use any browser you want to view solutions to the exercises in this text, as long as the browser is compatible with the standardized version of the DOM that is recommended by the World Wide Web Consortium (W3C). At the time of this writing, Firefox and Internet Explorer 5.0 and higher are compatible with the W3C DOM; other browsers are also compatible.

- **A text-based HTML editor**, such as Macromedia Dreamweaver, or a text editor such as Notepad on Windows, GNU Emacs on UNIX/Linux, or SimpleText on the Macintosh.

To the Instructor

To complete the exercises and chapters in this book, your users must work with a set of data files and download software from Web sites. The data files are on the Instructor Resources CD, and may also be obtained electronically at *login.cengage.com* and *www.cengagebrain.com*. Have students follow the instructions in Chapter 1 to install the data files.

Course Technology Data Files

You are granted a license to copy the data files to any computer or computer network used by people who have purchased this book.

Visit Our World Wide Web Site

Additional materials designed especially for this book might be available for your course. Periodically search *www.cengage.com/ coursetechnology* for more information and materials to accompany this text.

Acknowledgements

A text such as this represents the hard work of many people, not just the author. I would like to thank all the people who helped make this book a reality. First and foremost, I want to thank the following people for helping me get the job done: Dan Seiter, Development Editor; Alyssa Pratt, Senior Product Manager; Amy Jollymore, Acquisitions Editor; Chris Scriver, Manuscript Quality Assurance Lead; and Lisa Weidenfeld, Content Product Manager. I would also like to thank Ann Shaffer for her editorial work on earlier versions of material in this book.

Many thanks to the reviewers who provided plenty of comments and positive direction during the development of this book: Judy Woodruff, Indiana University/Purdue University Indianapolis and Yejun Wu, Louisiana State University.

On the personal side, I would like to thank my family and friends for supporting me in my career; I don't see many of you nearly as often as I'd like, but you are always in my thoughts. My most important thanks always go to my wonderful wife Kathy for her never-ending support and encouragement, and to Noah the wonder dog, my best (non-human) friend.

CHAPTER 1

Introduction to Web Page Development

In this chapter you will:

◎ Study the history of the World Wide Web

◎ Learn about the basics of Extensible Markup Language (XML)

◎ Learn how to create structured Web pages

This book teaches you how to use HTML to develop Web pages. HTML was the first language used for creating traditional Web pages that are displayed in Web browsers on desktop computers and workstations. However, because the Web is expanding to other types of media such as mobile phones and iPads, you need to use XHTML so that your Web pages are compatible with these devices. XHTML is a stricter form of HTML that requires Web page syntax to adhere to a specific set of rules and XML standards. HTML and XHTML will continue to coexist for some time, so you need to understand both languages and the differences between them. The good news is that XHTML is almost identical to HTML, which means that the techniques you use in both languages are virtually interchangeable.

Which language should you use to develop your Web pages? Ideally, you would always use XHTML because its stricter rules will make your Web pages compatible with devices other than traditional Web browsers. XHTML also makes your Web pages compatible with the Americans with Disabilities Act (ADA), allowing handicapped people to read them. For this reason, many corporate Web sites publish their Web pages using XHTML. However, for some smaller Web sites, it is sometimes easier to use HTML. HTML can be more flexible when it comes to Web page design, although virtually every HTML page can be reproduced with XHTML if you know the rules.

Introduction to the World Wide Web

The Internet is a vast network that connects computers all over the world. The original plans for the Internet grew out of a series of memos written by J.C.R. Licklider of the Massachusetts Institute of Technology (MIT) in August 1962, in which he discussed his concept of a "Galactic Network." Licklider envisioned a global computer network through which users could access data and programs from any site on the network. The Internet was actually developed in the 1960s by the Advanced Research Projects Agency (ARPA) of the U.S. Department of Defense, which later changed its name to Defense Advanced Research Projects Agency (DARPA). The goal of the early Internet was to connect the main computer systems of various universities and research institutions that were funded by ARPA. This first implementation of the Internet was referred to as the ARPANET. More computers were connected to the ARPANET in the years following its initial development in the 1960s, although access to the system was restricted by the U.S. government, primarily to academic researchers, scientists, and the military.

The 1980s saw the widespread development of local area networks (LANs) and the personal computer. Computers and networks soon became common in business and everyday life. By the end of the 1980s, businesses and individual computer users began to recognize the global communications capabilities and potential of the Internet, and they convinced the U.S. government to allow commercial access to it.

In 1990 and 1991, Tim Berners-Lee created what would become the **World Wide Web**, or the **Web**, at the European Laboratory for Particle Physics (CERN) in Geneva, Switzerland, as a way to easily access cross-referenced documents on the CERN computer network. When other academics and scientists saw the usefulness of access- ing cross-referenced documents using Berners-Lee's system, the Web as we know it was born. This method of accessing cross-referenced documents, known as **hypertext linking**, is probably the most impor- tant aspect of the Web because it allows you to open other Web pages quickly. A **hypertext link**, or **hyperlink** or **link**, contains a reference to a specific Web page that you can click to open that Web page.

If you want to learn more about the history of the Internet, the Internet Society (ISOC) maintains a list of links at *www.isoc.org/internet/history/*.

A common misconception is that the words *Web* and *Internet* are synony- mous. The Web is only one part of the Internet, and is a means of communi- cating on the Internet. The Internet is composed of other communication elements, such as e-mail systems that send and receive messages. However, because of its enormous influence on computing, communications, and the economy, the World Wide Web is arguably the most important part of the Internet today and is the primary focus of this book.

A document on the Web is called a **Web page** and is identified by a unique address called the **Uniform Resource Locator**, or **URL**. A URL is also commonly referred to as a **Web address**. A URL is a type of **Uniform Resource Identifier (URI)**, which is a generic term for many types of names and addresses on the Web. A **Web site** is a location on the Internet where an individual, company, or organization keeps its Web pages and related files (such as graphic and video files). You dis- play a Web page on your computer screen by using a program called a **Web browser**. A person can retrieve and open a Web page in a Web browser either by entering a URL in the Web browser's address box or by clicking a hypertext link. When a user wants to access a Web page using either method, the user's Web browser sends a Web server a **request** for the Web page. A **Web server** is a computer that delivers Web pages. The Web server's reaction to the user's request is called the **response**.

Understanding Web Browsers

You can choose from a number of different browsers, but at the time of this writing, Mozilla Firefox is the most popular browser on the market. The first browser, NCSA Mosaic, was created in 1993 at

4

Prior to version 6, the Netscape Web browser was called Navigator or Netscape Navigator. With the release of version 6, however, Netscape dropped *Navigator* from the browser name. In this book, therefore, *Navigator Web browser* refers to versions older than version 6, and *Netscape Web browser* refers to version 6 and later.

the University of Illinois and was the first program to allow users to navigate the Web by using a graphical user interface (GUI). In 1994, Netscape released Navigator, which soon controlled 75 percent of the market. Netscape maintained its control of the browser market until 1996, when Microsoft entered the competition with the release of Internet Explorer, and the so-called browser wars began between Microsoft and Netscape.

The browser wars began over **Dynamic Hypertext Markup Language (DHTML)**—a combination of various technologies, including HTML and JavaScript—which allows a Web page to change after it has been loaded by a browser. Examples of DHTML functionality include the ability to position text and elements, change document background color, and create effects such as animation. Early versions of Internet Explorer and Navigator included DHTML elements that were incompatible. Furthermore, Microsoft and Netscape each wanted its version of DHTML to become the industry standard. To settle the argument, the World Wide Web Consortium set out to create a platform-independent and browser-neutral version of DHTML. The **World Wide Web Consortium**, or W3C, was established in 1994 at MIT to oversee the development of Web technology standards. While the W3C was drafting a recommendation for DHTML, versions 4 of Internet Explorer and Navigator each added a number of proprietary DHTML elements that were completely incompatible with the other browser. As a result, when working with advanced DHTML techniques such as animation, a programmer had to write a different set of HTML code for each browser. Unfortunately for Netscape, the W3C adopted as the formal standard the version of DHTML in version 4 of Internet Explorer, which prompted many loyal Netscape users to defect to Microsoft.

DHTML is actually a combination of HTML, JavaScript, and Cascading Style Sheets (CSS). The style sheets in CSS refer to a standard set by the W3C for managing Web page formatting.

The W3C does not actually release a version of a particular technology. Instead, it issues a formal recommendation for a technology, which essentially means that the technology is (or will be) a recognized industry standard.

One benefit of the browser wars is that they forced the Web industry to rapidly develop and adopt advanced Web page standards (including JavaScript, CSS, and DHTML) that are consistent across browsers. In 2004, Internet Explorer appeared to be winning the browser wars, as it controlled 95 percent of the market. Yet, in the past few years, Internet Explorer has lost significant market share to Mozilla Firefox. The Firefox Web browser is open source software developed by the Mozilla organization (*www.mozilla.org*). **Open source** refers to software for which the source code can be freely used and modified. At the time of this writing, Internet Explorer usage has slipped to approximately 41 percent, while Firefox now controls about 47 percent of the market (according to the W3 Schools browser statistics page at *www.w3schools.com/browsers/browsers_stats.asp*). One of the most fascinating aspects of Firefox is that it's essentially an open source version of the Netscape browser. So, in a figurative sense, the original Netscape browser has risen from the ashes to resume battle with its arch nemesis, Internet Explorer—and it's winning at the time of this writing. Healthy competition is good for any market, so the renewed hostilities in the browser wars might encourage vendors to continue improving browser quality and capabilities, and to adopt and adhere to Web page standards.

Creating Web Pages

Originally, people created Web pages using a language called **Hypertext Markup Language (HTML)**. Web pages, therefore, are also commonly referred to as **HTML pages** or **HTML documents**. A **markup language** is a set of characters or symbols that defines a document's logical structure—that is, it specifies how a document should be printed or displayed. HTML is based on an older language called **Standard Generalized Markup Language**, or **SGML**, which defines the data in a document independent of how the data will be displayed. In other words, SGML separates the data in a document from the way that data is formatted. Each element in an SGML document is marked according to its type, such as paragraphs, headings, and so on. Like SGML, HTML was originally designed as a way of defining the elements in a document independent of how they would appear. HTML was not intended to be used for designing the actual appearance of the pages in a Web browser, but the language gradually evolved to have this capability.

This textbook uses the terms *Web pages* and *HTML documents* interchangeably.

Basic HTML Syntax

HTML documents are text documents that contain formatting instructions, called **tags**, which determine how data is displayed on a Web page. HTML tags range from formatting commands that make text appear in boldface or italics to controls that allow user input, such as option buttons and check boxes. Other HTML tags allow you to display graphic images and other objects in a document or Web page. Tags are enclosed in brackets (< >), and most consist of an opening tag and a closing tag that surround the text or other items they format or control. The closing tag must include a forward slash (/) immediately after the opening bracket. For example, to make a line of text appear in boldface, you use the opening tag <b> and the closing tag </b>. Any text between this pair of tags appears in boldface when you open the HTML document in a Web browser.

HTML documents must have a file extension of .htm or .html.

A tag pair and any data it contains are an **element**. The information within an element's opening and closing tags is its **content**. Some elements do not require a closing tag; they are called **empty elements** because you cannot use a tag pair to enclose text or other elements. For instance, the <hr> element, which inserts a horizontal rule on a Web page, does not include a closing tag. You simply place the <hr> element anywhere in an HTML document where you want the horizontal rule to appear.

HTML has literally hundreds of elements. Table 1-1 lists some of the more common elements.

HTML element	Description
<b></b>	Formats enclosed text in a bold typeface
<body></body>	Encloses the body of the HTML document
 	Inserts a line break
<center>	Centers a paragraph in the middle of a Web page
<head></head>	Encloses the page header and contains information about the entire page
<h*n*></h*n*>	Indicates heading level elements, where *n* represents a number from 1 to 6
<hr>	Inserts a horizontal rule
<html></html>	Begins and ends an HTML document; these are required elements
<i></i>	Formats enclosed text in an italic typeface
<img>	Inserts an image file
<p></p>	Identifies enclosed text as a paragraph
<u></u>	Formats enclosed text as underlined

Table 1-1   Common HTML elements

All Web pages must use the <html> element as the root element. A **root element** contains all the other elements in a document, and tells a Web browser to assemble any instructions between the tags into a Web page. The opening and closing <html>...</html> tags are required and contain all the text and other elements that make up the HTML document.

Two other important elements are the <head> element and the <body> element. The <head> element contains information used by the Web browser; you place it at the beginning of a document, after the opening <html> tag. You place several elements within the <head> element to help manage a document's content, including the <title> element, which contains text that appears in a browser's title bar.

A <head> element must contain a <title> element. With the exception of the <title> element, elements in the <head> element do not affect the display of the HTML document. The <head> element and the elements within it are referred to as the **document head**. Next comes the <body> element; the text and elements it contains are the **document body**.

When you open an HTML document in a Web browser, the document is assembled and formatted according to the instructions contained in its elements. The process by which a Web browser assembles and formats an HTML document is called **parsing** or **rendering**. The following example shows how to make a phrase appear in boldface in an HTML document:

```
<p>Receive <b>50% off</b> your next purchase!</p>
```

HTML is not case sensitive, so you can use <B> in place of <b>. However, XHTML is case sensitive, and you must use lowercase letters for elements. Therefore, this book uses lowercase letters for all elements. (You will learn about XHTML shortly.)

You use various parameters, called **attributes**, to configure many HTML elements. You place an attribute before the closing bracket of the opening tag, and separate it from the tag name or other attributes with a space. You assign a value to an attribute using the syntax *attribute*="*value*". For example, you can configure the <img> element, which embeds an image in an HTML document, with a number of attributes, including src. The src attribute specifies the filename of an image file or video clip. To include the src attribute within the <img> element, you type <img src="mygraphic.gif">.

When a Web browser parses or renders an HTML document, it ignores nonprinting characters such as tabs and line breaks; the final document that appears in the Web browser includes only recognized HTML elements and text. You cannot use line breaks in the body of an HTML document to insert spaces before and after a paragraph; the browser recognizes only paragraph <p> and line break <br> elements for this purpose. In addition, most Web browsers ignore multiple, contiguous spaces on a Web page and replace them with a single space. The following code shows the document head and a portion of the document body for the Web page shown in Figure 1-1.

```
<html>
<head>
    <title>Home</title>
    <meta http-equiv="Content-Type"
        content="text/html; charset=utf-8">
    <link href="style.css" rel="stylesheet"
        type="text/css">
</head>
```

```
<body>
    <table width="100%" border="0" cellspacing="0"
        cellpadding="0" style="height: 100%">
        <tr>
            <td valign="top"> </td>
. . .
```

 Most screen captures of Web pages in this book were taken in Mozilla Firefox 3.5, running on the Windows XP operating system. Different Web browsers might render the parts of a Web page slightly differently from other browsers. The appearance of a Web browser itself can also vary across platforms. If you are not using Firefox and Windows XP, your Web pages and browser might not match the figures in this book. 

Figure 1-1   Global Warming Web page

Creating an HTML Document

Because HTML documents are text files, you can create them in any text editor, such as Notepad or WordPad, or any word-processing application capable of creating simple text files. If you use a text editor to create an HTML document, you cannot view the final result until you open the document in a Web browser. Instead of a text editor or word processor, you could choose to use an HTML editor, which is an application designed specifically for creating HTML documents. Some popular HTML editors, such as Macromedia Dreamweaver and Microsoft Expression Web, have graphical interfaces that allow you to create Web pages and immediately view the results, similar to the WYSIWYG (what-you-see-is-what-you-get) interface in word-processing programs. In addition, many current word-processing applications, including Microsoft Word, allow you to save files as HTML documents.

Like text editors, HTML editors create simple text files, but they automate the process of applying elements. For example, suppose you are creating a document in Word. You can add boldface to a heading in the document simply by clicking a toolbar button. Then, when you save the file as an HTML document, Word automatically adds the <b> element to the text in the HTML document.

Any HTML editor can greatly simplify the task of creating Web pages. However, HTML editors automatically add many unfamiliar elements and attributes to documents that might confuse you and distract from the learning process. Therefore, in this book you create Web pages using a simple text editor.

Before you begin the first exercise, be certain to extract the data files, which you can download from Course Technology's Web site at *www.course.com.* Use the 474610_Data.exe file to install the data files on Windows operating systems and the 474610_Data.jar file to install the data files on UNIX/Linux operating systems. The 474610_Data.exe and 474610_Data.jar files automatically create directories where you can store the exercises and projects you create in this book and install any necessary data files. By default, the directories and data files are installed for Windows platforms in C:\Course Technology\Programming\HTML\Data Files and for UNIX/Linux platforms in *usr/local/course/programming/html/ data_files.* The data file directories contain separate directories for each chapter, which in turn contain the Chapter, Exercises, and Projects directories.

Many people who are new to creating Web pages are surprised that you cannot use a Web browser to create an HTML document.

9

The Course Technology directory might also contain data files for other books you have used from Course Technology.

Save the exercises and projects you create in the main body of each chapter within the Chapter directory. Save the Reinforcement Exercises and Discovery Projects you create at the end of each chapter in the Exercises and Projects directories, respectively.

Next, you will create a simple HTML document that contains some of the tags you have seen in this section. You can use any text editor, such as Notepad or WordPad.

To create an HTML document:

1. Start your text editor and create a new document, if necessary.

2. Type the following tags to begin the HTML document. Remember that all HTML documents must begin and end with the <html>...</html> tag pair.

```
<html>
</html>
```

3. Add the following <head> and <title> tags between the <html>...</html> tag pair. The title will appear in your Web browser's title bar. Remember that the <head>...</head> tag pair must include the <title>...</title> tag pair.

    ```
    <head>
    <title>Web Page Example</title>
    </head>
    ```

4. Next, add the following document body tags above the closing </html> tag:

    ```
    <body>
    </body>
    ```

5. Type the following tags and text between the <body>... </body> tag pair to create the body of the HTML document.

    ```
    <h1>This line uses the heading 1 tag</h1>
    <p>This line includes <br> a line break</p>
    <p>The following line is a horizontal rule</p>
    <hr>
    <h2>This line uses the heading 2 tag</h2>
    <h3>This line uses the heading 3 tag</h3>
    <p>This <b>line</b> <i>contains</i> <sup>text</sup>
    <sub>formatting</sub></p>
    ```

6. Save the file as **FirstWebPage.html** in your Chapter folder for Chapter 1. Some text editors automatically add their own extension to a document. Notepad, for instance, adds an extension of .txt. Be sure your document is saved with the extension .html.

    Some Web servers do not correctly interpret spaces within the names of HTML files—for example, Hello World.html has a space between *Hello* and *World*. Therefore, filenames in this book do not include spaces.

7. Close the **FirstWebPage.html** file and then open it in Firefox or another Web browser. (You open a local HTML file in Firefox by selecting Open File from the File menu; other Web browsers use similar commands.) Figure 1-2 displays the FirstWebPage.html file as it appears in Firefox.

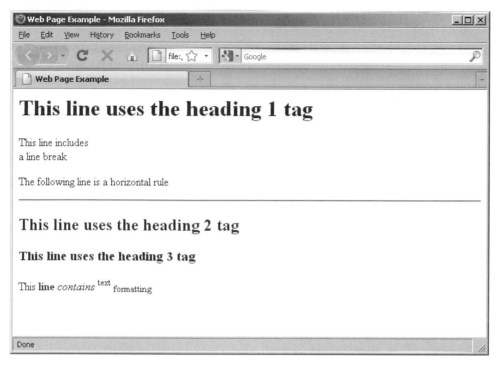

Figure 1-2   FirstWebPage.html in Firefox

8.   Close your Web browser window.

Understanding Web Development

Web page design, or **Web design**, refers to the visual design and creation of the documents that appear on the World Wide Web. Most businesses today—both prominent and small—have Web sites. To attract and retain visitors, and to stand out from the crowd, Web sites must be exciting and visually stimulating. High-quality Web design plays an important role in attracting first-time and repeat visitors. However, the visual aspect of a Web site is only one part of the story. Equally important is the content of the Web site and how that content is structured.

Web design is an extremely important topic. However, this book is not about Web design, even though you will certainly learn many Web design concepts and techniques as you work through the chapters ahead. Instead, this book touches on both Web page authoring and Web development. **Web page authoring** (or **Web authoring**) refers to the creation and assembly of the tags, attributes, and data that make up a Web page. There is a subtle but important distinction between Web design and Web page authoring: Web design refers

Another term that you might often see in relation to Web development is *Webmaster*. Although there is some dispute over exactly what the term means, typically a Webmaster is responsible for the day-to-day maintenance of a Web site, including the monitoring of Web site traffic and ensuring that the site's hardware and software are running properly. The duties of a Webmaster often require knowledge of Web page design, authoring, and development.

to the visual and graphical design aspects of creating Web pages, whereas Web page authoring refers to the physical task of assembling the Web page tags and attributes. **Web development**, or **Web programming**, refers to the design of software applications for a Web site. Generally, a Web developer works "behind the scenes" to develop software applications that access databases and file systems, communicate with other applications, and perform other advanced tasks. The programs created by a Web developer will not necessarily be seen by a visitor to a Web site, although the visitor will certainly use the developer's programs, particularly if the Web site writes and reads data to and from a database.

There are countless ways of combining the hundreds of HTML tags to create interesting Web pages. One technique that professional Web authors use to increase their HTML skill is examining the underlying HTML tags of a Web page that they admire. All Web browsers contain commands that allow you to view the underlying HTML code for a Web page; in Firefox you select Page Source from the View menu, and in Internet Explorer you select the Source command from the View menu.

The open nature of HTML makes it possible for anyone to easily see how another Web author created a Web page. However, you should *never* copy another Web page author's work and attempt to pass it off as your own. As a responsible member of the Web community, you should examine the HTML code behind a Web page only to improve your own skills. The potential theft of another Web page author's hard work and intellectual property is no small concern. Not only is it unscrupulous to steal another Web page author's code and page designs, in many cases it is illegal, especially if the work is copyrighted. Throughout this book, you will examine the underlying HTML code from various published Web sites. However, you will examine this code only to understand the techniques used to create specific elements on a Web page and to improve your own skills, not to hijack someone else's hard work.

Working with Well-Formed Web Pages

HTML first became an Internet standard in 1993 with the release of version 1.0. The next version, HTML 2.0, was released in 1994 and included many core HTML features, such as forms and the ability to bold and italicize text. However, many of the standard features that are widely used today, such as using tables to organize text and graphics on a page, were not available until the release of HTML 3.2 in 1996. The current version of HTML, 4.01, was released in 1999. A few years ago, the W3C's stated goal was that HTML 4.01 would be the last version and would be replaced with **Extensible Hypertext Markup Language**, or **XHTML**, which is the next-generation markup language for creating Web pages. XHTML version 1.0 was introduced in 2000. However, browser vendors were reluctant to implement the new XHTML features because they did not feel that the specifications served the needs of modern Web development. For this reason, in 2004 the Web Hypertext Application Technology Working Group (WHATWG) was formed independently of the W3C to promote the development of HTML separately from XHTML. The standard that WHATWG developed eventually became known as HTML 5, and includes an XHTML implementation. In 2007, the W3C voted to recognize WHATWG's HTML 5 specification as the standard for the next generation of HTML. Then, in 2009 the W3C stopped work on XHTML 2.0 and officially recognized that HTML 5 would be the next-generation standard for both HTML and XHTML.

XHTML was developed because earlier versions of HTML were useful only for rendering documents in traditional Web browsers like Firefox or Internet Explorer. This approach worked well as long as browsers running on computers were the main source of requests for files over the Web. These days, however, many types of devices besides computers use the Web. For example, mobile phones are commonly used to browse the Web. An application that can retrieve and process HTML and XHTML documents is called a **user agent**. A user agent can be a traditional Web browser, a mobile phone, or even an application such as a crawler for a search engine that simply collects and processes data instead of displaying it. Although user agents other than browsers can process HTML, they are not ideally suited to the task, primarily because HTML is more concerned with how data appears than with the data itself. As Web browsers have evolved over the years, they have added extensions (elements and attributes) to HTML to provide functionality for displaying and formatting Web pages. For instance, one extension to the original HTML language is the <font> element, which allows you to specify the font for data in an HTML document. The <font> element has nothing to do with the type of data in an HTML document. Instead, its sole purpose is to display data in a specific typeface within a Web browser.

For two primary reasons, HTML is not suitable for user agents other than Web browsers. First, as discussed earlier, HTML originally evolved into a markup language that focuses more on the appearance of data than with the data itself. Recall that HTML is based on SGML, which defines the data in a document independently of how it will be displayed. Tags like the <font> tag violate this rule.

13

This book primarily focuses on HTML 5 techniques, although keep in mind that it may take years before some of the techniques are available in all major Web browsers.

14

Second, most Web browsers allow you to write sloppy HTML code. For instance, earlier you learned that all HTML documents *should* begin with <html> and end with </html>, and *should* include <head>. . . </head> and <body>. . . </body> tag pairs. In practice, however, you can omit any of these tags from an HTML document and a Web browser will still render the page correctly. In fact, although many tags require a closing tag, you can often omit it and the Web page will usually render properly.

To illustrate the point, you will create an HTML document that does not include the <html>, <head>, and <body> tags, which are technically required.

To create an HTML document that does not include all of the required tags:

1. Create a new document in your text editor.

2. Without including any <html>, <head>, or <body> tags, type the following statements. Notice that the closing tags are missing for the <p> tags and the last <b> tag.

    ```
    <h1>Understanding Client/Server Architecture</h1>
    <p>To be successful in Web development, you need to
    understand the basics of client/server architecture.
    There are many definitions of the terms <i>client</i>
    and <i>server</i>. In traditional client/server
    architecture, the <b>server</b> is usually some sort
    of database from which a client requests information.
    <p>from <i>JavaScript 5th Edition</i><br>
    by <b>Don Gosselin
    ```

3. Save the file as **Architecture.html** in the Chapter folder for Chapter 1.

4. Close the **Architecture.html** file and then open it in Firefox or another Web browser. Even though the HTML document does not include all of the required tags, the Web browser displays it properly, as shown in Figure 1-3.

Figure 1-3   Architecture.html file in Firefox

5.   Close your Web browser window.

Languages based on SGML use a **Document Type Definition**, or
DTD, to define the tags and attributes that you can use in a document and the rules the document must follow when it includes them.
When a document conforms to an associated DTD, it is said to be
valid. When a document does not conform to an associated DTD,
it is **invalid**. For example, you may have a DTD that defines tags and
elements in a document that will be used by a Human Resources
department. The DTD may include tags such as <employee_name>,
<position>, and <salary>. The DTD may also define attributes
such as employeeID that can be used in the <employee_name> tag.
Additionally, the Human Resources DTD may define rules about how
the tags and attributes can be used in a document. For instance, it
may require that the <employee_name>, <position>, and <salary>
tags be contained within a <department> tag.

You can check
whether a docu-
ment conforms
to an associated
DTD by using a
program called a validat-
ing parser. You will use a
validating parser later in
this chapter.

Some languages that are based on SGML are not required to use DTDs. XML
documents, for instance, can be created with or without a DTD. You will
study XML in the next section.

Because earlier versions of HTML were based on SGML, it requires
a DTD, and the HTML DTD is built directly into Web browsers. The
HTML DTD defines tags such as <html>, <head>, and <body> and

HTML 5 is the first version of the language that is not based on SGML.

defines rules that you must follow when authoring your documents. For instance, one rule in the HTML DTD states that you must include a `<title>` tag with a `<head>` tag. However, because most Web browsers allow you to write sloppy code, this rule—and almost every other rule defined in the HTML DTD—is usually ignored. Note that you cannot edit the HTML DTD or create your own version, although other SGML-based languages do allow you to create your own DTDs.

When a Web browser opens an HTML document, it first compares the document to the DTD. If an HTML document is missing any required tags, the HTML DTD supplies them, allowing the Web browser to render the page correctly. However, if an HTML document uses any tags that are not defined in the HTML DTD, the browser ignores them. Because Web browsers operate on a standard computer, they have plenty of processing power to determine the missing required tags in a poorly written document and render the document into a Web page. Additionally, the DTD in a Web browser can be as large as necessary to define the W3C-approved tags and attributes, along with any extensions implemented by the browser. But again, user agents such as mobile phones do not have the processing power to interpret sloppy code or the ability to process any extensions that handle the display and formatting of data.

To ensure backward compatibility with older browsers, you should save XHTML documents with an extension of .html or .htm, just like HTML documents.

To address these issues and provide a common standard for Web page development, the W3C created XHTML, which combines the tags and attributes of HTML with the structure of a language called XML. To be successful with XHTML, you must first understand a little about XML, which you will study next. Later in this chapter, you will study how XHTML differs from HTML and how to create XHTML documents.

Short Quiz 1

1. How and why was the Internet first developed?

2. What were the "browser wars"?

3. Explain basic HTML syntax.

4. What are the differences between Web page design, Web page authoring, and Web development?

5. Why was XHTML developed?

Understanding the Basics of XML

Extensible Markup Language, or **XML**, is a text-based format for organizing data. Like HTML, XML is based on SGML. Version 1.0 of XML achieved recommendation status by the W3C in 1998 and was still current at the time of this writing. Although XML is a markup language like HTML, it is not a replacement for HTML. XML is primarily a way of defining and organizing data, and does not include the display capabilities of HTML. The user agent that receives the XML document decides how to display it. In fact, a user agent may not display an XML document at all, but instead may store the information in a database or use it to perform a calculation.

In XML, as in HTML, you refer to a tag pair and the data it contains as an element. All elements must have an opening and a closing tag, and the data within these tags is called its content. One concept that can be difficult to grasp is that XML does not specify any elements or attributes. Instead, you define your own elements and attributes to describe the data in your document. The following code is an example of an XML document that defines several elements to describe the data associated with an automobile:

```
<auto>
    <make manufacturer="GM">Chevrolet</make>
    <model>Corvette</model>
    <year>1967</year>
    <color>Red</color>
</auto>
```

The preceding code is the most basic form of an XML document. In order for your XML documents to be properly structured, they must also include an XML declaration and adhere to XML's syntax rules. You will study these requirements in the rest of this section.

The XML Declaration

XML documents should begin with an **XML declaration**, which specifies the version of XML being used. You are not required to include an XML declaration because currently only one version of XML exists (1.0). However, it's a good practice to always include the XML declaration because XML will almost certainly evolve into other versions that contain features not found in version 1.0. Specifying the version with the XML declaration will help ensure that any user agent or application that parses an XML document will know which version to use (assuming that newer versions will be released).

You can use three attributes with the XML declaration: `version`, `standalone`, and `encoding`. All three are optional, but you should at

XML 1.0 has undergone some minor revisions since 1998, although the version number hasn't changed. A second edition of XML, 1.1, was published in February 2004 and contains features that make some XML tasks easier to implement. However, XML 1.1 is not widely supported and is recommended only for users who need its unique features.

17

The XML declaration is not actually a tag, but a **processing instruction**, which is a special statement that passes information to the user agent or application that is processing the XML document. You can easily recognize processing instructions because they begin with <? and end with ?>.

least include the version attribute, which designates the XML version number (currently "1.0"). The following statement is an XML declaration that includes only the version attribute:

```
<?xml version="1.0"?>
```

The encoding attribute of the XML declaration designates the language used by the XML document. Although English is the primary language used on the Web, it is not the only one. As a considerate resident of the international world of the Web, use the encoding attribute of the XML declaration to designate the character set for your XML document. English and many western European languages use the iso-8859-1 character set. Therefore, you should use the following XML declaration in your documents:

```
<?xml version="1.0" encoding="iso-8859-1"?>
```

The standalone="yes" attribute indicates that the document does not require a DTD to be rendered correctly. Unlike HTML, XML documents do not require a DTD for proper rendering. Because XML does not include predefined elements, it does not need a DTD to define them. However, some XML documents may benefit from a DTD, especially if multiple XML documents share the same elements. If your XML document requires a DTD, you assign the standalone attribute a value of "no". However, if you are certain that your XML document will not require a DTD, you assign the standalone attribute a value of "yes". For instance, you use the following XML declaration for any XML documents that do not require a DTD:

```
<?xml version="1.0" encoding="iso-8859-1"
    standalone="yes"?>
```

Next you create a simple XML document that contains your mailing address.

To create an XML document that contains your mailing address:

1. Start your text editor and create a document.

2. Add the following XML declaration that includes the version, encoding, and standalone attributes:

   ```
   <?xml version="1.0" encoding="iso-8859-1"
       standalone="yes"?>
   ```

3. Type the following opening tag to begin the document:

   ```
   <Mailing_Address>
   ```

4. Next, add the following elements that contain your mailing address. Be sure to replace the text within each tag pair with your own information.

   <Name>*your name***</Name><Address>***your address***</Address>**
   <City>*your city***</City><State>***your state***</State>**
   <Zip>*your zip code***</Zip>**

5. Type the closing mailing address tag, as follows:

   `</Mailing_Address>`

6. Save the file as **MailingAddress.xml** in the Chapter folder for Chapter 1.

7. Close the **MailingAddress.xml** file in your text editor.

Be sure to type an extension of .xml and not .html or .txt.

Parsing XML Documents

When a Web browser opens an HTML document that is not written properly, such as a document without the closing </html> tag, the browser ignores the error and renders the page. In contrast, XML documents must adhere to strict rules. The most important rule is that all elements must be closed. When a document adheres to XML's syntax rules, it is said to be **well formed**. You will study XML's rules for writing well-formed documents in the next section.

The W3C uses the term *well formedness*, although grammatically it sounds strange, so this book uses the term *well formed*.

You use a program called a **parser** to check whether an XML document is well formed. There are two types of parsers: non-validating and validating. A non-validating parser simply checks whether an XML document is well formed; if it is, the parser displays the document's XML elements and data. A validating parser checks whether an XML document is well formed and whether it conforms to an associated DTD. Firefox and other browsers have the capability to act as non-validating parsers. For instance, if you open the automobile XML document in Firefox and the document is well formed, Firefox will correctly parse and display it, as shown in Figure 1-4.

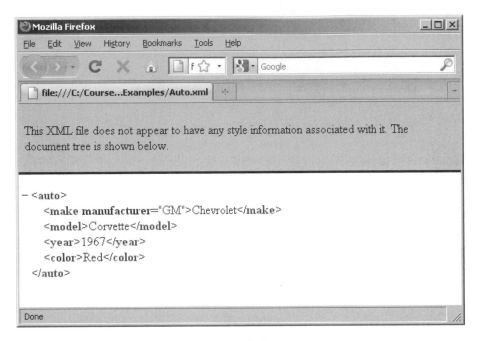

This XML file does not appear to have any style information associated with it. The document tree is shown below.

```
- <auto>
    <make manufacturer="GM">Chevrolet</make>
    <model>Corvette</model>
    <year>1967</year>
    <color>Red</color>
  </auto>
```

Done

Figure 1-4   Well-formed XML document in Firefox

Web browsers use Extensible Stylesheet Language, or XSL, to format and display XML. A style sheet is a file that defines the layout of a document. The message shown at the top of Figure 1-4 explains that the XML document does not have an associated style sheet.

If an XML document is not well formed, the parser displays the error. For example, if the automobile XML document is missing the closing </auto> tag, it is not well formed. In this case, most Web browsers will point to the error, as shown in Figure 1-5.

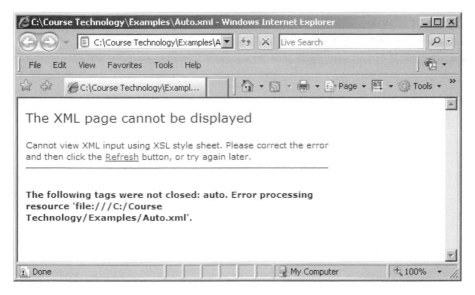

Figure 1-5 XML document that is not well formed in Internet Explorer

Next, you will parse the mailing address XML document you created in the last exercise.

To parse a document:

1. Open the **MailingAddress.xml** file in Firefox or another browser that can be used as a non-validating parser. The easiest way to open an XML document in Firefox is to type the complete path to the file, as shown in Figure 1-6. If you created the document correctly, your Web browser window should look like the figure. If you did not create the document correctly, fix any errors that appear in the browser window and reload the document.

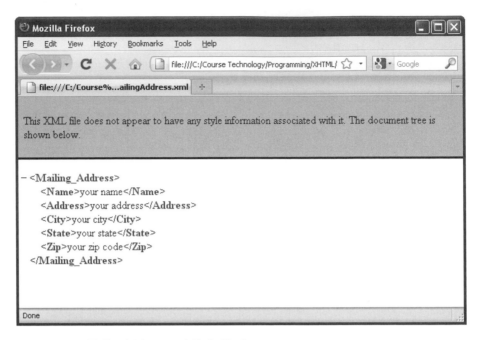

Figure 1-6   MailingAddress.xml file in Firefox

   2.   Close your Web browser window.

Writing Well-Formed Documents

Well-formed XML documents allow user agents to read the document's data easily. User agents expect XML data to be structured according to specific rules, which allows the user agent to read data quickly without having to decipher the data structure.

In this section, you will study the syntax, or rules, for writing well-formed XML documents. The most important of these rules are:

- All XML documents must have a root element.
- XML is case sensitive.
- All XML elements must have a closing tag.
- XML elements must be properly nested.
- Attribute values must appear within quotation marks.
- Empty elements must be closed.

Next, you will study each of these rules.

All XML Documents Must Have a Root Element

A root element contains all the other elements in a document. The
<html>. . . </html> element is the root element for HTML docu-
ments, although most Web browsers do not require a document to
include it. XML documents, however, require a root element that
you define yourself. For instance, the root element for the XML
automobile data document is the <auto> element. If you do not
include a root element, the XML document will not be well formed.
The following version of the XML automobile data document is not
well formed because it is missing the <auto> root element:

```
<?xml version="1.0" encoding="iso-8859-1"
    standalone="yes"?>
<make>Ford</make><model>Mustang</model>
<year>1967</year><color>Red</color>
```

Next, you will start creating an XML document that stores data associated with fiction books. You will develop a simple example of an
XML document that a bookstore or publisher might use to organize
its inventory.

To create an XML document that stores data:

1. Create a new document in your text editor.

2. Type the XML declaration, as follows:

   ```
   <?xml version="1.0" encoding="iso-8859-1"
       standalone="yes"?>
   ```

3. Next, type the opening and closing tags for a root element
   named <books>:

   ```
   <books>
   </books>
   ```

4. Save the file as **Books.xml** in the Chapter folder for Chapter 1,
   and then open the file in Firefox. Your Web browser should
   look like Figure 1-7.

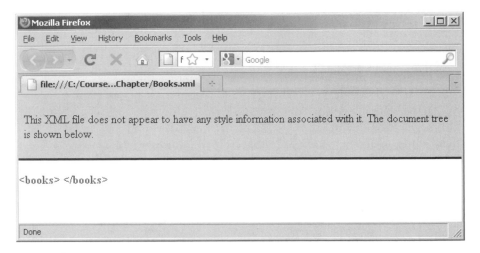

Figure 1-7   Books.xml in Firefox

    5.   Close your Web browser.

XML Is Case Sensitive

Unlike HTML tags, XML tags are case sensitive. For instance, it makes no difference whether the bold tag is uppercase or lowercase in an HTML document. Both of the following HTML statements will be rendered properly in a Web browser:

```
<B>This line is bold.</B>
<b>This line is also bold.</b>
```

You can even mix and match the case tags in an HTML document, as in the following statements:

```
<B>This line is bold.</b>
<b>This line is also bold.</B>
```

With XML, however, you cannot mix the case of elements. For instance, if you have an opening tag named `<color>` that is all lowercase, you must also use lowercase letters for the closing tag, as follows:

```
<color>Red</color>
```

If you use a different case for the opening and closing tags, they will be treated as separate tags, resulting in a document that is not well formed. The following statement is incorrect because the case of the opening and closing tags does not match:

```
<color>Red</COLOR>
```

For practice, you will introduce a case error into your sample XML document to see the error that appears in your non-validating parser (Firefox).

To introduce a case error into the Books.xml document:

1. Return to the **Books.xml** file in your text editor.

2. Modify the closing **</books>** tag so it is uppercase. Your file should appear as follows:

```
<?xml version="1.0" encoding="iso-8859-1"
    standalone="yes"?>
<books>
</BOOKS>
```

3. Save the **Books.xml** file and then open it in Firefox. You should receive an error like the one shown in Figure 1-8. As you can see, the closing **</BOOKS>** tag does not match the **<books>** start tag.

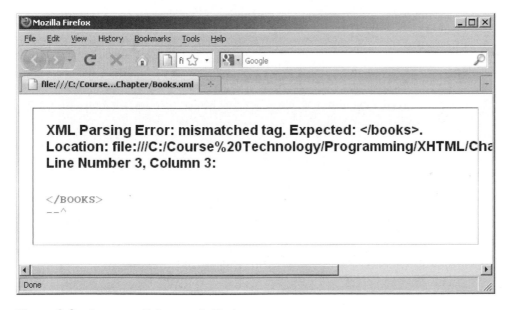

Figure 1-8   Case sensitivity error in Firefox

4. Return to the **Books.xml** file in your text editor and change the closing **</BOOKS>** tag back to lowercase letters, then save the file.

5. Return to the Web browser window that displays the Books.xml file and refresh the window. You can refresh Firefox by clicking the **Refresh** button. The file should open correctly.

6. Close your Web browser.

All XML Elements Must Have a Closing Tag

As mentioned earlier, most Web browsers usually ignore errors in an HTML document that is not properly structured and is missing closing tags. One common example is the paragraph element (<p>).

The <p> element should be used to mark a block of text as a single paragraph by enclosing the text within a <p>. . . </p> tag pair, as follows:

```
<p>All roads lead to Rome.</p>
```

Many Web authors, however, do not follow this convention and place a <p> tag at the end of a block of text to create a new paragraph as follows:

```
All roads lead to Rome.<p>
```

One reason you can omit closing tags is that Web browsers usually treat HTML documents as text that contains formatting elements. XML, however, is designed to organize data, not display it. As a result, instead of documents consisting of text that contains elements, as is the case with HTML, XML documents consist of elements that contain text. All elements must have a closing tag or the document will not be well formed. For instance, in the automobile data XML document you saw earlier, each element had a corresponding closing tag. The following version of the document is illegal because there are no corresponding closing tags for the <make>, <model>, <year>, and <color> elements:

```
<?xml version="1.0" encoding="iso-8859-1"
    standalone="yes"?>
<auto>
    <make>Ford<model>Mustang
    <year>1967<color>Red
</auto>
```

 You may have noticed that the XML declaration does not include a closing tag. This is because the XML declaration is not actually part of the document; it only declares the document as an XML document.

Next, you will add two <book> elements to the Books.xml file. Each <book> element will contain the title of a book.

To add two <book> elements to the Books.xml file:

1. Return to the **Books.xml** file in your text editor.

2. Modify the document as follows to include two <book> elements. Be sure to add the elements within the <books> root element. For now, do not include the closing </book> tag.

    ```
    <?xml version="1.0" encoding="iso-8859-1"
        standalone="yes"?>
    <books>
        <book>A Farewell to Arms
        <book>Of Mice and Men
    </books>
    ```

3. Save the **Books.xml** file, and then open it in Firefox. You should receive an error like the one shown in Figure 1-9. The error is raised because Firefox cannot find the ending tag for the <book> elements.

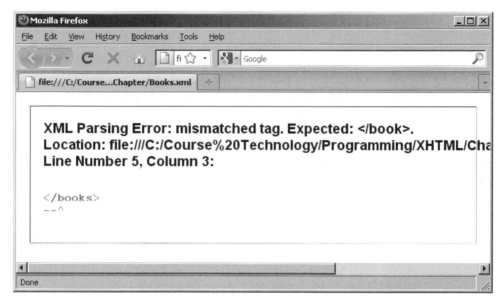

Figure 1-9 Missing closing tag error raised in Firefox

4. Return to the **Books.xml** file in your text editor and add the closing </book> tags to each of the <book> elements, then save the file.

```
<?xml version="1.0" encoding="iso-8859-1"
    standalone="yes"?>
<books>
    <book>A Farewell to Arms</book>
    <book>Of Mice and Men</book>
</books>
```

5. Return to the Web browser window that displays the Books.xml file and refresh the window. Your Web browser should look like Figure 1-10.

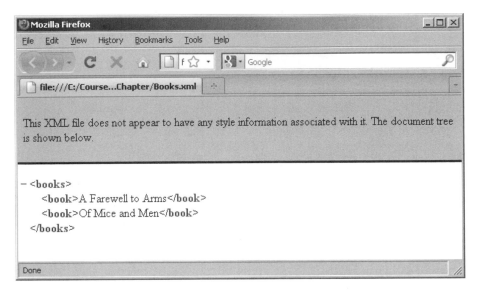

Figure 1-10   Books.xml after adding the closing </book> tags

6.   Close your Web browser.

XML Elements Must Be Properly Nested

Nesting refers to how elements are placed inside other elements. For example, in the following code, the <i> element is nested within the <b> element, while the <b> element is nested within the <p> element.

```
<p><b><i>This paragraph is bold
and italicized.</i></b></p>
```

In an HTML document, it makes no difference how the elements are nested. Examine the following HTML statement, which applies bold and italics to the text within a paragraph:

```
<p><b><i>This paragraph is bold
and italicized.</b></p></i>
```

In the preceding code, the opening <i> element is nested within the <b> element, which in turn is nested within the <p> element. Notice, however, that the closing </i> element is outside the closing </p> element. This <i> element is the innermost element. In XML, each innermost element must be closed before another element is closed. In the preceding statement, the <b> and <p> elements are closed before the <i> element. Although the order in which elements are closed makes no difference in HTML, the statement must be written as follows to be correct in XML:

```
<p><b><i>This paragraph is bold and italicized.</i></b></p>
```

As another example, consider the following version of the automobile data XML document. The code is not well formed because the <make> and <model> elements are not properly nested.

```
<?xml version="1.0" encoding="iso-8859-1"
    standalone="yes"?>
<auto>
    <make>Ford
        <model>Mustang</make>
    </model>
    <year>1967</year><color>Red</color>
</auto>
```

For the preceding XML code to be well formed, the <model> element must be closed before the <make> element, as follows:

```
<?xml version="1.0" encoding="iso-8859-1"
    standalone="yes"?>
<auto>
    <make>Ford
        <model>Mustang</model>
    </make>
    <year>1967</year><color>Red</color>
</auto>
```

Next, you will modify the <book> elements in the Books.xml file to include nested elements that describe more detailed information about each book.

To modify the Books.xml file to include nested elements:

1. Return to the **Books.xml** file in your text editor.

2. Replace the <book> element for *A Farewell to Arms* with the following nested elements that contain information on the book's title and author. Notice that the <title> and <author> elements are nested within the <book> element, and that the <first_name> and <last_name> elements are nested within the <author> element.

```
<book>
    <title>A Farewell to Arms</title>
    <author>
        <first_name>Ernest</first_name>
        <last_name>Hemingway</last_name>
    </author>
</book>
```

3. Next, replace the <book> element for *Of Mice and Men* with the following nested elements:

```
<book>
    <title>Of Mice and Men</title>
    <author>
        <first_name>John</first_name>
```

```
            <last_name>Steinbeck</last_name>
        </author>
    </book>
```

4. Save the **Books.xml** file, and then open it in Firefox. Your Web browser should look like Figure 1-11.

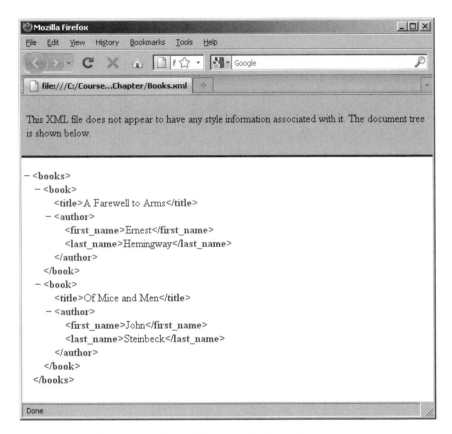

Figure 1-11   Books.xml after adding nested elements

5. Close your Web browser.

Attribute Values Must Appear Within Quotation Marks

The value assigned to an attribute in an HTML document can be either contained in quotation marks or assigned directly to the attribute, provided there are no spaces in the value being assigned. For example, recall that a common HTML attribute is the src attribute of the image element (<img>). You assign to the src attribute the name of an image file that you want to display in your document.

The following code shows two <img> elements. Even though the first element includes quotation marks around the value assigned to the src attribute and the second element does not, both statements will function correctly.

```
<img src="dog.gif">Image of a dog</img>
<img src=cat.gif>Image of a cat</img>
```

With XML, you must place quotation marks around the values assigned to an attribute. An example is the company attribute of the <manufacturer> element you saw earlier in the automobile data XML document. You must include quotation marks around the value assigned to the company attribute using a statement similar to <manufacturer company="General Motors"/>. Omitting the quotation marks from this statement results in a document that is not well formed.

Next, you will add an attribute named publisher to each of the <book> elements in your example XML document. The publisher attribute stores a value containing the name of each book's publisher.

To add a publisher attribute to each of the <book> elements:

1. Return to the **Books.xml** file in your text editor.

2. Modify the opening tag for the *A Farewell to Arms* <book> element so it includes the publisher attribute with an assigned value of "Scribner":

   <book publisher="Scribner">

3. Modify the opening tag for the *Of Mice and Men* <book> element so it includes the publisher attribute with an assigned value of "Penguin":

   <book publisher="Penguin">

4. Save the **Books.xml** file, and then open it in Firefox. Your Web browser should look like Figure 1-12.

You also cannot include an empty attribute in an element. You must assign a value to an attribute or exclude the attribute from the element. For instance, the statement <manufacturer company /> is incorrect because no value is being assigned to the company attribute.

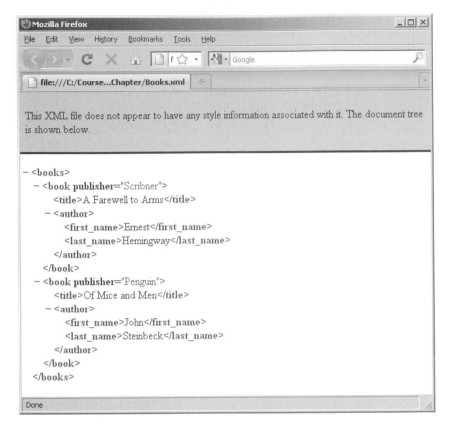

Figure 1-12   Books.xml after adding attributes

    5. Close your Web browser.

Empty Elements Must Be Closed

Several elements in HTML do not have corresponding ending tags, including the <hr> element, which inserts a horizontal rule into the document, and the <br> element, which inserts a line break. Elements that do not require an ending tag are called **empty elements** because you cannot use them as a tag pair to enclose text or other elements. You can create an empty element in an XML document by adding a single slash (/) before the tag's closing bracket to close the element. Most often, you use an empty element for an element that does not require content, such as an image. For instance, in the XML document of automobile data, you may create a <photo> element with a single attribute that stores the name of an image file. This image file contains a photograph of the automobile. An example of the <photo> empty element is shown in the following XML code:

```
<?xml version="1.0" standalone="yes"?>
<auto>
     <photo image_name="mustang.jpg"/>
     <make>Ford</make><model>Mustang</model>
     <year>1967</year><color>Red</color>
</auto>
```

Next, you will add an empty element named publication to the Books.xml file. This element contains a single attribute that stores the original publication year for each book.

To add an empty element to an XML document:

1. Return to the **Books.xml** file in your text editor.

2. Add a nested empty publication element to the *A Farewell to Arms* <book> element, as follows:

```
<book publisher="Scribner">
     <publication year="1929" />
     <title>A Farewell to Arms</title>
     <author>
          <first_name>Ernest</first_name>
          <last_name>Hemingway</last_name>
     </author>
</book>
```

3. Now add an empty publication element to the *Of Mice and Men* <book> element, as follows:

```
<book publisher="Penguin">
     <publication year="1937" />
     <title>Of Mice and Men</title>
     <author>
          <first_name>John</first_name>
          <last_name>Steinbeck</last_name>
     </author>
</book>
```

4. Save the **Books.xml** file, and then open it in Firefox. Your Web browser should look like Figure 1-13.

Remember that the primary purpose of XML is to define and organize data. An empty image element like the one shown in the XML automobile document only provides the name of the associated image file—it does not display the image. However, you can display an image from an XML document if you use CSS and XSL.

33

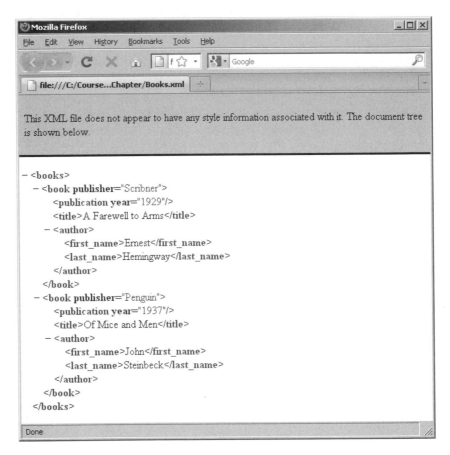

Figure 1-13   Books.xml after adding empty elements

5.   Close your Web browser.

Combining XML and HTML

In this section, you studied how XML is used for defining data. Although XML was designed primarily to define data, you can also use it to create Web pages. You can create formatted Web pages using XML and **Extensible Stylesheet Language**, or **XSL**, which is a specification for formatting XML in a Web browser.

With the growing need to create Web pages that can be easily displayed in *all* user agents, it is clear that an alternative to HTML is needed. For a number of reasons, however, it is not clear that XML and XSL currently provide an adequate alternative to HTML. First, getting Web page authors and developers to abandon existing HTML techniques is asking a lot. Second, learning XML and XSL is more difficult than learning HTML. Finally, many older browsers simply do not support XML.

To make the transition to XML-based Web pages easier, the W3C combined XML and HTML to create XHTML, which is almost identical to HTML, except that it uses strict XML syntax to describe the parts of a document. XHTML is actually considered to be an XML application because it is written in XML, and the XHTML language must adhere to the same requirements as XML. One of XHTML's chief advantages is that XHTML documents are backward compatible with older browsers, provided you follow several simple rules that you will study next.

Short Quiz 2

1. What is an XML declaration and how is it defined?

2. How do you ensure that an XML document is well formed?

3. What is a root element in XML and HTML documents?

4. What does it mean that XML documents must be properly nested?

5. How do you close an empty XML element?

Structuring Web Pages

Although you will work primarily with HTML 5 documents in this book, this section explains how to structure both HTML 5 and XHTML documents. Both HTML 5 and XHTML require a <!DOCTYPE> declaration and the <html>, <head>, and <body> elements. The **<!DOCTYPE> declaration** states the XHTML version of the document. The <!DOCTYPE> declaration for HTML 5 is simply <!DOCTYPE HTML>. The following elements are all you need to write a well-formed HTML 5 Web page:

```
<!DOCTYPE HTML>
<html>
<head>
<title>title</title>
</head>
<body>
. . .
</body>
</html>
```

36

One big difference between XML and XHTML is that XML does not contain any predefined elements, while XHTML contains almost all the elements that are available in HTML. However, because XHTML is based on XML, you need to follow the XML rules for creating well-formed documents.

For some newer browsers and certain types of XHTML documents, you must use the .xml or .xhtml extension to execute the XML contained within the document. You will use the .xhtml extension when you study multimedia and executable content in Chapter 7.

The <!DOCTYPE> declaration for XHTML is a little more complex and requires one of three DTDs: Transitional, Frameset, or Strict. Recall that a DTD defines the elements and attributes that you can use in a document. By writing your Web pages so that they use only the elements and attributes that are defined in one of the XHTML DTDs, you can ensure that your document is well formed.

Understanding Backward Compatibility

To be backward compatible with older browsers, XHTML documents must have an extension of .html or .htm, just like HTML documents. You must also follow several rules to ensure that the code within your XHTML documents is backward compatible. Recall that XML requires empty elements to include a slash before the closing bracket to close the element. This rule also applies to XHTML. However, older browsers that do not support XML ignore the element when they see the slash immediately following the element name in an empty element. You can ensure that older browsers are able to read empty elements in a well-formed XHTML document by adding a space between the element name and the closing slash. Older browsers simply ignore the space and the slash and render the element normally. Browsers that support XHTML recognize the slash as closing the empty element. For instance, to properly close the horizontal rule (<hr>) empty element and ensure that it is backward compatible with older browsers, you use the statement <hr />. Be sure to include the space and slash for all empty elements, including the often-used <br> and <img> elements.

Defining the XHTML <!DOCTYPE> Declaration

The syntax for the XHTML <!DOCTYPE> declaration is <!DOCTYPE html *type* "*public identifier*" "*URL*">. The html attribute of the <!DOCTYPE> declaration identifies the root element of the document; for XHTML documents this attribute value should always be html. You replace the *type* attribute of the <!DOCTYPE> declaration with PUBLIC or SYSTEM. You use a type of PUBLIC if the DTD is available on the Web or SYSTEM if the DTD is available on the local computer. If you use a type of PUBLIC, you must also include the public identifier attribute within quotation marks. A **public identifier** is a text string used to identify a DTD on the Web. For instance, the public identifier for one of the XHTML DTDs is "-//W3C//DTD XHTML 1.0 Strict//EN". The final attribute in the <!DOCTYPE> declaration is the Universal Resource Locator (URL) of the DTD. If you use a <!DOCTYPE> declaration of PUBLIC, the user agent first attempts to use the DTD identified by the public identifier.

The public identifiers for XHTML 1.0 are built into current Web browsers and other user agents. However, if the user agent does not recognize the public identifier, it attempts to locate the DTD using the URL.

Here is a simple XHTML document.

```
<!DOCTYPE html
PUBLIC "-//W3C//DTD XHTML 1.0 Strict//EN"
"http://www.w3.org/TR/xhtml1/DTD/xhtml1-strict.dtd">
<html>
<head>
<title>Basic XHTML Document</title>
</head>
<body>
<p>President Obama is from Hawaii.</p>
</body>
</html>
```

<aside>If an XHTML document is missing the <!DOCTYPE> declaration, it automatically reverts to a standard HTML document.</aside>

<aside>37</aside>

Understanding XHTML DTDs

As you learned earlier, the World Wide Web Consortium (W3C) created XHTML to make the transition to XML-based Web pages easier. To facilitate the transition, the W3C provided three types of XHTML DTDs: Transitional, Frameset, and Strict.

Transitional DTD

One goal of XHTML is to separate the way a document is structured from the way it is displayed. To accomplish this, several common HTML formatting and display elements and attributes have been deprecated in XHTML 1.0. Elements and attributes that are considered to be obsolete and that will eventually be eliminated are said to be **deprecated**. The **Transitional DTD** allows you to continue using deprecated elements along with the well-formed document requirements of XML. Table 1-2 lists the elements that are deprecated in XHTML 1.0, but that are still available in the Transitional DTD.

Element	Description
`<applet>`	Executes Java applets
`<basefont>`	Specifies the base font size
`<center>`	Centers text
`<dir>`	Defines a directory list
`<font>`	Specifies a font name, size, and color
`<s>` or `<strike>`	Formats strikethrough text
`<u>`	Formats underlined text

Table 1-2 HTML elements that are deprecated in XHTML 1.0

38

You should use the Transitional DTD only if you need to create Web pages that use the deprecated elements listed in Table 1-2.

The `<basefont>`, `<center>`, `<font>`, `<s>`, `<strike>`, and `<u>` elements are deprecated in favor of Cascading Style Sheets (CSS). The `<applet>` element is deprecated in favor of the `<object>` element; the `<dir>` and `<menu>` elements are deprecated in favor of unordered lists; and the `<isindex>` element is deprecated in favor of the `<input>` element. In later chapters, you will study all of the elements that replace the deprecated elements.

The `<!DOCTYPE>` declaration for the Transitional DTD is as follows:

```
<!DOCTYPE html PUBLIC
"-//W3C//DTD XHTML 1.0 Transitional//EN"
"http://www.w3.org/TR/xhtml1/DTD/xhtml1-transitional.dtd">
```

Next, you create a document containing a paragraph from the draft of a fiction novel. You use the Transitional DTD along with the deprecated `<s>` and `<u>` elements. You use the `<s>` element to strike out portions of the paragraph that will be deleted and the `<u>` element to underline new text that will be inserted.

To create a document that uses the Transitional DTD:

1. Start your text editor and create a new document.

2. Type the opening `<!DOCTYPE>` declaration that uses the Transitional DTD, as follows:

   ```
   <!DOCTYPE html PUBLIC "-//W3C//DTD XHTML 1.0
   Transitional//EN"
   "http://www.w3.org/TR/xhtml1/DTD/
       xhtml1-transitional.dtd">
   ```

3. Type the `<html>` element, as follows. Remember that all Web pages must begin and end with the `<html>...</html>` tag pair.

   ```
   <html>
   </html>
   ```

4. Within the `<html>` element, add the following `<head>` and `<title>` elements to the document. The title appears in the Web browser's title bar. Remember that the `<head>` element must include a `<title>` element. The `<title>` element cannot exist outside the `<head>` element.

   ```
   <head>
   <title>Great American Novel</title>
   </head>
   ```

5. Next, add the following `<body>` element above the closing `</html>` tag:

   ```
   <body>
   </body>
   ```

6. Type the following elements and text between the <body>. . . </body> tag pair to create the body of the document.

```
<p>It was a <s>dark and stormy night</s> <u>bright
and sunny day</u>. <s>Lightning streaked the sky,
followed by an angry explosion of thunder.</s> <u>High,
soft clouds accented the sky and a soft wind gently
swayed the trees.</u></p>
```

7. Save the file as **Novel.html** in your Chapter folder for Chapter 1. Be sure your document is saved with an extension of .html.

8. Open the **Novel.html** file in your Web browser. Figure 1-14 displays the Novel.html file as it appears in Firefox.

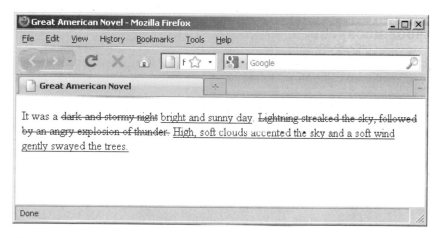

Figure 1-14 Novel.html in Firefox

9. Close your Web browser window.

Frameset DTD

The **Frameset DTD** is identical to the Transitional DTD, except that it includes the <frameset> and <frame> elements, which allow you to split the browser window into two or more frames. Frames are independent, scrollable portions of a Web browser window, with each frame capable of displaying a separate URL. The <!DOCTYPE> declaration for the Frameset DTD is as follows:

```
<!DOCTYPE html PUBLIC
"-//W3C//DTD XHTML 1.0 Frameset//EN"
"http://www.w3.org/TR/xhtml1/DTD/xhtml1-frameset.dtd">
```

You should understand that frames have been deprecated in favor of tables, but frameset documents are still widely used and you may find them useful. Additionally, you should be able to recognize and work with frameset documents if you need to modify an existing Web page that was created with frames. See the appendices for information on how to work with frames.

Strict DTD

The **Strict DTD** eliminates the elements that were deprecated in the Transitional DTD and Frameset DTD. The <!DOCTYPE> declaration for the Strict DTD is as follows:

```
<!DOCTYPE html PUBLIC
"-//W3C//DTD XHTML 1.0 Strict//EN"
"http://www.w3.org/TR/xhtml1/DTD/xhtml1-strict.dtd">
```

Throughout this book, you will primarily use the Strict DTD to learn about the most current Web page authoring techniques.

Next, you start creating the home page for the Don's Pizza Web site. You create the XHTML document using the Strict DTD. The home page simply lists the daily special.

To start creating the home page for the Don's Pizza Web site:

1. Create a new document in your text editor and type the opening <!DOCTYPE> declaration that uses the Strict DTD, as follows:

    ```
    <!DOCTYPE html
    PUBLIC "-//W3C//DTD XHTML 1.0 Strict//EN"
    "http://www.w3.org/TR/xhtml1/DTD/xhtml1-strict.dtd">
    ```

2. Type the <html> element, as follows.

    ```
    <html>
    </html>
    ```

3. Within the <html> element, add the following <head> and <title> elements to the document.

    ```
    <head>
    <title>Don's Pizza Home Page</title>
    </head>
    ```

4. Next, add the following document <body> element within the <html> element:

    ```
    <body>
    </body>
    ```

5. Add the following elements to the document body between the <body>. . .</body> tags.

    ```
    <p><b>Today's special</b>: buy a large meat lover's
    or vegetarian pizza and receive a free Caesar salad
    and two liters of Diet Pepsi! Our meat lover's pizza
    ```

is covered with loads of pepperoni, savory Italian sausage, smoked bacon, hamburger, mushrooms, and extra cheese. Our vegetarian pizza has lots of mushrooms, black olives, bell peppers, onions, artichoke hearts, and fresh tomatoes.</p>

6. Save the file as **DonsPizza.html** in your Chapter folder for Chapter 1.

7. Open the **DonsPizza.html** file in your Web browser. Figure 1-15 displays the file as it appears in Firefox.

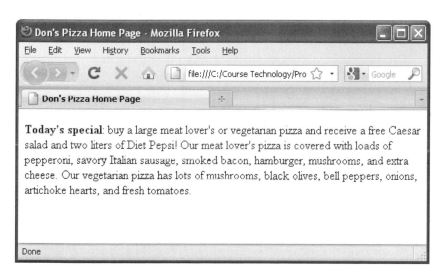

Figure 1-15   DonsPizza.html in Firefox

8. Close your Web browser window.

Working with Required Elements

To explain how an XHTML document is structured, this section discusses the three elements that must be included in every XHTML document: the <html>, <head>, and <body> elements.

The <html> Element

All HTML documents must include an <html> element, which tells a Web browser that the instructions between the opening and closing <html> tags are to be assembled into an HTML document. The <html> element is required and contains all the text and other elements that make up the HTML document. The <html> element is also the root element for XHTML documents and is required for XHTML documents to be well formed.

You may be wondering why XHTML documents do not use a root element of <xhtml>. The <html> element is necessary for backward compatibility with older browsers that do not recognize the <!DOCTYPE> element, which declares the DTD used by an XHTML element.

All of the predefined elements in an XHTML document are orga-nized within the **XHTML namespace** that you declare in the <html> element. To understand a namespace, recall that you must define your own elements and attributes in an XML document. Because you define your own elements, an XML document that combines multiple other XML documents can cause conflicts among elements. For instance, two separate XML documents may both define an ele-ment named <company>. If you combine both XML documents into a single document, how does a Web browser know which version of the <company> element to use? To address this problem, you iden-tify each <company> element by the namespace to which it belongs. A **namespace** organizes the elements and attributes of an XML document into separate groups. You have already used the XML namespace with an attribute. Because the lang attribute exists in both HTML and XHTML, you differentiate the two by preceding the XHTML version of the attribute with *xml* and then a colon to identify the XML namespace. Use a statement similar to xml:lang"en".

For elements, you add the namespace and colon before the tag name in both the opening and closing tags. For instance, if one of two ver-sions of the <company> element exists in a namespace named *invest-ments*, you would ensure that a Web browser uses the investments namespace version of the element by using a statement similar to the following:

```
<investments:company>Oracle</investments:company>
```

The xml and investments namespaces are examples of **local namespaces** that you specifically apply to individual elements and attributes. In this book, you use local namespaces only when you define a document or element's language using the value xml:lang.

A **default namespace** is applied to all of the elements and attributes in an XHTML document, with the exception of elements and attri-butes to which local namespaces have been applied. With a default namespace, you do not precede element and attribute names with a namespace and colon, as you do with local namespaces, because the namespace is applied by default to all of the elements and namespaces in the document. You specify a default namespace for an XHTML document by using the **xmlns namespace attribute** in the <html> ele-ment. Namespaces are identified by a unique URI, which you assign as a value to the xmlns attribute. All XHTML documents, regardless of whether they use the Transitional, Frameset, or Strict DTD, use the namespace identified by the following URI: *www.w3.org/1999/xhtml*. The following statement shows how to assign the URI to the xmlns attribute in the <html> element:

```
<html xmlns="http://www.w3.org/1999/xhtml">
```

According to the W3C XHTML recommendation, the xmlns attribute is required in the <html> element and must be assigned the preceding URI. To ensure that the elements and attributes in your document are correctly referenced in the XHTML namespace, you should always include the xmlns attribute in your <html> element.

Next, you modify the <html> element for the DonsPizza.html file so it includes the xmlns attribute.

You are not required to use the xmlns namespace attribute with HTML 5.

To modify the <html> element to include the xmlns attribute:

1. Return to the **DonsPizza.html** file in your text editor.

2. Modify the <html> element so it includes the xmlns attribute, as follows:

   ```
   <html xmlns="http://www.w3.org/1999/xhtml">
   ```

3. Save the **DonsPizza.html** file and open it in your Web browser. It should render the same as it did before you modified the <html> element.

4. Close your Web browser window.

The Document Head

Web pages consist of two types of information: the content *displayed* by the Web page and information *about* the Web page. The elements within the document body contain the content that the Web page displays. The elements within a document's head section contain information about the Web page itself. The document head does not actually display any information in a browser. Rather, it is a **parent element**, an element that contains other elements known as **child elements**. Table 1-3 lists the child elements that can appear in the <head> element.

Do not confuse the document head with heading elements such as <h1> and <h2>.

You learn how to work with most of the child elements of the <head> element in later chapters.

Element	Description
<base>	Specifies a base URL for all of a document's relative links
<link>	Defines the relationship between linked documents
<meta>	Defines metadata about a Web page
<script>	Contains commands for scripting languages such as JavaScript and VBScript
<style>	Defines the style information for a specific element
<title>	Contains text that appears in a browser's title bar

Table 1-3   Child elements of the <head> element

44

You are already familiar with one child element of the <head> element—the <title> element, which contains text that appears in a browser's title bar. Every page in a Web site must have its own title, and you should choose these titles carefully. For instance, for Don's Pizza, you may be tempted to use *Don's Pizza* as the title for each page on the Web site. Although that title is acceptable for the home page, good Web authoring practice dictates that you use titles that accurately describe the purpose or content of each Web page. Some examples of good titles for the Don's Pizza Web pages might include:

- Don's Pizza Produce
- Don's Pizza Schedule
- Don's Pizza Vendor Directory
- Don's Pizza Contact Information

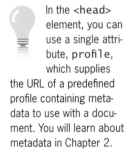

In Windows operating systems, the title of a Web page also appears as the title of a taskbar icon when a Web browser window is minimized.

In the <head> element, you can use a single attribute, profile, which supplies the URL of a predefined profile containing metadata to use with a document. You will learn about metadata in Chapter 2.

Another important reason to create a good title for each Web page is that the title becomes the default text used when a bookmark is added in a Web browser. (In Internet Explorer, bookmarks are called *favorites*.) For instance, if a Web page has the title *Don's Pizza*, the browser will suggest the same text as the description for the bookmark. Users can change a bookmark description to anything they want, but they will appreciate being able to use a title that also makes sense as a bookmark name. For instance, if you have a Web site for a shoe repair shop, you would not want to use a bare-bones title such as *Shoe Repairs.* Instead, you would want to include the name of the shop along with a description of the page, such as *Old World Shoe Repairs Price List.*

The Document Body

Recall that the document body is represented by the <body> element and contains other elements that define all of the content a user sees rendered in a browser. Although this book focuses on how to write well-formed XHTML documents, it is worth noting the differences in the use of the <body> element in HTML and XHTML.

Earlier in this chapter you learned that HTML was designed primarily to display data. With HTML, you can write the content that you want the browser to render, and add to the content any formatting elements you need. XHTML documents consist of elements that contain content, as opposed to HTML documents, which consist of content that contains elements. Understanding this distinction is important because it has a great deal to do with how browsers render content, especially text. In HTML, you can type text within the <body> element—or eliminate the <body> element entirely—and the browser still renders the text. For instance, the following code is perfectly acceptable for an HTML document:

```
<body>
<b>Llamas</b> are from South America, <br />
<b>kangaroos</b> are from Australia, <br />
and <b>pandas</b> are from China.
</body>
```

In HTML, you can also use various attributes in the <body> element that affect the appearance of the document, such as the bgcolor attribute for setting the background color and the text attribute for setting the default color of text. The document formatting attributes of the <body> element were deprecated in XHTML Strict and replaced by CSS, although document formatting attributes are still used frequently on many Web sites.

Comments

When you work with any type of programming language, whether it is a simple markup language like HTML or an advanced language like Java or C++, it is considered good practice to add comments to your code. **Comments** are nonprinting lines that you place in programming code to contain various types of remarks, including your name and the date you wrote the code, notes to yourself, copyright information, or instructions to future Web page authors and developers who may need to modify your work. When you are working with long documents, comments can make it easier to decipher how the document is structured.

HTML comments begin with an opening comment tag <!-- and end with a closing comment tag -->, as shown in the following example. The browser does not render any text located between opening and closing comment tags.

```
<!DOCTYPE html PUBLIC
"-//W3C//DTD XHTML 1.0 Strict//EN"
"http://www.w3.org/TR/xhtml1/DTD/xhtml1-strict.dtd">
<html lang="EN" xml:lang = "EN" dir="ltr">
<head>
<title>Comments</title>
</head>
<body>
<p>The browser renders this line normally because it is
located before the opening comment tag.</p>
<!-- Text on this line does not appear
Text on this line does not appear
This line does not appear either -->
<p>The browser renders this line normally because
it is located after the closing comment tag.</p>
</body>
</html>
```

Next, you add comments to the DonsPizza.html file.

To add comments to the DonsPizza.html file:

1. Return to the **DonsPizza.html** file in your text editor.

2. At the top of the file, above the <!DOCTYPE> declaration, add the following comments. Be sure to use your name and today's date.

```
<!--
Home page for Don's Pizza
your name
today's date
-->
```

3. Save and close the **DonsPizza.html** file and then open it in your Web browser to confirm that the comments do not appear.

4. Close your Web browser window.

Validating Web Pages

When you open an XHTML document in a Web browser, the browser does not parse the code as it would an XML document. Instead, if the XHTML document is not well formed, the browser simply ignores the errors, as it would with an HTML document, and renders the Web page. To ensure that an XHTML document is well formed and that its elements are valid, you need to use a **validating parser**. **Validation** checks that your XHTML document is well formed, and that the elements in your document are written correctly according to the element definitions in an associated DTD. You are not required to validate XHTML documents. If you do not validate an XHTML document and it contains errors, most Web browsers will probably treat it as an HTML document, ignore the errors, and render the page anyway. However, validation can help you spot errors in your code. Even the most experienced Web authors frequently introduce typos or some other error into XHTML documents that prevent the document from being well formed and valid. Remember that if your XHTML document is not well formed, user agents such as mobile phones may have trouble rendering it.

Many XHTML validating parsers exist. One of the best available is the W3C Markup Validation Service, a free service that validates both HTML and XHTML. The W3C Markup Validation Service is located at *http://validator.w3.org*. The main Web page for the service allows you to validate a Web page by entering its URI in the Address box and selecting various options in the form shown in Figure 1-16.

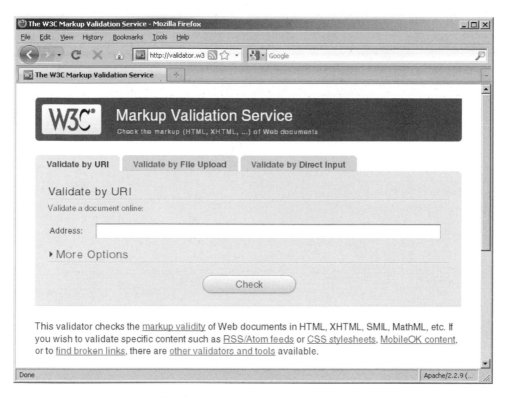

Figure 1-16   W3C Markup Validation Service main page

Once you validate a document, the W3C Markup Validation Service displays a results page that lists warnings or errors found in the document.

The W3C Markup Validation Service also includes a separate page that you can use to validate XHTML files by uploading them from your computer. You can open the File Upload page of the W3C Markup Validation Service by clicking the Validate by File Upload tab at the top of the main page or by entering the following URL in your browser's Address box: *http://validator.w3.org/#validate_by_upload.* Figure 1-17 shows an example of the File Upload page.

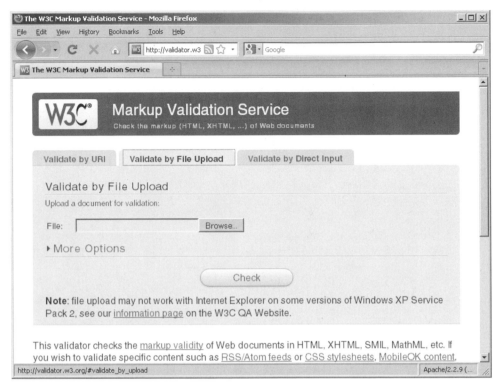

Figure 1-17   W3C Markup Validation Service upload page

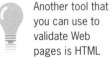

Another tool that you can use to validate Web pages is HTML Tidy, a popular stand-alone program that you can download to your computer. In addition to validating HTML and XHTML documents, HTML Tidy also assists in converting HTML documents to XHTML. HTML Tidy is available for numerous platforms and can be downloaded at *http://tidy.sourceforge.net/*.

Before you can validate a Web page, you must designate its character encoding by including a `<meta>` element in the document head. Although you will learn more about the `<meta>` element in Chapter 2, for now you should understand that it is used to inform search engines and Web servers about the information in your Web page. You use the following `<meta>` element to specify character encoding in your Web pages:

```
<meta http-equiv="Content-Type"
    content="text/html; charset=iso-8859-1" />
```

The preceding statement specifies that the document is created with the character set that is used in English and many Western languages.

Next, you validate the DonsPizza.html file using the W3C Markup Validation Service.

To validate a file:

1. Return to the **DonsPizza.html** file in your text editor.

2. Add the following `<meta>` element immediately above the closing `</head>` tag:

    ```
    <meta http-equiv="Content-Type"
        content="text/html; charset=iso-8859-1" />
    ```

3. Start your Web browser and enter the URL for the W3C Markup Validation Service upload page in the Address box: **http://validator.w3.org/#validate_by_upload**.

4. Click the **Browse** button to display the Choose file dialog box.

5. In the Choose file dialog box, navigate to where you saved the **DonsPizza.html** file. Locate and open the file. The drive, folder path, and filename should appear in the File text box on the upload page.

6. Click the **Validate this file** button. The W3C Markup Validation Service validates the document and returns the results displayed in Figure 1-18.

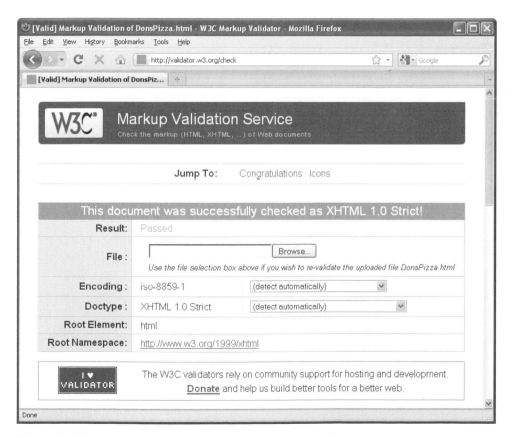

Figure 1-18 W3C Markup Validation Service results page after successfully validating a strict Web page

7. Close your Web browser window.

Short Quiz 3

1. How do XHTML documents maintain compatibility with HTML documents?

2. Explain how to use the `<!DOCTYPE>` declaration.

3. What are the differences between the three XHTML DTDs?

4. What elements are required for all XHTML documents?

5. How do you validate an XHTML document?

Summing Up

- In 1990 and 1991, Tim Berners-Lee created what would become the World Wide Web, or the Web, at the European Laboratory for Particle Physics (CERN) in Geneva, Switzerland, as a way to easily access cross-referenced documents on the CERN computer network. This method of access, known as hypertext linking, is probably the most important aspect of the Web because it allows you to open other Web pages quickly.

- A document on the Web is called a Web page and is identified by a unique address called the Uniform Resource Locator, or URL. A URL is a type of Uniform Resource Identifier (URI), which is a generic term for many types of names and addresses on the World Wide Web.

- The World Wide Web Consortium, or W3C, was established in 1994 at MIT to oversee the development of Web technology standards.

- Hypertext Markup Language, or HTML, is a markup language used to create the Web pages that appear on the World Wide Web. HTML documents are text documents that contain formatting instructions, called tags, which determine how data is displayed on a Web page. A tag pair and any data it contains are referred to as an element.

- The process by which a Web browser assembles and formats an HTML document is called parsing or rendering.

- Web page authoring (or Web authoring) refers to the creation and assembly of the tags, attributes, and data that make up a Web page.

- Web development, or Web programming, refers to the design of software applications for a Web site.

- User agents are devices capable of retrieving and processing HTML and XHTML documents.

- Languages based on SGML use a Document Type Definition, or DTD, to define the tags and attributes that you can use in a document.

- Extensible Markup Language, or XML, is used for creating Web pages and for defining and transmitting data between applications.

- In XML, as in HTML, you refer to a tag pair and the data it contains as an element.

- The data contained within an element's opening and closing tags is referred to as its content.

- XML documents should begin with an XML declaration, which specifies the version of XML being used.

- You use a program called a parser to check whether an XML document is well formed.

- A root element contains all the other elements in a document.

- Elements that do not require a closing tag are called empty elements.

- Extensible Hypertext Markup Language, or XHTML, is a combination of XML and HTML that is used to author Web pages.

- The `<!DOCTYPE>` declaration states the XHTML version of the document and the XHTML DTDs with which the document complies.

- The Transitional DTD allows you to continue using deprecated elements along with the well-formed document requirements of XML.

- The Frameset DTD is identical to the Transitional DTD, except that it includes the `<frameset>` and `<frame>` elements, which allow you to split the browser window into two or more frames.

- The Strict DTD eliminates the elements that were deprecated in the Transitional DTD and Frameset DTD.

- All XHTML documents, regardless of whether they use the Transitional, Strict, or Frameset DTD, use the namespace identified by the following URI: *www.w3.org/1999/xhtml.*

- The \<head\> element represents the document head and contains other elements that store information about the Web page or are used by the Web page.

- The \<body\> element represents the document body and contains other elements that store all of the content a user sees rendered in a browser.

- Comments are nonprinting lines that you place in programming code to contain various types of remarks, including your name and the date you wrote the code, notes to yourself, copyright information, or instructions to future Web page authors and developers who may need to modify your work.

- Validation checks that your XHTML document is well formed and that the elements in your document are correctly written according to the element definitions in an associated DTD.

Comprehension Check

1. The Internet was originally designed as a communications network capable of surviving a nuclear attack. True or False?

2. URL stands for _____.

    a. Unique Resource List

    b. Unnamed Reference Locator

    c. Uniform Resource List

    d. Uniform Resource Locator

3. A Web browser's process of assembling and formatting an HTML document is called _____. (Choose all that apply.)

    a. parsing

    b. painting

    c. rendering

    d. compiling

4. What does the term *Web site programming* refer to?

5. Your goal should be to create Web pages that are compatible with as many browser types and versions as possible. True or False?

6. What happens when a browser does not support a specific HTML tag?

    a. The browser attempts to render the tag anyway.

    b. The browser ignores the tag.

    c. The browser contacts the W3C for the correct definition of the tag.

    d. The browser displays an error message.

7. With which tag pair should all HTML documents begin and end?

    a. `<body>...</body>`

    b. `<head>...</head>`

    c. `<html>...</html>`

    d. `<xml>...</xml>`

8. Even though an HTML document may omit the `<html>...</html>`, `<head>...</head>`, and `<body>...</body>` tag pairs, the code will render properly in a browser. True or False?

9. DTD stands for _____.

    a. Data Transfer Display

    b. Digital Technology Definition

    c. Document Test Descriptor

    d. Document Type Definition

10. Which of the following devices can be user agents? (Choose all that apply.)

    a. Mobile phones

    b. iPads

    c. Internet Explorer

    d. Netscape

11. What is the correct syntax for an XML declaration that does not require a DTD in order to be rendered correctly?

    a. `<xml version="1.0" standalone="yes">`

    b. `<xml version="1.0" standalone="no">`

c. `<?xml version="1.0" standalone="yes"?>`

d. `<?xml version="1.0" standalone="no"?>`

12. A _____ element contains other elements on a page.

    a. master

    b. source

    c. base

    d. root

13. Which of the following statements is considered to be well formed?

    a. `<name>Rajesh Singh</name>`

    b. `<name>Rajesh Singh</NAME>`

    c. `<NAME>Rajesh Singh</name>`

    d. `<Name>Rajesh Singh</name>`

14. Which of the following is the correct way to write a well-formed element with an attribute?

    a. `<organization name=General Motors>`

    b. `<organization name="General Motors">`

    c. `<organization "name=General Motors">`

    d. `<"organization name=General Motors">`

15. How do you close the empty `<hr>` element in an XHTML document to make it backward compatible with older browsers?

    a. `<hr\>`

    b. `<hr \>`

    c. `<hr/>`

    d. `<hr />`

16. Explain when you should use PUBLIC and when you should use SYSTEM as the type attribute of the `<!DOCTYPE>` declaration.

17. What must you place on the first line of an XHTML document?

    a. an `<html>` tag

    b. an `<xhtml>` tag

    c. a `<title>` tag

    d. a `<!DOCTYPE>` declaration

18. Which XHTML DTD(s) allows you to continue using deprecated elements? (Choose all that apply.)

    a. XML

    b. Transitional

    c. Strict

    d. Frameset

19. All of the predefined elements in XHTML are organized within the _____ namespace.

    a. XML

    b. XHTML

    c. HTML

    d. Browser

20. The `xmlns` attribute is required in the `<html>` element in order for an HTML 5 document to be well formed. True or False?

Reinforcement Exercises

 Exercise 1-1

In this exercise, you create an XML document that contains the name and price per pound of different types of coffee beans.

1. Create a new document in your text editor and type the opening XML declaration. Be sure to use all three attributes of the XML declaration.

2. Type the opening and closing tags for a root element named `<coffee_beans>`.

3. Within the <coffee_beans> element, create at least three <coffee> elements. Each <coffee> element should contain nested <name> and <price> elements. For the content of the <name> elements, enter the names of different types of coffees, such as Kona and Colombian. For the content of the <price> element, enter the current price per pound for each type of coffee.

4. Save the document as **Coffee.xml** in the Exercises folder for Chapter 1.

5. Open the **Coffee.xml** document in your Web browser. If you receive any parsing errors, fix them and reopen the document.

 Exercise 1-2

In this exercise, you identify and fix the problems in an XML document that is not well formed.

1. Create a document in your text editor. Type the following XML document, but identify and fix each of the errors that prevent it from being well formed.

```
<?xml version="1.0" standalone="yes"?>
<travel>
    <transportation mode=airplane>
        <destination>Paris</destination>
        <depart_date>June 1</depart_date>
        <carrier company=United>
    <transportation mode=train>
        <destination>New Orleans</destination>
        <depart_date>April 15</depart_date>
        <railroad company=Amtrak>
    <transportation mode=automobile>
        <destination>Vancouver</destination>
        <depart_date>August 3</depart_date>
</travel>
```

2. Save the document as **Travel.xml** in the Exercises folder for Chapter 1.

3. Open the **Travel.xml** document in your Web browser. If you receive any parsing errors, fix them and reopen the document.

Exercise 1-3

In this exercise, you create an XML document that contains airline flight information.

1. Create a new document in your text editor and type the opening XML declaration. Be sure to use all three attributes of the XML declaration.

2. Create a root element named `<airlines>`.

3. Within the `<airlines>` root element, create three nested `<carrier>` elements for three different airlines. Each `<carrier>` element should include a name attribute that stores the name of the airline. You can use fictional or actual airline names.

4. Within each `<carrier>` element, nest at least two `<flight>` elements that contain the following elements: `<departure_city>`, `<destination_city>`, `<flight_number>`, and `<departure_time>`. You can use fictional information for the content of each element.

5. Save the document as **Airlines.xml** in the Exercises folder for Chapter 1.

6. Open the **Airlines.xml** document in your Web browser. If you receive any parsing errors, fix them and reopen the document.

Exercise 1-4

In this exercise, you create an XML document that contains grading information for an elementary school class.

1. Create a new document in your text editor and type the opening XML declaration. Be sure to use all three attributes of the XML declaration.

2. Create a root element named `<report_cards>`.

3. Within the `<report_cards>` root element, create at least three `<student>` elements.

4. Within each `<student>` element, create the following nested elements. Be sure to nest the `<history_grade>`, `<math_grade>`, `<geography_grade>`, and `<english_grade>` elements within the `<grades>` element. Make up fictitious names and grades for at least three students.

```
<name>content</name>
<grades>
      <history_grade>content</history_grade>
      <math_grade>content</math_grade>
      <geography_grade>content</geography_grade>
      <english_grade>content</english_grade>
</grades>
```

5. Save the document as **ReportCards.xml** in the Exercises folder for Chapter 1.

6. Open the **ReportCards.xml** document in your Web browser. If you receive any parsing errors, fix them and then reopen the document.

Discovery Projects

In the following projects, be sure that each XML document includes an XML declaration and is well formed.

Discovery Project 1-1

Create an XML document that contains elements you would find in a business letter. Use a root element named `<business_letter>`. Include elements such as company name, logo, company address, subject, salutation, and body. Nest the recipient's name, title, company name, and address within another element named `<to>`. Also, nest the sender's name and title within another element named `<from>`. Save the document as **Letter.xml** in the Projects folder for Chapter 1.

Discovery Project 1-2

Create an XML version of your resume. Use a root element named `<resume>`. Include elements such as your name, contact information, and objective. Create an `<employment>` element that includes nested `<employer>` elements for each of your former employers. Each `<employer>` element should include nested elements for the following data: employer name, employer location, position held, employment dates, and responsibilities. Also, create an <education> element that includes nested <school> elements for your educational experience. Each <school> element should include the following nested elements: school name, dates attended, and degree obtained. Create any other elements that you deem appropriate, such as <references> or <special_skills>. Save the document as **Resume.xml** in the Projects folder for Chapter 1.

 Discovery Project 1-3

Create an XML document that outlines the table of contents for a software reference manual. You can write the table of contents based on any software with which you are proficient. Use a root element named <reference>. Within the <reference> root element, create a <manual> element that contains the name of the manual along with an <author> element that contains the author name. Also include elements named <chapter> for each chapter of the manual. The <chapter> element should include a number attribute that is assigned the chapter number. Within each <chapter> element, create an empty <name> element that includes a title attribute that is assigned the chapter title. Also, within each <chapter> element, create elements for a chapter summary and for the names of the chapter's major sections. Save the document as **TOC.xml** in the Projects folder for Chapter 1.

Building, Linking, and Publishing Basic Web Pages

In this chapter you will:

◎ Work with basic elements and attributes

◎ Learn how to organize your pages with section and content-grouping elements

◎ Add links to Web pages

◎ Publish Web pages

You were introduced to basic structural elements such as the <head> and <body> elements in Chapter 1, and in this chapter you study them in greater detail. As you work through the chapter, remember that the goal of XHTML is to write Web pages that are well formed and to separate a document's content from the way it is displayed.

In Chapter 1, you also learned that hypertext linking is likely the most important aspect of the Web because it allows you to open other Web pages quickly. So far you have studied only the basic structural requirements for creating the elements and attributes within a single Web page. In this chapter, you will begin expanding the capabilities of your Web pages by learning how to create links. You will also study how to publish your completed Web pages so that others can access them on the Web. Finally, you will learn how to use metadata to provide information to search engines and Web servers about the data in your Web page.

Working with Basic Elements and Attributes

In Chapter 1 you learned that XML defines a tag pair and the data it contains as an element. You can think of elements as the basic building blocks of all HTML pages. All elements must have an opening tag and a closing tag; otherwise, the document is not well formed. The data within an element's opening and closing tags is called the content. In this section, you will learn about the basic elements and attributes that are used with all Web pages. First, you will study the different types of elements.

Understanding the Different Types of Elements

HTML 5 includes many different types of elements that are organized into the categories listed in Table 2-1.

Element Category	Description
Content grouping	Organizes the majority of the content within the various document sections.
Edits	Used for identifying inserted or deleted text on a Web page.
Embedded content	Imports another type of resource, such as a video file, into an HTML document.
Forms	Creates user input fields for gathering data. Form content is contained within the <form> element.

Table 2-1   Element categories *(continues)*

(continued)

Element Category	Description
Interactive	Creates elements for interacting with users, such as a menu element.
Metadata	Refers to data that describes the definition and structure of information. Metadata in HTML is enclosed within the `<head>` element.
Root	Contains all the other elements in a document. The root element for HTML is `<html>`.
Scripting	Used for controlling a Web page with JavaScript or another scripting language. Scripting code is contained within the `<script>` element.
Sections	Used for organizing the primary sections of an HTML document. All section elements are contained within the `<body>` element.
Tables	Organizes content into a tabular format. Table content is contained within the `<table>` element.
Text-level	Describes the format of the text that appears on a Web page. These elements do not appear on their own lines; they appear within the line of the content-grouping element that contains them.

Table 2-1　Element categories

As you progress through this book, you will work with all element categories listed in Table 2-1.

Two basic types of elements can appear within a document's `<body>` element: block-level and inline. **Block-level elements** give a Web page its structure. Most Web browsers render block-level elements so they appear on their own line. Block-level elements can contain other block-level elements or inline elements. The `<p>` element and heading elements (`<h1>`, `<h2>`, and so on) are examples of common block-level elements. **Inline**, or **text-level**, **elements** describe the text that appears on a Web page. Unlike block-level elements, inline elements do not appear on their own lines; they appear within the line of the block-level element that contains them. Examples of inline elements include the `<b>` (bold) and `<br>` (line break) elements.

According to the Strict DTD, inline elements must be placed inside a block-level element; otherwise, your document is not well formed. Additionally, any text displayed by your document must also be placed within a block-level element. For instance, if you attempt to validate a document that contains the following line against the Strict DTD, the document will be declared invalid because the text, `<b>` element, and `<br>` element are not contained within a block-level element:

```
This line contains <b>bold</b> text and <br />
a line break.
```

The code must be contained within a block-level element such as the <p> element.

```
<p>This line contains <b>bold</b> text and <br />
a line break.</p>
```

Next, you will start creating the home page for the Central Valley Farmers' Market Web site. You will create the HTML document using the HTML DTD because you will add some HTML 5 elements to the page later in this chapter. The home page contains general information about the farmers' market, including contact information, hours of operation, and a featured vendors list. You will work on the Central Valley Farmers' Market Web site throughout this chapter to learn how to author well-formed HTML documents.

To start creating the home page for the Central Valley Farmers' Market Web site:

1. Create a new document in your text editor and type the opening <!DOCTYPE> declaration that uses the HTML DTD, as follows:

   ```
   <!DOCTYPE HTML>
   ```

2. Type the <html> element, as follows:

   ```
   <html>
   </html>
   ```

3. Within the <html> element, add the following <head> and <title> elements to the document.

   ```
   <head>
   <title>Central Valley Farmers' Market Web</title>
   </head>
   ```

4. Next, add the following document <body> element within the <html> element:

   ```
   <body>
   </body>
   ```

5. Add the following elements to the document body (between the <body>. . .</body> tags). Notice that the text and inline <b> element are contained within a block-level <p> element.

   ```
   <p>The <b>Central Valley Farmers' Market</b> offers
   plenty of fresh picked fruits, vegetables, herbs,
   and flowers. Local artisans bring wonderful hand-
   made arts and crafts. You will also find lots of
   baked goods, jams, honey, cheeses, and other
   products.</p>
   ```

6. Save the file as **index.html** in your Chapter folder for Chapter 2.

7. Open the **index.html** file in your Web browser. Figure 2-1 displays the file as it appears in Firefox.

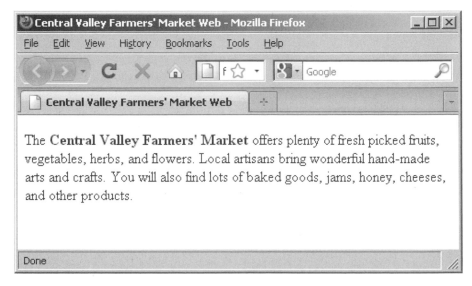

Figure 2-1   Central Valley Farmers' Market home page in Firefox

8. Close your Web browser window.

Working with Attributes

In this section, you will learn how to work with attributes, starting with standard attributes.

Using Standard Attributes

As you learned in Chapter 1, you use various parameters called attributes to configure many elements. You use an equal sign to assign a value to an attribute, and the attribute must be enclosed within quotation marks. You place attributes before the closing bracket of the starting tag, and you separate them from the tag name or other attributes with a space. Many HTML attributes are unique to a specific element or can only be used with certain types of elements. For instance, the src attribute of the <img> element is used for specifying the URL of an image file you want to display. The src attribute is available only for two other elements: <input> and <script>. However, HTML also includes several **standard**, or **common**, **attributes** that are available to almost every element. The standard HTML attributes are listed in Table 2-2.

Attribute	Description
accesskey	Designates a key that visitors can use to select an element
class	Identifies various elements as part of the same group
contenteditable (HTML 5)	Allows users to edit the content of an element
contextmenu (HTML 5)	Specifies an element's context menu
dir	Specifies the direction of text
draggable (HTML 5)	Allows an element to be draggable
hidden (HTML 5)	Determines whether an element is hidden
id	Uniquely identifies an individual element in a document
lang	Specifies the language in which the contents of an element were originally written
spellcheck (HTML 5)	Checks the spelling and grammar of an element's content
style	Defines the style information for a specific element
tabindex	Determines an element's tab order
title	Provides descriptive text for an element

Table 2-2   Standard attributes

Of the HTML 5 attributes listed in Table 2-2, only the contenteditable, draggable, and spellcheck attributes are currently implemented in a Web browser. The contenteditable attribute is available in all current Web browsers; the draggable attribute is available in Firefox, Safari, and Chrome; and the spellcheck attribute is available in Firefox.

Although English is the primary language of the Web, it is certainly not the only language used. To be a considerate resident of the international world of the Web, you should designate the language of your elements using the lang attribute. Be aware that the lang attribute simply states the original language in which an element was written; it is up to the user agent that renders the element to decide what to do with the information.

You will learn how to use the class, id, and style attributes when you study CSS in Chapter 3. You will learn how to use the accesskey attribute when you study forms in Chapter 6. You will learn how to use the draggable attribute when you study JavaScript in Chapter 8.

You assign to the lang attribute a two-letter code that represents a language. For instance, the language code for English is en. Therefore, to assign English as the language for a particular element, you add the attributes lang="en" and xml:lang="en" to the element's opening tag. Table 2-3 lists some other examples of two-letter language codes.

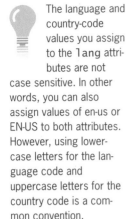

The language and country-code values you assign to the lang attributes are not case sensitive. In other words, you can also assign values of en-us or EN-US to both attributes. However, using lowercase letters for the language code and uppercase letters for the country code is a common convention.

You can find a complete list of language and country codes in the appendices.

Code	Language
af	Afrikaans
el	Greek
fr	French
it	Italian
ja	Japanese
sa	Sanskrit
zh	Chinese

Table 2-3   Examples of two-letter language codes

The language code assigned to the lang attributes can be further defined to specify the language spoken in a particular country if you add a hyphen and a two-letter country code. For instance, the two-letter country code for the United Kingdom is UK. To specify an element's language as the type of English spoken in the United Kingdom, use the attribute lang="en-UK". Similarly, the two-letter country code for the United States is US. Therefore, you can specify an element's language as the type of English spoken in the United States using the attribute lang="en-US".

You must also consider the direction in which a language is read when you define elements. Although you read most Western languages from left to right, languages such as Arabic and Hebrew are read from right to left. For this reason, you should always include the dir attribute along with the lang attribute. You can assign one of two values to the dir attribute: ltr (for left to right) and rtl (for right to left). For Western languages such as English, you assign the dir attribute a value of left to right, as follows: dir="ltr".

Another critical attribute to consider is the title attribute, which provides descriptive text for an element, similar to the text that appears in a Web browser's title bar. With newer Web browsers, the value assigned to the title attribute appears as a ToolTip when you hold your mouse over the element that includes it.

In the following simple HTML document, the <p> element in the body includes the lang attributes to specify French (as it is spoken in France) as the element's language, along with the dir attribute to specify a text direction of left to right. The title attribute in the paragraph includes the English translation of the French phrase

contained within the <p> element. Figure 2-2 shows how the ToolTip
appears in Firefox.

```
<!DOCTYPE HTML>
<html>
<head>
<title>French Phrase</title>
<meta http-equiv="content-type"
    content="text/html; charset=iso-8859-1" />
</head>
<body>
<p title="The English translation of this phrase is↵
    'Those who laugh on Friday will cry on Sunday.'"
lang="fr-FR" xml:lang="fr-FR" dir="ltr">
Ceux qui rient le vendredi, pleureront le
dimanche</p>
</body>
</html>
```

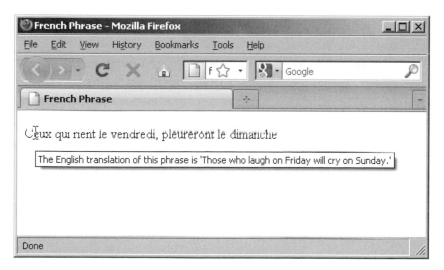

Figure 2-2 HTML document demonstrating the `lang`, `dir`, and `title` attributes

Next, you will add a paragraph containing an Italian phrase to the
Central Valley Farmers' Market home page. You will include the
`lang` attributes in the <p> element to specify Italian as the element's
language. You also will add a `dir` attribute that specifies a text
direction of left to right and a `title` attribute that includes the
English translation of the Italian phrase.

To add standard attributes to the Central Valley Farmers' Market home page:

1. Return to the **index.html** file in your text editor.

2. Just above the closing </body> tag, add the following <p> element that contains the Italian phrase. The <p> element also includes the `lang`, `dir`, and `title` attributes.

   ```
   <p title="What one puts into a dish, one finds!"
   lang="it" dir="ltr"><i>Quello che ci mette, ci
   trova!</i></p>
   ```

3. Save the **index.html** file and then open it in your Web browser. Figure 2-3 displays the index.html file as it appears in Firefox.

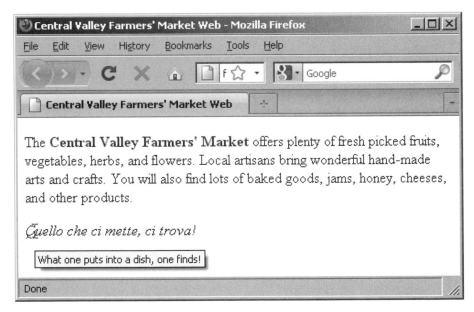

Figure 2-3   Central Valley Farmers' Market home page after adding standard attributes

4. Close your Web browser window.

The `contenteditable` attribute allows users to edit the content of an element; this attribute is currently available in all major Web browsers. As an example of when you would use this attribute, suppose that a user submits a form containing order information. You can use the `contenteditable` attribute to allow users to correct any errors in the data they submitted. By default, elements cannot be edited. To create an editable element, assign a value of true to the contenteditable attribute. The following code demonstrates how to create <span> elements that the user can edit. Figure 2-4 shows the code opened in Firefox with the address portion of the shipping information selected and editable.

```
<p>Please verify your shipping information:</p>
<p><span contenteditable="true">
Don Gosselin</span><br />
<span contenteditable="true">14 West 85th
Street</span><br />
<span contenteditable="true">Brooklyn, NY 10024</p>
```

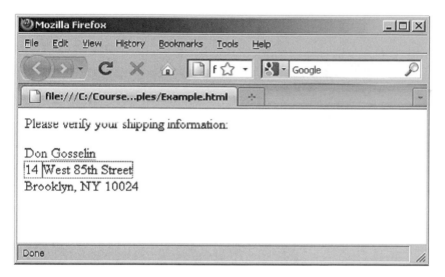

Figure 2-4 Web page with editable elements in Firefox

The spellcheck attribute specifies that the Web browser should check the spelling and grammar of an element's content. This attribute is only partially supported in Firefox. You should be able to turn spell checking on and off for any element by assigning a value of true or false to the spellcheck attribute. However, Firefox does not appear to support this functionality yet. Currently, spell checking is only available when you assign a value of true to the contenteditable attribute. If you right-click a misspelled word in an editable element, a shortcut menu appears and suggests some correct spellings, as shown in Figure 2-5.

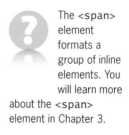

The <span> element formats a group of inline elements. You will learn more about the <span> element in Chapter 3.

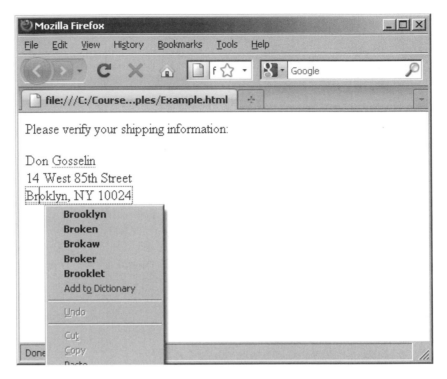

Figure 2-5 Web page with spell-check functionality in Firefox

Defining Boolean Attributes

Several elements in HTML include special Boolean attributes that do not need a value assigned to them. A **Boolean attribute** specifies one of two values: true or false. The presence of a Boolean attribute in an element's opening tag indicates a value of "true", whereas its absence indicates a value of "false". For example, in Chapter 6 you will learn how to use the empty `<input>` element to create a check box control that can be used on a form. In HTML, you can specify that the check box control is selected, or checked, by default by including the Boolean `checked` attribute within the `<input>` element, as follows:

```
<input type="checked" checked />
```

When a Boolean attribute is not assigned a value, as in the preceding code, it is referred to as having a **minimized form**. However, recall from Chapter 1 that all attribute values must appear within quotation marks. This syntax also means that an attribute must be assigned a value. For this reason, minimized Boolean attributes are illegal in HTML. You can still use Boolean attributes in HTML if you use their full form. You create the **full form** of a Boolean attribute by assigning the name of the attribute itself as the attribute's value. For example, to use the `<input>` element's `checked` Boolean attribute in HTML, you use the full form of the attribute as follows:

```
<input type="checked" checked="checked" />
```

Remember that to specify a value of false for a Boolean attribute, you simply exclude the attribute from the element. If you do not want a check box control to be selected by default, for instance, you simply exclude the checked attribute from the <input> element, as follows:

```
<input type="checked" />
```

Short Quiz 1

1. Explain the differences between block-level elements and inline elements.

2. How do you designate the language and text direction of your elements?

3. Explain how to define the minimized and full form of a Boolean attribute.

Organizing with Section and Content-Grouping Elements

Section elements are used for organizing the primary sections of an HTML document. Table 2-4 describes the HTML 5 section elements that are available at the time of this writing.

Element	Description
<address>	Defines contact information, typically for the owner or author of an <article> or <body> element
<article>	Defines a link to external content such as a news article or Web log (blog)
<aside>	Creates content that is related to the surrounding content
<body>	Contains all elements, text, and other content that comprise the document body
<footer>	Defines owner and copyright information for the preceding section
<h1>...<h6>	Defines a document's headings and subheadings
<header>	Defines an introduction to a document or section
<hgroup>	Defines the heading elements for a document or section
<nav>	Defines a navigation section that contains links to other parts of the current page or to other pages
<section>	Organizes a logical group of content, usually with a heading

Table 2-4   HTML 5 section elements

With the exception of the `<h1>`...`<h6>` elements, you can't actually see any of the elements listed in Table 2-4. Instead, their main purpose is to provide a logical order and grouping to the primary parts of a Web page. Although few browsers currently support all of the section elements—and some elements are not yet supported at all—you can still use them to organize your Web pages. However, be sure to use the `<!DOCTYPE HTML>` declaration to ensure that your Web pages validate successfully with the W3C Markup Validation Service.

The main section element is the `<body>` element, which contains all other section elements. Next, you will learn about the other section elements, starting with headings created with the `<h1>`...`<h6>` elements.

Creating Headings

Heading elements are used to emphasize a document's headings and subheadings, which helps provide structure by hierarchically organizing the document's content. XHTML has six heading elements, `<h1>` through `<h6>`. The highest level of importance is `<h1>`, and the lowest is `<h6>`. The following code shows how to create the six heading elements in the document body:

Each heading element is a block-level element.

```
<body>
<h1>Heading 1</h1>
<h2>Heading 2</h2>
<h3>Heading 3</h3>
<h4>Heading 4</h4>
<h5>Heading 5</h5>
<h6>Heading 6</h6>
</body>
```

You should choose a heading element based on how the sections of your document fit together rather than how the headings appear in a Web browser—different user agents render the output of heading elements differently. Although many Web page authors use heading elements as a formatting tool, their real purpose is to provide a way of outlining the content of your document, much as you would create an outline or a table of contents. In those formats you would not use a higher-numbered heading unless it was nested under a lower-numbered heading, but this is not a requirement for writing well-formed HTML documents.

There are several rules of thumb for using headings. Generally, most Web pages should include only a single `<h1>` element as the main heading for a page. You can think of the `<h1>` element as being equivalent to the title of a document, and a document should contain only one title. Second-level headings should use the `<h2>` element, and additional higher-numbered headings should be nested beneath lower-numbered headings. As an example, the following code displays several heading styles associated with a Web page for a flight school named DRG Aviation. The code begins with a single <h1> element that contains the title of the document, "DRG Aviation". A single <h2> element defines a heading named Flight Training. Within the <h2> element are two <h3> elements: Requirements and Flight Experience. Figure 2-6 shows the headings in Firefox.

```
<h1>DRG Aviation</h1>
<h2>Flight Training</h2>
<h3>Requirements</h3>
<p>Applicants need to meet standards in three
separate areas to qualify for FAA pilot
certificates: Flight experience, Flight skill, and
Theoretical understanding.</p>
<h3>Flight Experience</h3>
<p>An applicant for the Private Pilot certificate
must have 40 hours flight time, to include a
minimum of 20 hours dual instruction and 10 hours
solo.</p>
```

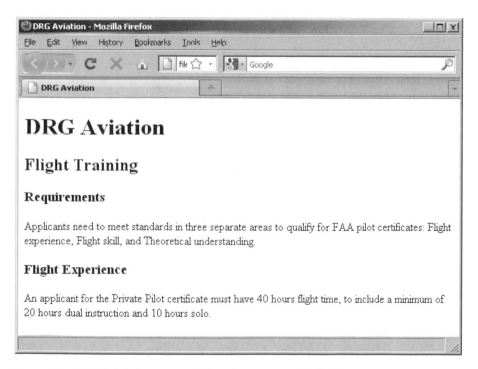

Figure 2-6 DRG Aviation page with heading elements in Firefox

In practice, few Web page authors use heading elements properly. As long as your heading elements are properly constructed, your Web pages will be valid regardless of how they are nested.

Next, you add heading elements to the Central Valley Farmers' Market home page. The file includes a single <h1> element that contains the Web page title "Central Valley Farmers' Market". Major sections of the Web page, such as Hours of Operation and a Featured Vendor List, are contained within <h2> elements. The Featured Vendor List also contains <h3> headings that identify each vendor.

To add heading elements to the Central Valley Farmers' Market home page:

1. Return to the **index.html** file in your text editor.

2. Add the following <h1> and <h2> elements as the first elements in the body section, after the opening <body> tag but before the first <p> tag:

```
<h1>Central Valley Farmers' Market</h1>
<h2>About the Market</h2>
```

3. At the end of the body section, add the following <h2> element that lists the hours of operation:

```
<h2>Hours of Operation</h2>
<p>The Central Valley Farmers' Market is held every
Tuesday, Thursday, and Saturday from April through
October, then Saturdays only in November until
Thanksgiving. The Market is open from 7 a.m.- 1
p.m. <i>The vendors will be there rain or
shine</i>!</p>
```

4. At the end of the body section, add the following <h2> and <h3> elements that list this week's featured vendors:

```
<h2>Featured Vendor List</h2>
<p>Be sure to visit this week's featured
vendors.</p>
<h3>Big Creek Produce</h3>
<p>Offers a diverse selection of produce including
restaurant-quality vegetables and edible flowers.
</p>
<h3>Blue Sky Gardens</h3>
<p>Grows a variety of organic vegetables including
French slenderette green beans, spinach, salad
greens, squash, pumpkins, and cherry tomatoes, as
well as a vast array of fresh-cut and dried
flowers.</p>
<h3>Maple Ridge Farms</h3>
<p>Specializes in organically grown lettuces,
arugula, red mustard, and other greens.</p>
```

```
<h3>Manzi Produce</h3>
<p>Hand picks, hand washes, and hand sorts all of
their products, which include nuts, plants, herbs,
perennials, flowers, wild-gathered items, meat,
fruit, and vegetables.</p>
<h3>Lee Family Farms</h3>
<p>Produces organically grown traditional Asian
vegetables such as bok choy, lemon grass, and hot
chili peppers.</p>
```

5. Save the **index.html** file and open it in your Web browser. Figure 2-7 shows how some of the new headings appear in Firefox.

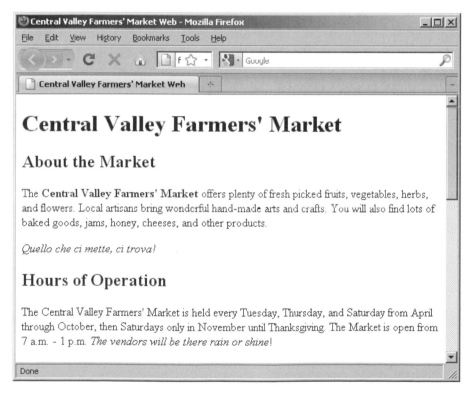

Figure 2-7   Central Valley Farmers' Market home page after adding heading elements

6. Close your Web browser window.

Defining Document Sections (HTML 5)

Sections created with the `<section>` element usually define specific types of organized content such as chapters or other types of logical groupings. The following example demonstrates how to define the Flight Training content as a section of the DRG Aviation page:

```
<section>
<h2>Flight Training</h2>
<h3>Requirements</h3>
<p>Applicants need to meet standards in three
separate areas to qualify for FAA pilot
certificates: Flight experience, Flight skill, and
Theoretical understanding.</p>
<h3>Flight Experience</h3>
<p>An applicant for the Private Pilot certificate
must have 40 hours flight time, to include a
minimum of 20 hours dual instruction and 10 hours
solo.</p>
</section>
```

The `<section>` element is only supported in Safari and Chrome Web browsers.

Note that `<section>` elements are not meant for visually formatting content, but are used to *define* organized types of content. The W3C's rule of thumb is that content should only be enclosed within a `<section>` element if it would appear in the document's table of contents.

One element that is used with the `<section>` element is the `<hgroup>` element, which defines the headings for a document or section. In most cases, you only need to use the `<hgroup>` element for sections that include multiple contiguous headings, such as the Flight Training heading on the DRG Aviation page.

The `<hgroup>` element is not yet supported by any current Web browsers.

```
<section>
<hgroup>
<h2>Flight Training</h2>
<h3>Requirements</h3>
</hgroup>
...
</section>
```

Next, you will add section elements to the Central Valley Farmers' Market home page.

To add section elements to the Farmers' Market home page:

1. Return to the **index.html** file in your text editor.

2. Enclose the Hours of Operation and Featured Vendor List `<h2>` heading elements and the paragraphs that follow them within section elements, as follows:

```
<section>
<h2>Hours of Operation</h2>
<p>The Central Valley Farmers' Market is held every
Tuesday, Thursday, and Saturday from April through
October, then Saturdays only in November until
Thanksgiving. The Market is open from 7 a.m.- 1
p.m. <i>The vendors will be there rain or
shine</i>!</p>
<h2>Featured Vendor List</h2>
<p>Be sure to visit this week's featured
vendors.</p>
</section>
```

3. Enclose the <h3> elements and paragraph elements that follow them in a section element, as follows:

```
<section>
<h3>Big Creek Produce</h3>
<p>Offers a diverse selection of produce including
restaurant-quality vegetables and edible flowers.
</p>
<h3>Blue Sky Gardens</h3>
<p>Grows a variety of organic vegetables including
French slenderette green beans, spinach, salad
greens, squash, pumpkins, and cherry tomatoes, as
well as a vast array of fresh-cut and dried
flowers.</p>
. . .
</section>
```

4. Save the **index.html** file and open it in your Web browser. The page should look the same as it did before you added the section elements.

5. Close your Web browser window.

Working with Headers and Footers (HTML 5)

The <header> and <footer> elements are not yet supported by any current Web browsers.

A **header** section defines an introduction to a document or section. A **footer section** usually is placed immediately after a section element and contains information about that section, such as when it was created or last updated, the author, and copyright information.

The following example of the DRG Aviation page demonstrates how to use header and footer sections. In this case, the header contains the <h1> element and introductory text that explains the goal of flight training. The footer contains copyright information.

```
<header>
<h1>DRG Aviation</h1>
<p>The goal of flight training is to earn your
Private Pilot Certificate, which permits you to fly
a wide variety of aircraft and to carry passengers
virtually anywhere. New Private Pilots are
restricted from flying in non-visual conditions
(clouds and other "bad" weather).</p>
</header>
<section>
<hgroup>
<h2>Flight Training</h2>
<h3>Requirements</h3>
</hgroup>
<p>Applicants need to meet standards in three
separate areas to qualify for FAA pilot
certificates: Flight experience, Flight skill, and
Theoretical understanding.</p>
```

77

```
<h3>Flight Experience</h3>
<p>An applicant for the Private Pilot certificate
must have 40 hours flight time, to include a
minimum of 20 hours dual instruction and 10 hours
solo.</p>
</section>
<footer>Copyright 2011 DRG Aviation. All rights
reserved.</footer>
```

Next, you will add header and footer elements to the Central Valley Farmers' Market home page.

To add header and footer elements to the Farmers' Market home page:

1. Return to the **index.html** file in your text editor.

2. Enclose the first <h2> heading elements and the two paragraphs that follow them in a header element, as follows:

```
<header>
<h2>About the Market</h2>
<p>The <b>Central Valley Farmers' Market</b> offers
plenty of fresh picked fruits, vegetables, herbs,
and flowers. Local artisans bring wonderful hand-
made arts and crafts. You will also find lots of
baked goods, jams, honey, cheeses, and other
products.</p>
<p title="What one puts into a dish, one finds!"
lang="it" dir="ltr"><i>Quello che ci
mette, ci trova!</i></p>
</header>
```

3. Add the following footer element to the end of the document body:

```
<footer>Copyright 2011 Central Valley Farmers'
Market. All rights reserved.</footer>
```

4. Save the **index.html** file.

Linking to External Articles (HTML 5)

The <article> element is only supported in Safari and Chrome.

The <article> element defines a link to external content such as a news article or Web log (blog). Although there are no requirements for what you place in an <article> element, it should normally include a brief description of the article, a link to the external URL, and the date of publication.

The following code contains an <article> element that links to the Airplane Flying Handbook, which is published by the FAA. Figure 2-8 shows how the element appears on the DRG Aviation page in Google Chrome.

```
<article cite="http://www.faa.gov/library/manuals/ ↵
    aircraft/airplane_handbook/" pubdate="2004">
<p><a href="http://www.faa.gov/library/manuals/↵
    aircraft/airplane_handbook/">Airplane Flying
Handbook</a>, published by the FAA.<br />
Last updated: 12:55PM EST August 16, 2005.</p>
</article>
```

79

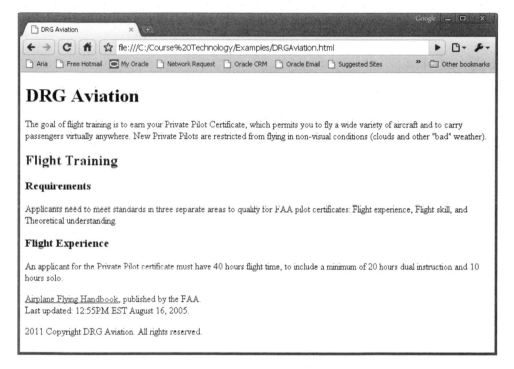

DRG Aviation

The goal of flight training is to earn your Private Pilot Certificate, which permits you to fly a wide variety of aircraft and to carry passengers virtually anywhere. New Private Pilots are restricted from flying in non-visual conditions (clouds and other "bad" weather).

Flight Training

Requirements

Applicants need to meet standards in three separate areas to qualify for FAA pilot certificates: Flight experience, Flight skill, and Theoretical understanding.

Flight Experience

An applicant for the Private Pilot certificate must have 40 hours flight time, to include a minimum of 20 hours dual instruction and 10 hours solo.

Airplane Flying Handbook, published by the FAA.
Last updated: 12:55PM EST August 16, 2005.

2011 Copyright DRG Aviation. All rights reserved.

Figure 2-8   DRG Aviation page with an article element in Google Chrome

Defining Addresses

The <address> element defines contact information, typically for the owner or author of an <article> or <body> element. This element should not describe a postal address unless it is part of the actual contact information. Instead, the <address> element should define an e-mail address or Web page of the owner or author. Typically, the <address> element is placed within a <footer> element.

The following code shows an <address> element in the <footer> element on the DRG Aviation page.

```
...
<footer>Copyright 2011 DRG Aviation. All rights
reserved. <address>DRG Aviation.
(707) 555-1212.</address></footer>
</body>
</html>
```

 Most Web browsers render the <address> element in italics, with a line break before and after the element.

Next, you will add an address to the footer element of the Central Valley Farmers' Market home page.

To add an address to the footer element of the Farmers' Market home page:

1. Return to the **index.html** file in your text editor.

2. Add an address element to the footer element, as follows:

```
<footer>Copyright 2011 Central Valley Farmers'
Market. All rights reserved.
<address>CVFM Inc. (650) 777-1234.</address>
</footer>
```

3. Save the **index.html** file and open it in your Web browser. Figure 2-9 shows how the footer appears in Firefox.

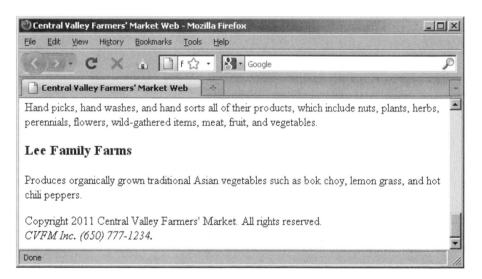

Figure 2-9   Central Valley Farmers' Market home page with footer and address elements

4. Close your Web browser window.

Grouping Navigation Elements (HTML 5)

You use the <nav> element to define a navigation section that contains links to other parts of the current page or to other pages. Any major navigation blocks should be placed inside the <nav> element. For example, the following code demonstrates how to create a navigation section for the DRG Aviation page. Figure 2-10 shows the output in Firefox.

```
. . .
<body>
<nav><a href="index.html">Home</a> 
<a href="training.html">Training</a> 
<a href="charter.html">Charters</a> 
<a href="contact.html">Contact Info</a> 
<a href="about.html">About</a></nav>
<header>
<h1>DRG Aviation</h1>
. . .
```

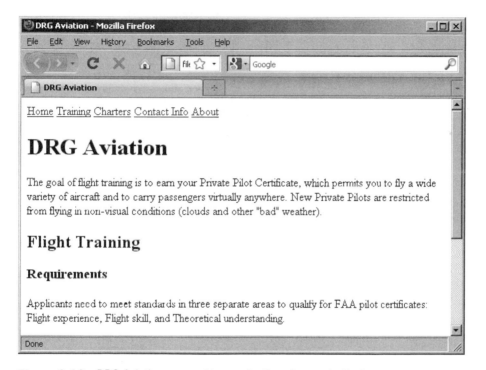

Figure 2-10 DRG Aviation page with a navigation element in Firefox

 Footers often contain links to other pages on a Web site. If you include a list of navigation links in your footers, you do not need to use the `<nav>` element because the `<footer>` element is sufficient for organizing the links.

 The `<nav>` element is only supported in Safari and Chrome Web browsers.

You will add a navigation element to the Central Valley Farmers' Market home page later in this chapter.

Creating Asides (HTML 5)

An aside refers to a comment or remark about the main theme or topic. You can use the `<aside>` element to create content that is related to the surrounding content. The following example demonstrates how to create an aside for the DRG Aviation page. Figure 2-11 shows the output in Firefox.

```
. . .
<h3>Flight Experience</h3>
<p>An applicant for the Private Pilot certificate
must have 40 hours flight time, to include a minimum
of 20 hours dual instruction and 10 hours solo.</p>
</section>
<aside><strong>Although the FAA requires 40 hours of
flight time to apply for the Private Pilot
certificate, most students take almost 100 hours of
instruction before they apply.</strong></aside>
. . .
```

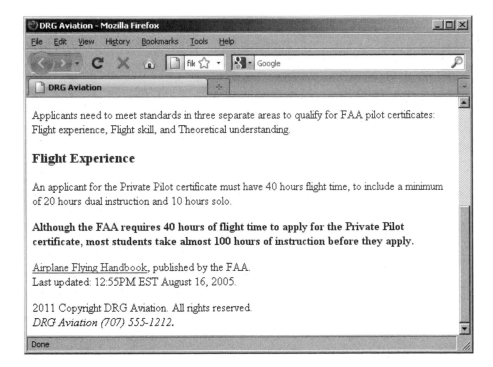

Figure 2-11   DRG Aviation page with an aside in Firefox

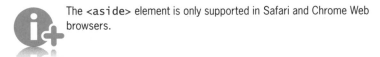

The <aside> element is only supported in Safari and Chrome Web browsers.

Working with Content-Grouping Elements

Content-grouping elements organize the majority of the content within the various document sections. Table 2-5 describes the available content-grouping elements.

Element	Description
`<blockquote>`	Defines long quotations
` `	Inserts a line break
`<dd>`	Creates an inline element that defines a definition list item
`<div>`	Formats a group of block-level and inline elements with styles
`<dl>`	Defines a block-level element that creates a definition list
`<dt>`	Creates an inline element that defines a definition list term
`<hr />`	Inserts a horizontal rule
`<li>`	Identifies an item within an ordered or unordered list
`<ol>`	Creates an ordered list
`<p>`	Creates a paragraph element
`<pre>`	Tells a Web browser that text and line breaks contained between the opening and closing tag must be rendered exactly as they appear
`<ul>`	Creates an unordered list

Table 2-5   Content-grouping elements

Basic body elements such as the `<p>` and `<br />` elements are some of the most frequently used elements in Web page authoring. In this section, you will study paragraphs, line breaks, and horizontal rules.

Paragraphs and Line Breaks

The paragraph (`<p>`) and line-break (`<br />`) elements provide the simplest way of adding white space to a document. **White space** is an important design element that refers to the empty areas on a page. It makes a page easier to read and enhances visual appeal. Beginning Web page authors are often tempted to pack each page with as much information as possible, but experienced authors know that white space is critical to the success both of Web pages and traditional printed pages. However, you cannot add white space to a Web page simply by including spaces or carriage returns in a document. As you learned in Chapter 1, most Web browsers ignore multiple, contiguous spaces on a Web page and replace them with a single space. Web browsers also ignore carriage returns. For instance, the following code shows the exotic animals example you saw in Chapter 1. Although the document body is properly formed because the content is contained within a `<p>` element, the browser runs the lines together because the carriage returns that separate the lines are ignored by Web browsers, as Figure 2-12 shows in Firefox.

```
<body>
<p><b>Llamas</b> are from South America,
<b>kangaroos</b> are from Australia,
and <b>pandas</b> are from China.</p>
</body>
```

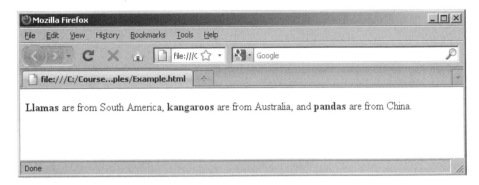

Figure 2-12   Paragraph without line breaks in Firefox

To enable the line breaks to be rendered by the browser, you must add <br /> elements. Figure 2-13 shows how a Web browser renders the following code.

```
<body>
<p><b>Llamas</b> are from South America, <br />
<b>kangaroos</b> are from Australia, <br />
and <b>pandas</b> are from China.</p>
</body>
```

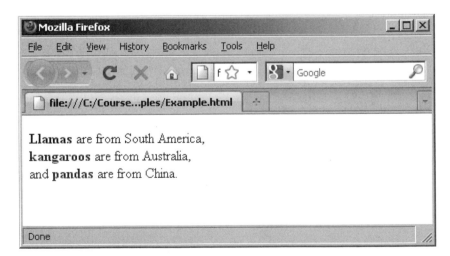

Figure 2-13   Paragraph with line breaks in Firefox

Notice that the <br /> element only inserts a line break in an existing paragraph. To create separate paragraphs, the content for each paragraph must exist within its own <p> element. The following code shows a modified version of the Exotic Animals page that includes three separate paragraphs. Figure 2-14 shows the output. Notice the additional white space between the lines when they are enclosed in paragraph elements, compared with when each line ends in a <br /> element. The <br /> element simply creates a new line within the current paragraph. In comparison, the <p> element creates individual paragraphs that are separated by a single line.

```
<body>
<p><b>Llamas</b> are from South America.</p>
<p><b>Kangaroos</b> are from Australia.</p>
<p><b>Pandas</b> are from China.</p>
</body>
```

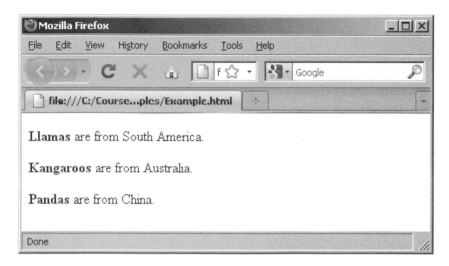

Figure 2-14 Separate paragraphs in Firefox

 Remember that because the <br /> element is an inline element, it must be placed within a block-level element such as the <p> element.

Horizontal Rules

The empty **horizontal-rule (<hr />) element** draws a horizontal rule on a Web page to act as a section divider. Horizontal rules are useful visual elements for breaking up long documents. Although the <hr /> element is technically a block-level element, it cannot contain any content because it is an empty element. However, because it is a block-level element, it can exist on its own line in the document body without being contained within another block-level element.

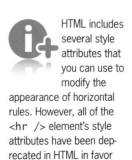 HTML includes several style attributes that you can use to modify the appearance of horizontal rules. However, all of the <hr /> element's style attributes have been deprecated in HTML in favor of CSS.

The following document body includes an example of a horizontal rule:

```
<body>
<p>The following element is a horizontal rule.</p>
<hr />
</body>
```

Next, you add horizontal rules to the Central Valley Farmers' Market home page.

To add horizontal rules to the Farmers' Market home page:

1. Return to the **index.html** file in your text editor.

2. Add horizontal rules above each of the <h2> elements. You should add three <hr /> elements in all.

3. Save the **index.html** file and open it in your Web browser. Figure 2-15 shows how the horizontal rules appear above the About the Market and Hours of Operation headings.

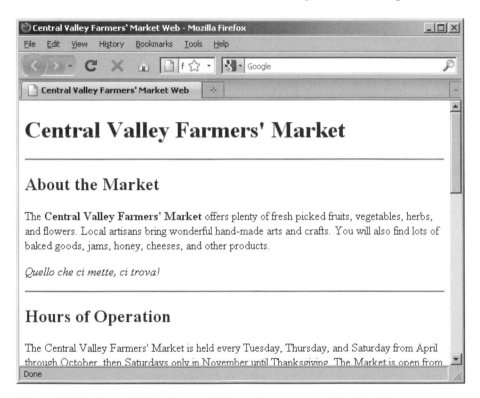

Figure 2-15   Central Valley Farmers' Market home page with horizontal rules

4. Close your Web browser window.

Short Quiz 2

1. Explain how you should use heading elements in your documents.

2. Why should you use <section>, <header>, and <footer> elements in your Web pages?

3. What type of content should you normally place inside an <article> element?

4. How do you define a navigation section that contains links to other parts of the current page or to other pages?

5. What is white space and why is it important to Web page design?

Linking and Publishing Your Web Pages

Almost every Web page contains hypertext links, which are used to open files or navigate to other documents on the Web. You activate a hypertext link by clicking it with your mouse button. A hypertext link in an HTML document is underlined and often displayed in a vivid color. A hypertext link uses text to describe the target of the link; you can click the text to move to the link's target. The target of a link can be another location on the same Web page, an external Web page, an image, or some other type of document. Other types of elements, such as images, can also be hypertext links to other Web pages, images, or files. The text or image used to represent a link on a Web page is called an **anchor**.

Different Web browsers use different default colors for visited and unvisited links. You can change the default link colors on a Web page by using Cascading Style Sheets (CSS).

You create a basic hypertext link using the **<a> element** (the *a* stands for anchor). Although you can use a variety of attributes with the <a> element, the most common one is the href (for hypertext reference) attribute, which specifies the link's target URL. The following code shows how to use the <a> element to create a link to the W3C Markup Validation Service. Figure 2-16 shows the output in Internet Explorer.

```
<p>To validate your HTML documents, visit the
<a href="http://validator.w3.org/">
W3C Markup Validation Service</a>.</p>
```

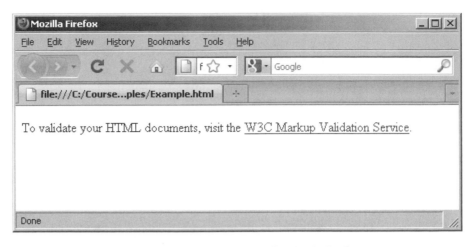

Figure 2-16   Link to the W3C Markup Validation Service in Firefox

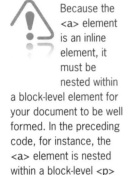

Because the <a> element is an inline element, it must be nested within a block-level element for your document to be well formed. In the preceding code, for instance, the <a> element is nested within a block-level <p> element.

When you write the descriptive content that will be used as the text for a link, be sure to clearly describe the target of the link. The preceding code, for instance, uses *W3C Markup Validation Service* as the descriptive text for a link. It is considered bad form to use text such as *click* or *click here* as the descriptive text, as shown in the following example:

```
<p>To validate your HTML documents,
<a href="http://validator.w3.org/">
click here</a> to visit the W3C Markup Validation
Service</p>
```

You can easily use an image as a link anchor by replacing the content of an <a> element with a nested <img> element. For instance, the following code creates the image link shown in Figure 2-17. Notice that the link consists of both descriptive text and an image file. Although descriptive text is not required when you create an image link, the text can make it easier for users to identify the image links on your Web page.

```
<p><a href="Noah.html"><img src="Noah.jpg"
height="120" width="120" /><br />
Click the image to open Noah's Web page</a></p>
```

Figure 2-17 Web page with an image link

You may have seen many types of hypertext links represented by images in the form of buttons. For instance, the Gosselin Motors Web page shown in Figure 2-18 allows users to find more information about a particular model of automobile by clicking its image link. These image links are quite effective, and help make a well-designed Web page.

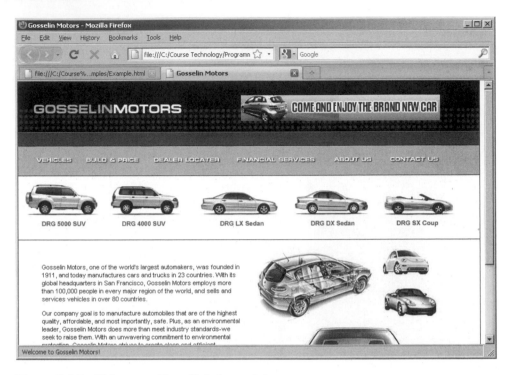

Figure 2-18   Web page with multiple image links

Using images for links is not always necessary; basic text links, if properly placed on a Web page, can be just as effective. Plus, creating a text-based hyperlink takes much less time than designing an image to use as a hyperlink. To see how effective basic text links can be, look at a page from the popular eBay online auction site, shown in Figure 2-19. eBay constantly revises its links to represent an ever-changing variety of merchandise. To create (or even locate) new images for eBay's many items would be incredibly time-consuming and cost-inefficient. As shown in Figure 2-19, even the home page contains many text-based hyperlinks that represent various categories or items currently offered as specials. Also notice, however, that the page includes images for links that do not change frequently, such as the Sign In and Registration buttons, and images for various types of products.

Figure 2-19   Link examples on eBay

Next, you will add a contact information page to the Central Valley
Farmers' Market Web site that users will access from the home page
via a text link.

**To add a contact information page to the Farmers' Market
Web site:**

1. Create a new document in your text editor.

2. Type the `<!DOCTYPE>` declaration, `<html>` element, docu-
    ment head, and the `<body>` element. Use the HTML DTD and
    "Contact Information for the Central Valley Farmers' Market"
    as the content of the `<title>` element. Your document should
    appear as follows:

    ```
    <!DOCTYPE HTML>
    <html>
    <head>
    <title>Contact Information for the Central Valley
    Farmers' Market</title>
    </head>
    ```

```
<body>
</body>
</html>
```

3. In the document body, add the following headings and address element that list the contact information for the Central Valley Farmers' Market.

```
<h1>Central Valley Farmers' Market</h1>
<h2>Contact Information</h2>
<address>
<p>If you have any questions or concerns about the
Central Valley Farmers' Market, please call (908)
626-3764.<br />
You can also send mail to the Central Valley
Farmers' Market at the following address:</p>
<p>P.O. Box 135<br />
Central Valley, CA 94359</p>
</address>
```

4. At the end of the body section, add the following statement that creates a link back to the home page for the Central Valley Farmers' Market:

```
<p><a href="index.html">Home</a></p>
```

5. Save the file as **contact.html** in your Chapter folder for Chapter 2.

Next, you add a link from the Central Valley Farmers' Market home page to the contact information page.

To add a link from the Farmers' Market home page to the contact information page:

1. Return to the **index.html** file in your text editor.

2. Place the insertion point after the closing </h1> tag, press **Enter**, and then type the following elements that create a link to the contact.html document:

```
<p><a href="contact.html">Contact
Information</a></p>
```

3. Save the **index.html** file, and then open it in a Web browser and click the **Contact Information** link. The contact.html file should open in your browser window.

4. Click the **Home** link to return to the home page for the Central Valley Farmers' Market.

5. Close your Web browser window.

To better understand how to work with hypertext links, you need to understand more about URLs, which you will study next.

Understanding Uniform Resource Locators

As you learned in Chapter 1, a Web page is identified by a unique address called the Uniform Resource Locator (URL). A Web page's URL is similar to a telephone number. Each URL consists of two basic parts: a protocol (usually Hypertext Transfer Protocol, or HTTP) and either the domain name for a Web server or a Web server's Internet Protocol (IP) address. **Hypertext Transfer Protocol (HTTP)** manages the hypertext links that are used to navigate the Web. HTTP ensures that Web browsers correctly process and display the various types of information contained in Web pages (text, graphics, audio, and so on). The protocol portion of a URL is followed by a colon, two forward slashes, and a host. A **host** refers to a computer system that is being accessed by a remote computer. The host portion of a URL is usually *www* for "World Wide Web." A **domain name** is a unique address used for identifying a computer (often a Web server) on the Internet. The domain name consists of two parts separated by a period. The first part of a domain name is usually text that easily identifies a person or an organization, such as DonGosselin or Course. The last part of a domain name, known as the **domain identifier**, identifies the type of institution or organization. Common domain identifiers include .biz, .com, .edu, .info, .net, .org, .gov, .mil, and .int. Each domain identifier briefly describes the type of business or organization it represents. For instance, .com (for *company*) represents private companies, .gov (for *government*) represents government agencies, and .edu (for *educational*) represents educational institutions. Therefore, the domain name consists of descriptive text for the Web site, combined with the domain identifier. For example, oracle.com is the domain name for Oracle Corporation. An entire URL would be http://www.oracle.com.

An Internet Protocol, or IP, address is another way to uniquely identify computers or devices connected to the Internet. An IP address consists of four groups of numbers separated by periods. Each Internet domain name is associated with a unique IP address.

In a URL, a specific filename—or a combination of directories and a filename—can follow the domain name or IP address. If the URL does not specify a filename, the requesting Web server looks for a default Web page located in the root or specified directory. Default Web pages usually have names similar to index.html or default.html. For instance, if you enter *www.howstuffworks.com* in your browser's Address box, the Web server automatically opens a file named index.htm.

When a URL does not specify a filename, the index.html file or other file that opens automatically may not appear in your Address box after the document renders.

Although HTTP is probably the most widely used protocol on the Internet, it is not the only one. Another common protocol is Hypertext Transfer Protocol Secure (HTTPS), which provides secure Internet connections used in Web-based financial transactions and other types of communication that require security and privacy. For instance, to use a Web browser to view your account information through Wells Fargo bank, you need to access the following URL:

```
https://banking.wellsfargo.com/
```

Notice that the preceding URL uses the HTTPS protocol. You can either enter this URL in the Address box of your browser window or use it in a link, as follows:

```
<p><a href="https://banking.wellsfargo.com/">
Wells Fargo Online Banking
</a></p>
```

Table 2-6 lists additional protocols that are used with links.

Note that the file:/// protocol is followed by three slashes, not two.

Protocol	Description
file:///	Accesses a file from a local hard drive
ftp://	Accesses a file from a File Transfer Protocol (FTP) server
gopher://	Accesses a file from a Gopher server
telnet://	Connects a computer to a network server

Table 2-6   Common protocols used with links

Unlike other protocols, the `mailto` and `news` protocols are followed only by a colon. The `mailto` protocol is most frequently used in links to provide a quick way to send an e-mail message to a specified address. The syntax for using the `mailto` protocol is mailto:*name@domain*.com. Using this syntax with an `<a>` element, you could create a link in the following statement that sends an e-mail to the President of the United States:

```
<p><a href="mailto:president@whitehouse.gov">
Send a message to the president</a></p>
```

Next, you will add a `mailto` link to the Central Valley Farmers' Market contact page.

To add a `mailto` link to the Farmers' Market contact page:

1. Return to the **contact.html** file in your text editor.

2. Place the insertion point above the closing `</address>` tag, press **Enter**, and then add the following statement that creates a `mailto` link. Be sure to enter your e-mail address.

   ```
   <p>You can send an e-mail to
   <a href="mailto:your_email_address">
   Your e-mail address</a>.</p>
   ```

3. Save the **contact.html** file, and then open the **index.html** file in Internet Explorer. Click the **Contact Information** link, then click the mailto link on the contact.html page and try sending yourself an e-mail message.

4. Close your Web browser window.

Working with Absolute and Relative Links

An anchor uses the URL to specify the name and location of a Web page. You can use two types of URLs on a Web page: absolute and relative. An **absolute URL** refers to the full Web address of a Web page or to a specific drive and directory. The following elements display an anchor and contain an absolute reference to a Web page named index.html.

```
<p><a href="http://www.aaai.org/index.html">
American Association for Artificial Intelligence
(AAAI)</a></p>
```

An absolute URL can also refer to a file on a local computer, as in the following code.

```
<p><a href="c:\MyWebPages\HomePage.html">
My Web Site</a></p>
```

A **relative URL** specifies the location of a file relative to the location of the currently loaded Web page. You use relative URLs to load Web pages located on the same computer as the currently displayed Web page. If the currently displayed Web page is located at *www. MyWebSite.com/WebPages*, then the following relative URL looks in the WebPages folder for the AnotherWebPage.html file:

```
<p><a href="AnotherWebPage.html">
Another Web Page</a></p>
```

You can also use a URL that locates subfolders that are relative to the location of the current Web page folder. In the following example, the link opens a Web page named YetAnotherWebPage.html from the MoreWebPages subfolder within the current folder:

```
<p><a href="MoreWebPages/YetAnotherWebPage.html">
Yet Another Web Page</a></p>
```

When all of your documents are in the same folder, relative URLs are convenient because you do not have to include the entire location of each file. In addition, if you rename the folder that contains the primary document and linked documents or move the folder to a different computer, you do not have to update the location of relative URLs. For example, suppose you have a primary document that contains 10 links to documents located in the same directory. If you move the primary document and the 10 linked documents to a new location, you do not have to update the relative links. However, if you created each of the 10 links as absolute URLs, you would need to update each URL before the links would function properly.

Linking Within the Same Web Page

The <a> element can create either a link to another document or to a bookmark within the current document. **Bookmarks** are internal links within the current document and can be an effective tool for helping users navigate through a long Web page. For instance, examine the Web page shown in Figure 2-20, which displays a portion of a Wikipedia page for HTML 5. In the Contents section of the page, you can see a group of text links to other bookmarks (internal links) within the current document. These internal links make it much easier for visitors to navigate through the Web page's contents.

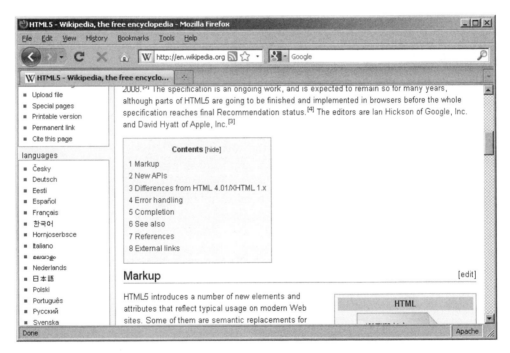

Figure 2-20   Wikipedia's HTML 5 page with internal links

You create bookmark links by using the id attribute. Recall that the standard id attribute uniquely identifies an individual element in a document. Any element that includes an id attribute can be the target of a link. For instance, you may have a long Web page with an <h2> element near the bottom that reads "Summary of

Qualifications". To create the element with an `id` attribute of sq1, you use the following statement:

```
<h2 id="sq1">Summary of Qualifications</h2>
```

To create a bookmark, you assign an id value to the `href` attribute of an `<a>` element, preceded by the # sign. For instance, to create a bookmark to the `<h2>` element with the `id` of sq1, you use the following statement:

```
<p><a href="#sq1">
Read the Summary of Qualifications</a></p>
```

To create a bookmark to any other element, including heading elements, you nest an `<a>` element inside another element. If an `<a>` element does not include an `href` attribute (it shouldn't when you are creating a bookmark), its contents are treated as normal text and are subject to the rules of the parent element. Therefore, if the content of an `<a>` element does not include an `href` attribute and is nested inside a heading element, it will be formatted in a browser with the style of the parent heading element. Use the following statement to create the `<h2>` element with the `id` of sq1 so it will function both in older and new browsers:

```
<h2><a id="sq1">
Summary of Qualifications</a></h2>
```

Next, you will create bookmarks on the Central Valley Farmers' Market home page by adding links to the `<h2>` elements. The bookmarks will allow visitors to quickly jump from the top of the index.html file to the About the Market, Hours of Operation, and Featured Vendor List headings.

To add links to the `<h2>` elements on the Farmers' Market home page:

1. Return to the **index.html** file in your text editor.

2. Place the insertion point after the closing `</p>` tag in the statement that creates the Contact Information link, press **Enter**, and then add the following bookmark links to the document's heading level 2 elements. Also, enclose all four paragraphs in a `<nav>` section.

    ```
    <nav>
    <p><a href="contact.html">Contact
    Information</a></p>
    <p><a href="#am1">About the Market</a></p>
    <p><a href="#ho1">Hours of Operation</a></p>
    <p><a href="#fvl1">Featured Vendor List</a></p>
    </nav>
    ```

3. Modify the About the Market heading element so it includes an <a> element with the same id attribute that you added to the bookmark element:

   `<h2><a id="am1">About the Market</a></h2>`

4. Modify the Hours of Operation heading element so it includes an <a> element with the same id attribute that you added to the bookmark element:

   `<h2><a id="ho1">Hours of Operation</a></h2>`

5. Modify the Featured Vendor List heading element so it includes an <a> element with the same id attribute that you added to the bookmark element:

   `<h2><a id="fvl1">Featured Vendor List</a></h2>`

6. Save the **index.html** file, and then open it in a Web browser and test the new links. Figure 2-21 shows how the new bookmark links should appear.

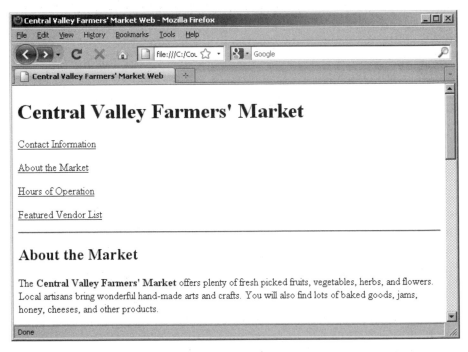

Figure 2-21   Bookmark links on the Central Valley Farmers' Market home page

7. Close your Web browser window.

Publishing Your Web Pages

Before you publish your Web pages, you need to decide where the Web site will be hosted, create and register a domain name for the site, and post the files via FTP to the Web server. The process of publishing Web pages is often confusing for new Web authors. **Web hosting** refers to the publication of a Web site for public access. You can use your own computer to host your Web site, provided it is connected to the Internet. However, using your own computer is usually not a good idea for several reasons. First, hosting a Web site involves many security and maintenance issues and may require skills and time you do not have. Second, the speed of your Internet access is a significant factor. Although broadband Internet access is still growing in the form of cable modems, digital subscriber lines (DSL), and satellite systems, some users still access the Internet through slower dial-up modems. If you use a dial-up modem, your Internet connection will have nowhere near enough speed to allow multiple users to access a Web site hosted on your computer. A final consideration is the speed of your computer. Even if you have a state-of-the-art desktop computer, it will probably still be slower than a professional-strength **Web server**, which is a special type of computer used for hosting Web sites.

Most people use an Internet Service Provider to host their Web sites. An **Internet Service Provider (ISP)** provides access to the Internet and other types of services, including e-mail. Some of the more popular ISPs include Yahoo!, Google, America Online, and EarthLink, although many others exist. Almost every ISP offers Web site hosting. Often, an account with an ISP such as America Online automatically includes a limited amount of Web server space (usually 5-10 megabytes) that you can use to host your Web site. Check with your ISP to find out if your account includes Web hosting.

Having an ISP host your Web site offers many advantages. Most ISPs have extremely fast Internet connections using advanced fiber optics that are far more powerful than a dial-up modem. ISPs also have large and powerful Web servers, along with the expertise and manpower to maintain and manage them. Using a professional Web hosting service allows you to concentrate on authoring your Web pages without having to worry about the requirements of hosting.

Registering Domain Names

Choosing a domain name for your site is an important decision. You should pick a name that is close to your business name or that describes your Web site. However, you cannot choose a domain name that is already in use, such as microsoft.com or harvard.edu. Also, you cannot use a domain name that infringes on another company's trademarked brand name.

To find out if a domain name is available and register it, you must contact a **domain name registrar**. Domain names are stored in a master database that is maintained by **InterNIC**, the organization responsible for the registration of domain names and IP addresses.

Any computer can act as a Web server, although special types of computers with extremely large hard drives and memory are specifically designed for that purpose.

99

Five to ten megabytes is not enough storage space to host professional Web sites. However, you may find this amount of storage space sufficient to create a personal Web site with a limited number of pages.

You can find a comprehensive list of ISPs at *www.thelist.com*.

You can view a list of InterNIC-accredited domain name registrars at *www.internic.net/alpha.html*.

Any domain name registrar that is accredited by InterNIC is permitted to access and modify the master domain name database. A domain name registrar's Web site helps you search the database to find out if your proposed domain name is available. If it is, for a fee the registrar will help you register the domain name for a specified period of time (usually one to two years).

Once you register your domain name, you need to notify your ISP of your domain information. Usually, it is easiest to register your domain name through the ISP you intend to use (assuming they are a domain name registrar) because they can automatically set up the domain for you. If you have an existing domain that you want to transfer to another ISP, or if you register your domain name with a different registrar, your ISP usually has a form or some other procedure to help you transfer your domain.

Advertising Your Web Site

Another option is to use a commercial service that automatically submits your site to multiple search engines for a fee. One service promises to submit your Web site to more than 1000 search engines. However, most people could probably not name 10 search engines. Rather than spending money, you may want to submit your site to the most popular search engines yourself.

You are undoubtedly familiar with Web sites such as Yahoo! and Google that help you locate Web sites that match search criteria. To draw visitors to your Web site, your best bet is to get listed on these search sites. Two types of sites allow users to search for Web pages: Web directories and search engines. **Web directories** are listings of Web sites that have been manually compiled. **Search engines** use software to "crawl" or "spider" their way through the Web and automatically compile an index of Web sites. Yahoo! is an example of a manually compiled Web directory, and HotBot is a search engine that finds Web sites automatically.

If you publish your Web site and do nothing else, most search engines will eventually find it. Directories may also find your site, although it may take some time. Waiting for search engines and directories to come to you, however, is not the best way of advertising your site. Your best bet is to submit your site to a search engine or Web directory when you first publish the site or whenever you make major changes to it. Most search engines and directories have a button that allows you to submit a site. For instance, AltaVista's tools page at *www.altavista.com/web/tools* includes a Submit A Site link at the bottom of the page.

A Web site you might find useful is Search Engine Watch at *www.searchenginewatch.com*. Search Engine Watch monitors and provides information about search engines and directories, and it lists the major search engines in various categories.

Manually compiled directories such as Yahoo! require that you include a description of your Web site when you submit it. In comparison, a search engine's "spider" (or "crawler" or "robot") will visit a Web page on the site, record information about the page in an index, and then follow any links to other pages within the site and index their information. The spider will revisit the site on a regular basis to see if its information has changed. The search engine relies on special software to sort through the information indexed by the spider and return a set of results to a user. The information that a spider indexes about a Web page varies by search engine. Some search engines index the entire page or only the first few lines of a page. Other search engines rely on a Web page's metadata.

Understanding Metadata

The term **metadata** refers to data that describes the definition and structure of information. Metadata in HTML is enclosed within the <head> element. In a Web page, you use the <meta> element to inform search engines and Web servers about the information in your Web page. You must place the <meta> element within the <head> element. You can use three primary attributes with the <meta> element: name, content, and http-equiv. You use the content attribute to provide information that is required by both the name and http-equiv attributes. Therefore, the only required attribute in the <meta> element is the content attribute.

Defining the name Attribute

You use the **name attribute** to define a name for the information you want to provide about the Web page. You can use any text you want as the value of the name attribute. For instance, you may want to include a <meta> element that contains the author of the document and copyright information about it. To do this, you create two <meta> elements in a document's head. You would assign a value of "author" to the name attribute in the first <meta> element and a value of "copyright" to the name attribute in the second <meta> element. Both elements must include a content attribute that contains the associated value for each name attribute. The following statements illustrate this use of the <meta> element:

```
<html lang="EN" xml:lang="EN" dir="ltr">
<head>
<title>Publishing Information</title>
<meta name="author" content="Don Gosselin" />
<meta name="copyright"
content="(c) 2011, Course Technology" />
</head>
```

Some search engines use two values called *description* and *keyword*. Many search engines create a description of a Web page based on the first 200 characters following the opening <body> tag, unless the Web page includes a description <meta> element. You can think of this element as equivalent to the description you might submit for a particular Web page to a directory such as Yahoo!. Keywords are words that describe the type of Web page a user is looking for; the user probably will type these keywords into a Web directory or search engine. You can create a keyword <meta> element that lists the keywords you want a search engine to associate with your Web page. You separate the keywords you assign to the content attributes with commas.

```
<html lang="EN" xml:lang="EN" dir="ltr">
<head><title>Publishing Information</title>
<meta name="description" content="Frank's Fishery⏎
    offers a large selection of fishing gear at low⏎
    prices." />
<meta name="keywords" content="fishing tackle, ⏎
    fishing equipment, fishing rods, fishing poles, ⏎
    ocean fishing, fresh water, tackle box, fishing⏎
    lures, tackle shops, sport fishing, angler, ⏎
    fishing, tackle, bait, hooks, lures" />
<meta http-equiv="content-type"
    content="text/html; charset=iso-8859-1" />
</head>
```

In an attempt to trick search engines into returning their Web pages more often during searches, some Web page authors pack their keywords list with repetitious or unrelated words. Some search engines will not index a document that contains too many repetitious words, and other search engines will ban sites if they list keywords that are unrelated to the site. Most spiders will ignore the entire keyword list if it repeats a keyword more than seven times. Additionally, most search engines will truncate a description that is longer than 200 characters and will only process the first 1000 characters in a keywords list.

Next, you will add keyword and description <meta> elements to the home page for the Central Valley Farmers' Market.

To add keywords and description meta elements to the Central Valley Farmers' Market home page:

1. Return to the **index.html** file in your text editor.

2. Above the closing </head> tag, add the following <meta> element that creates the description meta element:

   ```
   <meta name="description" content="The Central Valley⏎
       Farmers' Market sells fresh produce, hand-made⏎
       crafts, baked goods, and a variety of other⏎
       products." />
   ```

3. After the description <meta> element, add the following keyword <meta> element:

   ```
   <meta name="keywords" content="market, farmers'⏎
       market, organic produce, fresh produce,⏎
       vegetables, fruit, herbs, crafts, baked goods" />
   ```

4. Save the **index.html** file.

Hiding Web Pages from Search Engines

Recall that a search engine's spider will visit a Web page, index its information, follow any links to other pages within the site, and index the resulting information. However, your Web site may include pages that you want to exclude from search engine indexes. For instance, you may have a page that stores personal information or private data; this data is not private enough to encrypt using special security software or a protocol such as HTTPS, but it should not be returned to a user who performs a search with a search engine. Or, your site may include test pages or pages under construction that do not need to be posted in search engine indexes. To inform search-engine spiders that you do not want certain pages on your site to be indexed, you can place a file named robots.txt in the root directory of the Web server that hosts your Web site. This technique is called the Robots Exclusion Protocol (recall that spiders are also called "robots"). For example, you could place the following statements in the robots.txt file to inform search-engine spiders not to index certain directories and files:

```
User-agent: *
Disallow:/personal/
Disallow:/development/
```

The first statement in the preceding code specifies that the file instructions apply to all spiders that access the Web site. The second two statements specify the names of folders that the spiders should skip when indexing the Web site.

Although the robots.txt file is effective in preventing spiders from indexing certain pages on your Web site, it is not very useful for typical Web page authors, because they do not have access to the root directory of the hosting ISP's Web server. Only an ISP's Webmaster or someone with administrative rights would have access to the Web server's root directory. An alternate method for preventing spiders from indexing certain Web pages is to create a robots <meta> element for each Web page. You create this element by assigning a value of *robots* to the <meta> element's name attribute. You then assign one or more of the following values to the content attribute: *index*, *noindex*, *nofollow*, or *none*. The index value instructs a spider to index the page, the noindex value instructs a spider not to index the page, and the nofollow value instructs a spider not to follow any links on the page. For instance, the following <meta> element instructs a robot to index the page, but not to follow any links on the page.

```
<meta name="robots" content="index, nofollow" />
```

Assigning a value of none to the content attribute is the equivalent of assigning both the noindex and nofollow values, as shown in the following example:

```
<meta name="robots" content="none" />
```

Next, you will revise the home page for the Central Valley Farmers' Market to add a robots <meta> element that allows spiders to index the page, but not to follow any links on the page.

To add a robots <meta> element to the Central Valley Farmers' Market home page:

1. Return to the **index.html** file in your text editor.

2. Above the closing </head> tag, add the following <meta> element to create a robot <meta> element that allows spiders to index the page, but not to follow any links on the page:

   ```
   <meta name="robots" content="index, nofollow" />
   ```

3. Save the **index.html** file.

Specifying Content Type with the *http-equiv* Attribute

Another important part of a Web page response is the **response header**, which is sent to the Web browser before the Web page to provide information that the browser needs to render the page. A key piece of information in the response header is the type of data, or content-type, that the server is sending. For Web pages, you create a **content-type <meta> element** to specify a content type that the document uses. A Web server will use this element to construct the response header.

Multipurpose Internet Mail Extensions (MIME) is a protocol that was originally developed to allow different file types to be transmitted as attachments to e-mail messages. MIME has become a standard method of exchanging files over the Internet, although the technology is still evolving. You specify MIME types with two-part codes separated by a forward slash (/). The first part specifies the MIME type and the second part specifies the MIME subtype.

One important use of the <meta> element is to specify a document's character encoding. Although you can do this when you validate the document with the W3C Markup Validation Service, you should specify the character encoding within the document to allow a Web server to construct the response header. A requesting browser will use the content type in the response header to properly render the Web page. To create a content-type <meta> element, you assign a value of *content-type* to the http-equiv attribute in a <meta> element. You then assign to the content attribute a value of *text/html; charset = utf-8*, which specifies that the document's MIME type is "text/html" and that the document uses the UTF-8 character set. The following statement shows how to construct the same content-type meta elements that you have created since Chapter 1:

```
<meta http-equiv="content-type"
   content="text/html; charset=utf-8" />
```

The most recent version of HTTP that is commonly used today is 1.1. The specifications for this version state that you should use the ISO-8859-1 character set, which represents Western European languages. However, because ISO-8859-1 is limited to only these languages, you should instead specify the UTF-8 character set, which can represent any Unicode character set. **Unicode** is a standardized set of characters from many of the world's languages.

The W3C strongly encourages the use of `content-type` `<meta>` elements to specify an HTML document's character set. However, these elements are not required because most current Web browsers can figure out the character set of an HTML document. For HTML documents you create in this book, you will include the `content-type` `<meta>` elements.

The `content-type` `<meta>` element is one of many response-header `<meta>` elements that you can construct with the `http-equiv` attribute. For a complete list, go to *www.vancouver-webpages.com/META/*.

Next, you will add the `content-type` `<meta>` element to the documents you created in this chapter and validate them with the W3C Markup Validation Service.

To add the `content-type` `<meta>` element and then validate the documents:

1. Return to the **index.html** file. Above the closing `</head>` tag, add the following `<meta>` element to create a content-type meta tag that specifies a MIME type of text/html and a character set of UTF-8:

   ```
   <meta http-equiv="content-type"
         content="text/html; charset=utf-8" />
   ```

2. Save and close the **index.html** file.

3. Return to the **contact.html** file and add a `content-type` `<meta>` element above its closing `</head>` tag.

4. Save and close the **contact.html** file.

5. Start your Web browser and enter the URL for the upload page of the W3C Markup Validation Service: **http://validator.w3.org/#validate_by_upload**. Open and validate the **index.html** and **contact.html** files. If you receive any warnings or errors, fix them and then revalidate the documents.

6. Close your Web browser.

Short Quiz 3

1. Explain the difference between absolute and relative URLs.

2. How do you link within the same Web page?

3. What steps are involved in publishing a Web page?

4. What is metadata and how do you add it to your Web pages?

5. Explain why you would use a robots `<meta>` element instead of the robots.txt file to inform search-engine spiders of the directories and files you do not want indexed.

Summing Up

- Block-level elements are elements that give a Web page its structure.

- Inline, or text-level, elements describe the text that appears on a Web page.

- HTML includes several standard, or common, attributes that are available to almost every element.

- A Boolean attribute specifies one of two values: true or false.

- Heading elements are used for emphasizing a document's headings and subheadings, which helps provide structure by hierarchically organizing a document's content.

- Sections created with the `<section>` element usually define specific types of organized content such as chapters or other types of logical groupings.

- A header section defines an introduction to a document or section. A footer section usually is placed immediately after a section element and typically contains information about that section, such as when it was created or last updated, the author, and copyright information.

- The `<article>` element defines a link to external content such as a news article or Web log (blog).

- The `<address>` element defines contact information, typically for the owner or author of an `<article>` or `<body>` element.

- You use the <nav> element to define a navigation section that contains links to other parts of the current page or to other pages.

- You can use the <aside> element to create content that is related to the surrounding content.

- Content-grouping elements organize the majority of the content within the various document sections.

- White space is an important design element that refers to the empty areas on a page.

- The empty horizontal-rule (<hr />) element draws a horizontal rule on a Web page to act as a section divider.

- The text or image used to represent a link on a Web page is called an anchor.

- You create a basic hypertext link using the <a> element (the *a* stands for anchor).

- Hypertext Transfer Protocol (HTTP) manages the hypertext links that are used to navigate the Web.

- A host refers to a computer system that is being accessed by a remote computer.

- A domain name is a unique address used for identifying a computer (often a Web server) on the Internet.

- The last part of a domain name, known as the domain identifier, identifies the type of institution or organization.

- An absolute URL refers to the full Web address of a Web page or to a specific drive and directory.

- A relative URL specifies the location of a file relative to the location of the currently loaded Web page.

- Bookmarks are internal links within the current document. They can be an effective tool for helping users navigate through a long Web page.

- Web hosting refers to the publication of a Web site for public access.

- An Internet Service Provider (ISP) provides access to the Internet and other types of services, including e-mail.

- To find out if a domain name is available and register it, you must contact a domain name registrar. Domain names are stored in a master database that is maintained by InterNIC, the organization responsible for the registration of domain names and IP addresses.

- Web directories are manually compiled listings of Web sites. Search engines use software to "crawl" or "spider" their way through the Web and automatically compile an index of Web sites.

- The term *metadata* refers to data that describes the definition and structure of information. In a Web page, you use the `<meta>` element to inform search engines and Web servers about the information in your Web page.

- To inform search-engine spiders that you do not want certain pages on your site to be indexed, you create a robots `<meta>` element for each Web page. You create this element by assigning a value of *robots* to the `<meta>` element's `name` attribute. You then assign one or more of the following values to the `content` attribute: *index*, *noindex*, *nofollow*, or *none*. The index value instructs a spider to index the page, the noindex value instructs a spider not to index the page, and the nofollow value instructs a spider not to follow any links on the page.

- The response header is another important part of a Web page response. It is sent to the Web browser before the Web page to provide information that the browser needs to render the page.

- You use the `http-equiv` attribute to create a `content-type` `<meta>` element, which a Web server will use to construct a response header.

Comprehension Check

1. _____ elements give a Web page its structure.

    a. XHTML

    b. Block-level

    c. Inline

    d. Meta

2. According to the Strict DTD, inline elements must be placed within block-level elements. True or False?

3. You should designate the language of your elements using the _____ and `xml:lang` attributes.

    a. `country`

    b. `local`

    c. `lang`

    d. `language`

4. Which of the following values can you assign to the `dir` attribute? (Choose all that apply.)

   a. ltr

   b. rtl

   c. left

   d. right

5. Which standard attribute can you use to create a ToolTip for an element?

   a. `ToolTip`

   b. `Description`

   c. `Help`

   d. `Title`

6. Which of the following is the correct full form of a Boolean attribute named `selected`?

   a. `selected`

   b. `selected="true"`

   c. `selected=""`

   d. `selected="selected"`

7. Most Web browsers render `<address>` elements as _____ text.

   a. blue

   b. boldface

   c. italicized

   d. superscript

8. You do not need to use a `<nav>` element inside a `<footer>` element. True or False?

9. Which elements can you use to add white space to a document? (Choose all that apply.)

   a. `<b>`

   b. `<p>`

   c. `<br />`

   d. `<hr />`

10. Horizontal rules are empty elements. True or False?

11. The last part of a domain name, known as the _____, identifies the type of institution or organization.

    a. domain

    b. domain identifier

    c. protocol

    d. IP address

12. What protocol do you use to automatically send an e-mail message to a specified address?

    a. ftp://

    b. mail:

    c. mailto:

    d. telnet://

13. Domain names are stored in a master database that is maintained by _____.

    a. Microsoft

    b. Netscape

    c. the W3C

    d. InterNIC

14. You can register a domain name yourself. True or False?

15. Explain the differences between search engines and Web directories.

16. Which attribute is required in all `<meta>` elements?

    a. `description`

    b. `content`

    c. `name`

    d. `http-equiv`

17. How many characters are you limited to in a description `<meta>` element?

    a. 50

    b. 100

    c. 200

    d. 300

18. How many characters are you limited to in a keyword `<meta>` element?

    a. 250

    b. 500

    c. 1000

    d. You can use as many characters as you like.

19. To get search engines to return your Web pages more often during searches, you should pack the keyword list with repetitious or unrelated words. True or False?

20. Which of the following values can you assign to the `content` attribute in a robots `<meta>` element? (Choose all that apply.)

    a. index

    b. noindex

    c. nofollow

    d. none

Reinforcement Exercises

 Exercise 2-1

In this exercise, you create the home page for a shoe repair service.

1. Create a new HTML 5 document in your text editor, and type the opening `<!DOCTYPE>` declaration, `<html>` element, `<head>` element, `content-type` `<meta>` element, and `<body>` element. Use "Olde World Shoe Repair" as the content of the `<title>` element. Your document should appear as follows:

```
<!DOCTYPE html>
<html>
<head>
<title>Olde World Shoe Repair</title>
<meta http-equiv="content-type"
    content="text/html; charset=utf-8" />
</head>
<body>
</body>
</html>
```

2. Add the following code to the document body:

```
<h1>Olde World Shoe Repair</h1>
<p>Specialists in the care of fine shoes since
1905.</p>
<p><a href="ContactUs.html">Contact
Information</a></p>
<p><a href="#sr1">Shoe Repair</a></p>
<p><a href="#lr1">Leather Repair</a></p>
<hr />
<h2><a id="sr1">Shoe Repair</a></h2>
<p>We have been repairing designer shoes and
refurbishing boots for almost 100 years. Because of
our great success and reasonable pricing we service
over 2000 pairs of shoes every week. Most of our
repairs are completed within five working days and
cost less than $45.00.</p>
<hr />
<h2><a id="lr1">Leather Repair</a></h2>
<p>We specialize in repair of briefcases, handbags,
and luggage. Our total repair service not only
includes handles, locks, straps, relining, hinges,
and zippers, but the refinishing of the color and
replacing corners and rivets. Remember, we have
almost 100 years of fine service on leather
repairs.</p>
```

3. Save the document as **OldeWorldShoeRepair.html** in your Exercises folder for Chapter 2.

Exercise 2-2

In this exercise, you add a new Web page to the Olde World Shoe Repair Web site.

1. Create a new HTML 5 document in your text editor, and type the opening `<!DOCTYPE>` declaration, header information, and opening `<body>` tag. Use "Contact Information" as the content of the `<title>` element. (You will find it easiest to copy the existing elements in the OldeWorldShoeRepair.html file and paste them into the new file, then simply change the contents of the `<title>` element.)

2. In the document body, add an `<h1>` element that reads "Olde World Shoe Repair" and an `<h2>` element that reads "Contact Information", as follows:

   ```
   <h1>Olde World Shoe Repair</h1>
   <h2>Contact Information</h2>
   ```

3. Add the following contact information to the document:

   ```
   <p>123 Main Street<br />
   Anywhere, USA 12345<br />
   Phone: (565) 555-1212</p>
   <p>You can send us an e-mail at
   <a href="mailto:info@oldworldshoes.com>info@oldworld
   shoes.com"</a>.</p>
   ```

4. Type the following link that returns to the Olde World Shoe Repair home page:

   ```
   <p><a href="OldeWorldShoeRepair.html">Home</a></p>
   ```

5. Save the file as **ContactUs.html** in your Exercises folder for Chapter 2.

6. Use the W3C Markup Validation Service to validate the **OldeWorldShoeRepair.html** and **ContactUs.html** files, and then open the **OldeWorldShoeRepair.html** file in your Web browser and test the links. Because the file does not contain much text, it will not be obvious that the links to the book-mark elements work unless your browser window is sized to be fairly small.

Exercise 2-3

In this exercise, you create a page for an employment Web site that includes a mailto link so job seekers can receive new job postings via e-mail.

1. Create a new HTML 5 document in your text editor, and type the opening `<!DOCTYPE>` declaration, `<html>` element, `<head>` element, `content-type` `<meta>` element, and `<body>` element. Use "Job Postings" as the content of the `<title>` element.

2. Type the following header elements and mailto link:

```
<h1>Coast City Employment Opportunities</h1>
<h2>Job Postings</h2>
<p><a href="mailto:jobpostings@coastcity.gov">
Send us a message to receive new job postings via
e-mail.</a></p>
```

3. Save the file as **JobPostings.html** in your Exercises folder for Chapter 2.

4. Use the W3C Markup Validation Service to validate the **JobPostings.html** file, and then open it in your Web browser and test the mailto link.

Exercise 2-4

Although the bookmark links you created in this chapter jumped only to elements on the current page, you can also create bookmark links to specific elements on other pages. You create a link to a bookmark on another page by appending the # sign to the page's URL, followed by the value assigned to the `id` attribute of the element that is the target of the link. For example, to jump to an element with an `id` attribute of "mh2" on a Web page named MedicalHistory.html, you would use the following `<a>` element:

```
<a href="MedicalHistory.html#mh2">Serious
Illnesses</a>
```

In this exercise, you create a main Web page that lists some hiking destinations in the San Francisco Bay area. Each destination includes a link to a heading on another Web page that describes information about the hike.

1. Create a new HTML 5 document in your text editor, and type the opening `<!DOCTYPE>` declaration, `<html>` element, `<head>` element, content-type `<meta>` element, and `<body>` element. Use "San Francisco Bay Area Hiking Guide" as the content of the `<title>` element.

2. In the document body, add the following heading elements and hiking destination links to bookmarks on a Web page named HikingDestinations.html.

```html
<h1>San Francisco Bay Area</h1>
<h2>Hiking Guide</h2>
<p><a href="HikingDestinations.html#hd1">
    Fort Funston</a></p>
<p><a href="HikingDestinations.html#hd2">
    Rodeo Beach</a></p>
<p><a href="HikingDestinations.html#hd3">
    Mission Peak</a></p>
```

3. Save the file as **HikingGuide.html** in your Exercises folder for Chapter 2.

4. Create another HTML 5 document in your text editor, and type the opening `<!DOCTYPE>` declaration, `<html>` element, `<head>` element, content-type `<meta>` element, and `<body>` element. Use "San Francisco Bay Area Hiking Destinations" as the content of the `<title>` element.

5. In the document body, add the following heading and paragraph elements that list information about each hiking destination. Notice that the `<h3>` elements include `id` attributes.

```html
<h1>San Francisco Bay Area</h1>
<h2>Hiking Destinations</h2>
<h3><a id="hd1">Fort Funston</a></h3>
<p>Distance: 1.5 Miles<br />
Elev. (low/high): 0/183 ft.<br />
Difficulty: Easy</p>
<h3><a id="hd2">Rodeo Beach</a></h3>
<p>Distance: 4.3 Miles<br />
Elev. (low/high): 20/850 ft.<br />
Difficulty: Easy</p>
<h3><a id="hd3">Mission Peak</a></h3>
<p>Distance: 5.6 Miles<br />
Elev. (low/high): 425/2453 ft.<br />
Difficulty: Moderate</p>
```

6. Type the following link that returns to the San Francisco Bay Area Hiking Guide home page:

```
<p><a href="HikingGuide.html">Hiking Guide</a></p>
```

7. Save the file as **HikingDestinations.html** in your Exercises folder for Chapter 2.

8. Use the W3C Markup Validation Service to validate the **HikingGuide.html** and **HikingDestinations.html** files, and then open the **HikingGuide.html** file in your Web browser and test the links. Because the file does not contain much text, it will not be obvious that the links to the bookmark elements work unless your browser window is sized to be fairly small.

 Exercise 2-5

In this exercise, you create a simple Web page for a ballroom dancing studio that includes description and keyword <meta> elements.

1. Create a new HTML 5 document in your text editor, and type the opening <!DOCTYPE> declaration, <html> element, <head> element, content-type <meta> element, and <body> element. Use "Ballroom Dancing" as the content of the <title> element.

2. Add the following description and keyword <meta> elements above the closing </head> tag:

```
<meta name="description" content="San Francisco ↵
Bay Area's best place to learn to dance. Private ↵
lessons and group classes available in Swing, Salsa, ↵
Lindy Hop, Cha Cha, Rumba, Samba, Waltz, Foxtrot, ↵
Tango, Hip Hop, Hustle, Two-Step, and many others."/>
<meta name="keywords" content="dance, dancing, ↵
ballroom, ballroom dance, ballroom dancing, dance ↵
lessons, swing, salsa, lindy hop, cha cha, rumba, ↵
samba, waltz, foxtrot, tango, hip hop, hustle, two-step" />
```

3. In the document body, add the following heading and paragraph elements:

```
<h1>Coast City</h1>
<h2>Ballroom Dancing</h2>
<p>Private lessons and group classes available in
Swing, Salsa, Lindy Hop, Cha Cha, Rumba,
Samba, Waltz, Foxtrot, Tango, Hip Hop, Hustle, Two-
Step, and many others.</p>
```

4. Save the file as **BallroomDancing.html** in your Exercises folder for Chapter 2.

5. Use the W3C Markup Validation Service to validate the **BallroomDancing.html** file.

Exercise 2-6

In this exercise, you create a family's Web page that contains a robots `<meta>` element to prevent spiders from indexing its content.

1. Create a new HTML 5 document in your text editor, and type the opening `<!DOCTYPE>` declaration, `<html>` element, `<head>` element, `content-type` `<meta>` element, and `<body>` element. Use "The Tanaka Family Web Page" as the content of the `<title>` element.

2. Add the following robots `<meta>` element above the closing `</head>` tag. The `content` attribute is assigned a value of "none" to instruct spiders not to index the page and not to follow any links on the page.

```
<meta name="robots" content="none" />
```

3. In the document body, add the following heading and paragraph elements:

```
<h1>The Tanaka Family</h1>
<h2>Welcome to Our Web Page</h2>
<p>This page is dedicated to keeping our friends and
family up to speed on what's going on in our busy
lives!</p>
<p>Feel free to <a
href="mailto:tanakas@coastcity.com">
send us a message</a>.</p>
```

117

4. Save the file as **TanakaFamily.html** in your Exercises folder for Chapter 2.

5. Use the W3C Markup Validation Service to validate the **TanakaFamily.html** file.

Discovery Projects

For the following projects, save the files you create in your Projects folder for Chapter 2. Create the files so they are well formed according to HTML 5. Be sure to validate the files with the W3C Markup Validation Service.

 Discovery Project 2-1

Create a Book of the Month Club Web site. The home page should describe the current month's selection, including book title, author, publisher, ISBN number, and number of pages. Create separate Web pages for book selections in each of the last three months. Add links to the home page that open each of the three Web pages. Save the home page as **BookClub.html**, and save the Web pages for previous months using the name of the month.

 Discovery Project 2-2

Create a Web site for a boat rental company. On the home page, describe the company and the types of boats it rents. Create separate Web pages for rental rates and reservations. On the rental rates page, list the types of boats available and their rental rates according to the length of the boat. Include rates for 1 day, 3 to 6 days, and 7 or more days. On the reservations page, include a mailto link that visitors can use to send a message that reserves a boat. Give visitors instructions on what types of information to include in their message, including the boat length, rental dates, and contact information. Save the home page as **BoatRentals.html**, the rental rates page as **Rates.html**, and the reservations page as **Reservations.html**.

Discovery Project 2-3

Create a Web site for the Central Valley Pottery Studio. On the home page, describe the studio, including what it teaches and the types of classes it offers. Create separate Web pages for Adult Classes, Kids' Classes, and Workshops. Within each Web page, include the day, time, dates, instructor, and cost of each class. Save the home page as **PotteryStudio.html**. Save the Adult Classes Web page as **Adults.html**, the Kids' Classes Web page as **Kids.html**, and the Workshops Web page as **Workshops.html**.

 Discovery Project 2-4

Create a Web site for a bug extermination company. On the home page, describe the company's general services and include links to other pages that explain the company's procedures for exterminating different types of bugs. Include pages for cockroaches, fleas, and ticks. Also include a page that contains information on ordering an inspection. Add links from the inspection Web page to each of the other four pages. Save the home page as **Exterminator.html**. Save the other pages as **Cockroaches.html**, **Fleas.html**, **Ticks.html**, and **Inspection.html**.

Cascading Style Sheets

In this chapter you will:

- ◎ Study basic Cascading Style Sheets (CSS) syntax
- ◎ Work with internal and external style sheets
- ◎ Set color and background properties
- ◎ Set text properties
- ◎ Set font properties
- ◎ Validate style sheets

So far, you have studied the importance of organizing your Web pages using logical and semantic elements. This organization enables all user agents to correctly render the contents of a Web page, even if the user agent does not support formatting characteristics such as fonts, colors, or images.

Although you should always strive to create Web pages that are compatible with all user agents, you should also design and format pages so they are visually pleasing when rendered in a traditional Web browser. To design and format the display of Web pages for traditional browsers, you use Cascading Style Sheets (CSS), which are covered in this chapter. As you work through the chapter, notice that CSS design and formatting techniques are independent of the content of a Web page, unlike text-formatting elements such as the <b> and <i> elements. Cascading Style Sheets allow you to provide design and formatting specifications for well-formed documents that are compatible with all user agents.

Remember as you work through this chapter that although CSS are a vital part of Web page design, this book teaches Web page authoring, not design. Therefore, this chapter focuses on the skills necessary for using CSS to format Web pages, not on design techniques and concepts.

Introduction to Styles and Properties

In Chapter 1 you learned that Hypertext Markup Language (HTML) was originally designed to define the elements in a document independently of how they would appear. This approach was similar to that of HTML's predecessor, Standard Generalized Markup Language (SGML). However, HTML has gradually evolved into a language that can define how elements should appear in a Web browser. This evolution became possible when display and formatting extensions to HTML were added to each Web browser to provide functionality for displaying and formatting Web pages.

To ensure that future Web page authoring separates the definition of document elements from how they appear, many display and formatting extensions that were added to HTML, such as the <font> element, were deprecated in HTML 4.0 and in XHTML 1.0 in favor of CSS. **Cascading Style Sheets (CSS)** are a standard set of styles from the World Wide Web Consortium (W3C) for managing the design and formatting of Web pages in a browser. A single piece of CSS formatting information, such as text alignment or font size, is referred to as a **style**. CSS allows you to change fonts, backgrounds, and colors, and to modify the layout of elements as they appear in a Web browser. CSS information can be added directly to documents or stored in separate documents and shared among multiple Web pages. The term *cascading* refers to the Web pages' ability to use CSS information from multiple sources. When a Web page has access to multiple CSS sources, the styles "cascade," or "fall together," based on rules that you will study later in this chapter.

It bears repeating that your primary goal as a Web page author is to write well-formed documents that separate content from the way it appears in a user agent. Your first step in achieving this goal was to learn how to create well-formed documents that focus on content instead of design. Your second step is to learn how to apply styles using CSS. Today, almost every professionally designed Web site is created with CSS. CSS not only separates a Web page's content from its appearance, it provides much more extensive design and formatting capabilities than those of standard HTML and XHTML elements and attributes.

Understanding CSS Properties

CSS styles are created with two parts separated by a colon: the **property**, which refers to a specific CSS style, and the value assigned to the property, which determines the style's visual characteristics. Together, a CSS property and its assigned value are referred to as a **declaration** or **style declaration**. The following example demonstrates a simple style declaration for the `color` property that changes the color of an element's text to blue.

You can find a listing of CSS1 properties in Appendix D.

`color: blue`

Table 3-1 contains descriptions and examples of some common CSS properties.

CSS Property	Description	Code Example
background-color	Specifies a background color for the document	background-color: blue
color	Specifies the text color of an element	color: blue
font-family	Specifies the font name	font-family: arial
font-style	Specifies the font style: normal, italic, or oblique	font-style: italic
margin-left	Adjusts the left margin	margin-left: 2in
margin-right	Adjusts the right margin	margin-right: 2in
text-align	Determines the alignment of text: center, justify, left, or right	text-align: center

Table 3-1   Common CSS properties

You can define numerous properties for a single element, and you can format each CSS property with different values, depending on the property. For example, the <p> element can use any of the properties listed in Table 3-1, and many others.

The W3C published its first CSS recommendation, Level 1, in 1996; it is commonly referred to as CSS1. Current Web browsers provide excellent support for most properties in CSS1, which are grouped into the following categories:

- Color and background properties

- Font properties

- Text properties

- Box properties

- Classification properties

CSS recommendation Level 2 (CSS2) was released in 1998. CSS2 builds on the properties in CSS1 and includes new features such as table properties and the ability to change the appearance of the mouse pointer.

In this chapter you will focus on learning how to add CSS styles to documents and how to work with styles in three of the most commonly used property categories: color and background, text, and font and list. Once you understand the basics of CSS, it's fairly easy to use the various properties because the ways in which you use CSS are limited. Its properties are used almost exclusively for setting two primary aspects of your Web pages: the display of elements and their position on the screen.

You can apply CSS styles to a document in three ways: using inline styles, internal style sheets, and external style sheets. First, you learn how to use inline styles to apply style information to individual elements on a Web page.

Applying Inline Styles

When you design a Web page, you often want its elements to share the same formatting. For example, you may want all of the headings to be formatted in a specific font and color. Later in this chapter, you learn how to use internal and external style sheets to apply the same formatting to multiple elements on a Web page. However, you sometimes want to change the style of a single element on a Web page. The most basic method of applying styles is to use **inline styles**, which allow you to add style information to a single

At the time of this writing, CSS recommendation Level 3 (CSS3) is in final draft form and should be released as soon as a recommendation is made by the W3C. You may need to wait a while before Web browsers that support all of the new properties and features in CSS3 are available.

Entire books are devoted to CSS. This chapter provides enough information to get you started. For books that cover CSS more fully, search for "css" on the Course Technology Web site at http://www.course.com. You can also find the latest information on CSS at the W3C Web site: http://www.w3.org/Style/CSS/.

element in a document. You use the **style attribute** to assign inline style information to an element. You assign to the style attribute a property declaration enclosed in quotation marks. For example, suppose you want to modify a single paragraph in a document so it uses the Verdana font instead of the browser's default font. You can modify the default font using the following statement, which uses an inline style declaration for the font-family property. Figure 3-1 shows how the paragraph appears in a Web browser.

```
<p>This paragraph does not use CSS.</p>
<p style="font-family: Verdana">Paragraph formatted
with inline styles.</p>
```

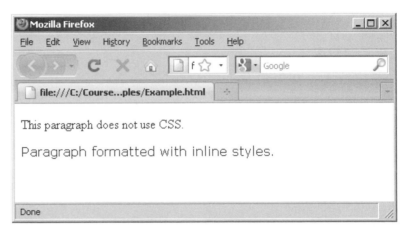

Figure 3-1   Paragraph formatted with an inline style declaration

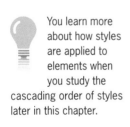

You learn more about how styles are applied to elements when you study the cascading order of styles later in this chapter.

The styles you assign to an element are automatically passed to any nested elements it contains. For example, if you use the font-family style to assign a font to a paragraph, that font is automatically assigned to any nested elements the paragraph contains, such as <strong> or <em> elements.

Next, you start working on the home page for a fictional company named Western Kayak Adventures. Your Chapter folder for Chapter 3 contains an existing copy of the home page, WesternKayak.html, but it has no style formatting. You add style formatting to the file throughout this chapter. First, you use inline styles to add the font-family property to each element in the file.

To add inline styles:

1. In your text editor, open the **WesternKayak.html** file, which is in your Chapter folder for Chapter 3. Immediately save the file as **WesternKayakInline.html**.

2. Add the following inline style declaration to the file's `<h1>` and `<h2>` tags: **style="font-family: Tahoma"**. For example, the opening tag for the `<h1>` element should read as follows:

    ```
    <h1 style="font-family: Tahoma">Western Kayak
    Adventures</h1>
    ```

3. Add the following inline style declaration to each of the file's `<p>` tags and to the `<footer>` tag: **style="font-family: Trebuchet MS"**. The modified opening tags for each of the paragraph elements should read as follows:

    ```
    <p style="font-family: Trebuchet MS">
    ```

4. Save the file and then open it in your Web browser. Your file should look like Figure 3-2.

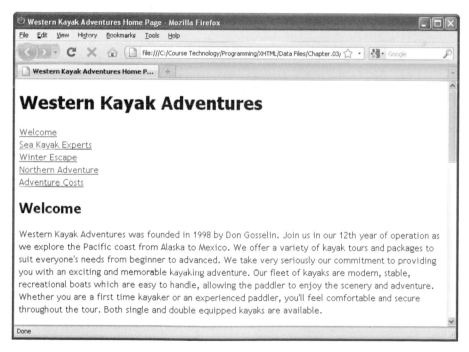

Figure 3-2   Western Kayak Adventures home page after adding inline styles

5. Close your Web browser window.

You can include multiple style declarations in an inline style by separating each declaration with a semicolon. The following statement shows the paragraph element you saw earlier, but this time with two additional style declarations: one for the `color` property, which sets an element's text color to blue, and one for the `text-align` property, which centers the paragraph in the middle of the page. Notice that the `<strong>` element, which is nested in the paragraph element, automatically takes on the paragraph element's styles. Figure 3-3 shows how the paragraph appears in a Web browser.

```
<p>This paragraph does not use CSS.</p>
<p style="font-family: Verdana; color: blue;
    text-align: center">Paragraph formatted with
    <strong>inline styles</strong>.</p>
```

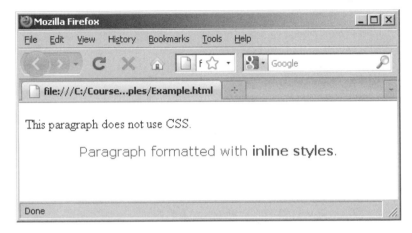

Figure 3-3   Paragraph formatted with multiple inline style declarations

Next, you will add `color` property declarations to the inline styles in the Western Kayak Adventures home page.

To add `color` property declarations to the inline styles in the sample home page:

1. Return to the **WesternKayakInline.html** file in your text editor.

2. Add the following `color` property declaration to the inline styles for each of the six heading elements: **color: maroon**. The modified opening tag for the `<h1>` element should appear as follows:

    ```
    <h1 style="font-family: Tahoma; color: maroon">
    ```

3. Add the following `color` property declaration to the inline styles for each of the nine paragraph elements: **color: blue**. The modified opening tags for each of the paragraph elements should read as follows:

    ```
    <p style="font-family: Trebuchet MS; color: blue">
    ```

4. Save the **WesternKayakInline.html** file and open it in your Web browser. The file should look the same, except for the new colors of the heading and paragraph elements.

5. Close your Web browser window.

A great advantage to using CSS is that you can share styles among multiple Web pages, making it easier to maintain a common look and feel for an entire Web site. Inline styles, however, cannot be shared by other Web pages or other elements on the same page (except by elements that are nested within other elements). Plus, it is extremely time-consuming to add inline styles to every element on a Web page. Inline styles are only useful if you need to make a one-time change to a single element on a page. If you want to apply the same formatting to multiple elements on a page or share styles with other Web pages, you need to use internal or external style sheets, which you will study later in this chapter.

Applying Styles with the `<div>` and `<span>` Elements

Two elements that are commonly used for applying styles are the `<div>` and `<span>` elements. The **`<div>` element** formats a group of block-level and inline elements with styles, whereas the **`<span>` element** formats a group of inline elements. The only difference between these two elements is that the `<div>` element can contain block-level elements and adds a line break after its closing tag. The following code contains `<div>` and `<span>` elements with inline elements. The `<div>` element contains block-level elements (`<h2>` and `<p>`), while the `<span>` element contains only text and another inline element. Figure 3-4 shows the code in a Web browser.

```
...
<body style="color: black; font-family: arial; ⏎
     font-size: .8em; font-weight: normal">
<h1>Don's Bicycle Tours</h1>
<h2>Bicycle Tours</h2>
<p>A bicycle tour allows you to pedal through the
world's most scenic highways and byways, where a
ribbon of new sights, scents, and sounds are
revealed. <span style="color: olive"><strong>Head
off on your own or ride with fellow travelers if
you choose!</strong></span></p>
<div style="color: blue"><h2>Walking Tours - New!</h2>
<p>Our new walking tours transform the small details
of the region into a mosaic of unforgettable
encounters and cultural revelations. There's simply
no better way to discover the simple beauty of a
landscape, the friendliness of the locals, or the
camaraderie of fellow travelers than by
walking.</p></div>
</body>
</html>
```

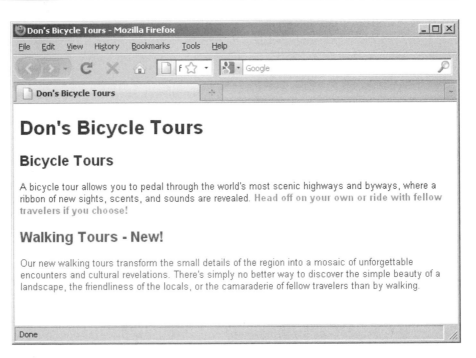

Figure 3-4   Document with `<div>` and `<span>` elements

Understanding Length Units

The values you can assign to a CSS property depend on what type of property you use. Some properties can be assigned a range of values. For instance, you can assign any font name that is available on a user's system to the `font-family` property. For other properties, you must assign a value from a specific set of values. For example, you can only assign one of the following five values to the `text-align` property: left, center, right, justify, or inherit. (You will learn more about the `font-family` and `text-align` properties later in this chapter.) Three types of common values are assigned to properties: length units, percentage units, and color units.

Length units refer to the units of measure that you can use in a style declaration to determine the size or positioning of an element. Whether a length unit is used for sizing or positioning depends on the property and the element to which it is assigned. For example, the length unit value you assign to the `font-size` property determines the font size for an element. The length unit value you assign to the `text-indent` property adjusts positioning by determining how far to indent an element from the document's left margin. Table 3-2 lists the length units you can use with CSS.

Unit	Name	Description
cm	Centimeters	Measures values in centimeters
em	Em space	Measures values according to the width of the uppercase letter *M* for the selected font
ex	x-height	Measures values according to the height of the lowercase letter *x* for the selected font
in	Inches	Measures values in inches
mm	Millimeters	Measures values in millimeters
pc	Picas	Measures values in picas, which are equal to 1/6 of an inch
pt	Points	Measures values in points, which are equal to 1/72 of an inch
px	Pixels	Measures values in pixels

Table 3-2 CSS length units

Although an em space length unit is usually defined as being equal to the width of a font's uppercase letter *M*, in practice it actually represents the point size of the current font. For example, if the font size for a paragraph is set to 12 points, then 1 em is equal to 12 points, 2 em is equal to 24 points, and so on.

You assign a measurement value to a property by entering the number that represents the measurement, immediately followed by the unit of measure. For instance, the second paragraph in the following code increases an element's font size to 16 points and indents its first line by 1.5 inches. Notice that there is no space between "16" and "pt" or between "1.5" and "in". Figure 3-5 shows how the styles appear in a Web browser.

```
<p>This paragraph does not use CSS.</p>
<p style="font-size: 16pt; text-indent: 1.5in">
Paragraph is formatted with length units.</p>
```

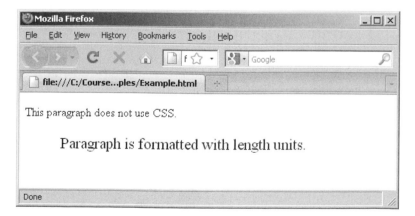

Figure 3-5 Paragraph formatted with length units

Do not include a space between the number and length unit assigned to a property; if you include a space, most browsers will ignore the style. For instance, the styles in the following code include spaces between the number and the length unit assigned to the properties. As you can see in Figure 3-6, the Web browser ignores the styles.

```
<p>This paragraph does not use CSS.</p>
<p style="font-size: 16 pt; text-indent: 1.5 in">
This paragraph is incorrectly formatted with length
units.</p>
```

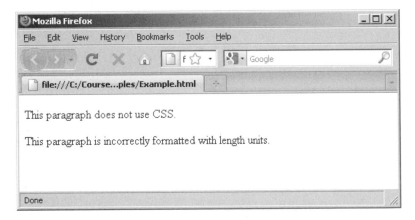

Figure 3-6   Paragraph with incorrectly formatted length units

Next, you will modify the point sizes of the heading and paragraph elements in the Western Kayak Adventures home page.

To modify the point sizes for the heading and paragraph elements:

1. Return to the **WesternKayakInline.html** file in your text editor.

2. Add the following `font-size` property declaration to the inline style for the `<h1>` tag: **font-size: 16pt**. Be sure not to include a space between "16" and "pt".

3. Add the following `font-size` property declaration to the inline styles for the `<h2>` tags: **font-size: 14pt**. Be sure not to include a space between "14" and "pt".

4. Add the following `font-size` property declaration to the inline styles for each of the paragraph elements: **font-size: 10pt**.

5. Save the **WesternKayakInline.html** file and open it in your Web browser. The point sizes of the heading and paragraph elements should appear smaller, as shown in Figure 3-7.

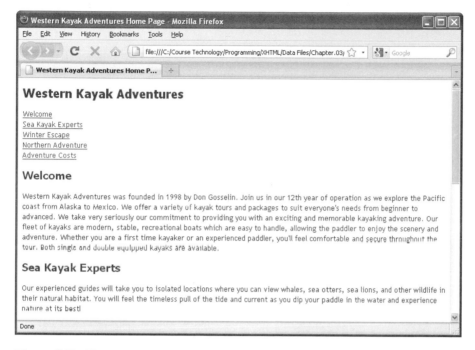

Figure 3-7   Western Kayak Adventures home page after modifying the point sizes of the heading and paragraph elements

6. Close your Web browser window.

CSS length units are either absolute or relative. **Absolute length units** use an exact measurement to specify the size or placement of an element. The following CSS length units are absolute:

- cm (centimeters)
- in (inches)
- mm (millimeters)
- pc (picas)
- pt (points)

Absolute length units are not a good choice for Web page design because they do not automatically adjust to different screen sizes.

132

Relative length units are preferred because they adjust properties according to screen size or user preferences. The following CSS length units are relative:

- em (em space)
- ex (x-height)
- px (pixels)

Consider the em and ex length units, which adjust font size in relation to the font size of the current element or the default font size of an element that is set by a browser. If a user with visual disabilities sets his or her monitor to display larger fonts, any elements with font sizes that are assigned with the em and ex units will automatically be sized larger for that user's monitor. However, if the font sizes are assigned values with the absolute pt measurement, the elements will not be resized.

The following code shows an example of a paragraph with a `font-size` property set to 18 points. The paragraph includes a nested `<strong>` element with a `font-size` property set to 1.5em. Because the paragraph's font is set to 18 points, assigning a value of 1.5em to the nested `<strong>` element formats the content to 27 points, as shown in Figure 3-8.

```
<p style="font-family: Arial; font-size: 18pt">
We're having a <strong
style="font-size: 1.5em">sale</strong>!</p>
```

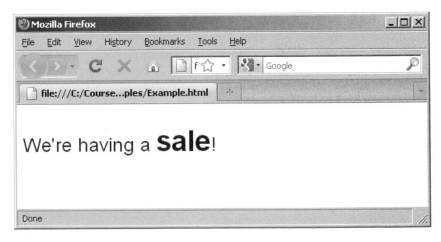

Figure 3-8　Paragraph formatted with pt and em length units

Next, you will modify the pt length units in the inline styles to em length units for each of the heading and paragraph elements.

To use em length units in the inline styles for each of the heading and paragraph elements:

1. Return to the **WesternKayakInline.html** file in your text editor.

2. Change the value assigned to the font-size property for the `<h1>` tag from 16pt to **1.3em**.

3. Change the value assigned to the font-size properties for the `<h2>` tags from 14pt to **1.2em**.

4. Change the value assigned to the font-size properties in each paragraph element's inline style from 10pt to **.8em**.

5. Save the **WesternKayakInline.html** file and open it in your Web browser. The point size of the heading and paragraph elements should look the same as they did before you modified the length units assigned to the font-size properties.

6. Close your Web browser window.

Using Percentage Units

An alternative to relative length units is **percentage units**, which adjust properties relative to other values. You assign a percentage unit value to a property by entering a percentage number immediately followed by the percent symbol (%). The following code shows two paragraph elements that contain nested `<strong>` elements. The font of the `<strong>` element in the first paragraph is reduced to 50 percent of the size of the paragraph font, whereas the font of the `<strong>` element in the second paragraph is increased to 150 percent of the size of the paragraph font. Figure 3-9 shows the resulting styles in a Web browser.

```
<p style="font-family: Arial; font-size: 18pt">
Are you feeling <strong
style="font-size: 50%">down</strong>?</p>
<p style="font-family: Arial; font-size: 18pt">
We're having a <strong
style="font-size: 150%">sale</strong>!</p>
```

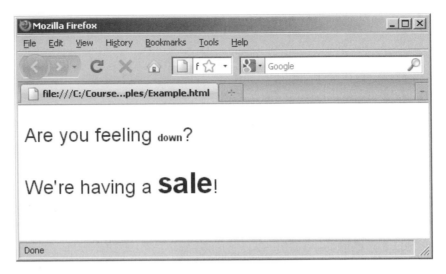

Figure 3-9   Elements resized with percentage units

Next, you will modify the em length units in the inline styles to percentage units for each of the heading and paragraph elements.

To modify the em length units to percentage units for the heading and paragraph elements:

1. Return to the **WesternKayakInline.html** file in your text editor.

2. Change the value assigned to the font-size property of the <h1> tag from 1.3em to **130%**.

3. Change the value assigned to the font-size properties of the <h2> tags from 1.2em to **120%**.

4. Change the value assigned to the font-size properties of the <p> tags from .8em to **80%**.

5. Save and close the **WesternKayakInline.html** file, and then open it in your Web browser. The point size of the heading and paragraph elements should look the same as they did before you modified the length units assigned to the font-size properties.

6. Close your Web browser window.

Specifying Color Units

A **color unit** represents a color value that you can assign to a property. You can assign a color unit to a property using any of the 16 color names defined in the CSS1 specification (see Table 3-3), or you can assign a red, green, blue (RGB) value.

aqua	gray	navy	silver
black	green	olive	teal
blue	lime	purple	white
fuchsia	maroon	red	yellow

Table 3-3   CSS1 color name values

You assign the color name to a property as shown in the following code. In this example, the `color` property specifies the text color of navy for an element:

```
<p style="color: navy">
```

The 16 color names in Table 3-3 are nowhere near sufficient for most professional Web page authors. Although most computer systems can display millions of colors, the colors displayed on a screen are the result of combining just three: red, green, and blue. Most graphical computer systems, such as Windows, use the **red**, **green**, **blue** or **RGB color system** for specifying colors. Using the RGB color system, you can assign a color unit in one of two ways: by using the color's RGB value or by using its hexadecimal value.

The syntax for assigning a color unit with an RGB value is `RGB(red, green, blue)`. Each color value is a number ranging from 0 to 255, which indicates its intensity. A value of 0 indicates that the color should include the minimum intensity of a primary color, and a value of 255 indicates that the color should include the maximum intensity. By combining different intensities of the red, green, and blue primary colors, you can come up with millions of different hues. You create primary colors of red, green, or blue by using a full intensity value of 255 for one of the primary colors, and values of 0 for the two other primary colors. For example, you use the following RGB value to assign the color red to the `color` property: `color: RGB(255, 0, 0)`.

The colors represented by RGB values can also be represented as hexadecimal numbers. The decimal numbers you are most familiar with are based on a value of 10. In contrast, **hexadecimal**, or **hex**, **numbers** are based on a value of 16. In the hexadecimal system, the numbers 0 through 9 are represented by the numerals 0 through 9, but the numbers 10 through 15 are represented by the letters A through F. A color represented by a hex number consists of the # symbol followed by six digits. The first two digits represent the red portion of the color, the second two digits represent the green portion, and the last two digits represent the blue portion. For example, the RGB value for yellow is represented as RGB(255, 255, 0). The decimal number 255 is equivalent to the hex number FF, and the decimal number 0 is equivalent to the hex number 0 or 00. Therefore, the hex number for yellow is #FFFF00. You use a hex number to assign yellow to the `color` property as follows: `color: #FFFF00`. In the following code, the color red is assigned to each paragraph. The first paragraph uses the RGB value for red, RGB(255, 0, 0), whereas the second paragraph uses the hex number for red, #FF0000.

```
<p style="color: RGB(255,0,0)">
Paragraph color formatted with an RGB value.</p>
<p style="color: #FF0000">
Paragraph color formatted with a hex number.</p>
```

Table 3-4 lists RGB values and hex values for the 16 color names defined in the CSS1 specification.

Color Name	RGB Value	Hex Value
aqua	0, 255, 255	#00FFFF
black	0, 0, 0	#000000
blue	0, 0, 255	#0000FF
fuchsia	255, 0, 255	#FF00FF
gray	128, 128, 128	#808080
green	0, 128, 0	#008000
lime	0, 255, 0	#00FF00
maroon	128, 0, 0	#800000
navy	0, 0, 128	#000080
olive	128, 128, 0	#808000
purple	128, 0, 128	#800080
red	255, 0, 0	#FF0000
silver	192, 192, 192	#C0C0C0
teal	0, 128, 128	#008080
white	255, 255, 255	#FFFFFF
yellow	255, 255, 0	#FFFF00

Table 3-4   CSS1 color names and their corresponding RGB and hex values

CSS can generate millions of colors. However, the problem with being able to generate so many colors is that monitors differ in the number of colors they can display. Most computer platforms can display at least 256 colors. However, about 40 of these colors differ among platforms, which means you can't guarantee how those colors will look when your Web page renders. To ensure that colors on Web pages render the same on all monitors and platforms, most Web page authors only use colors that are part of the Web palette. The **Web palette**, also known as the **Web-safe palette** and **browser-safe palette**, is a set of 216 colors that display reliably across platforms and on most computer monitors.

You can find a list of browser-safe colors and their RGB and hex values at *http://www. w3schools.com/html/ html_colors.asp*.

Short Quiz 1

1. Explain how to use CSS styles and properties.

2. What is the difference between `<div>` and `<span>` elements?

3. Explain length units, percentage units, and color units and how they are used.

Structuring CSS

Now that you understand the basics of working with CSS, you can learn how to structure the CSS used by your documents. After this section, you will study the various types of properties available in CSS.

Creating Internal Style Sheets

As you learned earlier, inline styles are only useful if you want to add style information to a single element in a document. You use an **internal style sheet** to create styles that apply to an entire document. You create an internal style sheet within a `<style>` element placed within the document head. The `<style>` element must include a `type` attribute that is assigned a value of "text/css", as follows:

```
<style type="text/css">
style declarations
</style>
```

You can also use the optional `media` and `scoped` attributes with the `<style>` element. The `media` attribute allows you to select the destination medium for the style information. Valid values you can

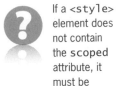

If a `<style>` element does not contain the `scoped` attribute, it must be placed in the `<head>` element in order for the page to be well formed.

assign to the `media` attribute are screen, tty, tv, projection, handheld, print, braille, aural, and all. The Boolean `scoped` attribute determines where the styles are applied. If you include the `scoped` attribute within a `<style>` element, the styles apply only to the parent element that contains the `<style>` element and to any child elements within the parent elements.

Within the `<style>` element, you create any style instructions for a specific element. These styles are applied to all instances of that element contained in the body of the document. The element to which specific style rules apply is called a **selector**. You create a style declaration for a selector in an internal style sheet by placing a list of declarations within a pair of braces { } following the name of the selector. Figure 3-10 shows a style declaration for the `<p>` selector that changes the `color` property to "blue".

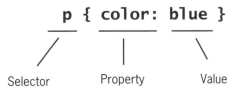

Figure 3-10 Selector style declaration

As with inline styles, you separate multiple properties for a selector using semicolons. The following code shows part of the head and body of a document that includes a style sheet for the `h1`, `h2`, and `p` selectors. A pair of braces containing style instructions follows each selector. All instances of the associated elements in the body of the document are formatted using these style instructions. Figure 3-11 shows how the document appears in a Web browser.

```
...
<head>
...
<style type="text/css">
h1 {color: navy; font-size: 2em;
    font-family: Arial }
h2 {color: navy; font-size: 1.5em;
    font-family: Arial }
body {color: blue; font-family: Arial;
    font-size: .8em; font-weight: normal }
</style>
</head>
<body>
<h1>Coast City Kites</h1>
<h2>Airfoils</h2>
<p>Supported by the wind itself, these kites have
nothing to break or assemble. They pack down small
enough to fit in a pack, purse, or pocket, so you
```

```
can always be ready to go fly a kite.</p>
<h2>Deltas</h2>
<p>Traditional Deltas are easy to fly and make great
first kites. Flying on the wind rather than against
it, they take off in the lightest of breezes and
soar with bird-like grace.</p>
</body>
```

Figure 3-11   Document formatted with an internal style sheet

You can group selectors so they share the same style declarations by separating each selector with a comma. For example, you use the following single declaration to format all of a document's <h1>, <h2>, and <h3> elements to use the same color and font:

```
<style type="text/css">
h1, h2, h3 {color: navy; font-family: Arial }
</style>
```

Next, you will create a new version of the Western Kayak Adventures home page, but with an internal style sheet instead of inline styles.

To create a version of the sample home page using an internal style sheet:

1.   Open the **WesternKayakInline.html** file in your Chapter folder for Chapter 3 and immediately save it as **WesternKayakInternal.html** in your text editor.

140

2. Above the closing `</head>` tag, add a `<style>` element, as follows:

```
<style type="text/css">
</style>
```

3. To the `<style>` element, add the following grouped selectors and declaration for the `<h1>` and `<h2>` elements, which format the headings using the Tahoma font and the color maroon:

```
h1, h2 { font-family: Tahoma; color: maroon }
```

4. To the end of the `<style>` element, add the following selectors to format the font size of the `<h1>` and `<h2>` elements:

```
h1 { font-size: 130% }
h2 { font-size: 120% }
```

5. To the end of the `<style>` element, add the following selector and declaration for the `<p>` element, which sets the font to Trebuchet MS, the color to navy, and the font size to 80%:

```
p { font-family: Trebuchet MS; color: blue;
      font-size: 80% }
```

6. Delete the inline styles from all of the heading and paragraph elements, but leave the inline style for the `<footer>` element.

7. Save the **WesternKayakInternal.html** file and open it in your Web browser. The style formatting for each of the elements should look the same as they did in the inline styles version of the document.

8. Close your Web browser window.

Defining Contextual Selectors

A **contextual selector** allows you to specify formatting for an element, but only when it is contained within another element. You create a contextual selector by including two or more selectors in a declaration within a `<style>` element separated by spaces. For example, the following `<style>` element creates a contextual selector that formats any `<em>` elements contained within a `<div>` element with the hex color #A00000 (green) and in bold. The `<div>` elements themselves are formatted with the hex color #F00000. Figure 3-12 shows how the document appears in a Web browser. Notice in the figure that the `<em>` element in the paragraph does not include the formatting in the contextual selector; only the `<em>` element within the `<div>` element contains the formatting.

```
...
<style type="text/css">
...
div { color: #F00000 }
```

```
div em { color: #A00000; font-weight: bold }
</style>
</head>
<body>
<h1>Coast City Kites</h1>
<h2>Where to Fly a Kite</h2>
<p>Choose an open, treeless area. <em>Hills can be
great places to fly kites.</em> Stand on the
windward side to avoid turbulence created by the
hill itself.</p>
<div><p>Trees or buildings upwind can cause
ground turbulence and make your kite hard to
launch. Downwind, these <em>kite eating</em>
obstacles can cause turbulence that attracts
kites.</p>
</div>
</body>
</html>
```

Figure 3-12   Document with a contextual selector

Next, you will add a contextual selector to the Western Kayak
Adventures home page. The contextual selector consists of a
<strong> element inside a <div> element. Whenever the <strong>
element appears within a <div> element, it is formatted in green.

To add a contextual selector to the Western Kayak Adventures home page:

1. Return to the **WesternKayakInternal.html** file in your text
    editor.

2. Above the closing `<style>` element, add the following declaration for a contextual selector that formats the `<strong>` element in the hex color #66CC00 whenever it appears within a `<div>` element.

```
div strong { color: #66CC00 }
```

3. Next, add the following `<div>` element immediately above the Sea Kayak Experts `<h2>` element. Notice that the `<div>` element contains several `<strong>` elements.

```
<div><p>"My trip with Western Kayak
Adventures is one of the <strong>memorable
experiences of my life</strong>. Their kayak
equipment is of the <strong>highest
quality</strong>, their employees are <strong>well
trained</strong> and <strong>personable</strong>,
and their safety record is
<strong>impeccable</strong>."</p></div>
```

4. Save the **WesternKayakInternal.html** file and open it in your Web browser. Figure 3-13 shows how the `<div>` element appears.

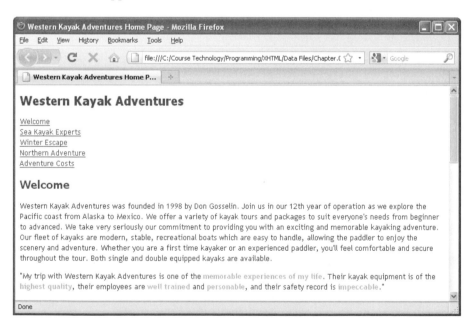

Figure 3-13 `<div>` element formatted with a contextual selector

5. Close your Web browser window.

Organizing with Class Selectors

Another method of applying styles is to use **class selectors**, which allow you to create different groups of styles for the same element. You create a class selector within a `<style>` element by appending a class name to a selector with a period. You then assign the class name to the standard `class` attribute of elements in the document that you want to format with the class's style definitions.

The following code defines a class selector named "danger" that formats paragraph text as red and bold. The class selector is applied to two of the paragraphs in the document body.

```
...
<style type="text/css">
...
p.danger { color: red; font-weight: bold }
</style>
</head>
<body>
<h1>Coast City Kites</h1>
<h2>Safety Tips</h2>
<p>Never fly over people.</p>
<p>Never fly near trees or buildings.</p>
<p>Never fly near the airport.</p>
<p class="danger">Never fly in rain or
thunderstorms.</p>
<p>Never fly near busy streets or roadways.</p>
<p class="danger">Never fly near power lines.</p>
</body>
```

Next, you will return to the Western Kayak Adventures home page and add a class selector for the `<h2>` element. The class selector formats any `<h2>` elements that include the class selector name to be displayed in red. You will apply the new class selector to the Winter Escape and Northern Adventure headings to draw more attention to them.

To add a class selector for the <h2> element:

1. Return to the **WesternKayakInternal.html** file in your text editor.

2. To the end of the `<style>` element, add the following class selector declaration for the `<h2>` element, which formats any `<h2>` elements that include the class selector to be displayed in red:

   ```
   h2.trip { color: red }
   ```

3. To the Winter Escape and Northern Adventure headings, add the following `class` attribute that specifies the "trip" class selector: **class="trip"**. The opening <h2> tag for both headings should read as follows:

```
<h2 class="trip">
```

4. Save the **WesternKayakInternal.html** file and open it in your Web browser. The Winter Escape and Northern Adventure headings should appear in red. The other <h2> headings in the document should still be formatted in maroon.

5. Close your text editor.

When you create a class selector by appending a class name to a selector with a period, you can only use that class selector with the element for which it was created. For instance, you can only use the danger class selector in the preceding example with <p> elements.

You can also create a generic class selector that is not associated with any particular element. You create a generic class selector to use with any element by defining a class name preceded by a period, but without appending it to an element. The following code shows an example of the danger class selector, but this time it is not appended to the p selector. Notice that in the document body, the danger class selector is now applied to two different elements: <p> and <strong>. Figure 3-14 shows the document in a Web browser.

```
...
<style type="text/css">
...
.danger { color: red; font-weight: bold }
</style>
</head>
<body>
<h1>Coast City Kites</h1>
<h2>Safety Tips</h2>
<p>Never fly over <strong
class="danger">people</strong>.
<p>
<p>Never fly near <strong
class="danger">trees</strong>
or <strong class="danger">buildings</strong>.</p>
<p>Never fly near the <strong class="danger">airport
</strong>.</p>
<p class="danger">Never fly in rain or
thunderstorms.</p>
<p>Never fly near busy <strong
class="danger">streets
</strong> or <strong
class="danger">roadways</strong>.</p>
<p class="danger">Never fly near power lines.</p>
</body>
```

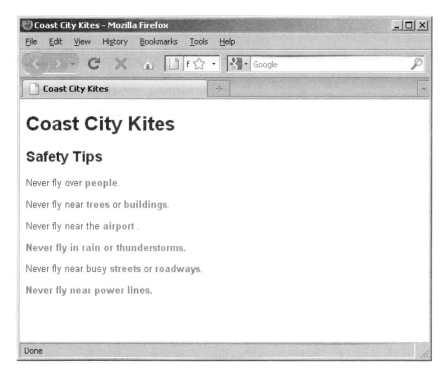

Figure 3-14   Document with a generic class selector

Next, you will modify the trip class selector you created in the last exercise so it is a generic class selector that is not associated with any particular element. You then apply the trip class selector to the paragraphs beneath the Winter Escape and Northern Adventure headings to draw more attention to both trips.

To modify the trip class selector so it is a generic class selector:

1. Return to the **WesternKayakInternal.html** file.

2. Remove the h2 selector from the declaration for the trip class selector. The modified class selector should read as follows:

    ```
    .trip { color: red }
    ```

3. To each of the paragraphs beneath the Winter Escape and Northern Adventure headings, add a `class` attribute with "trip" assigned as its value.

4. Save the **WesternKayakInternal.html** file and open it in your Web browser. The paragraphs beneath the Winter Escape and Northern Adventure headings should now appear in red.

5. Close your Web browser window.

Next, you will add a `<div>` element to the Western Kayak Adventures Web page. The `<div>` element will contain the anchor elements at the top of the page. You will also add a generic class selector to the style sheet that formats the anchor elements in the `<div>` element.

To add a `<div>` element to the Western Kayak Adventures Web page:

1. Return to the **WesternKayakInternal.html** file in your text editor.

2. Add the following class selector to the end of the `<style>` element. The class selector includes the `font-family` property to format the links with the same font properties as the paragraph elements.

   `.links { font-family: Trebuchet MS; font-size: 80% }`

3. Replace the `<p>` element that surrounds the links at the top of the page with a `<div>` element that includes the `class` attribute assigned a value of "links" for the class selector you just created. The elements should appear as follows:

   ```
   <div class="links">
   <a href="#wel">Welcome</a><br />
   <a href="#ske">Sea Kayak Experts</a><br />
   <a href="#we">Winter Escape</a><br />
   <a href="#na">Northern Adventure</a><br />
   <a href="#ac">Adventure Costs</a>
   </div>
   ```

4. Save the **WesternKayakInternal.html** file and open it in your Web browser. The file should look the same as it did before you added the `<div>` element.

5. Close your Web browser window.

Creating ID Selectors

An **ID selector** is similar to an inline style in that it allows you to create style declarations that are applied only to a single element in the document. As with inline styles, you use an ID selector when you want to change the style of a single element on your Web page. The benefit to using ID selectors over inline styles is that they allow you to maintain all of your style declarations in a single location within the `<style>` element. Inline style declarations must be created within each element.

Recall that the value assigned to an element's id attribute must be unique; it cannot be assigned to any other element's id attribute. You create an ID selector using the value assigned to an element's id attribute, but preceded by the # symbol. For example, the following code shows how to declare an ID selector for a paragraph with the value "p1" assigned to its id attribute:

```
...
<style type="text/css">
#p1 { font-family: Verdana; color: blue;
    text-align: center }
</style>
<p id="p1">Paragraph formatted with an ID
selector.</p>
```

Next, you will return to the Western Kayak Adventures home page and add an ID selector for a <div> element that contains the name, city, and state of the person who made the testimonial you added earlier. You create this additional <div> element to align the name, city, and state with the other <div> element. The ID selector formats the new <div> element so it is right-aligned with the text-align property.

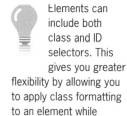

Elements can include both class and ID selectors. This gives you greater flexibility by allowing you to apply class formatting to an element while adding custom style declarations to the element using an ID selector.

147

To add an ID selector for a <div> element:

1. Return to the **WesternKayakInternal.html** file in your text editor.

2. To the end of the <style> element, add the following declaration for an ID selector named "b1". The selector includes a single style declaration that uses the text-align property to right-align the element.

   ```
   #b1 { text-align: right }
   ```

3. Add the following <div> element immediately after the existing <div> element. Notice that the opening <div> tag includes an id attribute that is assigned the value of the ID selector.

   ```
   <div id="b1"><p>Dan McClellen, Seattle,
   Washington</p></div>
   ```

4. Save the **WesternKayakInternal.html** file and open it in your Web browser. Figure 3-15 shows how the new <div> element appears.

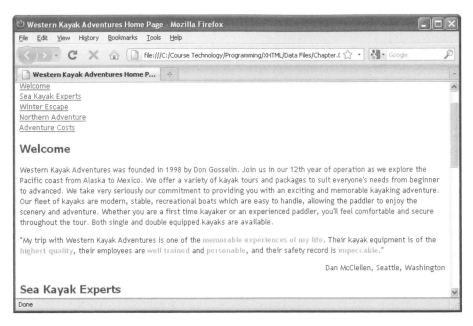

Figure 3-15 Western Kayak Adventures home page formatted with an ID selector

5. Close your Web browser window.

Working with External Style Sheets

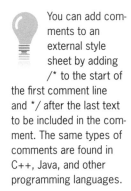

You can add comments to an external style sheet by adding /* to the start of the first comment line and */ after the last text to be included in the comment. The same types of comments are found in C++, Java, and other programming languages.

Inline styles are useful if you only need to format a single element, whereas internal style sheets are useful for creating styles that apply to an entire document. However, most companies want all of the documents on their Web site to have the same look and feel. For this reason, it's preferable to use **external style sheets**, which are separate text documents that contain style declarations used by multiple documents on a Web site. You should create an external style sheet whenever you need to use the same styles on multiple Web pages on the same site.

You create an external style sheet in a text editor, just as with XHTML documents. However, you should save the document with an extension of .css. The style sheet document should not contain XHTML elements, but only style declarations. Use the same rules for creating style declarations in an external style sheet as you use in an internal style sheet. The contents of a typical external style sheet may appear as follows. Notice that the code contains no XHTML elements.

```
h1 {color: navy; font-size: 2em;
     font-family: serif }
h2 {color: red; font-size: 1.5em;
     font-family: Arial }
body {color: blue; font-family: Arial;
     font-size: .8em; font-weight: normal }
```

You access the styles in an external style sheet by using the empty
`<link>` element to link a document to a style sheet. You place the
`<link>` element in the document head. You include three attributes
in the `<link>` element: an `href` attribute that is assigned the Uniform
Resource Locator (URL) of the style sheet, a `rel` attribute that is
assigned a value of "stylesheet" to specify that the referenced file is a
style sheet, and the `type` attribute, which is assigned the same "text/css"
value as the `type` attribute used in the `<style>` element. For example,
to link a document to a style sheet named company_styles.css, you
include a `<link>` element in the document head, as follows:

```
<head>
...
<link rel="stylesheet" href="company_styles.css"
type="text/css" />
</head>
```

When a Web browser formats a document that links to an external
style sheet, it uses style declarations for each selector in the external
style sheet, including contextual, class, and ID selectors.

Next, you will modify the Western Kayak Adventures home page so it
is formatted with an external style sheet.

To use an external style sheet with the Western Kayak Adventures home page:

1. Return to the **WesternKayakInternal.html** file in your text
   editor and immediately save it as **WesternKayakExternal.html**.

2. Cut the style declarations from the `<style>` element to your
   Clipboard and create a new document in your text editor. Be
   sure not to copy the `<style>` tags.

3. Paste the contents of your Clipboard into the new file.

4. Save the file as **adventure_styles.css** in your Chapter folder
   for Chapter 3.

5. Return to the **WesternKayakExternal.html** file in your text
   editor.

6. Replace the `<style>` element with the following `<link>` element
   that links to the adventure_styles.css external style sheet:

   ```
   <link rel="stylesheet" href="adventure_styles.css"
   type="text/css" />
   ```

7. Save the **WesternKayakExternal.html** file and open it in
   your Web browser. The file should look the same as it did
   before you linked it to the external style sheet.

8. Close your Web browser window.

Understanding Cascading Order

Earlier in this chapter, you learned that when a Web page has access to multiple CSS sources, the styles "cascade" or "fall together" based on certain rules. Styles from different sources (inline styles, internal style sheets, or external style sheets) that apply to the same selector fight for control over the element. A browser applies several rules to determine which style source wins the fight between competing style declarations from multiple sources. First, a more specific style declaration outweighs a more general one. For example, in the following code, two style declarations set the `color` property. The color declaration in the `<body>` element is more general than the one in the `<p>` element. Therefore, any `<p>` elements in the document are formatted in red instead of the blue declared in the `<body>` element. However, any other elements in the document that do not have a color specified through a style will be formatted in blue.

```
<style type="text/css">
body { color: blue }
p { color: red }
```

CSS also uses an order of precedence to determine which styles to apply when a selector is formatted in different sources. The least important style formatting is the browser's default style settings. The most important style formatting, or the one that wins out over other sources, is the inline styles that are applied to an element. The cascading order of precedence for styles, starting with the least important, is as follows:

1. Browser default

2. External style sheets

3. Internal style sheets

4. Inline styles

Short Quiz 2

1. How do you create an internal style sheet?

2. What is a contextual selector and how is it used?

3. How do you use class selectors?

4. How do you use ID selectors?

5. Explain how to create an external style sheet.

Setting Color and Background Properties

In this section, you study the color and background properties that are available in CSS. You already know that the color property sets the text color of an element. You have seen several examples of how to set the color for individual elements such as the <h1> and <p> elements. To set the text color for all of the text in a document, you add the color property to the <body> element, either as an inline style or using the body selector.

Background properties set the background color or image that appears behind an element. Table 3-5 lists the CSS1 background properties.

Property	Description	Values
background	Sets all the background properties in one declaration	*background-color* | *background-image* | *background-repeat* | *background-attachment* | *background-position*
background-attachment	Determines whether an image specified with the background-image property will scroll with a Web page's content or be in a fixed position	scroll | fixed
background-color	Sets the background color of an element	*color* | transparent
background-image	Sets the background image of an element	none | url(*url*)
background-position	Specifies the initial position of an image set with the background-image property	*percentage unit* | *length unit* | top | bottom | left | right | top left | top center | top right | center left | center center | center right | bottom left | bottom center | bottom right
background-repeat	Determines how an image specified with the background-image property is repeated on the page	repeat | repeat-x | repeat-y | no-repeat

Table 3-5   CSS1 background properties

In Table 3-5, the | symbol means "or" and is used to separate the different values that can be applied to a property. For instance, the background-attachment property can be assigned a value of "scroll" or "fixed". Values that appear in italics designate values that can vary. For example, the color value you assign to the background-color property will vary depending on the color you want to use.

Next, you will study each of the background properties.

Assigning Foreground and Background Color

You have already seen examples of how to use the `color` property to change the color of an element's text. The color you apply with the `color` property is also referred to as the **foreground color**. You can also add **background color** to elements using the `background-color` property. The foreground color that is applied to an element's text appears on top of an element's background color. For example, the following inline style formats a paragraph's foreground color (its text) as white and its background color as black:

```
p { color: white; background-color: black;
font-family: Arial }
```

The W3C strongly recommends that whenever you use the `color` property, you also include the `background-color` property to ensure that the foreground color text is placed on a suitable background. If you fail to include the `background-color` property, you could create some unpleasant results. For example, if you failed to include the black background color in the preceding example, the white foreground color would be unreadable in a Web browser.

Sometimes you do not need a background color for an element. For example, when you want to include an image as the document background (which you will study next), you would not want to set a color for an element's `background-color` property because the image would not be visible behind the element. In these cases, you can assign a value of "transparent" to the `background-color` property and still comply with the W3C's recommendation.

You have almost certainly seen Web pages with a background color or image. To set background properties for the Web page itself, you declare them for the `<body>` element. For example, the following code uses the `background-color` property to set the background color for the document body to gray.

```
body { background-color: gray }
```

Next, you will add aqua as a document background color to the Western Kayak Adventures home page. You also will add a value of transparent to the `background-color` properties for each of the style declarations that include `color` properties, to conform to the W3C's recommendation.

To add a background color to the Western Kayak Adventures home page:

1. Return to the **adventure_styles.css** file in your text editor.

2. Add the following declaration for the body selector to the end of the file. The declaration contains a single property, `color`, to which you assign the color aqua.

   ```
   body { background-color: aqua }
   ```

3. Add **background-color: transparent** to each of the other style declarations that include a color declaration. You should add four `background-color` properties in addition to the one you added for the body selector. For example, the style declaration for the p selector should appear as follows:

    ```
    p { font-family: Trebuchet MS; color: blue;
    font-size: 80%; background-color: transparent }
    ```

4. Save the **adventure_styles.css** file and then open the **WesternKayakExternal.html** file in your Web browser. The background of the Web page should appear in aqua.

5. Close your Web browser window.

Using Background Images

You have probably seen an image used as a document's background. To set an image to appear as the document background, you use the `background-image` property and assign it a URL using the format `url(url)`. For example, the following code sets the background image for a document to an image file named kite.jpg. Figure 3-16 shows how the background image appears in a Web browser.

```
body { color: blue; font-family: Arial;
    font-size: .8em; font-weight: normal;
    background-image: url(kite.jpg) }
```

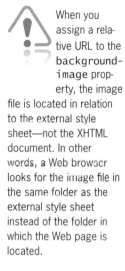

When you assign a relative URL to the background-image property, the image file is located in relation to the external style sheet—not the XHTML document. In other words, a Web browser looks for the image file in the same folder as the external style sheet instead of the folder in which the Web page is located.

Figure 3-16 Document with a background image

The kite image shown in Figure 3-16 is actually a single image. By default, CSS places the image in the top left of the screen and repeats it so that the image appears to be "wallpapering" the document. You can change where the image is initially placed using the `background-position` property, and you can determine how the image repeats using the `background-repeat` property. The following code shows how to place the image at the top-center part of the page and how to make it repeat along the y-axis only (from top to bottom). Figure 3-17 shows the document in a Web browser.

```
body { color: blue; font-family: Arial;
       font-size: .8em; font-weight: normal;
       background-image: url(kite.jpg);
       background-position: top center;
       background-repeat: repeat-y }
```

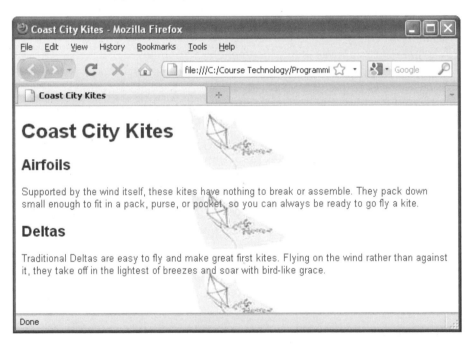

Figure 3-17 Document with a background image positioned at the top of the page and repeated along the y-axis

Next, you add a repeating background image to the Western Kayak Adventures home page. Your Chapter folder for Chapter 3 contains an image named kayak.gif that you can use.

To add a repeating background image to the Western Kayak Adventures home page:

1. Return to the **adventure_styles.css** file in your text editor.

2. Change the value assigned to the background-color property from aqua to transparent. Also, add a style declaration that assigns the kayak.gif file to the background-image property.

```
body { background-color: transparent;
background-image: url(kayak.gif) }
```

3. Save the **adventure_styles.css** file and then open the **WesternKayakExternal.html** file in your Web browser. Figure 3-18 shows how the file appears after the background image is added.

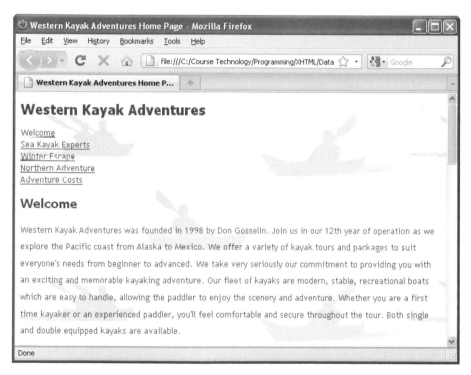

Figure 3-18 Western Kayak Adventures home page after adding a background image

4. Close your Web browser window.

Setting the background Shorthand Property

Several of the property categories include a special **shorthand property** that allows you to set all of the properties in a category using one declaration. The shorthand property for the background properties category is the background property. Many of the properties for each category have unique values you can assign. The background-attachment property, for instance, can be assigned the values "scroll" or "fixed"; neither of these values can be assigned to any other background property. With this in mind, you can set any background property by assigning just its property value to the shorthand background property. Multiple property values are separated by spaces. For example, to use the background property to set the background-image, background-position, and background-repeat properties from the preceding example, you would use the following declaration:

```
background: url(kite.jpg) top center repeat-y
```

Next, you will replace some properties in the sample css file with the shorthand background property.

To replace the background-color and background-image properties in the adventure_styles.css file with the background property:

1. Return to the **adventure_styles.css** file.

2. Replace the background-color and background-image properties in the style declaration for the body selector with the following background property:

   ```
   body { background: transparent url(kayak.gif) }
   ```

3. Save the **adventure_styles.css** file and then open the **WesternKayakExternal.html** file in your Web browser. The background color and image should look the same as they did before you added the background property.

4. Close your Web browser window.

Assigning a Background to Other Elements

Remember that background properties are not limited to the document background. You can also use them in other elements, as shown in the following declaration for the h2 selector. Figure 3-19 shows the document in a Web browser.

```
h2 { color: navy; font-size: 1.5em;
    font-family: Arial;
    background-image: url(kites.gif);
    background-position: center center;
    background-repeat: no-repeat }
}
```

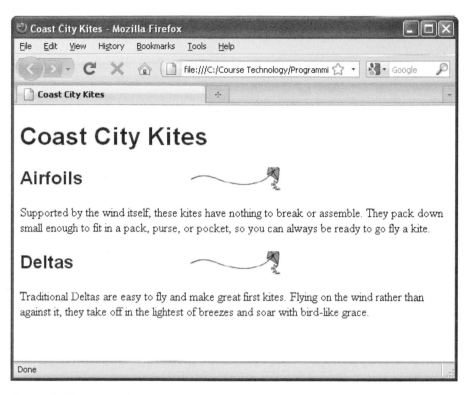

Figure 3-19 <h2> elements with a background image

Short Quiz 3

1. What is the difference between foreground and background colors when used with CSS?

2. Explain how to create a background image.

3. How do you set a background image's shorthand property?

Setting Text Properties

You use **text properties** to specify the placement and appearance of text. The difference between text properties and font properties (which you study next) is that text properties do not change the appearance of an element's font. Rather, text properties adjust visual aspects such as word and letter spacing, text alignment, and indentation. Table 3-6 lists the CSS1 text properties.

Property	Description	Values
word-spacing	Adjusts spacing between words	*length unit*
letter-spacing	Adjusts spacing between letters	*length unit*
text-decoration	Adds decorations to an element's text	none | underline | overline | line-through | blink
vertical-align	Determines the vertical positioning of an element	baseline | sub | super | top | text-top | middle | bottom | text-bottom | *percentage unit*
text-transform	Changes the letter case of an element's text	none | capitalize | uppercase | lowercase
text-align	Determines the horizontal alignment of an element's text	left | center | right | justify
text-indent	Specifies the indentation of an element's text	*length unit* | *percentage unit*
line-height	Determines the line height of an element's text	*length unit* | *percentage unit*

Table 3-6　CSS1 text properties

Next, you study the text properties.

Spacing Words and Letters

Word spacing and letter spacing refer to the amount of space between words and letters, respectively. You set word spacing with the word-spacing property and letter spacing with the letter-spacing property. Manipulating this spacing is common in publishing and typesetting. Increasing the space between words and letters can make text more readable, whereas decreasing the space can be useful for getting more text to fit within a line or paragraph. The amount of space between words and letters varies according to the typeface you are using. Therefore, you should always use a relative length unit, such as ems or percentages, when you assign a value for these items.

As an example of word and letter spacing, consider the paragraph in Figure 3-20, which does not include the word-spacing or letter-spacing properties. The paragraph is created with the following style declaration, which uses the Arial Narrow font:

```
<style type="text/css">
p { font-family: "Arial Narrow" }
</style>
```

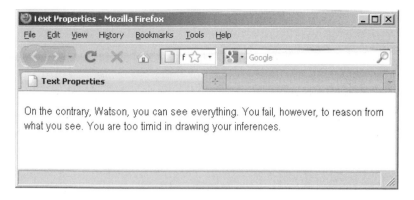

Figure 3-20   Paragraph that uses the Arial Narrow font

The word and letter spacing of the Arial Narrow font are fairly tight. You can expand the spacing of each by adding **word-spacing** and **letter-spacing** properties to the style declaration, as follows. Notice that only a small value, .1em, is assigned to each property. Figure 3-21 shows how the paragraph appears in a Web browser after the properties are added.

```
<style type="text/css">
p { font-family: "Arial Narrow";
word-spacing: .1em; letter-spacing: .1em }
</style>
```

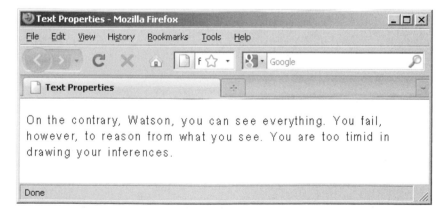

Figure 3-21   Paragraph that uses word-spacing and letter-spacing properties

Modifying Text Appearance

The **text-decoration** property modifies the appearance of text by adding the following "decorations": none, underline, overline, line-through, and blink. An underline value underlines the text, an

A value of "blink" should cause text to appear and disappear. Usability experts recommend that you avoid using blinking text because most people find it annoying. Additionally, some user agents, such as those for the visually impaired, have no way of rendering blinking text. Third, blinking text is not supported by Internet Explorer and other browsers.

You should avoid using underlined text on your Web pages because users may confuse the text with hyperlinks.

overline value places a line over the text, and a line-through value places a line through the text, the same as the <del> element.

A common use of the text-decoration property is to turn off the underline that appears beneath links for design purposes. To turn off the underline for a hyperlink, you assign a value of "none" to the text-decoration property for the anchor (<a>) element. For example, the a selector declaration in the following code turns off underlining for the document's <a> elements:

```
...
<style type="text/css">
p { font-family: Arial; color: olive }
a { text-decoration: none; color: blue }
</style>
...
<p><a href="http://abcnews.go.com">ABC News</a>
provides news around the globe.</p>
...
```

Next, you add a style declaration to the sample css file that turns off underlining for the anchor elements.

To add a style declaration to the adventure_styles.css file that turns off underlining for the anchor elements:

1. Return to the **adventure_styles.css** file in your text editor.

2. Add the following style declaration for the anchor elements to the end of the file:

   ```
   a { text-decoration: none }
   ```

3. Save the **adventure_styles.css** file and then open the **WesternKayakExternal.html** file in your Web browser. The anchor elements should no longer be underlined.

4. Close your Web browser window.

Setting Line Height

By default, the line height in a document is set to single space. You use the line-height property to change the line height of an element. The line-height property can accept a length unit or percentage unit value. If you use a length unit, be sure to use a relative unit such as ems or a percentage unit.

The following style declaration formats a document's paragraph elements to double space by assigning a value of 200% to the `line-height` property:

```
p { line-height: 200% }
```

Next, you will modify the style declaration for the p selector to change the spacing of paragraph text.

To modify the style declaration for the p selector so paragraph text is formatted with double spacing:

1. Return to the **adventure_styles.css** file in your text editor.

2. Modify the style declaration for the p selector so it includes a `line-height` property that changes the line height of the paragraph to double. The modified style declaration for the p selector should appear as follows:

    ```
    p { font-family: Trebuchet MS; color: blue;
    font-size: 80%; background-color: transparent;
    line-height: 200% }
    ```

3. Save the **adventure_styles.css** file and then open the **WesternKayakExternal.html** file in your Web browser. The paragraph text should appear double-spaced.

4. Close your Web browser window.

Indenting Elements

The `text-indent` property indents the first line of a paragraph according to the value you specify. You may be tempted to use an absolute measurement such as inches or centimeters with the `text-indent` property, but instead you should use a relative length unit or a percentage unit to allow the indent to scale according to the element's font. For example, the following p selector style declaration indents the paragraph text by 5 percent of the total width of the paragraph. The code also assigns a value of 200% to the `line-height` property. Figure 3-22 shows how the paragraphs appear for the Coast City Kites Web page when it includes the following declaration:

```
p { text-indent: 5%; line-height: 200% }
```

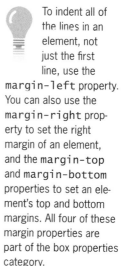

To indent all of the lines in an element, not just the first line, use the `margin-left` property. You can also use the `margin-right` property to set the right margin of an element, and the `margin-top` and `margin-bottom` properties to set an element's top and bottom margins. All four of these margin properties are part of the box properties category.

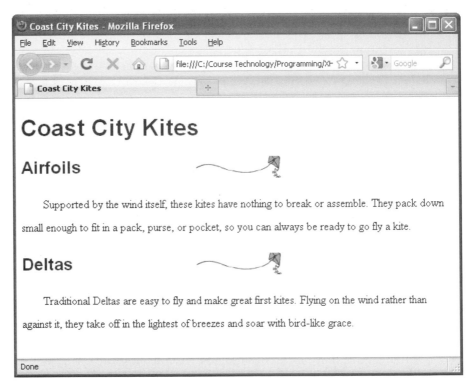

Figure 3-22   Coast City Kites Web page with paragraphs indented 5%

Next, you modify the style declaration for the p selector to indent text.

To modify the style declaration for the p selector so paragraph text is indented by 5 percent:

1. Return to the **adventure_styles.css** file in your text editor.

2. Modify the style declaration for the p selector so it includes a `text-indent` property that indents the first line of the paragraph by 5 percent. The modified style declaration for the p selector should appear as follows:

   ```
   p { font-family: Trebuchet MS; color: blue;
   font-size: 80%; background-color: transparent;
   line-height: 200%; text-indent: 5% }
   ```

3. Save the **adventure_styles.css** file and then open the **WesternKayakExternal.html** file in your Web browser. The first line of each paragraph should appear indented.

4. Close your Web browser window.

Aligning Text

You have seen how to align text horizontally using the `text-align` property. Although the previous examples have used inline styles, you can also use the `text-align` property with selectors. For example, to center-align a document's `<h1>` and `<h2>` elements, you include the following declarations for each element's selector:

```
h1 { text-align: center }
h2 { text-align: center }
```

The `vertical-align` property is a little more complicated in that it changes the vertical alignment of an element in relation to its parent element. One common use of the `vertical-align` property is to adjust the position of images, such as toolbar buttons, that are placed inside a line of text. For example, the following statement places an image named home.jpg within the paragraph. Figure 3-23 shows how the paragraph appears in a Web browser.

```
<p>In Firefox, you press the <img src="home.jpg"
style="vertical-align: bottom" /> button to return
to your home page.</p>
```

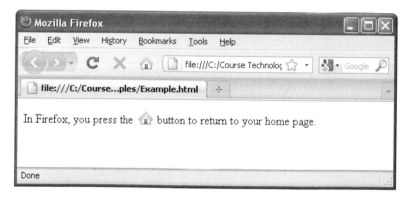

Figure 3-23   Paragraph with an inline image formatted with the `vertical-align` property

Notice in Figure 3-23 that the image is aligned to the bottom of the line, which is the default setting. To format the image so it is positioned in the middle of the line, you add the `vertical-align: middle` style declaration to the `<img>` element, as shown by the inline style in the following code:

```
<p>In Firefox, you press the <img style=
"vertical-align: middle" src="home.jpg" /> button to
return to your home page.</p>
```

Short Quiz 4

1. Explain how to adjust the spacing between words and letters.

2. How do you modify the appearance of text?

3. How do you set line height?

4. How do you indent elements?

5. How do you align text?

Setting Font Properties

You use **font properties** to specify the typeface, size, and style of an element's text. Table 3-7 lists the CSS1 font properties.

Property	Description	Values
font	Sets all the font properties in one declaration	*font-style* | *font-variant* | *font-weight* | *font-size* | *line-height* | *font-family* | inherit
font-family	Specifies a list of font names or generic font names	*font family* | serif | sans-serif | cursive | fantasy | monospace | inherit
font-size	Specifies the size of a font	xx-small | x-small | small | medium | large | x-large | xx-large | smaller | larger | *length unit* | *percentage unit* | inherit
font-style	Sets the style of a font	normal | italic | oblique | inherit
font-variant	Specifies whether the font should appear in small caps	normal | small-caps | inherit
font-weight	Sets the weight of a font	normal | bold | bolder | lighter | 100 | 200 | 300 | 400 | 500 | 600 | 700 | 800 | 900

Table 3-7   CSS1 font properties

Next, you will study each of the font properties.

Defining Font Names

The `font-family` property is critical because it sets the font that an element displays. When you select a font for an element, be sure to use a font that you know is installed on a user's computer. Your best bet is to assign a list of font names to the `font-family` property, separated by commas. When a Web browser renders the document, it looks for the first font name in the list, and uses it if the font is available. If the first font in the list is not available, the browser looks for the second name in the list, and so on. The following code specifies that the `<p>` element should use the Arial typeface if it is available. If Arial is not available, the Helvetica typeface is used.

```
p { font-family: Arial, Helvetica }
```

For font names that do not include spaces, as in the preceding example, assign the names directly to the `font-family` property. However, you must place any font names that include spaces in quotation marks, as follows:

```
p { font-family: "Times New Roman",
    "New Century Schoolbook", Garamond }
```

If you use an inline style to specify a font name with spaces, place the font name in single quotation marks, as follows:

```
<p style="font-family: 'Times New Roman'">
Paragraph formatted with Times New Roman.</p>
```

Generic font families represent the five major font families available in typography: serif, sans serif, cursive, fantasy, and monospace. Serif fonts include short lines and strokes, called serifs, like the ones found in the Times New Roman and New Century Schoolbook typefaces. Sans-serif fonts are plainer and do not include text adornments. Examples of sans-serif fonts include Arial and Helvetica. Cursive fonts look like cursive writing or handwriting. Fantasy fonts include various types of artistic fonts, like Algerian or Impact. Monospace fonts such as Courier and Courier New resemble typewriter fonts. The W3C recommends that you end a font list with one of the five generic font names. If the fonts you specify in the font list are not available on a user's machine, the Web browser will find the first font in the user's font list that is part of the generic font family. For example, a font list that specifies serif fonts, such as Times New Roman, should end with the serif generic font family, as follows:

```
p { font-family: "Times New Roman", "New Century
Schoolbook", Garamond, serif }
```

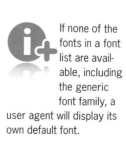 If none of the fonts in a font list are available, including the generic font family, a user agent will display its own default font.

166

Next, you will add font lists and a generic font family to each of the style declarations in adventure_styles.css that include a `font-name` property.

To add font lists and a generic font family to the style declarations that include a `font-name` property:

1. Return to the **adventure_styles.css** file in your text editor.

2. For the h1 and h2 selectors, add Arial and sans-serif to the `font-family` property list. The modified style declaration should appear as follows:

   ```
   h1, h2 { font-family: Tahoma, Arial, sans-serif;
   color: maroon; background-color: transparent }
   ```

3. For the p and links selectors, place the Trebuchet MS font in quotation marks, and add Arial, Helvetica, and sans-serif to the `font-family` property list. The modified style declarations for both selectors should appear as follows:

   ```
   p { font-family: "Trebuchet MS", Arial, Helvetica,
   sans-serif; color: blue; background-color:
   transparent; font-size: 80%; line-height: 200%;
   text-indent: 5% }
   .links { font-family: "Trebuchet MS", Arial,
   Helvetica, sans-serif; font-size: 80% }
   ```

4. Save the **adventure_styles.css** file and then open the **WesternKayakExternal.html** file in your Web browser. The Web page should look the same as it did before you added the font lists.

5. Close your Web browser window.

Selecting Font Size

You have seen examples of how to specify font size using the `font-size` property. When specifying font size, be sure to use a relative length unit such as ems or a percentage unit. Alternatively, you can use one of the following predefined values to set font size: xx-small, x-small, small, medium, large, x-large, xx-large, smaller, or larger. These predefined values are called absolute sizes and are somewhat limited because they do not adjust automatically to the browser or parent font, as do font sizes specified with relative length units. Figure 3-24 shows how each of the absolute sizes appears in a Web browser; each line shown is created using a statement similar to the following:

```
<p style="font-size: xx-small">Paragraph formatted
with the <code>xx-small</code> absolute value.</p>
```

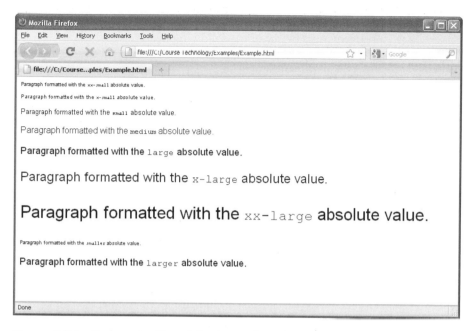

Figure 3-24 Paragraph with an inline image formatted with the `font-size` property

Defining Font Appearance

In addition to the font family and the font size, you can change the appearance of a font using the `font-style`, `font-variant`, and `font-weight` properties. The `font-style` property allows you to make text italicized or oblique (which is slanted, similar to italics). The `font-variant` property causes text to appear as small capital letters, LIKE THIS. The `font-weight` property determines how bold or light the text appears.

Using the `font` Shorthand Property

Just as the `background` property is the shorthand property for the background properties category, the `font` property is the shorthand property for the font properties category. Using the `font` shorthand property, you can set values for all of the font properties in a single declaration. In addition to setting the `font-style`, `font-variant`, `font-weight`, `font-size`, and `font-family` properties, you can also use the `font` shorthand property to set the `line-height` property from the text properties category. As with the `background` property, you can set any `font` property or the `line-height` property by assigning just the property value to the `font` property. You separate multiple property values with spaces. Note that the values for the font property must be set in the following order:

- font-style (optional)

- font-variant (optional)

- font-weight (optional)

- font-size (required)

- line-height (optional)

- font-family (required)

You must include the font-size and font-family property values, although you can safely exclude the rest. However, if you include the optional property values, be sure that the properties you use follow the correct order.

 Do not include spaces on either side of the forward slash that separates the font-size and line-height values. If you include spaces, Internet Explorer and other browsers will ignore the line-height value.

Note that the font-size and line-height property values must be separated by a forward slash (/). For example, to use the font property to set the font-weight, font-size, line-height, and font-family properties, you use the following declaration. Notice that although the declaration does not include the font-style or font-variant properties, the values still follow the correct order.

```
p { font: normal 1em/200% Arial, Verdana, sans-serif
}
```

Next, you replace the font-family, font-size, and line-height properties in the style declaration for the p selector with the font shorthand property.

To use the font shorthand property in the style declaration for the p selector:

1. Return to the **adventure_styles.css** file in your text editor.

2. Replace the font-family, font-size, and line-height properties in the style declaration for the p selector with the font shorthand property, as follows:

   ```
   p { color: blue; background-color: transparent;
   text-indent: 5%; font: 80%/200% "Trebuchet MS",
   Arial, Helvetica, sans-serif }
   ```

3. Save and close the **adventure_styles.css** file and then open the **WesternKayakExternal.html** file in your Web browser. The Web page should look the same as it did before you added the font shorthand property.

4. Close your Web browser window and text editor.

Validating Style Sheets

Next, you will validate the WesternKayakExternal.html file.

To validate the WesternKayakExternal.html file:

1. Start your Web browser and enter the URL for the upload page of the W3C Markup Validation Service: **http://validator.w3.org/#validate-by-upload**.

2. Open and validate the **WesternKayakExternal.html** file. If you receive any errors, fix them and then revalidate the document.

3. Close your Web browser window.

The W3C also offers a utility called the W3C CSS Validation Service for validating CSS code. This service is primarily used for external style sheets. You can download a copy of the utility or validate your CSS code online, just as you validate XHTML code with the W3C Markup Validation Service. You can access the W3C CSS Validation Service at *http://jigsaw.w3.org/css-validator/*. The upload page for the service is at *http://jigsaw.w3.org/css-validator/#validate_by_upload*.

You choose the external style sheet file you want to validate by clicking the Browse button. The Warnings option allows you to select the severity of warnings to display when your style sheet is validated. The Profile option allows you to select the type of styles used in your style sheet (CSS1, CSS2, and so on). Use the Medium option to select the medium your styles are designed for, such as the screen, aural and Braille browsers, and handheld devices.

Now you will validate the adventure_styles.css file.

To validate the adventure_styles.css file:

1. Start your Web browser and enter the URL for the upload page of the W3C CSS Validation Service: **http://jigsaw.w3.org/css-validator/#validate_by_upload**.

2. Open the **adventure_styles.css** file. Leave the Warnings box at the default setting of Normal report and the Medium box at the default setting of all. Change the setting in the Profile box from CSS version 2 to **CSS version 1**.

3. Click the **Submit this CSS file for validation** button to validate the file. You should receive the message "No error or warning found". If you receive any errors, fix them and then revalidate the style sheet.

4. Close your Web browser window.

Short Quiz 5

1. How do you specify the font names to use with an element?

2. How do you set font size?

3. How do you define a font's appearance?

4. Explain how to use the font shorthand property.

Summing Up

- Cascading Style Sheets (CSS) are a standard set of styles from the W3C for managing the design and formatting of Web pages in a Web browser.

- A single piece of CSS formatting information, such as text alignment or font size, is referred to as a style.

- The term *cascading* refers to the ability of Web pages to use CSS information from multiple sources.

- CSS styles are created in two parts separated by a colon: the property, which refers to a specific CSS style, and the value assigned to the property, which determines the style's visual characteristics.

- A CSS property and its assigned value are referred to as a declaration or style declaration.

- Inline styles allow you to add style information to a single element in a document.

- Length units refer to the units of measure that you can use in a style declaration to determine the size or positioning of an element.

- Percentage units adjust properties relative to other values.

- A color unit represents a color value that you can assign to a property.

- You use an internal style sheet to create styles that apply to an entire document.

- The element to which specific style rules apply in a style sheet is called a selector.

- A contextual selector allows you to specify formatting for an element, but only when it is contained within another element.

- A class selector allows you to create different groups of styles for the same element.

- An ID selector allows you to create style declarations that are applied only to a single element in the document.

- External style sheets are separate text documents containing style declarations that can be used by multiple documents on a Web site.

- The `<div>` element formats a group of block-level and inline elements with styles, whereas the `<span>` element formats a group of inline elements.

- The `color` property sets the text color of an element.

- Background properties set the background color or image that appears behind an element.

- Several property categories include a special shorthand property that allows you to set all of the properties in a category using one declaration.

- You use text properties to specify the placement and appearance of text.

- You use font properties to specify the typeface, size, and style of an element's text.

Comprehension Check

1. What is the correct syntax for creating an inline style that assigns Arial to the `font-family` property?

   a. `style="font-family, Arial"`

   b. `font-family=Arial`

   c. `style="font-family: Arial"`

   d. `font-family; Arial`

2. You can include multiple style declarations in an inline style by separating each declaration with a _____.

   a. colon

   b. semicolon

   c. comma

   d. forward slash

3. Which of the following length units are relative? (Choose all that apply.)

   a. em (em space)

   b. ex (x height)

   c. px (pixels)

   d. pt (points)

4. The number and unit of measure you assign as a value to a property must be separated by a space. True or False?

5. Which element do you use to create an internal style sheet?

   a. `<css>`

   b. `<link>`

   c. `<style>`

   d. `<styles>`

6. Explain when you should use an internal style sheet.

7. The element to which specific style rules apply in a style sheet is called a _____.

   a. selector

   b. variable

   c. style

   d. style declaration

8. A contextual selector allows you to specify formatting for an element, but only when it is contained within another element. True or False?

9. What is the correct syntax for creating a class selector named "emphasis" that can be used with any element?

   a. `styles.emphasis { color: green; font-weight: bolder }`

   b. `all.emphasis { color: green; font-weight: bolder }`

   c. `emphasis { color: green; font-weight: bolder }`

   d. `.emphasis { color: green; font-weight: bolder }`

10. The declaration for an ID selector must be preceded by a
    _____ symbol.

    a. #

    b. $

    c. %

    d. @

11. What value is assigned to the `rel` attribute in the `<link>`
    element?

    a. css

    b. external

    c. stylesheet

    d. stylesheets

12. Which of the following elements allows you to apply style
    information to a group of elements? (Choose all that apply.)

    a. `<div>`

    b. `<css>`

    c. `<span>`

    d. `<styles>`

13. Which of the following style sources has the highest level of
    precedence?

    a. internal style sheets

    b. external style sheets

    c. inline styles

    d. browser defaults

14. What is the default value applied to the `background-repeat`
    property?

    a. repeat

    b. repeat-x

    c. repeat-y

    d. no-repeat

174

15. Background properties can be applied only to the document body. True or False?

16. What is the correct format for assigning an image to the `background-image` property?

    a. `background-image: image.jpg`

    b. `background-image: "url(image.jpg)"`

    c. `background-image: url("image.jpg")`

    d. `background-image: url(image.jpg)`

17. Explain how you assign values to a shorthand property.

18. Which of the following values can be assigned to the `text-align` property? (Choose all that apply.)

    a. left

    b. center

    c. right

    d. justify

19. You must place any font names that include spaces in quotation marks. True or False?

20. If you create a `font-family` property that includes the Arial and Helvetica fonts in its font list, what should be the last entry in the font list?

    a. serif

    b. sans-serif

    c. script

    d. fantasy

Reinforcement Exercises

 Exercise 3-1

In this exercise, you use inline styles to format a Web page for a relocation service. The file to which you will add the style information, Relocation.html, is in your Exercises folder for Chapter 3.

1. In your text editor, open the **Relocation.html** file from your Exercises folder for Chapter 3. The document body contains two heading elements and three paragraph elements.

2. To the `<body>` element, add the following inline style declaration to change the background color of the page to gray:

   ```
   style="background-color: aqua"
   ```

3. Next, modify the two heading elements so they contain inline style formatting, as follows:

   ```
   <h1 style="font-family: 'Times New Roman', ↵
     Times, serif; font-size: 2em; color: navy; ↵
     background-color: transparent">Central Valley</h1>
   <h2 style="font-family: 'Times New Roman', Times, ↵
     serif; font-size: 1.5em; text-spacing: 80%; ↵
     color: navy; background-color: transparent">
   Relocation Service</h2>
   ```

4. Add the following inline style declaration to each of the paragraph elements:

   ```
   style="font-family: 'Times New Roman', Times, ↵
     serif; font-size: .8em; color: navy; ↵
     background-color: transparent"
   ```

5. Save the **Relocation.html** file.

6. Use the W3C Markup Validation Service to validate the **Relocation.html** file. Once the file is valid, open it in your Web browser and see how the new style formatting appears.

7. Close your Web browser window.

 ## Exercise 3-2

In this exercise, you use an internal style sheet to add style information to a Web page that contains customer testimonials for an auto body shop. The file to which you add the style information, AutoBodyShop.html, is in your Exercises folder for Chapter 3.

1. In your text editor, open the **AutoBodyShop.html** file from your Exercises folder for Chapter 3. The document body contains three `<blockquote>` elements, each of which includes text and `<em>` elements.

2. Add the following internal style sheet above the document's closing </head> element. The style sheet includes declarations for the h1, h2, and blockquote selectors, along with a contextual selector for the <em> element when located within a <div> element.

```
<style type="text/css">
h1 { font-family: Verdana, Helvetica, sans-serif;
font-size: 1.5em; color: navy }
h2 { font-family: Verdana, Helvetica, sans-serif;
font-size: 1.2em; color: red }
blockquote { font-family: Verdana, Helvetica,
sans-serif; font-size: 1em; color: blue }
div em { font-weight: bold; color: purple }
</style>
```

3. Save and close the **AutoBodyShop.html** file.

4. Use the W3C Markup Validation Service to validate the **AutoBodyShop.html** file. Once the file is valid, open it in your Web browser.

5. Close your Web browser window.

Exercise 3-3

In this exercise, you use inline styles to add background color, foreground color, and line height formatting to a paragraph on a sailing school's Web page. The file to which you add the style information, SailingSchool.html, is in your Exercises folder for Chapter 3.

1. In your text editor, open the **SailingSchool.html** file from your Exercises folder for Chapter 3. The document body contains a single paragraph with information about the school.

2. Add inline styles to the paragraph so it matches Figure 3-25. Use any fonts you like, but be sure to create a font list. Format the paragraph so it is double-spaced. The background color should be navy and the foreground color should be the hex value equivalent of white.

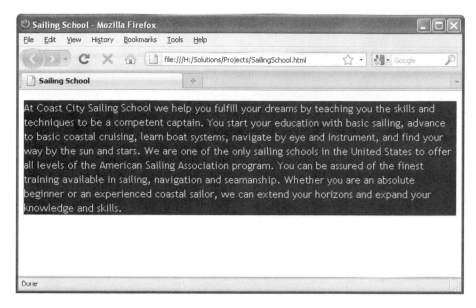

Figure 3-25   Sailing School Web page

3. Save the **SailingSchool.html** file.

4. Use the W3C Markup Validation Service to validate the **SailingSchool.html** file. Once the file is valid, open it in your Web browser and see how the colors look.

5. Close your Web browser window.

Exercise 3-4

In this exercise, you create a Web page for a petting zoo that includes an internal style sheet.

1. Create a new document in your text editor.

2. Type the `<!DOCTYPE>` declaration, `<html>` element, document head, and `<body>` element. Use the Strict DTD and "Noah's Ark Petting Zoo" as the content of the `<title>` element.

3. Create the document shown in Figure 3-26. Format the document using an internal style sheet. Create two class selectors in the style sheet for the `<p>` element: one for the first two indented paragraphs and another for the boldface, centered

paragraph at the bottom of the page. Use the closest fonts you have to the fonts displayed in the figure, but be sure to create a font list.

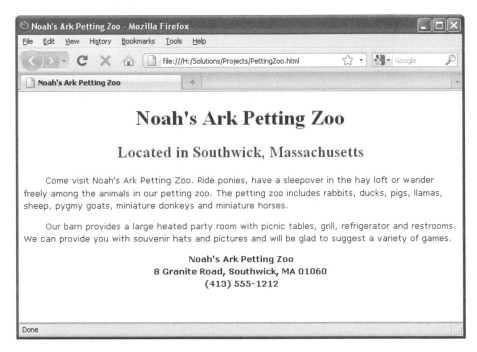

Figure 3-26 Noah's Ark Petting Zoo Web page

4. Save the file as **PettingZoo.html** in the Exercises folder for Chapter 3.

5. Close the **PettingZoo.html** file in your text editor, and then use the W3C Markup Validation Service to validate it. Once the file is valid, open it in your Web browser.

6. Close your Web browser window.

 Exercise 3-5

In this exercise, you create a document that uses an ID selector to align a toolbar button in the middle of a line.

1. Create a new document in your text editor.

2. Type the `<!DOCTYPE>` declaration, `<html>` element, document head, and `<body>` element. Use the Strict DTD and "Free Shipping" as the content of the `<title>` element.

3. To the document body, add the following paragraph and inline image:

```
<p><img src="dollars.gif"
   alt="Graphic of a price tag with a dollar symbol." />
   Free shipping until January 1!</p>
```

4. Save the document as **FreeShipping.html** in your Exercises folder for Chapter 3 and open the file in your Web browser window. The image should be raised too high on the line.

5. Close your Web browser window and return to the **FreeShipping.html** file in your text editor.

6. Add an internal style sheet to the document that includes an ID selector with the appropriate style declaration to align the image in the middle of the line. Assign the ID selector to the `<img>` element that displays the image.

7. Save and close the **FreeShipping.html** file.

8. Use the W3C Markup Validation Service to validate the **FreeShipping.html** file. Once the file is valid, open it in your Web browser.

9. Close your Web browser window.

 ## Exercise 3-6

In this exercise, you use class selectors to add yellow highlighting to sections of a paragraph. The file to which you will add the highlighting, Highlighter.html, is in your Exercises folder for Chapter 3.

1. In your text editor, open the **Highlighter.html** file from your Exercises folder for Chapter 3. The document body contains a single paragraph from Leo Tolstoy's *Anna Karenina*.

2. Use an internal style sheet to add the yellow highlighting shown in Figure 3-27.

179

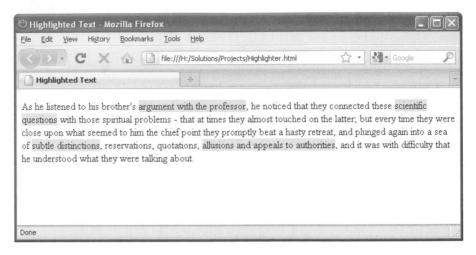

Figure 3-27   Paragraph with yellow highlighting

3. Save and close the **Highlighter.html** file.

4. Use the W3C Markup Validation Service to validate the **Highlighter.html** file. Once the file is valid, open it in your Web browser to see how the highlighted text appears.

5. Close your Web browser window.

Exercise 3-7

In this exercise, you create a document for a company that sells baseball team uniforms.

1. Create a new document in your text editor.

2. Type the `<!DOCTYPE>` declaration, `<html>` element, document head, and `<body>` element. Use the Strict DTD and "Team Uniform Sales" as the content of the `<title>` element.

3. Create the table shown in Figure 3-28. The three image files you need for the document—marlins.gif, braves.gif, and yankees.gif—are in your Exercises folder for Chapter 3. Add the text formatting using an internal style sheet. For the text formatting in the right column, create three generic class selectors and apply them to each line using a `<div>` element.

Name the class selector for the first line .team, the class selector for the second line .shipping, and the class selector for the third line .price. Use the closest fonts you have to the fonts displayed in the figure, but be sure to create a font list. Also, use different colors for each of the three generic class selectors.

Figure 3-28 Team Uniform Sales Web page

4. Save the file as **TeamUniforms.html** in the Exercises folder for Chapter 3.

5. Close the **TeamUniforms.html** file in your text editor, and then use the W3C Markup Validation Service to validate it. Once the file is valid, open it in your Web browser.

6. Close your Web browser window.

Exercise 3-8

In this exercise, you add a background image to the document body of a Web page for a chimney repair company. The files you need, ChimneyRepair.html and chimney.gif, are in your Exercises folder for Chapter 3.

1. In your text editor, open the **ChimneyRepair.html** file from your Exercises folder for Chapter 3. The document body contains a heading and several paragraphs. The document head contains a `<style>` element that contains some font and color formatting properties for the heading and paragraphs.

2. Add the appropriate style declaration to the `<style>` element that will place the **chimney.gif** file in the document's background. The image should repeat.

3. Save and close the **ChimneyRepair.html** file.

4. Use the W3C Markup Validation Service to validate the **ChimneyRepair.html** file. Once the file is valid, open it in your Web browser. Your file should look similar to Figure 3-29.

Figure 3-29   Chimney Repairs Web page

5. Close your Web browser window.

Discovery Projects

For the following projects, save the files you create in the Projects folder for Chapter 3. Use external style sheets to add CSS formatting to each of the projects. Create the files so they are well formed according to the Strict DTD. Be sure to validate the Web pages you create with the W3C Markup Validation Service.

Discovery Project 3-1

Create a Web page for a copy center. Format the heading level styles in olive and the paragraphs in blue. Format the heading and body elements using sans-serif fonts such as Arial and Helvetica. Include headings such as Services Offered, Hours of Operation, Copy Charges, and Accepted Forms of Payment. Within the Copy Charges heading, create a table that lists the costs of different types of copies such as black and white, color, and transparencies. Format the rows in the table so they alternate from white to gray. Within the gray rows, format the text to be white. Within the white rows, format the text to be black. You will need to set the `color` and `background-color` properties for the table's `<tr>` elements using class selectors. Save the Web page as **CopyCenter.html** and the style sheet as **copies.css**.

Discovery Project 3-2

Create a Web page for a company that rents snowmobiles. Format the heading elements in navy and the paragraphs in black. Use the body selector to format all of the text in the body using serif fonts such as Garamond and Times New Roman. Also, include the snow.gif image as a repeating background image; this image file is in your Projects folder for Chapter 3. Use any size you want for the heading and paragraph font sizes. Include at least three paragraphs that describe the services the company offers. Format each paragraph so its line height is spaced at 150%. Also, format the first word in every paragraph so it is 30 percent larger than the surrounding text, is formatted in blue, and uses a sans-serif font such as Arial. Save the Web page as **SnowmobileRentals.html** and the style sheet as **snowmobile.css**.

Discovery Project 3-3

Create a Web site for a tanning salon. Include a home page, a services page, and an FAQ (frequently asked questions) page. Create the Web page using a table that simulates a frame. Use white as the background color for the Web site. Format the heading elements in Arial with a font weight of bold and a color of lime. Also format the anchor elements in Arial and using the color lime, but with a font weight of normal. Format paragraph and table elements in Arial with a background color of black. Save the home page as **TanningSalon.html**, the services page as **Services.html**, the FAQ page as **FAQ.html**, and the style sheet as **tanning.css**.

Adding Images and Text

In this chapter you will:

◎ Add images to your Web pages

◎ Learn how to work with text-formatting elements

◎ Study phrasing elements

◎ Study block-level text elements

◎ Work with quotations

◎ Add special characters to your Web pages

◎ Create image maps

Many commercial services on the Web offer images that you can purchase for your Web pages. Many public-domain images can be used for free. You can find images by searching for "images" or "clip art". One particularly useful place to search is the Images tab at *http://www.google.com*. Once you find an image you want to use on your Web page, you can download it to your computer by right-clicking the image and selecting the Save command from the shortcut menu. Be sure to observe any copyright or licensing requirements before using an image.

In Chapter 2, you learned about some of the basic structural elements, and in Chapter 3 you learned how to use CSS to enhance the appearance of your Web pages. However, the most important part of a Web page is the content it displays. The text and images represent information that interests visitors to your Web page. That information may include a schedule of classes, a price list, company earnings, or directions to a particular location. Although the visual display of text is important to today's Web browsers, the *type* of information represented by the text will likely become more important as the Web evolves to other types of user agents. For this reason, HTML includes numerous elements for working with text, along with several elements and techniques for working with images. In this chapter, you study how to work with text and image elements and how to create an image map, which allows users to navigate to different Web pages by clicking various images.

Understanding the Image Element

One of the more visually pleasing parts of a Web page is its images. Web pages today include company logos, photographs of products and works of art, drawings, animation, image maps, and other types of graphics. Commerce-oriented Web pages that do not include images would be hard pressed to attract—and keep—visitors.

From Chapter 2, you already know the basics of including images on Web pages, including how to use images as links. Recall that the src attribute specifies the filename of an image file. To include the src attribute within the <img> element, you type <img src="mygraphic.gif">. The <img> element also includes other attributes, as listed in Table 4-1.

Attribute	Description
src	Specifies the filename of the image file
alt	Specifies alternate text to display in place of the image file
longdesc	Identifies the URL of a Web page with a long description of an image
width	Defines the width of an image
height	Defines the height of an image
usemap	Identifies an image to be used as a client-side image map
ismap	Identifies an image to be used as a server-side image map

Table 4-1   Attributes of the <img> element

Specifying Alternate Text

For a Web page to be well formed, the <img> element must include the src and alt attributes. The alt attribute, which specifies alternate text to display in place of the image file, is important for user agents that do not display images, such as the text-based Lynx browser and Web browsers designed for users of Braille and speech devices. Additionally, alternate text will be displayed if an image has not yet downloaded, if users have turned off the display of images in their Web browsers, or if the image is not available for some reason. The following <img> element displays a photo of an ambulance; the element's alt attribute is assigned an appropriate value, *Photo of an ambulance.* If the image has not yet been downloaded or if users have turned off the display of images in their Web browsers, they will see the alternate text shown in Figure 4-1.

```
<img src="ambulance.jpg" alt="Photo of an ambulance." />
```

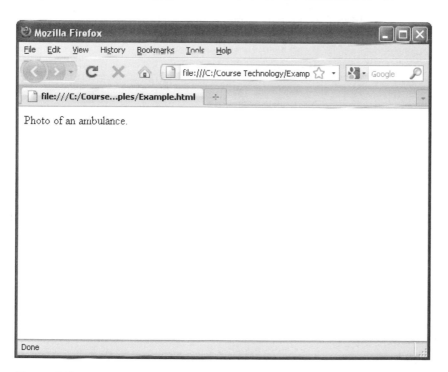

Figure 4-1   Alternate text displayed in a Web browser

Specifying Image Height and Width

When you create an <img> element that includes only the src and alt attributes, a Web browser needs to examine the image and determine the number of pixels to reserve for it. This process can significantly

188

You can find the height and width of an image using almost any graphics program such as Adobe Photoshop or PaintShop Pro. You can also quickly determine the height and width of an image by right-clicking the image in Firefox or Internet Explorer and then selecting Properties from the shortcut menu. Both browsers display a Properties dialog box that shows the selected image's height and width in pixels.

slow down the time required for a Web page to render. However, if you use the `height` and `width` attributes to specify the size of an image, the Web browser will use the values to reserve enough space on the page for the image. This allows the browser to render all of the text on the page and then go back and render each image after it finishes downloading. Each image placeholder displays the specified alternative text until the image itself is rendered.

In Figure 4-1, you saw the placeholder displaying alternative text for the ambulance.jpg image. Because the `<img>` element did not include `height` and `width` attributes, the Web browser reserved only enough space to display the alternative text. The image itself is actually 225 pixels in height and 350 pixels in width. The following code shows a modified version of the `<img>` element for the ambulance.jpg image; this time it includes `height` and `width` attributes. Figure 4-2 shows the placeholder that the Web browser now reserves for the image.

```
<img src="ambulance.jpg" alt="Photo of an ambulance."
    height="225" width="350" />
```

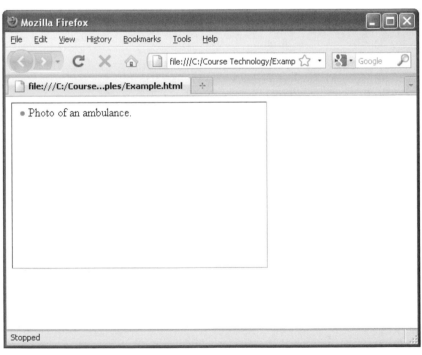

Figure 4-2   Placeholder for the ambulance.jpg image

You should always assign `height` and `width` attribute values that are the exact dimensions of the original image. Do not use the `height` and `width` attributes to resize an image on your Web page. If you want an image to have a different size, use an image-editing program to create a new, smaller version of the image. (Most image-editing programs include commands that automatically reduce the size of an image by a specified percentage or number of pixels.) Using the `height` and `width` attributes to resize an image on a Web page results in a poor-quality rendering. For one thing, unless you calculate the new dimensions so that the `height` and `width` attributes remain proportional to each other, the image will appear stretched or "squished." Figure 4-3 shows how the ambulance.jpg image appears using the `height` and `width` of the original image. Figure 4-4 shows the image resized to a height of 150 pixels and a width of 400 pixels. As you can see, the image in Figure 4-4 is significantly out of proportion from the original.

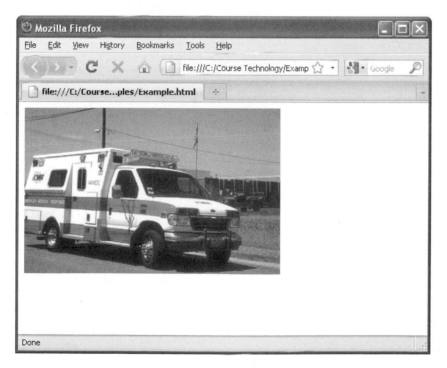

Figure 4-3   ambulance.jpg scaled to its original size

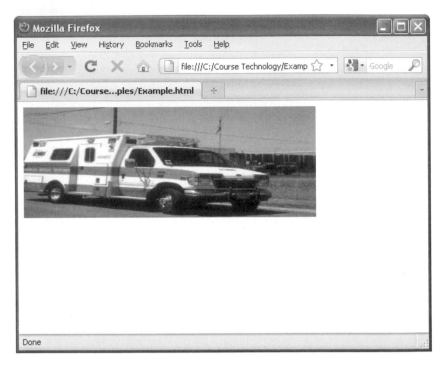

Figure 4-4   ambulance.jpg scaled to 150 pixels high by 400 pixels wide

Another reason not to resize an image using the `height` and `width` attributes is that the browser still needs to download the original image in its original size, which may make the page render more slowly than necessary. This can be especially problematic for slow dial-up modem connections. One solution that developers use for image-intensive Web sites is to create small "thumbnail" versions of images that visitors can view to get an idea of what the images look like. If visitors want to see a larger version of an image, they can click the thumbnail version, which is usually contained in an `<a>` element. Note that the thumbnail version is not the original image reduced using the `height` and `width` attributes of the `<img>` element. Rather, the thumbnail images are entirely separate images that have been resized using image-editing software.

Real estate agents commonly use thumbnails on their Web sites to display pictures of homes and other types of property. If visitors are interested in a particular property, they can click a thumbnail image to view the image in a larger size, along with information about the property. Figure 4-5 shows a Web page from realtor.com that displays thumbnail images of homes for sale in Riverside, California. Each thumbnail image is fairly small—only about 5 kilobytes, 110 pixels in height, and 165 pixels in width. Clicking the first thumbnail image opens the Web page shown in Figure 4-6, which displays a larger version of the image along with several other images. In this case, the larger image is about 12 kilobytes, 310 pixels in width, and 233 pixels in height—about three times the size of the thumbnail version.

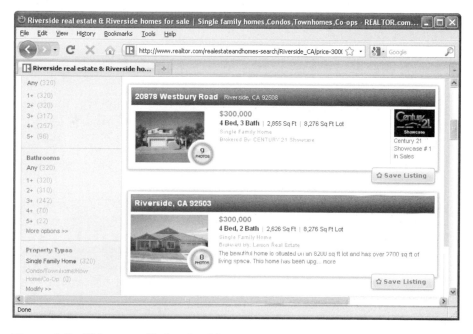

Figure 4-5   Web page with thumbnail images

Figure 4-6   Larger version of thumbnail images

Remember that this book is about Web page authoring, not Web page development, so you will not study the design techniques used to create the newYou Health Club Web page.

Next, you start working on the home page for a company named newYou Health Club. Your Chapter folder for Chapter 4 contains a CSS file named style.css that contains some existing styles you can use for this project. The Chapter folder also contains a folder named images, where you can find the graphic files for the project. First, you will use <div> and <img> elements to create the Web page design.

To start creating the home page for the newYou Health Club Web site:

1. Create a new document in your text editor and type the opening <!DOCTYPE> declaration that uses the HTML DTD, as follows:

   ```
   <!DOCTYPE HTML>
   ```

2. Type the <html> element, as follows:

   ```
   <html>
   </html>
   ```

3. Within the <html> element, add the following <head>, <title>, and <meta> elements to the document:

   ```
   <head>
   <title>newYou Health Club</title>
   <meta http-equiv="content-type"
         content="text/html; charset=utf-8" />
   <link href="style.css" rel="stylesheet"
         type="text/css" />
   </head>
   ```

4. Next, add the document <body> element within the <html> element:

   ```
   <body>
   </body>
   ```

5. Add the following code to the document body. Each <div> element is assigned an ID for which a style containing a background image exists in the style.css document.

   ```
   <div id="wrapper">
       <div id="top">
           <div id="nav">
               <a href="index.html"><img src="images/
                   b1.gif" width="83"
                   height="30" style="border-style: none"
                   alt="Visual formatting element" /></a>
               <img src="images/b2.gif"
                   alt="Visual formatting element"
                   width="83" height="30" hspace="1" />
               <img src="images/b3.gif" width="83"
                   height="30"
   ```

```
                    alt="Visual formatting element" /></div>
        </div>
        <div id="content">
            <div id="left">
                <img src="images/logo.gif" width="277"
                    height="133"
                    alt="Visual formatting element"
                        /><br /><br />
            </div>
            <div id="right">
                <div id="header">
                </div>
                <div class="greenbg">
                </div>
            </div>
            <div id="bottom2"><br /><br />
                Copyright newYou Health Club. All Rights
                    Reserved.
            </div>
        </div>
    </div>
```

6. Save the file as **index.html** in your Chapter folder for Chapter 4.

7. Open the **index.html** file in your Web browser. Figure 4-7 displays the index.html file as it appears in Firefox.

Figure 4-7 newYou Health Club home page in Firefox

Using Images from Other Locations

The image files you have used so far have been relative, meaning they are located on the same computer as the currently displayed document. For instance, the src attribute of the following <img> element is relative because it assumes that the ambulance.jpg file exists within the same folder as the Web page:

```
<img src="ambulance.jpg"
    alt="Photo of an ambulance."
    height="225" width="350" />
```

You can also place images in subfolders that are relative to the location of the current Web page folder. For instance, the following <img> element assumes that the ambulance.jpg file is located in a subfolder named graphics:

```
<img src="graphics/ambulance.jpg"
    alt="Photo of an ambulance."
    height="225" width="350" />
```

You can link to images at other locations on the Web by assigning an absolute URL to the src attribute of the <img> element. You can see an example of linking to an image on the Web at the W3C Web page for validating XHTML documents. After you successfully validate a Web page using the W3C Markup Validation Service, you can add the W3C XHTML image to your Web page to show that your document is valid. The instructions for adding the W3C XHTML image are shown at the bottom of the W3C Markup Validation Service Web page. You can download the image, place it in a folder on your Web site, and use it as a relative file, or you can link directly to the image at the W3C site. The Validation Service's validation page includes the following code that you can use to add the image by accessing it directly from the W3C Web site. Figure 4-8 shows how the image appears in a Web browser.

```
<p>
    <a href="http://validator.w3.org/check?uri=referer">
    <img src="http://www.w3.org/Icons/valid-xhtml10"
        alt="Valid XHTML 1.0 Strict" height="31"
        width="88" /></a>
</p>
```

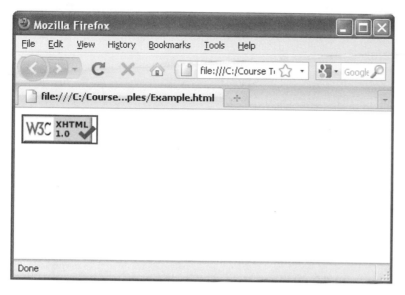

Figure 4-8   W3C XHTML markup validation image in a Web browser

Short Quiz 1

1. Explain the basic requirements for creating a well-formed alt attribute.

2. What should you do if you want to resize an image on a Web page?

3. How do you link to images in other locations?

Understanding Text-Level Semantics

Recall that early in the Web browser wars, browser makers began to add their own extensions to HTML, such as the bold and font elements, to provide functionality for displaying and formatting Web pages. These extensions did nothing to describe the type of data being presented, but only instructed a Web browser how to display and format the data. Consider the bold element. Although it works fine for visually displaying text in boldface type, how should it be handled by a user agent for the visually impaired that reads the contents of a Web page aloud? Should the user agent shout the content within the bold element? To address these types of issues, you need to understand HTML 5's text-level semantic elements. The term *semantics* refers to the study of meaning—in this case, the meaning of the elements that format and define text on a Web page. The text-level semantic elements are divided into two categories: formatting elements and phrasing elements.

Formatting Elements

Formatting elements provide specific instructions for how their content should be displayed. For instance, the <i> element instructs user agents to display its content in italics. **Phrasing elements**, however, primarily identify or describe their content. Consider the <em> element, which emphasizes text, similar to a quotation. How the <em> element is rendered is decided by each user agent, although most current Web browsers display the contents of the <em> element using italics. However, a user agent for the visually impaired may use the <em> element to pronounce the text it contains with more emphasis, to convey the meaning to the visually impaired user. Generally, you should strive to use only Cascading Style Sheets (CSS) to manage the display of elements on your Web pages. However, because several of the basic formatting elements are so commonly used, they are not deprecated in XHTML or HTML 5.

As discussed in Chapter 1, several elements that were popular in earlier versions of HTML are deprecated in favor of CSS. These elements include the <basefont>, <center>, <font>, <s>, <strike>, and <u> elements.

Table 4-2 lists the text-formatting elements.

Element	Description
<b>	Formats text in boldface type
<big>	Formats text in a larger font
<i>	Formats text in italic type
<small>	Formats text in a smaller font
<sub>	Formats enclosed text as a subscript
<sup>	Formats enclosed text as a superscript

Table 4-2   Text-formatting elements

You are probably already familiar with the elements listed in Table 4-2. However, to be sure you understand the formatting produced by each element, examine the following code for a simple Web page that uses each element. Figure 4-9 shows the output in a Web browser.

```
<!DOCTYPE HTML>
<html>
<head>
<title>Text Formatting Elements</title>
<meta http-equiv="content-type"
      content="text/html; charset=utf-8" />
```

```
</head>
<body>
<p><b>Bold text</b></p>
<p><big>Big text</big></p>
<p><i>Italicized text</i></p>
<p><small>Small text</small></p>
<p><sub>Subscripted</sub> text</p>
<p><sup>Superscripted</sup> text</p>
</body>
</html>
```

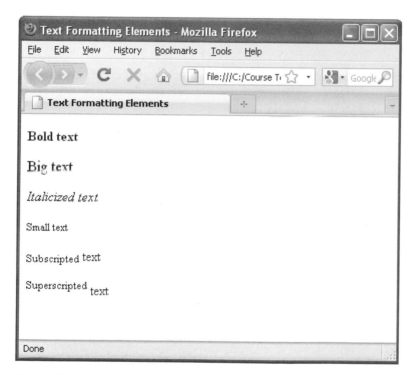

Figure 4-9 Web page with text-formatting elements

Most of the text-formatting elements in Figure 4-9 are self-explanatory. The <b> element is the equivalent of applying bold in a word-processing program. The <big> element renders its content in a slightly larger font than that used for the other elements on a page. Similarly, the <small> element renders its content in a slightly smaller font than that used for the other elements on the page.

Next, you will add some text to the newYou Health Club Web site.

To create a home page using text-formatting elements:

1. Return to the **index.html** file in your text editor.

2. Within the `<div>` element that has an ID of "header", add the following elements that contain the company's motto. The motto uses text-formatting elements to create boldface and italicized text. The motto is a French phrase that translates to "to your health." The statement is missing two French characters; you will add them later in this chapter when you learn how to add special characters to your Web pages.

    ```
    <p style="font-size: 20px; color: red">
    <b>Our motto is <i>A votre sante!</i></b></p>
    ```

3. At the end of the `<div>` element that has an ID of "greenbg", add the following elements to create the Today's Health Tip heading and section:

    ```
    <h2>Today's Health Tip</h2>
    <p>Caryn Honig wrote in the online edition of
    <i>Health & Fitness Sports Magazine</i> the
    following advice about energy bars:</p>
    <p>Energy bars can contain high amounts
    of calories and fat. Many contain palm
    kernel oil, which is saturated enough to
    stay solid at room temperature, preventing
    the coating from melting. Palm kernel oil is
    twice as saturated as lard. Try to avoid the
    bars that are high in saturated fat. When
    looking for an energy bar, read the labels.
    Stay away from bars with ma huang, ephedra,
    large amounts of caffeine and large amounts of
    ginseng. Stick to the natural ingredients, such
    as oats, fruit juice, and nuts. Often times, you
    are better off with an apple, a handful of nuts,
    or some other type of snack that fills you up with
    less calories, fat and artificial additives.</p>
    ```

4. Save the **index.html** file and then open it in your Web browser. Figure 4-10 displays the index.html file as it appears in Firefox.

Figure 4-10 newYou Health Club home page after adding formatting elements

    5. Close your Web browser window.

Using Phrasing Content

Although text-formatting elements are commonly used and work well for displaying text with a specific style of formatting, it is much better to format the text on your Web pages using a phrasing element that more adequately describes its content. Using phrasing elements helps ensure that your Web pages are compatible with user agents that may not be capable of handling formatting elements. Table 4-3 lists the phrasing elements that are available in HTML 5, and indicates how each element is rendered by most Web browsers.

Element	Description	Renders As
`<abbr>`	Specifies abbreviated text or acronyms	Default text
`<cite>`	Defines a citation	Italics
`<code>`	Identifies computer code	Monospace font
`<dfn>`	Marks a definition	Italics
`<em>`	Defines emphasized text	Italics

Table 4-3   Phrasing elements *(continues)*

(continued)

Element	Description	Renders As
`<figcaption>` HTML 5	Defines a caption for a group of elements	Not applicable
`<figure>` HTML 5	Used for grouping elements that explain parts of the document	Not applicable
`<kbd>`	Indicates text that is to be entered by a visitor to a Web site	Monospace font
`<mark>` HTML 5	Highlights text	Not applicable
`<meter>` HTML 5	Defines measurements with known minimum and maximum values	Not applicable
`<progress>` HTML 5	Identifies progress of time	Not applicable
`<samp>`	Identifies sample computer code	Monospace font
`<strong>`	Defines strongly emphasized text	Bold
`<time>` HTML 5	Defines date and time	Not applicable
`<var>`	Defines a variable	Italics

Table 4-3   Phrasing elements

The HTML 5 elements listed in Table 4-3 were not supported by any browsers at the time of this writing.

Current Web browsers use similar conventions for displaying the content of phrasing elements. For instance, most Web browsers render the `<em>` element in italics.

Phrasing elements are preferred over text-formatting elements for handling simple types of formatting (such as bold and italics) on a Web page. However, CSS is preferable for managing the display of elements on your Web pages.

The following example contains the code for a simple Web page that uses each phrasing element. Figure 4-11 shows the output in a Web browser.

```
<!DOCTYPE HTML>
<html>
<head>
<title>Phrasing elements</title>
<meta http-equiv="content-type"
      content="text/html; charset=utf-8" />
</head>
<body>
<p><abbr>Abbreviation</abbr></p>
<p><cite>Citation</cite></p>
<p><code>Code</code></p>
<p><dfn>Definition</dfn></p>
<p><em>Emphasis</em></p>
<p><kbd>Keyboard</kbd></p>
<p><samp>Sample</samp></p>
<p><strong>Strong</strong></p>
<p><var>Variable</var></p>
</body>
</html>
```

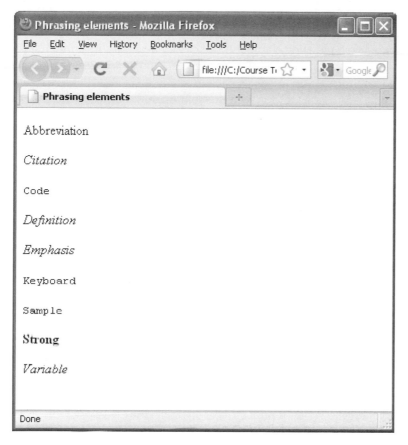

Figure 4-11   Web page with phrasing elements

The two most common text-formatting elements are the <b> and <i> elements. You should use the <strong> phrasing element in place of the <b> text-formatting element, and the <em> phrasing element in place of the <i> text-formatting element. This allows user agents other than Web browsers to better understand the meaning of each element, although current Web browsers still render the <strong> element as boldface and the <em> element in italics. Consider the following code written with the <b> and <i> elements:

```
<p><b>Yogi Berra said</b><br />
<i>When you come to a fork in the road,
    take it.</i></p>
```

Now consider the following version of the code that uses the <strong> and <em> elements instead of the <b> and <i> elements:

```
<p><strong>Yogi Berra said</strong><br />
<em>When you come to a fork in the road,
    take it.</em></p>
```

Both versions render identically in a Web browser. The version that uses the phrasing elements, however, is preferred (see Figure 4-12) because each phrasing element more clearly describes its contents, rather than simply determining how text should appear in a browser, as do text-formatting elements such as <i> and <b>. Recall the earlier example of a user agent for the visually impaired that reads the contents of a Web page aloud. This type of user agent may have difficulty rendering the bold element, whose primary purpose is to make text appear in boldface. However, the same user agent may be able to handle the <strong> element more easily by speaking its content with a louder intonation. In other words, the <strong> element specifies that the user agent should speak the text in a stronger voice. Similarly, the user agent may speak the contents of an <em> element with greater inflection to provide more emphasis.

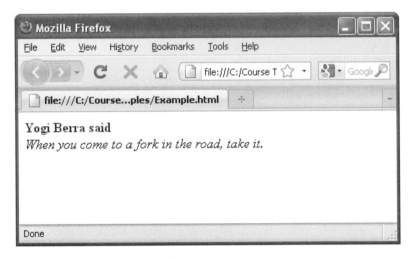

Figure 4-12   Output of text-formatting elements and phrasing elements

Next, you modify the paragraph that contains the motto in the index.html file so it uses the <strong> and <em> phrasing elements instead of the <b> and <i> text-formatting elements.

To use the <strong> and <em> phrasing elements instead of the <b> and <i> text-formatting elements:

1. Return to the **index.html** file in your text editor.

2. Modify the paragraph that contains the motto so it uses the <strong> and <em> phrasing elements instead of the <b> and <i> text-formatting elements. The modified statement should read as follows:

```
<p style="font-size: 20px; color: red"><strong>
Our motto is <em>A votre sante!</em></strong></p>
```

3. Save the **index.html** file and then open it in your Web browser. The paragraph that contains the motto should look the same as it did before you changed the text-formatting elements to phrasing elements.

4. Close your Web browser window.

You use the other phrasing elements to clearly identify specific types of content in your Web pages. Several phrasing elements, such as the `<cite>` and `<dfn>` elements, are designed for formal documents or technical documents. However, you should use phrasing elements when they best describe the type of content you are using. For instance, if one of your Web pages includes a formal definition of a term, you should use the `<dfn>` element to mark the first instance of the term in your document. Similarly, all citations within your documents should be marked with the `<cite>` element.

In the Today's Health Tip section, the paragraph that contains the author's name and publication should include a `<cite>` element. You will modify the paragraph so that it contains a `<cite>` element.

To modify the paragraph so that it contains a `<cite>` element:

1. Return to the **index.html** file in your text editor.

2. Go to the paragraph that lists the author's name and publication. Modify the paragraph so it contains a citation that lists the author's name and publication date within a `<cite>` element. Also change the `<i>` elements around the magazine name to `<em>` elements. The modified paragraph should read as follows:

```
<p>Caryn Honig wrote in the online edition
of <em>Health & Fitness Sports Magazine</em>
the following advice about energy bars
<cite>(Honig 2002)</cite>:</p>
```

3. Save the **index.html** file and then open it in your Web browser. The portion of the paragraph within the `<cite>` element should appear in italics, as shown in Figure 4-13.

204

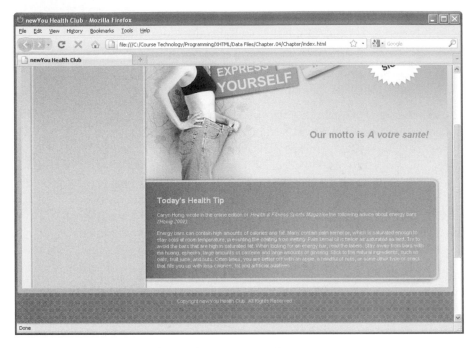

Figure 4-13   index.html after adding a `<cite>` element

    4. Close your Web browser window.

Next, you create the three Web pages that are the target of the links in the left margin: chest.html, arms.html, and legs.html. Each Web page contains definitions of various weightlifting exercises. You use the `<dfn>` element to identify each definition and the `<strong>` element to make each defined term appear in boldface. First, you will add links to the index.html page for each new page.

To add links to the index.html page for each new page and then create the pages:

    1. Return to the **index.html** file in your text editor. Locate the `<div>` element with the ID of "left" and add the following code to the end of the element, above the closing `</div>` tag:

```
<div class="leftbox">
    <h2>Online Trainer</h2>
    <p style="font-size: 20px">
        <a href="chest.html">
            Chest Exercises</a><br />
        <a href="arms.html">Arms Exercises</a><br />
        <a href="legs.html">Leg Exercises</a></p>
</div>
```

2. Copy the entire contents of the **index.html** file and paste them into a new file named **chest.html** in your Chapter folder for Chapter 4.

3. Use the following code to replace the contents of the <div> element that includes an ID of "greenbg":

```
<h2>Chest Exercises</h2>
<h3>Bench Press</h3>
<p>To perform the <dfn><strong>bench press</strong>
</dfn>, lie on a horizontal bench and hold a
barbell over your chest with your arms extended to
form a right angle with your chest. Lower the
barbell to your chest and then push upwards until
your arms are completely extended again.</p>
```

4. Copy the entire contents of the **chest.html** file and paste them into a new file named **arms.html** in your Chapter folder for Chapter 4.

5. Use the following code to replace the contents of the <div> element that includes an ID of "greenbg":

```
<h2>Arm Exercises</h2>
<h3>Bicep Curls</h3>
<p>Perform <dfn><strong>bicep curls</strong></dfn>
with a barbell in the standing position by
contracting your biceps to raise the barbell to the
level of your chest and then lowering the barbell
until your arms are completely extended.</p>
<h3>Dumbbell Curls</h3>
<p>Perform <dfn><strong>dumbbell
curls</strong></dfn> by holding a dumbbell in each
hand, either in the seated or standing position,
contracting your biceps one at a time to raise the
dumbbell to the level of your chest, and then
lowering the dumbbell until your arm is completely
extended.</p>
```

6. Copy the entire contents of the **arms.html** file and paste them into a new file named **legs.html** in your Chapter folder for Chapter 4.

7. Use the following code to replace the contents of the <div> element that includes an ID of "greenbg":

```
<h2>Leg Exercises</h2>
<h3>Leg Curls</h3>
<p>Perform <dfn><strong>leg curls</strong></dfn>
using a leg curl machine by extending your legs
until they are parallel with the floor and then
lowering them.</p>
<h3>Squats</h3>
```

```
<p>Perform <dfn><strong>squats</strong></dfn> by
placing a barbell on your shoulders, squatting
until your thighs are parallel with the floor,
and then returning to the standing position.</p>
```

8. Save the **legs.html** file.

9. Open the **index.html** file in your Web browser and test the links. Figure 4-14 shows the legs.html file in Firefox.

Figure 4-14   legs.html file in Firefox

10. Close your Web browser window.

Recall that you use the `<abbr>` phrasing element to specify abbreviated text or acronyms. Most Web browsers render the `<abbr>` element using default text. You can use the `title` attribute in conjunction with this phrasing element to provide Web site visitors with the long form of each element's content in a ToolTip. Figure 4-15 shows the output of the following code and the ToolTip that appears when you hold your mouse over one of the `<abbr>` elements.

```
<p>The <abbr title="Aquatic Ecosystem Health and
Management Society">AEHMS</abbr> was established
in 1989 to promote holistic, ecosystemic, and
integrated initiatives for the conservation and
management of global aquatic resources. This year's
annual conference will take place in Chicago,
<abbr title="Illinois">IL</abbr>.</p>
```

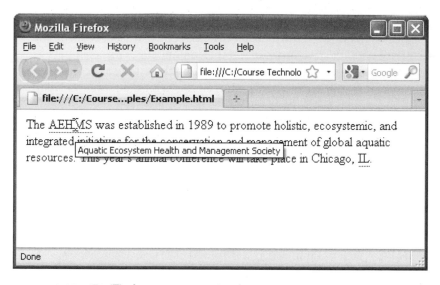

The AEHMS was established in 1989 to promote holistic, ecosystemic, and integrated initiatives for the conservation and management of global aquatic resources. This year's annual conference will take place in Chicago, IL.

Aquatic Ecosystem Health and Management Society

Figure 4-15   ToolTip for an <abbr> element

Short Quiz 2

1. What does the term *semantics* mean when working with text elements?

2. What is the difference between formatting elements and phrasing elements?

3. How do you use the <abbr> element?

Using Block-Level Text Elements

In Chapter 2 you learned about the various types of block-level elements that are available, including the paragraph and heading elements. In this section, you study the following block-level text elements:

- <del>
- <ins>
- <pre>

Using the <del> and <ins> Elements

The <del> and <ins> elements are used for marking changes to a document. The <del> element marks text to be deleted, and the <ins> element marks text to be inserted into a document. You most often

208

see these elements used in drafts of legal documents or other types of formal documents. Most Web browsers render the contents of <del> elements with strikeout text and the contents of <ins> elements as underlined text. The following code shows how to use the <del> and <ins> elements to mark up a paragraph in a legal document. Figure 4-16 shows how the code renders in a Web browser.

```
<h2>ARTICLE V: STRUCTURE OF THE BOARD OF
DIRECTORS</h2>
<h3>Section 1. INITIAL BOARD</h3>
<p>The initial Board of Directors of the Corporation
("Initial Board") shall <del>consist of nine At
Large members, the President (when appointed) and
those</del> <ins>be the Board that exists prior to
the time of the seating of</ins> Directors that
have been selected in accordance with these bylaws
by any Supporting Organization(s) that exists under
Section 3(a) of Article VI <del>during the term of
any of such</del>, <ins>and shall consist of
nine</ins> At Large members<ins> and the
President</ins>.</p>
```

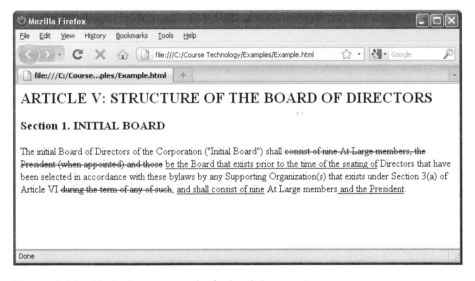

Figure 4-16   Marked-up paragraph of a legal document

The only purpose of these attributes is to identify a URL that contains an explanation for a change and the date and time the change was made; they are not rendered by a browser or visible in a ToolTip.

When using the <del> and <ins> elements to mark up documents, especially legal documents and other types of formal documents, it is important to know why and when a change was made. For this reason, the <del> and <ins> elements include two optional attributes: cite and datetime. The cite attribute is assigned the URL of a Web page that contains an explanation for the change. The datetime attribute specifies the date and time a change was made.

The value you assign to the `datetime` attribute must be in the following format:

```
YYYY-MM-DDThh:mm:ssTZD
```

In the preceding format, *YYYY* represents the year, *MM* represents the month, and *DD* represents the day of the month, from 1 to 31. *T* is a required character that represents the beginning of the time portion of the attribute. In the time portion, *hh* is the hour, *mm* represents the minutes, and *ss* represents the seconds. *TZD* represents the time zone, which can be one of three values: Z, which indicates that the time is in Coordinated Universal Time (UTC); the number of hours and minutes ahead of UTC in the format *+hh:mm*; or the number of hours and minutes behind UTC in the format *-hh:mm*. If you use the Z value, it must be uppercase.

The following time value is in UTC format and represents July 27, 2002, at 9:30:45 P.M. Pacific Standard Time:

```
2002-07-27T21:30:45Z
```

The preceding value represents any time in the world. The example just uses Pacific Standard Time for reference. You can also use the following format to create a more localized time value. Because the West Coast of the United States is eight hours earlier than UTC format, the following time value subtracts eight hours from the UTC time:

```
2002-07-27T21:30:45-08:00
```

The following code shows an example of an `<ins>` element that includes the `cite` attribute (assigned a fictitious URL) and the `datetime` attribute:

```
<p><ins cite="http://draftrevisions.newcorporation.com"
datetime="2002-11-05T14:30:32Z">The authorized
number of Directors shall be no less than nine (9)
and no more than nineteen (19).</ins></p>
```

Unlike most elements, the `<ins>` and `<del>` elements can act as both inline and block-level elements. However, when used as block-level elements, the `<ins>` and `<del>` elements do not appear on their own line, as do most other block-level elements. You must separate block-level `<del>` and `<ins>` elements using `<p>` or `<br>` elements. For instance, the following block-level `<ins>` and `<del>` elements are separated by an empty `<p>` element. Figure 4-17 shows the output.

```
<ins>The Board of Directors shall elect the Chairman
annually.</ins>
<p></p>
<del>The regular term of office of a Director of
the Board shall be three (3) years.</del>
```

Instead of using the `cite` attribute, you can provide a brief explanation of why a change was made using the `title` attribute, which allows readers of the document to view the reason for the change through an element's ToolTip.

When used as block-level elements, the `<del>` and `<ins>` elements cannot contain other block-level elements.

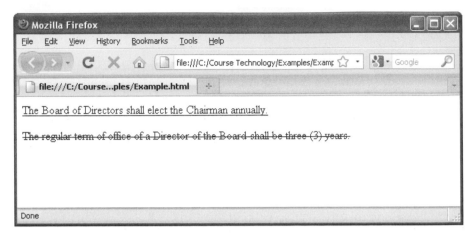

Figure 4-17   Block-level `<del>` and `<ins>` elements

Using the `<pre>` Element

The **`<pre>` element** (short for preformatted text) tells a Web browser that any text and line breaks contained between the opening and closing tags are to be rendered exactly as they appear. The user agent should display the contents of a `<pre>` element in a monospace font, leave any white space intact, and should not wrap long lines of text. Current Web browsers follow these rules, although some types of nonvisual user agents do not recognize white space.

The `<pre>` element was originally designed as a way of preserving column alignment and line spacing. In current browsers, it is much easier to use tables to manage column alignment. However, the `<pre>` element is still typically used to contain computer output or programming code that needs to be rendered in a monospace font and must retain the original line breaks, spaces, and white space. The following code uses a `<pre>` element to manage some JavaScript code. Notice that the `<p>` elements also use the `<strong>`, `<dfn>`, `<var>`, and `<code>` phrasing elements. Figure 4-18 shows the output.

Because the `<pre>` element is primarily designed as a way of providing constant formatting in a monospace font, the W3C strongly discourages using CSS to modify the display of `<pre>` elements.

```
<p>An <dfn><strong>infinite loop</strong></dfn> is a
situation in which a loop statement never ends
because its conditional expression is never updated
or is never <var>false</var>. Consider the following
<code>while</code> statement:</p>
<pre>
var count = 1;
while (count <= 10) {
    window.alert("The number is " + count);
}
```

```
</pre>
<p>Although the <code>while</code> statement in the
preceding example includes a conditional expression
that checks the value of a count variable, there is
no code within the <code>while</code> statement
body that changes the count variable value.</p>
```

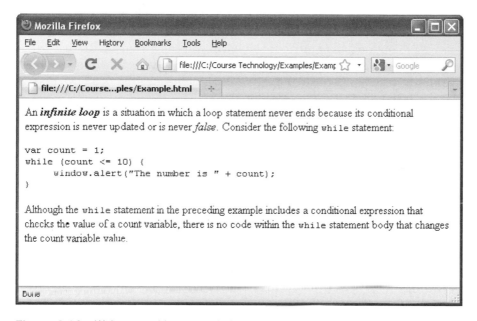

Figure 4-18   Web page with a <pre> element

Short Quiz 3

1. Explain the use of the <del> and <ins> elements.

2. Explain the use of the <pre> element.

Using Quotations

Quotations represent another type of data commonly found on Web pages. In this section, you study the two elements used for describing quotations: <blockquote> and <q>. Quotations are no more or less important than other types of data you find on Web pages, but because the <blockquote> element is a block-level element and the `<q>` element is an inline element, it is easier to discuss both elements in the same section. First you will learn about the `<blockquote>` element.

Using the `<blockquote>` Element

The **`<blockquote>` element** is a block-level element that defines long quotations on Web pages. The `<blockquote>` element includes an optional `cite` attribute to which you can assign a URL that cites the quotation, provided you found it on the Web. The only purpose of the `cite` attribute is to identify the location of a URL that is the original source of a quotation; the value assigned to it is not rendered by a browser or visible in a ToolTip. For users to see the value assigned to the `cite` attribute, they must view the Web page's HTML code.

The following code uses the `<blockquote>` element to define a quotation from Abraham Lincoln. Readers can find the quotation at the URL for The Quotations Page, which is assigned to the `cite` attribute. Figure 4-19 shows the output in a browser.

```
<p>Abraham Lincoln once wrote:</p>
<blockquote
cite="http://www.quotationspage.com/quotes/↵
Abraham_Lincoln"><p>When the conduct of men is
designed to be influenced, persuasion, kind
unassuming persuasion, should ever be adopted. It is
an old and true maxim that 'a drop of honey catches
more flies than a gallon of gall.' So with men. If
you would win a man to your cause, first convince
him that you are his sincere friend. Therein is a
drop of honey that catches his heart, which, say
what he will, is the great highroad to his reason,
and which, once gained, you will find but little
trouble in convincing him of the justice of your
cause, if indeed that cause is really a good
one.</p></blockquote>
```

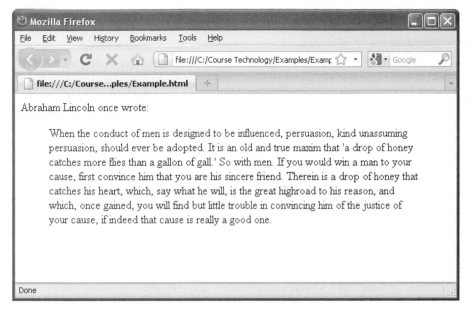

Figure 4-19 A `<blockquote>` element displayed in a Web browser

Most Web browsers indent `<blockquote>` elements on both sides, as shown in Figure 4-19.

Next, you modify the long quotation in the Today's Health Tip section in index.html so that it is defined by a `<blockquote>` element.

To modify the long quotation so it is defined by a `<blockquote>` element:

1. Return to the **index.html** file in your text editor.

2. Add a `<blockquote>` element to the long quotation in the Today's Health Tip section. Within the opening `<blockquote>` tag, include the `cite` attribute and assign it a value of **http://www.healthandfitnessmag.com/hw_col1.htm**, which is the URL where the quotation can be found on the Web. The modified quotation should appear as follows:

```
<blockquote
cite="http://www.healthandfitnessmag.com/hw_col1.htm">
<p>Energy bars can contain ... and artificial
additives.</p></blockquote>
```

3. Save the **index.html** file and then open it in your Web browser. Figure 4-20 shows how the modified quotation appears in a Web browser.

Figure 4-20   newYou Health Club home page after adding a `<blockquote>` element

    4.   Close your Web browser window.

Using the `<q>` Element

The **`<q>` element** is an inline element that you use to specify short quotations on your Web pages. You can also include the `cite` attribute with the `<q>` element. Recall that you can assign the source of the quotation to the `cite` attribute. For instance, the following code uses the `<q>` element to define a shorter quotation by Abraham Lincoln from The Quotations Page Web site:

```
<p>Abraham Lincoln once said, <q
cite="http://www.quotationspage.com/quotes/Abraham_Lincoln">
   Whatever you are, be a good one.</q></p>
```

The preceding code renders on one line if you run it in a Web browser, and the text is surrounded by quotation marks.

Next, you modify the motto near the top of the index.html file so that it is defined by a `<q>` element.

To modify the motto so it is defined by a <q> element:

1. Return to the **index.html** file in your text editor.

2. Add a <q> element to the motto near the top of the page. Within the opening <q> element, include the `cite` attribute and assign it a value of **http://babelfish.yahoo.com/**, which is the URL to Yahoo's Babel Fish Web site. You can use this site to translate words and phrases to and from multiple languages. Also include a `title` attribute that contains the English translation of the phrase. The modified paragraph should read as follows:

```
<p style="font-size: 20px; color: red">
<strong>Our motto is <em>
<q cite=http://babelfish.yahoo.com/"
title="The English translation of this phrase, ↵
    provided by Babel Fish at babelfish.yahoo.com, ↵
    is 'To your health'.">A votre sante!</q></em></strong>
</p>
```

3. Save the **index.html** file and then open it in your Web browser. The motto should now be contained within quotation marks.

4. Close your Web browser window.

Short Quiz 4

1. Explain the use of the <blockquote> element.

2. Explain the use of the <q> element.

Adding Special Characters

You will often need to add special characters to your Web pages, such as a copyright symbol (©) or a foreign-language character. You add these special characters using numeric character references or character entity references. You will learn about both in this section.

Using Numeric Character References

A **numeric character reference** inserts a special character using its numeric position in the Unicode character set. **Unicode** is a standardized set of characters from many of the world's languages.

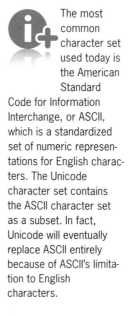

The most common character set used today is the American Standard Code for Information Interchange, or ASCII, which is a standardized set of numeric representations for English characters. The Unicode character set contains the ASCII character set as a subset. In fact, Unicode will eventually replace ASCII entirely because of ASCII's limitation to English characters.

215

A number represents each character in the Unicode character set. To display a character using a numeric character reference, place an ampersand (&) and the number sign (#) before the character's Unicode number and a semicolon after the Unicode number. For instance, the Unicode numbers for the uppercase letters *A*, *B*, and *C* are 65, 66, and 67, respectively. You can display these letters using the following numeric character references:

```
<p>&#65;</p>
<p>&#66;</p>
<p>&#67;</p>
```

Clearly, you do not need to use numeric character references for letters or numbers. However, you use the preceding syntax to display special characters in the Unicode character set. For instance, the Unicode number for the copyright symbol is 169. Therefore, you can display the copyright symbol on a Web page using a numeric character reference of ©.

Numeric character references and character entity references are both defined using an ampersand. For this reason, a Web browser may be confused if it encounters an ampersand within the text of a Web page. Therefore, you should use a numeric character reference of & in place of any ampersands in your document. The home page for the newYou Health Club contains an ampersand in the title of *Health & Fitness Sports Magazine*, which is in the Today's Health Tip section. Also, the French phrase should be written as *À votre santé*. The numeric character reference for the *À* character is À, and the numeric character reference for the *é* character is é. You now add each numeric character reference to the index.html file.

You can find a complete list of numeric character references at *www.macchiato.com/unicode/charts.html*.

To add numeric character references to the index.html file:

1. Return to the **index.html** file in your text editor.

2. Modify the motto within the <q> element so it includes the numeric character references for the two foreign letters. The modified paragraph should read as follows:

```
<p style="font-size: 20px; color: red">
<strong>Our motto is <em>
<q cite="http://babelfish.yahoo.com/"
title="The English translation of this phrase, ↵
    provided by Babel Fish at babelfish.yahoo.com, ↵
    is 'To your health'.">&#192; votre sant&#233;!</q>
    </em></strong>
</p>
```

3. Add the numeric character reference for the ampersand to *Health & Fitness Sports Magazine* in the first paragraph of the Today's Health Tip section:

```
<p>Caryn Honig wrote in the online edition
of <em>Health &#038; Fitness Sports Magazine</em>
the following advice about energy bars
<cite>(Honig 2002)</cite>:</p>
```

4. Save the **index.html** file and then open it in your Web browser. Although the ampersands will look the same, you should now see the foreign characters in the French phrase, as shown in Figure 4-21.

Figure 4-21 newYou Health Club home page after adding foreign characters to the French phrase

5. Close your Web browser window.

Using Character Entities

Using numeric character references can be difficult because you must know a character's exact number within the Unicode character set, and Unicode can represent more than 65,000 characters. Therefore, you may find it easier to use a **character entity reference**, or **character entity**, which uses a descriptive name for a special character instead of its Unicode number. For instance, the descriptive name for the copyright symbol is *copy*. Therefore, you can display the copyright symbol on a Web page using a character entity of ©. Note that you do not include the number sign (#) after the ampersand as you do with numeric character references. Also note that character entities are case-sensitive. For instance, if you use an uppercase *C* in

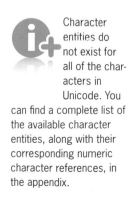

Character entities do not exist for all of the characters in Unicode. You can find a complete list of the available character entities, along with their corresponding numeric character references, in the appendix.

the copyright character entity, a Web browser will not recognize it as a character entity and will display the text *&Copy;* instead of the copyright symbol.

Table 4-4 lists the numeric character references and character entities for commonly used special characters.

Character	Description	Numeric Character Reference	Character Entity
	Non-breaking space		
¢	Cent	&#162;	&cent;
£	Pound	&#163;	&pound;
¥	Yen	&#165;	&yen;
©	Copyright	&#169;	&copy;
®	Registered trademark	&#174;	&reg;
<	Less than	&#60;	&lt;
>	Greater than	&#62;	&gt;
&	Ampersand	&#38;	&amp;
"	Quotation	&#34;	&quot;

Table 4-4   Commonly used special characters

The non-breaking space, less-than, greater-than, and quotation symbols listed in Table 4-4 require a little more explanation. Most Web browsers ignore multiple, contiguous spaces on a Web page and replace them with a single space. For instance, if you include two spaces between the abbreviation for a state and the zip code in a mailing address, most Web browsers will automatically render the two spaces as a single space. To force Web browsers to render multiple spaces, you must add a non-breaking space using the   character entity. The following code shows how to use two   character entities to force two spaces between the state and zip code in a mailing address:

```
<p>Elvis Presley<br />
Graceland Mansion<br />
3734 Elvis Presley Blvd.<br />
Memphis, TN  38116</p>
```

As you know, the less-than and greater-than symbols mark the beginning and end of HTML tags. However, if you add either symbol to the text of your Web page as part of a mathematical equation or for some other purpose, a Web browser will interpret the symbol as the beginning or ending bracket of an HTML tag, which will cause problems in how your page renders. The solution is to use the appropriate character entity.

Earlier you saw an example of a `<pre>` element with some JavaScript code that contained a less-than symbol. If you tried to validate the code using the W3C Markup Validation Service, the code would be declared invalid because the service assumes that the less-than symbol is the starting bracket of a tag that does not include a closing bracket. To make the code valid, you can use the character entity for the less-than symbol (<), as follows:

```
<pre>
var count = 1;
while (count &lt;= 10) {
    window.alert("The number is " + count);
}
</pre>
```

You should use character entities for any quotations you want to include in your Web pages. Because quotation marks are used for assigning values to element attributes, a Web browser may be confused if it encounters quotations within the text of a Web page. For example, the following code displays a heading element for a construction company's Web page, along with the company's motto. For the motto to appear within quotation marks, it is enclosed within " character entities. Note also that the & character entity is used instead of the ampersand symbol.

```
<h1>Sanders &amp; Sons Construction, Inc.</h1>
<h2>Our motto is &quot;Pride before profit&quot;</h2>
```

Next, you replace the numeric character references with character entities in the French phrase in the index.html file. The character entity for the uppercase *A* with a grave accent is À, and the character entity for the lowercase *e* with an acute accent is é.

To replace the numeric character references with character entities in the French phrase in the index.html file:

1. Return to the **index.html** file in your text editor.

2. Modify the numeric character references in the motto to read as follows:

```
<p><strong>Our motto is <em><q
cite="http://babelfish.yahoo.com/"
title="The English translation of this phrase, ↵
    provided by Babel Fish at babelfish.yahoo.com, is ↵
    'To your health'.">&Agrave; votre sant&eacute;
    </q></em>
    </strong>!
</p>
```

3. Save the **index.html** file and open it in your Web browser. The foreign characters in the motto should look the same as they did before you replaced the numeric character references with the character entities.

4. Close your Web browser window.

The only purpose of the elements and text in the code at left is to correctly render the JavaScript code in a browser—not to actually execute the code. The JavaScript code would not execute properly with a character entity replacing the less-than symbol.

219

Short Quiz 5

1. What is a numeric character reference?

2. What is Unicode?

3. What is a character entity reference?

Creating Image Maps

Image maps allow users to navigate to different Web pages by clicking an image. An image map consists of an image that is divided into regions. Each region is then associated with a URL; these regions are called **hot zones**. You can open the URL associated with each region by clicking the hot zone with your mouse. One of the most common uses of image maps is to create graphical menus that you can use for navigation. Using an image to create links to other Web pages gives you more flexibility than using just hypertext links, and allows for much more creativity. For instance, Figure 4-22 displays the home page for eBay. The image displaying Father's Day gifts is an image map that links to more information about each item.

Figure 4-22 Image map on eBay's home page

To create an image map, you must include the following elements on your Web page:

- An <img> element that contains a src attribute specifying the name of the image file and a usemap attribute specifying the value assigned to the id and name attributes of the <map> element.

- A <map> element that specifies mapping coordinates and includes id and name attributes that have the same values as those used in the <img> element usemap attribute.

- <area> elements nested within the <map> element that identify the coordinates within the image that will be recognized as hot zones.

There are two types of image maps: server-side image maps created with the ismap attribute of the <img> element, and client-side image maps created with the usemap attribute of the <img> element. With server-side image maps, the code that maps each region of an image is located on a server. In comparison, with client-side image maps, the code that maps each region of an image is part of an HTML document that renders in a browser. This section covers client-side image maps.

The value you assign to the usemap attribute is preceded in the <img> element by a number sign (#). The usemap attribute is the value assigned to the id and name attributes of the <map> element. For instance, the eBay image map uses an <img> element like the following one to load an image named MERC-FathersDay-Q210-613x290.jpg, which references a <map> element named FathersDayBB_Map1:

```
<img src="http://rtm.ebaystatic.com/0/RTMS/Image/MERC↵
    -FathersDay-Q210-613x290.jpg" usemap="#FathersDayBB_Map1"
    width="613" border="0" height="290">
```

The **<map> element** defines the coordinates used to create an image map's hot zones. In addition to the standard attributes available to all elements, the <map> element also includes the name attribute to make it backward compatible with older browsers. (Recall that in XHTML the id attribute replaces the name attribute that was used in HTML.) The values of the id and name attributes specify the name of the map; you assign the same value to both the id and name attributes. For example, to create a <map> element named navigationMap, you use the statement <map id="navigationMap" name="navigationMap">.

The **<area> element** defines a region within an image map, and is nested within a <map> element. The <area> element is empty, so you must include a space and a slash (/) at the end of the <area> tag. Table 4-5 lists attributes of the <area> element.

 As with the `<img>` element, the `alt` attribute is required with the `<area>` element to provide alternative text if the image map cannot be displayed.

Attribute	Description
coords	The coordinates of the shape in pixels; the coordinates you enter depend on the shape you specify with the `shape` attribute
href	The URL associated with the area
nohref	A placeholder for areas that will not be associated with a URL
shape	The shape of the defined region
alt	Alternate text to display in place of the area

Table 4-5 Common `<area>` element attributes

When you use the `<area>` element to define a region as a hot zone on an image map, you use the `shape` attribute to specify the shape of the region and the `coords` attribute to specify the coordinates of the shape's pixels. The `shape` attribute can be set to circle, rect (for rectangle), or poly (for polygon). The coordinates you specify depend on the value you assign to the `shape` attribute. For example, the following code shows the syntax for assigning coordinates for each type of shape. You assign four coordinates for the rect shape, one for each corner of the rectangle. For the circle shape, you include the x and y coordinates to specify where to place the center of the circle, and you include the radius to determine the size of the circle. Because a polygon can be any type of shape, you can use as many x, y pairs as necessary to define the shape of the object.

```
shape="rect" coords="upper-left x, upper-left y,
     lower-right x, lower-right y"
shape="circle" coords="center-x, center-y, radius"
shape="poly" coords="x1,y1, x2,y2, x3,y3,..."
```

The image map on the eBay home page has `shape` attributes of "poly". Here's an example of one of the hot zones defined on the eBay image map:

```
<area alt="PING Drivers" shape="poly"
coords="170,288,228,220,227,218,232,213,234,210,
     240,198,248,190,260,183,270,179,279,177,286,
     177,304,184,309,188,313,194,316,201,317,208,
     317,214,314,223,306,233,299,238,293,240,284,
     242,276,242,270,241,260,236,250,229,242,222,
     239,219,233,225,232,225,179,288"
href="http://srx.main.ebayrtm.com/clk?RtmClk&amp;
     lid=721082&amp;m=153900&amp;pi=3907&amp;aii=
     8048600698588488638&amp;u=1H4sIAAAAAAAAFN2K8pU
     8CrNUzAwUTAOsTIysTIxVvANDlEwMjA04OXKzEyxtTAws
     TAzMDCztDC1sDCxsDAztuDlAgB34QZ30AAAAA%3D%3D&amp;
     i=-9999&amp;g=ef9522971280a0aad2507a00fedb5fcd&amp;uf=0"
target="_top" />
```

Figure 4-23 shows another example of an image map; this one is created using an image of a pie chart. The code uses polygon shape attributes to create hot zones associated with each wedge of the pie chart.

```
<p>Click a piece of the pie chart to learn more about each
source of income.</p>
<p><img usemap="#income_chart" src="income.jpg"
alt="Pie chart of income broken down by category"
width="468" height="321" />
<map id="income_chart" name="income_chart">
<area shape="poly"
coords="253,160,252,22,355,69,381,118,384,195,318,278"
href="tuition.html" alt="Tuition fees" />
<area shape="poly" coords="253,160,318,278,217,291,147,246"
href="Endowments.html" alt="Endowments" />
<area shape="poly" coords="253,160,147,245,117,185,120,126"
href="Investments.html" alt="Investment income" />
<area shape="poly" coords="253,160,119,125,141,80,185,40"
href="Research.html" alt="Research grants" />
<area shape="poly" coords="253,160,185,40,253,22"
   href="Other.html"
alt="Other income" /></map>
```

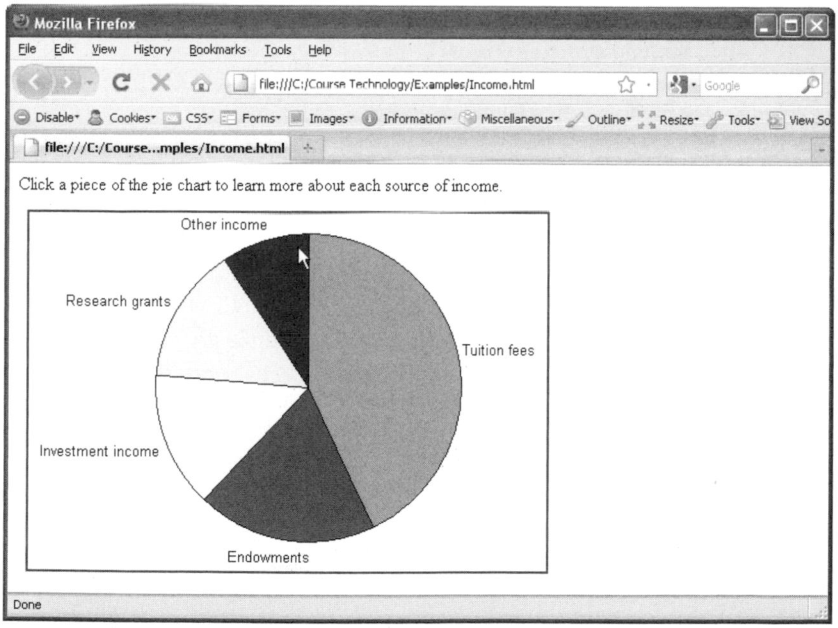

Figure 4-23   Pie chart image map

Next, you will add an image map to the Online Trainer section of the newYou Health Club home page. The image is a picture of Leonardo da Vinci's Vitruvian Man; it is in the images folder in your Chapter folder for Chapter 4. Clicking an area of the body in the image (chest, arms, or legs) will open the associated Web page.

To add an image map to the newYou Health Club home page:

1. Return to the **index.html** file in your text editor.

2. Replace the first paragraph after the Online Trainer heading with the following paragraph:

   ```
   <p>Click the muscle group that you want to work on.</p>
   ```

3. Next, add the following <p> element that displays an image named DaVinci.jpg, which will be used as an image map. The image map is named "vitruvian_man".

   ```
   <p><img usemap="#vitruvian_man" src="images/DaVinci.jpg"
   alt="Image of Leonardo da Vinci's Vitruvian Man."
   width="205" height="205" /></p>
   ```

4. After the <img> element, add the following <map> element, which uses shape attributes of "rect" to map each of the muscle groups:

   ```
   <p><map id="vitruvian_man" name="vitruvian_man">
   <area shape="rect" coords="0, 0, 78, 49" href="Arms.html"
   alt="Right arm" />
   <area shape="rect" coords="128, 0, 205, 49" href="Arms.html"
   alt="Left arm" />
   <area shape="rect" coords="76, 33, 128, 55"
   href="Chest.html" alt="Chest" />
   <area shape="rect" coords="40, 100, 175, 205"
   href="Legs.html" alt="Legs" />
   </map></p>
   ```

5. Copy the elements and text that you added in the preceding steps into the **arms.html**, **chest.html**, and **legs.html** files.

6. Save and close your files. Next, validate the **arms.html**, **chest.html**, and **legs.html** files with the W3C Markup Validation Service at *http://validator.w3.org/#validate_by_upload*. If you receive any errors, fix them and then revalidate the document.

7. Open the **index.html** file in your Web browser. Test the image map to see if all of the links work. Figure 4-24 shows how the map appears in a browser.

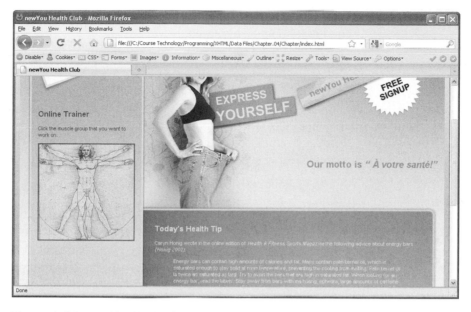

Figure 4-24   newYou Health Club home page after adding an image map

8. Close your Web browser window.

Short Quiz 6

1. What are the basic requirements for creating an image map?

2. Explain the different types of image maps.

3. What are the requirements for defining the usemap attribute?

Summing Up

- The <img> element must include the src and alt attributes for a Web page to be well formed.

- When you use the height and width attributes with the <img> element to specify the size of your images, the Web browser will use their values to reserve enough space on the page for each image.

- The values you assign to the height and width attributes of the <img> element should always be the exact dimensions of the original image.

- Formatting elements provide specific instructions for how their contents should be displayed.

- Phrasing elements primarily describe their contents.

- The `<del>` and `<ins>` elements are used for marking changes to a document.

- The `<pre>` element (short for preformatted text) tells a Web browser that any text and line breaks contained between the opening and closing tags are to be rendered exactly as they appear.

- The `<blockquote>` element is a block-level element that you use to define long quotations on your Web pages.

- The `<q>` element is an inline element that you use to define short quotations on your Web pages.

- A numeric character reference inserts a special character using its numeric position in the Unicode character set.

- Unicode is a standardized set of characters from many of the world's languages.

- Character entity references, or character entities, use a descriptive name for a special character instead of its Unicode number.

- Image maps allow users to navigate to different Web pages by clicking an image. An image map consists of an image that is divided into regions. Each region is then associated with a URL; these regions are called hot zones.

- The `<map>` element defines the coordinates used to create an image map's hot zones.

- The `<area>` element defines a region within an image map, and is nested within a `<map>` element.

Comprehension Check

1. Which of the following attributes of the `<img>` element are required for a Web page to be well formed? (Choose all that apply.)

    a. `alt`

    b. `longdesc`

    c. `usemap`

    d. `width`

2. Why should you use the `height` and `width` attributes with the `<img>` element?

3. How do you create thumbnail images?

4. Explain how to link to images using both relative and absolute URLs.

5. You should use text-formatting elements over phrasing elements. True or False?

6. Which of the following are text-formatting elements? (Choose all that apply.)

   a. `<b>`

   b. `<small>`

   c. `<sup>`

   d. `<sub>`

7. Which of the following are phrasing elements? (Choose all that apply.)

   a. `<big>`

   b. `<i>`

   c. `<code>`

   d. `<dfn>`

8. Which element should be used in place of the `<b>` element?

   a. `<big>`

   b. `<strong>`

   c. `<bold>`

   d. `<cite>`

9. Which element should be used in place of the `<i>` element?

   a. `<var>`

   b. `<samp>`

   c. `<em>`

   d. `<dfn>`

10. How do most Web browsers render the `<abbr>` element?

    a. as default text

    b. as boldface

    c. in italics

    d. in a slightly larger font

11. When marking up the draft of a legal document, when should you use the `cite` and `datetime` attributes?

12. What is the correct format for the value you assign to the `datetime` attribute?

    a. *YYYY-MM-DDhh:mm:ssTZD*

    b. *YY-MM-DDThh:mm:ssTZD*

    c. *YY-MM-DDThh:mm:ss*

    d. *YYYY-MM-DDThh:mm:ssTZD*

13. The `<del>` and `<ins>` elements can act as both inline and block-level elements. True or False?

14. Why would you use the `<pre>` element, and how does a user agent display its contents?

15. How are the contents of the `<blockquote>` element displayed in a Web browser?

    a. as default text

    b. indented on both sides

    c. as italicized text

    d. in quotation marks

16. What is the numeric character reference for an ampersand?

    a. $

    b. %

    c. &

    d. '

17. What is the character entity for a quotation mark?

    a. &q;

    b. "

    c. &quotation;

    d. &qt;

18. Each clickable region on an image map is referred to as a(n) _____.

    a. dynamic link

    b. enhanced anchor

    c. hot zone

    d. map link

19. Which attribute do you include with the `<img>` element to create a client-side image map?

    a. `ismap`

    b. `usemap`

    c. `map`

    d. `getmap`

20. Which of the following values can you apply to the `<area>` element's `shape` attribute? (Choose all that apply.)

    a. circle

    b. square

    c. poly

    d. rect

Reinforcement Exercises

Exercise 4-1

In this exercise, you create a document that uses text-formatting elements for a mobile oil change company named Grease and Go.

1. Create a new document in your text editor.

2. Type the `<!DOCTYPE>` declaration, `<html>` element, document head, and the `<body>` element. Use the Strict DTD and "Grease and Go" as the content of the `<title>` element.

3. Add the following heading elements to the document body:

   ```
   <h1>Grease and Go</h1>
   <h2>Mobile Oil Change Service</h2>
   ```

4. Use text-formatting elements to create the paragraphs shown in Figure 4-25.

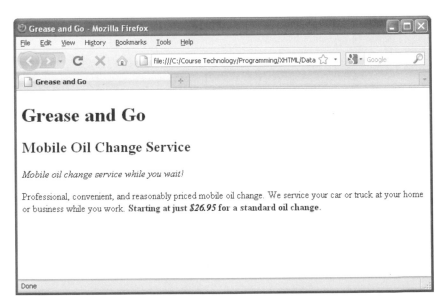

Figure 4-25   Mobile oil change Web page

5. Save the file as **MobileOilChange.html** in the Exercises folder for Chapter 4.

6. Close the **MobileOilChange.html** file in your text editor and then use the W3C Markup Validation Service to validate it. Once the file is valid, open it in your Web browser.

7. Close your Web browser window.

Exercise 4-2

In this exercise, you create a document that uses phrasing elements for a stunt-training school named Freefall Stunt School.

1. Create a new document in your text editor.

2. Type the <!DOCTYPE> declaration, <html> element, document head, and the <body> element. Use the Strict DTD and "Freefall Stunt School" as the content of the <title> element.

3. Add the following heading elements to the document body:

```
<h1>Freefall Stunt School</h1>
<h2>General Information</h2>
```

4. Use phrasing elements to create the paragraph shown in Figure 4-26.

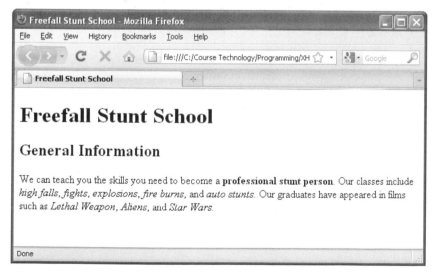

Figure 4-26 Stunt school Web page

5. Save the file as **StuntSchool.html** in the Exercises folder for Chapter 4.

6.   Close the **StuntSchool.html** file in your text editor and then use the W3C Markup Validation Service to validate it. Once the file is valid, open it in your Web browser.

7.   Close your Web browser window.

 Exercise 4-3

In this exercise, you create a document that uses a `<pre>` element to contain a phrase spoken by the robot in the 1960s television series *Lost in Space*.

1.   Create a new document in your text editor.

2.   Type the `<!DOCTYPE>` declaration, `<html>` element, document head, and the `<body>` element. Use the Strict DTD and "Lost in Space" as the content of the `<title>` element.

3.   Add the following elements and text to the document body:

```
<pre>Danger, danger Will Robinson!
My sensors indicate an intruder present.</pre>
<p>Robot, from the 1960s television series,
<cite>Lost in Space</cite>.</p>
```

4.   Save the file as **Robot.html** in the Exercises folder for Chapter 4.

5.   Close the **Robot.html** file in your text editor and then use the W3C Markup Validation Service to validate it. Once the file is valid, open it in your Web browser.

6.   Close your Web browser window.

 Exercise 4-4

In this exercise, you create a document that lists the month and year that the *New York Times Book Review* published its review of Victor Villaseñor's novel *Children of Another Revolution*. You will use the `<cite>` element for the *New York Times Book Review* and *Children of Another Revolution*. For the ñ character, use the ñ character entity.

1.   Create a new document in your text editor.

2.   Type the `<!DOCTYPE>` declaration, `<html>` element, document head, and the `<body>` element. Use the Strict DTD and "New York Times Book Review" as the content of the `<title>` element.

3. Add the following elements and text to the document body:

```
<p>In September, 1991, the <cite>New York
Times Book Review</cite> gave its review
of Victor Villase&ntilde;or's
<cite>Children of Another Revolution</cite>.</p>
```

4. Save the file as **BookReview.html** in the Exercises folder for Chapter 4.

5. Close the **BookReview.html** file in your text editor and then use the W3C Markup Validation Service to validate it. Once the file is valid, open it in your Web browser.

6. Close your Web browser window.

Exercise 4-5

In this exercise, you create a document that quotes the first paragraph from Chapter 1 of John Jakes' novel *Heaven and Hell*.

1. Create a new document in your text editor.

2. Type the <!DOCTYPE> declaration, <html> element, document head, and the <body> element. Use the Strict DTD and "Heaven and Hell" as the content of the <title> element.

3. Add the following elements and text to the document body:

```
<p>The first chapter in John Jakes' novel
<cite>Heaven and Hell</cite> begins as follows:</p>
<blockquote><p>All around him, pillars of fire shot
skyward. The fighting had ignited the dry underbrush,
then the trees. Smoke brought tears to his eyes
and made it hard to see the enemy
skirmishers.</p></blockquote>
```

4. Save the file as **JohnJakes.html** in the Exercises folder for Chapter 4.

5. Close the **JohnJakes.html** file in your text editor and then use the W3C Markup Validation Service to validate it. Once the file is valid, open it in your Web browser.

6. Close your Web browser window.

234

Exercise 4-6

In this exercise, you create a document that uses character entities to provide the Greek spelling of *Prometheus*.

1. Create a new document in your text editor.

2. Type the <!DOCTYPE> declaration, <html> element, document head, and the <body> element. Use the Strict DTD and "Prometheus" as the content of the <title> element.

3. Add the following elements and text to the document body. Notice that the name Prometheus is described using the <em> element. Also notice that the attributes in the <p> element identify the element as written in the Greek language (the language code is "el") with a direction of left to right.

   ```
   <p>In Greek, <em>Prometheus</em> is spelled</p>
   <p lang="el" xml:lang="el"
   dir="ltr">&Pi;&rho;&omicron;&mu;&eta;&theta;&epsilon;
   &alpha;&sigma;</p>
   ```

4. Save the file as **Prometheus.html** in the Exercises folder for Chapter 4.

5. Close the **Prometheus.html** file in your text editor and then use the W3C Markup Validation Service to validate it. Once the file is valid, open it in your Web browser.

6. Close your Web browser window.

Exercise 4-7

In this exercise, you create a document that contains an image of a professor. The Exercises folder for Chapter 4 contains an image file named professor.jpg that you can use for this exercise.

1. Create a new document in your text editor.

2. Type the <!DOCTYPE> declaration, <html> element, document head, and the <body> element. Use the Strict DTD and "Professor" as the content of the <title> element.

3. Add the `<img>` element to the document body.

    `<p><img src="professor.jpg" /></p>`

4. Modify the `<img>` element so it includes alternate text along with the `height` and `width` attributes. Use a Web browser or an image-editing program to find the height and width of the image.

5. Save the file as **Professor.html** in the Exercises folder for Chapter 4.

6. Close the **Professor.html** file in your text editor and then use the W3C Markup Validation Service to validate it. Once the file is valid, open it in your Web browser.

7. Close your Web browser window.

Exercise 4-8

In this exercise, you create a document that includes an image map of a person's head. Clicking each part of the head, such as an eye, ear, or nose, will open another Web page that contains a photo and definition of the selected body part.

1. Search the Internet for an image of a head that you can use as an image map, along with images of different parts of the head, such as an image of an eye, an image of an ear, and so on.

2. Create a new document in your text editor.

3. Type the `<!DOCTYPE>` declaration, `<html>` element, document head, and the `<body>` element. Use the Strict DTD and "Head Map" as the content of the `<title>` element.

4. In the document body, add a map of the head image you found. Use the appropriate shape for each hot zone. For example, use rect shapes for the ears and circle shapes for the eyes.

5. Save the file as **HeadMap.html** in your Exercises folder for Chapter 4.

6. Next, create Web pages for each of the hot zones you added to the head image. In each hot zone's Web page, include the image of the associated body part, along with a formal definition of it. (You can find a formal definition of each body part at *http://dictionary.reference.com*.) Be sure to cite the source

of each definition. Add links to each Web page to return to the **HeadMap.html** document. Save each Web page you create using the name of the body part, such as **Ear.html** or **Eye.html**.

7. Use the W3C Markup Validation Service to validate the files you created. Once the files are valid, open the **HeadMap.html** file in your Web browser and test the image map.

8. Close your Web browser window.

Discovery Projects

For the following projects, save the files you create in the Projects folder for Chapter 4. Create the files so they are well formed according to the Strict DTD. Be sure to validate the files you create with the W3C Markup Validation Service.

Discovery Project 4-1

Create a Web site for a pet photography service named Central Valley Pet Photography. On the home page, include a description of the service and contact information. Create the contact information using appropriate phrasing elements. In the address, use the acronym CVPP for the company name. Include a Samples page and a Pricing page. Search the Internet for images of pets that you can include on the Samples page. Save the home page as **PetPhotos.html**, the Samples page as **Samples.html**, and the Pricing page as **Pricing.html**.

Discovery Project 4-2

Create a Web site that contains photos and biographical information of your favorite actors. Place thumbnail images of each actor along with his or her name on the site's home page. Then, use the thumbnail images and actor names to create links to separate pages for each actor. Each actor's page should display a larger version of the same photo along with biographical information, including film and television credits. You can find thumbnail and full-sized versions of photos, along with biographical information for many actors, by searching *http://movies.yahoo.com/*. Save the home page as **ActorBios.html** and save each actor's Web page using his or her first and last name as the filename. For instance, Robert DeNiro's Web page should be named **RobertDeNiro.html**.

Discovery Project 4-3

Create a Web site that sells natural rocks, gems, minerals, and crystals. Include links on the home page for different categories such as amethyst, geodes, quartz, and fossils. Search the Internet for image files of different types of precious and semiprecious stones. The Web page for each category should include a picture and name of the item, along with price, weight, size, and a description. Save the home page as **RocksAndGems.html**, and save the Web page for each category using the category name.

Discovery Project 4-4

Search the Internet for an image of a sports team photo. Use the image to create an image map that uses each player as a hot zone. Clicking a hot zone should open a separate Web page that displays the player's statistics for the associated sport. For instance, if you use a photo of a baseball team, clicking a player should open a page that displays the player's batting average, number of errors, and so on. You can make up any statistical information you want. Save the home page as **SportsTeam.html**, and save each team member's Web page using his or her first and last name. You can make up names for each team member.

Using Tables and Lists

In this chapter you will:

- ◎ Create basic tables
- ◎ Structure tables
- ◎ Format tables
- ◎ Create lists

When HTML was first introduced, it provided no way to create tables, which are essentially rows and columns of tabular data. Tables were introduced in HTML 3.2, and Web authors quickly realized how useful they were. Tables provide an effective way of structuring and displaying data in an organized format that is difficult to achieve using standard text-formatting elements such as the <p> element. Additionally, tables are replacing frames, which are used for designing effective navigation systems and laying out pages.

You can also use lists to structure and display data in an organized format. You will study lists later in this chapter.

Creating Basic Tables

Tables are collections of rows and columns that you use to organize and display data. In a table, the intersection of a row and column is called a **cell**. You are probably familiar with traditional tables, which are widely used for displaying data on Web pages. However, Web page tables are not limited to displaying simple text. Tables are also commonly used to display images and to lay out Web pages, much like frames have been used. Recall from Chapter 1 that frames are deprecated in XHTML, although they are still useful for navigation, document layout, and other functionality.

The W3C discourages using tables for document layout because they can be difficult for nonvisual user agents such as Braille and speech devices to interpret. Also, browsers that use large fonts and other user agents with small monitors, such as cell phones, may have difficulty rendering a Web page that is laid out using tables. Instead, the W3C encourages the use of Cascading Style Sheets (CSS) for document layout. However, using CSS can be difficult and time-consuming, so many Web page authors continue to use tables for layout. Nevertheless, if you anticipate that users with disabilities will frequently visit your Web site, you should seriously consider avoiding the use of tables for document layout.

Using Basic <table> Elements

You create tables using the **<table> element**. Within the <table> element, you can nest a number of other elements that specify the content of each cell along with the table's structure and appearance. The elements you use to build a table are listed in Table 5-1.

To help ensure that your Web pages are well formed, you should always type the opening `<table>` tag and the closing `</table>` tag at the same time, and then go back and fill in the table elements and content.

Element	Description
`<caption>`	A table caption
`<col>`	A table column
`<colgroup>`	A table column group
`<tbody>`	A table body
`<td>`	Table data
`<tfoot>`	A table footer
`<th>`	A table heading
`<thead>`	A table header
`<tr>`	A table row

Table 5-1 Table elements

Using the `<td>` Element

Cells are the most basic parts of a table. You create a cell within the `<table>` element using the **`<td>` element**. The `<td>` element stands for "table data". The content of each `<td>` element is the data that appears in the table cell. Each `<td>` element essentially represents a column in the table. You declare table cells within table row elements that you create with the **`<tr>` element**. Each `<tr>` element you include within a `<table>` element creates a separate row. The following code shows the basic syntax for creating a table that consists of three columns and two rows:

By default, tables are displayed without borders. The preceding code includes a style section with the short-hand **border** property that creates a solid 1-pixel border around the table, rows, and cells so you can see them more clearly in a Web browser. You will learn more about borders later in this chapter.

```
...
<style type="text/css">
table, td {
    border: 1px solid black;
}
</style>
</head>
<body>
<table>
    <!-- Row 1 -->
    <tr>
        <td>column 1</td>
        <td>column 2</td>
        <td>column 3</td>
    </tr>
    <!-- Row 2 -->
    <tr>
        <td>column 1</td>
        <td>column 2</td>
        <td>column 3</td>
    </tr>
</table>
```

Figure 5-1 shows how the preceding table appears in a Web browser.

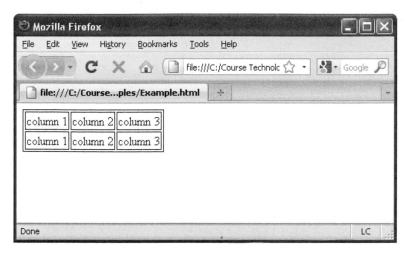

Figure 5-1 Simple table

As another example, consider Table 5-2, which lists the days of the week in English, French, and German.

Sunday	Dimanche	Sonntag
Monday	Lundi	Montag
Tuesday	Mardi	Dienstag
Wednesday	Mercredi	Mittwoch
Thursday	Jeudi	Donnerstag
Friday	Vendredi	Freitag
Saturday	Samedi	Samstag

Table 5-2 Days of the week in English, French, and German

To display Table 5-2 as a table on a Web page, you use the following table elements. Figure 5-2 shows how the table appears in a Web browser.

```
...
<style type="text/css">
table, td {
    border: 1px solid black;
}
</style>
</head>
<body>
<table>
<tr><td>Sunday</td><td>Dimanche</td>
<td>Sonntag</td></tr>
<tr><td>Monday</td><td>Lundi</td>
<td>Montag</td></tr>
```

```
<tr><td>Tuesday</td><td>Mardi</td>
<td>Dienstag</td></tr>
<tr><td>Wednesday</td><td>Mercredi</td>
<td>Mittwoch</td></tr>
<tr><td>Thursday</td><td>Jeudi</td>
<td>Donnerstag</td></tr>
<tr><td>Friday</td><td>Vendredi</td>
<td>Freitag</td></tr>
<tr><td>Saturday</td><td>Samedi</td>
<td>Samstag</td></tr>
</table>
```

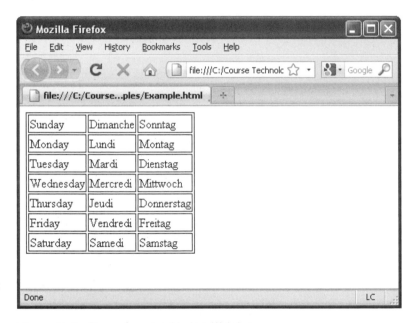

Figure 5-2 Days of week table in a Web browser

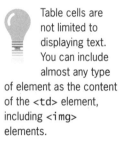

Table cells are not limited to displaying text. You can include almost any type of element as the content of the `<td>` element, including `<img>` elements.

Next, you start creating the weekly schedule for a commuter railroad. Because a schedule's data is tabular, it makes sense to create the data in a table instead of using heading and text elements. First, you will create the style sheet and main page.

To create a style sheet for the commuter railroad Web page:

1.   Start your text editor and create a new document.

2.   Add the following style declarations. Notice that several of the styles include background images that will be used to format the document:

   ```
   body
   {
       font: 11px tahoma, arial;
   ```

```
        margin: 0px;
        padding: 0px;
        background: #e4e5ec
            url(images/bg1.gif) repeat-x;
    }
table {
        border: 1px solid black;
    }
td {
        border: 1px solid black;
    }
#header1
    {
        background: url(images/top01.gif) no-repeat;
            height: 225px;
    }
#header2
    {
        background: url(images/top02.gif)
            no-repeat;
        height: 40px;
        text-align: left;
        font-weight: bold;
        text-transform: uppercase;
        color: #FFFFFF;
        padding-left: 300px;
        padding-top: 10px;
    }
#header2 a:link
    {
        color: #FFFFFF;
    }
#content
    {
        background: url(images/bg.gif)
            repeat-y;
        margin-left: 25px;
        color: #7b7b7b;
        margin: 25px;
    }
#footer
    {
        background: url(images/bottombg.gif)
            repeat-x;
        height: 27px;
        color: #AAAEC4;
        padding-top: 16px;
        padding-left: 10px;
    }
```

3. Save the document as **railroad.css** in your Chapter folder for Chapter 5.

Next, you will create the weekly schedule for the commuter railroad.

To start creating the weekly schedule for the commuter railroad:

1. Create a new document in your text editor.

2. Type the <!DOCTYPE> declaration, <html> element, document head, and <body> element, as follows:

```
<!DOCTYPE HTML>
<html>
<head>
    <title>Metropolitan Rail</title>
    <meta http-equiv="content-type"
        content="text/html;
        charset=utf-8" />
     <link href="railroad.css"
      rel="stylesheet" type="text/css" />
</head>
<body>
</body>
</html>
```

3. Add the following content elements to the document body:

```
<div id="header1">
</div>
<div id="header2">
    <a href="schedule.html">
    SCHEDULE</a> |
    <a href="fares.html">FARES</a> |
    <a href="rules.html">RULES</a>
</div>
<div id="content">
</div>
<div id="footer">
    &copy; 2011. Metropolitan Rail.
    All Rights Reserved.
</div>
```

4. Within the empty <div> element (with an ID of "content") in the document body, add the following simple table, which includes the railroad's departure and arrival times from Pleasantville to Coast City:

```
<h1>Pleasantville to Coast City</h1>
<table>
<tr><td>6:00 a.m.</td>
<td>7:00 a.m.</td></tr>
```

```
<tr><td>7:00 a.m.</td>
<td>8:00 a.m.</td></tr>
<tr><td>8:00 a.m.</td>
<td>9:00 a.m.</td></tr>
<tr><td>4:00 p.m.</td>
<td>5:00 p.m.</td></tr>
<tr><td>5:00 p.m.</td>
<td>6:00 p.m.</td></tr>
<tr><td>6:00 p.m.</td>
<td>7:00 p.m.</td></tr>
</table>
```

5. Save the file as **schedule.html** and then open it in your Web browser. Figure 5-3 shows how the file should appear in your Web browser.

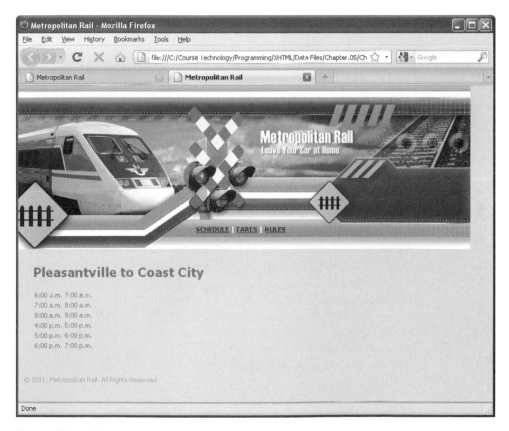

Figure 5-3 Schedule table

6. Close your Web browser window.

Using the `<th>` Element

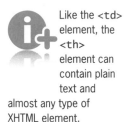

Like the `<td>` element, the `<th>` element can contain plain text and almost any type of XHTML element.

Table cells can contain two types of information: data that you define with the `<td>` element and heading information that you define with the **`<th>` element**. Heading information usually describes the contents of one or more columns within a table. The content of a `<th>` element will appear as the heading for one or more columns. User agents render the content of a `<th>` element distinctly; most Web browsers display heading information in a bold typeface and align it in the center of the column.

Consider the table you saw earlier that listed the days of the week. The table would be more useful if it included heading information that displayed each column's language, as shown in Table 5-3.

English	French	German
Sunday	Dimanche	Sonntag
Monday	Lundi	Montag
Tuesday	Mardi	Dienstag
Wednesday	Mercredi	Mittwoch
Thursday	Jeudi	Donnerstag
Friday	Vendredi	Freitag
Saturday	Samedi	Samstag

Table 5-3   Days of the week with heading information

Place the data you want to use as a column's heading information within the beginning and ending `<th>` tags. The following code shows how to add the heading information shown in Table 5-3 to the XHTML code for the table. Notice that the th selector has been added to the style section to ensure that borders are displayed around the table headings. Figure 5-4 shows the output.

```
...
<style type="text/css">
table, td, th {
    border: 1px solid black;
}
</style>
</head>
<body>
<table>
<tr><th>English</th><th>French</th>
<th>German</th></tr>
<tr><td>Sunday</td><td>Dimanche</td>
<td>Sonntag</td></tr>
<tr><td>Monday</td><td>Lundi</td>
<td>Montag</td></tr>
<tr><td>Tuesday</td><td>Mardi</td>
<td>Dienstag</td></tr>
```

```
<tr><td>Wednesday</td><td>Mercredi</td>
<td>Mittwoch</td></tr>
<tr><td>Thursday</td><td>Jeudi</td>
<td>Donnerstag</td></tr>
<tr><td>Friday</td><td>Vendredi</td>
<td>Freitag</td></tr>
<tr><td>Saturday</td><td>Samedi</td>
<td>Samstag</td></tr>
</table>
```

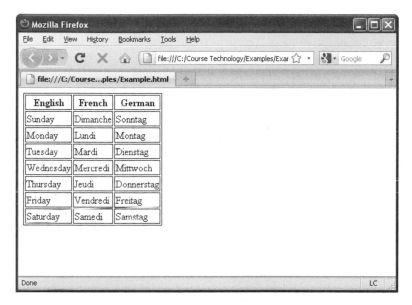

Figure 5-4 Days of the week table after adding heading information

Next, you will add table headings to the schedule.html file.

To add heading information to the schedule.html file:

1. Return to the **railroad.css** file in your text editor and add the following style declaration for the th selector immediately after the td declaration:

```
th {
    border: 1px solid black;
}
```

2. Save the **railroad.css** file and then return to the **schedule.html** file in your text editor.

3. Add the following heading elements immediately after the opening <table> tag:

```
<tr><th>Depart Pleasantville</th>
<th>Arrive Coast City</th></tr>
```

4. Save the **schedule.html** file and then open it in your Web browser. The heading information you entered should appear as the first row in the table. The heading should be in a bold typeface and centered.

5. Close your Web browser window.

Adding Table Captions

Most tables include a caption that describes the data in the table. You create a caption for a Web page table using the **<caption> element**. The <caption> element must be the first element following the <table> element; you can include only a single <caption> element per table. A caption should provide a short phrase or title that clearly describes the contents of the table. Most Web browsers center the <caption> element above the table. The following code creates a table that lists Major League Baseball players who have had 10 or more runs batted in (RBIs) in a single game. The table includes a caption and headings. Figure 5-5 shows how the table appears in a Web browser.

```
...
<style type="text/css">
table, td, th {
    border: 1px solid black;
}
</style>
</head>
<body>
<table>
<caption>10+ RBI in a Game</caption>
<tr><th>Player</th><th>Team</th>
<th>Date</th><th>RBI</th></tr>
<tr><td>Jim Bottomley</td>
<td>Cardinals</td>
<td>9/24/1924</td><td>12</td></tr>
<tr><td>Mark Whiten</td>
<td>Cardinals</td>
<td>9/7/1993</td><td>12</td></tr>
<tr><td>Wilbert Robinson</td>
<td>Orioles</td>
<td>6/10/1892</td><td>11</td></tr>
<tr><td>Tony Lazzeri</td>
<td>Yankees</td>
<td>5/24/1936</td><td>11</td></tr>
<tr><td>Phil Weintraub</td>
<td>Giants</td>
<td>4/30/1944</td><td>11</td></tr>
<tr><td>Rudy York</td><td>Red Sox</td>
<td>7/27/1946</td><td>10</td></tr>
```

```
<tr><td>Walker Cooper</td><td>Reds</td>
<td>7/6/1949</td><td>10</td></tr>
<tr><td>Norm Zauchin</td>
<td>Red Sox</td>
<td>5/27/1955</td><td>10</td></tr>
<tr><td>Reggie Jackson</td><td>A's</td>
<td>6/14/1969</td><td>10</td></tr>
<tr><td>Fred Lynn</td><td>Red Sox</td>
<td>6/18/1975</td><td>10</td></tr>
<tr><td>Nomar Garciaparra</td>
<td>Red Sox</td>
<td>5/10/1999</td><td>10</td></tr>
<tr><td>Alex Rodriguez</td>
<td>Yankees</td>
<td>4/26/2005</td><td>10</td></tr>
<tr><td>Garret Anderson</td>
<td>Angels</td>
<td>8/21/2007</td><td>10</td></tr>
</table>
```

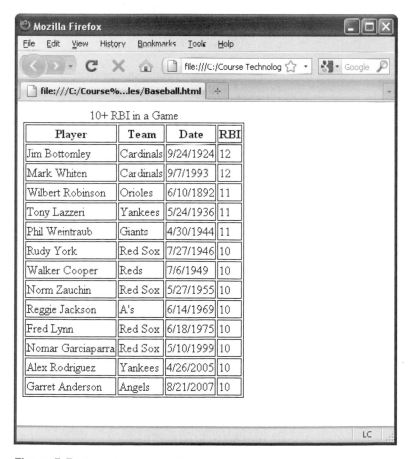

Figure 5-5   RBI table with caption

You may be tempted to provide a caption for tables simply by using heading elements instead of the <caption> element. However, the <caption> element is important because it allows nonvisual user agents to understand the purpose of a table. Because heading elements are not directly associated with a table, a user agent has no way of knowing whether one is used for a table caption. If you want to change the appearance of a table caption, you can include elements such as the <strong> element within the <caption> element, or you can use CSS.

By default, table captions are placed above the table. You can also place a caption below the table by assigning a value of "bottom" to the caption-side property of a caption selector, as follows:

```
<style type="text/css">
table, td, th {
    border: 1px solid black;
}
caption {
    caption-side: bottom;
}
</style>
```

 By default, the caption-side property of a caption selector is assigned a value of "top", which places a caption above a table.

Next, you add a table caption to the schedule.html file.

To add a caption to the schedule.html file:

1. Return to the **railroad.css** file in your text editor and add the following style declaration to the end of the file.

   ```
   caption {
       font-weight: bold;
   }
   ```

2. Save the **railroad.css** file and return to the **schedule.html** file in your text editor.

3. Modify the table so it includes the <caption> element shown below in boldface:

   ```
   <table>
   <caption>Weekday Schedule</caption>
   <tr><th>Depart Pleasantville</th>
   <th>Arrive Coast City</th></tr>
   <tr><td>6:00 a.m.</td><td>7:00 a.m.</td></tr>
   ...
   ```

4. Save the **schedule.html** file and then open it in your Web browser. Figure 5-6 shows how the file should appear in your Web browser.

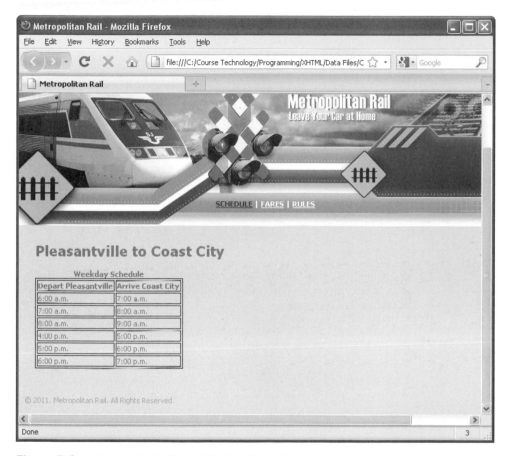

Figure 5-6 schedule.html after adding heading information and a `<caption>` element

5. Close your Web browser window.

Formatting Table Widths

Even though a Web author creates a table and determines its content, the user agent determines how wide the table should be. Web browsers size each column to be as wide as the widest item in each cell, up to the width of the browser window. However, for design purposes you may want to specify that your table takes up a certain width (in pixels) or a percentage of the Web browser window. You use the CSS **width property** to format the size of elements, including `<table>`

elements. You can assign a fixed value in pixels or a percentage that represents the size of the block-level element that contains an inline element you want to resize. If you are resizing a block-level element, you can assign a value that represents the width of the visible browser window. For instance, the `table` selector (a block-level element) in the following code includes a `width` property that specifies the RBI table should take up 100 percent of the visible Web browser window.

```
...
<style type="text/css">
table {
    border: 1px solid black;
    width: 100%;
}
td, th {
    border: 1px solid black;
}
</style>
</head>
<body>
<table>
<caption>10+ RBI in a Game</caption>
<tr><th>Player</th><th>Team</th>
<th>Date</th><th>RBI</th></tr>
<tr><td>Jim Bottomley</td>
<td>Cardinals</td>
<td>9/24/1924</td><td>12</td></tr>
<tr><td>Mark Whiten</td>
<td>Cardinals</td>
<td>9/7/1993</td><td>12</td></tr>
...
```

Next, you modify the railroad.css file so the table takes up 100 percent of the `<div>` element that contains it.

To modify the railroad.css file so the table takes up 100 percent of the `<div>` element that contains it:

1. Return to the **railroad.css** file in your text editor.

2. Add the `width` property to the `table` selector, as follows:

```
table {
    border: 1px solid black;
    width: 100%;
}
```

3. Save the **railroad.css** file, and then open the **schedule.html** file in your Web browser. Your table should take up 100 percent of the visible Web browser window.

4. Close your Web browser window.

Formatting Horizontal Alignment

You can use the CSS **text-align property** to adjust the horizontal alignment of elements, including the contents of all table elements except the <table> and <caption> elements. You can assign left, center, right, and justify values to the align property. For example, the following code shows the RBI table with the heading row alignment changed to left; a text-align: left property has been assigned to the style attribute in the row's opening <tr> element. (Recall that heading information is center-aligned by default.) Figure 5-7 shows the output.

```
...
<style type="text/css">
table {
    border: 1px solid black;
    width: 100%;
}
td, th {
    border: 1px solid black;
}
</style>
</head>
<body>
<table>
<caption>10+ RBI in a Game</caption>
<tr style="text-align: left">
<th>Player</th><th>Team</th>
<th>Date</th><th>RBI</th></tr>
<tr><td>Jim Bottomley</td>
<td>Cardinals</td>
<td>9/24/1924</td><td>12</td></tr>
<tr><td>Mark Whiten</td>
<td>Cardinals</td>
<td>9/7/1993</td><td>12</td></tr>
...
```

254

10+ RBI in a Game

Player	Team	Date	RBI
Jim Bottomley	Cardinals	9/24/1924	12
Mark Whiten	Cardinals	9/7/1993	12
Wilbert Robinson	Orioles	6/10/1892	11
Tony Lazzeri	Yankees	5/24/1936	11
Phil Weintraub	Giants	4/30/1944	11
Rudy York	Red Sox	7/27/1946	10
Walker Cooper	Reds	7/6/1949	10
Norm Zauchin	Red Sox	5/27/1955	10
Reggie Jackson	A's	6/14/1969	10
Fred Lynn	Red Sox	6/18/1975	10
Nomar Garciaparra	Red Sox	5/10/1999	10
Alex Rodriguez	Yankees	4/26/2005	10
Garret Anderson	Angels	8/21/2007	10

You can align individual `<td>` or `<th>` elements, although if you want an entire row to have the same alignment, it is easier to place the `align` attribute in the row's opening `<tr>` tag.

Figure 5-7   Table that includes an `align` attribute in the heading row

Next, you modify the railroad.css file to center the data in the table cells.

To modify the railroad.css file so the data in the table cells is centered:

1. Return to the **railroad.css** file in your text editor.

2. Add `text-align: center` to the `td` selector in the style section, as follows:

```
td {
    border: 1px solid black;
    text-align: center;
}
```

3. Save the **railroad.css** file and then open the **schedule.html** file in your Web browser. Figure 5-8 shows how the file should appear in your Web browser.

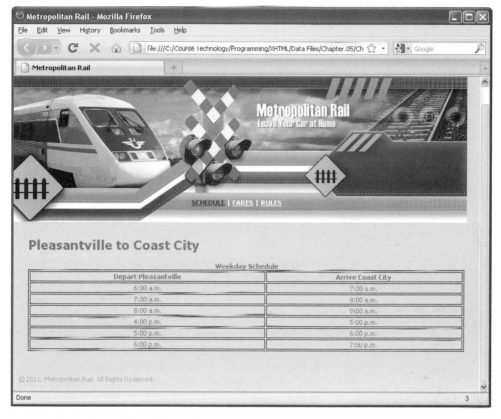

Figure 5-8 schedule.html after adjusting the table width to 100% and centering the contents of each cell

4. Close your Web browser window.

Short Quiz 1

1. Explain how to use basic table elements.

2. How and why would you use the <caption> element?

3. How do you set table widths?

4. Explain how to set a table's horizontal alignment.

Structuring Tables

The last section described the basic table elements that are necessary for a document to be well formed. However, you sometimes might want to have more control over parts of a table, such as the columns, to make it easier to apply formatting. In this section you study elements that give a table its structure and that give you more control. Although table structure elements are not required for your documents to be well formed, including them will help to clearly identify the different parts of your tables. Table structure elements also allow you to apply default alignment and CSS styles to entire sections of a table, and to adjust the width of individual columns.

Creating Row Groups

You can create table **row group elements** that consist of a table header, table body, and table footer. A table header refers to the rows of <th> elements that make up the table headings. The table body refers to the rows of data that make up the body of a table. The table footer refers to information that should be placed at the bottom of a table. To define a table header, you use the **<thead> element**; to define the table body, you use the **<tbody> element**; and to define the table footer, you use the **<tfoot> element**. These elements allow user agents to scroll through the body of a table independent of its header and footer. At the time of this writing, however, most Web browsers do not support table scrolling; this is expected to change as new browser versions are released that provide greater support for XHTML. Nevertheless, it is a good practice to include row group elements to provide a clear structure for your tables. Additionally, you can set the alignment for all the elements in a row group because each row group element supports the align attribute.

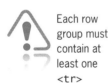

Each row group must contain at least one <tr> element.

The next section discusses the specific syntax for each row group element.

Using a Table Header

You must place the <thead> element after any <caption>, <colgroup>, and <col> elements and before the <tbody> and <tfoot> elements. Typically, you place table heading information (created with the <th> element) within the <thead> element, as follows:

```
...
<style type="text/css">
table {
    border: 1px solid black;
    width: 100%;
}
```

```
td, th {
    border: 1px solid black;
}
</style>
</head>
<body>
<table>
<caption>10+ RBI in a Game</caption>
<thead style="text-align: left">
<tr><th>Player</th><th>Team</th>
<th>Date</th><th>RBI</th></tr>
</thead>
<tr><td>Jim Bottomley</td>
<td>Cardinals</td>
<td>9/24/1924</td><td>12</td></tr>
<tr><td>Mark Whiten</td>
<td>Cardinals</td>
<td>9/7/1993</td><td>12</td></tr>
...
```

Next, you modify the schedule.html file so it includes a
<thead> element.

**To modify the schedule.html file to include a <thead>
element:**

1. Return to the **schedule.html** file in your text editor.

2. Add a <thead> element so it encloses the heading information
   row, as follows:

   ```
   <table>
   <caption>Weekday Schedule</caption>
   <thead><tr><th>Depart Pleasantville</th>
   <th>Arrive Coast City</th></tr>
   </thead>
   ...
   ```

3. Save the **schedule.html** file.

Using Table Body Elements

The <tbody> element should contain the rows of data that make
up the body of a table. Although most browsers do not yet support
scrolling a table body independent of its header and footer, you
can use the <tbody> element to align a table body and apply CSS
formatting to it. You can also include multiple <tbody> elements
to control different parts of the table body. The following version
of the RBI table includes three <tbody> elements, each of which
includes a style attribute that specifies the color of the text within
each element. Each <tbody> element is assigned a different color that

distinguishes which players had 10, 11, or 12 RBIs in a single game. (Parts of the table are excluded from the code to save space.)

```
...
<style type="text/css">
table {
    border: 1px solid black;
    width: 100%;
}
td, th {
    border: 1px solid black;
}
</style>
</head>
<body>
<table>
<caption>10+ RBI in a Game</caption>
<thead style="text-align: left">
<tr><th>Player</th><th>Team</th>
<th>Date</th><th>RBI</th></tr>
</thead>
<tbody style="color:blue">
<tr><td>Jim Bottomley</td>
<td>Cardinals</td>
<td>9/24/1924</td><td>12</td></tr>
...
</tbody>
<tbody style="color:red">
<tr><td>Tony Lazzeri</td>
<td>Yankees</td>
<td>5/24/1936</td><td>11</td></tr>
...
</tbody>
<tbody style="color:green">
<tr><td>Walker Cooper</td><td>Reds</td>
<td>7/6/1949</td><td>10</td></tr>
...
</tbody>
</table>
```

Next, you modify the schedule.html file so it includes a <tbody> element that center-aligns the cells in the table body.

To add a <tbody> element to the schedule.html file:

1. Return to the **schedule.html** file in your text editor.

2. Add the following <tbody> element immediately after the closing </thead> tag. Notice that the element's align attribute is assigned a value of "center".

    ```
    <tbody style="text-align: center">
    ```

3. Add a closing **</tbody>** tag immediately above the closing </table> tag.

4. Save the **schedule.html** file and return to the **railroad.css** file in your text editor.

5. Delete the `text-align: center` property from the td selector in the style section.

6. Save the **railroad.css** file and then open the **schedule.html** file in your Web browser. Your file should look the same as it did when the `align` attributes were included in the `<td>` elements.

7. Close your Web browser window.

Using Table Footers

The `<tfoot>` element defines information that should be placed at the bottom of a table, such as additional information about the columns or about the table itself. The `<tfoot>` element must be placed before the `<tbody>` element to allow a user agent to render the table structure before it receives the potentially large amount of data that may appear in the table body. The following code shows the RBI table with a `<tfoot>` element. Figure 5-9 shows the table in a Web browser.

```
...
<style type="text/css">
table {
    border: 1px solid black;
    width: 100%;
}
td, th {
    border: 1px solid black;
}
</style>
</head>
<body>
<table>
<caption>10+ RBI in a Game</caption>
<thead style="text-align: left">
<tr><th>Player</th><th>Team</th>
<th>Date</th><th>RBI</th></tr>
</thead>
<tfoot style="text-align: left">
<tr><td>Statistics provided by <a href
="http://www.baseballimmortals.net/">
Baseball Immortals</a></td></tr>
</tfoot>
<tbody style="color:blue">
<tr><td>Jim Bottomley</td>
<td>Cardinals</td>
<td>9/24/1924</td><td>12</td></tr>
...
```

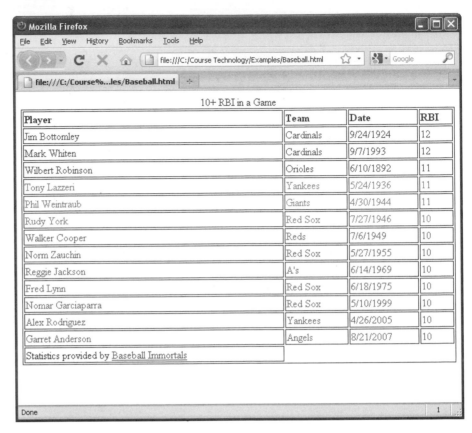

Figure 5-9 RBI table with `<thead>`, `<tbody>`, and `<tfoot>` elements in a Web browser

Next, you add a `<tfoot>` element to the schedule.html file.

To add a `<tfoot>` element to the schedule.html file:

1. Return to the **schedule.html** file in your text editor.

2. Add the following `<tfoot>` element immediately after the closing `</thead>` tag.

   ```
   <tfoot style="text-align: center">
   <tr><td>Please board at least 5 minutes
   prior to departure.</td>
   <td>Arrival times are approximate.</td></tr>
   </tfoot>
   ```

3. Save the **schedule.html** file and then open it in your Web browser. Figure 5-10 shows how the file should appear in a browser.

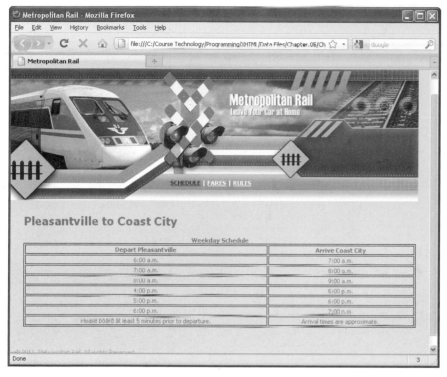

Figure 5-10 schedule.html after adding a table footer

4. Close your Web browser window.

Formatting Columns

Sometimes you might want to format the columns in your tables, either individually or as a group. In this section you study **column groups**, which are used for applying default alignment, width, and CSS styles to groups of columns within a table.

Using Column Groups

You use the **`<colgroup>` element** to create a column group in a table. You must place a `<colgroup>` element after a table's `<caption>` element and before its `<thead>` element. The `<colgroup>` element must be created as a tag pair that can contain `<col>` elements as its content. (You will study `<col>` elements shortly.) The `<colgroup>` element includes a `span` attribute that you use to specify the number of columns in the group. For example, consider the following modified version of the RBI table. The table now includes two column groups: one for each player's name and another for the player's statistics. The default value of the `span` attribute is "1", which means the first column group does not include the span attribute because it applies only to the player name column. The second column group includes a span attribute assigned a value of "3" so that it applies to the remaining columns in the table. The second column group also includes a style attribute with a background-color selector assigned a value of "red", which formats the background color of the columns to red. Figure 5-11 shows how the code appears in a Web browser.

```
...
<style type="text/css">
table {
    border: 1px solid black;
    width: 100%;
}
td, th {
    border: 1px solid black;
}
</style>
</head>
<body>
<table>
<caption>10+ RBI in a Game</caption>
<colgroup></colgroup>
<colgroup span="3"
    style="background-color: red"></colgroup>
<thead style="text-align: left">
...
```

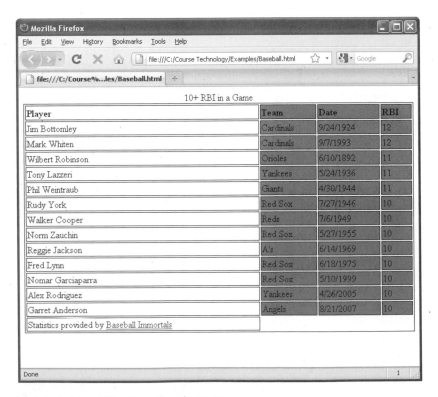

Figure 5-11   RBI table with column groups

The empty **<col> element** allows you to apply formatting to an individual column in a column group. You can also use the span attribute to format multiple columns in a column group. For instance, the second <colgroup> element in the following modified version of the RBI table now contains two <col> elements, one for each of the columns in the column group. The first <col> element formats the background color of the Team and Date columns to cyan, and the second <col> element formats the background color of the RBI column to red. Figure 5-12 shows how the table appears in a Web browser.

```
<style type="text/css">
table {
    border: 1px solid black;
    width: 100%;
}
td {
    border: 1px solid black;
}
</style>
<table>
<caption>10+ RBI in a Game</caption>
<colgroup></colgroup>
<colgroup span="3">
    <col span="2" style="background-color: cyan" />
    <col style="background-color: red" />
</colgroup>
<thead style="text-align: left">
...
```

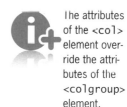

The attributes of the <col> element override the attributes of the <colgroup> element.

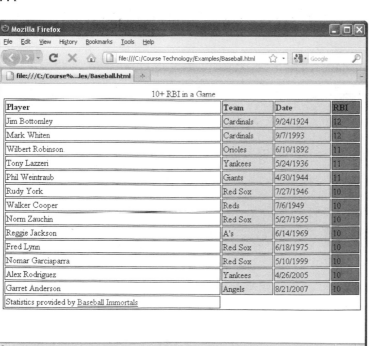

Figure 5-12 RBI table with column groups and <col> elements

Adjusting Column Widths

As you learned earlier, you use the CSS `width` property with the `table` selector to determine the width of a table. However, you cannot use this attribute to adjust the size of cells or columns in a table, which are determined automatically by each user agent. In addition, you cannot adjust the widths of individual table cells with the `<td>` and `<th>` elements. However, you can adjust the widths of columns using the CSS `width` property of the `<colgroup>` or `<col>` element.

Within the `width` property, you specify the width of a `<colgroup>` or `<col>` element by assigning a fixed value in pixels or a percentage representing a portion of the space that is available for the table. (This space is the visible width of a Web browser window.) In the following code, the first `<colgroup>` element specifies that the Player column of the RBI table must occupy 40 percent of the table width, and the second `<colgroup>` element specifies that the remainder of the columns must each occupy 100 pixels. Notice that the `table` selector in the style section does not include the `width` property. If you include the `width` property in a `<table>` element, it will override the `width` properties of any `<colspan>` or `<col>` elements defined within the table. Figure 5-13 shows how the table appears in a Web browser.

```
<style type="text/css">
table {
    border: 1px solid black;
}
td {
    border: 1px solid black;
}
</style>
<table>
<caption>10+ RBI in a Game</caption>
<colgroup style="width: 50%"></colgroup>
<colgroup span="3" style="width: 75px">
    <col span="2" style="background-color: cyan" />
    <col style="background-color: red" />
</colgroup>
<thead align="left">
<tr><th>Player</th><th>Team</th>
<th>Date</th><th>RBI</th></tr>
...
```

[Browser window screenshot]

Mozilla Firefox

File   Edit   View   History   Bookmarks   Tools   Help

file:///C:/Course Technology/Examples/Baseball.html

file:///C:/Course%...les/Baseball.html

10+ RBI in a Game

Player	Team	Date	RBI
Jim Bottomley	Cardinals	9/24/1924	12
Mark Whiten	Cardinals	9/7/1993	12
Wilbert Robinson	Orioles	6/10/1892	11
Tony Lazzeri	Yankees	5/24/1936	11
Phil Weintraub	Giants	4/30/1944	11
Rudy York	Red Sox	7/27/1946	10
Walker Cooper	Reds	7/6/1949	10
Norm Zauchin	Red Sox	5/27/1955	10
Reggie Jackson	A's	6/14/1969	10
Fred Lynn	Red Sox	6/18/1975	10
Nomar Garciaparra	Red Sox	5/10/1999	10
Alex Rodriguez	Yankees	4/26/2005	10
Garret Anderson	Angels	8/21/2007	10
Statistics provided by Baseball Immortals			

Done

Figure 5-13   RBI table with column groups that include width properties in a Web browser

When you do not assign widths for tables and columns, modern Web browsers automatically set the column widths to the widest unbreakable content in the cells. The problem with this approach is that large tables may render slowly because the browser needs to parse all of the table data before determining how to lay out the column widths. To speed up the rendering of tables, you can assign a value of "fixed" to the table-layout property of a table selector, which forces the browser to lay out the table based on the width of the table and its columns, not on the contents of its cells. The following code demonstrates how to assign a value of "fixed" to the table-layout property of a table selector:

```
table
{
    table-layout: fixed;
}
```

By default, the table-layout property of a table selector is assigned a value of "auto", which sets the column widths to the widest unbreakable content in the cells.

Next, you add a column group to the schedule.html file that formats the width and background color of the schedule table.

To add a column group to the schedule.html file:

1. Return to the **railroad.css** file in your text editor.

2. Delete the **width="100%"** property from the opening `table` selector.

3. Save the **railroad.css** file and return to the **schedule.html** file in your text editor.

4. Above the `<thead>` element, add the following column group that spans the arrival and departure columns and sets both columns to 360 pixels in width:

```
<colgroup span="2"
    style="width: 360px; background-color: silver" />
```

5. Save the **schedule.html** file and then open it in your Web browser. Figure 5-14 shows how the file should appear in a Web browser.

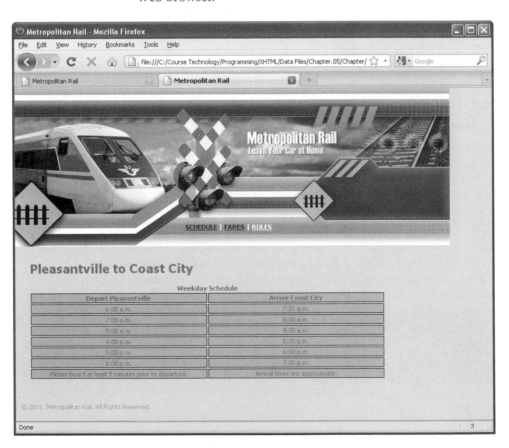

Figure 5-14   schedule.html after adding a column group

6. Close your Web browser window.

Using Tables to Simulate Frames

If you want to use tables to simulate frames, you create a table with the same number of cells as the number of frames you want. For instance, if you want to create two horizontal frames (one at the top of a page and one on bottom), you create a table with two rows, with each row containing a single <td> element. Similarly, if you want to create two vertical frames, you create a table with a single row containing two <td> elements. You can place almost any content you want within a cell—to create a navigation menu on the left and a content pane on the right, you would place a list of hyperlinks in the left cell and display each link's associated content in the right cell. You should take note of a significant difference between frames and tables that simulate frames: When you click a link in a table, the link opens a new page in the same browser window. It does not display a new URL in a different area of the same page, as do frames. Therefore, to get the same layout effect with a two-column table in which the left column contains a list of links, each document that is a target of the links must duplicate the table that simulates the frameset.

To help you understand how to use tables to simulate frames, consider the following code, which uses a table to simulate a page that displays car models for a company called Gosselin Motors. The table consists of a single row with two cells. The left cell contains a list of the links to each car model, and the right cell displays the information associated with the selected link. Notice that each link in the left cell opens a new Web page—clicking a link doesn't simply replace the contents of the right cell. The following document is for the DRG 5000 SUV; Figure 5-15 shows how the document appears in a Web browser.

```
<table><colgroup style="width: 250px" /></colgroup>
<tr><td style="border-right: thin solid black; text-
align: center; vertical-align: top">
<a href="DRG5000.html"><img src="images/drg5000.gif"
width="154" height="108" alt="Formatting element"
class="NoBorder" /></a><br />
<a href="DRG4000.html"><img src="images/drg4000.gif"
width="154" height="108" alt="Formatting element"
class="NoBorder" /></a><br />
<a href="DRGLX.html"><img src="images/drglx.gif"
width="154" height="108" alt="Formatting element"
class="NoBorder" /></a><br />
<a href="DRGDX.html"><img src="images/drgdx.gif"
width="154" height="108" alt="Formatting element"
class="NoBorder" /></a><br />
<a href="DRGSX.html"><img src="images/drgsx.gif"
```

```
width="154" height="108" alt="Formatting element"
class="NoBorder" /></a><br /></td>
<td style="margin-left: 250px; vertical-align: top">
<h2>DRG 5000 SUV</h2>
<p>MSRP: <strong>$37,900</strong><br />
Seats: <strong>7</strong><br />
Horsepower: <strong>310</strong><br />
EPA Est. Fuel Economy City:
<strong>14 MPG</strong><br />
EPA Est. Fuel Economy Highway: <strong>20
MPG</strong><br />
Cargo Capacity: <strong>137 cu. ft.</strong><br />
Engine type: <strong>4.0L SOHC 12V V6 </strong><br />
Engine electronics: <strong>PTEC - Powertrain Electronic
Controller</strong><br />
Displacement: <strong>4.0L (245 cu. in.) </strong><br />
Horsepower (SAE net@rpm): <strong>210 @ 5,100 </strong>
<br />
Torque (lb. ft. @ rpm): <strong>254 @ 3,700
</strong><br />
Compression ratio: <strong>9.7:1 </strong><br />
Bore x stroke (in.): <strong>3.95 x 3.32 </strong><br />
Main bearings: <strong>4 </strong><br />
Valve lifters: <strong>Hydraulic lash adjuster</strong>
<br />
Fuel delivery: <strong>Sequential multi port electronic
fuel injection </strong><br />
Recommended fuel: <strong>Unleaded regular </strong>
<br />
Exhaust: <strong>Single, stainless steel </strong>
<br />
Fuel economy: <strong>EPA-estimated mpg 14 city/20 hwy
(4x2) </strong><br />
Transmission type: <strong>5-speed automatic O/D
</strong><br />
Engine block material: <strong>Cast iron </strong><br />
Cylinder head material: <strong>Aluminum alloy </strong>
</p></td></tr></table>
```

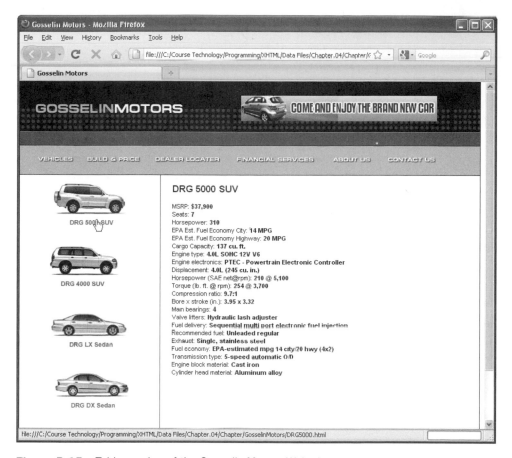

Figure 5-15 Table version of the Gosselin Motors Web site

Suppose you want one of the cells within a frame-simulation table to contain another table. Because table cells can include almost any content, you can nest a table within a table cell. This is not particularly complicated; all you need to do is place a `<table>` element and its text and child elements within a `<td>...</td>` tag pair in another table. For example, the following code contains a parent table that consists of one row with two cells. Each cell contains its own table that lists snow depths for this year and last year in areas of the Sierra Mountains in California. Figure 5-16 shows how the tables render in a browser. Because the parent table does not include a border `attribute`, the two nested tables appear to float next to each other.

```
...
<style type="text/css">
table {
    width: 100%;
}
}
```

```
td {
    border: 1px solid black;
}
</style>
</head>
<body>
<h1>Snow Depth</h1>
<table>
<tr>
<td>
<table>
<tr><th>Location</th><th>This
Year</th><th>Last Year</th></tr>
<tr><td>Bear Valley</td>
<td>17</td><td>28</td></tr>
<tr><td>Carson Pass</td>
<td>10</td><td>29</td></tr>
<tr><td>Donner Pass</td>
<td>10</td><td>46</td></tr>
</table>
</td>
<td>
<table>
<tr><th>Location</th><th>This Year</th>
<th>Last Year</th></tr>
<tr><td>Echo Summit</td>
<td>7</td><td>21</td></tr>
<tr><td>Mammoth</td><td>24</td>
<td>14</td></tr>
<tr><td>Pinecrest</td><td>13</td>
<td>12</td></tr>
</table>
</td>
</tr>
</table>
```

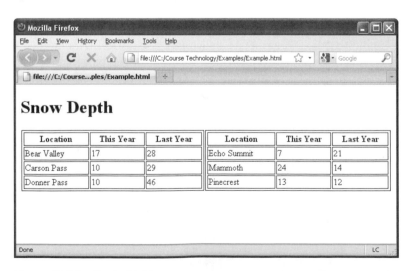

Figure 5-16   Nested tables

You will now modify the schedule.html file so it includes a one-row, two-cell table that simulates a frameset. The left table cell contains hyperlinks and the right cell displays each link's associated content.

To modify the schedule.html file to include a one-row, two-cell table that simulates a frameset:

1. Return to the **schedule.html** file in your text editor.

2. Immediately above the `<table>` tag, add the following elements for the parent table that simulates a frameset. The first `<td>` element includes two hyperlinks: one for schedule.html and another for a file named fares.html that you will create shortly. Notice that only two `<td>` elements are defined. The first `<td>` element contains the links. The second opening `<td>` tag includes the schedule table as its content.

```
<table border="1">
<colgroup span="1" style="width: 100px"></colgroup>
<colgroup span="1"></colgroup>
<tr><td><a href="schedule.html">Schedule</a><br />
<a href="fares.html">Fares</a></td>
<td>
```

3. To complete the new parent table, add the following closing `</td>`, `</tr>`, and `</table>` tags immediately after the closing `</table>` tag.

```
</td></tr></table>
```

4. Save the **schedule.html** file and then immediately save it as **fares.html** in your Chapter folder for Chapter 5.

5. In the **fares.html** file, replace the schedule table with the following fares table. Do not delete any of the tags for the parent table.

```
<table>
    <caption>One-Way Fares</caption>
    <colgroup span="3"
    style="width: 200px; background-color: silver">
    </colgroup>
    <thead>
<tr><th>Passenger</th><th>Weekdays</th>
<th>Weekends/Holidays</th></tr>
    </thead>
    <tbody>
        <tr><td>Adult (13-64)</td>
            <td>$3.25</td>
            <td>$5.60</td></tr>
        <tr><td>Youth (6-12)</td>
            <td>$2.45</td>
            <td>$4.20</td></tr>
```

```
<tr><td>Senior (65+)</td>
      <td>$1.60</td>
      <td>$2.80</td></tr>
<tr><td>Disabled</td>
      <td>$1.25</td>
      <td>$2.30</td></tr>
<tr><td>Child (0-5)</td>
      <td>FREE</td>
      <td>FREE</td></tr>
   </tbody>
</table>
```

6. Save the **fares.html** file and then open it in your Web browser. Figure 5-17 shows how the file should appear in your Web browser. Test the links to be sure that both files open correctly.

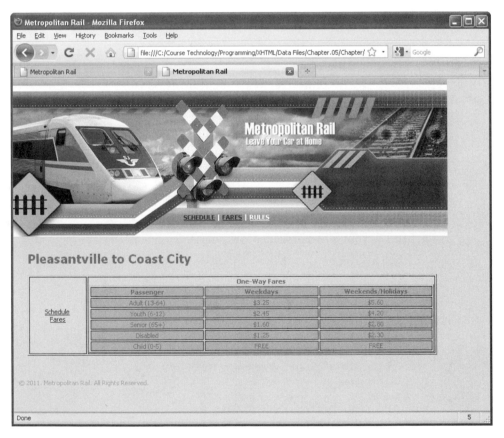

Figure 5-17   fares.html in a Web browser

7. Close your Web browser window.

Short Quiz 2

1. How do you define a table header?

2. How do you define a table body?

3. How do you define a table footer?

4. Explain how to use column groups.

5. How do you use tables to simulate frames?

Formatting Tables

As you learned in Chapter 3, you should handle the visual display of content with CSS. Nevertheless, you can use several types of built-in table formatting options without CSS. You study the following types of table formatting in this section:

- Table borders

- Collapsed borders

- Empty cells

- Cell margins

- Cells that span multiple rows or columns

- Vertical alignment

Prior to HTML 5, the majority of table formatting tasks were accomplished using attributes of the table elements. Most of these attributes are no longer available in HTML 5, so to ensure that your Web pages are well formed, use CSS for any table formatting.

Using Borders

As you learned earlier, tables are created without borders by default. You use the CSS shorthand **border property** to add borders to HTML elements. In addition to the `border` property, CSS includes many other properties that you can use to format borders and the rules (or lines) that separate table rows and columns. For example, CSS includes the following properties for formatting an element's right border:

- **border-right**—shorthand property for formatting an element's right border

- **border-right-color**—formats the color of an element's right border

- **border-right-style**—determines the style of an element's right border

- **border-right-width**—assigns the width of an element's right border

Similar properties exist for the top, bottom, and left sides of an element's border. The following code shows an American life expectancy table that uses the border-top shorthand property to display a border at the top of the table. Figure 5-18 shows the table in a Web browser.

```
...
<style type="text/css">
    td.tc {
        text-align: center;
    }
</style>
</head>
<body>
<table style="border-top: 2px solid red">
<caption><strong>American Life
Expectancy</strong></caption>
<colgroup span="3" width="100px"></colgroup>
<tr><th style="text-align: left">Group</th>
<th>At Birth</th><th>At Age 65</th></tr>
<tr><td>Males</td><td class="tc">74.1</td>
<td class="tc">16.3</td></tr>
<tr><td>Females</td><td class="tc">79.5</td>
<td class="tc">19.2</td></tr>
<tr><td>All Americans</td><td class="tc">76.9</td>
<td class="tc">17.9</td></tr>
</table>
```

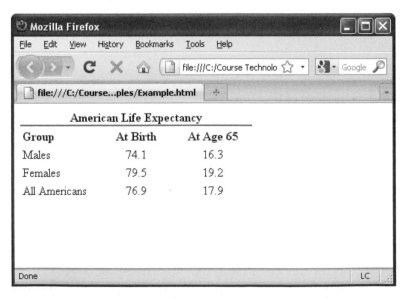

Figure 5-18 Table with a border-top shorthand property

Next, you modify the parent table in the schedule.html and fares.html files so that the border is visible only on the top and bottom of the table.

To modify the parent table so the table border is visible only on the top and bottom:

1. Return to the **railroad.css** file in your text editor.

2. Modify the `table` selector so it defines a class ID of "tmain". Also, replace the `border` property in the `table` selector with the following `border-top` and `border-bottom` properties:

```
table.tmain {
    border-top: 1px solid black;
    border-bottom: 1px solid black;
}
```

3. Delete the `border` properties from the `td` and `th` selectors.

4. Save the **railroad.css** file and then return to the **schedule.html** file in your text editor.

5. Add `class="tmain"` to the opening `<table>` tag for the first table. Be sure not to add the code to the second table.

6. Save the **schedule.html** file and return to the **fares.html** file. Make the same change in the fares.html file that you made to the schedule.html file in the preceding step.

7. Save the **fares.html** file and then open the **schedule.html** file in your Web browser. As you can see, the document is starting to look more like a frameset document. Open the **fares.html** document by clicking the **Fares** link, and make sure that the parent table looks the same as it does in the schedule.html file.

8. Close your Web browser window.

Collapsing Borders

By default, Web browsers display the borders for both the table itself and the elements it contains, as shown in Figure 5-19. The figure is rendered by the following version of the life expectancy table:

```
...
<style type="text/css">
table {
    border: 1px solid black;
}
}
```

```
td, th {
    border: 1px solid black;
}
td.tc {
    text-align: center;
}
</style>
</head>
<body>
<table>
<caption><strong>American Life
Expectancy</strong></caption>
<colgroup span="3" width="100px"></colgroup>
<tr><th style="text-align: left">Group</th>
<th>At Birth</th><th>At Age 65</th></tr>
<tr><td>Males</td><td class="tc">74.1</td>
<td class="tc">16.3</td></tr>
<tr><td>Females</td><td class="tc">79.5</td>
<td class="tc">19.2</td></tr>
<tr><td>All Americans</td><td class="tc">76.9</td>
<td class="tc">17.9</td></tr>
</table>
```

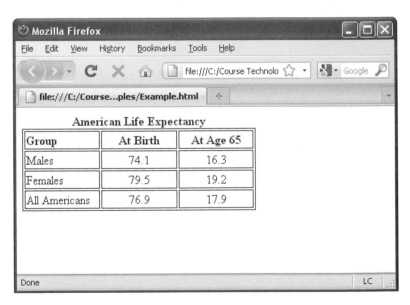

Figure 5-19   Table with separate, detached borders

To prevent table border elements from being displayed as separate, detached borders, use the CSS border-collapse property. By default, the border-collapse property is assigned a value of "separate", which displays the table borders as detached. To display the borders as a single border, you assign a value of "collapse" to the border-collapse property. For example, if you add a style declaration of `border-collapse: collapse` to the `table` selector in the preceding code, the table will be displayed with collapsed borders, as shown in Figure 5-20.

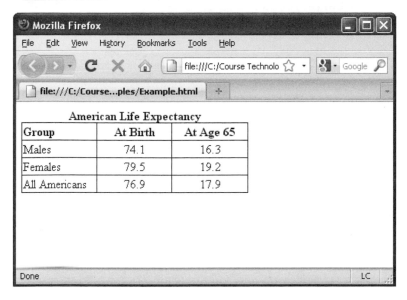

Figure 5-20　Table with collapsed borders

Displaying Empty Cells

Tables often must include empty cells. For instance, the following code shows a table that tracks the retail cost of barrels of diesel fuel and gasoline for several months in 2010. Let's assume that you do not yet have the data for several weeks, but you still want to include rows in the table for them. The following code does not include cells (`<td>` elements) for the gas and diesel prices in the missing weeks, but it does include cells that contain the dates.

```
...
<style type="text/css">
table {
    border: 1px solid black;
    border-collapse: collapse;
    width: 100%;
}
td {
    border: 1px solid black;
}
</style>
</head>
<body>
<table border="1">
```

```
<caption>Retail Diesel and Gasoline
Prices</caption>
<tr><th>Week Ending</th>
<th>Diesel</th><th>Gasoline</th></tr>
<tr><td>4/26/2010</td><td>307.8</td>
<td>281.5</td></tr>
<tr><td>5/3/2010</td><td>312.2</td>
<td>286.4</td></tr>
<tr><td>5/10/2010</td><td>312.7</td>
<td>287.0</td></tr>
<tr><td>5/17/2010</td><td>309.4</td>
<td>282.3</td></tr>
<tr><td>5/24/2010</td></tr>
<tr><td>5/31/2010</td></tr>
<tr><td>6/7/2010</td></tr>
<tr><td>6/14/2010</td></tr>
<tr><td>6/21/2010</td></tr>
</table>
```

Unfortunately, most Web browsers do not render the borders around empty cells. For example, Figure 5-21 shows that the borders are missing around the empty cells in the preceding code.

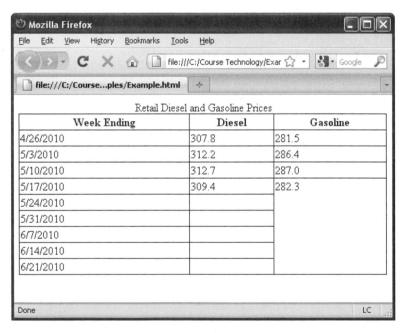

Figure 5-21   Missing borders around empty cells

XHTML offers two alternatives to fix this problem. With the first method, you add a <td> element for each empty cell, and include a nonbreaking space character entity ( ) as each cell's content. For instance, the following code shows the rows in the diesel and gasoline prices table that contains empty cells created with nonbreaking space character entities. Figure 5-22 shows the output in a Web browser.

```
...
<tr><td>5/24/2010</td><td> </td></tr>
<tr><td>5/31/2010</td><td> </td></tr>
<tr><td>6/7/2010</td><td> </td></tr>
<tr><td>6/14/2010</td><td> </td></tr>
<tr><td>6/21/2010</td><td> </td></tr>
</table>
```

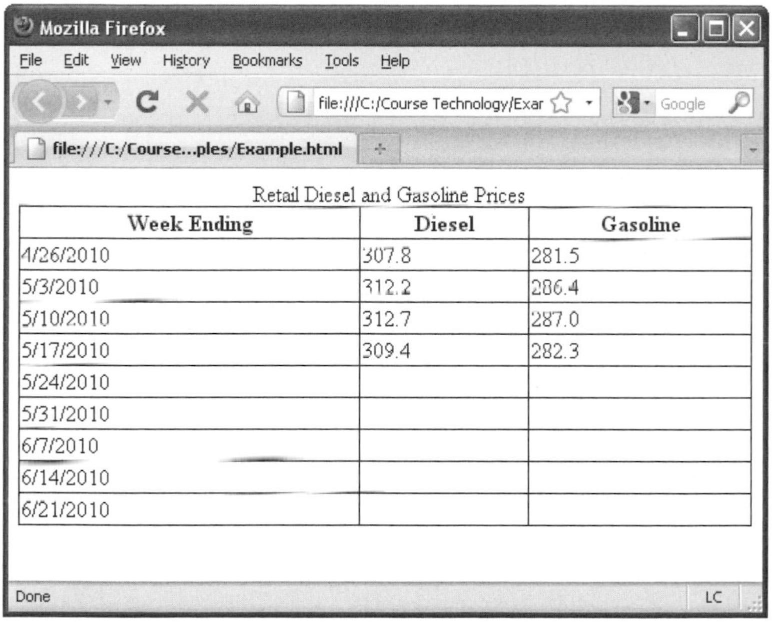

Figure 5-22 Table with empty cells created with nonbreaking space character entities

Next, you will add a new column to the train schedule table for stops in the city of Central Valley, which lies between Pleasantville and Coast City. However, only some trains stop in Central Valley. Therefore, you will add empty cells to represent times that the trains do not stop at the Central Valley station.

To add empty cells for times that trains do not stop in Central Valley:

1. Return to the **schedule.html** file in your text editor.

2. As shown in the following code, change the value assigned to the span attribute in the nested schedule table's <colgroup>

element from "2" to **"3"**, and decrease the width in the `style` attribute to **200px**. Add the bold statements shown in the following code to the nested schedule table. Notice that the empty cells include the nonbreaking space character entity.

```
<table border="1">
  <caption>Weekday Schedule</caption>
  <colgroup span="3"
  style="width: 200px; background-color:
silver"></colgroup>
  <thead>
     <tr><th>Depart Pleasantville</th>
     <th>Central Valley</th>
     <th>Arrive Coast City</th></tr>
  </thead>
  <tfoot>
     <tr><td>Please board at least 5
        minutes prior to departure.</td>
<td> </td>
<td>Arrival times are approximate.</td></tr>
  </tfoot>
  <tbody>
  <tr><td>6:00 a.m.</td>
     <td>6:30 a.m.</td>
     <td>7:00 a.m.</td></tr>
  <tr><td>7:00 a.m.</td>
     <td> </td>
     <td>8:00 a.m.</td></tr>
  <tr><td>8:00 a.m.</td>
     <td>8:30 a.m.</td>
     <td>9:00 a.m.</td></tr>
  <tr><td>4:00 p.m.</td>
     <td> </td>
     <td>5:00 p.m.</td></tr>
  <tr><td>5:00 p.m.</td>
     <td>5:30 p.m.</td>
     <td>6:00 p.m.</td></tr>
  <tr><td>6:00 p.m.</td>
     <td> </td>
     <td>7:00 p.m.</td></tr>
  </tbody>
</table>
```

3. Save the **schedule.html** file and then open it in your Web browser. Figure 5-23 shows how the file should appear in a Web browser.

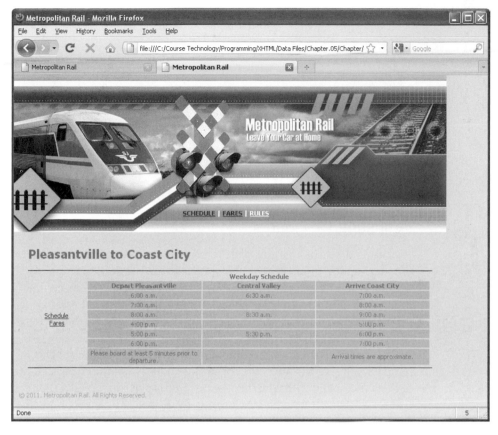

Figure 5-23 schedule.html after adding a new column with empty cells

4. Close your Web browser window.

The second method to fix the problem of browsers not rendering the borders around empty cells is to use the CSS **empty-cells property**, which determines whether to show or hide the background and borders of empty cells. By default, the empty-cells property is assigned a value of "hide", which hides the background and borders of empty cells. To display the background and borders of empty cells, you assign a value of "show" to the empty-cells property, as shown in the following example of the diesel and gasoline prices table. The following code displays the same table shown in Figure 5-22.

```
...
<style type="text/css">
table {
    border: 1px solid black;
    width: 100%;
    empty-cells: show;
}
```

```
td {
    border: 1px solid black;
}
</style>
</html>
<body>
<table>
<caption>Retail Diesel and Gasoline Prices</caption>
<tr><th>Week Ending</th>
<th>Diesel</th><th>Gasoline</th></tr>
<tr><td>4/26/2010</td><td>307.8</td>
<td>281.5</td></tr>
...
```

Adjusting Cell Margins

You can adjust the margins of cells in a table by using the CSS
border-spacing and padding properties. The **border-spacing
property** specifies a pixel value that represents the amount of
horizontal and vertical space between table cells. You can assign one
or two values to the border-spacing property; a single value specifies
the same amount of both horizontal and vertical spacing, while two
values specify separate amounts of horizontal and vertical spacing,
respectively. For instance, the following code shows the American life
expectancy table with a border-spacing property assigned a single
value of 10 pixels between the table cells. Figure 5-24 shows how the
table appears in a Web browser.

```
...
<style type="text/css">
table {
    border: 1px solid black;
    border-spacing: 10px;
}
td {
    border: 1px solid black;
}
</style>
</head>
<body>
<table>
<caption><b>American Life
Expectancy</b></caption>
<tr><th>Group</th>
<th>At Birth</th><th>At Age 65</th></tr>
<tr><td>Males</td><td>74.1</td>
<td>16.3</td></tr>
<tr><td>Females</td><td>79.5</td>
<td>19.2</td></tr>
<tr><td>All Americans</td>
<td>76.9</td><td>17.9</td></tr>
</table>
```

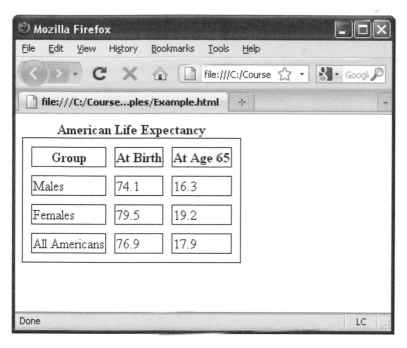

Figure 5-24 Table with 10 pixels between the table cells

If you assign a value of "collapse" to the border-collapse property, the border-spacing property is ignored.

In comparison, the **CSS padding properties** specify the amount of horizontal and vertical space between each cell's border and the contents of the cell. You use the CSS shorthand **padding property** to add horizontal and vertical space to a table. In addition to the padding property, CSS includes the following properties for padding an element:

- **padding-bottom**—formats an element's bottom padding
- **padding-left**—formats an element's left padding
- **padding-right**—formats an element's right padding
- **padding-top**—formats an element's top padding

The following code shows the American life expectancy table with the shorthand padding property that specifies 20 pixels between each cell's border and content. Figure 5-25 shows how the table appears in a Web browser.

The CSS padding properties can be used with elements other than table elements.

```
...
<style type="text/css">
table {
    border: 1px solid black;
    padding: 20px;
}
td {
    border: 1px solid black;
}
</style>
</head>
<body>
<table>
<caption><strong>American Life
Expectancy</strong></caption>
<tr><th>Group</th>
<th>At Birth</th><th>At Age 65</th></tr>
<tr><td>Males</td><td>74.1</td>
<td>16.3</td></tr>
<tr><td>Females</td><td>79.5</td>
<td>19.2</td></tr>
<tr><td>All Americans</td>
<td>76.9</td><td>17.9</td></tr>
</table>
```

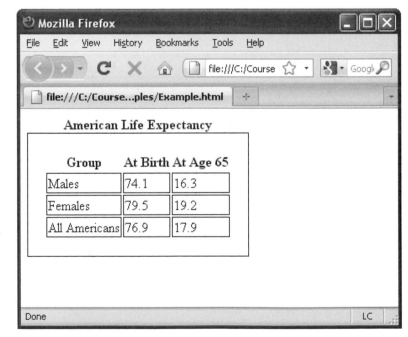

You can use the border-spacing and **padding** properties together to create different combinations of spacing and padding within your tables.

Figure 5-25   Table with 20 pixels between each cell's border and content

Making Cells Span Multiple Rows or Columns

You can cause cells to span multiple rows or columns by including the **rowspan** or **colspan attribute** in the <td> or <th> elements. As an example of the rowspan attribute, the following table shows a breakdown of the animal kingdom into phylum and class. Figure 5-26 shows the table in a Web browser.

```
...
<style type="text/css">
table {
    border: 1px solid black;
    width: 100%;
}
td, th {
    border: 1px solid black;
}
</style>
</head>
<body>
<table><tr><th>Kingdom</th>
<th>Phylum</th><th>Class</th></tr>
<tr><td rowspan="4">Animalia</td><td rowspan="2">
Chordata</td><td>Mammalia</td></tr>
<tr><td>Amphibia</td></tr>
<tr><td rowspan="2">Arthropoda</td>
<td>Insecta</td></tr>
<tr><td>Arachnida</td></tr>
</table>
```

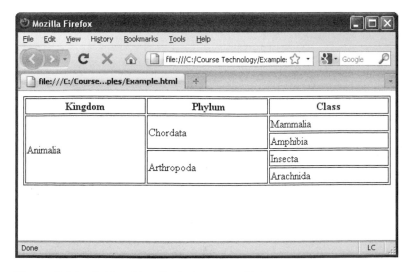

Figure 5-26 Table with cells that span multiple rows

The following table shows an alternate version of the animal kingdom table, but this time with cells that span multiple columns. Figure 5-27 shows the table in a Web browser.

```
...
<style type="text/css">
table {
    border: 1px solid black;
    width: 100%;
    text-align: center;
}
td, th {
    border: 1px solid black;
}
</style>
</head>
<body>
<table>
<tr><td><strong>Kingdom</strong></td>
<td colspan="4">
Animalia</td></tr>
<tr><td><strong>Phylum</strong></td>
<td colspan="2">Chordata</td>
<td colspan="2">Arthropoda</td></tr>
<tr><td><strong>Class</strong></td>
<td>Mammalia</td>
<td>Amphibia</td>
<td>Insecta</td>
<td>Arachnida</td></tr>
</table>
```

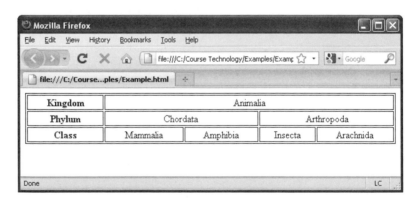

Figure 5-27   Table with cells that span multiple columns

Next, you modify the schedule.html file so the schedule table includes cells that span multiple rows and columns.

To modify the schedule table so cells span multiple rows and columns:

1. Return to the **schedule.html** file in your text editor.

2. Modify the span attribute in the nested schedule table's `<colgroup>` element so it is assigned a value of **"4"** instead of "3". The modified element should appear as follows:

```
<colgroup span="4" width="200px"></colgroup>
```

3. Modify the `<thead>` section in the nested table, as follows, so the heading information includes a new "Rush Hour" column:

```
<thead>
    <tr><th>Rush Hour</th>
<th>Depart Pleasantville</th>
    <th>Central Valley</th>
<th>Arrive Coast City</th></tr>
</thead>
```

4. Within the nested table body, add the following `<td>` elements highlighted in boldface, which create two new cells that span several rows:

```
<tbody>
    <tr style="text-align: center">
    <td rowspan="3">Morning</td>
    <td>6:00 a.m.</td>
    <td>6:30 a.m.</td>
    <td>7:00 a.m.</td></tr>
    <tr><td>7:00 a.m.</td>
    <td> </td>
    <td>8:00 a.m.</td></tr>
    <tr><td>8:00 a.m.</td>
    <td>8:30 a.m.</td>
    <td>9:00 a.m.</td></tr>
    <tr><td rowspan="3">Evening</td>
    <td>4:00 p.m.</td>
...
```

5. Finally, edit the `<tfoot>` element to add the following statements, which create a single footer cell that spans the other columns in the table:

```
<tfoot>
    <tr><td colspan="4">Please board at least 5 minutes
    prior to departure. Arrival times are approximate.
    </td></tr>
</tfoot>
```

6. Save the **schedule.html** file and then open it in your Web browser. Figure 5-28 shows how the file should appear in a Web browser.

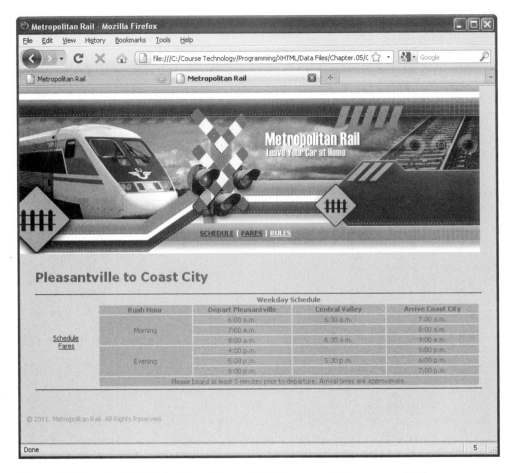

Figure 5-28   schedule.html after adding cells that span multiple rows and columns

7. Close your Web browser window.

Vertically Aligning Table Contents

In addition to using the CSS text-align property to horizontally align columns, you can use the **vertical-align property** to adjust the vertical alignment of the contents of all table elements except the <table> and <caption> elements. The values you can assign to the vertical-align property are baseline, sub, super, top, text-top, middle, bottom, text-bottom, and inherit. The default vertical-align property is "baseline". You can also assign positive and negative lengths and percentages to raise or lower an element.

If you examine the animal kingdom table in Figure 5-26, which originally included cells that spanned multiple rows, you will see that by default the contents of the cells are aligned in the middle of each cell. If you add `vertical-align: top` to the `td, th` selector, as shown in the following code, the cell contents are aligned at the top of the cells, as shown in Figure 5-29.

```
<style type="text/css">
table {
    border: 1px solid black;
    width: 100%;
}
td, th {
    border: 1px solid black;
    vertical-align: top;
}
</style>
```

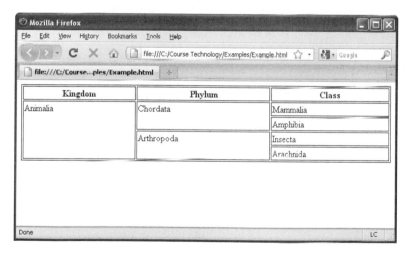

Figure 5-29 Table with data vertically aligned at the tops of each cell

Next, you modify the schedule.html and fares.html files so cell contents are vertically aligned at the top instead of the middle by default.

To modify the schedule.html and fares.html files so the links in the left cell of the parent table are vertically aligned at the top:

1. Return to the **schedule.html** file in your text editor.

2. Add `style="vertical-align: top"` to the first `<td>` tag in the parent table.

3. Save the **schedule.html** file, then return to the **fares.html** file and add the same style attribute to the first `<td>` tag in the parent table.

4. Save the **fares.html** file, then open **schedule.html** in a Web browser and examine the vertical alignment of its cell contents. Click the **Fares** link and examine the vertical alignment of the cell contents. Figure 5-30 shows how the fares.html file should appear in a Web browser.

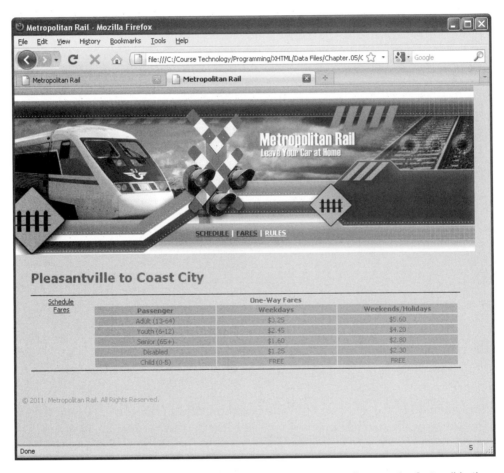

Figure 5-30 fares.html after adding the `vertical-align` attribute to the first cell in the parent table

5. Close your Web browser window.

Short Quiz 3

1. Explain how to use borders.

2. Why would you need to collapse borders?

3. How do you display borders for empty cells?

4. How do you create cells that span multiple rows or columns?

5. Explain how to adjust vertical alignment.

Creating Lists

Lists are an important tool in proper Web page authoring because they provide a way to logically order a series of words or numbers. They also provide a simple yet effective design technique for allowing Web site visitors to locate information more easily. You can add three types of lists to a Web page: unordered lists, ordered lists, and definition lists. Table 5-4 lists the elements used to create these lists.

Element	Description
`<ul>`	Block-level element that creates an unordered list
`<ol>`	Block-level element that creates an ordered list
`<li>`	Inline element that defines a list item
`<dl>`	Block-level element that creates a definition list
`<dt>`	Inline element that defines a definition list term
`<dd>`	Inline element that defines a definition list item

Table 5-4   List elements

This section presents basic information for working with lists. To change the formatting and appearance of lists, you must use CSS.

Creating Unordered Lists

An **unordered list** is a series of bulleted items. To define the items that will appear in the bulleted list, you nest `<li>` elements within a `<ul>` element. The following code creates the unordered list shown in Figure 5-31.

```
<h1>Meatloaf Recipe</h1>
<h2>Ingredients</h2>
<ul>
<li>1 1/2 pounds ground beef</li>
<li>1 egg</li>
<li>1 onion, chopped</li>
<li>1 cup milk</li>
<li>1 cup dried bread crumbs</li>
<li>2 tablespoons brown sugar</li>
<li>2 tablespoons prepared mustard</li>
<li>1/3 cup ketchup</li>
</ul>
```

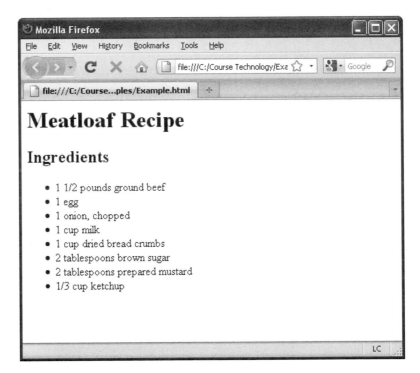

Figure 5-31   Unordered list

Next, you add an unordered list to your sample Web site.

To add a Courtesy Rules page with an unordered list to the Metropolitan Commuter Railroad Web site:

1. Return to the **schedule.html** file in your text editor and modify the first cell in the parent table as follows so it includes a new link to a page named rules.html:

```
<td style="vertical-align: top">
    <a href="schedule.html">Schedule</a><br />
    <a href="fares.html">Fares</a><br />
    <a href="rules.html">Courtesy Rules</a>
</td>
```

2. Save and close the **schedule.html** file.

3. Return to the **fares.html** file in your text editor and make the same change that you made to the schedule.html file in Step 1.

4. Save the **fares.html** file and immediately save it as **rules.html** in your Chapter folder for Chapter 5.

5. Replace the nested fares table with the following unordered rules list:

```
<ul style="text-align: left">
<li>Smoking is not permitted on
Metropolitan Commuter Railroad
trains.</li>
<li>No seats are reserved. Please do not
inconvenience other customers by
holding seats or blocking seats with
parcels or wraps.</li>
<li>Please refrain from placing feet on
seats or upper deck railings.</li>
<li>Please do not block the doors,
making it difficult for passengers to
board or disembark at their
stations.</li>
<li>Please be considerate of others and
keep volume on head sets low.</li>
<li>Help us to maintain a clean
environment by not leaving litter
on trains, in stations, or in stairwells
and walkways.</li>
<li>Passengers whose conduct is
disorderly or unsafe will not be
allowed on the train.</li>
<li>Obscene language is prohibited.</li>
</ul>
```

6. Save the file as **rules.html** and then open it in your Web browser. Figure 5-32 displays the document in a Web browser.

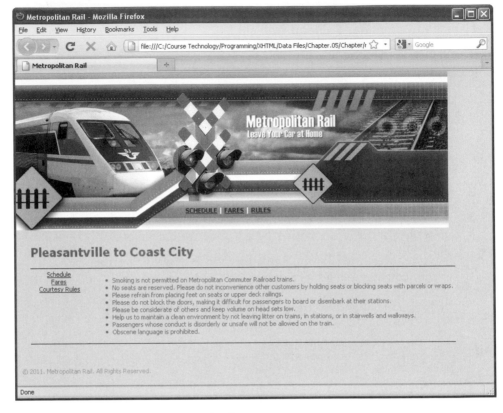

Figure 5-32   Unordered courtesy rules list

> **7.** Close your Web browser window.

Creating Ordered Lists

An **ordered list** is a series of numbered items. To define the items that will appear in the numbered list, you nest <li> elements within an <ol> element. The following code creates the ordered list shown in Figure 5-33.

```
<h1>Meatloaf Recipe</h1>
<h2>Directions</h2>
<ol>
    <li>Preheat oven to 350 degrees Fahrenheit.</li>
    <li>In a large bowl, combine the beef, egg, onion,
    milk, and breadcrumbs. Season with salt and pepper
    to taste and place in a lightly greased 5x9 inch
    loaf pan. </li>
    <li>In a separate small bowl, combine the brown
    sugar, mustard and ketchup. Mix well and pour
    over the meatloaf.</li>
     <li>Bake at 350 degrees Fahrenheit for 1 hour.</li>
</ol>
```

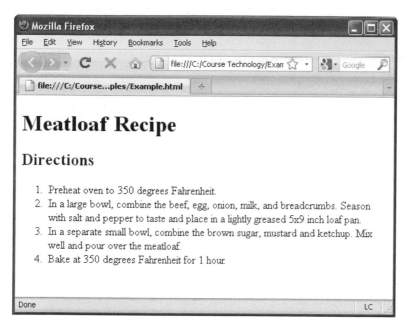

Figure 5-33 Ordered list

Next, you modify the unordered courtesy rules list from the previous exercise so that it becomes an ordered list.

To change the unordered courtesy rules list to an ordered list:

1. Return to the **rules.html** file in your text editor.

2. Change the `<ul>` and `</ul>` tags to `<ol>` and `</ol>` tags, as follows:

```
<ol style="text-align: left">
<li>Smoking is not permitted on Metropolitan Commuter
Railroad trains.</li>
<li>No seats are reserved. Please do not
inconvenience other customers ...
</ol>
```

3. Save the **rules.html** file and validate it with the W3C Markup Validation Service at **http://validator.w3.org/#validate_by_upload**.

4. Close the **rules.html** file, and then validate the schedule.html and fares.html files with the W3C Markup Validation Service. If you receive any errors, fix them and then revalidate the documents.

5. Open **rules.html** in your Web browser. Figure 5-34 displays the document in a browser.

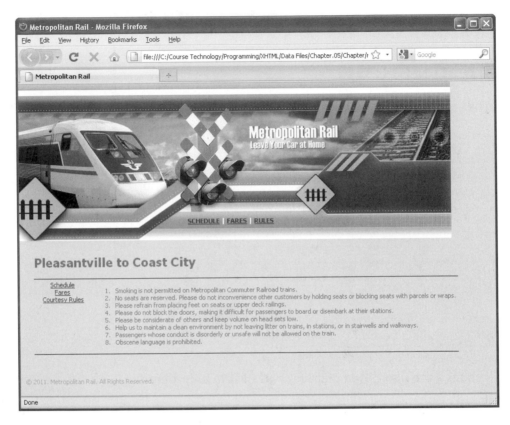

Figure 5-34   Ordered courtesy rules list

6. Close your text editor and Web browser window.

Creating Definition Lists

A **definition list** is a series of terms and their definitions. Web browsers render each term and its definition on separate lines with an indented left margin. You create a definition list by using the <dl> element. Within the <dl> element, you nest <dt> elements for term names and <dd> elements for term definitions. The following code creates the definition list shown in Figure 5-35.

```
<h1>Electrical Terms</h1>
<h2>Beginning with the Letter
<em>'O'</em></h2>
<dl>
        <dt><b>Ohm</b></dt>
        <dd>Measurement unit for electrical
```

```
        resistance or impedance.</dd>
    <dt> <b>Ohmmeter</b></dt>
    <dd>An instrument used for measuring resistance
        in Ohms.</dd>
    <dt><b>Overcurrent</b></dt>
    <dd>An electrical current that
        is in excess of an appliance's
        rated current or the ampacity
        of a conductor.</dd>
    <dt><b>Overload</b></dt>
    <dd>A load that exceeds the rating
        of a system or mechanism.</dd>
</dl>
```

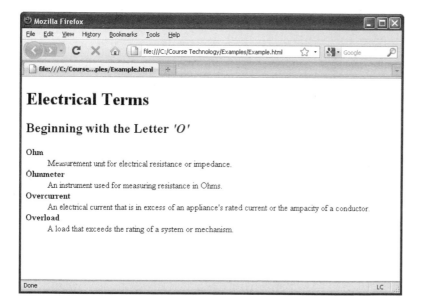

Figure 5-35   Definition list

Short Quiz 4

1.   Explain how to create unordered lists.

2.   Explain how to create ordered lists.

3.   Explain how to create definition lists.

Summing Up

- Tables are collections of rows and columns that you use to organize and display data.

- In a table, the intersection of a row and column is called a cell.

- You create tables using the `<table>` element.

- You create a cell within the `<table>` element using the `<td>` element.

- Table cells are declared within table row elements that you create with the `<tr>` element.

- Table cells can contain two types of information: data that you define with the `<td>` element and heading information that you define with the `<th>` element.

- You create a caption for a Web page table using the `<caption>` element.

- You use the CSS `width` property to format the size of elements, including `<table>` elements.

- You can use the CSS `text-align` property to adjust the horizontal alignment of elements, including the contents of all table elements except the `<table>` and `<caption>` elements.

- You can create row groups in a table that consist of a table header, table body, and table footer.

- The `<thead>` element defines a table header.

- The `<tbody>` element defines the table body.

- The `<tfoot>` element defines the table footer.

- Column groups are used for applying default alignment, width, and CSS styles to groups of columns within a table.

- You use the `<colgroup>` element to create a column group in a table.

- The `<col>` element allows you to apply formatting to an individual column in a column group.

- You can adjust the widths of columns using the CSS `width` property of the `<colgroup>` or `<col>` element.

- You use the CSS border properties to add borders to a table and its elements.

- To prevent table border elements from being displayed as separate, detached borders, use the CSS border-collapse property.

- You can use a <td> element to create an empty cell, but you must include the nonbreaking space character entity ( ) as content for each empty cell.

- The CSS empty-cells property determines whether to show or hide the background and borders of empty cells.

- The border-spacing property specifies a pixel value that represents the amount of horizontal and vertical space between table cells.

- The CSS padding properties specify the amount of horizontal and vertical space between each cell's border and the contents of the cell.

- You can cause cells to span multiple rows or columns by including the rowspan or colspan attribute in the <td> or <th> elements.

- You can use the vertical-align property to adjust the vertical alignment of the contents of all table elements except the <table> and <caption> elements.

- An unordered list is a series of bulleted items.

- An ordered list is a series of numbered items.

- A definition list is a series of terms and their definitions.

Comprehension Check

1. Tables are limited to displaying simple text. True or False?

2. Explain why the W3C discourages the use of tables to simulate frames and achieve other types of document layout.

3. Which of the following elements do you use to create table cells? (Choose all that apply.)

   a. <table>

   b. <cell>

   c. <td>

   d. <th>

4. Which of the following elements do you use to create table rows?

   a. <row>

   b. <table_row>

   c. <tr>

   d. <rt>

5. How do most Web browsers display a table's heading information?

6. Which of the following elements do you use to create a table caption?

   a. <tc>

   b. <caption>

   c. <th>

   d. <heading>

7. A Web browser automatically sizes a table's width to 100 percent of the visible browser window. True or False?

8. Which values can you assign to the text-align property? (Choose all that apply.)

   a. left

   b. center

   c. right

   d. justify

9. You must include row group elements in a table. True or False?

10. Which elements are required when you include row groups in a table? (Choose all that apply.)

    a. <thead>

    b. <trows>

    c. <tbody>

    d. <tfoot>

11. Where must you place the <colgroup> element?

12. Which attribute of the <colgroup> and <col> elements determines the number of columns that are part of the group?

     a. group

     b. cols

     c. span

     d. colspan

13. Explain how you use a table to simulate frames.

14. Explain how to assign borders to just the left and right sides of a table.

15. Explain how to format an empty cell so it appears in a Web browser.

16. Which of the following properties determines whether to show or hide the background and borders of empty cells?

     a. display-empty

     b. show-empty

     c. empty-cells

     d. show-nbsp

17. Which properties adjust the margins of a table's cells? (Choose all that apply.)

     a. border-spacing

     b. padding

     c. space-border

     d. margin-border

18. In which elements can you use the rowspan and colspan attributes? (Choose all that apply.)

     a. <table>

     b. <th>

     c. <td>

     d. <tr>

19. What property adjusts the vertical alignment of cell contents?

   a. `vertical-align`

   b. `valign`

   c. `span`

   d. `rowspan`

20. Which of the following elements is used with both unordered and ordered lists?

   a. `<ul>`

   b. `<ol>`

   c. `<li>`

   d. `<dl>`

Reinforcement Exercises

 Exercise 5-1

In this exercise, you create a document that contains a price list for a barbershop.

1. Create a new HTML 5 document in your text editor and use **Bernie's Barbershop Prices** as the title.

2. Add the following style section to the document head:

```
<style type="text/css">
      table
      {
            border: 1px solid black;
            width: 100%;
      }
      td, th
      {
            border: 1px solid black;
      }
</style>
```

3. Add the following heading element to the document body.

```
<h1>Bernie's Barbershop</h1>
```

4. Add the following table after the heading element.

```
<table>
  <caption>Haircut Price
List</caption>
  <tr>
    <th> </th>
    <th>Haircut</th>
    <th>Crew Cut</th>
    <th>Trim</th>
  </tr>
  <tr>
    <td>Men</td>
    <td>$11.99</td>
    <td>$9.99</td>
    <td>$6.99</td>
  </tr>
  <tr>
    <td>Boys</td>
    <td>$8.99</td>
    <td>$6.99</td>
    <td>$4.99</td>
  </tr>
</table>
```

5. Save the file as **HaircutPrices.html** in your Exercises folder for Chapter 5.

6. Close the **HaircutPrices.html** file in your text editor, and then use the W3C Markup Validation Service to validate the file. Once the file is valid, open it in your Web browser.

7. Close your Web browser window.

Exercise 5-2

In this exercise, you create a document that contains a table of dog breeds by group, such as hounds and terriers.

1. Create a new HTML 5 document in your text editor and use **Dog Breeds** as the title.

2. Add the following style section to the document head:

```
<style type="text/css">
    table
    {
        border: 1px solid black;
        width: 100%;
    }
}
```

```
                    td, th
                    {
                            border: 1px solid black;
                    }
        </style>
```

304

3. Add the following heading element to the document body.

   ```
   <h1>Dog Breeds</h1>
   ```

4. Add the following table after the heading element:

   ```
   <table>
     <caption>Dogs Organized by
   Group</caption>
     <tr>
       <td>Herding Group</td>
       <td>Hound Group</td>
       <td>Terrier Group</td>
       <td>Sporting Group</td>
     </tr>
     <tr>
       <td>Collie</td>
       <td>Afghan Hound</td>
       <td>Bull Terrier</td>
       <td>Chesapeake Bay Retriever</td>
     </tr>
     <tr>
       <td>German Shepherd</td>
       <td>Basset Hound</td>
       <td>Cairn Terrier</td>
       <td>Golden Retriever</td>
     </tr>
     <tr>
       <td>Welsh Corgi</td>
       <td>Beagle</td>
       <td>Fox Terrier</td>
       <td> </td>
     </tr>
     <tr>
       <td> </td>
       <td>Bloodhound</td>
       <td>Scottish Terrier</td>
       <td> </td>
     </tr>
     <tr>
       <td> </td>
       <td>Greyhound</td>
       <td> </td>
       <td> </td>
     </tr>
   </table>
   ```

5. Save the file as **DogBreeds.html** in your Exercises folder for Chapter 5.

6. Close the **DogBreeds.html** file in your text editor, and then use the W3C Markup Validation Service to validate the file. Once the file is valid, open it in your Web browser.

7. Close your Web browser window.

Exercise 5-3

In this exercise, you create a document that contains three empty tables.

1. Create a new HTML 5 document in your text editor and use **Empty Tables** as the title.

2. Add three tables to the document body. Create the first table with one column and three rows; create the second table with one row and three columns; and create the third table with three rows and three columns. Use an internal style sheet to place a simple border around each table, and size each table so it fills 60 percent of the screen. Also, format the tables so they display the empty cells.

3. Save the file as **EmptyTables.html** in your Exercises folder for Chapter 5.

4. Close the **EmptyTables.html** file in your text editor, and then use the W3C Markup Validation Service to validate the file. Once the file is valid, open it in your Web browser.

5. Close your Web browser window.

Exercise 5-4

In this exercise, you create a document with a table that lists major medical health insurance rates.

1. Create a new HTML 5 document in your text editor and use **Insurance Rates** as the title.

2. Within the document body, add the headings and table shown in Figure 5-36. Use styles to align the insurance rate columns

and column groups to adjust their widths. Be sure that the first column and its heading are left-aligned. Also add row groups to the table.

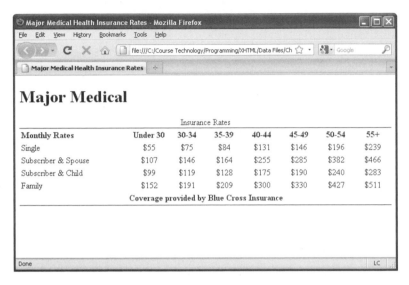

Figure 5-36 Insurance rates table

3. Save the file as **InsuranceRates.html** in your Exercises folder for Chapter 5.

4. Close the **InsuranceRates.html** file in your text editor, and then use the W3C Markup Validation Service to validate the file. Once the file is valid, open it in your Web browser.

5. Close your Web browser window.

Exercise 5-5

In this exercise, you create a document with a table that lists the prices of exterior latex paint according to its sheen (flat, semi-gloss, and so on).

1. Create a new HTML 5 document in your text editor and use **Exterior Latex Satin Paint Prices** as the title.

2. Within the document body, add the headings and table shown in Figure 5-37. Use styles, column groups, and row groups to achieve the formatting shown in the figure.

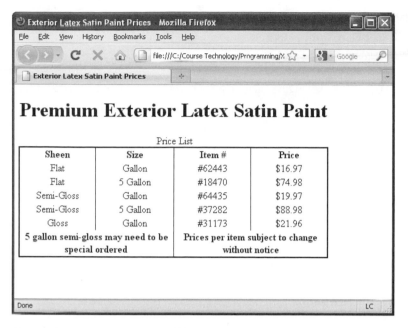

Figure 5-37 Exterior latex satin paint prices table

3. Save the file as **PaintPrices.html** in your Exercises folder for Chapter 5.

4. Close the **PaintPrices.html** file in your text editor, and then use the W3C Markup Validation Service to validate the file. Once the file is valid, open it in your Web browser.

5. Close your Web browser window.

Exercise 5-6

In this exercise, you create a document with a table that lists the credit terms for a credit card company.

1. Create a new HTML 5 document in your text editor and use **Credit Terms** as the title.

2. Within the document body, add the headings and table shown in Figure 5-38. Use styles and row groups to achieve the formatting shown in the figure.

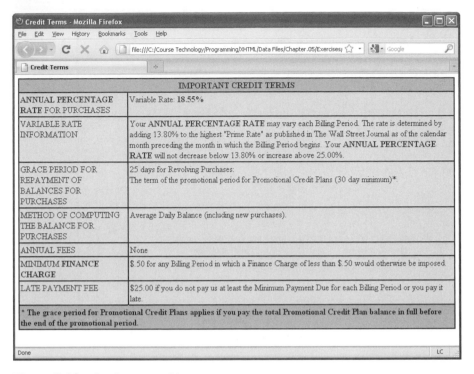

Figure 5-38   Credit terms table

3. Save the file as **CreditTerms.html** in your Exercises folder for Chapter 5.

4. Close the **CreditTerms.html** file in your text editor, and then use the W3C Markup Validation Service to validate the file. Once the file is valid, open it in your Web browser.

5. Close your Web browser window.

Exercise 5-7

In this exercise, you use tables to simulate a frameset document for a construction company. The frame simulation tables list information about home styles that the company offers. The tables simulate a two-column frameset. The left frame lists home styles, and the right frame displays an image of the home style along with available features. Your Exercises folder for Chapter 5 contains three images—cottage.jpg, ranch.jpg, and chalet.jpg—that you can use for this exercise.

1. Create a new HTML 5 document in your text editor and use **Home Styles** as the title.

2. Within the document body, add the headings and table shown in Figure 5-39. Use styles and column groups to achieve the formatting shown in the figure.

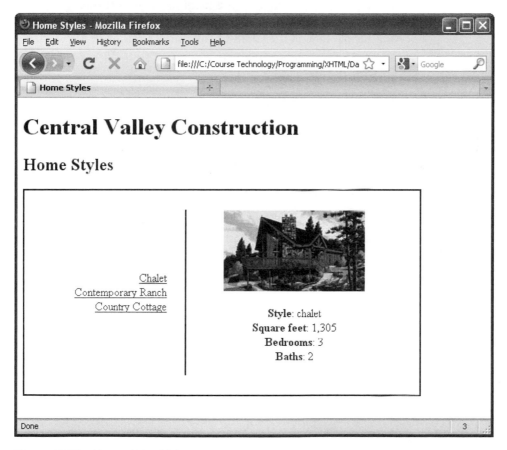

Figure 5-39 Home styles Web page

3. Save the file as **Chalet.html** in your Exercises folder for Chapter 5, then immediately save the file as **Ranch.html** in your Exercises folder for Chapter 5.

4. Replace the image in the table's second cell with **ranch.jpg** and change the image dimensions to 200 pixels wide by 53 pixels high. Also, change the style to **ranch**, the square feet to **1,670**, the number of bedrooms to **4**, and the number of bathrooms to **3**.

5. Save the **Ranch.html** file, then immediately save it as **Cottage.html** in your Exercises folder for Chapter 5.

6. Also, change the style to **cottage**, the square feet to **1,400**, the number of bedrooms to **2**, and the number of bathrooms to **1**.

7. Save and close the **Cottage.html** file in your text editor, and then use the W3C Markup Validation Service to validate the file along with the **Chalet.html** and **Ranch.html** files. Once the files are valid, open one of them in your Web browser and test the links.

8. Close your Web browser window.

Exercise 5-8

In this exercise, you create a document that contains a definition list of weather-related terms.

1. Create a new HTML 5 document in your text editor and use **Weather Terms** as the title.

2. Add the following heading elements to the document body.

```
<h1>Weather Terms</h1>
<h2>Definition List</h2>
```

3. At the end of the document body, add the following definition list:

```
<dl>
     <dt><b>Anemometer</b></dt>
     <dd>An instrument that measures the
     speed or force of
     the wind.</dd>
     <dt><b>Baroclinity</b></dt>
     <dd>The state of stratification in
     a fluid in which
     surfaces of constant pressure
     intersect surfaces
     of constant density. </dd>
     <dt><b>Celestial Equator</b></dt>
     <dd>The projection of the plane of
     the geographical
     equator upon the celestial
     sphere.</dd>
</dl>
```

4. Save the file as **WeatherTerms.html** in your Exercises folder for Chapter 5.

5. Close the **WeatherTerms.html** file in your text editor, and then use the W3C Markup Validation Service to validate the file. Once the file is valid, open it in your Web browser.

6. Close your Web browser window.

Discovery Projects

For the following projects, save the files you create in your Projects folder for Chapter 5.

Discovery Project 5-1

Create a set of documents that use tables to simulate frames for a metric conversion Web site. Include pages that contain conversion tables for common measurements such as centimeters, inches, miles, kilometers, and so on. One page should present tables for converting from inches to centimeters, another should present tables for converting from gallons to liters, and so on. Use document names that describe the conversion tables. For instance, the inches-to-centimeters page should be named **InchesToCentimeters.html**, the gallons-to-liters page should be named **GallonsToLiters.html**, and so on.

Discovery Project 5-2

Create a set of documents that use tables to simulate frames for a math tables Web site. Include pages that contain math tables such as multiplication tables, prime number tables, and square root tables. Use document names that describe the math tables. For instance, the multiplication tables page should be named **Multiplication.html**, the prime number tables page should be named **PrimeNumbers.html**, and so on.

Discovery Project 5-3

Create a set of documents that use tables to simulate frames for an online photo calendar. The parent table should contain a single row with two cells. The left cell should display a list of links for the 12 months of the year. The right cell should display a calendar created with a table for the currently selected month. Create the first row in the calendar table so it spans all of the other rows in the table, and include an image that is appropriate for the current month. For example, the image for April may be some spring flowers. Search the Internet for images you can use for each month. Use the name of each month as the document names. For example, the January document should be named **January.html**.

Discovery Project 5-4

Create a document that contains a list of hyperlinks to your favorite recipes. Clicking each hyperlink should open another document that displays the selected recipe. Use unordered lists for the recipe ingredients and ordered lists for the preparation instructions. Name the main document **Recipes.html**, and name each recipe document according to the recipe name. For example, if you have a recipe for apple pie, name its associated document **ApplePie.html**.

Working with Forms

In this chapter you will:

- ◎ Study the basics of forms
- ◎ Create selection lists
- ◎ Work with button controls
- ◎ Define labels, access keys, and field sets

Many Web sites use forms to collect information from users and transmit it to a server for processing. Typical forms you may encounter on the Web include order forms, surveys, and applications. Another common type of Web form gathers search criteria from a user. This search data is sent as a query to a database on a Web server, which then returns the results to a Web browser. In this chapter, you learn the basics of creating forms that a user submits to a server.

Introduction to Forms

A **form** is used primarily to gather data from Web users. Forms are usually set up so that the collected data is transmitted either to a server-side scripting language program on a Web server or to an e-mail address. A **server-side scripting language program** processes data that is transmitted from a form to a server. Some of the more popular server-side scripting languages include PHP, Active Server Pages (ASP), and Java Server Pages (JSP). The programs you create with server-side scripting languages are called **scripts**. Because the main focus of this book is XHTML, you will not study server-side scripting languages. Later in this chapter, you will learn how to submit form data to an e-mail address.

You use the following primary elements to create forms in XHTML:

With the exception of the `<form>` element, all of the elements used to create forms are inline elements that must be contained within a block-level element such as `<p>`.

- `<form>`
- `<input>`
- `<textarea>`
- `<button>`
- `<select>`
- `<label>`

First, you will learn how to use the `<form>` element.

To help ensure that your Web pages are well formed, you should always type the opening `<form>` tag and the closing `</form>` tag at the same time, and then go back and fill in the elements and content that you want to display in the form.

Using the `<form>` Element

The **`<form>` element** designates a form within a Web page and contains all the text and elements that make up a form. You can include as many forms as you want on a Web page, although you cannot nest one form inside another. Table 6-1 lists the attributes you can use with the `<form>` element.

Attribute	Description
`action`	Specifies a URL to which form data will be submitted. If this required attribute is excluded, the data is sent to the URL that contains the form. Typically you would specify the URL of a program on a server or specify an e-mail address.
`autocomplete` (HTML 5)	Determines whether the browser should store a form's input values and automatically fill the form when a user returns to the page. You can assign a value of "on" to store input values or a value of "off" to prevent input values from being stored.
`method`	Determines how form data will be submitted. The two options for this attribute are "get" and "post". The default option, "get", appends form data as one long string to the URL specified by the `action` attribute. The "post" option sends form data as a transmission separate from the URL specified by the `action` attribute. Although "get" is the default selection, "post" is considered the preferred option because it allows the server to receive the data separately from the URL.
`enctype`	Specifies the Multipurpose Internet Mail Extensions (MIME) type of the data being submitted. The default value is "application/x-www-form-urlencoded".
`accept-charset`	Specifies a comma-separated list of possible character sets that the form supports.
`autocomplete`	If a browser's auto-fill feature is turned on, this attribute stores values that are input into a form if a user returns to the page.
`novalidate` (HTML 5)	Prevents a form from being validated when it is submitted.

Table 6-1   Attributes of the `<form>` element

The `enctype` attribute is important because a server-side scripting program uses its value to determine how to process the form data. The default MIME type of *application/x-www-form-urlencoded* specifies that form data should be encoded as one long string. The only other MIME types allowed with the `enctype` attribute are multipart/form-data, which encodes each field as a separate section, and text/plain, which is used to upload a file to a Web server or to submit form data to an e-mail address. Unless you are submitting form data to an e-mail address, you should use the default MIME type.

The `autocomplete` attribute is available in all current browsers. The `novalidate` attribute is only available in Safari and Chrome Web browsers.

The following code shows an example of how to send data to a URL. The document contains a simple form with a single text box that you use to subscribe to "The Plant Report" newsletter. The `<form>` element also contains an `action` attribute that sends the form data to the URL *subscribe.asp*, which specifies an ASP script that will process the form data. The method attribute of the <form> element specifies that the form data will be sent using the post method instead of the default get method. Because the enctype attribute is omitted, the form data will be encoded with the default *application/ x-www-form-urlencoded* format.

```
<form name="subscribe" action="subscribe.asp"
method="post">
<p>Your e-mail address: <input type="hidden"
     name="frmaction" value="yes">
...
</form>
```

In this chapter you will work on a simple Web site for a company named Central Valley Technology. The goal of the chapter is to create a subscription form for the company's technology journal. Your Chapter folder for Chapter 6 includes a folder named CVTech that contains the files you need for the project. First, you will start creating a subscription form on a prewritten Web page named subscription.html.

To start creating the technology journal subscription page for Central Valley Technology:

1. Open your text editor, and then open the **subscription.html** document in the CVTech folder in your Chapter folder for Chapter 6.

2. Locate <!--[Add code here]--> in the document body and replace it with the following heading elements:

   ```
   <h1>Technology Journal Subscription Form</h1>
   <h2>Customer Information</h2>
   ```

3. Add the following two tags after the <h2> element to create the form section. Throughout the rest of this chapter, you will add form elements between these tags. Notice that the form's action attribute submits the form data to an empty string. You will modify this later in the chapter to submit the data to an e-mail address.

   ```
   <form action="" method="post"
   enctype="application/x-www-form-urlencoded">
   </form>
   ```

4. Save the document and open it in a Web browser. The page should look similar to Figure 6-1.

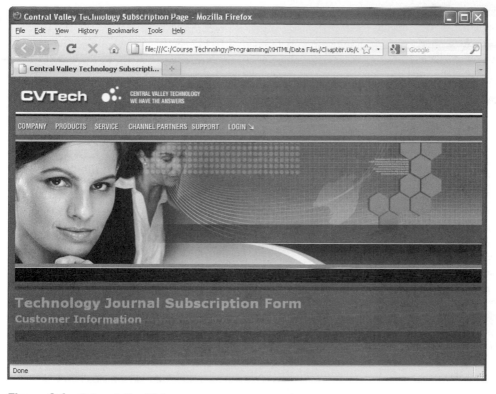

Figure 6-1 Subscription Web page

5. Close your Web browser window.

Using Form Controls

Four primary elements are used within the `<form>` element to create form controls: `<input>`, `<button>`, `<select>`, and `<textarea>`. The `<input>` and `<button>` elements are used to create input fields with which users interact. The `<select>` element displays choices in a drop-down menu or scrolling list known as a selection list. The `<textarea>` element is used to create a text field in which users can enter multiple lines of information. Any form element into which a user can enter data, such as a text box, or that a user can select or change, such as a radio button, is called a **field**.

The `<input>`, `<textarea>`, and `<select>` elements can include `name` and `value` attributes. The `name` attribute defines a name for an element, and the `value` attribute defines a default value. When you submit a form to a Web server, the form data is submitted in name=value pairs, based on the `name` and `value` attributes of each tag. For example, for a text `<input>` field created with the statement `<input type="text" name="company_info" value="ABC Corp.">`,

You are not required to include a `value` attribute or enter a value into a field before the form data is submitted.

Rendering of form controls varies based on the Web browser and the operating system used. You may notice differences in how form controls appear in Windows and Macintosh operating systems and even in different versions of the same operating system. For instance, form controls look noticeably different in Windows Vista and Linux.

a name=value pair of *company_info=ABC Corp.* will be sent to a Web server (unless the user types something else into the field). If you intend to submit your form to a Web server, you must include a `name` attribute for each `<input>`, `<textarea>`, and `<select>` element.

Gathering Data with Input Fields

The empty `<input>` element is used to create **input fields**, which in turn create different types of interface elements to gather information. Table 6-2 lists common attributes of the `<input>` element.

Attribute	Description
alt	Provides alternate text for an image submit button
checked	Determines whether a radio button or a check box is selected; a Boolean attribute
maxlength	Accepts an integer value that determines the number of characters that can be entered into a field
name	Designates a name for the element; part of the name=value pair that is used to submit data to a Web server
size	Accepts an integer value that determines how many characters wide a text field is
src	Specifies the URL of an image
type	Specifies the type of element to be rendered; `type` is a required attribute. Valid values include text, password, radio, checkbox, reset, button, submit, image, file, and hidden.
value	Sets an initial value in a field or a label for buttons; part of the name=value pair that is used to submit data to a Web server

Table 6-2   Common attributes of the `<input>` element

One of the most important attributes of the `<input>` element is the required `type` attribute, which determines the type of element to be rendered. Valid values for the `type` attribute are shown in Table 6-2. You will study the `type` attributes next.

Using Text Boxes

An `<input>` element with a type of *text* (`<input type="text" />`) creates a simple **text box** that accepts a single line of text. You can include the `name`, `value`, `maxlength`, and `size` attributes with the `<input type="text">` element. When you include the `value` attribute in a text <input> element, the specified text is used as the default value when the form first loads. The following code contains several examples of text boxes:

```
<form action="whitehouse.html" method="get">
<p>Name<br />
<input type="text" name="name"
    value="The White House" size="50" /></p>
<p>Address<br />
<input type="text" name="address"
    value="1600 Pennsylvania Ave." size="50" /></p>
<p>City, State, Zip<br />
<input type="text" name="city"
    value="Washington" size="38" />
<input type="text" name="state"
    value="DC" size="2" maxlength="2" />
<input type="text" name="zip"
    value="20500" size="5" maxlength="5" /></p>
</form>
```

Next, you add text <input> elements to the Subscription form to collect basic customer data.

To add text <input> elements to the Subscription form:

1. Return to the **subscription.html** document in your text editor.

2. Above the closing </form> tag, add the following table to contain the billing and shipping information text boxes. The table will consist of a single row that contains two cells.

   ```
   <table>
   </table>
   ```

3. Within the table, add the following text <input> elements, which will be used to gather a customer's billing information.

   ```
   <tr>
       <td>
           <h3>
               Billing Information</h3>
           <p>
               Name<br />
               <input type="text" name="name"
                   size="56" /></p>
           <p>
               Address<br />
               <input type="text" name="address"
                   size="56" /></p>
           <p>
               City, State, Zip<br />
               <input type="text" name="city" size="34" />
               <input type="text" name="state" size="2"
                   maxlength="2" />
   ```

```
                                <input type="text" name="zip" size="10"
                                    maxlength="10" /></p>
                </td>
        </tr>
```

4. Above the closing </form> tag, add the following elements for the telephone number:

```
<p>
    Telephone</p>
<p>
    (<input type="text" name="area" size="3"
        maxlength="3" />)
    <input type="text" name="exchange" size="3"
        maxlength="3" />
    <input type="text" name="phone" size="4"
        maxlength="4" /></p>
```

5. Save the **subscription.html** document and then open it in your Web browser. The text <input> elements you entered should appear as shown in Figure 6-2.

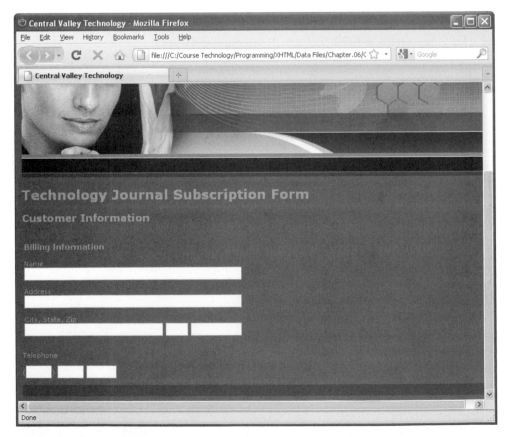

Figure 6-2   Subscription form after adding text <input> elements

6. Close your Web browser window.

Using Password Boxes

An <input> element with a type of *password* (<input
type="password" />) creates a **password box** for entering passwords
or other sensitive data. Each character that a user enters in a password
box appears as an asterisk or bullet, depending on the operating
system and Web browser, to hide the password from anyone who
may be looking over the user's shoulder. The following code creates a
password box with a maximum length of eight characters. Figure 6-3
shows how the password box appears in a Web browser after the user
enters some characters.

```
<form action="app.html" method="get"
enctype="application/x-www-form-urlencoded">
<p>Please enter a password of <br />
8 characters or less:<br />
<input type="password" name="password"
    maxlength="8" /></p>
</form>
```

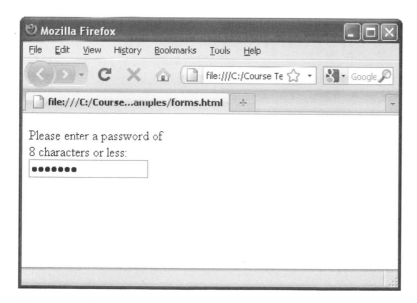

Figure 6-3 Password box in a Web browser

Next, you add a user name field and password <input> element to
the subscription.html document. Users will be prompted to enter a
password to manage their subscriptions online.

To add a password <input> element to the subscription.html document:

1. Return to the **subscription.html** document in your
    text editor.

2. Above the closing `</form>` tag, add the following lines for a user name text box and the password `<input>` element, which prompts users to enter a password:

```
<p>User name<br />
<input type="text" name="userName" size="50" /></p>
<p>Password<br />
<input type="password" name="password"
    size="50" /></p>
```

3. Save the **subscription.html** document and then open it in your Web browser. Test the password field to see whether the password you enter appears as asterisks or bullets. Figure 6-4 shows how the form appears after you type a password in Firefox.

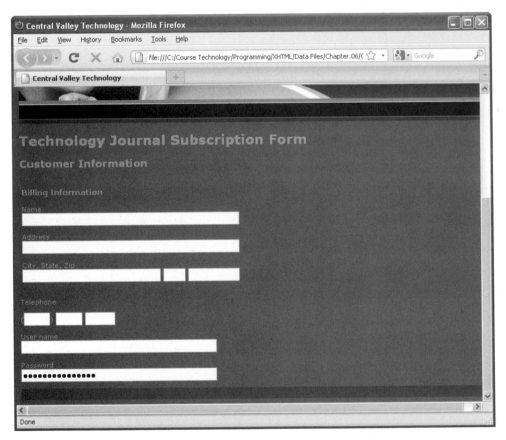

Figure 6-4 Subscription form after adding a password `<input>` element

4. Close your Web browser window.

Using File Boxes

An `<input>` element with a type of *file* (`<input type="file" />`) creates a **file box**—a text box control with a Browse button that you can use to upload a file to a Web server. You can type the name of the drive, folder, or file you want to upload into the text box or you can search for the file on your computer by clicking the Browse button. To see an example of a file box, go to the upload page of the W3C Markup Validation Service, which you have used thus far to validate your documents. A <form> element that contains a file box control must have a method attribute with a value of "post" and an enctype attribute with a value of "multipart/form-data". The following code shows a form with a file box that a job candidate might use to upload a resume to an employer's Web site. Figure 6-5 shows how the form appears in a Web browser.

```html
<h2>Resume Submission Form</h2>
<form action="apply.html" method="post"
enctype="multipart/form-data">
<p>Please attach your resume and press
the Submit button.<br />
<input type="file" />
<input type="submit" value="Submit" /></p>
</form>
```

Figure 6-5   File box in a Web browser

 You can use the value attribute to specify a default filename to include in the file box, although most current browsers ignore this attribute for security reasons. If you use the value attribute with a file <input> element, a persistent hacker could determine who visited your Web site and then access files on their computers without their knowledge.

Using Hidden Form Fields

A special type of form element called a **hidden form field** allows you to hide information from users. You create hidden form fields with the <input> element. Hidden form fields temporarily store data that needs to be sent to a server with the rest of a form, but that a user does not need to see. Examples of data stored in hidden fields include the result of a calculation or some other type of information that a program on the Web server might need. You create hidden form fields using the same syntax used for other fields created with the <input>

element: `<input type="hidden" />`. The only attributes that you can include with a hidden form field are the `name` and `value` attributes.

As an example of a hidden form field, you may have a form that a script on a Web server processes. Once the script processes the form fields, you want it to send the results to an e-mail address (probably your own) contained within the form. However, you do not want people who access the form to view your private e-mail address, so you could place it in a hidden form field, as follows:

```
<form action="subscribe.html" method="get"
enctype="application/x-www-form-urlencoded">
...form fields...
<input type="hidden" name="email"
    value="your_email_address@domain.com" />
<input type="submit" /></p>
</form>
```

A hidden form field is invisible within a browser that renders the Web page. In other words, a visitor to the Web page that contains the preceding elements will not see the hidden form field with the e-mail address. However, visitors to the Web page can view the default value assigned to a hidden form field by viewing the source file.

Using Multiline Text Fields

The `<textarea>` element is used to create a field in which users can enter multiple lines of information. Fields created with `<textarea>` elements are known as **multiline text fields** or **text areas**. Table 6-3 lists the attributes of the `<textarea>` element.

Attribute	Description
name	Designates a name for the text area
cols	Specifies the number of columns to be displayed in the text area
rows	Specifies the number of rows to be displayed in the text area

Table 6-3   Attributes of the `<textarea>` element

You can create the `<textarea>` element either as an empty element or using the `<textarea>...</textarea>` tag pair. The only items you include within this tag pair are default text and characters you want to display in the text area. Any characters placed between this tag pair, including tab marks and paragraph returns, will be displayed as the text area default value. For example, a line of text that is indented with two tabs and placed between the `<textarea>...</textarea>` tags will be indented with two tabs when it appears in the text area on the Web page. Any XHTML elements you place within a `<textarea>` element will be rendered as plain text within the text area. Note that any text displayed in a text area when a form is submitted will be part of the control's name=value pair.

The following elements create a text area control consisting of 50 columns and 10 rows, with the default text of *Enter additional information here*. Figure 6-6 shows the output in a Web browser.

```
<form action="feedback.html" method="get"
enctype="application/x-www-form-urlencoded">
<h3>Comments</h3>
<p><textarea cols="50" rows="10">
Enter additional information here
</textarea></p>
</form>
```

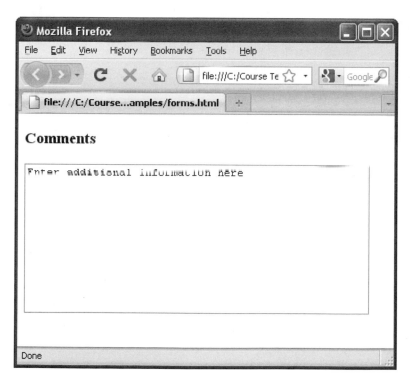

Figure 6-6   Multiline text field in a browser

Next, you add a text area element to the subscription.html file so that subscribers can provide directions to their home or special delivery instructions.

To add a text area element to the subscription.html file:

1.   Return to the **subscription.html** file in your text editor.

2. Above the closing `</form>` tag, add the following elements to create the text area:

```
<p>Directions or special instructions<br />
<textarea name="directions" cols="50" rows="10">
Enter directions to your home or any special
instructions.
</textarea></p>
```

3. Save the **subscription.html** file and then open it in your Web browser. Figure 6-7 shows how the text area appears in a Web browser.

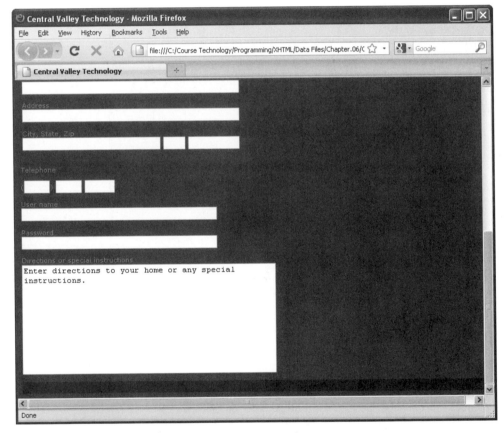

Figure 6-7 Subscription form after adding a `<textarea>` element

4. Close your Web browser window.

Short Quiz 1

1. Explain how to use the form element.

2. How do you specify default text to display in a text `<input>` element?

3. What is the purpose of a password box?

4. What attributes are required with hidden form fields?

5. How do you define the number of columns and rows in a multiline text field?

Using Selection Lists

The **<select> element** creates a **selection list** from which users can choose listed options. The options displayed in a selection list are created with <option> elements, which you will study next. As with other form elements that create controls, the <select> element must appear within a block-level element such as the <p> element. The selection list can appear as an actual list of choices or as a drop-down menu. Depending on the number of options in the list, a selection list can also include a scroll bar. Table 6-4 lists the attributes of the <select> element.

Attribute	Description
disabled	Disables the selection list
multiple	Specifies whether a user can select more than one option from the list; a Boolean attribute
name	Designates a name for the selection list
size	Determines how many lines appear in the selection list

Table 6-4   Attributes of the <select> element

Like other form controls, the <select> element includes a name attribute that is submitted to a Web server. However, the value portion of a <select> element's name=value pair is the value assigned to an option that is created with the <option> element. If a <select> element includes the Boolean multiple attribute, which specifies whether a user can select more than one option from the list, and a visitor does select more than one option, then multiple name=value pairs for the <select> element are submitted with the form. Each instance of a <select> element's name=value pair includes a value assigned to one of the list options created with the <option> element.

The size attribute designates how many lines appear in the selection list when the form is rendered in a Web browser. If this attribute is excluded or set to 1, and the <select> element does not include the multiple attribute, then the selection list is a drop-down menu. The first <option> element is automatically selected in a drop-down menu.

Specifying Menu Options

You use **<option> elements** to specify menu options that appear in a selection list. Table 6-5 lists the attributes of the <option> element.

Attribute	Description
disabled	Disables the option
label	Designates alternate text to display in the selection list for an individual option
selected	Determines if an option is initially selected in the selection list when the form first loads; a Boolean attribute
value	Specifies the value submitted to a Web server

Table 6-5   Attributes of the <option> element

You specify the menu options in a selection list using <option> elements placed within a <select> element. A selection list must contain at least one <option> element. For example, the following code creates two selection lists. Figure 6-8 shows the code in a Web browser. Notice that because the <select> element in the first list includes the multiple attribute, you can select multiple options, as shown in the figure. Also notice that "All" is selected in the first list and "$2,000 to $2,999" is selected in the second list.

```
<h1>Central Valley Appliances</h1>
<h2>Televisions</h2>
<form action="cva.html" method="get"
enctype="application/x-www-form-urlencoded">
<table border="0">
<tr><td style="background: white; border: 0">
<strong>Brand</strong></td>
<td style="background: white; border:0">
<strong>Price Range</strong></td></tr>
<tr><td>
<select name="brand" multiple="multiple" size="6">
<option value="all" selected="selected">All</option>
<option value="hitachi">Hitachi</option>
<option value="magnavox">Magnavox</option>
<option value="panasonic">Panasonic</option>
<option value="samsung">Samsung</option>
<option value="sharp">Sharp</option>
<option value="sony">Sony</option>
</select></td>
<td>
<select name="price" size="6">
<option value="199">Under $200</option>
<option value="499">$200 to $499</option>
<option value="999">$500 to $999</option>
<option value="1999">$1,000 to
```

```
$1,999</option>
<option value="2999" selected="selected">
$2,000 to $2,999</option>
<option value="3000_plus">Over $3,000</option>
</select></td></tr></table></form>
```

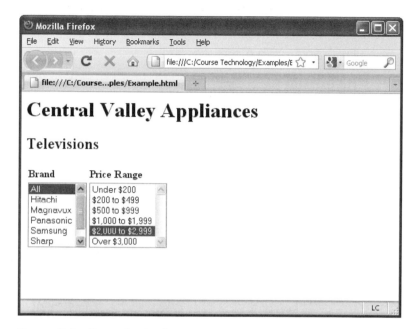

Figure 6-8　Two selection lists

Next, you add a selection list and some text <input> elements to the subscription.html file. A subscriber uses these elements to enter payment information.

To add a selection list to the subscription.html file:

1. Return to the **subscription.html** file in your text editor.

2. Above the closing </form> tag, add the following elements to create the selection list:

```
<p>Payment Method<br />
<select name="payment">
<option value="check">Check</option>
<option value="moneyorder">Money Order</option>
<option value="visa">Visa</option>
<option value="mastercard">MasterCard</option>
<option value="amex">American Express</option>
<option value="discover">Discover</option>
<option value="dinersclub">Diners Club</option>
</select></p>
```

3. After the closing `</p>` tag that follows the closing `</select>` tag, add the following text `<input>` elements for the subscriber's credit card information:

```
<p>Name as it appears on credit card<br />
<input type="text" name="cc_name"
    size="50" /><br /></p>
<p>Credit card number<br />
<input type="text" name="cc_num"
    size="50" /><br /></p>
<p>Expiration date<br />
<input type="text" name="expires"
    size="50" /><br /></p>
```

4. Save the **subscription.html** file and then open it in your Web browser. Figure 6-9 shows how the selection list appears in a Web browser.

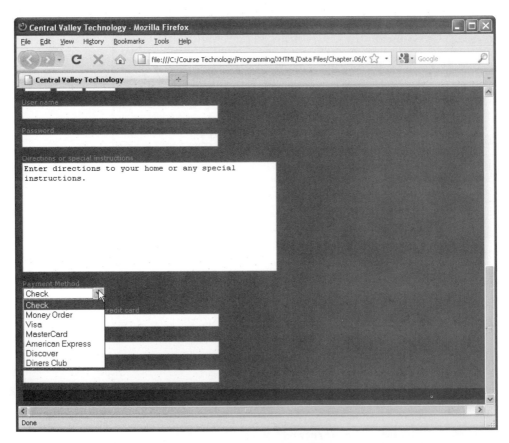

Figure 6-9   Subscription form after adding a selection list

5. Close your Web browser window.

Using Option Groups

You use the **<optgroup> element** to create **option groups** that organize option elements in a selection list. The <optgroup> element includes two attributes: disabled and label. The optional Boolean disabled attribute disables an option group, whereas the required label attribute defines the heading that will identify a specific option group. You nest the <option> elements of an option group within the <optgroup>...</optgroup> tag pair. For example, the following code combines two threatened and endangered Florida species lists and organizes them according to animal type. Figure 6-10 shows how the combined selection list appears in a Web browser.

```
<h1>U.S. Fish and Wildlife Service</h1>
<h2>Threatened and Endangered Florida Species</h2>
<form action="floridastate.html" method="get"
enctype="application/x-www-form-urlencoded">
<p><select name="species" size="12">
<optgroup label="Mammals">
<option value="panther">Florida Panther</option>
<option selected="true" value="manatee">West Indian
Manatee</option>
</optgroup>
<optgroup label="Birds">
<option value="jay">Florida Scrub Jay</option>
<option value="sparrow">Cape Sable Seaside
Sparrow</option>
</optgroup>
<optgroup label="Reptiles">
<option value="alligator">American
Alligator</option>
<option value="sea_turtle">Hawksbill Sea
Turtle</option>
</optgroup>
<optgroup label="Amphibians">
<option value="salamander">Flatwoods
Salamander</option>
</optgroup>
</select></p>
</form>
```

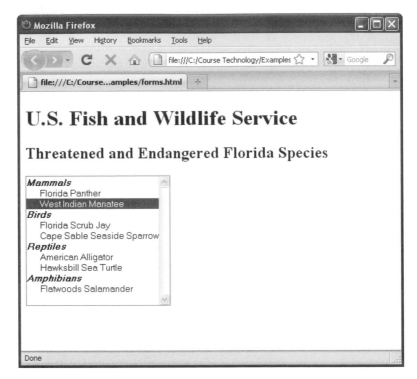

Figure 6-10   Selection organized by option groups

Next, you add a single option group of credit card names to the payment method selection list in the subscription.html file.

To add an option group to the payment method selection list:

1. Return to the **subscription.html** file in your text editor.

2. Modify the selection list as follows so the credit card names are contained within an `<optgroup>` element with a label of "Credit Cards":

    ```
    <p><select name="payment">
    <option value="check">Check</option>
    <option value="moneyorder">Money Order</option>
    <optgroup label="Credit Cards">
    <option value="visa">Visa</option>
    <option value="mastercard">MasterCard</option>
    <option value="amex">American Express</option>
    <option value="discover">Discover</option>
    <option value="dinersclub">Diners Club</option>
    </optgroup>
    </select></p>
    ```

3. Save the **subscription.html** file and then open it in your Web browser. Figure 6-11 shows how the selection list appears in a Web browser.

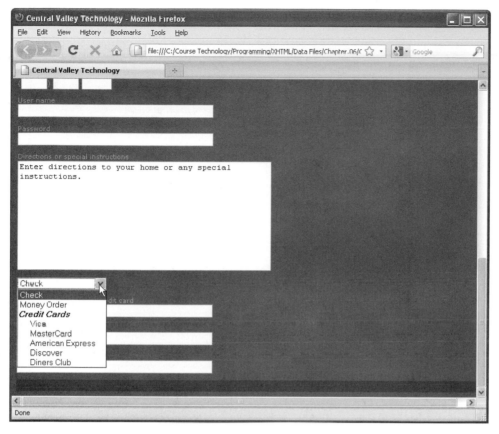

Figure 6-11 Payment method selection list after adding an option group

4. Close your Web browser window.

Creating a Data List (HTML 5)

Data lists are only available in Opera Web browsers.

In HTML 5, the `<input>` element includes a new `list` attribute that allows you to create a **data list**, which is a list of values for a text box that are displayed when the text box is selected.

To create a data list, you assign a unique value to the `list` attribute of the `<input>` element. Then, you identify which data list values you want to include in the text box by nesting `<option>` elements within a `<datalist>` element. To identify which data list contains the values for a specific text box, you assign the unique value of the text box's `list` element to the `id` attribute of the `<datalist>` element. For example, the following elements create a data list of credit card names. Figure 6-12 shows the output in Opera.

```
<input list="creditcards" />
<datalist id="creditcards">
<option value="Visa" />
<option value="MasterCard" />
```

```
<option value="American Express" />
<option value="Discover" />
<option value="Diners Club" />
</datalist>
```

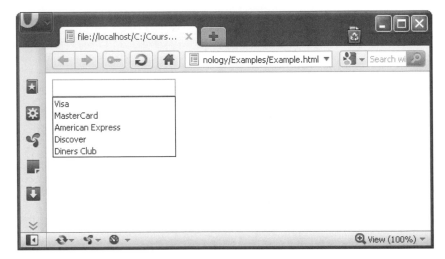

Figure 6-12   Data list in Opera

Short Quiz 2

1. How do you define a drop-down selection list?

2. How do you define a multiline selection list?

3. Describe how to use <option> elements in a selection list.

4. How do you determine the initially selected value in a selection list?

5. Why do you use option groups?

Working with Button Controls

In this section, you will learn how to work with form button controls, starting with radio buttons.

Working with Radio Buttons

An <input> element with a type of *radio* (<input type="radio" />) is used to create a group of **radio buttons**, or **option buttons**, from which you can select only one value. To create a group of radio buttons, all of them must have the same name attribute. Each radio button requires a value attribute. Only one selected radio button in a group creates a name=value pair when a form is submitted to a Web server. You can also include the checked attribute in a radio <input> element to select an initial value for a group of radio buttons. If the checked attribute is not included in any of the radio button elements, none of the buttons will be selected when the form loads.

The following code creates a group of five radio buttons. Because the "18-30" radio button includes the checked attribute, it will be selected when the form first loads. Figure 6-13 shows how the radio buttons appear in a Web browser.

```
<form action="quote.html" method="get"
enctype="application/x-www-form-urlencoded">
<p>Please select your age range:<br />
<input type="radio" name="age_range"
    value="Under 18" />Under 18<br />
<input type="radio" name="age_range"
    value="18-30" checked="checked" />18-30<br />
<input type="radio" name="age_range"
    value="31 45" />31-45<br />
<input type="radio" name="age_range"
    value="46-64" />46-64<br />
<input type="radio" name="age_range"
    value="65 and older" />65 and older</p>
</form>
```

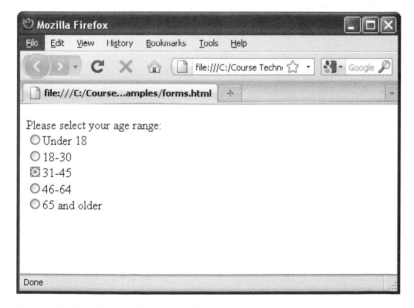

Figure 6-13   Form with radio buttons

Next, you add radio buttons to the subscription.html file to allow users to select a delivery option. The radio buttons are created within a table to make it easier to align them on the page.

To add radio buttons to the subscription.html file:

1. Return to the **subscription.html** file in your text editor.

2. Above the closing `</form>` tag, add the following `<p>` element along with the opening `<table>` element and the table's header information:

```
<p>Delivery Rates</p>
<table>
<colgroup style="text-align: center; ↵
    width: 200px"></colgroup>
<colgroup span="4" style="text-align: center; ↵
    width: 140px"></colgroup>
<tr style="text-align: left"><th> </th>
<th>4 weeks</th>
<th>13 weeks</th>
<th>26 weeks</th>
<th>52 weeks</th></tr>
```

3. Next, add the following table row elements that include payment options for deliveries made Monday through Saturday. Notice that each radio button's name attribute is assigned the same name of "delivery" so that the radio buttons are part of the same group.

```
<tr><td><strong>Mon-Sat</strong></td>
<td><input type="radio" name="delivery"
    value="12.60" />$12.60</td>
<td><input type="radio" name="delivery"
    value="40.95" />$40.95</td>
<td><input type="radio" name="delivery"
    value="81.90" />$81.90</td>
<td><input type="radio" name="delivery"
    value="156.00" />$156.00</td></tr>
```

4. Next, add the following table row elements that include payment options for deliveries made every day of the week:

```
<tr><td><strong>Every Day</strong></td>
<td><input type="radio"
    name="delivery" value="13.56" />$13.56</td>
<td><input type="radio"
    name="delivery" value="44.07" />$44.07</td>
<td><input type="radio" name="delivery"
    value="88.14" />$88.14</td>
<td><input type="radio" name="delivery"
    value="159.74" />$159.74</td></tr>
```

5. Type the closing `</table>` tag.

6. Save the **subscription.html** file and then open it in your Web browser. Test the radio buttons to see if you can select only a single button at a time. Figure 6-14 shows how the radio buttons appear in a Web browser.

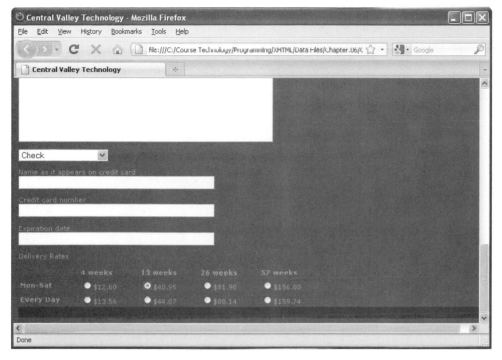

Figure 6-14 Subscription form after adding radio buttons

7. Close your Web browser window.

Using Check Boxes

An <input> element with a type of *checkbox*
(<input type="checkbox" />) creates a box that can be set to
yes (checked) or no (unchecked). You use **check boxes** to allow
users to select certain items and to select multiple values from a
list of items. Include the Boolean checked attribute in a check box
<input> element to set the initial value of the check box to *yes*. You
can also include the name and value attributes with the check box
<input> element. If a check box is selected (checked) when a form
is submitted, the check box name=value pair is included in the form
data. If a check box is not selected, a name=value pair will not be
included in the data submitted from the form.

The following code creates several check boxes. Note that the Science
Fiction check box will be checked when the form first loads because
it includes the checked attribute. Figure 6-15 shows how the check
boxes appear in a Web browser.

```
<form action="books.html" method="get"
enctype="application/x-www-form-urlencoded">
<h3>What type of books do you like to read?</h3>
```

338

```
<p><input type="checkbox" name="books"
    value="fiction" />Fiction<br />
<input type="checkbox" name="books"
    value="science_fiction"
    checked="checked" />Science
Fiction<br />
<input type="checkbox" name="books"
    value="romance" />Romance<br />
<input type="checkbox" name="books"
    value="mysteries" />Mysteries</p>
</form>
```

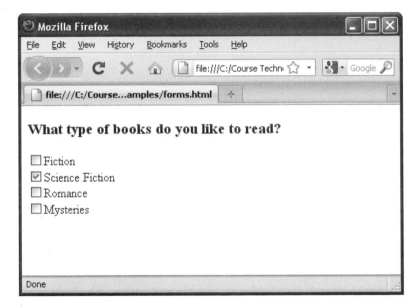

Figure 6-15   Form with check boxes

Like radio buttons, you can group check boxes by giving each one the same name value, although each check box can have a different value. Unlike radio buttons, users can select as many check boxes in a group as they want. When multiple check boxes on a form share the same name, then multiple name=value pairs, each using the same name, are submitted to a Web server. In the preceding example, if the Fiction and Romance check boxes are selected, then two name=value pairs—books=fiction and books=romance—are submitted. Note that you are not required to group check boxes with the same name attribute. Although a common group name helps identify and manage groups of check boxes, it is often easier to keep track of individual values when each check box has a unique name attribute.

Next, you add check boxes to the subscription.html file to allow users to select any other newspapers to which they are currently subscribed.

To add check boxes to the subscription.html file:

1. Return to the **subscription.html** file in your text editor.

2. Above the closing </form> tag, add the following check box elements:

```
<p>Do you subscribe to any other newspapers?</p>
<p><input type="checkbox" name="newspapers"
    value="nytimes" />The New York Times<br />
<input type="checkbox" name="newspapers"
    value="bostonglobe" />The Boston Globe<br />
<input type="checkbox" name="newspapers"
    value="sfchronicle" />San Francisco
Chronicle<br />
<input type="checkbox" name="newspapers"
    value="miamiherald" />The Miami Herald<br />
<input type="checkbox" name="newspapers"
    value="other" />Other</p>
```

3. Save the **subscription.html** file and then open it in your Web browser. Figure 6-16 shows how the check boxes appear in a Web browser.

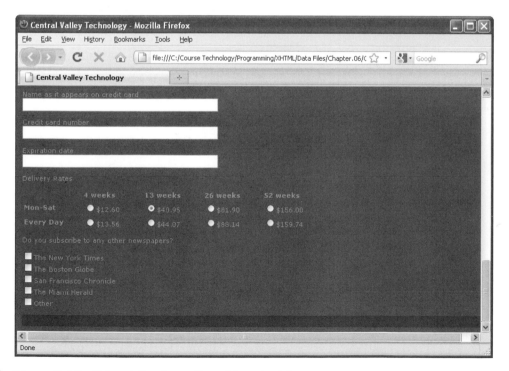

Figure 6-16 Subscription form after adding check boxes

4. Close your Web browser window.

Working with Reset Buttons

An <input> element with a type of *reset* (<input type="reset" />) creates a **reset button** that clears all form entries and resets each form element to the initial value specified by its value attribute. Although you can include the name attribute for a reset button, it is not required because reset buttons do not have values that are submitted to a Web server as part of the form data. The text you assign to the reset button's value attribute will appear as the button label. If you do not include a value attribute, the default label of the reset button, *Reset*, appears. The width of a button created with the reset <input> element depends on the number of characters in its value attribute.

The following code creates a form with a reset button. Figure 6-17 shows the resulting Web page after some data is entered.

```
<form action="billing.html" method="get"
enctype="application/x-www-form-urlencoded">
<h3>Billing Information</h3>
<p><strong>Name</strong><br />
<input type="text" name="name" size="50" /></p>
<p><strong>Address</strong><br />
<input type="text" name="address" size="50" /></p>
<p><strong>City, State, Zip</strong><br />
<input type="text" name="city" size="34" />
<input type="text" name="state" size="2"
maxlength="2" />
<input type="text" name="zip" size="5"
    maxlength="5" /></p>
<p><strong>Credit Card</strong><br />
<input type="radio" name="creditcard"
checked="checked" />Visa
<input type="radio" name="creditcard" />MasterCard
<input type="radio" name="creditcard" />American
Express<br />
<input type="radio" name="creditcard" />Discover
<input type="radio" name="creditcard" />Diners
Club</p>
<p><strong>Credit Card Number</strong><br />
<input type="text" name="cc" size="50" /></p>
<p><strong>Expiration Date</strong><br />
<input type="text" name="expdate" size="50" /></p>
<p><input type="reset" /></p>
</form>
```

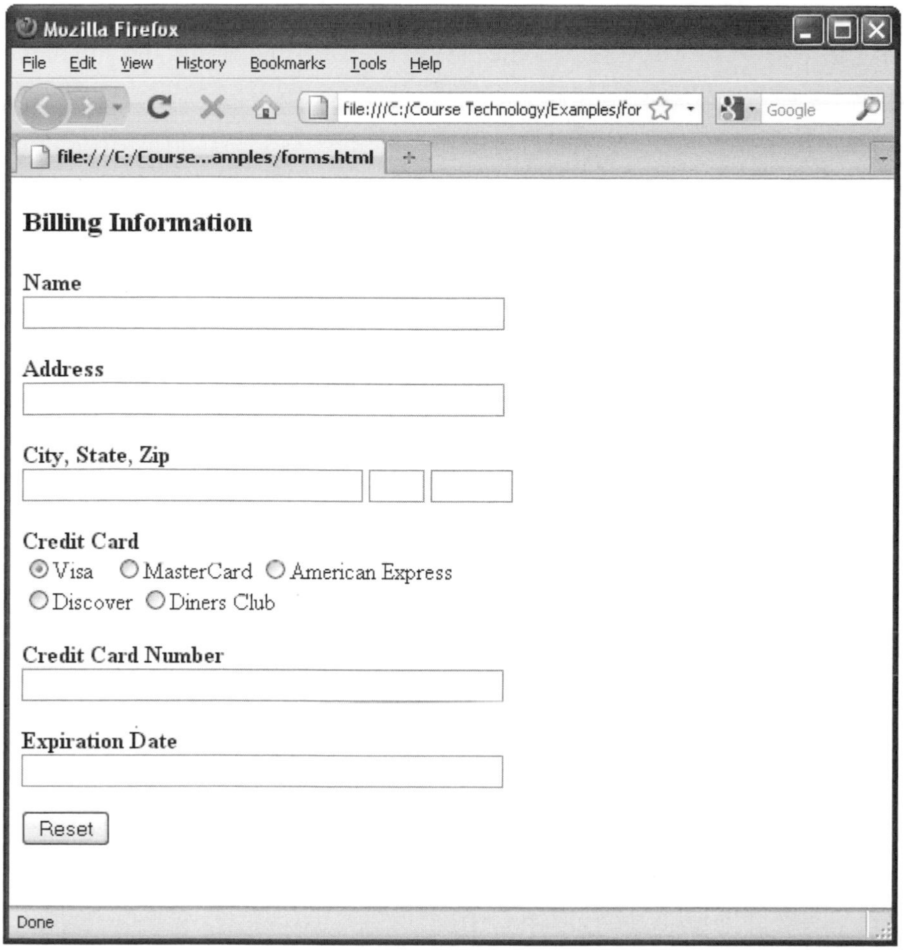

Figure 6-17 Form with a reset button

If you click the reset button in the form shown in Figure 6-17, the content of each field clears or resets to its default value.

Next, you add a reset button to the subscription.html file.

To add a reset button to the subscription.html file:

1. Return to the **subscription.html** file in your text editor.

2. Above the closing `</form>` tag, add the following element to create the reset button:

   ```
   <p><input type="reset" /></p>
   ```

3. Save the **subscription.html** file and then open it in your Web browser. Enter some data in the form's fields and test the reset button to see how it works. You should see the reset button at the bottom of the form.

4. Close your Web browser window.

Using Push Buttons

Push buttons are also called command buttons.

An <input> element with a type of *button* (<input type="button" />) creates a **push button** that is similar to the OK and Cancel buttons you see in dialog boxes. Push buttons do not submit form data to a Web server, as submit buttons do, nor do they clear the data entered into form fields, as reset buttons do. (You will learn about submit buttons next.) Instead, push buttons execute JavaScript code that performs some type of function, such as a calculation. Because the main purpose of push buttons is to execute JavaScript code, they are essentially useless unless you know how to use JavaScript.

You can use the name and value attributes with a push button <input> element. The text you assign to the value attribute is the text that will appear on the button. The width of a push button is based on the number of characters in its value attribute.

You are not required to include the name and value attributes because a user cannot change the value of a push button. If you include the name and value attributes, the default value set with the value attribute is transmitted to a Web server with the rest of the form data. The following code creates a push button that uses JavaScript code to display a simple dialog box:

```
<p><input type="button" name="push_button"
    value="Click Here"
    onClick=
        "alert('You clicked a push button');" />
</p>
```

The code for the <input> element creates a button with a value of *Click Here* and a name of *push_button*. As shown in Figure 6-18, if you click the push button, you will see a dialog box that contains the text *You clicked a push button*.

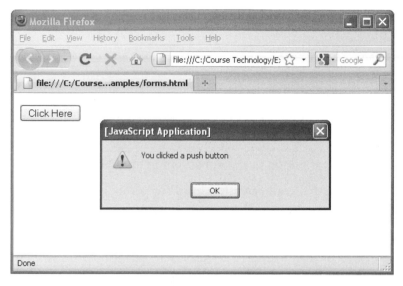

Figure 6-18   A push button after being clicked in a Web browser

Using Submit Buttons

An <input> element with a type of *submit* (<input type="submit" />)
creates a **submit button** that transmits form data to a Web server. The
action attribute of the <form> element that creates the form deter
mines the URL to which the form is submitted. You can include the
name and value attributes with the submit <input> element, as you can
with a push button <input> element. The width of a submit button is
based on the number of characters in its value attribute. If you do not
include a value attribute, the default label of the submit button, *Submit
Query*, appears.

The following code creates a Web page with a submit button:

```
<h1>DVD of the Month Club</h1>
<h2>Select the types of movies you like to see and
click the Join button.<br />
A new movie will be sent to you every month.</h2>
<form action="dvd.html" method="get"
enctype="application/x-www-form-urlencoded">
<p><input type="checkbox" name="genre"
value="action" />
Action<input type="checkbox" name="genre"
value="adventure" />
Adventure<br />
<input type="checkbox" name="genre"
    value="comedy" />Comedy
<input type="checkbox" name="genre" value="drama" />
Drama<br />
<input type="checkbox" name="genre"
    value="sci_fi" />
```

```
Science Fiction
<input type="checkbox" name="genre"
    value="western" />
Westerns</p>
<p><input type="submit" name="submit_button"
value="Join" /></p>
</form>
```

Next, you add a submit button to the subscription.html file.

To add a submit button to the subscription.html file:

1. Return to the **subscription.html** file in your text editor.

2. Before the reset <input> element's closing paragraph tag, add the following elements shown in boldface to create the submit button:

   ```
   <p><input type="reset" />
   <input type="submit" value="Subscribe" /></p>
   ```

3. Save the **subscription.html** file and then open it in your Web browser. You should see the submit button.

4. Close your Web browser window.

Working with Image Submit Buttons

An <input> element with a type of *image* (<input type="image" />) creates an **image submit button** that displays a graphical image and transmits form data to a Web server. The image <input> element performs the same function as the submit <input> element. You include the src attribute to specify the image to display on the button. You can also include the name and value attributes with the image <input> element, and use the alt attribute to define alternate text for user agents that do not display images. The following code creates a Web page with an image <input> element, as shown in Figure 6-19. Notice that the image <input> element also includes the alt attribute.

```
<h1>DVD of the Month Club</h1>
<h2>Select the types of movies you like to see and
click the image.<br />
A new movie will be sent to you every month.</h2>
<form action="dvd.html" method="get"
enctype="application/x-www-form-urlencoded">
<p><input type="checkbox" name="genre"
value="action" />
Action<input type="checkbox" name="genre"
value="adventure" />
Adventure<br />
<input type="checkbox" name="genre"
    value="comedy" />Comedy
<input type="checkbox" name="genre" value="drama" />
```

```
Drama<br />
<input type="checkbox" name="genre"
    value="sci_fi" />
Science Fiction
<input type="checkbox" name="genre"
    value="western" />
Westerns</p>
<p><input type="image" alt="Graphical image of a
DVD" src="dvd.jpg" /></p>
</form>
```

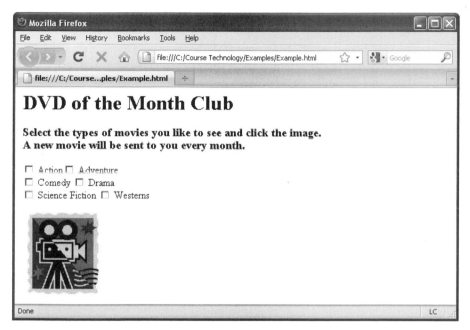

Figure 6-19   Form with an image submit button

Using the <button> Element

Because the <input> element is an empty element, you must use the value attribute to define the text that appears as the label for push buttons, submit buttons, and reset buttons. You can create the same types of buttons using the **<button> element**. Table 6-6 lists the attributes of the <button> element.

Attribute	Description
name	Designates a name for the button.
type	Specifies the button type to be rendered. Valid values are submit, reset, and button.
value	Assigns a value that will be submitted to a Web server.

Table 6-6   Attributes of the <button> element

You specify the type of button to create by assigning the appropriate value to the `type` attribute. The buttons you create with the `<button>` element are virtually identical to the buttons you create with the `<input>` element. The big difference, however, is that you create the `<button>` element using an opening and closing tag pair, which allows more flexibility in the labels you can create for a button. You can include the `name` and `value` attributes with the `<button>` element, the same as with the submit and push button `<input>` elements. However, the value you assign to the `value` attribute is not used as the button's label (although it will be sent to the Web server as part of the control's name=value pair). Instead, the content placed within the `<button>` element tag pair determines the button label. You can embed an `<img>` element within the `<button>` tag or use text formatting and phrasing elements to modify the appearance of the text that appears as a button's label. For instance, the following code uses the `<strong>` element to add emphasis to the label in a `<button>` element and adds an `<img>` element to the button label.

```
<form action="flightinfo.html" method="get"
enctype="application/x-www-form-urlencoded">
<p><button type="button">Click for <strong>Flight
Information</strong><br /><br />
<img src="airplane.gif" alt="Graphical image of an
airplane." />
</button></p>
</form>
```

Next, you modify the subscription.html file's reset and submit buttons so they are created with the `<button>` element instead of the `<input>` element. The images folder in your CVTech folder contains two image files, erase.jpg and save.jpg, that you use to create the reset and submit buttons.

To modify the subscription.html file's reset and submit buttons:

1. Return to the **subscription.html** file in your text editor.

2. Replace the `<p>` and `<input>` elements that make up the reset and submit buttons with the following elements:

```
<p><button type="reset"><strong>Reset Form</strong>
    <br /><br /><img src="images\erase.jpg"
    alt="Graphical image of an eraser." />
</button>
<button type="submit"><strong>Subscribe</strong>
<br /><br />
<img src="images\save.jpg" alt="Graphical image
of a floppy disk." />
</button></p>
```

3. Save the **subscription.html** file and then open it in your Web browser. Figure 6-20 shows how the buttons appear. Enter some data in the form fields, and then test the Reset Form button.

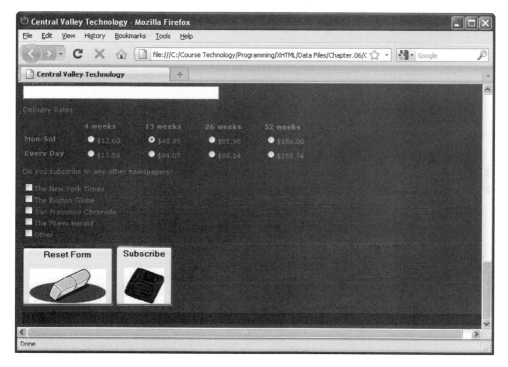

Figure 6-20 Subscription form after adding button elements

4. Close your Web browser window.

E-Mailing Form Data

Most of the forms you have seen so far are set up so that the collected data is transmitted to a Web server. As an alternative, you can set up a form to send data to an e-mail address, which is much simpler than creating and managing a script on a Web server. Instead of relying on a complex script on a Web server to process the data, you rely on the e-mail's recipient to process the data. For instance, a Web site may contain an online order form for a product. After the user clicks the Submit button, the order data can be e-mailed to the person responsible for filling the order. For large organizations that deal with hundreds or thousands of orders a day, e-mailing each order to a single person is not an ideal solution. However, for smaller companies or Web sites that do not have a high volume of orders, e-mailing form data is a good solution.

To e-mail form data, you replace the Web server script's URL in the <form> element's action attribute with mailto:*email_address*.

You add the mailto protocol and any optional mailto properties to the URL, just as you did when you added it to an anchor element in Chapter 3. For instance, the following code generates an RSVP form for a fictitious wedding-planning company. The form's data is e-mailed to a fictitious e-mail address, rsvp@CentralValleyWeddings.com. Notice that the mailto attribute is placed at the start of the URL, separated by a colon, and that the optional subject property is appended to the end of the URL with a question mark. Figure 6-21 shows the form in a Web browser.

```
<h1>Jose and Melinda's Wedding</h1>
<h2>RSVP Form</h2>
<p><strong>Please send your reply by
3/15/2012.</strong></p>
<form action="mailto:rsvp@CentralValleyWeddings.com
    ?subject=RSVP" method="post"
    enctype="text/plain">
<h3>Your Name</h3>
<p><input type="text" size="50" /></p>
<p><input type="radio" name="attending"
    value="yes" />Will attend<br />
<input type="radio" name="attending"
    value="no" />Will not</p>
<p><input type="hidden" name="wedding"
    value="Jose and Melinda" /></p>
<p><button type="reset">Reset</button>
<button type="submit">RSVP</button></p>
</form>
```

Notice that the code at right includes a hidden element that stores the names of the people who are getting married.

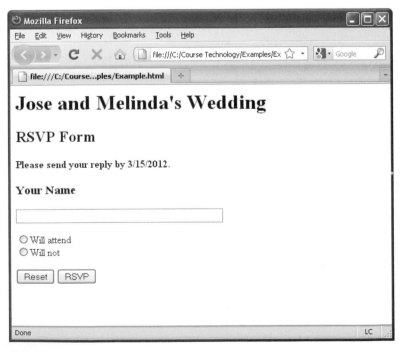

Figure 6-21   RSVP form that is sent to an e-mail address

When you send form data to an e-mail address, use the enctype of *text/plain*, which ensures that the data arrives at the e-mail address in a readable format.

The drawback to e-mailing form data is that the mailto:*email_address* option is unreliable. Some Web browsers that support the e-mailing of form data do not properly place the data within the body of an e-mail message. If you write a Web page that e-mails form data, be sure to test it thoroughly before using it.

Data that is transferred between Web browsers and Web servers cannot include spaces or certain special characters such as a percent sign (%). When you transmit data, most Web browsers will convert spaces to plus signs (+) and convert special characters into their equivalent hexadecimal American Standard Code for Information Interchange (ASCII) values, preceded by a percent sign. Hexadecimal ASCII is a special code for representing English characters as numbers. For example, 25 is the hexadecimal ASCII equivalent of a percent sign (%). Most e-mail programs, including Microsoft Outlook, will convert the plus signs back into spaces and any hexadecimal ASCII values back into their character equivalents. However, some e-mail programs do not perform this conversion. If you see any plus symbols or hexadecimal ASCII characters in data that is e-mailed from a form, your e-mail program does not automatically perform this conversion. You will either need to write a special program to perform the conversion or use a different e-mail program.

When users click the Submit button for a form that is e-mailed, they may receive a security warning or be given a chance to edit the e-mail, depending on how their e-mail application is configured.

Next, you change the `<form>` element of the Subscription form so that the form data is sent to your e-mail address whenever it is submitted.

To change the Subscription form so that the form data is sent to your e-mail address:

1. Return to the **subscription.html** file in your text editor.

2. Modify the opening `<form>` element as follows; be sure to replace *email_address* with your own e-mail address:

   ```
   <form action="mailto:email_address" method="post"
   enctype="text/plain">
   ```

3. Save the **subscription.html** file and then open it in your Web browser. Fill in the form fields and then submit the form. Depending on your e-mail configuration, you may see warnings or be given a chance to edit the e-mail message.

4. Wait several minutes before retrieving the new message from your e-mail application, because transmission times on the Internet can vary. After you receive the e-mail, examine the message to see how the form data appears.

5. Close your Web browser window.

Short Quiz 3

1. How do you define a group of radio buttons?

2. How do you define a group of check boxes?

3. What is the purpose of the reset button?

4. Explain the differences between push buttons, submit buttons, image submit buttons, and the <button> element.

5. How do you send form data to an e-mail address?

Defining Labels, Access Keys, and Field Sets

In this section, you learn how to make the controls on your forms more accessible by using labels and access keys. You also learn how to visually organize your controls with field sets.

Defining Labels

So far, the labels you have created for your form controls have consisted of text that is unrelated to the control itself, except that it happens to appear next to the control when rendered in a browser. In other types of programming languages, the label for a control is actually part of the control itself. This allows you to select the control by clicking the control's label instead of clicking the control. In XHTML, you use the **<label> element** to associate a label with a form control. You can associate a particular <label> element and its content with only one form control. You can include other elements such as <strong> and <em> within the <label> element to modify the label's appearance. Also, the <label> element allows you to select and deselect controls such as check boxes by clicking the control label. Another benefit is that the <label> element provides control descriptions to nonvisual browsers, helping ensure that a Web page is compatible with the greatest number of user agents.

You can use two attributes with the <label> element: accesskey and for. (The accesskey attribute is discussed later in this section.) You use the for attribute to associate a <label> element with a target form control; the for attribute is assigned the same value that is assigned to the target control's id attribute. Throughout this chapter, you have used only name attributes with your form controls, but to associate a label with a form control, the control must include an id attribute.

The following code shows an example of the White House form you saw earlier. This time each <input> element includes a <label> element. In addition, each form control now includes an id attribute that is assigned the same value as the control's name attribute. Note that you are not required to assign the same value to the name and id attributes. In fact, if you want to associate a <label> element with a particular radio button or check box that is assigned the same name value as other radio buttons or check boxes in the same group, you must assign a unique value to the control's id attribute in order for the code to be valid. However, for controls that have a unique value assigned to their name attributes, you can safely use the same value for the control's id attribute.

```
<form action="FormProcess.html" method="get"
enctype="application/x-www-form-urlencoded">
<p><label for="name">Name</label><br />
<input type="text" name="name" id="name"
    value="The White House" size="50" /></p>
<p><label for="address">Address</label><br />
<input type="text" name="address" id="address"
    value="1600 Pennsylvania Ave." size="50" /></p>
<p><label for="city">City</label>, <label
for="state">State</label>, <label
for="zip">Zip</label><br />
<input type="text" name="city" id="city"
    value="Washington" size="30" />
<input type="text" name="state" id="state"
    value="DC" size="2" maxlength="2" />
<input type="text" name="zip" id="zip"
    value="20500" size="5" maxlength="5" /></p>
</form>
```

For a document with a form to be valid, a <label> element must either include a for attribute or contain as a nested element the form control with which it is associated. The following code shows the first two controls of the White House form nested within their associated <label> elements.

```
<form action="FormProcess.html" method="get"
enctype="application/x-www-form-urlencoded">
<p><label>Name<br />
<input type="text" name="name" id="name"
    value="The White House" size="50" /></label></p>
```

```
<p><label for="address">Address<br />
<input type="text" name="address" id="address"
    value="1600 Pennsylvania Ave."
    size="50" /></label></p>
...
```

Next, you add <label> elements to controls in the Subscription form. To keep the exercise simple, you add <label> elements only for the name, address, city, state, and zip controls.

To add <label> elements to controls in the Subscription form:

1. Return to the **subscription.html** file in your text editor.

2. Modify the name, address, city, state, and zip controls so they include <label> elements. The code you need to add is shown in boldface. Be sure to add id attributes to each of the <input> elements.

```
<p><label for="name">Name</label><br />
<input type="text" name="name" id="name" size="56" />
<br /></p>
<p><label for="address">Address</label><br />
<input type="text" name="address" id="address"
size="56" /></p>
<p><label for="city">City</label>,
<label for="state">State</label>,
<label for="zip">Zip</label><br />
<input type="text" name="city" id="city"
size="34" />
<input type="text" name="state" id="state" size="2"
maxlength="2" />
<input type="text" name="zip" id="zip" size="10"
maxlength="10" /></p>
```

3. Save the **subscription.html** file and then open it in your Web browser. The labels for the <input> elements should look the same as they did before you added the <label> elements. Test the page by clicking the labels to ensure that the correct field is selected.

4. Close your Web browser window.

Defining Access Keys

All of the form control elements except for the <select> element can also include the **accesskey attribute**, which designates a key that visitors to your Web site can press to jump to a control, or to select and deselect a control such as a check box. You assign to the accesskey attribute the keyboard character that you want to use as a control's access key. How you execute an access key depends on the platform and Web browser you are using. In Firefox, you select an access key by holding down the Shift+Alt keys and simultaneously pressing the access key, while in Internet Explorer you only need to press Alt and the access key. On Macintosh systems, you select an access key by pressing it and holding down the Control key simultaneously. For instance, if you assign an access key of 'W' to a control, you can access the control by pressing Alt+W in Internet Explorer on a Windows system or Ctrl+W on a Macintosh system. The following code shows access keys assigned to the first two elements in the White House form:

```
<form action="whitehouse.html" method="get"
enctype="application/x-www-form-urlencoded">
<p><label for="name">Name</label><br />
<input type="text" name="name" id="name"
    accesskey="N"
    value="The White House" size="50" /></p>
<p><label for="address">Address</label><br />
<input type="text" name="address" id="address"
    accesskey="A"
    value="1600 Pennsylvania Ave." size="50" /></p>
...
```

The <label> element can also be assigned an access key, which either jumps to the label's associated control or selects and deselects controls such as a check box. One benefit to assigning access keys to <label> elements is that they allow you to assign an access key to a <select> element, which cannot use the accesskey attribute on its own. To assign an access key for a control to its label, the <label> element must include the for attribute. The following code shows access keys assigned to the first two <label> elements in the White House form:

```
<form action="whitehouse.html" method="get"
enctype="application/x-www-form-urlencoded">
<p><label for="name" accesskey="N">
    Name</label><br />
<input type="text" name="name" id="name"
    value="The White House" size="50" /></p>
<p><label for="address" accesskey="A">
    Address</label><br />
<input type="text" name="address" id="address"
    value="1600 Pennsylvania Ave." size="50" /></p>
...
```

Regardless of whether you assign an access key directly to a control or to its associated <label> element, you should identify the access key for Web page visitors. Windows platforms use underscores or underlines to identify access keys. However, in Web page authoring, you should not use underscores because visitors to your Web site may

Be sure not to assign an access key that is already used by the Web browser. For instance, 'f' is the access key that opens the File menu in the Windows version of Internet Explorer. If you assign 'f' as an access key to one of your form controls, the control's access key overrides the File menu's 'f' access key. You can tell what access keys are assigned to a Web browser menu by holding down your Alt key and examining the menu names. Each menu's access key appears as an underlined letter in the menu name.

Access keys are not case sensitive.

confuse them with links. An alternative is to use an element such as `<strong>` to make the access key stand out, as shown in the following code for the first two elements of the White House form.

```
<form action="whitehouse.html" method="get"
enctype="application/x-www-form-urlencoded">
<p><label for="name"
accesskey="N"><strong>N</strong>ame</label><br />
<input type="text" name="name" id="name"
    value="The White House" size="50" /></p>
<p><label for="address"
accesskey="A"><strong>A</strong>ddress</label><br />
<input type="text" name="address" id="address"
    value="1600 Pennsylvania Ave." size="50" /></p>
...
```

Access keys are of limited use due to the mouse-oriented nature of Web pages. With long or complex forms, you may find it counterproductive to assign access keys to every control. Therefore, you may want to consider using access keys only on short or simple forms, where they would provide the most benefit. In this chapter's Subscription form, access keys would help users select the check boxes for newspapers to which they already have subscriptions.

Next, you add `<label>` elements and access keys to the check boxes in the Subscription form.

To add `<label>` elements and access keys to the Subscription form:

1. Return to the **subscription.html** file in your text editor.

2. Modify the check box `<input>` elements so they include `<label>` elements and `accesskey` attributes. The code you need to add is shown in boldface. Also add `<strong>` elements to identify the access key for each control. Notice that new `id` attributes have been added to the `<input>` elements. Because all of the check box `<input>` elements have the same value ("newspapers") assigned to their `name` attributes, each `id` attribute is assigned a unique name to clearly identify each `<label>` element with its associated control.

```
<p><input type="checkbox" name="newspapers" id="nyt"
    value="nytimes" /><label for="nyt"
    accesskey="n">The <strong>N</strong>ew York
Times</label><br />
<input type="checkbox" name="newspapers" id="bg"
    value="bostonglobe" /><label for="bg"
    accesskey="b">The <strong>B</strong>oston
Globe</label><br />
```

```
<input type="checkbox" name="newspapers" id="sfc"
    value="sfchronicle" /><label for="sfc"
    accesskey="s"><strong>S</strong>an Francisco
Chronicle</label><br />
<input type="checkbox" name="newspapers" id="mh"
    value="miamiherald" /><label for="mh"
    accesskey="m">The <strong>M</strong>iami
Herald</label><br />
<input type="checkbox" name="newspapers" id="ot"
    value="other" /><label for="ot"
    accesskey="o"><strong>O</strong>ther</label></p>
```

3. Save the **subscription.html** file and then open it in your Web browser. Test the access keys for the newspaper check boxes. Also, try clicking the label for each check box to see if it selects and deselects the associated check box control. The check boxes should look the same, except that the access key for each control should be bold.

4. Close your Web browser window.

Defining Field Sets

If you want to clearly identify controls in a form as being part of the same group, you can use a **field set** to visually group the controls. A field set draws a box around a group of controls. You create a field set by nesting a group of related controls within the <fieldset> element. The first element in a <fieldset> must be a <legend> element, which provides a caption or description for the group of controls.

The following code shows how to place a group of check boxes within a field set that is identified by the caption "What type of books do you like to read?"

```
<fieldset>
<legend>What type of books do you like to
read?</legend>
<p><input type="checkbox" name="books"
    value="fiction" />Fiction<br />
<input type="checkbox" name="books"
    value="science_fiction" checked="checked" />
    Science Fiction<br />
<input type="checkbox" name="books"
    value="romance" />Romance<br />
<input type="checkbox" name="books"
    value="mysteries" />Mysteries<br /></p>
</fieldset>
```

The radio buttons for the Subscription form's delivery rates would be easier to read if they were part of the same field set. Therefore, you will add a field set to these radio buttons in the Subscription form.

 Like option groups, field sets are not widely supported in older browsers, so use them only for Web pages that will be viewed in current browsers.

To add a field set to the delivery rate radio buttons:

1. Return to the **subscription.html** file in your text editor.

2. Replace the `<p>Delivery Rates</p>` statement that starts the delivery rates radio button group with the following `<fieldset>` and `<legend>` elements:

   ```
   <fieldset>
   <legend>Delivery Rates</legend>
   ```

3. Add a closing `</fieldset>` tag after the closing `</table>` tag for the table that contains the delivery rates.

4. Save the **subscription.html** file and then validate it with the W3C Markup Validation Service at **http://validator.w3.org/#validate_by_upload**. If you receive any errors, fix them and then revalidate the document.

5. Close the **subscription.html** file in your text editor and then open the file in your Web browser. Figure 6-22 shows how the radio buttons appear in the field set.

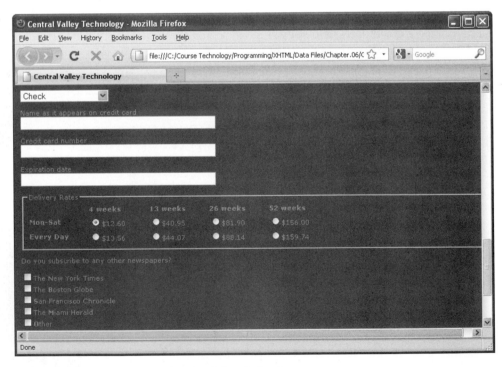

Figure 6-22 Field set added to the Subscription form

6. Close your Web browser window, text editor, and e-mail program.

Short Quiz 4

1. What is the primary purpose of the `<label>` element?

2. How do you define an access key?

3. Explain why a field set is used.

Summing Up

- Forms are used to collect information from users and transmit it to a server for processing.

- Server-side scripts process data that is transmitted from a form to a server.

- The `<form>` element designates a form within a Web page and contains all the text and elements that make up a form.

- Any form element into which a user can enter data, such as a text box, or that a user can select or change, such as a radio button, is called a field.

- The empty `<input>` element is used to create different types of input fields that gather information.

- An `<input>` element with a type of *text* (`<input type="text">`) creates a simple text box that accepts a single line of text.

- An `<input>` element with a type of *password* (`<input type="password">`) creates a password box for entering passwords or other sensitive data.

- An `<input>` element with a type of *file* (`<input type="file">`) creates a file box—a text box control with a Browse button that you can use to upload a file to a Web server.

- An `<input>` element with a type of *hidden* (`<input type="hidden">`) creates a special element called a hidden form field that allows you to hide information from users.

- The `<textarea>` element is used to create a multiline text field, or text area, in which users can enter multiple lines of information.

- The `<select>` element creates a selection list from which users can choose from fixed lists of values.

358

- You use <option> elements to specify the menu items that appear in a selection list.

- You use the <optgroup> element to create option groups that organize elements in a selection list.

- A data list is a list of values for a text box that are displayed when the text box is selected.

- An <input> element with a type of *radio* (<input type="radio">) is used to create a group of radio buttons, or option buttons, from which you can select only one value.

- An <input> element with a type of *checkbox* (<input type="checkbox">) creates a check box that allows users to select certain items and to select multiple values from a list of items.

- An <input> element with a type of *reset* (<input type="reset">) creates a reset button that clears all form entries and resets each form element to its initial value specified by the value attribute.

- An <input> element with a type of *button* (<input type="button">) creates a push button similar to the OK and Cancel buttons you see in dialog boxes.

- An <input> element with a type of *submit* (<input type="submit">) creates a submit button that transmits form data to a Web server.

- An <input> element with a type of *image* (<input type="image">) creates an image submit button that displays a graphical image and transmits form data to a Web server.

- You can use the <button> element to create push buttons, submit buttons, and reset buttons.

- Instead of submitting form data to a Web server, you can send the form data to an e-mail address.

- You use the <label> element to associate a label with a form control.

- The accesskey attribute designates a key that Web site visitors can press to jump to a control or to select and deselect a control such as a check box.

- A field set draws a box around a group of controls. You create a field set by nesting a group of related controls within the <fieldset> element.

- The first element in a <fieldset> must be a <legend> element, which provides a caption or description for the group of controls.

Comprehension Check

1. Explain how forms are used on Web pages.

2. Which of the following are server-side scripting languages? (Choose all that apply.)

    a. Common Gateway Interface (CGI)

    b. Active Server Pages (ASP)

    c. Java Server Pages (JSP)

    d. Extensible Markup Language (XML)

3. Which of the following are block-level elements? (Choose all that apply.)

    a. `<form>`

    b. `<input>`

    c. `<select>`

    d. `<textarea>`

4. You can nest one form inside another form. True or False?

5. What is the default value of the `<form>` element's `enctype` attribute?

    a. text/plain

    b. multipart/form-data

    c. application/x-www-form-urlencoded

    d. image/gif

6. Describe the two ways in which form data can be submitted to a Web server.

7. In what form is form data submitted to a Web server?

    a. in value,name pairs

    b. in name=value pairs

    c. as values separated by commas

    d. as values separated by paragraph marks

8. The text <input> element _____.

   a. displays a static label

   b. creates input fields that use different types of interface elements to gather information

   c. creates a simple text box that accepts a single line of text

   d. creates either a submit button or a reset button

9. The size attribute is used with the _____ <input> element.

   a. button

   b. image

   c. text

   d. submit

10. Each character entered into a text box that is created with a password <input> element appears _____.

    a. with the ampersand (&) symbol

    b. with the number (#) symbol

    c. as a percentage (%)

    d. as an asterisk (*)

11. Which of the following attributes designates a single button in a radio button group as the default selection?

    a. checked

    b. check

    c. selected

    d. default

12. Which of the following statements is true of check boxes?

    a. You can select only one check box in a group at a time.

    b. You can select as many check boxes as necessary.

    c. When you select one check box, all other check boxes in the same group are also selected.

    d. Check boxes are not used for user input.

13. What is the purpose of the reset `<input>` element?

    a. to reload the current Web page

    b. to reset the contents of a single form element to its default value

    c. to reset all form elements in the current form to their default values

    d. to close and restart the Web browser

14. What type of `<input>` element creates a button similar to the OK and Cancel buttons found in dialog boxes?

    a. radio

    b. ok_cancel

    c. dialog

    d. button

15. What is the default value of a submit button label?

    a. Submit

    b. Query

    c. Submit Query

    d. Execute

16. Which types of elements can be used to submit form data to a Web server? (Choose all that apply.)

    a. image `<input>` element

    b. radio `<input>` element

    c. submit `<input>` element

    d. submit `<button>` element

17. The contents of a selection list are determined by which element?

    a. `<select>`

    b. `<contents>`

    c. `<items>`

    d. `<option>`

18. Which of the following is the correct syntax for creating a text area?

    a. `<text cols="50" rows="10">default text</text>`

    b. `<textarea cols="50" rows="10">default text</textarea>`

    c. `<text size="50">default text</text>`

    d. `<textarea size="50">default text</textarea>`

19. Explain the benefits of using a `<label>` element to associate a label with a form control.

20. The first element in a `<fieldset>` must be a `<legend>` element. True or False?

Reinforcement Exercises

 Exercise 6-1

In this exercise, you create a contact information form for an online company that sells patio furniture.

1. Create a new HTML 5 document in your text editor and use "Contact Us" as the content of the `<title>` element.

2. Add the following heading elements to the document body:

```
<h1>Coast City Patio Furniture</h1>
<h2>Contact Us</h2>
```

3. Add the following `<form>` element to the end of the document body so that you can submit the form to your e-mail address:

```
<form action="mailto:email_address" method="post"
enctype="text/plain">
</form>
```

4. Add the following `<input>` and `<textarea>` fields to the `<form>` element. The text `<input>` fields are created in a table to make them easier to lay out on the page.

```
<table>
<colgroup span="1" style="width: 100px"></colgroup>
<colgroup span="1" style="width: 150px">
</colgroup>
<tr><td>Name</td><td><input type="text"
```

```
size="75" name="name" /></td></tr>
<tr><td>Address</td><td><input type="text"
size="75" name="address" /></td></tr>
<tr><td>City</td><td><input type="text"
size="75" name="city" /></td></tr>
<tr><td>State</td><td><input type="text"
size="75" name="state" /></td></tr>
<tr><td>Zip</td><td><input type="text"
size="75" name="zip" /></td></tr>
<tr><td>Telephone</td><td><input type="text"
size="75" name="phone" /></td></tr>
</table>
<p>Question or comment<br />
<textarea rows="6" cols="70">Enter your
question or comment here</textarea></p>
```

5. Add the following reset and submit buttons using `<input>` elements:

   ```
   <p><input type="reset" /><input type="submit" /></p>
   ```

6. Save the file as **ContactUs.html** in the Exercises folder for Chapter 6.

7. Close the **ContactUs.html** file in your text editor, and then use the W3C Markup Validation Service to validate the file. Once the file is valid, open it in your Web browser. Test the form and submit the data to your e-mail address.

8. Close your Web browser window.

Exercise 6-2

In this exercise, you create an airline survey form.

1. Create a new HTML 5 document in your text editor and use "Airline Survey" as the content of the `<title>` element.

2. Create the airline survey form shown in Figure 6-23. Design the form using a table and `<input>` elements to create the radio buttons. The `<input>` elements in each row of radio buttons should be assigned the same name attribute, which enables them to be part of the same group. Assign the appropriate value (Excellent, Good, Fair, Poor, No Opinion) to the value attribute of each `<input>` element. For example, you create the radio button for the first "Excellent" option using the statement `<input type="radio" name="wait_time" value="Excellent" />`.

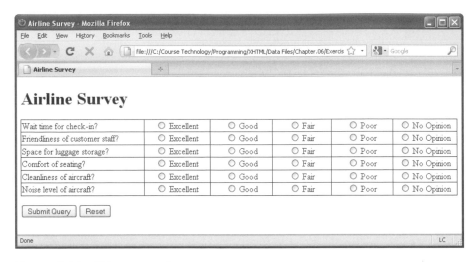

Figure 6-23   Airline survey form

3. Add reset and submit buttons to the airline survey form. The submit button should submit the survey data to your e-mail address.

4. Save the file as **AirlineSurvey.html** in the Exercises folder for Chapter 6.

5. Close the **AirlineSurvey.html** file in your text editor, and then use the W3C Markup Validation Service to validate the file. Once the file is valid, open it in your Web browser. Test the form and submit some data to your e-mail address.

6. Close your Web browser window.

Exercise 6-3

Forms on Web pages commonly use selection lists to allow users to select dates. In this exercise, you create a simple form that uses selection lists to create date fields.

1. Create a new HTML 5 document in your text editor and use "Date Fields" as the content of the `<title>` element.

2. Within the document body, add the following `<form>` element that submits the form to your e-mail address:

```
<form action="mailto:email_address" method="post"
enctype="text/plain">
</form>
```

3. Within the `<form>` element, add the following selection list with `<label>` elements that allows users to select a month:

```
<label for="month">Month </label>
<select name="month" id="month">
<option selected="selected" value="Jan">Jan</option>
<option value="Feb">Feb</option>
<option value="Mar">Mar</option>
<option value="Apr">Apr</option>
<option value="May">May</option>
<option value="Jun">Jun</option>
<option value="Jul">Jul</option>
<option value="Aug">Aug</option>
<option value="Sep">Sep</option>
<option value="Oct">Oct</option>
<option value="Nov">Nov</option>
<option value="Dec">Dec</option>
</select>
```

4. At the end of the `<form>` element, add the following selection list for the date of the month:

```
<label for="date">Date </label><select
name="date" id="date">
<option selected="selected"
value="01">01</option>
<option value="02">02</option>
<option value="03">03</option>
<option value="04">04</option>
<option value="05">05</option>
<option value="06">06</option>
<option value="07">07</option>
<option value="08">08</option>
<option value="09">09</option>
<option value="10">10</option>
<option value="11">11</option>
<option value="12">12</option>
<option value="13">13</option>
<option value="14">14</option>
<option value="15">15</option>
<option value="16">16</option>
<option value="17">17</option>
<option value="18">18</option>
<option value="19">19</option>
<option value="20">20</option>
<option value="21">21</option>
<option value="22">22</option>
<option value="23">23</option>
<option value="24">24</option>
<option value="25">25</option>
<option value="26">26</option>
<option value="27">27</option>
<option value="28">28</option>
<option value="29">29</option>
```

```
        <option value="30">30</option>
        <option value="31">31</option>
</select>
```

5.   At the end of the `<form>` element, add the following `<label>`
     and text `<input>` elements for the year, along with submit and
     reset buttons created with the `<button>` element:

```
<label for="year">Year </label>
<input type="text" name="year" id="year"
value="Year" size="4" /></p>
<p><button type="reset">Reset</button>
<button type="submit">Submit</button></p>
```

6.   Save the file as **DateFields.html** in the Exercises folder for
     Chapter 6.

7.   Close the **DateFields.html** file in your text editor, and then
     use the W3C Markup Validation Service to validate the file.
     Once the file is valid, open it in your Web browser. Test the
     form and submit it to your e-mail address.

8.   Close your Web browser window.

 ## Exercise 6-4

In this exercise, you create a reservation form for a surfboard rental
company.

1.   Create a new HTML 5 document in your text editor and
     use "Coast City Surfboard Rentals" as the content of the
     `<title>` element.

2.   Add the following heading elements to the document body:

```
<h1>Coast City Surfboard Rentals</h1>
<h2>Reservations</h2>
```

3.   At the end of the document body, add the following `<form>`
     element that submits the form to your e-mail address:

```
<form action="mailto:email_address" method="post"
enctype="text/plain">
</form>
```

4. Use `<input>` elements to create contact information fields in the `<form>` element, including name, address, and telephone number.

5. Use the date selection lists you created in Exercise 6-3 to add two date reservation fields to the end of the form: one for the date the user will pick up the surfboard and another for the return date.

6. Add two selection lists from which users can select the number of guests needing surfboards. One selection list is for the number of adults and the other is for the number of children.

7. Add a text area where users can enter questions or comments.

8. Use `<button>` elements to add reset and submit buttons to the document.

9. Save the file as **SurfboardRentals.html** in the Exercises folder for Chapter 6.

10. Close the **SurfboardRentals.html** file in your text editor, and then use the W3C Markup Validation Service to validate the file. Once the file is valid, open it in your Web browser. Test the form and submit it to your e-mail address.

11. Close your Web browser window.

 ## Exercise 6-5

In this exercise, you create a product survey form with some radio button fields for a software company.

1. Create a new HTML 5 document in your text editor and use "Product Survey" as the content of the `<title>` element.

2. Create the form with the radio buttons shown in Figure 6-24. Use `<label>` elements and create access keys for each of the radio button options.

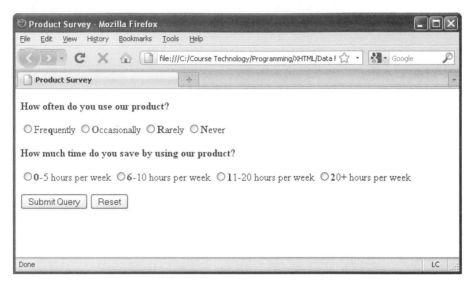

Figure 6-24   Product survey form

3. Use <button> elements to add reset and submit buttons to the product survey form. The submit button should submit the survey data to your e-mail address.

4. Save the file as **ProductSurvey.html** in the Exercises folder for Chapter 6.

5. Close the **ProductSurvey.html** file in your text editor, and then use the W3C Markup Validation Service to validate the file. Once the file is valid, open it in your Web browser. Test the form and submit some data to your e-mail address.

6. Close your Web browser window.

 Exercise 6-6

In this exercise, you create a fitness survey form for a health club.

1. Create a new HTML 5 document in your text editor and use "Fitness Survey" as the content of the <title> element.

2. Create the form shown in Figure 6-25.

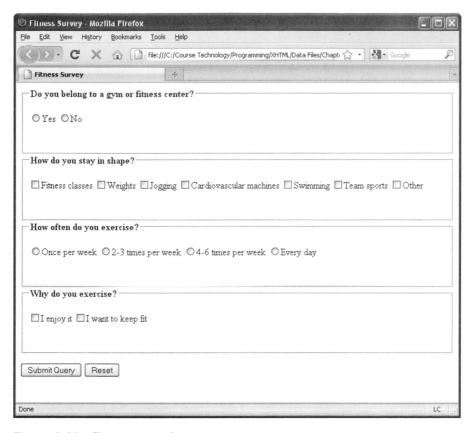

Figure 6-25 Fitness survey form

3. Use <button> elements to add reset and submit buttons to the product survey form. The submit button should submit the survey data to your e-mail address.

4. Save the file as **FitnessSurvey.html** in the Exercises folder for Chapter 6.

5. Close the **FitnessSurvey.html** file in your text editor, and then use the W3C Markup Validation Service to validate the file. Once the file is valid, open it in your Web browser. Test the form and submit some data to your e-mail address.

6. Close your Web browser window.

Discovery Projects

For the following projects, save the files you create in the Projects folder for Chapter 6 and be sure to validate them with the W3C Markup Validation Service.

Discovery Project 6-1

Create a form to be used as a software development bug report. Create two radio buttons labeled "Open" and "Closed" for the status of a bug. Include fields such as short and long descriptions of the bug, severity, the date the bug was opened, diagnosis of the problem, and actions taken to fix the bug. Use <label> elements for each control, and create the date fields using selection lists. Place the radio buttons within a field set. Submit the form to your e-mail address. Save the document as **BugReport.html**.

Discovery Project 6-2

Create a form to be used for tracking, documenting, and managing the process of interviewing candidates for professional positions. Create three field sets: Interviewer Information, Candidate Information, and Candidate's Skills/Presentation. Within the Interviewer Information field set, include fields for the interviewer's first name, last name, position, and date of interview. Create the date field using selection lists. Within the Candidate Information field set, include fields for the candidate's first name and last name, a selection list for the interviewer's overall recommendation (Don't Hire, Maybe Hire, and so on), and a comment field. Within the Candidate's Skills/Presentation field set, include the following selection lists: Intellect, Communication Skills, Business Knowledge, and Computer Skills. Within each selection list, include values such as Average, Above Average, and so on. Use <label> elements for each of the form controls. Submit the form to your e-mail address. Save the document as **Interview.html**.

Discovery Project 6-3

Create a consent form for a school trip. The form should contain three field sets: Description of Trip, Student Information, and Parental Information. Within the Description of Trip field set, include fields for the destination, date of the trip, and purpose of the trip. Also include three radio buttons for the duration of the trip: Half Day, Full Day, and Overnight. Within the Student Information field set, include fields for the student's name, home telephone, physician's name and telephone, and any special medical requirements. Within the Parental Information field set, include fields for the names of the student's mother and father, along with their work telephone numbers. Include two radio buttons labeled "Permission is Granted" and "Permission is NOT Granted" that parents can use to grant or deny permission for the field trip. Use <label> elements for each of the form controls. Also assign access keys to each of the form's radio buttons. Submit the form to your e-mail address. Save the document as **ConsentForm.html**.

Discovery Project 6-4

Create a documentation evaluation form for a software company. Include check boxes to allow visitors to select the documents to which their comments apply, along with a text area where they can type their comments. Also, include a survey that allows visitors to rate the documents they selected. The survey should include questions to rate the document's technical accuracy, clarity of writing, usefulness, and so on. Use radio buttons that allow users to select one of five choices to answer each survey question. The five answer choices should be Excellent, Good, Fair, Poor, and Very Poor. Also include a section in the form that allows visitors to enter their contact information. Submit the form to your e-mail address. Save the document as **DocEval.html**.

CHAPTER 7

Incorporating Multimedia and Executable Content

In this chapter you will:

- ◎ Learn the basics of multimedia and executable content
- ◎ Incorporate multimedia images into your Web pages
- ◎ Add sounds to a Web page
- ◎ Add videos and Java applets to a Web page

Many Web sites today use audio, video, and other multimedia for entertainment, educational, and training purposes. Animation, another component of multimedia, is a popular way of enlivening a Web site. Embedded objects such as Adobe Flash presentations can add even more types of multimedia and business functionality to a Web site through games, advertisements, and other types of interactivity. In this chapter, you will learn the basics of how to add multimedia and embedded objects to your Web pages.

Introduction to Multimedia

Multimedia refers to any type of data format that you can see, hear, or interact with, including images, video, sound, games, and animation. Before you start filling your pages with multimedia, you need to understand some basic ground rules. First, you should only add multimedia to your Web pages if it serves one of two purposes: presenting information or providing entertainment. If you add multimedia for any other reason, you risk annoying visitors to your Web site. How many times have you visited a Web page that immediately began playing an irritating song for no other reason than the author thought it was cool? Your goal when using multimedia should always be to provide information (such as an instructional video) or to entertain. You don't want to drive your visitors away. News sites such as *www.cnn.com* and *www.msnbc.com* make excellent use of multimedia by including audio and video clips to present current news topics.

Web pages that incorporate multimedia and executable content require visitors to have a broadband Internet connection, such as a cable modem or Digital Subscriber Line (DSL).

Another important consideration for multimedia is the way in which the content is delivered. Multimedia effects such as sound, video, and animation are contained in separate files that are accessible from a Web page. The two main methods of executing a multimedia file on a Web page are to download the file to the user's computer or to use a streaming media technology. The first option requires the entire file to download before it can execute, which can result in annoying delays across slow Internet connections. In **streaming media technology**, media files begin executing while the download is occurring, thanks to a process called **buffering**. For instance, the first few seconds of a streaming audio file will be downloaded (or "buffered") and then start playing before the rest of the file finishes downloading. Once the Web browser finishes playing the first few seconds of the file, it plays the next few seconds that downloaded while the first few seconds were playing. This sequence continues until the entire file finishes playing. As you might imagine, streaming media technology is a great boon to users with slow Internet connections.

You will not study streaming media in this chapter because it has substantial hardware and software requirements. Instead, you will work with downloadable multimedia files. The next few sections focus on the types of multimedia files and some popular multimedia applications.

Understanding Add-Ons

Web browsers display two basic types of media: text contained within HTML documents, and graphics such as Graphic Interchange Format (GIF) and Joint Photographic Experts Group (JPG) images. However, many other types of media are available, including word-processing documents, Adobe Acrobat files, and audio, video, and animation formats. To display and execute these additional types of media on a Web page, browsers use helper applications called **add-ons**. *Add-on* is a generic term; for example, some browsers support a specific type of add-on called **plug-ins**, which are external software components that display a particular type of media.

Each media type is contained in a different file format. A Web page identifies a file format by its extension and associated Multipurpose Internet Mail Extensions (MIME) type. Recall that MIME is a protocol that was originally developed to allow different file types to be transmitted as attachments to e-mail messages. In XHTML, you usually assign MIME types to attributes. You specify MIME types with two-part codes separated by a forward slash (/). The first part specifies the MIME type, and the second part specifies the MIME subtype. For example, you have assigned the common "text/css" MIME type to a `<style>` element's `type` attribute to identify the element content as CSS. Web browsers also use MIME types to identify file formats contained within Web pages. For example, the MIME type for a JPG image is "image/jpeg". A Web browser uses the first part of this MIME type to identify the file format as an image, and then uses the second part to render it as a JPG file.

Although Web browsers have been able to recognize file formats such as GIF and JPG for some time, new types of file formats are constantly being developed. Given the range of media now available, Web browsers cannot possibly support every conceivable file format. Add-on technology allows a Web browser to support newly developed file types without having to be continually updated.

Not long ago, if you did not have the necessary add-on installed, you had to download it before you could play its associated multimedia files on a Web page. This tedious task often resulted in visitors leaving the Web site rather than installing the add-on. Thankfully, newer versions of current browsers include the most popular add-ons as part of their basic installations. If a browser does not include the add-on for a particular file format, it will still prompt you to download it. For example, Figure 7-1 shows the Atkins Web page in Firefox if the Adobe Shockwave Flash plug-in is not installed. Notice the prompt at the top of the document window and the prompts for each Flash object.

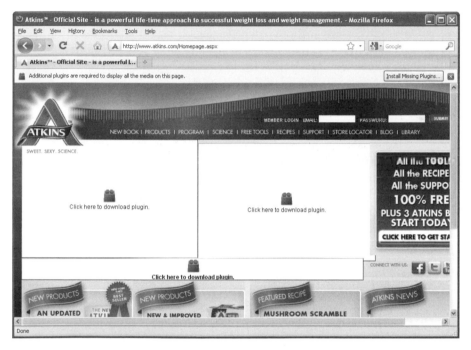

Figure 7-1 Firefox with prompts to install missing plug-ins

Plug-ins were originally created by Netscape for use with the Navigator Web browser. Although Internet Explorer supports plug-ins, it primarily uses ActiveX controls to execute embedded objects. **ActiveX controls** are objects that are executed within Web pages or within other programs. The term **embedded object** refers to any type of multimedia file or program that you can add to your Web pages. Even though plug-ins and ActiveX controls are separate technologies, ActiveX controls are commonly referred to as plug-ins when discussed in the context of a Web page. When working with multimedia files, you don't need to worry about whether your Web page is using a Netscape plug-in or an ActiveX control "plug-in"

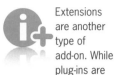

Extensions are another type of add-on. While plug-ins are external software components, **extensions** provide access to different types of media by integrating with the browser itself. In other words, extensions are internal to the browser, not external. Most browsers prompt you to install extensions when necessary, like other types of add-ons.

376

because there is little difference between the installation and execution of each type of component.

Understanding Popular Multimedia Applications

Add-ons are designed to execute within the confines of a Web page. However, many add-ons are actually a way to provide Web pages with access to stand-alone multimedia applications (that is, applications that play media independently of a browser). You can install a wide variety of multimedia applications on your computer, and most are also available as add-ons. This section discusses the most popular multimedia applications; each is available as a Web page add-on and as a free, downloadable player that can be used without a Web browser.

Apple QuickTime

Apple's QuickTime was originally created as a video add-on for Macintosh systems, and it is now available on Windows platforms. QuickTime is popular because it supports more than 200 file types and offers excellent cross-platform performance and compression technology. It is also popular for streaming media, and is the base multimedia technology for all Apple products, including the Mac OS operating system, iTunes, iPhones, and iPads. You can download the QuickTime player from *www.apple.com/quicktime/*.

Windows Media Player

In the past, Microsoft released versions of Windows Media Player for the Mac OS, Mac OS X, and Solaris operating systems, but it no longer does so for these operating systems.

Microsoft's Windows Media Player is widely used because it is part of all current Windows platforms. It also supports a wide variety of file types, including audio and video formats, and is available for the Macintosh. Windows Media Player offers powerful streaming media capabilities. You can download it from *www.microsoft.com/windows/windowsmedia/*.

RealPlayer

RealPlayer, produced by RealNetworks, was the industry leader in streaming media technology during the early years of the Internet, but it has since been surpassed by Windows Media Player and Apple's iTunes. RealPlayer supports a number of popular multimedia formats, along with proprietary formats such as RealAudio (RA) and RealVideo (RV). You can download RealPlayer from *www.real.com/realplayer/*.

Flash

Macromedia's Flash is considered the industry leader in Web page animation and interactive graphics. Unlike audio and video clips, which are created with a variety of hardware and software, Flash files, called "movies," are created with the Flash authoring tool. Flash movies are essentially animations, although they can include audio and video. Flash is a descendent of Macromedia Director, an old and respected tool for creating traditional interactive, multimedia presentations that execute on CD-ROMs and in other types of interactive formats. To allow Director files to run on the Web, Macromedia created Shockwave, another popular multimedia format. Flash was then created as a less expensive, easier-to-use alternative to Shockwave; Flash has become extremely popular over the past two decades. Flash files are actually created in the Shockwave file format. You can download the Flash player from *www.adobe.com/downloads/*.

Apple products such as the iPad and iPhone are the most popular devices for playing music, videos, and other multimedia. However, Apple restricts the use of technologies such as Flash on its multimedia devices in favor of its own QuickTime format. Ironically, this means that the most popular multimedia format cannot be used on the most popular multimedia devices.

Respecting Copyright Issues

The requirements for creating multimedia data files vary greatly with the file format. Animation files can be created with some fairly inexpensive software, but the creation of audio and video files requires additional software, knowledge of audiovisual techniques and concepts, and additional hardware that allows you to transfer audio and video to a computer format. Regardless of the type of multimedia you want to create, you will face a steep learning curve and additional purchases of software and hardware. Your next option is to use existing multimedia files, which brings up the important issue of copyrights.

You can copy almost any type of image or multimedia data file that you find on the Internet, but that does not mean you can legally use it. Legally, you can only use images or data files that are clearly marked as public domain. Otherwise, you must contact the creator and either pay a licensing fee or obtain permission to use the file. You are allowed to experiment with a copyrighted multimedia file for learning purposes without permission, but you cannot broadcast, distribute, reproduce, or include the file on an Internet Web site.

Musicians, artists, filmmakers, and designers spend a great deal of time and artistic effort creating the audio, video, and animation that end up as multimedia files. As a good citizen of the Internet, you should respect their legal rights and intellectual property by observing all copyright requirements. A few years ago, the Napster Web site made headlines by essentially allowing anyone to freely download copyrighted music files without paying a royalty to the original artists. Napster was eventually shut down by a court order, which has led to a general crackdown on the illegal use of copyrighted material on the Internet. So be warned: If you illegally use copyrighted material on your Web site, you do so at your own risk.

Public-domain audio files are fairly easy to find, although you will have trouble finding useful public-domain animation and video. To find multimedia files on the Internet, search for "animation files," "audio files," "video files," or for a specific type of multimedia format, such as the "midi" audio format. Again, however, keep copyright issues in mind. To avoid problems, your best bet is to learn how to create your own animation, audio, and video files. Creating professional multimedia files for your Web pages requires extensive study and practice, so use this chapter as a starting point for learning basic techniques, and then look into the requirements for creating the types of multimedia that interest you.

378

You can also purchase collections of royalty-free clip art and multimedia files from online sites such as Clipart.com (*www.clipart.com*) and from almost any store that sells software, such as Best Buy or OfficeMax.

Working with Multimedia Elements

Table 7-1 lists the standard multimedia elements that you can use in HTML.

Element	Description
`<audio>` (added in HTML 5)	Defines audio content such as music or audio streams
`<embed>` (added in HTML 5)	Defines audio, video, and other types of multimedia content
`<object>`	Defines audio, video, and other types of multimedia content and allows you to specify data, parameters, and code
`<param>`	Used with the `<object>` element to identify additional parameters
`<source>`	Used with multimedia elements such as the `<audio>` and `<video>` elements to define media content
`<video>` (added in HTML 5)	Defines video content such as movie clips or video streams
inline MathML (added in HTML 5)	An XML application for describing mathematical notations and capturing both its structure and content
inline SVG (added in HTML 5)	An XML-based file format for describing two-dimensional vector graphics

Table 7-1   HTML multimedia elements

Many of the multimedia elements can perform the same task. For example, the <video>, <embed>, and <object> elements can all display video. So which element should you use for each multimedia type? For basic multimedia objects, the <embed> element is the easiest to use. However, if you want to display or hide controls for starting and stopping multimedia content, such as a video, you should use a more specific element, such as <video>. For multimedia objects that require more control, you can use the <object> element to specify additional data, parameters, and code.

In this chapter, you will study each of the elements listed in Table 7-1, starting with the <embed> element.

Using the <embed> Element (HTML 5)

Older versions of HTML required proprietary, browser-specific elements to execute multimedia files. With Internet Explorer, you used the <bgsound> element to add audio files to Web pages. The <embed> element, which was originally created by Netscape, is used to add audio, video, images, and other types of multimedia content to Web pages. The <bgsound> element has been deprecated, but the <embed> element, which was not part of the XHTML recommendation, has been added to the HTML 5 recommendation.

Table 7-2 lists the attributes of the <embed> element.

Newer HTML 5 elements, such as <video> and <audio>, are not widely supported in older browser versions. For this reason, you should use the <embed> and <object> elements as your primary means of incorporating multimedia objects into your Web pages. Later in this chapter, you will learn how to nest the newer multimedia elements inside the <object> element for modern browsers that support them.

379

Attribute	Description
height	Defines the height of the element
source	Identifies the URL of the multimedia content
type	Identifies the MIME type of the multimedia content
width	Defines the width of the element

Table 7-2   Attributes of the <embed> element

The only required attribute of the <embed> element is source, which identifies the URL of the embedded content. Although you can use the type attribute to specify the MIME type, it is usually unnecessary because the browser can automatically determine the type of add-on from the file extension of the embedded object. The following example demonstrates how to use the <embed> element to define a Flash animation of a break dancer, as shown in Figure 7-2.

The <embed> element is supported by all current browsers.

```
<embed src="breakdancer.swf"
    type="application/x-shockwave-flash" />
```

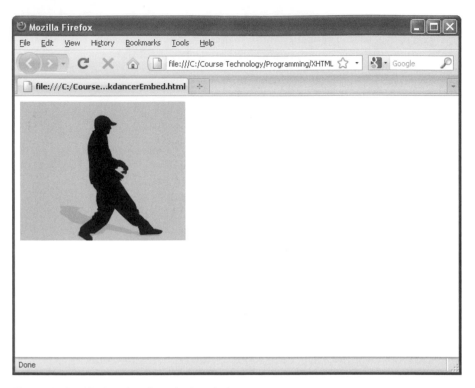

Figure 7-2   Flash animation of a break dancer

The `height` and `width` attributes determine the size of an add-on's **bounding box**—a rectangular area on a Web page in which an object executes. Recall from Chapter 4 that you use the `height` and `width` attributes of the `<img>` element to assign the exact dimensions of the original image so that the Web browser will reserve enough space on the page for the image. If you use the `height` and `width` attributes to resize an image, it may appear stretched or "squished," and its quality will be poor. In contrast, the `height` and `width` attributes of the `<embed>` object are used to resize the multimedia content on the screen, and do not affect quality in any way. For example, the following `<embed>` object assigns the `height` attribute a value of 400 and the `width` attribute a value of 100, which causes the Flash animation to appear in a strip along the left side of the screen, as shown in Figure 7-3.

```
<embed src="breakdancer.swf"
    type="application/x-shockwave-flash"
    height="400" width="100" />
```

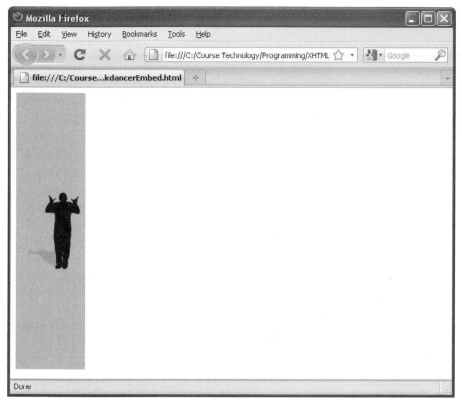

Figure 7-3 Flash animation of a break dancer with values assigned to the height and width attributes of the <embed> object

 Although the height and width properties of the <embed> object will not distort add-ons such as Flash movies, they will distort standard image files such as GIF and JPG images. Also note that the height and width properties will distort the display of add-ons in Internet Explorer if they are not set properly.

 Do not append px to the values you assign to the height and width attributes; otherwise, the <embed> element will be invalid.

In this chapter, you will work on a Web site for a martial arts studio named DRG Karate. The goal of the chapter will be to add multimedia elements to the Web site. Your Chapter folder for Chapter 7 includes a folder named DRGKarate that contains the files you will need for the project. First, you will add a Flash animation to the home page using the <embed> element.

 Your Examples folder for Chapter 7 includes a file named BreakdancerEmbed.html that contains an example of the break dancer animation files with an <embed> element.

To add a Flash animation to the DRG Karate home page:

1. Open your text editor, and then open the **index.html** document in the DRGKarate folder in your Chapter folder for Chapter 7.

2. Locate `<!-- Add Flash code here -->` in the document body and replace it with the following table cell and `<embed>` element:

```
<td valign="top">
    <embed src="kickboxer.swf"
        type="application/x-shockwave-flash"
        height="90" width="128" />
</td>
```

3. Save the document and open it in a Web browser. The Flash animation should begin to play. Your page should look similar to Figure 7-4.

Figure 7-4   DRG Karate home page after adding a Flash animation

4. Close your Web browser window.

Using the `<object>` Element

Although the `<embed>` element is available in HTML 5 for adding various types of multimedia content to Web pages, you can also use the `<object>` element. Both types of elements can display and run many of the same types of content, although the `<object>` element is more powerful because it allows you to specify data, parameters, and code for a multimedia object. The `<embed>` element only allows you to specify the source, type, height, and width of the object.

Table 7-3 lists the attributes of the `<object>` element.

Attribute	Description
data	Identifies the absolute or relative URL of the object's data file
form (HTML 5)	Defines one or more forms to which the `<object>` element belongs
height	Specifies the height of the object using pixels or a percentage of the screen height
name	Assigns a name to the object
type	Specifies the MIME type of the object
usemap	Identifies the location of an image map to use with the object
width	Specifies the width of the object using pixels or a percentage of the screen width

Table 7-3 Attributes of the `<object>` element

The required syntax for working with the `<object>` element varies according to the type of content being displayed or executed. To be valid in HTML 5, the `<object>` element requires either the `data` or `type` attribute. The following code demonstrates how to use the `<object>` element to define the break dancer Flash animation:

```
<object data="breakdancer.swf"
    type="application/x-shockwave-flash"
    height="400" width="100" /></object>
```

 Do not append *px* to the values you assign to the `height` and `width` attributes; otherwise, the `<object>` element will be invalid.

Although the `<embed>` element is new to HTML 5, it has been supported in most Web browsers for a long time. In fact, the `<embed>` element is more widely supported than the `<object>` element. To ensure that your multimedia elements will run in all browsers, you should nest the `<embed>` element inside the `<object>` element. Web browsers that do not support the `<object>` element will ignore it and instead execute the nested `<embed>` element. The following example demonstrates how to nest an `<embed>` element inside an `<object>` element for the break dancer Flash animation:

```
<object data="breakdancer.swf"
    type="application/x-shockwave-flash"
    height="400" width="100">
    <embed src="breakdancer.swf"
        type="application/x-shockwave-flash"
        height="400" width="100" />
</object>
```

Next, you will modify the DRG Karate home page so the `<embed>` element is nested within an `<object>` element.

To modify the DRG Karate home page so the `<embed>` element is nested within an `<object>` element:

1. Return to the **index.html** Web file in your text editor.

2. Enclose the `<embed>` element within an `<object>` element, as follows:

```
<object data="kickboxer.swf"
    type="application/x-shockwave-flash"
    height="90" width="128">
    <embed src="kickboxer.swf"
    type="application/x-shockwave-flash"
    height="90" width="128" />
</object>
```

3. Save the document and open it in a Web browser. The Flash animation should work the same as it did before you added the `<object>` element.

4. Close your Web browser window.

Setting Parameters

When working with multimedia elements, you can set parameters for both the `<object>` and `<embed>` elements. With the `<object>` element, you use the empty `<param>` element to identify additional parameters, or information, that an embedded object needs to run. The required parameters will vary according to the type of embedded object. You can usually obtain parameter information directly from the developer or software manufacturer who created the embedded object. The `<param>` element supports two attributes: `name` and `type`. The `name` attribute defines a unique name for the parameter and the `type` attribute identifies the parameter value.

Your Examples folder for Chapter 7 includes a file named BreakdancerObject.html that contains an example of the break dancer animation files with `<object>` and `<embed>` elements.

384

You add <param> elements as the content of an <object> element. The following code shows an example of an <object> element with parameters that plays the break dancer animation. Flash requires that you specify the name of the multimedia file to play, using the movie parameter. The embedded object also includes two additional Flash parameters: wmode and quality. The value of "transparent" assigned to the wmode parameter removes the background from the animation. The value of "high" assigned to the quality parameter plays the animation with high quality. Figure 7-5 shows how the animation appears after the background is set to transparent.

```
<object data="breakdancer.swf"
    type="application/x-shockwave-flash"
    height="400" width="100">
    <param name="movie" value="breakdancer.swf" />
    <param name="wmode" value="transparent" />
    <param name="quality" value="high" />
</object>
```

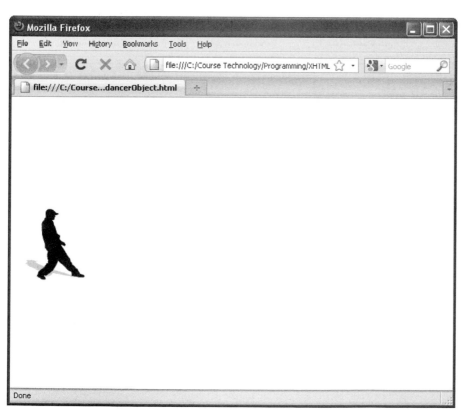

Figure 7-5   Break dancer Flash animation after setting the background to transparent

To use parameters with the <embed> element, you assign them as attributes in the opening <embed> tag. For example, to ensure that the break dancer animation is compatible with all browsers, you can nest an <embed> element in an <object> element and use the same parameters as attributes, as follows:

```
<object data="breakdancer.swf"
    type="application/x-shockwave-flash"
    height="400" width="100">
    <param name="movie" value="breakdancer.swf" />
    <param name="wmode" value="transparent" />
    <param name="quality" value="high" />
    <embed src="breakdancer.swf"
        type="application/x-shockwave-flash"
        height="400" width="100"
        movie="breakdancer.swf" wmode="transparent"
        quality="high" />
</object>
```

Short Quiz 1

1. What are add-ons and how do they work?

2. Why should you be aware of copyright issues?

3. Explain how to use the <embed> element.

4. Explain how to use the <object> element.

5. How do you set parameters for both the <embed> and <object> elements?

Incorporating Multimedia Images

As you learned earlier, the term *multimedia* refers to any type of data format that you can see or hear, including images, video, sound, and animation. Because images are considered to be multimedia elements, you should be able to use the <embed> and <object> elements to display images, along with any other type of multimedia or embedded object. As a simple example of how to use the <object>

element with an image file, consider the following code, which displays an image file named postcard.jpg:

```
<object data="postcard.jpg" type="image/jpeg"
    height="246" width="350"></p></object>
```

In the preceding code, the data attribute identifies the image file and the type attribute identifies the file as having a MIME type of "image/jpeg". Figure 7-6 shows how the object appears in Firefox.

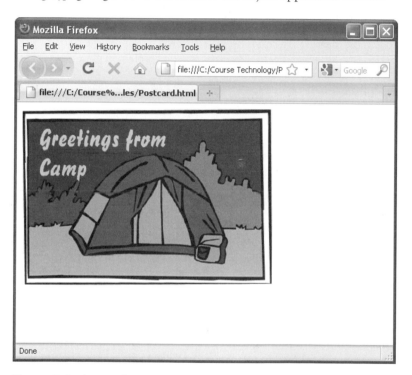

Figure 7-6 Image displayed with <object> element in Firefox

The problem with using the <embed> and <object> elements to display images is that some Web browsers, including older versions of Internet Explorer, will not properly display them. For example, consider the image shown in Figure 7-7, which is rendered in Internet Explorer. Even though sufficient space is assigned to the height and width attributes, the image is still surrounded by a box and includes a scroll bar, and getting rid of these unwanted display characteristics is difficult. Because many current Web browsers do not properly render images using <embed> and <object> elements (Internet Explorer adds scroll bars, for instance), you should continue using the <img> element to add images to your Web pages.

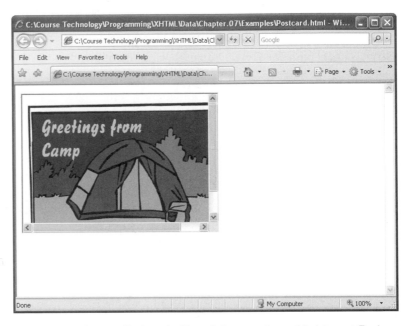

Figure 7-7   Image displayed with `<object>` element in Internet Explorer

Using Animated GIFs

Throughout this book you have used both JPG and GIF files to add images to your Web pages. In addition to being used as static images, GIF files can also include animation. An **animated GIF** is a single file containing a series of individual images that creates simple animation. It's debatable whether animated GIFs are considered "multimedia." However, because this chapter defines multimedia as any type of data format that you can see or hear, animated GIFs are discussed here. It's important to keep in mind that animated GIFs do not include sound or any user interactivity. However, they are extremely popular on the Web. If you search for "animated gif" in a search engine, you will find thousands of animated GIF images. Numerous animated GIF editors are also available, including commercial applications such as Paint Shop Pro and various Adobe products. Search for "animated gif editor" or "animated gif tool" in a search engine to find listings of additional editors.

You will not actually create animated GIFs in this chapter. However, you should have no trouble learning how to work with an animated GIF editor. All animated GIF files use the same animation technique, in which multiple images are swapped after a given time interval to create the effect of animation. For example, Figure 7-8 shows the individual frames that make up an animated GIF file named penguin.gif. You can find a copy of the penguin.gif file in your Chapter folder for Chapter 7. When displayed one after another, these images create an animation of a waddling penguin.

Figure 7-8   Animated GIF of a penguin

You add animated GIFs to your Web page in exactly the same way you add static images: by using the <img> element. Most Web browsers will automatically start the animation once the file finishes loading. The following code shows the <img> element that displays the waddling penguin animated image:

```
<img src="penguin.gif" height="200" width="200"
     alt="Animated GIF image of waddling penguin." />
```

Next, you will add an animated GIF to the kickboxing.html page of the DRG Karate Web site.

To add an animated GIF to the kickboxing.html page of the DRG Karate Web site:

1. In your text editor, open the Web page named **kickboxing.html** from your Chapter folder for Chapter 7.

2. Locate `<!-- Add animated GIF code here -->` in the document body and replace it with the following table elements and `<img>` element:

```
<tr>
    <td>
        <img src="images/karate.gif"
            alt="Animated image of a martial artist↵
                executing a side kick."
            height="140" width="105" />
    </td>
</tr>
```

3. Save the **kickboxing.html** file and open it in your Web browser. Figure 7-9 shows how the Web page appears. The animated GIF should start executing as soon as the page loads.

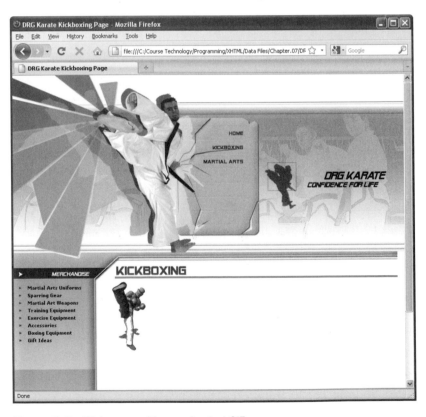

Figure 7-9 Web page with an animated GIF

4. Close your Web browser window.

Using Inline SVG (HTML 5)

Scalable Vector Graphics (SVG) is an XML specification for defining static and dynamic two-dimensional **vector graphics**, which are made up of simple objects. These objects include shapes such as polygons and circles, and objects such as lines, points, and curves. In comparison, **raster graphics**, such as photographs, are made up of arrays of pixels. Even though they are made up of simple objects, vector graphics can be extremely complex. While raster graphics typically represent a static image, vector graphics can be edited with programs such as Adobe Illustrator. SVG allows you to define a vector image using XML; you do not need to include an accompanying image file to display an SVG image. Inline SVG refers to the ability to render SVG XML elements from inside a Web page. Note that because inline SVG is an XML application, Web pages that include inline SVG must use a file extension of .xhtml or .xml for Web browsers to recognize the page as XML.

SVG is defined by the SVG 1.1 specification, which is published by the W3C at *www.w3.org/TR/SVG11/*.

Inline SVG is available in all major browsers except for Internet Explorer. Support for Inline SVG is expected to be added in Internet Explorer 9.

You define an SVG image with the `<svg>` element, and you must include the `xmlns="http://www.w3.org/2000/svg"` namespace within the opening `<svg>` tag. You can also use the attributes listed in Table 7-4.

Attribute	Description
height	Defines the height of the object using pixels or a percentage of the screen height
width	Defines the width of the object using pixels or a percentage of the screen width
version	Identifies the SVG language version
baseProfile	Identifies the minimum SVG language profile
x	Specifies the horizontal location of the upper-left corner of the object box
y	Specifies the vertical location of the upper-left corner of the object box

Table 7-4   Attributes of the `<svg>` element

To define the content of an SVG image, you use a variety of SVG XML elements, such as the `<circle>` element to create circles and the `<text>` element to create text. For example, the following code defines the Olympic rings shown in Figure 7-10. The `height` and `width` attributes define the graphic size as 300 by 650 pixels. The `<circle>` elements include several attributes: `cx`, `cy`, `r`, `stroke`, `stroke-width`, and `fill`. The `cx` and `cy` attributes define the horizontal and vertical location of the circle, and the `r` attribute (for radius) defines the size of each circle. The stroke attribute defines the color of the circle's border, the stroke-width attribute defines the width of the border, and the fill attribute determines whether the circles will be filled with a color.

```
<svg xmlns="http://www.w3.org/2000/svg"
    height="300px" width="650px">
<circle cx="150" cy="120" r="80" stroke="blue"
    stroke-width="15" fill="none" />
<circle cx="250" cy="200" r="80" stroke="orange"
    stroke-width="15" fill="none" />
<circle cx="350" cy="120" r="80" stroke="black"
    stroke-width="15" fill="none" />
<circle cx="450" cy="200" r="80" stroke="green"
    stroke-width="15" fill="none" />
<circle cx="550" cy="120" r="80" stroke="red"
    stroke-width="15" fill="none" />
</svg>
```

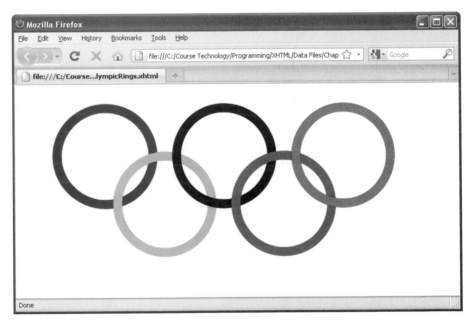

Figure 7-10 Olympic rings created with inline SVG

Using Inline MathML (HTML 5)

Mathematical Markup Language (MathML) is an XML specification for mathematical notations. Inline MathML refers to the ability to render MathML XML elements from inside a Web page. Inline MathML is similar to inline SVG; any Web pages that contain inline MathML must use a file extension of .xhtml or .xml for Web browsers to recognize the page as XML.

Inline MathML is available in all major browsers except for Internet Explorer. Support for Inline MathML is expected to be added in Internet Explorer 9.

Unlike internal SVG, when using MathML you must include the following <!DOCTYPE> declaration in your XHTML documents:

```
<!DOCTYPE html PUBLIC
    "-//W3C//DTD XHTML 1.1 plus MathML 2.0//EN"
    "http://www.w3.org/Math/DTD/mathml2/
        xhtml-math11-f.dtd">
```

You define a MathML object with the <math> element, and you must include the xmlns="http://www.w3.org/1998/Math/MathML" namespace within the opening <math> tag. The <math> object also includes a number of different attributes that are listed in the W3C MathML specification. One attribute of note is the display attribute, which determines how the MathML object will be rendered. You can assign one of two values to the display attribute: block or inline. A value of "block" renders the MathML object in a separate vertical block; a value of "inline" renders the object aligned with the adjacent text.

Using MathML is beyond the scope of this book, but to give you an idea of how it works, the following code renders a mathematical concept known as Taylor's Theorem. Notice that the <math> element includes the display attribute assigned a value of "inline," which aligns the object with the adjacent text. Figure 7-11 shows the output in a Web browser.

```
<p style="font-family: Arial; font-size: 14pt">
Taylor's Theorem reads
<math xmlns="http://www.w3.org/1998/Math/MathML"
    display="inline"><mrow>
    <mrow><mo>f</mo><mfenced>
    <mrow><mi>x</mi></mrow></mfenced>
    </mrow><mo>=</mo><mrow>
    <msubsup><mo>?</mo><mrow>
    <mrow><mi>j</mi></mrow><mo>=</mo>
    <mrow><mn>0</mn></mrow></mrow>
    <mi>8</mi></msubsup><mrow><mspace/>
    <mfenced open=" " close=" "><mrow>
    <mfrac><mrow><msup><mrow><mo>f</mo>
    </mrow><mrow><mfenced><mrow>
    <mi>j</mi></mrow></mfenced></mrow></msup>
    <mfenced><mrow><mi>0</mi></mrow></mfenced>
    </mrow><mrow><mi>j</mi><mo>!</mo></mrow></mfrac>
    <mo></mo><msup><mrow><mi>x</mi></mrow>
    <mrow><mi>j</mi></mrow></msup></mrow></mfenced>
    </mrow></mrow></mrow>
</math></p>
```

MathML is defined by the MathML Version 3.0 specification, which is published by the W3C at *www.w3.org/TR/MathML3/*.

393

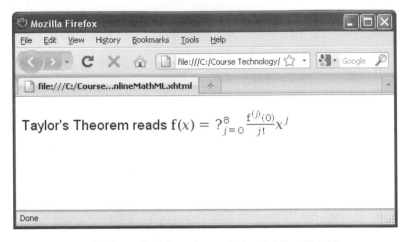

Figure 7-11   Mathematical formula created with inline MathML

Short Quiz 2

1. What are animated GIFs and how do you use them?

2. Explain how to incorporate inline SVG into your Web pages.

3. Explain how to incorporate inline MathML into your Web pages.

Adding Sounds to a Web Page

Unless they are used for the right reasons, sounds on a Web page can be annoying. When used correctly, however, they can significantly add to the value of your Web page. For example, users can listen to songs at online music sites. Or, you can offer users the chance to listen to a speech or other type of recording. Online games often include sound effects. Finally, a legitimate and important use of audio is to help a visually impaired person use your Web site. Remember that you should only add sounds to your Web pages if they provide information, provide valid entertainment, or increase a site's accessibility.

In this section, you will study the different types of audio formats and the techniques involved in adding sound to your Web pages.

Understanding Audio Formats

Numerous audio formats can be used in Web pages. Table 7-5 lists the most common audio formats and their file extensions.

Format	Extension
Advanced Audio Coding (AAC)	.aac
Audio Interchange File Format (AIFF)	.aif, .aiff
MP3	.mp3
Musical Instrument Digital Interface (MIDI)	.mid
RealAudio	.ra
Waveform Audio File Format (WAV)	.wav
Windows Media Audio	.wma, .asf
Vorbis	.ogg

Table 7-5   Common audio formats

Next, you will be introduced to each of the audio formats listed in Table 7-5.

AIFF

The Audio Interchange File Format (AIFF) was originally developed by Apple for the Macintosh OS. While other platforms now support AIFF, it is not as widely supported as other audio file types. AIFF files can be very large because the format does not support data compression.

MPEG Files (MP3)

The Moving Picture Experts Group Layer-3 Audio (MP3) format was originally developed by the Moving Picture Experts Group (MPEG) as a video format. However, because of its extremely high quality and small size due to excellent data compression, the MP3 format has become very popular for digitally recording music that can be transferred across the Internet. Unfortunately, its popularity has led to a dramatic increase in the piracy of copyrighted music.

AAC

Advanced Audio Coding (AAC) is a standardized audio format with compression and coding schemes for digital audio. AAC was designed to be the successor to MP3 and has been standardized by ISO and IEC as part of the MPEG-2 and MPEG-4 specifications.

AAC may be one of the most popular audio formats in use because it is the standard audio format for Apple products, including iTunes, iPhones, iPods, and iPads. It is also used on the Sony PlayStation Portable, Nintendo's Wii platform, and Android-based phones.

MIDI

The Musical Instrument Digital Interface (MIDI) format was originally developed in 1982 by the music industry as a way of recording and controlling sounds in electronic musical devices, such as synthesizers, and transferring those files to computers. MIDI files are fairly small, and remain a popular format for composing and editing digital music.

RealAudio

RealAudio (RA) is a proprietary format created by RealNetworks for streaming audio across the Internet. Although sounds recorded in the RA format can be downloaded and played in the same way as other audio files, the format is still mostly used for streaming audio. Unlike other types of audio formats, you can only play RA files in RealPlayer.

WAV

The Waveform Audio File Format (WAV) was developed jointly by Microsoft and IBM. WAV is considered the standard audio format for personal computers (PCs) and is one of the most popular formats on the Internet. Although the WAV format offers good quality, it is greatly reduced when WAV files are compressed. For this reason, they are not well suited for digitally recorded sounds. However, WAV files remain popular for recorded music and for short audio clips such as a sound effect or greeting.

Windows Media Audio

Windows Media Audio is the proprietary format of Windows Media Player. Windows Media Audio files are available in two formats: downloadable files saved with an extension of .wma and Active Streaming File format, which has an extension of .asf. Like RA files that can only be played in RealPlayer, Windows Media Audio files can only be played in Windows Media Player, which is widely distributed with Windows operating systems.

Vorbis

Vorbis is a free and open source audio format that is growing in popularity, primarily because it is not covered by any patents, as are most of the other audio technologies discussed here. Vorbis files run within the Ogg container format, which is a free and open technology used for executing local and streaming multimedia content.

Which Sound Format Should You Use?

Unless you are actually recording sound files, the sound format you use depends on the format of the audio files you find that suit your needs. One issue you need to consider is the add-on or multimedia application that executes the file. Recall that a Web page identifies a file format by its extension and associated MIME type, which also determine which add-on will execute the file. Some audio formats, such as WAV and MIDI files, will automatically execute in the user's default multimedia add-on or multimedia application. However, you may want to ensure that an audio file on your Web page is executed by a particular multimedia add-on so that the sound quality will be consistent from one user to the next. Or, you may need to ensure that the add-on is available for a proprietary format such as RA. To use the RA format, for instance, you need to ensure that the user's Web browser has the RealPlayer add-on installed. Next, you will learn how to play sounds on a Web page.

Playing Sounds on a Web Page

You can add a sound to a Web page by using a simple link, or by embedding the sound in the Web page using the `<object>` or `<audio>` elements. First, you will learn how to use links to sound files on your Web pages.

Linking to Sound Files

The easiest way to add a sound file to a Web page is to provide a link that the user can click to play the sound. You can add a link to a sound file in the same way you add a link to another Web page. For example, the following link plays a WAV file named laugh.wav:

```
<p><a href="laugh.wav">Need a good laugh?</a></p>
```

Using a link to add sound to a Web page is the most user-friendly option because users control when they want to play the sound. However, this option gives you no control over how the sound is played; it may be executed from an add-on within the browser or with a stand-alone multimedia application. It all depends on which software and add-ons are installed on the user's system and how the system is set up. Or, the user's computer may not be configured to play the sound format at all. More than likely, the user's computer will be set up with a common multimedia application, such as Windows Media Player or QuickTime, in which case the browser will open the stand-alone application and play the file. Your Examples folder for Chapter 7 contains a file named LaughLink.html that you can use to test the preceding link. If you have Windows Media Player installed as your default multimedia application, it will open and play the sound file, which is a short clip of people laughing. If you do not have Windows Media Player installed, you will be prompted to install the add-on. Figure 7-12 shows how the Web page and Windows Media Player appear when the file is executing.

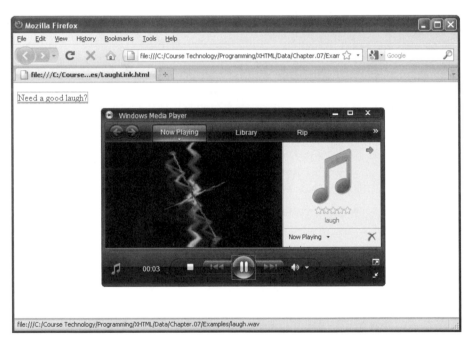

Figure 7-12 Link to an audio file

Next, you will add a MIDI sound clip of DRG Karate's theme song to the home page.

To add a MIDI sound clip of the studio's theme song to the DRG Karate home page:

1. Return to the **index.html** Web file in your text editor.

2. Add the following paragraph and link immediately above the `<div>` element containing the paragraph that begins with "Welcome to DRG Karate Studio":

```
<p style="line-height: 12px; text-align: center">
    Listen to our <a href="theme.mid">
    Theme Song</a></p>
```

3. Save the **index.html** file and open it in your Web browser.

4. Click the **Theme Song** link to play the MIDI file. You should hear the song start playing. How the file is played depends on how your system is configured.

5. Close your Web browser window. If necessary, close your multimedia application.

Embedding Sound Files with the `<object>` Element

If you want to have control over which multimedia application or add-on plays your sound file, or if you want to give users control options over the file within the Web page itself, you can use the `<object>` element. Recall that the required parameters you use will vary according to the type of embedded object. For example, Table 7-6 lists common parameters of the QuickTime add-on.

Parameter	Description
src	A string value that specifies the name of the file to be executed
autoplay	Boolean parameter that determines whether the file should start automatically after it loads
controller	Boolean parameter that specifies whether to show the QuickTime controls
loop	Boolean parameter that determines whether to play the file continuously

Table 7-6 Parameters of the QuickTime add-on

You can get the required parameters for other add-ons from the software company that created the add-on.

The following `<object>` and `<embed>` elements demonstrate how to play the laugh.wav file. The elements include the `src`, `autoplay`, and `controller` parameters. The `src` parameter is assigned the laugh.wav file, and the `autoplay` and `controller` parameters are set to true.

```
<object type="application/wmf">
<param name="src" value="laugh.wav">
<param name="controller" value="true">
<param name="autoplay" value="true">
<embed src="laugh.wav" type="application/wmf"
controller="true" autoplay="true"
autostart="true" />
</object>
```

Your Examples folder for Chapter 7 contains a file named LaughObject.html that you can use to test the preceding code. Figure 7-13 shows how a version of the document appears in Chrome.

400

When you include a sound file on your Web page that automatically executes when the page opens, be sure to add the `<object>` element as the last element on the page. Otherwise, if your sound file is very large, visitors to your Web site will stare at a blank page while the sound file finishes downloading.

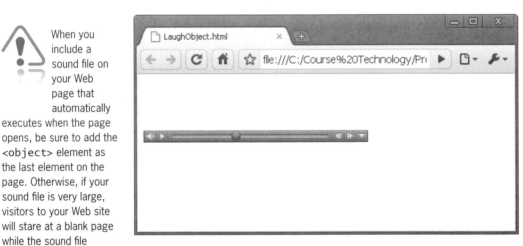

Figure 7-13 Audio file embedded with the `<object>` element

Next, you will modify the DRG Karate home page so the studio's theme song plays automatically when the Web page opens.

To modify the DRG Karate home page so the studio's theme song plays automatically when the Web page opens:

1. Return to the **index.html** Web file in your text editor.

2. Modify the paragraph that contains the link to the MIDI file so it uses an embedded link, as follows:

```
<p style="line-height: 12px; text-align: ↵
center">Listen to our Theme Song<br />
<object type="application/wmf">
    <param name="src" value="theme.mid" />
    <param name="type" value="audio/mid" />
    <param name="showcontrols" value="true" />
```

```
<param name="autostart" value="true" />
<embed src="theme.mid" type="application/wmf"
    height="15" showcontrols="true"
    autostart="true" />
</object></p>
```

3. Save the **index.html** file and open it in your Web browser. The theme song should begin playing as soon as the Web page loads, and you should see the audio controller.

4. Close your Web browser window.

Playing Sounds with the `<audio>` Element (HTML 5)

The `<audio>` element embeds audio content, such as music or audio streams, in a Web page. One of the biggest advantages the `<audio>` element has over other elements that play sound, such as the `<object>` and `<embed>` elements, is that it plays native audio within the browser and does not rely on add-ons such as plug-ins and extensions.

The `<audio>` element is available in all major browsers except Internet Explorer, although Microsoft is expected to add support in Internet Explorer 9.

Table 7-7 lists the attributes of the `<audio>` element.

Parameter	Description
autoplay	Determines whether the file should start automatically after it loads
controls	Displays audio controls
preload	Determines whether the audio will load when the page starts; this attribute is ignored if `autoplay` is present
src	Identifies the URL of the audio file

Table 7-7   Attributes of the `<audio>` element

The following `<audio>` element demonstrates how to play the laugh.wav file and includes the `src`, `autoplay`, and `controls` parameters. The `src` parameter is assigned the laugh.wav file, and the `autoplay` and `controls` parameters are set to true.

```
<audio src="laugh.wav" controls="true"
autoplay="true">
<p>Your browser does not support the audio
element.</p>
</audio>
```

Your Examples folder for Chapter 7 contains a file named LaughAudioObject.html that you can use to test the preceding link. Figure 7-14 shows how the file appears in Internet Explorer. The sound should execute as soon as the Web page loads. You can play the file again by clicking the play button.

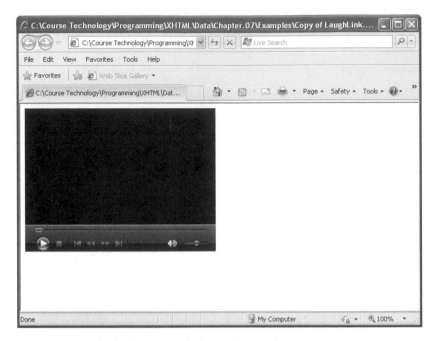

Figure 7-14   Audio file embedded with the `<audio>` element

One problem with using the `<audio>` element is that even the most current browsers do not always support other browsers' native audio formats. For example, the `<audio>` element in Firefox will not play MP3 files, while the `<audio>` element in Safari and Chrome will not play WAV files. To get around this problem, you can use the `<source>` element within the `<audio>` element to identify multiple audio sources. The two primary attributes of the `<source>` element are `src`, which identifies the URL of the audio file, and `type`, which specifies the MIME type. The following code demonstrates how to use the `<source>` element to specify WAV and MP3 versions of the laugh audio file:

For a free online utility that converts your media files, go to *http://media.io*.

```
<audio autoplay="true" controls="true">
    <source src="laugh.wav" type="audio/wav" />
    <source src="laugh.mp3" type="audio/mp3" />
<p>Your browser does not support the audio
element.</p>
</audio>
```

Next, you will modify the DRG Karate home page so it plays the studio's theme song with an `<audio>` element. Your DRGKarate folder contains MP3 and WAV versions of the theme song.

To modify the DRG Karate home page so the studio's theme song plays automatically when the Web page opens:

1. Return to the **index.html** Web file in your text editor.

2. Replace the <object> element with the following <audio> element:

```
<audio autoplay="true" controls="controls"
    style="width: 200px">
    <source src="theme.mp3" type="audio/mp3" />
    <source src="theme.wav" type="audio/wav" />
Your browser does not support the audio element.
</audio>
```

3. Save the **index.html** file and open it in your Web browser. The theme song should begin playing as soon as the Web page loads, and you should see the <audio> element controller.

4. Close your Web browser window.

Short Quiz 3

1. Explain how to link to sound files.

2. Explain how to play sound files with the <object> element.

3. Explain how to play sound files with the <audio> element.

Adding Video and Applets to a Web Page

Video is another type of multimedia format that can degrade the value of a Web site if used incorrectly. However, when used appropriately, video can make your Web site useful and interesting. Many types of video can be used on a Web site, ranging from entertainment to news clips. The big challenge is that video files can become enormous. If you are using streaming media, you should limit your video to short clips unless you are certain that the visitors to your site have high-speed Internet access. If your Web pages are restricted to a corporate site with a fast internal network, for example, then video can be an invaluable tool for providing employees with online training or other types of information. As with audio, be sure that you only add video to your Web pages if it provides useful information or serves valid entertainment purposes.

Understanding Video Formats

Table 7-8 lists the most common Web video formats and their file extensions.

Format	Extension
Audio Video Interleave (AVI)	.avi
Flash	.swf
Moving Picture Experts Group (MPEG)	.mpg, .mpeg
QuickTime	.mov
RealVideo	.rv
Theora	.ogg
Windows Media Video	.wmv, .asf

Table 7-8   Common video formats

Next, you will learn a little about each of the video formats listed in Table 7-8.

AVI

The Audio Video Interleave (AVI) format was developed by Microsoft and is commonly used on the Internet. However, AVI is not always supported on other platforms or browsers, and it is being replaced on most Windows platforms by the proprietary Windows Media Video (WMV) format of Windows Media Player. Even so, you will find that many of the video clips on the Internet use the AVI format.

Flash/Shockwave

The Flash/Shockwave movie format has become one of the most popular multimedia formats in recent years. Flash movies are really animations that can contain other types of video. One of the great benefits of Flash movies is that they are extremely compact, allowing for fast downloads and execution via the Web. They are also popular for creating Web page intros, interactive navigational tools, and other types of multimedia effects.

MPEG

The Moving Picture Experts Group (MPEG) format offers videos of extremely high quality and small size. MPEG-4 Part 14 (MP4) is a related technology based on Apple's QuickTime technology; it is considered by many to be the next global multimedia standard. The MPEG format is one of the best choices for video files because of its high quality, small file size, and compatibility across many types of platforms and browsers.

Apple QuickTime

Apple's QuickTime format (MOV) is also one of the most popular video formats on the Internet. QuickTime is broadly supported by many Web browsers and platforms other than Macintosh.

RealVideo

The RealVideo (RV) format is the video version of the proprietary format created by RealNetworks for streaming audio across the Internet. As with the RA format, RV files can be downloaded and played just like other video files, although the format is still mostly used for streaming audio. RV files can only be played in RealPlayer. Note that because this format is designed to be streamed, video quality is often reduced.

Theora

Theora is a free and open source video format that is growing in popularity, primarily because it is not covered by any patents, as are most of the other video technologies discussed here. Theora files can be used locally and streamed. As with the Vorbis audio format, Theora runs within the Ogg free and open container format.

Windows Media Video

The Windows Media Video format is the video version of the proprietary format of Windows Media Player. As with Windows Media Audio files, Windows Media Video files are available in two formats: downloadable files saved with an extension of .wmv and streaming files saved with an extension of .asf. Windows Media Video files can only be played in Windows Media Player, which is widely distributed with Windows operating systems.

Which Video Format Should You Use?

As with sound formats, unless you are actually recording your own videos, the video formats you use depend on your particular needs. The two most common types of downloadable video files are the QuickTime and AVI/WMV formats. For animation, there is little competition for the Flash/Shockwave format. For streaming video, QuickTime, Windows Media Player, and RealPlayer are all excellent choices.

Playing Video on a Web Page

Adding video to a Web page is similar to adding audio. You can add a simple link or embed the video in the Web page using the `<object>` and `<video>` elements. You will examine these methods in the next three sections.

Linking to Video Files

Linking to video files works exactly like linking to audio files. Using a link to add video to a Web page is especially user-friendly given the large size of many videos. Plus, because links open the video file on another page or in an external multimedia application, you do not need to worry about leaving enough space on your Web page to accommodate the multimedia player. For example, the following link plays an AVI file named babycha3.avi:

```
<p><a href="babycha3.avi">The Dancing Baby</a></p>
```

The preceding code shows an example of one of the most ubiquitous pieces of multimedia animation ever developed for the Internet: the "dancing baby," sometimes referred to as "Oogachaka." There have been many variations of Oogachaka since it was first released on the Internet in 1998; the preceding file is one of the originals. Figure 7-15 shows a frame from the animation in Windows Media Player. The purpose of this example is only to show you how to use video; it is not an example of good Web page design. While Oogachaka is entertaining, it serves little purpose, so please do not use it on your Web pages. (Even one of the original designers of the dancing baby, Ron Lussier, states on his Web site that the baby video "…needs to evolve or die".)

Figure 7-15   Dancing baby animation playing in Windows Media Player

Next, you will add links to the DRG Karate kickboxing page that play video clips of sparring matches in the kickboxing class. The four video clips you will need are in the DRGKarate Chapter folder for Chapter 7. The folder also contains four image files that you will use to create image links to each of the video clips.

Depending on your system configuration, you may need to install a multimedia application before performing the next exercise.

To add links to the DRG Karate kickboxing page that play video clips of sparring matches in the kickboxing class:

1. Return to the **kickboxing.html** file in your text editor.

2. Immediately after the row that contains the karate.gif image, add the following table that will contain links to the video clips:

    ```
    <tr><td><table style="border: 0px;
        margin-left: 40px; border-spacing: 0px 20px">
    <colgroup span="2" style="width: 200px">
    </colgroup>
    <tr>
        <td> </td>
        <td> </td>
    </tr>
    <tr>
        <td> </td>
        <td> </td>
    </tr>
    </table></tr>
    ```

3. Replace the nonbreaking space character ( ) in the first cell with the following image link, which plays the alyson_kevin.mov video clip:

    ```
    <h3><a href="alyson_kevin.mov">
    Alyson &amp; Kevin</a></h3>
    <a href="alyson_kevin.mov">
    <img src="images/alyson_kevin.jpg"
    height="140" width="160" alt="Video frame of
        Alyson and Kevin sparring." /></a>
    ```

4. Replace the nonbreaking space character ( ) in the second cell with the following image link, which plays the juan_kevin.mov video clip:

    ```
    <h3><a href="juan_kevin.mov">Juan &amp;
    Kevin</a></h3>
    <a href="juan_kevin.mov">
    <img src="images/juan_kevin.jpg"
    height="140" width="160" alt="Video frame
        of Juan and Kevin sparring." /></a>
    ```

5. Replace the nonbreaking space character ( ) in the third cell with the following image link, which plays the kamau_yahoteh.mov video clip:

    ```
    <h3><a href="kamau_yahoteh.mov">Kamau &amp;
    Yahoteh</a></h3>
    ```

```
<a href="kamau_yahoteh.mov">
<img src="images/kamau_yahoteh.jpg"
height="140" width="160" alt="Video frame↵
    of Kamau and Yahoteh sparring." /></a>
```

6. Replace the nonbreaking space character ( ) in the fourth cell with the following image link, which plays the kevin_steve.mov video clip:

```
<h3><a href="kevin_steve.mov">Kevin &amp;
Steve</a></h3>
<a href="kevin_steve.mov">
<img src="images/kevin_steve.jpg"
height="140" width="160" alt="Video frame↵
    of Kevin and Steve sparring." /></a>
```

7. Save the **kickboxing.html** file and then validate it with the W3C Markup Validation Service at **http://validator. w3.org/#validate_by_upload**. If you receive any errors, fix them and then revalidate the document. Once the document is valid, close it in your text editor and then open it in your Web browser and test the video links. How the file plays depends on how your system is configured. Figure 7-16 shows the index.html file with the new video links.

Figure 7-16   Kickboxing.html page after adding video links

8. Close your Web browser window. If necessary, close your multimedia application.

Embedding Video Files with the `<object>` Element

Video links suffer from the same liability as audio links, in that you have no control over how the sound is played. Video may be executed from an add-on within the browser or from a stand-alone multimedia application; it all depends on how the user's system is set up. Although visual display is not so important when playing sound files, it is very important when playing a video. If you want to create a custom Web page for playing videos, you must be able to specify the type of add-on that will play the video in order for your page to display properly. For example, Figure 7-17 shows a Web page from Yahoo! Movies that plays a video trailer from the film *Clash of the Titans*. Without knowing which add-on will execute the file, it would be nearly impossible to know if the Web page would render as expected in a user's browser.

Figure 7-17 Video trailer from Yahoo! Movies

There is little difference between how you embed a sound file and a video file, with the exception of the parameters you specify. The following <object> and <embed> elements play a video file named car.wmv that shows a car racing through a desert. The code includes three parameters: filename, which specifies the URL of the video file, autostart, which determines whether the video starts automatically, and showcontrols, which determines whether to show the video controls.

```
<object type="application/wmf"
    height="480" width="640">
    <param name="filename" value="car.wmv" />
    <param name="autostart" value="true" />
    <param name="showcontrols" value="true" />
    <embed src="car.wmv" type="application/wmf"
        height="480" width="640"
        autostart="true" showcontrols="true"
        loop="true" />
</object>
```

Your Chapter folder for Chapter 7 contains a file named Car.html that you can use to test the preceding code. Figure 7-18 shows how the video appears in a Web browser.

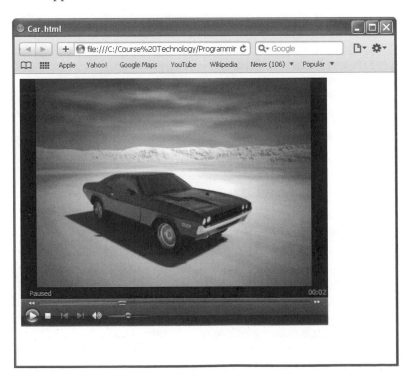

Figure 7-18   Output of car.wmv executed with the <object> and <embed> elements

In the next exercise, you will use the QuickTime add-on to play an embedded QuickTime file. Table 7-9 lists common QuickTime parameters.

Parameter	Description
autoplay	Boolean parameter that determines whether the file should start automatically after it loads.
controller	Boolean parameter that specifies whether to show the QuickTime controls.
loop	Boolean parameter that determines whether the movie should play continuously. You can also assign a value of "palindrome" to this parameter, which specifies that the movie should play alternately forward and backward.
src	A string value that specifies the filename to execute.

Table 7-9 Common parameters of the QuickTime add-on

Next, you will add embedded videos to the martial_arts.html page of the DRG Karate Web site. The videos play clips of other martial art techniques. The four video clips you will need are in your Chapter folder for Chapter 7.

The video clips you will add are from the American Independent Karate Instructor's Association at *www.aikia.net.*

411

To add embedded video clips of other martial art techniques to the DRG Karate home page:

1. Return to your text editor and open the **martial_arts.html** file in the DRGKarate folder in your Chapter folder for Chapter 7.

2. Locate `<!-- Add QuickTime here -->` in the document body and replace it with the following table elements:

```
<tr><td><table style="border: 0px; ↵
    margin-left: 40px; border-spacing: 0px 20px">
<colgroup span="2" style="width: 200px">
</colgroup>
<tr>
    <td> </td>
    <td> </td>
</tr>
<tr>
    <td> </td>
    <td> </td>
</tr>
</table></td></tr>
```

3. Replace the nonbreaking space character ( ) in the first cell with the following heading element and `<object>` element, which plays an aikido video clip:

```
<h3>
    Aikido</h3>
<object type="application/quicktime"
width="160" height="140">
<param name="src" value="aikido.mov" />
<param name="controller" value="true" />
<param name="autoplay" value="false" />
<embed src="aikido.mov"
    type="application/quicktime"
    width="160" height="140" controller="true"
    autoplay="false" />
</object>
```

4. Replace the nonbreaking space character ( ) in the second cell with the following heading element and `<object>` element, which plays a judo video clip:

```
<h3>
    Judo</h3>
<object type="application/quicktime"
width="160" height="140">
<param name="src" value="judo.mov" />
<param name="controller" value="true" />
<param name="autoplay" value="false" />
<embed src="judo.mov" type="application/ ↵
    quicktime"
    width="160" height="140" controller="true"
    autoplay="false" />
</object>
```

5. Replace the nonbreaking space character ( ) in the third cell with the following heading element and `<object>` element, which plays a ju-jutsu video clip:

```
<h3>
    Ju-Jutsu</h3>
<object type="application/quicktime"
width="160" height="140">
<param name="src" value="jujutsu.mov" />
<param name="controller" value="true" />
<param name="autoplay" value="false" />
<embed src="jujutsu.mov"
    type="application/quicktime"
    width="160" height="140" controller="true"
    autoplay="false" />
</object>
```

6. Replace the nonbreaking space character ( ) in the fourth cell with the following heading element and <object> element, which plays a kendo video clip:

```
<h3>
    Kendo</h3>
    <object type="application/quicktime"
    width="160" height="140">
    <param name="src" value="kendo.mov" />
    <param name="controller" value="true" />
    <param name="autoplay" value="false" />
    <embed src="kendo.mov"
        type="application/quicktime"
        width="160" height="140" controller="true"
        autoplay="false" />
</object>
```

7. Save the **martial_arts.html** file and then validate it with the W3C Markup Validation Service at **http://validator .w3.org/#validate_by_upload**. If you receive any errors, fix them and then revalidate the document. Once the document is valid, close it in your text editor and then open it in your Web browser and test the embedded videos. Figure 7-19 shows an example of how your screen should appear.

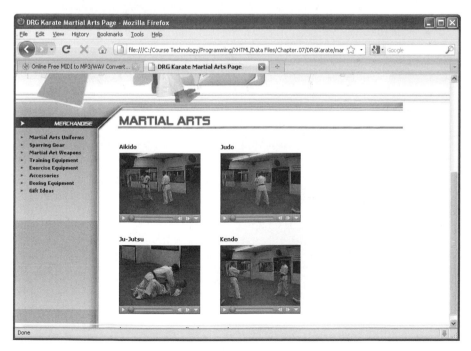

Figure 7-19 martial_arts.html file after adding embedded video objects

8. Close your Web browser window.

Playing Videos with the `<video>` Element (HTML 5)

The `<video>` element defines video content such as movie clips or video streams. Unlike the HTML 5 `<audio>` element, the `<video>` element has a long way to go before it is ready for prime time. The main challenge has been that browser companies have not agreed on which video formats the `<video>` element should support. For example, Firefox supports the Theora format, but not MPEG-4. Internet Explorer supports MPEG-4, but not Theora. Until there is more uniform support for video standards, you should avoid using this element and instead use the `<object>` or `<embed>` elements.

When the `<video>` element is more widely supported, it will include the attributes listed in Table 7-10.

Attribute	Description
autoplay	Determines whether the file should start automatically after it loads
controls	Displays video controls
height	Determines the height of the object
loop	Determines whether the video will play once or keep looping
preload	Determines whether the video will load when the page starts; this attribute is ignored if `autoplay` is present
src	Identifies the URL of the audio file
width	Determines the width of the object

Table 7-10   Attributes of the `<video>` element

You use code similar to the following to execute a Theora version of the cars video with the `<video>` element:

```
<video src="car.ogg" autoplay="autoplay"
    controls="true" />
```

Your Chapter folder for Chapter 7 contains a file named CarVideo.html that you can use to test the preceding code. Keep in mind that the code will not run in Internet Explorer.

Embedding Java Applets

In this section, you will learn how to add Java applets and ActiveX controls to your Web pages. An **applet** is a Java program that runs within a Web page. Applets function the same way as the multimedia files that you embed in your Web pages. However, in addition to being able to display multimedia files, applets are often used to create "mini-programs" that run within the confines of a Web page.

Applets were once the most popular tool for data embedded in Web pages; however, JavaScript, DHTML techniques, and add-ons such as Flash movies have been gaining ground on applets. Because they are written in the powerful Java language, applets are still useful if you need to create interactivity that is a little too complicated for JavaScript and DHTML. For example, advanced scientific calculators, complex games, and networking functionality are all easier to create in Java than in JavaScript. The downside to creating applets is that they require a strong knowledge of Java, which is considerably more difficult to master than JavaScript.

You use the `<object>` element to add applets to your Web pages. Adding applets with `<object>` elements is similar to adding other types of multimedia elements, except that you declare a MIME type of "application/x-java-applet" and a parameter named `code` to identify the applet file. The following code shows an example of an `<object>` element that displays a rotating, twisting, three-dimensional clock. The element also contains several `<param>` elements that control the display of the applet. Figure 7-20 shows how the applet appears in a Web browser.

```
<object type="application/x-java-applet"
    height="200" width="300">
    <param name="code" value="Clock3D.class" />
    <param name="fps value="18">
    <param name="a1" value="12500">
    <param name="pixd" value="29">
    <param name="pixangle" value="5">
    <param name="radius" value="26">
    <param name="roty" value="-4">
    <param name="rotx" value="0">
    <param name="rotz" value="0.401">
    <param name="irotx" value="0">
    <param name="iroty" value="0">
    <param name="irotz" value="00">
    <param name="style" value="1">
    <param name="color" value="#00ff66">
    <param name="bgcolor" value="#000000">
    <param name="12hour" value="0">
</object>
```

415

Very few new applets are being developed today because programmers favor more modern techniques using JavaScript and add-ons. Applets you find on the Internet are usually quite old.

Many people think that JavaScript is related to Java or is a simplified version of it. However, the languages are considerably different. JavaScript was created by Netscape and was originally called LiveScript. With the release of Navigator 2.0, the name was changed to JavaScript to take advantage of the rising popularity of Java, which was created by Sun Microsystems.

Your Examples folder for Chapter 7 contains a working version of the three-dimensional clock in a file named 3DClock.html.

The three-dimensional clock applet is free for noncommercial use. For information on the developer and how to configure the applet parameters, refer to the 3DClock.html file in your Examples folder for Chapter 7.

416

 Applets will only run in a browser if Java is enabled. To enable Java applets in Firefox, click the Tools menu and then click Options. In the Options dialog box, click the Content tab and ensure that the Java box is selected, then click OK. To enable Java applets in Internet Explorer, click the Tools menu and then click Internet Options. In the Internet Options dialog box, click the Security tab and then click Custom level. In the Security Settings dialog box, locate the Scripting section and ensure that the Scripting of Java applets section is set to "Enable". Click OK to close each dialog box, and then restart Internet Explorer.

To complete the following steps, your Web browser must be configured to run Java applets.

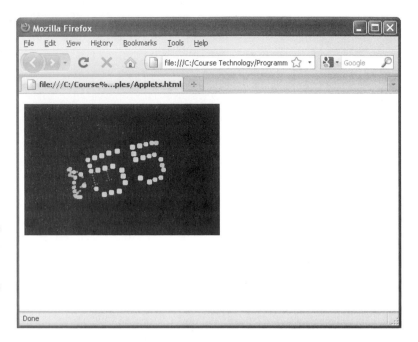

Figure 7-20   Three-dimensional Java applet in a Web browser

Next, you will use the `<object>` element to add a simple applet named PulseText to the DRG Karate home page. The PulseText applet is written by David Coldwell; it is freely available on the Java Boutique Web site at *www.javaboutique.com*, although you can also find a copy of the class file, PulseText.class, in your Chapter folder for Chapter 7. The PulseText applet creates a banner with some animated text. You will replace the `<h1>` element in the DRG Karate home page with the PulseText applet. The following exercise uses some basic parameters that are available with the PulseText applet. You can find a complete listing of parameters for the applet on the Java Boutique Web site.

To add a simple applet named PulseText to the DRG Karate home page:

1. Return to the **index.html** Web file in your text editor.

2. Locate `<!-- Add applet code here -->` and replace it with a table row and cell that contains the Flash animation.

```
<tr><td>
<object type="application/x-java-applet" width="604"
height="24">
<param name="code" value="PulseText" />
<param name="text" value="DRG Karate Studio" />
<param name="bkd-color" value="#003333" />
```

```
<param name="text-color" value="#CCFFFF" />
<param name="pulse-color" value="#FFCC99" />
<param name="font"
    value="ComicSans-bolditalic-20" />
</object>
</td></tr>
```

3. Save the **index.html** file and then validate it with the W3C Markup Validation Service at **http://validator .w3.org/#validate_by_upload**. If you receive any errors, fix them and then revalidate the document. Once the document is valid, close it in your text editor and then open it in your Web browser. Figure 7-21 shows how the applet appears.

417

Figure 7-21 DRG Karate home page after adding an applet

4. Close your Web browser window and text editor.

Short Quiz 4

1. What happens when a user clicks a video file link?

2. Explain how to play video files with the `<object>` element.

3. Explain how to play sound files with the `<video>` element.

4. How do you embed Java applets in Web pages?

Summing Up

- Multimedia refers to any type of data format that you can see, hear, or interact with, including images, video, sound, games, and animation. You should only add multimedia to your Web pages if it serves a purpose. Your goal in providing multimedia should always be to provide information (such as an instructional video) or to entertain.

- To display and execute multimedia within a Web page, browsers use helper applications called add-ons. Add-ons can include plug-ins, which are external software components that display particular types of media, and extensions, which provide access to multimedia by integrating with the browser itself.

- A Web page identifies a file format by its extension and associated MIME type.

- The term *embedded object* refers to any type of multimedia file or program that you can add to your Web pages.

- If an image or data file is not identified as public domain, you must contact the creator and either pay a licensing fee or obtain permission to use the file.

- The `<embed>` and `<object>` elements are used to add audio, video, images, and other types of multimedia content to Web pages. When working with multimedia elements, you can set parameters for both the `<object>` and `<embed>` elements.

- The `height` and `width` attributes determine the size of an add-on's bounding box—a rectangular area on a Web page in which an object executes.

- An animated GIF is a single file of individual images that create simple animation.

- Scalable Vector Graphics (SVG) is an XML specification for defining static and dynamic two-dimensional vector graphics such as polygons, circles, lines, points, and curves.

- Mathematical Markup Language (MathML) is an XML specification for mathematical notations.

- The easiest way to add a sound or video file to a Web page is to provide a link to it.

- The `<audio>` element embeds audio content such as music or audio streams in a Web page.

- The `<video>` element defines video content such as movie clips or video streams.

- An applet is a Java program that runs within a Web page.

- You use the `<object>` element to add applets to your Web pages.

Comprehension Check

1. The term *multimedia* refers to which of the following data formats? (Choose all that apply.)

   a. images

   b. video

   c. sound

   d. animation

2. Describe some valid reasons for adding multimedia to your Web pages.

3. Explain how Internet connection speed affects multimedia.

4. With streaming media technology, the entire file must download before it can execute. True or False?

5. Plug-ins are also known as _____.

   a. sub applications

   b. batch files

   c. help applications

   d. extensions

6. Internet Explorer primarily uses ActiveX controls to execute embedded objects. True or False?

7. ActiveX controls are also referred to as _____.

   a. plug-ins

   b. applets

   c. libraries

   d. parameters

8. Explain the copyright issues involved with multimedia data files that you find on the Internet.

9. The only required attribute of the `<embed>` element is _____.

   a. `href`

   b. `class`

   c. `src`

   d. `source`

10. Why don't you need to specify the MIME type with the `<embed>` element?

11. What is a bounding box and how do you use it?

12. How do you ensure that your multimedia elements will run in all browsers?

13. Which attributes does the `<param>` element support in HTML 5? (Choose all that apply.)

   a. `name`

   b. `type`

   c. `value`

   d. `valuetype`

14. Explain how to use parameters with the `<embed>` element.

15. Animated GIFs consist of a single file. True or False?

16. Which of the following elements are deprecated in XHTML? (Choose all that apply.)

    a. `<bgsound>`

    b. `<embed>`

    c. `<param>`

    d. `<applet>`

17. You should use the `<object>` element to add images to your Web pages. True or False?

18. Which of the following parameters is common to all plug-ins? (Choose all that apply.)

    a. `autoplay`

    b. `src`

    c. `file`

    d. `loop`

19. Explain how a Web page determines which multimedia plug-in to execute when a multimedia file is the target of a link.

20. Where should you place an `<object>` element that executes a sound as soon as a Web page loads?

    a. at the start of the document head

    b. at the end of the document head

    c. at the start of the document body

    d. at the end of the document body

Reinforcement Exercises

 Exercise 7-1

In this exercise you will create a Web page with a Flash intro for a company called GossComm. A Flash intro is typically used when a visitor first enters your Web site; the intro usually includes marketing content, animation, and sound. Your Exercises folder for Chapter 7 contains the files you need for this exercise.

1. Create a new HTML 5 document in your text editor and use "GossComm" as the content of the `<title>` element.

2. Add the following `<div>` element to the document body:

    ```
    <div style="text-align: center">
    </div>
    ```

3. Next, add the following `<object>` element to the `<div>` element:

    ```
    <object data="GossComm.swf"
        type="application/x-shockwave-flash"
        height="230" width="450">
        <param name="movie" value="GossComm.swf" />
        <param name="loop" value="false" />
        <param name="menu" value="false" />
        <param name="quality" value="high" />
    </object>
    ```

4. Finally, add the following `<embed>` element above the closing `</object>` tag:

    ```
    <embed src="GossComm.swf"
        type="application/x-shockwave-flash"
        height="230" width="450" loop="false"
        menu="false" quality="high" />
    ```

5. Save the document as **FlashIntro.html** in your Exercises folder for Chapter 7, and validate the document with the W3C Markup Validation Service.

6. Open the **FlashIntro.html** file in your Web browser to ensure that the Flash animation runs correctly.

7. Close your Web browser window.

Exercise 7-2

In this exercise, you will create a Web page with links that play animal sounds. Your Exercises folder for Chapter 7 contains sound files that you can use.

1. Create a new HTML 5 document in your text editor and use "Animal Sounds" as the content of the `<title>` element.

2. Add the following heading element to the document body:

```
<h1>Animal Sounds</h1>
```

3. Next, add the following links that play animal sounds:

```
<p>Listen to a <a href="chimpanzee.wav">
chimpanzee</a>.<br />
Listen to a <a href="bird.wav">bird</a>.<br />
Listen to a <a href="cat.wav">cat</a>.<br />
Listen to a <a href="cow.wav">cow</a>.<br />
Listen to a <a href="dog.wav">dog</a>.<br />
Listen to a <a href="duck.wav">duck</a>.<br />
Listen to a <a href="horse.wav">horse</a>.</p>
```

4. Save the document as **AnimalSounds.html** in your Exercises folder for Chapter 7, and validate the document with the W3C Markup Validation Service.

5. Open the **AnimalSounds.html** file in your Web browser and test the sound links.

6. Close your Web browser window.

Exercise 7-3

In this exercise, you will create a Web page that uses <audio> elements to pronounce the letters of the alphabet and the numbers 1 through 10. Your Exercises folder for Chapter 7 contains WAV and MP3 sound files that you can use. You will create the Web page so it is valid and works in all current browsers.

1. Create a new HTML 5 document in your text editor and use "Pronunciation" as the content of the <title> element.

2. Add the following <h1> element to the document body:

```
<h1>Pronunciation</h1>
```

3. Add the following style section to the document head:

```
<style type="text/css">
    body
    {
        font-family: Tahoma;
        font-weight: bold;
    }
    table
    {
        table-layout: fixed;
        border-collapse: collapse;
        empty-cells: show;
    }
```

```
    tr, td, th
    {
        border: 1px solid black;
        text-align: center;
        vertical-align: middle;
    }
    td
    {
        line-height: 60px;
    }
</style>
```

4. Add the following heading element and table to the document body. The table will contain two columns: one for letters and one for numbers.

```
<h1>Pronunciation</h1>
<table>
    <tr>
        <th>
            Letters
        </th>
        <th>
            Numbers
        </th>
    </tr>
</table>
```

5. Add the following row to the end of the table. The first column displays an audio object that pronounces the letter *A* and the second column displays an audio object that pronounces the number *1*.

```
<tr>
    <td>
        A
        <audio controls="controls" style="width: ↵
            200px">
            <source src="A.wav" type="audio/wav" />
            <source src="A.mp3" type="audio/mp3" />
        </audio>
    </td>
    <td>
        1
        <audio controls="controls" style="width: ↵
            200px">
            <source src="1.wav" type="audio/wav" />
            <source src="1.mp3" type="audio/mp3" />
        </audio>
    </td>
</tr>
```

6. Continue building the table so the left column displays audio objects for the letters A through Z and the right column displays audio objects for the letters 1 through 10.

7. Save the document as **Pronunciation.html** in your Exercises folder for Chapter 7, and validate the document with the W3C Markup Validation Service.

8. Open the **Pronunciation.html** file in your Web browser and test the sound links.

9. Close your Web browser window.

Exercise 7-4

In this exercise, you will create a Web page with embedded videos of jungle animals. You will open the video files using the Windows Media Video plug-in. Your Exercises folder for Chapter 7 contains video files that you can use.

1. Create a new HTML 5 document in your text editor and use "The Jungle" as the content of the `<title>` element.

2. Add the following `<h1>` element to the document body:

   ```
   <h1>The Jungle</h1>
   ```

3. Add the following elements to the document body. These elements display a video of monkeys:

   ```
   <h2>
       Monkeys</h2>
   <object type="application/wmf" height="200"
       width="220">
       <param name="filename" value="monkeys.wmv" />
       <param name="autostart" value="true" />
       <param name="showcontrols" value="true" />
       <embed src="monkeys.wmv" type="application/wmf"
           height="200" width="220" autostart="false"
           showcontrols="true" loop="false" />
   </object>
   ```

4.   At the end of the document body, add the following elements, which display a video of crocodiles:

```
<h2>
    Crocodiles</h2>
<object type="application/wmf" height="200"
    width="220">
    <param name="filename" value="crocodiles.wmv" />
    <param name="autostart" value="true" />
    <param name="showcontrols" value="true" />
    <embed src="crocodiles.wmv"
        type="application/wmf" height="200"
        width="220" autostart="false"
        showcontrols="true" loop="false" />
</object>
```

5.   At the end of the document body, add the following elements, which display a video of a snake:

```
<h2>
    Snake</h2>
<object type="application/wmf" height="200"
    width="220">
    <param name="filename" value="snake.wmv" />
    <param name="autostart" value="true" />
    <param name="showcontrols" value="true" />
    <embed src="snake.wmv" type="application/wmf"
        height="200" width="220" autostart="false"
        showcontrols="true" loop="false" />
</object>
```

6.   Save the document as **Jungle.html** in your Exercises folder for Chapter 7, and validate the document with the W3C Markup Validation Service.

7.   Open the **Jungle.html** file in your Web browser and test the videos.

8.   Close your Web browser window.

Exercise 7-5

In this exercise, you will create a Web page with embedded videos of space exploration. You will open the video files using the QuickTime plug-in. Your Exercises folder for Chapter 7 contains video files that you can use.

1.   Create a new HTML 5 document in your text editor and use "Space Exploration" as the content of the <title> element.

2. Add the following <h1> element to the document body:

```
<h1>Space Exploration</h1>
```

3. Add the following table to the end of the document body:

```
<table style="width: 50%; table-layout: fixed ">
<colgroup span="2" style="width: 50%"></colgroup>
<tr><td></td><td></td></tr>
<tr><td></td><td></td></tr>
</table>
```

4. Add the following elements to the first table cell in the first row. These elements display a video of the space shuttle lifting off:

```
<h2>
    The Space Shuttle</h2>
    <object type="application/quicktime"
        width="250" height="220">
    <param name="src" value="space_shuttle.mov" />
    <param name="controller" value="true" />
    <embed src="space_shuttle.mov"
        type="application/quicktime"
        width="250" height="220" controller="true" />
</object>
```

5. Add the following elements to the second table cell in the first row. These elements display a video of the moon:

```
<h2>
    The Moon</h2>
    <object type="application/quicktime"
        width="250" height="220">
    <param name="src" value="moon.mov" />
    <param name="controller" value="true" />
    <embed src="moon.mov"
        type="application/quicktime"
        width="250" height="220" controller="true" />
</object>
```

6. Add the following elements to the first table cell in the second row. These elements display a video of the planet Jupiter:

```
<h2>
    Jupiter</h2>
    <object type="application/quicktime"
        width="250" height="220">
    <param name="src" value="jupiter.mov" />
    <param name="controller" value="true" />
    <embed src="jupiter.mov"
        type="application/quicktime"
        width="250" height="220" controller="true" />
</object>
```

7. Add the following elements to the second table cell in the second row. These elements display a video of the planet Saturn:

```
<h2>
    Saturn</h2>
    <object type="application/quicktime"
        width="250" height="220">
    <param name="src" value="saturn.mov" />
    <param name="controller" value="true" />
    <embed src="saturn.mov"
        type="application/quicktime"
        width="250" height="220" controller="true" />
</object>
```

8. Save the document as **SpaceExploration.html** in your Exercises folder for Chapter 7, and validate the document with the W3C Markup Validation Service.

9. Open the **SpaceExploration.html** file in your Web browser and test the videos.

10. Close your Web browser window.

Exercise 7-6

In this exercise, you will create a Web page that includes a Java applet named ChompMan, which includes a PacMan-like graphic eating the text you specify. ChompMan is a free applet that was downloaded from the Java Boutique. Your Exercises folder for Chapter 7 contains two files: a Java applet class named ChompText.class and an image it needs named chompani.gif.

1. Create a new HTML 5 document in your text editor and use "Chomp Man" as the content of the <title> element.

2. Add the following <applet> element to the document body. Be sure to enter your name as the value of the text parameter.

```
<object type="application/x-java-applet"
    width="250" height="55">
    <param name="code" value="ChompText.class" />
    <param name="text" value="your name" />
    <param name="textcolor" value="0000FF" />
    <param name="bgcolor" value="FFFFFF" />
</object>
```

3. Save the document as **ChompMan.html** in your Exercises folder for Chapter 7, and validate the document with the W3C Markup Validation Service.

4. Open the **ChompMan.html** file in your Web browser. You should see a PacMan-like character eat the letters in your name.

5. Close your Web browser window.

Discovery Projects

For the following projects, save the files you create in your Projects folder for Chapter 7 and validate them with the W3C Markup Validation Service.

Discovery Project 7-1

Your Projects folder for Chapter 7 contains a Flash intro animation named realestate.swf. Create a Web page that runs the animation. Save the Web page as **RealEstateFlash.html**.

Discovery Project 7-2

Your Projects folder for Chapter 7 contains two music files named DiscoDancer.wav and DiscoDancer.mp3. Create a Web page that uses the <audio> element to play music files. Save the Web page as **DiscoDancer.html** and ensure that it will run in multiple browsers.

Discovery Project 7-3

Your Projects folder for Chapter 7 contains six videos of a baseball umpire making various calls. Use embedded objects to create a Web page that displays all six videos using the Windows Media Player plug-in. Arrange the embedded objects in a table that is two rows long and three columns wide. Save the Web page as **UmpireSchool.html**.

Discovery Project 7-4

Your Projects folder for Chapter 7 contains two videos named santa_monica.mov and san_francisco.mov. Create a Web page that displays both videos using the QuickTime plug-in. Save the Web page as **California.html**.

Discovery Project 7-5

Your Projects folder for Chapter 7 contains two videos named welcome.mov and orientation.mov. Create a Human Resources Web page that displays both videos using the QuickTime plug-in. Save the Web page as **HumanResources.html**.

Introduction to JavaScript

In this chapter, you will:

◎ Learn about client/server architecture

◎ Add basic JavaScript code to your Web pages

◎ Learn about the JavaScript programming language

◎ Add structure to your JavaScript programs

The original purpose of the World Wide Web (WWW) was to locate and display information. However, once the Web grew beyond a small academic and scientific community, people began to recognize that greater interactivity would make the Web more useful. As commercial Web applications grew, the demand for more interactive and visually appealing Web sites also grew.

To respond to the demand for greater interactivity, an entirely new Web programming language was needed. Netscape filled this need in the mid-1990s by developing the JavaScript programming language. Originally designed for use in the Navigator Web browser, JavaScript is now used in most Web browsers, including Internet Explorer.

 For details on Web page design and authoring, see "Understanding Web Development" in Chapter 1.

Although JavaScript is considered a programming language, it is also a critical part of Web page design and authoring because JavaScript "lives" within a Web page's elements. In other words, the JavaScript code you write is usually placed within the elements that make up a Web page. JavaScript can turn static documents into applications such as games or calculators. JavaScript code can change the contents of a Web page after a browser has rendered it. JavaScript can also create visual effects such as animation, and it can control the Web browser window itself. None of this interactivity was possible before the creation of JavaScript.

Understanding Client/Server Architecture

To be successful in Web development, you need to understand the basics of client/server architecture. The terms *client* and *server* have many definitions. In traditional client/server architecture, the **server** is usually a database from which a client requests information. A server fulfills a request for information by managing the request, or "serving" the requested information to the client—hence the term *client/server*. A system consisting of a client and a server is known as a **two-tier system**.

A primary role of the **client**, or **front end**, in a two-tier system is to present an interface to the user. The user interface gathers information from the user, submits it to a server, or **back end**, and then receives, formats, and presents the results returned from the server. The main responsibility of a server is usually data storage and management. On client/server systems, heavy processing, such as calculations, usually takes place on the server. As desktop computers become increasingly powerful, however, many client/server systems have begun placing at least some of the processing responsibilities on the client. In a typical client/server system, a client computer might contain a front end that is used to request information from a database on a server. The server locates records that meet the client request, performs some sort of processing, such as calculations on the data, and then returns the information to the client. The client computer can also perform some processing, such as building the queries that are sent to the server or formatting and presenting the returned data. Figure 8-1 illustrates the design of a two-tier client/server system.

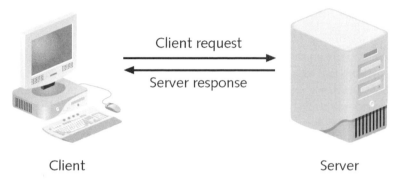

Client   Server

Figure 8-1   The design of a two-tier client/server system

The Web is built on a two-tier client/server system, in which a Web browser (the client) requests documents from a Web server. The Web browser is the client user interface. You can think of the Web server as a repository for Web pages. After a Web server returns the requested document, the Web browser (as the client user interface) is responsible for formatting and presenting the document to the user. HTTP handles the requests and responses through which a Web browser and Web server communicate. For example, if a Web browser requests the URL, *http://www.course.com*, the request is made with HTTP because the URL includes the HTTP protocol. The Web server then returns an HTTP response to the Web browser that contains the response header and the HTML code for Course Technology's home page.

After you start adding databases and other types of applications to a Web server, the client/server system evolves into what is known as a three-tier client architecture. A **three-tier**, or **multitier**, **client/server system** consists of three distinct pieces: the client tier, the processing tier, and the data storage tier. The client tier, or user interface tier, is still the Web browser. However, the database portion of the two-tier client/server system is split into a processing tier and the data storage tier. The **processing tier**, or **middle tier**, handles the interaction between the Web browser client and the data storage tier. (The processing tier is also sometimes called the processing bridge.) Essentially, the client

Two-tier client/server architecture is a physical arrangement in which the client and server are two separate computers. Three-tier client/server architecture is more conceptual than physical because the storage tier can be located on the same server.

tier makes a request of a database on a Web server. The processing tier performs any necessary processing or calculations based on the request from the client tier, and then reads information from or writes information to the data storage tier. The processing tier also handles the return of any information to the client tier. Note that the processing tier is not the only place where processing can occur. The Web browser (client tier) still renders Web page documents (which requires processing), and the database or application in the data storage tier might also perform some processing. Figure 8-2 illustrates the design of a three-tier client/server system.

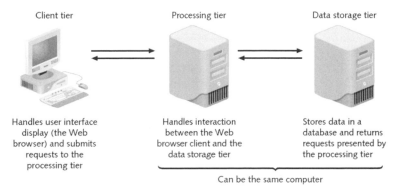

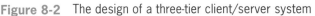

Client tier — Handles user interface display (the Web browser) and submits requests to the processing tier

Processing tier — Handles interaction between the Web browser client and the data storage tier

Data storage tier — Stores data in a database and returns requests presented by the processing tier

Can be the same computer

Multitier client/server architecture is also referred to as *n*-tier architecture.

Figure 8-2   The design of a three-tier client/server system

JavaScript and Client-Side Scripting

As mentioned earlier, HTML was not originally intended to control the appearance of pages in a Web browser. When HTML was first developed, Web pages were **static**—that is, they couldn't change after the browser rendered them. HTML could only be used to produce static documents, which were approximately equivalent to documents created in a word-processing or desktop publishing program; the only thing you could do was view or print these documents. Thus, to respond to the demand for greater interactivity, an entirely new Web programming language was needed. Netscape filled this need by developing JavaScript.

JavaScript is a client-side scripting language that allows Web page authors to develop interactive Web pages and sites. **Client-side scripting** refers to a scripting language that runs on a local browser (on the client tier) instead of on a Web server (on the processing tier). Originally designed for use in Navigator Web browsers, JavaScript is now also used in most other Web browsers, including Firefox and Internet Explorer.

The general term **scripting language** originally referred to fairly simple programming languages that did not contain the advanced capabilities of languages such as Java or C++. When it comes to Web development, the term *scripting language* refers to any type of language that can programmatically control a Web page or return a response to a Web browser. It's important to note that, although scripting languages originally were simple programming languages, today's Web-based scripting languages are anything but simple. The part of a browser that executes scripting language code is called the browser's **scripting engine**. A scripting engine is just one kind of interpreter; the term **interpreter** refers generally to any program that executes scripting language code. When a scripting engine loads a Web page, it interprets any programs written in scripting languages, such as JavaScript. A Web browser that contains a scripting engine is called a **scripting host**. Firefox and Internet Explorer are examples of scripting hosts that can run JavaScript programs.

JavaScript was first introduced in Navigator and was originally called LiveScript. With the release of Navigator 2.0, the name was changed to JavaScript 1.0. Subsequently, Microsoft released its own version of JavaScript in Internet Explorer 4.0 and named it JScript.

Microsoft's release of JScript created several major problems. First, the Netscape and Microsoft versions of the JavaScript language differed so greatly that programmers were required to write almost completely different JavaScript programs for Navigator and Internet Explorer. To avoid similar problems in the future, an international, standardized version of JavaScript, called **ECMAScript**, was created. The most recent version of ECMAScript is edition 3. Both Netscape JavaScript and Microsoft JScript conform to ECMAScript edition 3. Nevertheless, Netscape JavaScript and Microsoft JScript each include unique programming features that are not supported by the other language. In this book, you will learn to create JavaScript programs with ECMAScript edition 3, which is supported by all current Web browsers, including Firefox and Internet Explorer 4 and higher.

Although JavaScript is considered a programming language, it is also a critical part of Web page authoring because JavaScript "lives" within a Web page's elements. JavaScript gives you the ability to:

- Turn static Web pages into applications such as games or calculators.

- Change the contents of a Web page after a browser has rendered it.

- Create visual effects such as animation.

- Control the Web browser window itself.

Many people think that JavaScript is related to the Java programming language or is a simplified version of it. However, the languages are entirely different. Java is an advanced programming language that was created by Sun Microsystems and is considerably more difficult to master than JavaScript. Although Java can be used to create programs that can run from a Web page, Java programs are usually external programs that execute independently of a browser. In contrast, JavaScript programs always run within a Web page and control the browser.

For security reasons, the JavaScript programming language cannot be used outside of the Web browser. For example, to prevent mischievous scripts from stealing information, such as your e-mail address or credit card information used for an online transaction, or from causing damage by changing or deleting files, JavaScript does not allow any file manipulation. Similarly, JavaScript includes no mechanisms for creating a network connection or accessing a database. This limitation prevents JavaScript programs from infiltrating a private network or intranet from which information might be stolen or damaged. Another helpful limitation is that JavaScript cannot run system commands or execute programs on a client. The ability to read and write cookies is JavaScript's only type of access to a client. Web browsers, however, strictly govern cookies and do not allow access to cookies from outside the domain that created them. This security also means that you cannot use JavaScript to interact directly with Web servers that operate at the processing tier. Although the programmer can employ a few tricks (such as forms and query strings) to allow JavaScript to interact indirectly with a Web server, if you want true control over what's happening on the server, you need to use a server-side scripting language, as explained in the next section.

Understanding Server-Side Scripting

Server-side scripting refers to a scripting language that is executed from a Web server. Some of the more popular server-side scripting languages are PHP, Active Server Pages (ASP), and Java Server Pages (JSP). A primary reason for using a server-side scripting language is to develop interactive Web sites that communicate with a database. Server-side scripting languages work in the processing tier and have the ability to handle communication between the client tier and the data storage tier. At the processing tier, a server-side scripting language usually prepares and processes the data in some way before submitting it to the data storage tier. Server-side scripting languages have the following common uses, many of which you have probably already seen on the Web:

- Shopping carts
- Search engines
- Mailing lists and message boards
- Web-based e-mail systems
- Authentication and security mechanisms
- Web logs (blogs)
- Games and entertainment

Unlike JavaScript, a server-side scripting language can't access or manipulate a Web browser. In fact, a server-side scripting language cannot run on a client tier at all. Instead, a server-side scripting language exists and executes solely on a Web server, where it performs various types of processing or accesses databases. When a client requests a server-side script, the script is interpreted and executed by the scripting engine within the Web server software. After the script finishes executing, the Web server software translates the results of the script (such as the result of a calculation or the records returned from a database) into HTML, which it then returns to the client. In other words, a client will never see the server-side script, but only the HTML that the Web server software returns from the script. Figure 8-3 illustrates how a Web server processes a server-side script.

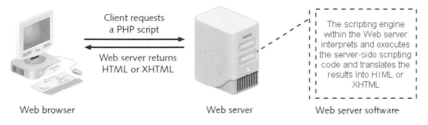

Figure 8-3   How a Web server processes a server-side script

Should You Use Client-Side or Server-Side Scripting?

An important question in the design of any client/server system is deciding how much processing to place on the client and how much to place on the server. In the context of Web site development, you must decide whether to use client-side JavaScript or a server-side script. This is an important choice because it can greatly affect the performance of your program. In some cases, the decision is simple. For example, if you want to control the Web browser, you must use JavaScript. If you want to access a database on a Web server, you must use a server-side script. However, both languages can accomplish some tasks, such as validating forms and manipulating cookies. Furthermore, both languages can perform the same types of calculations and data processing.

A general rule of thumb is to allow the client to handle the user interface processing and light processing, such as data validation, but to have the Web server perform intensive calculations and data storage. This division of labor is especially important when dealing with clients and servers over the Web. Unlike with clients on a private network, it's not possible to know in advance the computing capabilities of each client on the Web. You cannot assume that each client (browser) that accesses your client/server application (Web site) has the necessary power to perform the processing required by the application. For this reason, intensive processing should be performed on the server.

Because servers are usually much more powerful than client computers, your first instinct might be to let the server handle all processing and only use the client to display a user interface. Although you do not want to overwhelm clients with processing they cannot handle, it is important to perform as much processing as possible on the client for several reasons:

- Distributing processing among multiple clients creates applications that are more powerful, because the processing power is not limited to the capabilities of a single computer. Client computers become more powerful every day, and advanced capabilities such as JavaScript are now available in local Web browsers. Thus, it makes sense to use a Web application to harness some of this power and capability. A **Web application** is a program that executes on a server but that clients access through a Web page loaded in a browser.

- Local processing on client computers minimizes transfer times across the Internet and creates faster applications. If a client had to wait for all processing to be performed on the server, a Web application could be painfully slow over a busy Internet connection.

- Performing processing on client computers lightens the processing load on the server. If all processing in a three-tier client/server system is done on the server, the server for a popular Web site could become overwhelmed trying to process requests from numerous clients.

In this chapter, you will work on a home page for a company named Don's Cafe. Your Chapter folder contains a folder named DonsCafe that contains a style sheet and some image files you will need for this exercise.

To create the home page for Don's Cafe:

1. Create a new document in your text editor and type the opening <!DOCTYPE> declaration that uses the HTML DTD, as follows:

```
<!DOCTYPE HTML>
```

2. Type the <html> element, as follows.

```
<html>
</html>
```

3. Within the <html> element, add the following <head> and <body> elements:

```
<head>
    <meta http-equiv="content-type"
        content="text/html; charset=utf-8" />
    <title>Don's Cafe</title>
    <link href="style.css" rel="stylesheet"
        type="text/css" />
</head>
<body>
</body>
```

4. Add the following elements to the document body. This Web page uses <div> tags with associated styles to lay out and format the document.

```
<div id="mainbody">
    <div id="header">
        <img src="images/header.gif" width="761"
            height="345" alt="" /></div>
    <div id="contentarea">
        <img src="images/about_service.gif" />
        <p> </p>
        <img src="images/special_service.gif" />
        <p> </p>
        <br class="clearcols" />
    </div>
    <div id="copyright">
        <p>Copyrighted &copy; by 2011 Don's Cafe</p>
        <p class="copy">All Rights Reserved</p>
        <br class="clearcols" />
    </div>
</div>
```

5. Save the file as **index.html** in the **DonsCafe** folder within your Chapter folder for Chapter 8.

6. Open the **index.html** file in your Web browser. Figure 8-4 displays the index.html file as it appears in Firefox.

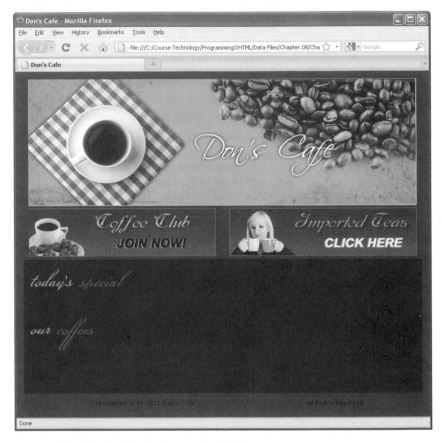

Figure 8-4   Don's Cafe home page in Firefox

7. Close your Web browser window.

Short Quiz 1

1. What are the differences among Web page design, Web page authoring, and Web development?

2. What are the primary roles of the client and the server in two-tier system architecture?

3. What is the purpose of the processing tier in three-tier system architecture?

4. Why are scripts written with the JavaScript programming language restricted to executing only within a Web browser?

Adding JavaScript to Your Web Pages

The following sections introduce basic procedures for adding JavaScript to your Web pages.

Using the `<script>` Element

JavaScript programs run from within a Web page. That is, you type the JavaScript code directly into the Web page code as a separate section. JavaScript programs contained within a Web page are often referred to as **scripts**. The **`<script>` element** tells the Web browser that the scripting engine must interpret the commands it contains. The `type` attribute of the `<script>` element tells the browser which scripting language and which version of the scripting language is being used. You assign a value of "text/javascript" to the `type` attribute to indicate that the script is written with JavaScript. You need to include the following code in a document to tell the Web browser that the statements that follow must be interpreted by the JavaScript scripting engine:

```
<script type="text/javascript">
statements
</script>
```

Next, you will add a script section to the Menu page for Don's Cafe.

To add a script section to the Menu page for Don's Cafe:

1. Return to the **index.html** document in your text editor.

2. Locate the first paragraph and nonbreaking space (` `) and replace it with the following script section:

   ```
   <script type="text/javascript">
   </script>
   ```

3. Save the **index.html** document.

The individual lines of code, or **statements**, that make up a JavaScript program in a document are contained within the `<script>` element. The following script contains a single statement that writes the text "We're having a sale!" to a Web browser window using the `write()` method of the `Document` object, which you will study shortly:

```
document.write("<p>We're having a sale!</p>");
```

Notice that the preceding statement ends in a semicolon. Many programming languages, including C++ and Java, require you to end all statements with a semicolon, although JavaScript does not. Semicolons are strictly necessary only when you want to separate

442

If you anticipate that your JavaScript programs will run only in Internet Explorer, you can specify "JScript" as your scripting language by using the statement `<script type="JScript">`. However, few browsers other than Internet Explorer recognize "JScript" as a valid `type` attribute for the `<script>` element; it is always safer to use "javascript."

HTML documents use the `language` attribute to tell the browser which scripting language and version of the scripting language is being used. However, the `language` attribute is deprecated, so be sure to use the `type` attribute with your documents.

statements that are placed on a single line. For example, the following script contains two statements on the same line, with each statement ending in a semicolon:

```
<script type="text/javascript">
document.write("<p>Can you "); document.write(
    "hear me now?</p>");
</script>
```

As long as you place each statement on its own line, separated from other lines with line breaks, you are not required to end statements with semicolons. The following code shows another example of the preceding script, but this time each statement is placed on its own line, without an ending semicolon:

```
<script type="text/javascript">
document.write("<p>Can you ")
document.write("hear me now?</p>")
</script>
```

Even though the statements do not end in semicolons, the preceding script is legal. However, that's not the entire story. Programmers often adopt conventions that make their code easier to read in a text editor. For example, it is considered good JavaScript programming practice to identify the end of each statement with a semicolon, making it easier for programmers to read their own code and for other programmers to read it later. You should follow this convention.

Although this book covers JavaScript, you can also use other scripting languages with Web pages. To use VBScript in your Web pages, you would use the following code: `<script type="text/vbscript">VBScript code</script>`. Do not confuse JScript with VBScript. As you have read, JScript is Microsoft's version of the JavaScript scripting language. To specify the JScript language, you specify JavaScript as the `type` attribute.

Understanding JavaScript Objects

Before you can use `<script>` elements to create a JavaScript program, you need to learn some basic terminology of JavaScript programming and other kinds of programming languages. In addition to being an interpreted scripting language, JavaScript is considered an object-based programming language. An **object** is programming code and data that can be treated as an individual unit or component. For example, you might create a StudentLoan object that calculates the number of payments required to pay off a student loan. The StudentLoan object may also store information such as the principal loan amount and the interest rate. Individual statements used in a computer program are often grouped into logical units called **procedures**, which are used to perform specific tasks.

For example, a procedure may contain a group of statements that calculate the sales tax based on sales total. The procedures associated with an object are called **methods**. A **property** is a piece of data, such as a color or a name, that is associated with an object. In the StudentLoan object example, the programming code that calculates the number of payments required to pay off the loan is a method. The principal loan amount and the interest rate are properties of the StudentLoan object.

To incorporate an object and an associated method in JavaScript code, you type the object's name, followed by a period, followed by the method. For example, the following code shows the StudentLoan object, followed by a period, followed by a method named calcPayments(), which calculates the number of payments required to pay off the loan:

```
studentLoan.calcPayments();
```

For many methods, you also need to provide some more specific information, called an **argument**, between the parentheses. Some methods require numerous arguments, whereas others don't require any. Providing an argument for a method is referred to as **passing arguments**. For example, the calcPayments() method may require an argument that specifies the amount paid each month toward the loan. In that case, the JavaScript statement would look like this:

```
studentLoan.calcPayments(800);
```

You use an object's properties in much the same way you use a method, by appending the property name to the object with a period. However, a property name is not followed by parentheses. One of the biggest differences between methods and properties is that a property does not actually do anything; you only use properties to store data. You assign a value to a property using an equal sign, as in the following example:

```
studentLoan.interest = .08;
```

The next part of this chapter focuses on the write() and writeln() methods as a way of helping you understand how to program with JavaScript.

Using the write() and writeln() Methods

JavaScript treats many things as objects. One of the most commonly used objects in JavaScript programming is the Document object, which represents the content of a browser's window. Any text, graphics, or other information displayed in a Web page is part of the Document object. One of its most common uses is to add new text to a Web page. You create new text on a Web page with the `write()` method or the `writeln()` method of the `Document` object. For example, you could use the `write()` method to render a Web page containing custom information such as a user's name or the result of a calculation.

You should understand that the only reason to use the `write()` and `writeln()` methods is to add new text to a Web page while it is being rendered. For example, you may want to display a new Web page based on information a user enters into a form. A user may enter, say, sales information into a form for an online transaction. Using the entered information, you can create a new Web page that displays the user's sales total, order confirmation, and so on. If you simply want to display text in a Web browser when the document is first rendered, there is no need to use anything but standard HTML elements. The procedures for dynamically gathering information are a little too complicated for this introductory chapter. However, in this chapter you will use the `write()` and `writeln()` methods to display text in a Web browser when the document is first rendered in order to learn the basics of creating JavaScript programs.

Different methods require different kinds of arguments. For example, the `write()` and `writeln()` methods of the `Document` object require a text string as an argument. A **text string**, or **literal string**, is text that is contained within double or single quotation marks. The text string argument of the `write()` and `writeln()` methods specifies the text that the `Document` object uses to create new text on a Web page. For example, `document.write("We're having a sale!");` displays the text "We're having a sale!" in the Web browser window (without the quotation marks). Note that you must place literal strings on a single line. If you include a line break within a literal string, you receive an error message.

The `write()` and `writeln()` methods perform essentially the same function that you perform when you manually add text to the body of a standard Web page document. Whether you add text to a document by using standard elements, such as the <p> element, or by using the `write()` or `writeln()` methods, the text is added according to the order in which the statements appear in the document.

The only difference between the `write()` and `writeln()` methods is that the `writeln()` method adds a line break after the line of text. Line breaks, however, are only recognized inside the <pre> element. In other words, in order to use line breaks with the `writeln()` method, you must place the method within a <pre> element. The following code contains a script that prints some text in a Web browser by using the `writeln()` method of the `Document` object.

If you are using a version of Internet Explorer that is later than 4, you need to turn on error notification by selecting Internet Options from the Tools menu and clicking the Advanced tab. In the Browsing category on the Advanced tab, make sure the "Display a notification about every script error" check box is selected, and click OK to close the dialog box. To view errors in Firefox, select Error Console from the Tools menu.

Programmers often talk about code that "writes to" or "prints to" a Web browser window. For example, you might say that a piece of code writes a text string to the Web browser window. This is just another way of saying that the code displays the text string in the Web browser window.

Notice that the <script> element is enclosed within a <pre> element. Figure 8-5 shows the output.

```
<pre style="color: blue; font-family: Arial;
    font-size: .8em; font-weight: normal">
<script type="text/javascript">
document.writeln("Leo Tolstoy wrote");
document.writeln("<em>War and Peace</em>");
</script>
</pre>
```

Note the use of semicolons at the end of each statement.
Remember that it is considered good JavaScript programming practice to end every statement with a semicolon.

445

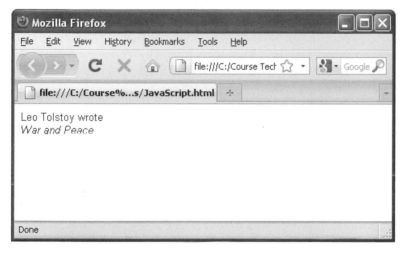

Figure 8-5 Output of a script that uses the writeln() method of the Document object

Notice that the second writeln() statement includes the element <em>. You can include any elements you want as part of an argument for the write() or writeln() methods, including elements such as <p> and <br>. This means that you can use write() statements to add line breaks to the text you create with a script instead of using writeln() statements within a <pre> element. The following code shows a modified version of the previous script, but this time it uses write() statements and does not include a <pre> element. The line break in the text is created by adding a <br /> element to the end of the first line of text.

```
<script type="text/javascript">
document.write("<p>Leo Tolstoy wrote<br />");
document.write("<em>War and Peace</em></p>");
</script>
```

Next, you will add text and elements to the index.html file by using write() methods of the Document object.

To add text and elements to the index.html file by using `write()` methods of the Document object:

1. Return to the **index.html** document in your text editor.

2. Add the following `document.write()` statements to the script section. These statements print the text and elements that display the daily special:

```
document.write("<p><strong>Buy two pounds</strong>");
document.write(" of any of our specialty coffees");
document.write(" and receive a third pound free!</p>");
```

3. Save the **index.html** document and open it in your Web browser. The image in your browser should look similar to Figure 8-6.

Figure 8-6 index.html displaying daily special generated with `document.write()` statements

4. Close your Web browser window.

446

Case Sensitivity in JavaScript

Like HTML, JavaScript is case sensitive, and within JavaScript code, object names must always be all lowercase. This can be a source of some confusion because in written explanations about JavaScript, the names of objects are usually referred to with an initial capital letter. For example, throughout this book, the Document object is referred to with an uppercase D. However, you must use a lowercase d when referring to the Document object in a script. The statement Document.write("We're having a sale!"); causes an error message because the JavaScript interpreter cannot recognize an object named Document with an uppercase D.

Similarly, the following statements will also cause errors:

```
DOCUMENT.write("We're having a sale!");
Document.Write("We're having a sale!");
document.WRITE("We're having a sale!");
```

Adding Comments to a JavaScript Program

When you create a program, whether in JavaScript or any other programming language, it is considered good programming practice to add comments to your code. In this section, you will learn how to create JavaScript comments. **Comments** are nonprinting lines that you place in your code to contain various types of remarks, including the name of the program, your name, the date you created the program, notes to yourself, or instructions to future programmers who may need to modify your work. When you are working with long scripts, comments make it easier to decipher how a program is structured.

JavaScript supports two kinds of comments: line comments and block comments. A **line comment** hides a single line of code. To create a line comment, add two slashes (//) before the text you want to use as a comment. The // characters instruct the JavaScript interpreter to ignore all text immediately following the slashes to the end of the line. You can place a line comment either at the end of a line of code or on its own line. **Block comments** hide multiple lines of code. You create a block comment by adding /* to the first line that you want included in the block, and you close a comment block by typing */ after the last character in the block. Any text or lines between the opening /* characters and the closing */ characters are ignored by the JavaScript interpreter. The following code shows a <script> element containing line and block comments. If you open a document that contains the following script in a Web browser, the browser does not render the text marked with comments.

```
<script type="text/javascript">
/*
This line is part of the block comment.
This line is also part of the block comment.
*/
document.writeln("<h1>Comments Example</h1>"); // Line ↵
comments can follow code statements
// This line comment takes up an entire line.
/* This is another way of creating a block comment. */
</script>
```

448

Comments in JavaScript use the same syntax as comments created in C++, Java, and other programming languages.

Next, you will add comments to the Menu page for Don's Cafe.

To add comments to the Menu page for Don's Cafe:

1. Return to the **index.html** document in your text editor.

2. Add the following block comment immediately after the opening <script> tag:

```
/*
JavaScript code for Chapter 8.
The purpose of this code is simply to demonstrate
how to add a script section to a Web page.
*/
```

3. Next, add the following line comments immediately after the block comment, taking care to replace "*your name*" with your first and last name and "*today's date*" with the current date:

```
// your name
// today's date
```

4. Save the **index.html** document, and then open it in your Web browser to confirm that the comments are not displayed.

5. Close your Web browser window.

Short Quiz 2

1. What element do you use to add JavaScript code to a Web page, and how is it structured?

2. What is an object, as the term is used in programming languages?

3. Explain how to include comments in your JavaScript code.

Writing Basic JavaScript Code

In this section, you will learn how to write basic JavaScript code, starting with variables.

Using Variables

The values a program stores in computer memory are commonly called **variables**. Technically speaking, though, a variable is actually a specific location in the computer's memory. Data stored in a specific variable often changes. You can think of a variable as similar to a storage locker—a program can put any value into it and then retrieve the value later for use in calculations. To use a variable in a program, you first have to write a statement that creates the variable and assigns it a name. For example, you may have a program that creates a variable named curTime and then stores the current time in that variable. Each time the program runs, the current time is different, so the value varies.

Programmers often talk about "assigning a value to a variable," which is the same as storing a value in a variable. For example, a shopping cart program might include variables that store customer names and purchase totals. Each variable will contain different values at different times, depending on the name of the customer and the items he or she is purchasing.

Assigning Variable Names

The name you assign to a variable is called an **identifier**. You must observe the following rules and conventions when naming a variable:

- Identifiers must begin with an uppercase or lowercase ASCII letter, dollar sign ($), or underscore (_).

- You can use numbers in an identifier but not as the first character.

- You cannot include spaces in an identifier.

- You cannot use reserved words for identifiers.

Reserved words (also called **keywords**) are special words that are part of the JavaScript language syntax. As noted, reserved words cannot be used for identifiers. Table 8-1 lists the JavaScript reserved words.

It's common practice to use an underscore (_) character to separate individual words within a variable name, as in my_variable_name. Another option is to use lowercase for the first letter of the first word in a variable name, with subsequent words starting with a capital letter, as in myVariableName.

abstract	else	instanceof	switch
boolean	enum	int	synchronized
break	export	interface	this
byte	extends	long	throw
case	false	native	throws
catch	final	new	transient
char	finally	null	true
class	float	package	try
const	for	private	typeof
continue	function	protected	var
debugger	goto	public	void
default	if	return	volatile
delete	implements	short	while
do	import	static	with
double	in	super	

Table 8-1   JavaScript reserved words

Variable names, like other JavaScript code, are case sensitive. Therefore, the variable name myVariable is a completely different variable than one named myvariable, MyVariable, or MYVARIABLE. If you receive an error when running a script, be sure that you are using the correct case when referring to any variables in your code.

Declaring and Initializing Variables

Before you can use a variable in your code, you have to create it. In JavaScript, you usually use the reserved keyword var to create variables. For example, to create a variable named myVariable, you use this statement:

```
var myVariable;
```

Using the preceding statement to create a variable is called **declaring** the variable. When you declare a variable, you can also assign a specific value to, or **initialize**, the variable using the following syntax. The equal sign in a variable declaration assigns a value to the variable.

```
var variable_name = value;
```

The equal sign (=) in the preceding statement is called an **assignment operator** because it assigns the value on the right side of the expression to the variable on the left side of the expression. The value you assign to a variable can be a literal string or a numeric value. For example, the following statement assigns the literal string "Don" to the variable myName:

```
var myName = "Don";
```

When you assign a literal string value to a variable, you must enclose the text in quotation marks, just as when you use a literal string with the `document.write()` or `document.writeln()` methods. However, when you assign a numeric value to a variable, do not enclose the value in quotation marks or JavaScript will treat the value as a string instead of a number. The following statement assigns the numeric value .05 to the `salesTax` variable:

```
var salesTax = .05;
```

You can declare multiple variables in the statement using a single var keyword followed by a series of variable names and assigned values separated by commas. For example, the following statement creates several variables using a single var keyword:

```
var orderNumber = "RP09030218", salesTotal = 47.58,
    salesTax = .05;
```

Notice in the preceding example that each variable is assigned a value. Although you can assign a value when a variable is declared, it is not required. Your script may assign the value later, or you may use a variable to store user input. However, your script will not run correctly if it attempts to use a variable that has not been initialized. Therefore, it is good programming practice to always initialize your variables when you declare them.

In addition to assigning literal strings and numeric values to a variable, you can also assign the value of one variable to another. For instance, in the following code, the first statement creates a variable named `salesTotal` without assigning it an initial value. The second statement creates another variable, named `curOrder`, and assigns it a numeric value of 27.52. The third statement then assigns the value of the `curOrder` variable to the `salesTotal` variable.

```
var salesTotal = 0;
var curOrder = 27.52;
salesTotal = curOrder;
```

Displaying Variables

To print a variable (that is, display its value on the screen), you pass the variable name to the `document.write()` or `document.writeln()` method without enclosing it in quotation marks, as follows:

```
document.write("<p>Your sales total is $"
       + salesTotal + ".</p>");
```

Notice in the preceding code that the `document.write()` method uses a plus sign (+) to combine a literal string with a variable containing a numeric value. You will learn more about performing similar operations as you progress through this chapter. However, you need to understand that using a plus sign to combine literal strings with variables containing numeric values does not add them together, as in an arithmetic operation. Rather, it combines the values to create a new string, which is then printed to the screen. Figure 8-7 shows how the script appears in a Web browser.

You are not required to use the var keyword to declare a variable. However, omission of the var keyword affects where a variable can be used in a script. Regardless of where you intend to use a variable in your script, it is good programming practice to always use the var keyword when declaring a variable.

451

452

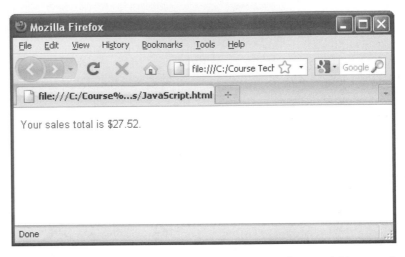

Figure 8-7   Results of script that assigns the value of one variable to another

In addition to using a plus sign to combine a literal string with the numeric value of a variable, you can use a plus sign to perform arithmetic operations involving variables that contain numeric values. For instance, the following code declares two variables and assigns numeric values to them. The third statement declares another variable and assigns it the sum of the values stored in the other variables. If you were to print the value of the grandTotal variable after assigning it the sum of the salesTotal and shipping variables, it would print a value of "37.64", as shown in Figure 8-8.

```
var salesTotal = 27.52;
var shipping = 10.12;
var grandTotal = salesTotal + shipping;
document.write("<p>Your sales total plus shipping is $"
     + grandTotal + ".</p>");
```

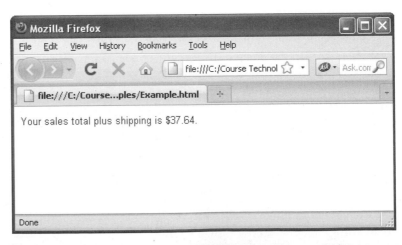

Figure 8-8   Results of script that adds the values of two variables

Modifying Variables

Regardless of whether you assign a value to a variable when it is declared, you can change the variable's value at any point in a script by using a statement that includes the variable's name, followed by an equal sign, followed by the value you want to assign to the variable. The following code declares a variable named `salesTotal`, assigns it an initial value of 27.52, and prints it using a `document.write()` method. The fourth statement changes the value of the `salesTotal` variable by adding its value to the value of another variable named `shipping`. The fifth statement prints the new value of the `salesTotal` variable. Notice that it's only necessary to declare the `salesTotal` variable (using the `var` keyword) once. Figure 8-9 shows the output in a Web browser.

453

```
var salesTotal = 27.52;
document.write("<p>Your sales total is $" + salesTotal
    + ".</p>");
var shipping = 10.12;
salesTotal = salesTotal + shipping;
document.write("<p>Your sales total plus shipping is $"
    + salesTotal + ".</p>");
```

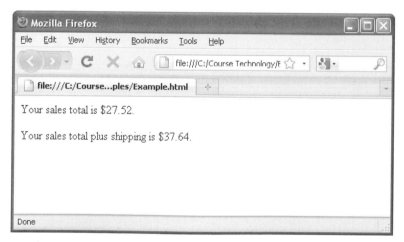

Figure 8-9   Results of script that includes a changing variable

Next, you will return to the index.html file and add some variables to the script that contain descriptions of various specialty coffees.

To add some variables to the script in index.html:

1. Return to the **index.html** file in your text editor.

2. Add the following variables to the end of the script section:

    ```
    var blueMountain = "This extraordinary coffee, ↵
        famous for its exquisite flavor and strong body, ↵
        is grown in the majestic Blue Mountain range ↵
        in Jamaica."
    var blueGrove = "This delightful coffee has an aroma ↵
    ```

```
                    that is captivatingly rich and nutty with a faint ↵
                    hint of citrus."
          var sumatra = "One of the finest coffees in the ↵
                    world, medium roasted to accentuate its robust ↵
                    character."
          var kona = "Grown and processed using traditional ↵
                    Hawaiian methods, then roasted in small batches ↵
                    to maintain peak freshness and flavor."
          var antigua = "An outstanding coffee with a rich, ↵
                    spicy, and smokey flavor."
```

3. Save the **index.html** document. Later in this section, you will add code that displays the values assigned to each of the variables you added in the last step.

Building Expressions

Variables and data become most useful when you use them in an expression. An **expression** is a literal value or variable or a combination of literal values, variables, operators, and other expressions that can be evaluated by the JavaScript interpreter to produce a result. You use operands and operators to create expressions in JavaScript. **Operands** are variables and literals contained in an expression. A **literal** is a value such as a literal string or a number. **Operators**, such as the addition operator (+) and multiplication operator (*), are symbols used in expressions to manipulate operands. You have worked with several simple expressions so far that combine operators and operands. Consider the following statement:

```
retirementAge = 67;
```

This statement is an expression that results in the value 67 being assigned to `retirementAge`. The operands in the expression are the `retirementAge` variable name and the integer value 67. The operator is the equal sign (=). The equal sign is a special kind of operator, called an assignment operator, because it assigns the value 67 on the right side of the expression to the variable (`retirementAge`) on the left side of the expression.

Understanding Events

Events are one of the primary ways in which JavaScript is executed on a Web page. An **event** is a specific circumstance (such as a user action or browser action) that is monitored by JavaScript and to which your script can respond in some way. As you will see in this section, you can use JavaScript events to allow users to interact with your Web pages. The most common events are actions that users perform. For example, when a user clicks a form button, a `click` event is generated. You can think of an event as a trigger that fires specific JavaScript code in response to a given situation. User-generated events, however, are not the only kinds of events monitored by JavaScript. Events that are not direct results of user actions, such as the load event, are also monitored. The load event, which is triggered automatically by a Web browser, occurs when a document finishes loading in a Web browser. Table 8-2 lists some JavaScript events and explains what triggers them.

Event	Triggered When
abort	The loading of an image is interrupted
blur	An element, such as a radio button, becomes inactive
change	The value of an element, such as a text box, changes
click	The user clicks an element once
error	An error occurs when a document or image is being loaded
focus	An element, such as a command button, becomes active
load	A document or image loads
mouseout	The mouse moves off an element
mouseover	The mouse moves over an element
reset	A form's fields are reset to its default values
select	A user selects a field in a form
submit	A user submits a form
unload	A document unloads

Table 8-2   JavaScript events

Working with Elements and Events

Events are associated with HTML elements. The events that are available to an element vary. The click event, for example, is available for the <a> element and form controls created with the <input> element. In comparison, the <body> element does not have a click event, but it does have a load event, which occurs when a Web page finishes loading, and an unload event, which occurs when a Web page is unloaded.

When an event occurs, your script executes the code that responds to that particular event. Code that executes in response to a specific event is called an **event handler**. You include event handler code as an attribute of the element that initiates the event. For example, you can add to a <button> element a click attribute that is assigned some JavaScript code, such as code that changes the color of some portion of a Web page. The syntax of an event handler within an element is:

```
<element event_handler ="JavaScript code">
```

 For a complete listing of HTML 5 events, visit w3schools.com/ html5/html5_ref_ eventattributes.asp.

456

Event handler names are the same as the name of the event itself, plus a prefix of "on". For example, the event handler for the click event is onclick, and the event handler for the load event is onload. Like all HTML code, event handler names are case sensitive and must be written using all lowercase letters in order for a document to be well formed.

The JavaScript code for an event handler is contained within the quotation marks following the name of the JavaScript event handler. The following code uses the <input> element to create a push button. The element also includes an onclick event handler that executes the JavaScript window.alert() method in response to a click event (which occurs when the button is clicked). The window.alert() method displays a pop-up dialog box with an OK button. You pass the window.alert() method a literal string containing the text you want to display. The syntax for the alert() method is window.alert(message);. The value of the literal string or variable is then displayed in the alert dialog box, as shown in Figure 8-10.

```
<input type="button"
       onclick="window.alert('You clicked a button!')" />
```

Figure 8-10 Alert dialog box

Typically, the code executed by the onclick event handler—the window.alert() method—is contained within double quotation marks. In the preceding example, however, the literal string being passed is contained in single quotation marks because the window.alert() method itself is already enclosed in double quotation marks.

The window.alert() method is the only statement being executed in the preceding event handler. You can, however, include multiple JavaScript statements in an event handler as long as semicolons separate the statements. To include two statements in the event handler example—a statement that creates a variable and another statement that uses the `window.alert()` method to display the variable—you would type the following:

```
<input type="button"
   onclick="var message='You clicked a button';
   window.alert(message)">
```

Referencing Web Page Elements

You can use JavaScript to access any element on a Web page by appending the element's name to the name of any elements in which it is nested, starting with the `Document` object. Specific properties of an element can then be appended to the element name. This allows you to retrieve information about an element or change the values assigned to its attributes. For example, form elements such as text boxes have `value` properties that you can use to set or retrieve the value entered into the field. Suppose you have a form with a `name` attribute that is assigned a value of "invoice"; also, suppose the form contains a text box with a `name` attribute that is assigned a value of "salesTotal". You can change the value of the text box by using a statement similar to `document.invoice.salesTotal.value = value;`.

Next, you will add a form to the index.html file that displays radio buttons for each of the specialty coffees that Don's Cafe sells: Jamaican Blue Mountain, Blue Grove Hawaiian Maui Premium, Sumatra Supreme, Pure Kona, and Guatemala Antigua. When a user clicks one of the radio buttons, the contents of one of the variables you added in the last exercise will be displayed in a `<textarea>` element.

To add a form to the index.html file:

1. Return to the **index.html** file in your text editor.

2. Locate the first paragraph and nonbreaking space (` `) and replace it with the following form:

   ```
   <form name="coffeeList" action="" method="get">
   </form>
   ```

3. Add the following text and elements to the form you just created. Each of the radio buttons includes an `onclick` event handler that assigns the value of the associated

variable (created earlier in this section) to a <textarea> element named coffeeDesc. You will create the coffeeDesc <textarea> element next.

```
<p>
   Click the buttons for a description of each
   coffee.</p>
<p>
   <input type="radio" name="coffees" onclick=
    "document.coffeeList.coffeeDesc.value=
       blueMountain" />
   Jamaican Blue Mountain <br />
   <input type="radio" name="coffees" onclick=
   "document.coffeeList.coffeeDesc.value=blueGrove" />
   Blue Grove Hawaiian Maui Premium<br />
   <input type="radio" name="coffees" onclick=
   "document.coffeeList.coffeeDesc.value=sumatra" />
   Sumatra Supreme<br />
   <input type="radio" name="coffees" onclick=
   "document.coffeeList.coffeeDesc.value=kona" />
   Pure Kona<br />
   <input type="radio" name="coffees" onclick=
   "document.coffeeList.coffeeDesc.value=antigua" />
   Guatemala Antigua</p>
```

4. Add the following text and elements to the end of the form to create the <textarea> element that will display the coffee descriptions. The <textarea> element contains a style attribute that formats it to appear as a label.

```
<p>
   <textarea name="coffeeDesc" cols="75" rows="20"
       style="background-color: Transparent;
       border: none; overflow: hidden"></textarea></p>
```

5. Save the **index.html** document, open it in your Web browser, and then test the radio buttons. Each coffee description should appear in the text area when you click the associated radio button. If the page doesn't load, or if you receive error messages, make sure that you typed all the JavaScript code in the correct case. (Remember that JavaScript is case sensitive.) Also make sure you entered all of the opening and closing tags for each element. Figure 8-11 shows how the page appears after a user selects the Jamaican Blue Mountain coffee.

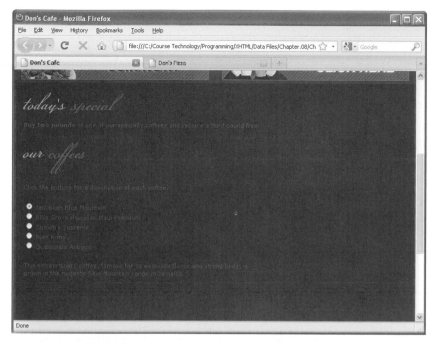

Figure 8-11 index.htrnl Web page after selecting the Jamaican Blue Mountain coffee

6. Close your Web browser window.

Short Quiz 3

1. What rules must you observe when naming a variable in JavaScript?

2. Why should you initialize a variable when you first declare it?

3. What is the difference between operands and operators?

4. How do you reference Web page elements with JavaScript?

Structuring JavaScript Code

When you add JavaScript code to a document, you need to follow certain rules that govern the code's placement and organization. The following sections describe some important rules to keep in mind when structuring your JavaScript code.

Including a `<script>` Element for Each Code Section

You can include as many script sections as you want within a document. However, when you include multiple script sections in a document, you must include a `<script>` element for each section. The following document includes two separate script sections. These script sections create the information that is displayed beneath the `<h2>` heading elements. Figure 8-12 shows the output.

```
<h1>Multiple Script Sections</h1>
<h2>First Script Section</h2>
<script type="text/javascript">
document.write("<p>Output from the first ↵
    script section.</p>");
</script>
<h2>Second Script Section</h2>
<script type="text/javascript">
document.write("<p>Output from the second ↵
    script section.</p>");
</script>
```

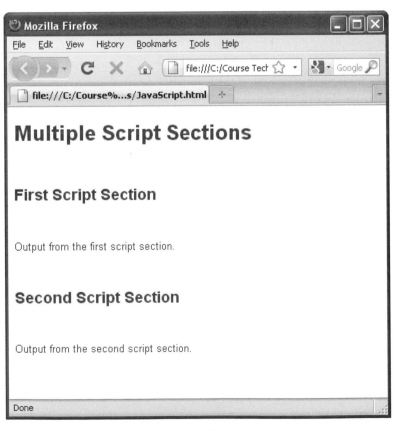

Figure 8-12   Output of a document with two JavaScript sections

Placing JavaScript in the Document Head or Document Body

You can place `<script>` elements in either the document head or document body. Where you place your `<script>` elements varies depending on the program you are writing. The statements in a script are rendered in the order in which they appear in the document. As a general rule, then, it is a good idea to place as much of your JavaScript code as possible in the document head, because it is rendered and processed before the main body of the document is displayed. It is especially important to place JavaScript code in the document head when your code performs behind-the-scenes tasks that are required by script sections in the document body.

Next, you will move the variable declarations in the index.html file to a script section in the document head.

To move the variable declarations to a script section in the document head:

1. Return to the **index.html** document in your text editor.

2. Create a new script section immediately above the closing `</head>` tag, as follows:

   ```
   <script type="text/javascript">
   </script>
   ```

3. Cut the variable declaration statements from the script section in the document body to your clipboard, and then paste them into the script section in the document head.

4. Save the **index.html** document, open it in your Web browser, and test the functionality. The script should work the same as it did before you moved the statements.

5. Close your Web browser window.

Creating a JavaScript Source File

JavaScript is often incorporated directly into a Web page. However, you can also save JavaScript code in an external file called a **JavaScript source** file. You can then write a statement in the document that executes (or calls) the code saved in the source file. When a browser encounters a line calling a JavaScript source file, it looks in the JavaScript source file and executes it.

A JavaScript source file is usually designated by the file extension .js and contains only JavaScript statements, although it can legally have any extension you want. It does not contain a `<script>` element. Instead, the `<script>` element is located within the document that calls the source file. To access JavaScript code that is saved in an external file, you use the `src` attribute of the `<script>` element. You assign the `src` attribute the URL of a JavaScript source file. For example, to call a JavaScript source file named scripts.js, you would include the following code in a document:

```
<script type="text/javascript" src="scripts.js">
</script>
```

JavaScript source files cannot include HTML elements. If you include an HTML element in a JavaScript source file, it will be ignored or an error message will be generated, depending on which Web browser you use. In addition, when you specify a source file in your document using the `src` attribute, the browser ignores any other JavaScript code located within the `<script>` element. For example, consider the following JavaScript code. In this case, the JavaScript source file specified by the `src` attribute of the `<script>` element executes properly, but the `write()` statement is ignored.

```
<script type="text/javascript" src="scripts.js">
document.write("<p>This statement will be ignored.</p>");
</script>
```

If the JavaScript code you intend to use in a document is fairly short, it is usually easier to include the code in a `<script>` element within the document itself. However, for longer JavaScript code, it is easier to include the code in a .js source file. For several reasons, you may want to use a .js source file instead of adding the code directly to a document:

- Your document will be neater. Lengthy JavaScript code in a document can be confusing. You may not be able to tell at a glance where the HTML code ends and the JavaScript code begins.

- The JavaScript code can be shared among multiple Web pages. For example, your Web site may contain pages that allow users to order an item. Each Web page displays a different item but uses the same JavaScript code to gather order information. Instead of re-creating this code within each document, the Web pages can share a central JavaScript source file. Sharing a single source file among multiple documents reduces disk space. In addition, when you share a source file among multiple documents, a Web browser needs to keep only one copy of the file in memory, which reduces system overhead.

- JavaScript source files hide JavaScript code from incompatible browsers. If your document contains JavaScript code, an incompatible browser displays that code as if it were standard text. By contrast, if you put your code in a source file, incompatible browsers simply ignore it.

You can use a combination of embedded JavaScript code and JavaScript source files in your documents. The ability to combine embedded JavaScript code and JavaScript source files in a single Web page is advantageous if you have multiple Web pages, each of which requires individual JavaScript code statements, but all of which also share a single JavaScript source file.

Suppose you have a Web site with multiple Web pages. Each page displays a product that your company sells. You may have a JavaScript source file that collects order information, such as a person's name and address, that is shared by each of the product Web pages. Each individual product page may also require other kinds of order information that you need to collect using JavaScript code. For example, one of your products may be a shirt, for which you need to collect size and color information. On another Web page, you may sell jellybeans, for which you need to collect quantity and flavor information. Each of these products can share a central JavaScript source file to collect standard information, but each may also include embedded JavaScript code to collect product-specific information.

Next, you will move the variable declaration statements from the script section in the document head of the index.html file to a JavaScript source file.

To move the variable declaration statements from the script section in the document head of the index.html file to a JavaScript source file:

1. Cut the variable declaration statements from the script section in the document head to your clipboard.

2. Create a new document in your text editor, and then paste the variable declaration statements into the file.

3. Save the document as **coffees.js** in the DonsCafe folder in your Chapter folder for Chapter 8, and then close the document.

4. Now return to the **index.html** document in your text editor.

5. Add a `src` attribute to the opening `<script>` tag in the document head, so it calls the external JavaScript source file:

   ```
   <script type="text/javascript" src="coffees.js">
   </script>
   ```

6. Save the **index.html** document, open it in your Web browser, and test the functionality. The script should work the same as it did before you created the JavaScript source file.

7. Close your Web browser window.

464

Writing Valid JavaScript Code

You should always strive to create Web pages that are well formed. However, JavaScript can prevent a document from being well formed because some JavaScript statements contain symbols such as the less-than symbol (<), greater-than symbol (>), and ampersand (&). This is not a problem with HTML documents, because the statements in a <script> element are interpreted as character data instead of markup. A section of a document that is not interpreted as markup is referred to as **character data**, or **CDATA**. If you were to validate an HTML document containing a script section, the document would validate successfully because the validator would ignore the script section and not attempt to interpret the text and symbols in the JavaScript statements as HTML elements or attributes. By contrast, with HTML documents, the statements in a <script> element are treated as **parsed character data**, or **PCDATA**, which identifies a section of a document that is interpreted as markup. Because JavaScript code in an HTML document is treated as PCDATA, if you attempt to validate an HTML document that contains a script section, it will fail the validation. To avoid this problem, you can do one of two things. One option is to move your code into a source file, which prevents the validator from attempting to parse the JavaScript statements. Alternatively, if you prefer to keep the JavaScript code within the document, you can enclose the code within a <script> element in a CDATA section, which marks sections of a document as CDATA. The syntax for including a CDATA section on a Web page is as follows:

```
/* <![CDATA[ */
statements to mark as CDATA
/* ]]> */
```

The following example contains JavaScript code that is enclosed within a CDATA section. Figure 8-13 shows the output.

```
...
<body>
<script type="text/javascript">
/* <![CDATA[ */
document.write("<h1>Order Confirmation</h1>");
document.write("<p>Your order has been received.</p>");
document.write("<p>Thank you for your business!</p>");
/* ]]> */
</script>
</body>
</html>
```

Figure 8-13 Output of Web page with hidden JavaScript code

Next, you will modify the script section in the index.html page so that it is hidden from incompatible browsers and is well formed.

To modify the script section in the index.html page so that it is hidden from incompatible browsers and well formed:

1. Return to the **index.html** document in your text editor.

2. Modify the script section in the document body as follows, so the code is contained within a CDATA section to ensure that the Web page can be validated:

```
<script type="text/javascript">
    /* <![CDATA[ */
    /*
    JavaScript code for Chapter 8.
    The purpose of this code is simply to demonstrate
    how to add a script section to a Web page.
    */
    // Don Gosselin
    // January 27, 2011
    document.write("<p><strong>Buy two pounds</
        strong>");
    document.write(" of any of our specialty
        coffees");
    document.write(" and receive a third pound
        free!</p>");
    /* ]]> */
</script>
```

3. Save the **index.html** document and then validate the file with the W3C Markup Validation Service, which is available at *http://validator.w3.org/*.

4. Once the document is valid, open it in your Web browser and test the functionality. The script should work the same as it did before you added the CDATA section.

5. Close your Web browser window and text editor.

Short Quiz 4

1. Why should you place `<script>` elements in the document head?

2. Why would you place JavaScript in a separate source file?

3. How should you format your JavaScript code so that it does not prevent a Web page from being valid?

Summing Up

- Web page authoring (or Web authoring) refers to the creation and assembly of the tags, attributes, and data that make up a Web page.

- Web development, or Web programming, refers to the design of software applications for a Web site.

- In traditional client/server architecture, the server is usually a database from which a client requests information.

- A system consisting of a client and a server is known as a two-tier system. The Web is built on a two-tier client/server system, in which a Web browser (the client) requests documents from a Web server.

- A three-tier, or multitier, client/server system consists of three distinct pieces: the client tier, the processing tier, and the data storage tier.

- JavaScript is a client-side scripting language that allows Web page authors to develop interactive Web pages and sites. Client-side scripting refers to a scripting language that runs on a local browser (on the client tier) instead of on a Web server (on the processing tier).

- The part of a browser that executes scripting language code is called the browser's scripting engine. A scripting engine is just one kind of interpreter; the term *interpreter* refers generally to any program that executes scripting language code. A Web browser that contains a scripting engine is called a scripting host. Firefox and Internet Explorer are examples of scripting hosts that can run JavaScript programs.

- For security reasons, the JavaScript programming language cannot be used outside of the Web browser.

- Server-side scripting refers to a scripting language that is executed from a Web server.

- A general rule of thumb is to allow the client to handle the user interface processing and light processing, such as data validation, but to have the Web server perform intensive calculations and data storage.

- The `<script>` element tells the Web browser that the scripting engine must interpret the commands it contains. The individual lines of code, or statements, that make up a JavaScript program in a document are contained within the `<script>` element.

- An object is programming code and data that can be treated as an individual unit or component. The procedures associated with an object are called methods. A property is a piece of data, such as a color or a name, that is associated with an object.

- Comments are nonprinting lines that you place in your code to contain various types of remarks, including the name of the program, your name, the date you created the program, notes to yourself, or instructions to future programmers who may need to modify your work.

- The values a program stores in computer memory are commonly called variables.

- Reserved words (also called keywords) are special words that are part of the JavaScript language syntax.

- An expression is a literal value or variable or a combination of literal values, variables, operators, and other expressions that can be evaluated by the JavaScript interpreter to produce a result.

- Operands are variables and literals contained in an expression.

- An event is a specific circumstance (such as a user action or browser action) that is monitored by JavaScript and to which your script can respond in some way. Code that executes in response to a specific event is called an event handler.

- You can save JavaScript code in an external file called a JavaScript source file.

- To ensure that you can validate an HTML document that contains a script section, you can move code into a source file or enclose the code within a `<script>` element in a CDATA section.

Comprehension Check

1. A system consisting of a client and a server is known as a _____.

   a. mainframe topology

   b. double-system architecture

   c. two-tier system

   d. wide area network

2. What is usually the primary role of a client?

   a. locating records that match a request

   b. heavy processing, such as calculations

   c. data storage

   d. the presentation of an interface to the user

3. Which of the following functions does the processing tier *not* handle in a three-tier client/server system?

   a. processing and calculations

   b. reading and writing of information to the data storage tier

   c. the return of any information to the client tier

   d. data storage

4. Which function can a client safely handle?

   a. data validation

   b. data storage

   c. intensive processing

   d. heavy calculations

5. What is ECMAScript and why was it developed?

6. JavaScript is a simplified version of the Java programming language. True or False?

7. What value do you assign to the `type` attribute of the `<script>` element to tell the browser to use JavaScript?

   a. `lang/javascript`

   b. `text/javascript`

   c. `javascript`

   d. `jscript`

8. JavaScript statements must end in semicolons. True or False?

9. Which of the following statements cause an error? (Choose all that apply.)

   a. `Document.write("The show must go on!");`

   b. `document.write("The show must go on!");`

   c. `document.Write("The show must go on!");`

   d. `Document.Write("The show must go on!");`

10. What rules and conventions must you observe when naming a variable?

11. Which of the following are valid identifiers? (Choose all that apply.)

    a. `var $InterestRate = .05;`

    b. `var 2008Interest Rate = .05;`

    c. `var interestRate = .05;`

    d. `var _interestRate = .05;`

12. Variables cannot be changed after they are first declared. True or False?

13. Which of the following statements correctly prints the value of a variable named profitMargin? (Choose all that apply.)

    a. `document.write(profitMargin);`

    b. `document.write("<p> Quarterly profits have ↵`
       `    increased by + profitMargin + </p>");`

    c. `document.write("<p>profitMargin</p>");`

    d. `document.write("<p>Quarterly profits have ↵`
       `    increased by " + profitMargin + "</p>");`

14. What is an expression?

15. What is one of the primary ways in which JavaScript is executed on a Web page?

16. Code that executes in response to a specific event is called a(n) _____.

    a. method

    b. event handler

    c. response

    d. procedure

17. Which of the following statements assigns *California* to a text box named state on a form named userInfo?

    a. `document.state.value`

    b. `userInfo.state.value`

    c. `document.userInfo.state`

    d. `document.userInfo.state.value`

18. JavaScript source files must use a file extension of .js. True or False?

19. What is the difference between character data and parsed character data? How is this relevant to JavaScript?

20. A section of a document that is not interpreted as markup is referred to as _____.

    a. PDATA

    b. CDATA

    c. PCDATA

    d. CPDATA

Reinforcement Exercises

 Exercise 8-1

In this exercise you will create a Web page that uses `document.write()` statements in a script section to print dietary recommendations for a healthy heart. The Web page will conform to the strict DTD.

1. Create a new HTML 5 document in your text editor and use "Dietary Recommendations" as the content of the `<title>` element.

2. Add the following text and elements to the document body:

```
<h1>Dietary Recommendations</h1>
<p>The American Heart Association recommends the
following dietary guidelines for a healthy heart:</p>
```

3. Add the following script section to the end of the document body. The script section contains a CDATA section to ensure that the Web page is valid, and includes block comments that will contain your name, the current date, and "Exercise 8-1". Be sure to add your name and the current date where indicated.

```
<script type="text/javascript">
/* <![CDATA[ */
/*
your name
current date
Exercise 8-1
*/
/* ]]> */
</script>
```

4. Add the following `document.write()` statements to the script section, immediately after the statement that contains the closing block comment characters (*/). These statements use an unordered list element to print dietary recommendations for a healthy heart.

```
document.write("<ul>");
document.write("<li>Eat less fat</li>")
document.write("<li>Avoid sugary and processed ↵
    foods</li>")
document.write("<li>Eat plenty of ↵
    fiber-rich foods</li>")
document.write("<li>Cut down on salt</li>")
document.write("<li>Eat at least 400g of fruit ↵
    and vegetables each day</li>")
document.write("<ul>");
```

5. Save the document as **HealthyHeart.html** in the Exercises folder for Chapter 8.

6. Use the W3C Markup Validation Service to validate the **HealthyHeart.html** document, and fix any errors in the document. Once the document is valid, close it in your text editor, open it in your Web browser, and examine how the elements are rendered.

7. Close your Web browser window.

Exercise 8-2

In this exercise, you will create a Web page that uses variables to display information about the five largest islands in the world.

1. Create a new HTML 5 document in your text editor and use "Largest Islands" as the content of the `<title>` element.

2. Add the following `<h1>` element to the document body:

```
<h1>Largest Islands</h1>
```

3. Add the following script section to the end of the document body:

```
<script type="text/javascript">
/* <![CDATA[ */
/* ]]> */
</script>
```

4. In the script section, type the following statements that declare variables containing the names and sizes of the world's five largest islands:

```
var island1Name = "Greenland";
var island2Name = "New Guinea";
var island3Name = "Borneo";
var island4Name = "Madagascar";
var island5Name = "Baffin";
var island1Size = 2175600;
var island2Size = 790000;
var island3Size = 737000;
var island4Size = 587000;
var island5Size = 507000;
```

5. Next, add the following statements to the end of the script section. These statements print the values stored in each of the variables you declared and initialized in the last step:

```
document.write("<p>The largest island in the world is "
    + island1Name + " with " + island1Size
    + " miles.</p>");
document.write(
    "<p>The second largest island in the world is "
    + island2Name + " with " + island2Size
    + " miles.</p>");
document.write(
    "<p>The third largest island in the world is "
    + island3Name + " with " + island3Size
    + " miles.</p>");
document.write(
    "<p>The fourth largest island in the world is "
    + island4Name + " with " + island4Size
    + " miles.</p>");
document.write(
    "<p>The fifth largest island in the world is "
    + island5Name + " with " + island5Size
    + " miles.</p>");
```

6. Save the document as **LargestIslands.html** in the Exercises folder for Chapter 8, and then open the document in your Web browser to examine how the elements are rendered.

7. Close your Web browser window.

Exercise 8-3

In this exercise, you will create a Web page that displays an alert dialog box when the user clicks a command button.

1. Create a new HTML 5 document in your text editor and use "Alert Box" as the content of the <title> element.

2. Add the following heading element and form to the document body:

    ```
    <h1>Alert Box</h1>
    <form action="" method="get">
    </form>
    ```

3. Add the following command button to the form. Notice that the button includes an onclick event handler that displays an alert dialog box with the text "Welcome to my Web site."

    ```
    <p><input type="button" value="Click Me"
    onclick="alert('Welcome to my Web site')" /></p>
    ```

4. Save the document as **AlertBox.html** in your Exercises folder for Chapter 8.

5. Use the W3C Markup Validation Service to validate the **AlertBox.html** document, and fix any errors in the document. Once the document is valid, close it in your text editor, open it in your Web browser, and click the **Click Me** button. You should see the alert dialog box that displays the text "Welcome to my Web site."

6. Click the **OK** button to close the alert dialog box, and then close your Web browser window.

Exercise 8-4

In this exercise, you will create a Web page that contains a list of news headlines in a list box. When a user clicks a headline, the associated story will be displayed in a <textarea> element.

1. Create a new HTML 5 document in your text editor and use "News Items" as the content of the <title> element.

474

2. Add the following form to the document body:

```
<form action="" name="newsHeadlines" method="get">
</form>
```

3. Add the following table to the form. Each item in the selection list displays a news headline. Clicking a headline assigns a variable for the associated news article to the <textarea> element named "news". You will create the variables next.

```
<table style="border: 0; width: 100%">
<tr valign="top">
<td>
<select name="headline" multiple="multiple"
    style="height: 93px">
    <option onclick="document.newsHeadlines ⏎
    .news.value=newsItem1">
    Investigation of building standards in
    quake zone</option>
    <option onclick="document.newsHeadlines ⏎
    .news.value=newsItem2">
    Obama sees signs of economic progress</option>
    <option onclick="document.newsHeadlines ⏎
    .news.value=newsItem3">
    Apple App Downloads Approach 1 Billion</option>
    <option onclick="document.newsHeadlines ⏎
    .news.value=newsItem4">
    Jones, Braves beat winless Nationals 8-5</option>
</select>
</td>
<td>
<textarea name="news" cols="50" rows="10"
style="background-color: Transparent"></textarea>
</td>
</tr>
</table>
```

4. Add the following script section to the end of the document head:

```
<script type="text/javascript">
/* <![CDATA[ */
/* ]]> */
</script>
```

5. Add the following variable declarations to the script section:

```
var newsItem1 = "L'AQUILA, ITALY (AP) - L'Aquila's ⏎
    chief prosecutor announced an investigation ⏎
    into allegations of shoddy construction as ⏎
    workers continued to scour the rubble for ⏎
    people still missing after a devastating ⏎
    earthquake five days ago. ⏎
    http://in.reuters.com/article/ ⏎
    idUSWBT01103020090411";
```

```
var newsItem2 = "WASHINGTON (Reuters) - President ↵
    Barack Obama said on Friday the recession- ↵
    hit US economy was showing 'glimmers of ↵
    hope' despite remaining under strain and ↵
    promised further steps in coming weeks to ↵
    tackle the financial crisis. ↵
    http://in.reuters.com/article/ ↵
    idUSWBT01103020090411";
var newsItem3 = "(eWeek.com) - Apple is close to ↵
    hitting 1 billion downloads from its App ↵
    Store and plans on a prize giveaway for ↵
    whoever downloads the billionth application ↵
    that includes a MacBook Pro and an iPod ↵
    Touch. http://www.eweek.com/c/a/ ↵
    Application-Development/eWeek-Newsbreak ↵
    -April-13-2009/";
var newsItem4 = "ATLANTA (AP) - Chipper Jones ↵
    drove in two runs, including a tiebreaking ↵
    single, and the Atlanta Braves beat ↵
    Washington 8-5 on Sunday to hand the ↵
    Nationals their sixth straight loss to ↵
    start the season. ↵
    http://www.newsvine.com/_news/2009/04/11/ ↵
    2667835-jones-braves-beat-winless ↵
    -nationals-8-5?category=sports";
```

6. Save the document as **NewsItems.html** in your Exercises folder for Chapter 8.

7. Use the W3C Markup Validation Service to validate the **NewsItems.html** document, and fix any errors in the document. Once the document is valid, close it in your text editor, open it in your Web browser, and test the script by clicking each new heading in the selection list. Each headline's associated story should appear in the <textarea> element.

8. Close your Web browser window.

 ## Exercise 8-5

In this exercise, you will move the variable declaration statements from the script section in the document head of the NewsItems.html file to a JavaScript source file.

1. Return to the **NewsItems.html** file in your text editor, and cut the variable declaration statements from the script section in the document head; the statements are placed on your clipboard.

2. Create a new document in your text editor, and then paste the variable declaration statements into the file.

3. Save the document as **newsitems.js** in your Exercises folder for Chapter 8, and then close the document.

4. Return to the **NewsItems.html** document in your text editor.

5. Add a `src` attribute to the opening `<script>` tag in the document head so that it calls the external JavaScript source file:

```
<script type="text/javascript" src="newsitems.js">
</script>
```

6. Save the **NewsItems.html** document, open it in your Web browser, and test the functionality. The script should work the same as it did before you created the JavaScript source file.

7. Close your Web browser window and the NewsItems.html document in your text editor.

Discovery Projects

Save your Discovery Projects files in the Projects folder for Chapter 8.

Discovery Project 8-1

Create a new HTML 5 document with three script sections: one in the document head and two in the document body. Be sure to include CDATA sections within the script sections. In the script section in the document head, include a `document.write()` statement that prints a line that reads "`<h1>Don's Jungle Tours</h1>`". Be sure to include the heading element. Add `<h2>Adventure</h2>` above the first script section and `<h2>Excellence</h2>` above the second script section. Add JavaScript comments with your name, today's date, and "Case Project 8-1". In the first script section in the document body, use five `document.write()` statements to print an unordered list that contains the following three lines: "Ecotourism is our specialty", "Get up close and personal with nature", and "Destinations include Africa, South America, and Asia". The second script section in the document body should call a JavaScript source file that prints the following two lines as list items: "Best quality and price" and "Authentic in-country experience". Save the Web page document as **JungleTours.html** and the JavaScript source file as **travel.js**.

Discovery Project 8-2

The Projects folder for Chapter 8 contains a Web page named **HighestWaterfalls.html** that uses document.write() statements to print a table that contains the names, locations, and heights of the 10 highest waterfalls in the world. The Web page contains errors that prevent it from being valid and prevent the document.write() statements from functioning. Save the document as **HighestWaterfalls_Corrected.html**, and identify and fix the problems in the file. Be sure that the document is valid; prints the names, locations, and heights for all 10 waterfalls; and does not generate any JavaScript errors.

Discovery Project 8-3

In this chapter you learned how to reference form elements by appending the form name, element names, and value property to the Document object. For example, to access the value in a text box named firstName on a form named customerInfo, you use the statement document.customerInfo.firstName.value. Using similar syntax, you can use the src property to dynamically change an image. For example, you can access an image (<img>) element named productImage through its src property using the statement document.productImage.src. Your Projects folder for Chapter 8 contains image files for the flags of 10 countries: argentina.jpg, australia.jpg, bolivia.jpg, cuba.jpg, finland.jpg, france.jpg, italy.jpg, peru.jpg, syria.jpg, and tunisia.jpg. Create a Web page that contains a table with two columns in a single row. In the first column, create a list of radio buttons that contains the name of each of the 10 countries. In the second column, display the flag of the selected country in an anchor element. Use onclick event handlers to display the flag image for each selected country. When the page first loads, the image should be blank. Save the Web page document as **Flags.html**.

CHAPTER 9

Working with Functions, Data Types, and Operators

In this chapter, you will:

◎ Learn how to use functions to organize your JavaScript code

◎ Study data types

◎ Use expressions and operators

◎ Study operator precedence

So far, the code you have written has consisted of simple statements placed within script sections. However, almost all programming languages, including JavaScript, allow you to group programming statements in logical units. In JavaScript, groups of statements that you can execute as a single unit are called functions. You'll learn how to use functions in this chapter.

In addition to functions, one of the most important aspects of programming is the ability to store values in computer memory and to manipulate those values. In the last chapter, you learned how to store values using variables. The values, or data, contained in variables are classified into categories known as data types. In this chapter, you will learn about JavaScript data types and the operations that can be performed on them.

Working with Functions

In Chapter 8, you learned that procedures associated with an object are called methods. In JavaScript programming, you can write your own procedures, called **functions**, which refer to a related group of JavaScript statements that are executed as a single unit. Functions are virtually identical to methods, except that they are not associated with an object the way the `write()` method is associated with the `Document` object. Functions, like all JavaScript code, must be contained within a `<script>` element. In the following section, you'll learn more about incorporating functions in your scripts.

Defining Functions

Before you can use a function in a JavaScript program, you must first create, or define, it. The lines that make up a function are called the **function definition**. The syntax for defining a function is:

```
function name_of_function(parameters) {
    statements;
}
```

Parameters are placed within the parentheses that follow a function name. A **parameter** is a variable that is used within a function. Placing a parameter name within the parentheses of a function definition is the equivalent of declaring a new variable. However, you do not need to include the `var` keyword. For example, suppose that you want to write a function named `calculate_square_root()` that calculates the square root of a number contained in a parameter named `number`. The function name would then be written as `calculate square root(number)`. In this case, the function declaration is declaring a new parameter (which is a variable) named `number`. Functions can contain multiple parameters separated by commas. To add three separate number parameters to the `calculate_square_root()` function, you would write the function name as `calculate_square_root(number1, number2, number3)`. Note that parameters receive their values when you call the function from elsewhere in your program. (You will learn how to call functions in the next section.)

A set of curly braces (called function braces) follows the parentheses that contain the function parameters. These braces contain the function statements, which do the actual work of the function, such as calculating the square root of the parameter or displaying a message on the screen. Function statements must be contained within the function braces. In the following example, a function prints the names of several students using the `write()` methods of the `Document` object. (Recall that functions are very similar to the methods associated with an object.)

```
function printStudentNames(student1, student2, student3) {
    document.write("<p>" + student1 + "</p>");
    document.write("<p>" + student2 + "</p>");
    document.write("<p>" + student3 + "</p>");
}
```

Notice how the preceding function is structured. The opening curly brace is on the same line as the function name, and the closing curly brace is on its own line following the function statements. Each statement between the curly braces is indented one-half inch. This structure is the preferred format among many JavaScript programmers. However, for simple functions it is sometimes easier to include the function name, curly braces, and statements on the same line. (Recall that JavaScript ignores line breaks, spaces, and tabs.) The only syntax requirement for spacing in JavaScript is that semicolons separate statements on the same line.

Always put your functions within the document head, and place calls to a function within the body section. As you recall, the document head is always rendered before the document body. Thus, placing functions in the head section and function calls in the body section ensures that functions are created before they are actually called. If your program attempts to call a function before it has been created, you will receive an error.

Next, you will work on an existing Web site for a wedding-hosting company named Don's Weddings. You can find the Don's Weddings

481

Functions do not have to contain parameters. Many functions only perform a task and do not require external data. For example, you might create a function that displays the same message each time a user visits your Web site; this type of function only needs to be executed and does not require any other information.

A JavaScript program is composed of all the `<script>` sections within a document; each individual `<script>` section is not necessarily its own individual JavaScript program, although it could be if the document has no other `<script>` sections.

files in a folder named DonsWeddings in your Chapter folder for Chapter 9. The Web site contains two pages: a page that can be used to estimate wedding costs and a guest book page. First, you will work on the guest book page. You won't actually be able to save the guest list by submitting it to a server-side script. Instead, you will just use the page to practice some of the techniques taught in this chapter.

To start working on the guest book page:

1. Open the **guestbook.html** file in your text editor. The file is located in a folder named DonsWeddings in your Chapter folder for Chapter 9.

2. Locate the text `<!-- Add visitor info form here -->` and replace it with the following form. You will use this form to add guests to a `<textarea>` element in another form.

```
<form action="" method="post" name="newGuest">
<p>Guest
    <input type="text" name="guestName"
        style="width: 180px" /></p>
    <p>Relationship
    <input type="text" name="relationship"
        style="width: 152px" /></p>
    <p><input type="button" value="Add Guest" /></p>
</form>
```

3. Locate the text `<!-- Add guestbook form here -->` and replace it with the following form, which contains a single `<textarea>` element to which you will add the names of guests who have signed the book:

```
<form action="" method="post" name="guestbook">
<p>Guest<br />
    <textarea name="guests" cols="40"
        rows="8"></textarea></p>
</form>
```

4. Add the following script section to the document head:

```
<script type="text/javascript">
/* <![CDATA[ */
/* ]]> */
</script>
```

5. Add the following function definition to the script section. The statements within the function definition build a text variable named `guestInfo`, which contains the guest name and relationship. This string is then assigned as the value of the `<textarea>` element.

```
function addGuest(){
    var guestInfo = document.newGuest.guestName. ↵
        value + ", ";
    guestInfo += document.newGuest.relationship. ↵
        value;
    document.guestbook.guests.value = guestInfo;
}
```

6. Save the **guestbook.html** file.

Calling Functions

A function definition does not execute automatically. Creating a function definition only names the function, specifies its parameters, and organizes the statements it will execute. To execute a function, you must invoke, or **call**, it from elsewhere in your program. The code that calls a function is referred to as a **function call**; it consists of the function name followed by parentheses, which in turn contain any variables or values to be assigned to the function parameters. The variables or values that you place in the parentheses of the function call statement are called **arguments** or **actual parameters** Sending arguments to the parameters of a called function is called **passing arguments**. When you pass arguments to a function, the value of each argument is then assigned to the value of the corresponding parameter in the function definition. (Again, remember that parameters are simply variables that are declared within a function definition.)

Next, you will add an onclick event handler to the Add Guest button.

To add an onclick event handler:

1. Return to the **guestbook.html** file in your text editor.

2. Locate the button control in the newGuest form, and add the following onclick event handler to the Add Guest button:

    onclick="**addGuest()**"

3. Save the **guestbook.html** file and open it in your Web browser. Add a name and relationship to the Guest and Relationship fields, and click the Add Guest button. Figure 9-1 shows how the page appears after adding a guest.

Figure 9-1 Guest book page after adding a guest

4. Close your Web browser window.

After you learn how to work with strings later in this chapter, you will be able to add multiple guests to the guest book page.

In many instances, you may want your program to receive the results from a called function and then use those results in other code. For example, consider a function that calculates the average of a series of numbers that are passed to it as arguments. Such a function would be useless if your program could not print or use the result elsewhere. As another example, suppose you have created a function that simply prints the name of a student. Now suppose that you want to alter the program to use the student name in another section of code. You can return a value from a function to a calling statement by assigning the calling statement to a variable. The following statement calls a function named `averageNumbers()` and assigns the return value to a variable named `returnValue`. The statement also passes three literal values to the function.

```
var returnValue = averageNumbers(1, 2, 3);
```

To actually return a value to a `returnValue` variable, the code must include a return statement within the `averageNumbers()` function. A **return statement** returns a value to the statement that called the function. To use a return statement, you use the `return` keyword with the variable or value you want to send to the calling statement.

The following script contains the `averageNumbers()` function, which calculates the average of three numbers. The script also includes a return statement that returns the value (contained in the `result` variable) to the calling statement:

```
function averageNumbers(a, b, c) {
    var sum_of_numbers = a + b + c;
    var result = sum_of_numbers / 3;
    return result;
}
```

 A function does not necessarily have to return a value.

485

Next, you will add a function call to the `onclick` event handler of the Add Guest button. You will also modify the `addGuest()` function so that the guest name and relationship are passed to it as arguments, and so the function returns a string to the function call.

To call the addGuest() function:

1. Return to the **guestbook.html** file in your text editor.

2. Modify the `addGuest()` function definition to include two parameters: `name` and `relationship`. Then, modify the statements that build the `guestInfo` variable so that they reference the parameters instead of the form values. Also, replace the last statement that assigns the `guestInfo` variable to the `<textarea>` element with a statement that returns the variable to the function. Your modified function should appear as follows:

```
function addGuest(name, relationship) {
    var guestInfo = name + ", ";
    guestInfo += relationship;
    return guestInfo;
}
```

3. Modify the `onclick` event handler in the button control so it includes two statements. The first statement in the event handler calls the `addGuest()` function and passes it the values of the name and relationship fields. The second statement then assigns the returned value to the `<textarea>` field. The modified event handler should appear as follows:

```
onclick="var newGuest=addGuest(↵
    document.newGuest.guestName.value, ↵
    document.newGuest.relationship.value); ↵
    document.guestbook.guests.value=newGuest"
```

 Be sure to type the preceding string on a single line.

4. Save the **guestbook.html** file, and open it again in your Web browser. The script should work the same as it did before you modified the function and event handler.

5. Close your Web browser window.

Understanding Variable Scope

When you use a variable in a JavaScript program, particularly a complex JavaScript program, you need to be aware of the variable's **scope**—that is, you need to think about where in your program a declared variable can be used. A variable's scope can be either global or local. A **global variable** is declared outside a function and is available to all parts of your program. A **local variable** is declared inside a function and is only available within that function. Local variables cease to exist when the function ends. If you attempt to use a local variable outside the function in which it is declared, you will receive an error message.

The parameters within the parentheses of a function declaration are local variables.

You must use the `var` keyword when you declare a local variable. However, when you declare a global variable, the `var` keyword is optional. For example, you can write the statement `var myVariable = "This is a variable.";` as `myVariable = "This is a variable.";`. If you declare a variable within a function and do not include the `var` keyword, the variable automatically becomes a global variable. Using the `var` keyword when declaring variables is considered good programming technique because it clarifies when and where you intend to start using the variable. Declaring a global variable inside of a function by not using the `var` keyword is considered poor programming technique because you make it harder to identify the global variables in your scripts. Using the `var` keyword forces you to explicitly declare your global variables outside of any functions and local variables within a function.

The following script includes a global variable named `salesPrice` and a function that contains two variable declarations. The first variable declaration in the function, for `shippingPrice`, is a global variable because it does not include the `var` keyword. The second variable declaration in the function, for `totalPrice`, is a local variable because it does include the `var` keyword. Both the global variable and the function are contained in a script section in the document head. When the function is called from the document body, the global variables and the local variable print successfully from within the function. After the call to the function, the global variables again print successfully from the document body. However, when the script tries to print the local variable from the document body, an error message is generated because the local variable ceases to exist when the function ends.

```
...
<head>
<title>Calculate Sales Price</title>
<meta http-equiv="content-type"
    content="text/html; charset=utf-8" />
<script type="text/javascript">
```

```
/* <![CDATA[ */
var salesPrice = 100.00;
function applyShipping() {
      shippingPrice = 8.95;
      var totalPrice = salesPrice + shippingPrice;
      document.write("<p>The sales price is $"
            + salesPrice + "<br />"); // prints successfully
      document.write("The shipping price is $"
            + shippingPrice + "<br />"); // prints ⏎
                successfully
      document.write("The sales price plus shipping is $"
            + totalPrice + "</p>"); // prints successfully
}
/* ]]> */
</script>
</head>
<body>
<script type="text/javascript">
/* <![CDATA[ */
applyShipping();
      document.write("<p>The sales price is $"
            + salesPrice + "<br />"); // prints successfully
      document.write("The shipping price is $"
            + shippingPrice + "<br />"); // error message
      document.write("The sales price plus shipping is $"
            + totalPrice + "</p>"); // prints successfully
/* ]]> */
</script>
</body>
</html>
```

Remember that intentionally declaring a global variable inside of a function by eliminating the var keyword is considered poor programming practice. The only intention of the shippingPrice variable in the preceding example is to illustrate variable scope. If shippingPrice needed to be a global variable, it should have been declared at the global level with the salesPrice variable.

When a program contains a global variable and a local variable with the same name, the local variable takes precedence when its function is called. However, even if the local variable and global variable have the same name, the value assigned to the variables is different. In the following code, the global variable pitcher is assigned a value of "Josh Beckett" before the function that contains a local variable of the same name is called. Once the function is called, the local pitcher variable is assigned a value of "Tim Lincecum". After the function ends, "Tim Lincecum" is still the value of the global pitcher variable. Figure 9-2 shows the output in a Web browser.

```
var pitcher = "Josh Beckett";
function duplicateVariableNames() {
      var pitcher = "Tim Lincecum";
          document.write("<p>" + pitcher + "</p>");
          // value printed is Tim Lincecum
}
duplicateVariableNames();
document.write("<p>" + pitcher + "</p>");
// value printed is Josh Beckett
```

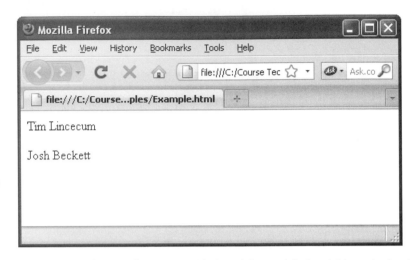

Although the code that displays the output shown in Figure 9-2 is syntactically correct, it is poor programming practice to use the same name for local and global variables because it makes your scripts confusing. Also, this practice makes it difficult to track which version of the variable is currently being used by the program.

Figure 9-2 Output of a program that contains a global variable and a local variable with the same name

Using Built-in JavaScript Functions

In addition to custom functions that you create yourself, JavaScript allows you to use the built-in functions listed in Table 9-1.

Function	Description
decodeURI(*string*)	Decodes text strings encoded with encodeURI()
decodeURIComponent(*string*)	Decodes text strings encoded with encodeURIComponent()
encodeURI(*string*)	Encodes a text string so that it becomes a valid URI
encodeURIComponent(*string*)	Encodes a text string so that it becomes a valid URI component
eval(*string*)	Evaluates expressions contained within strings
isFinite(*number*)	Determines whether a number is finite
isNaN(*number*)	Determines whether a value is the special value NaN (Not a Number)
parseFloat(*string*)	Converts string literals to floating-point numbers
parseInt(*string*)	Converts string literals to integers

Table 9-1   Built-in JavaScript functions

In this book, you will examine several of the built-in JavaScript functions as you need them. For now, you just need to understand that you call built-in JavaScript functions in the same way you call a custom function. For example, the following code calls the isNaN() function to determine whether the socialSecurityNumber variable is *not* a number. Because the Social Security number assigned to the socialSecurityNumber variable contains dashes, it is not a true number. Therefore, the isNaN() function returns a value of true to the checkVar variable.

```
var socialSecurityNumber = "123-45-6789";
var checkVar = isNaN(socialSecurityNumber);
document.write(checkVar);
```

Short Quiz 1

1. What is the difference between arguments and parameters?

2. How do you execute a function?

3. Why would you want to return a value from a function?

4. What is variable scope?

Working with Data Types

Variables can contain many different kinds of values—for example, the time of day, a dollar amount, or a person's name. A **data type** is the specific category of information that a variable contains. The concept of data types can be difficult for beginning programmers to grasp because in real life you don't often distinguish among different types of information. If someone asks for your name, your age, or the current time, you don't usually stop to consider that your name is a text string and that your age and the current time are numbers. However, a variable's specific data type is very important in programming because it helps determine how much memory the computer allocates for the data stored in the variable. The data type also governs the kinds of operations that can be performed on a variable.

Data types that can be assigned only a single value are called **primitive types**. JavaScript supports the five primitive data types described in Table 9-2.

Data type	Description
Number	Positive or negative numbers with or without decimal places, or numbers written using exponential notation
Boolean	A logical value of true or false
String	Text such as "Hello World"
Undefined	A variable that has never had a value assigned to it, has not been declared, or does not exist
Null	An empty value

Table 9-2 Primitive JavaScript data types

The null value is a data type as well as a value that can be assigned to a variable. Assigning the value "null" to a variable indicates that it does not contain a usable value. A variable with a value of "null" has a value assigned to it—null is really the value "no value." You assign the "null" value to a variable when you want to ensure that it does not contain any data. In contrast, an undefined variable has never had a value assigned to it (not even null), has not been declared, or does not exist. One use for an undefined variable is to determine whether a value is being used by another part of your script. As an example of an undefined variable, the following code declares a variable named stateTax without a value. When the second statement uses the document.write() method to print the stateTax variable, a value of "undefined" is printed because the variable has not yet been assigned a value. The variable is then assigned a value of 40 and printed to the screen, and then assigned a value of "null", which is also printed to the screen. Figure 9-3 shows the output in a Web browser.

```
var stateTax;
document.write("<p>Your state tax is $"
    + stateTax + ".</p>");
stateTax = 40;
document.write("<p>Your state tax is $"
    + stateTax + ".</p>");
stateTax = null;
document.write("<p>Your state tax is $"
    + stateTax + ".</p>");
```

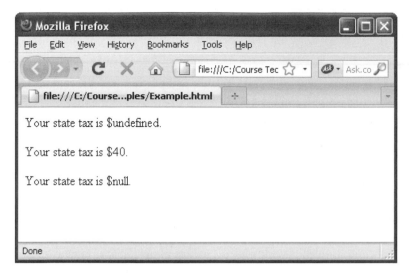

Figure 9-3 Variable assigned values of "undefined" and "null"

Many programming languages require that you declare the type of data that a variable contains; such languages are called **strongly typed programming languages**. Strong typing is also known as **static typing**, because data types do not change after they have been declared. Programming languages such as JavaScript that do not require you to declare the data types of variables are called **loosely typed programming languages**. Loose typing is also known as **dynamic typing** because data types can change after they have been declared. In JavaScript, you are not required to declare the data type of variables; in fact, you are not allowed to do so. Instead, the JavaScript interpreter automatically determines what type of data is stored in a variable and assigns its data type accordingly. The following code demonstrates how a variable's data type changes automatically each time the variable is assigned a new literal value:

```
diffTypes = "Hello World"; // String
diffTypes = 8;             // Integer number
diffTypes = 5.367;         // Floating-point number
diffTypes = true;          // Boolean
diffTypes = null;          // null
```

The next two sections focus on two especially important data types: numeric and Boolean data types.

Understanding Numeric Data Types

Numeric data types are an important part of any programming language and are particularly useful for arithmetic calculations. JavaScript supports two numeric data types: integers and

492

Floating-point values that exceed the largest positive value of $\pm1.7976931348623157 \times 10^{308}$ result in a special value of `Infinity`. Floating-point values that exceed the smallest negative value of $\pm5 \times 10^{-324}$ result in a value of `-Infinity`.

floating-point numbers. An **integer** is a positive or negative number with no decimal places. Integer values in JavaScript can range from -9007199254740990 (-2^{53}) to 9007199254740990 (2^{53}). The numbers -250, -13, 0, 2, 6, 10, 100, and 10000 are examples of integers. The numbers -6.16, -4.4, 3.17, $.52$, 10.5, and 2.7541 are not integers; they are floating-point numbers because they contain decimal places. A **floating-point number** contains decimal places or is written in exponential notation. **Exponential notation**, or **scientific notation**, is a shortened format for writing very large numbers or numbers with many decimal places. Numbers written in exponential notation are represented by a value between 1 and 10 multiplied by 10 raised to some power. The value of 10 is written with an uppercase or lowercase *E*. For example, the number 200,000,000,000 can be written in exponential notation as 2.0e11, which means "two times ten to the eleventh power." Floating-point values in JavaScript range from approximately $\pm1.7976931348623157 \times 10^{308}$ to $\pm 5 \times 10^{-324}$.

Next, you will create a script that uses variables containing integers, floating-point numbers, and exponential numbers to print the 20 prefixes of the metric system. A metric prefix, or SI prefix, is a name that precedes a metric unit of measure. For example, the metric prefix for centimeter is *centi*; it denotes a value of 1/100th. In other words, a centimeter is 1/100th of a meter.

To create a script that prints metric prefixes:

1. Create a new HTML 5 document in your text editor and use "Metric Prefixes" as the content of the `<title>` element. Add a link to a style sheet named js_styles.css, which is located in your Chapter folder for Chapter 9.

2. Add the following heading element to the document body:

   ```
   <h1>Metric Prefixes</h1>
   ```

3. Add the following script section to the end of the document body:

   ```
   <script type="text/javascript">
   /* <![CDATA[ */
   /* ]]> */
   </script>
   ```

4. In the script section, add the following variable declarations for the 20 metric prefixes:

   ```
   var yotta = 1e24;
   var zetta = 1e21;
   var exa = 1e18;
   var peta = 1e15;
   ```

```
var tera = 1e12;
var giga = 1e9;
var mega = 1e6;
var kilo = 1000;
var hecto = 100;
var deca = 10;
var deci = .1;
var centi = .01;
var milli = .001;
var micro = 1e-6;
var nano = 1e-9;
var pico = 1e-12;
var femto = 1e-15;
var atto = 1e-18;
var zepto = 1e-21;
var yocto = 1e-24;
```

5. At the end of the script section, add the following statements to print the value of each metric prefix variable as cells in a table:

```
document.write("<table border='1' ↵
    width='100%'><tr><th> ↵
    Prefix</th><th>Decimal Equivalent</th></tr>");
document.write("<tr><td>Yotta</td><td>"
    + yotta + "</td></tr>");
document.write("<tr><td>Zetta</td><td>"
    + zetta + "</td></tr>");
document.write("<tr><td>Exa</td><td>"
    + exa + "</td></tr>");
document.write("<tr><td>Peta</td><td>"
    + peta + "</td></tr>");
document.write("<tr><td>Tera</td><td>"
    + tera + "</td></tr>");
document.write("<tr><td>Giga</td><td>"
    + giga + "</td></tr>");
document.write("<tr><td>Mega</td><td>"
    + mega + "</td></tr>");
document.write("<tr><td>Kilo</td><td>"
    + kilo + "</td></tr>");
document.write("<tr><td>Hecto</td><td>"
    + hecto + "</td></tr>");
document.write("<tr><td>Deca</td><td>"
    + deca + "</td></tr>");
document.write("<tr><td>Deci</td><td>"
    + deci + "</td></tr>");
document.write("<tr><td>Centi</td><td>"
    + centi + "</td></tr>");
document.write("<tr><td>Milli</td><td>"
    + milli + "</td></tr>");
document.write("<tr><td>Micro</td><td>"
    + micro + "</td></tr>");
document.write("<tr><td>Nano</td><td>"
    + nano + "</td></tr>");
document.write("<tr><td>Pico</td><td>"
```

494

Most Web browsers automatically display very large numbers, such as the values represented by the zetta and yotta metric prefixes, in exponential format.

```
              + pico + "</td></tr>");
document.write("<tr><td>Femto</td><td>"
      + femto + "</td></tr>");
document.write("<tr><td>Atto</td><td>"
      + atto + "</td></tr>");
document.write("<tr><td>Zepto</td><td>"
      + zepto + "</td></tr>");
document.write("<tr><td>Yocto</td><td>"
      + yocto + "</td></tr>");
document.write("</table>");
```

6. Save the document as **MetricPrefixes.html** in the Chapter folder for Chapter 9, and then validate the document with the W3C Markup Validation Service at **http://validator.w3.org/**. Once the file is valid, close it in your text editor.

7. Open the **MetricPrefixes.html** document in your Web browser. Figure 9-4 shows how the document looks in a Web browser.

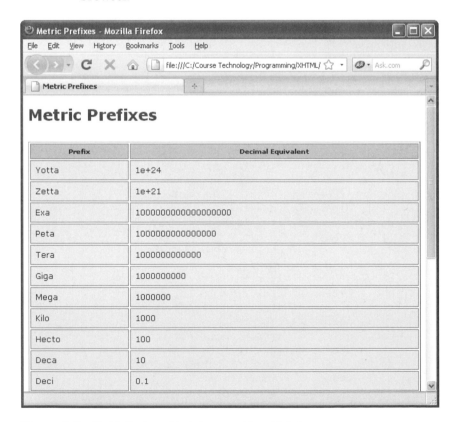

Figure 9-4   MetricPrefixes.html document in a Web browser

8. Close your Web browser window.

Using Boolean Values

A **Boolean value** is a logical value of true or false. You can also think of a Boolean value as meaning yes or no, or on or off. Boolean values are most often used for deciding which parts of a program should execute and for comparing data. In JavaScript programming, you can only use the words *true* and *false* to indicate Boolean values. In other programming languages, you can use the integer value of 1 to indicate true and 0 to indicate false. JavaScript converts the values true and false to the integers 1 and 0 when necessary. For example, when you attempt to use a Boolean variable of true in a mathematical operation, JavaScript converts the variable to an integer value of 1. In the following simple example, two variables are assigned Boolean values: one true and the other false. Figure 9-5 shows the output in a Web browser:

```
var newCustomer = true;
var contractorRates = false;
document.write("<p>New customer: "
    + newCustomer + "</p>");
document.write("<p>Contractor rates: "
    + contractorRates + "</p>");
```

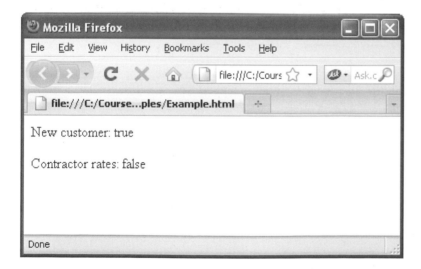

Figure 9-5   Boolean values

Next, you will add Boolean global variables to the planner.html page of the Don's Weddings site. The planner.html page will contain a calculator for estimating the cost of a wedding reception. The global variables you add will store the cost per guest, the limousine rental cost, the costs of live music and flowers, and the total estimate. You will complete the planner.html page later in this chapter.

To add five Boolean global variables to the planner.html page:

1. Open the **planner.html** file in your text editor. The file is in a folder named DonsWeddings in your Chapter folder for Chapter 9. Next, add a script section to the document head.

2. Within the script section, add the following global variables for the cost per guest, the limousine rental cost, the costs of live music and flowers, and the total estimate:

```
var guestsCost = 0;
var limousinesCost = 0;
var liveMusicCost = 0;
var flowersCost = 0;
var totalEstimate = 0;
```

3. Save the **planner.html** file.

Working with Strings

As you learned in Chapter 8, a text string contains zero or more characters surrounded by double or single quotation marks. For example, you can use company names, user names, comments, and other types of text as strings in a script. You can use text strings as literal values or assign them to a variable.

Literal strings can also be assigned a zero-length string value called an **empty string**. For example, the following statement declares a variable named customerName and assigns it an empty string:

```
var customerName = "";
```

Empty strings are valid values for literal strings and are not considered to be null or undefined. Why would you want to assign an empty string to a literal string? Think for a moment about the prompt() method, which displays a dialog box with a message, a text box, an OK button, and a Cancel button. You can pass two string arguments to the prompt() method. The first argument displays an instruction to the user, while the second argument is the default text that appears in the text box of the prompt dialog box. If you do not include the second argument, the value "undefined" appears as the default text of the prompt dialog box. To prevent this from happening, you pass an empty string as the second argument of the prompt() method.

When you want to include a quoted string within a literal string surrounded by double quotation marks, you surround the quoted string with single quotation marks. When you want to include a quoted string within a literal string surrounded by single quotation marks, you surround the quoted string with double quotation marks. Regardless of which method you use, a string must begin and end with the same type of quotation marks. For example, you can use either `document.write("Alexander Rodriguez is called 'A-Rod'.")` or `document.write('Alexander Rodriguez is called "A-Rod".')`. Thus, `document.write("This is a text string.");` is valid because it starts and ends with double quotation marks. However, the statement `document.write("This is a text string.');` is invalid because it starts with a double quotation mark and ends with a single quotation mark. In the second case, you would receive an error message because the Web browser cannot tell where the literal strings begin and end. The following code shows an example of a script that prints strings. Figure 9-6 shows the output.

```
document.write("<p>This is a literal ↵
    string.<br />");
document.write("This string contains a ↵
    'quoted' string.<br />");
document.write('This is another example of a ↵
    "quoted" string.<br />');
var firstString = "This literal string was ↵
    assigned to a variable.<br/>";
var secondString = 'This literal string was ↵
    also assigned to a variable.</p>';
document.write(firstString);
document.write(secondString);
```

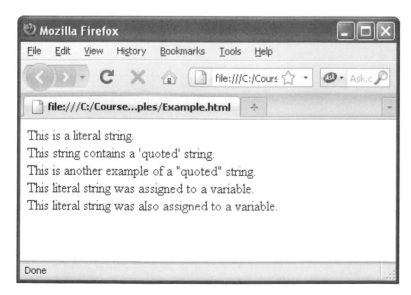

Figure 9-6 String examples in a Web browser

Unlike other programming languages, JavaScript includes no special data type for a single character, such as the `char` data type in the C, C++, and Java programming languages.

String Operators

JavaScript has two operators that can be used with strings: + and +=. When used with strings, the plus sign is known as the concatenation operator. The **concatenation operator** (+) is used to combine two strings. You have already learned how to use the concatenation operator. For example, the following code combines a string variable and a literal string, and assigns the new value to another variable:

```
var destination = "Honolulu";
var location = "Hawaii";
destination = destination + " is in " + location;
```

The combined value of the location variable and the string literal assigned to the destination variable is "Honolulu is in Hawaii".

You can also use the compound assignment operator (+=) to combine two strings. The following code combines the two text strings, but without using the location variable:

```
var destination = "Honolulu";
destination += " is in Hawaii";
```

Note that the same symbol—a plus sign—serves as the concatenation operator and the addition operator. When used with numbers or variables containing numbers, expressions that use the concatenation operator return the sum of the two numbers. As you learned earlier in this chapter, if you use the concatenation operator with a string value and a number value, the two values are combined into a new string value, as shown in the following example:

```
var textString = "The legal voting age is ";
var votingAge = 18;
newString = textString + votingAge;
```

Escape Characters and Sequences

You need to take extra care when using single quotation marks with possessives and contractions in strings, because the JavaScript interpreter always looks for the first closing single or double quotation mark to match an opening single or double quotation mark. For example, consider the following statement:

```
document.write('<p>My city's zip code is 94558.</p>');
```

This statement causes an error. The JavaScript interpreter assumes that the literal string ends with the apostrophe following *city* and looks for the closing parentheses for the document.write() statement immediately following *city's*. To get around this problem, you include an escape character before the apostrophe in *city's*.

An **escape character** tells the compiler or interpreter that the character after it has a special purpose. In JavaScript, the escape character is the backslash (\). Placing a backslash in front of an apostrophe tells the JavaScript Interpreter to treat the apostrophe as a regular keyboard character, such as "a", "b", "1", or "2", and not as part of a single quotation mark pair that encloses a text string. The backslash in the following statement tells the JavaScript interpreter to print the apostrophe following the word *city* as an apostrophe:

```
document.write('<p>My city\'s zip code is 94558.</p>');
```

You can also use the escape character in combination with other characters to insert a special character into a string. Such a combination is called an **escape sequence**. The backslash followed by an apostrophe (\') and the backslash followed by a double quotation mark (\") are both examples of escape sequences. Most escape sequences carry out special functions; for example, the escape sequence \t inserts a tab into a string. Table 9-3 describes the escape sequences that can be added to a string in JavaScript.

 If you place a backslash before any character other than those listed in Table 9-3, the backslash is ignored.

Escape sequence	Character
\\	Backslash
\b	Backspace
\r	Carriage return
\"	Double quotation mark
\f	Form feed
\t	Horizontal tab
\n	Newline
\0	Null character
\'	Single quotation mark
\v	Vertical tab
\XX	Latin-1 character specified by the XX characters, which represent two hexadecimal digits
\XXXXX	Unicode character specified by the XXXX characters, which represent four hexadecimal digits

Table 9-3   JavaScript escape sequences

Notice that the backslash is one of the characters generated by an escape sequence. Because the escape character itself is a backslash, you must use the escape sequence \\ to include a backslash as a character in a string. For example, to include the path

C:\JavaScript_Projects\Files\ in a string, you must include two backslashes for every single backslash you want to include in the string, as in the following statement:

```
document.write("<p>My JavaScript files are located in
    C:\\JavaScript_Projects\\Files\\</p>");
```

The following code shows an example of a script containing strings with several escape sequences. Figure 9-7 shows the output.

```
<pre>
<script type="text/javascript">
/* <![CDATA[ */
document.write("<p>This line is printed \non
    two lines.</p>"); // New line
document.write("<p>\tThis line includes a
    horizontal tab.</p>"); // Horizontal tab
document.write("<p>My personal files are
    in c:\\personal.</p>"); // Backslash
document.write(("<p>My cousin's nickname
    is \"Bubba.\"</p>")); // Double quotation mark
document.write('<p>India\'s capital
    is New Delhi.</p>'); // Single quotation mark
/* ]]> */
</script>
</pre>
```

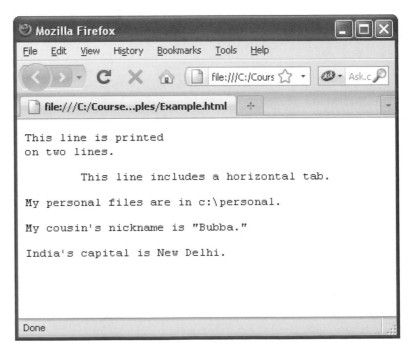

Figure 9-7 Output of script with strings containing escape sequences

The current version of the guest book page only allows you to add a single guest to the `<textarea>` element. To add multiple guests on individual lines, you need to add a carriage return escape sequence (`\r`) to the end of each line.

To modify the guest book page so you can add multiple guests:

1. Return to the **guestbook.html** file in your text editor.

2. Modify the statement in the `addGuest()` method that assigns the relationship argument to the `guestInfo` variable so that it also includes a carriage return escape sequence, as follows:

   ```
   guestInfo += relationship + "\r";
   ```

3. Modify the last statement in the Add Guest button element's `onclick` event handler so that it adds the new guest string to the existing value in the `<textarea>` element, as follows:

   ```
   onclick="var newGuest=addGuest( ↵
       document.newGuest.questName.value, ↵
       document.newGuest.relationship.value); ↵
       document.guestbook.guests.value ↵
           = document.guestbook.guests.value + newGuest"
   ```

4. Save the **guestbook.html** file, and then validate it with the W3C Markup Validation Service at **http://validator.w3.org/**. Once the file is valid, close it in your text editor. Open the file again in your Web browser and test the script to ensure that you can add multiple guests.

5. Close your Web browser window.

Several escape sequences, including the newline and horizontal tab escape sequences, are only recognized inside a container element such as the `<pre>` element.

Short Quiz 2

1. What is the difference between loosely typed and strongly typed programming languages?

2. Explain exponential notation.

3. What are Boolean values and how do you use them?

4. Explain how to use the concatenation and compound assignment operators with strings.

5. What are escape characters and escape sequences?

Using Operators to Build Expressions

In Chapter 8, you learned how to create expressions using basic operators, such as the addition operator (+) and multiplication operator (*). In this section, you will learn about additional types of operators you can use with JavaScript. Table 9-4 lists these operator types.

Operator type	Operators	Description
Arithmetic	addition (+)	Used for performing mathematical calculations
	subtraction (–)	
	multiplication (*)	
	division (/)	
	modulus (%)	
	increment (++)	
	decrement (– –)	
	negation (–)	
Assignment	assignment (=)	Assigns values to variables
	compound addition assignment (+=)	
	compound subtraction assignment (–=)	
	compound multiplication assignment (*=)	
	compound division assignment (/=)	
	compound modulus assignment (%=)	
Comparison	equal (==)	Compares operands and returns a Boolean value
	strict equal (===)	
	not equal (!=)	
	strict not equal (!==)	
	greater than (>)	
	less than (<)	
	greater than or equal (>=)	
	less than or equal (<=)	

Table 9-4   JavaScript operator types *(continues)*

(continued)

Operator type	Operators	Description
Logical	and (&&)	Used for performing Boolean operations on Boolean operands
	or (| |)	
	not (!)	
String	concatenation operator (+)	Performs operations on strings
	compound assignment operator (+=)	
Special	property access (.)	Used for various purposes; these operators do not fit within other operator categories
	array index ([])	
	function call (())	
	comma (,)	
	conditional expression (?:)	
	delete (delete)	
	property exists (in)	
	object type (instanceof)	
	new object (new)	
	data type (typeof)	
	void (void)	

Table 9-4   JavaScript operator types

JavaScript operators are binary or unary. A **binary operator** requires an operand before and after the operator. The equal sign in the statement myNumber = 100; is an example of a binary operator. A **unary operator** requires a single operand either before or after the operator. For example, the increment operator (++), an arithmetic operator, is used for increasing an operand by a value of one. The statement myNumber++; changes the value of the myNumber variable to 101.

In the following sections, you will learn more about the different types of JavaScript operators.

Using Arithmetic Operators

Arithmetic operators are used in JavaScript to perform mathematical calculations such as addition, subtraction, multiplication, and division. You can also use an arithmetic operator to return the modulus of a calculation, which is the remainder left when you divide one number by another number.

Another type of JavaScript operator, bitwise operators, are used on integer values. However, these are a fairly complex topic. Bitwise operators and other complex operators are beyond the scope of this book.

The operand to the left of an operator is known as the left operand, and the operand to the right of an operator is known as the right operand.

Arithmetic Binary Operators

JavaScript binary arithmetic operators and their descriptions are listed in Table 9-5.

Name	Operator	Description
Addition	+	Adds two operands
Subtraction	–	Subtracts one operand from another operand
Multiplication	*	Multiplies one operand by another operand
Division	/	Divides one operand by another operand
Modulus	%	Divides one operand by another operand and returns the remainder

Table 9-5   Arithmetic binary operators

The following code shows examples of expressions that include arithmetic binary operators. Figure 9-8 shows how the expressions appear in a Web browser:

```
var x = 0, y = 0, arithmeticValue = 0;
// ADDITION
x = 400;
y = 600;
arithmeticValue = x + y; // arithmeticValue changes to 1000
document.write("<p>arithmeticValue after addition ↵
   expression: " + arithmeticValue + "</p>");
// SUBTRACTION
x = 14;
y = 6;
arithmeticValue = x - y; // arithmeticValue changes to 8
document.write("<p>arithmeticValue after subtraction ↵
   expression: " + arithmeticValue + "</p>");
// MULTIPLICATION
x = 20;
y = 4;
arithmeticValue = x * y; // arithmeticValue changes to 80
document.write("<p>arithmeticValue after multiplication ↵
    expression: " + arithmeticValue + "</p>");
// DIVISION
x = 99;
y = 3;
arithmeticValue = x / y; // arithmeticValue changes to 33
document.write("<p>arithmeticValue after division ↵
    expression: " + arithmeticValue + "</p>");
// MODULUS
x = 5;
y = 3;
arithmeticValue = x % y; // arithmeticValue changes to 2
document.write("<p>arithmeticValue after modulus ↵
    expression: " + arithmeticValue + "</p>");
```

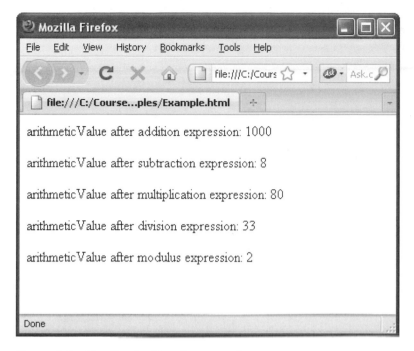

Figure 9-8   Results of arithmetic expressions

Notice in the preceding code that JavaScript performs an arithmetic calculation on the right side of the assignment operator and then assigns the value to a variable on the left side of the assignment operator. For example, in the statement arithmeticValue = x + y;, the operands x and y are added, and then the result is assigned to the arithmeticValue variable on the left side of the assignment operator.

You may be confused by the difference between the division (/) operator and the modulus (%) operator. The division operator performs a standard mathematical division operation. For example, dividing 15 by 6 results in a value of 2.5. By contrast, the modulus operator returns the remainder from the division of two integers. The following code, for instance, uses the division and modulus operators to return the result of dividing 15 by 6. The result is a value of 2.5 because 6 goes into 15 exactly 2.5 times. But, if you only allow for whole numbers, 6 goes into 15 only 2 times, with a remainder of 3. Thus, the modulus of 15 divided by 6 is 3, because 3 is the remainder following the division. Figure 9-9 shows the output.

```
var divisionResult = 15 / 6;
var modulusResult = 15 % 6;
document.write("<p>15 divided by 6 is "
    + divisionResult + ".</p>"); // prints '2.5'
document.write("<p>The whole number 6 goes into 15 twice, ↵
    with a remainder of "+ modulusResult + ".</p>"); // ↵
        prints '3'
```

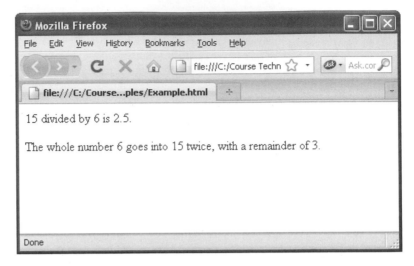

Figure 9-9   Division and modulus expressions

You can include a combination of variables and literal values on the right side of an assignment statement. For example, any of the following addition statements are correct:

```
arithmeticValue = 250 + y;
arithmeticValue = x + 425;
arithmeticValue = 250 + 425;
```

However, you cannot include a literal value as the left operand because the JavaScript interpreter must have a variable to which it can assign the returned value. Therefore, the statement 362 = x + y; causes an error.

When performing arithmetic operations on string values, the JavaScript interpreter attempts to convert the string values to numbers. The variables in the following example are assigned as string values instead of numbers because they are contained within quotation marks. Nevertheless, the JavaScript interpreter correctly performs the multiplication operation and returns a value of 20.

```
x = "4";
y = "5";
arithmeticValue = x * y; // the value returned is 20
```

The JavaScript interpreter does not convert strings to numbers when you use the addition operator. The strings are combined instead of being added together. In the following example, the operation returns a value of 54 because the x and y variables contain strings instead of numbers:

```
x = "5";
y = "4";
arithmeticValue = x + y; // a string value of 54 is returned
```

Arithmetic Unary Operators

Arithmetic operations can also be performed on a single variable using unary operators. Table 9-6 lists the arithmetic unary operators in JavaScript.

Name	Operator	Description
Increment	++	Increases an operand by a value of one
Decrement	--	Decreases an operand by a value of one
Negation	-	Returns the opposite value (negative or positive) of an operand

Table 9-6   Arithmetic unary operators

The increment (++) and decrement (--) unary operators can be used as prefix or postfix operators. A **prefix operator** is placed before a variable, and a **postfix operator** is placed after a variable. For example, the statements ++count; and count++; both increase the count variable by one. However, the two statements return different values. When you use the increment operator as a prefix operator, the value of the operand is returned *after* it is increased by a value of one. When you use the increment operator as a postfix operator, the value of the operand is returned *before* it is increased by a value of one. Similarly, when you use the decrement operator as a prefix operator, the value of the operand is returned *after* it is decreased by a value of one, and when you use the decrement operator as a postfix operator, the value of the operand is returned *before* it is decreased by a value of one. If you intend to assign the incremented or decremented value to another variable, it makes a difference whether you use the prefix or postfix operator.

You use arithmetic unary operators whenever you want to use a more simplified expression for increasing or decreasing a value by 1. For example, the statement count = count + 1; is identical to the statement ++count;. As you can see, if your goal is only to increase a variable by 1, it is easier to use the unary increment operator. But remember that with the prefix operator, the value of the operand is returned *after* it is increased or decreased by a value of 1. By contrast, with the postfix operator, the value of the operand is returned *before* it is increased or decreased by a value of 1.

As an example of when you would use the prefix operator or postfix operator, consider an integer variable named studentID that is used for assigning student IDs in a class registration script. One way of creating a new student ID number is to store the last assigned student ID in the studentID variable. When it's time to assign a new student ID, the script could retrieve the last value stored in the studentID variable and then increase its value by 1. In other words, the last value stored in the studentID variable will be the next number used for a student ID number. In this case, you would use the postfix operator to return the value of the expression *before* it is incremented, using a statement similar to `currentID = studentID++;`. If you are storing the last assigned student ID in the `studentID` variable, you would want to increment the value by 1 and use the result as the next student ID. In this scenario, you would use the prefix operator, which returns the value of the expression after it is incremented using a statement similar to `currentID = ++studentID;`.

Figure 9-10 shows a simple script that uses the prefix increment operator to assign three student IDs to a variable named `curStudentID`. The initial student ID is stored in the `studentID` variable and initialized to a starting value of 100. Figure 9-11 shows the output.

```
var studentID = 100;
var curStudentID;
CurStudentID = ++studentID; // assigns '101'
document.write("<p>The first student ID is "
    + curStudentID + "</p>");
curStudentID = ++studentID; // assigns '102'
document.write("<p>The second student ID is "
    + curStudentID + "</p>");
curStudentID = ++studentID; // assigns '103'
document.write("<p>The third student ID is "
    + curStudentID + "</p>");
```
— perfix increment operator

Figure 9-10 Script that uses the prefix increment operator

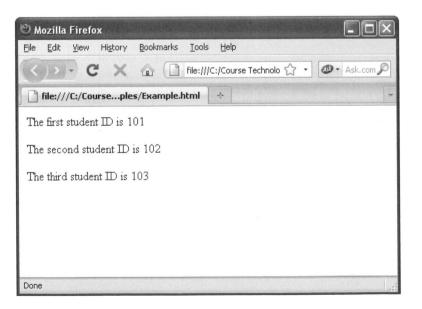

Figure 9-11 Output of the prefix version of the student ID script

The script in Figure 9-12 performs the same tasks, but uses a postfix increment operator. Notice that the output in Figure 9-13 differs from the output in Figure 9-11. Because the first example of the script uses the prefix increment operator, which increments the studentID variable *before* it is assigned to curStudentID, the script does not use the starting value of 100. Rather, it first increments the studentID variable and uses 101 as the first student ID. By contrast, the second example of the script uses the initial value of 100 because the postfix increment operator increments the studentID variable *after* it is assigned to curStudentID.

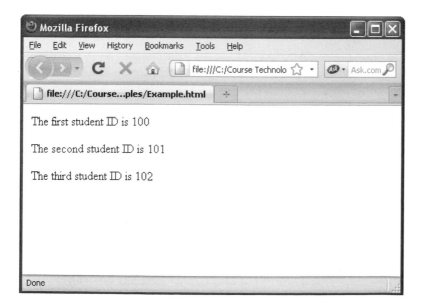

```
var studentID = 100;
var curStudentID;
CurStudentID = studentID++; // assigns '100'
document.write("<p>The first student ID is "
       + curStudentID + "</p>");
curStudentID = studentID++; // assigns '101'
document.write("<p>The second student ID is "
       + curStudentID + "</p>");
curStudentID = studentID++; // assigns '102'
document.write("<p>The second student ID is "
       + curStudentID + "</p>");
```

postfix increment operator

Figure 9-12   Script that uses a postfix increment operator

Mozilla Firefox

File   Edit   View   History   Bookmarks   Tools   Help

file:///C:/Course Technolo   ·   Ask.com

file:///C:/Course...ples/Example.html

The first student ID is 100

The second student ID is 101

The third student ID is 102

Done

Figure 9-13   Output of the postfix version of the student ID script

Next, you will modify the planner.html file of the Don's Weddings site so that it calculates the cost of a wedding.

To modify the planner.html file so that it calculates the cost of a wedding:

1. Return to the **planner.html file** in your text editor.

2. Locate the text [Add details form here] and replace it with the following form, which allows users to enter the number of guests and limousines for a wedding. Notice that the numGuests and numLimousines text boxes use onchange events to call the calcGuests() and calcLimousines() functions, respectively. You will add these functions next.

```
<form action="" name="details">
<table>
  <tr>
    <td>Guests<br />
      ($65 each)</td>
    <td><input type="text"
      name="numGuests" size="3"
      onchange="calcGuests()" /></td>
  </tr>
  <tr>
    <td>Limousines<br />
      ($125 each)</td>
    <td><input type="text"
      name="numLimousines" size="3"
      onchange="calcLimousines()"/></td>
  </tr>
</table>
</form>
```

3. Locate the text [Add estimate form here] and replace it with the following form, which simply displays the calculated estimate.

```
<form action="" name="estimate">
<p>
    Estimated total cost:
    <input type="text" name="cost" size="5"
        style="border-style: none; border-color: ↵
        inherit; border-width: medium; ↵
        background-color: Transparent" /></p>
</form>
```

4. Add the following `calcGuests()` function to the end of the script section. The first statement subtracts the current guest cost from the `totalEstimate` variable. The second and third statements calculate the new guest cost, and the fourth statement assigns the new estimate to the text box in the estimate form.

```
function calcGuests() {
    totalEstimate -= guestsCost;
    guestsCost = document.details.numGuests.value
        * 65;
    totalEstimate += guestsCost;
    document.estimate.cost.value = "$"
        + totalEstimate;
}
```

5. Add the following `calcLimousines()` function to the end of the script section. This function contains the same statements as the `calcGuests()` function, except that it calculates the limousine cost instead.

```
function calcLimousines() {
    totalEstimate -= limousinesCost;
    limousinesCost =
        document.details.numLimousines.value * 125;
    totalEstimate += limousinesCost;
    document.estimate.cost.value = "$"
        + totalEstimate;
}
```

6. Save the **planner.html** file and open it in your Web browser. Test the form by entering values in the Guests and Limousines text boxes. Figure 9-14 shows how the page appears after a user enters some values.

Figure 9-14　Wedding Planner page

> **7.** Close your Web browser window.

Using Assignment Operators

Assignment operators are used for assigning a value to a variable. You have already used the most common assignment operator, the equal sign (=), to assign values to variables you declared using the var statement. The equal sign assigns an initial value to a new variable or assigns a new value to an existing variable. For example, the following code creates a variable named favoriteBook, uses the equal sign to assign it an initial value, then uses the equal sign again to assign the variable a new value:

```
var favoriteBook = "A Farewell to Arms";
favoriteBook = "The Kite Runner";
```

JavaScript includes other assignment operators in addition to the equal sign. These additional operators, called **compound assignment operators**, perform mathematical calculations on variables and literal values in an expression, and then assign a new value to the left operand. Table 9-7 displays a list of common JavaScript assignment operators.

Name	Operator	Description
Assignment	=	Assigns the value of the right operand to the left operand
Compound addition assignment	+=	Combines the value of the right and left operands, or adds the value of the right and left operands and assigns the new value to the left operand
Compound subtraction assignment	-=	Subtracts the value of the right operand from the value of the left operand and assigns the new value to the left operand
Compound multiplication assignment	*=	Multiplies the values of the right and left operands and assigns the new value to the left operand
Compound division assignment	/=	Divides the value of the left operand by the value of the right operand and assigns the new value to the left operand
Compound modulus assignment	%=	Divides the value of the left operand by the value of the right operand and assigns the remainder (the modulus) to the left operand

Table 9-7   Assignment operators

You can use the += compound addition assignment operator to combine two strings and to add numbers. In the case of strings, the string on the left side of the operator is combined with the string on the right side, and the new value is assigned to the left operator. Before combining operands, the JavaScript interpreter attempts to convert a nonnumeric operand, such as a string, to a number. If the conversion is not possible, you receive a value of "NaN", which stands for "Not a Number"; this value is returned when a mathematical operation does not result in a numerical value. The following code shows examples of the different assignment operators:

```
var x, y;
x = "Hello ";
x += "World"; // x changes to "Hello World"
document.write("<p>" + x + "<br />");
x = 100;
y = 200;
x += y;        // x changes to 300
document.write(x + "<br />");
x = 10;
y = 7;
x -= y;        // x changes to 3
document.write(x + "<br />");
x = 2;
y = 6;
x *= y;        // x changes to 12
document.write(x + "<br />");
```

The comparison operator (==) consists of two equal signs and performs a different function from that of the assignment operator, which consists of a single equal sign (=). As their names suggest, the comparison operator *compares* values, while the assignment operator *assigns* values.

Comparison operators are often used with two kinds of special statements: conditional statements and looping statements. You'll learn how to use comparison operators in such statements in Chapter 10.

```
x = 24;
y = 3;
x /= y;        // x changes to 8
document.write(x + "<br />");
x = 3;
y = 2;
x %= y;        // x changes to 1
document.write(x + "<br />");
x = "100";
y = 5;
x *= y;        // x changes to 500
document.write(x + "<br />");
x = "one hundred";
y = 5;
x *= y;        // x changes to NaN
document.write(x + "</p>");
```

Using Comparison and Conditional Operators

Comparison operators are used to compare two operands and determine if one numeric value is greater than another. A Boolean value of true or false is returned after two operands are compared. For example, the statement 5 < 3 would return a Boolean value of false because 5 is not less than 3. Table 9-8 lists the JavaScript comparison operators.

Name	Operator	Description
Equal	==	Returns true if the operands are equal
Strict equal	===	Returns true if the operands are equal and of the same type
Not equal	!=	Returns true if the operands are not equal
Strict not equal	!==	Returns true if the operands are not equal or not of the same type
Greater than	>	Returns true if the left operand is greater than the right operand
Less than	<	Returns true if the left operand is less than the right operand
Greater than or equal	>=	Returns true if the left operand is greater than or equal to the right operand
Less than or equal	<=	Returns true if the left operand is less than or equal to the right operand

Table 9-8   Comparison operators

You can use number or string values as operands with comparison operators. When two numeric values are used as operands, the JavaScript interpreter compares them numerically. For example, the statement `arithmeticValue = 5 > 4;` returns true because 5 is numerically greater than 4. When two nonnumeric values are used as operands, the JavaScript interpreter compares them in alphabetical order. The statement `arithmeticValue = "b" > "a";` returns true because *b* is alphabetically greater than *a*. When one operand is a number and the other is a string, the JavaScript interpreter attempts to convert the string value to a number. If the string value cannot be converted to a number, a value of false is returned. For example, the statement `arithmeticValue = 10 == "ten";` returns false because the JavaScript interpreter cannot convert the string "ten" to a number.

The comparison operator is often used with another kind of operator, the conditional operator. The **conditional operator** executes one of two expressions based on the results of a conditional expression. The syntax for the conditional operator is *conditional expression ? expression1: expression2;*. If the conditional expression evaluates to true, then `expression1` executes. If the conditional expression evaluates to false, then `expression2` executes.

The following code shows an example of the conditional operator. The conditional expression checks to see if the `intVariable` variable is greater than 100. If it is, the text "intVariable is greater than 100" is assigned to the `result` variable. If `intVariable` is not greater than 100, the text "intVariable is less than or equal to 100" is assigned to `result`. Because `intVariable` is equal to 150, the conditional statement returns a value of true, the first expression executes, and "intVariable is greater than 100" prints to the screen.

```
var intVariable = 150;
var result;
(intVariable > 100) ? result =
    "intVariable is greater than 100" : result =
    "intVariable is less than or equal to 100";
document.write(result);
```

Next, you will add fields and code to the Wedding Planner form that allow users to select live music and flowers. Conditional operators in associated functions for each field will determine whether to add or subtract the cost of each item.

To add fields and code to the Wedding Planner form that allow users to select live music and flowers:

1. Return to the **planner.html** file in your text editor.

2. Add the following elements and fields to the end of the table in the details form. Radio buttons allow users to select

whether to include live music and flowers. The radio buttons use onchange event handlers to call associated functions for each of the radio buttons.

```
<tr>
    <td>Live music<br />
        ($500)</td>
    <td>
        <input type="radio" name="music"
            onclick="addMusic()" />Yes
        <input type="radio" name="music"
            checked="checked"
            onclick="removeMusic()" />No
    </td>
</tr>
<tr>
    <td>Flowers<br />
        ($400)</td>
    <td>
        <input type="radio" name="flowers"
            onclick="addFlowers()" />Yes
        <input type="radio" name="flowers"
            checked="checked"
            onclick="removeFlowers()"/>No</td>
</tr>
```

3. Add the following global variables above the calcGuests() function. These variables will be used to determine whether the user has selected live music and flowers.

```
var liveMusic = false;
var flowers = false;
```

4. Add the following functions to the end of the script section. The addMusic() function uses a conditional operator to determine whether the liveMusic variable is set to false. If it is, then the liveMusicCost variable is assigned a value of 500. If not, it is assigned a value of 0. The liveMusicCost variable is then assigned to the totalEstimate variable with an addition assignment operator. The last two statements assign the liveMusic variable a value of true and the value of the totalEstimate variable to the text box in the estimate form. The removeMusic() function uses the same syntax as the addMusic() function, except that it assigns a value of –500 to the liveMusicCost variable, which causes the addition assignment expression to subtract the value from the totalEstimate variable.

```
function addMusic() {
    (liveMusic == false) ? liveMusicCost = 500
        : liveMusicCost = 0;
    totalEstimate += liveMusicCost;
```

```
        liveMusic = true;
        document.estimate.cost.value = "$"
            + totalEstimate;
    }
    function removeMusic() {
        (liveMusic == true) ? liveMusicCost = -500
            : liveMusicCost = 0;
        totalEstimate += liveMusicCost;
        liveMusic = false;
        document.estimate.cost.value = "$"
            + totalEstimate;
    }
```

5. Add the following addFlowers() and removeFlowers()
   functions to the end of the script section. These functions are
   identical to the addMusic() and removeMusic() functions,
   except that they update the total estimate to include flower
   costs instead of the music cost.

```
    function addFlowers() {
        (flowers == false) ? flowersCost = 400
            : flowersCost = 0;
        totalEstimate +- flowersCost;
        flowers = true;
        document.estimate.cost.value = "$"
            + totalEstimate;
    }
    function removeFlowers() {
        (flowers == true) ? flowersCost = -400
            : flowersCost = 0;
        totalEstimate += flowersCost;
        flowers = false;
        document.estimate.cost.value = "$"
            + totalEstimate;
    }
```

6. Save the **planner.html** file, and then validate it with the W3C
   Markup Validation Service at **http://validator.w3.org/**. Once
   the file is valid, close it in your text editor and open it in your
   Web browser. Test the functionality of the Live music and
   Flowers fields. Figure 9-15 shows how the page appears after
   adding the Live music and Flowers fields.

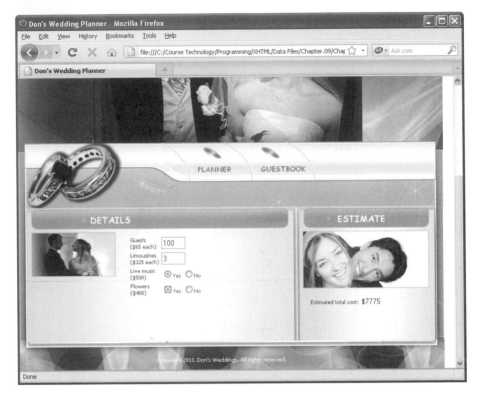

Figure 9-15 Wedding Planner page after adding the Live music and Flowers fields

7. Close your Web browser window and text editor.

Using Logical Operators

Logical operators are used for comparing two Boolean operands for equality. For example, a script for an automobile insurance company may need to determine whether a customer is male *and* under 21 in order to determine the correct insurance quote. As with comparison operators, a Boolean value of true or false is returned after two operands are compared. Table 9-9 lists the JavaScript logical operators.

Name	Operator	Description
And	&&	Returns true if both the left operand and right operand return a value of true; otherwise, it returns a value of false
Or	||	Returns true if either the left operand or right operand returns a value of true; if neither operand returns a value of true, the expression containing the Or (||) operator returns a value of false
Not	!	Returns true if an expression is false, and returns false if an expression is true

Table 9-9 Logical operators

The Or (||) and And (&&) operators are binary operators (requiring two operands), whereas the Not (!) operator is a unary operator (requiring a single operand). Logical operators are often used with comparison operators to evaluate expressions, allowing you to combine the results of several expressions into a single statement. For example, the And (&&) operator is used for determining whether two operands return an equivalent value. The operands themselves are often expressions. The following code uses the And operator to compare two separate expressions:

```
var gender = "male";
var age = 17;
var riskFactor = gender=="male" && age<=21; // returns true
```

In the preceding example, the gender variable expression evaluates to true because it is equal to "male", and the age variable expression evaluates to true because its value is less than or equal to 21. Because both expressions are true, riskFactor is assigned a value of true. The statement containing the And (&&) operator essentially says, "If variable gender is equal to "male" *and* variable age is less than or equal to 21, then assign a value of true to riskFactor. Otherwise, assign a value of false to riskFactor." In the following code, riskFactor is assigned a value of false because the age variable expression does not evaluate to true:

```
var gender = "male";
var age = 28;
var riskFactor = gender=="male" && age<=21; // returns false
```

The logical Or (||) operator checks to see if either expression evaluates to true. For example, the statement in the following code says, "If the variable speedingTicket is greater than 0 *or* variable age is less than or equal to 21, then assign a value of true to riskFactor. Otherwise, assign a value of false to riskFactor."

```
var speedingTicket = 2;
var age = 28;
var riskFactor = speedingTicket>0
    || age<=21; // returns true
```

The riskFactor variable in the preceding example is assigned a value of true because the speedingTicket variable expression evaluates to true, even though the age variable expression evaluates to false. This result occurs because the Or (||) statement returns true if *either* the left *or* right operand evaluates to true.

Logical operators are often used within conditional and looping statements such as the if...else, for, and while statements. You will learn about conditional and looping statements in Chapter 10.

The following code is an example of the Not (!) operator, which returns true if an operand evaluates to false and returns false if an operand evaluates to true. Notice that because the Not operator is unary, it requires only a single operand.

```
var trafficViolations = true;
var safeDriverDiscount
    = !trafficViolations; // returns false
```

Using Special Operators

JavaScript also includes the special operators that are listed in Table 9-10. These operators are used for various purposes, and do not fit within any other category.

Name	Operator	Description
Property access	.	Appends an object, method, or property to another object
Array index	[]	Accesses an element of an array
Function call	()	Calls up functions or changes the order in which individual operations are evaluated in an expression
Comma	,	Allows you to include multiple expressions in the same statement
Conditional expression	?:	Executes one of two expressions based on the results of a conditional expression
Delete	delete	Deletes array elements, variables created without the var keyword, and properties of custom objects
Property exists	in	Returns a value of true if a specified property is contained within an object
Object type	instanceof	Returns true if an object is of a specified object type
New object	new	Creates a new instance of a user-defined object type or a predefined JavaScript object type
Data type	typeof	Determines the data type of a variable
Void	void	Evaluates an expression without returning a result

Table 9-10   Special operators

You will be introduced to the special JavaScript operators as necessary throughout the remaining chapters. One special operator is typeof, which is useful because the data type of variables can change during the course of program execution. This can cause problems if you attempt to perform an arithmetic operation and one of the variables is a string or the null value. To avoid such problems, you can use the typeof operator to determine the data type of a variable. The syntax for the typeof operator is typeof(variablename);.

You should use the `typeof` operator whenever you need to be sure that a variable is the correct data type. The values that can be returned by the `typeof` operator are listed in Table 9-11.

Return value	Returned for
Number	Integers and floating-point numbers
String	Text strings
Boolean	True or false
Object	Objects, arrays, and null variables
Function	Functions
Undefined	Undefined variables

Table 9-11   Values returned by `typeof` operator

Short Quiz 3

1. What is the difference between the division (/) operator and the modulus (%) operator?

2. How do you use prefix and postfix operators?

3. Explain how to use the += compound addition assignment operator.

4. Explain how the JavaScript interpreter compares nonnumeric values.

5. Explain how to use logical operators.

Understanding Operator Precedence

When using operators to create expressions in JavaScript, you need to be aware of the precedence of the operators. The term **operator precedence** refers to the order in which operations are evaluated in an expression. Table 9-12 shows the order of precedence for JavaScript operators. Operators in the same grouping in Table 9-12 have the same order of precedence. When performing operations with operators in the same precedence group, the order of precedence is determined by the operator's **associativity**—that is, the order in which operators of equal precedence execute. Associativity is evaluated from left to right or right to left depending on the operators involved, as you will learn shortly.

Operators	Description	Associativity
.	Objects—highest precedence	Left to right
[]	Array elements—highest precedence	Left to right
()	Functions/evaluation—highest precedence	Left to right
new	New object—highest precedence	Right to left
++	Increment	Right to left
--	Decrement	Right to left
-	Unary negation	Right to left
+	Unary positive	Right to left
!	Not	Right to left
typeof	Data type	Right to left
void	Void	Right to left
delete	Delete object	Right to left
* / %	Multiplication/division/modulus	Left to right
+ -	Addition/concatenation and subtraction	Left to right
< <= > >=	Comparison	Left to right
instanceof	Object type	Left to right
in	Object property	Left to right
== != === !==	Equality	Left to right
&&	Logical And	Left to right
||	Logical Or	Left to right
?:	Conditional	Right to left
=	Assignment	Right to left
= += -= *= /= %=	Compound assignment	Right to left
,	Comma—lowest precedence	Left to right

Table 9-12 Operator precedence

The preceding list does not include bitwise operators because they are beyond the scope of this book.

Operators in a higher grouping have precedence over operators in a lower grouping. For example, the multiplication operator (*) has a higher precedence than the addition operator (+). Therefore, in the expression 5 + 2 * 8, the numbers 2 and 8 are multiplied first for a total of 16, and then the number 5 is added, resulting in a total of 21. If the addition operator had a higher precedence than the multiplication operator, the statement would evaluate to 56, because 5 would be added to 2 for a total of 7, which would then be multiplied by 8.

As an example of how associativity is evaluated, consider the multiplication and division operators, which have an associativity of left to right. Thus, the expression 30 / 5 * 2 results in a value of 12. Although the multiplication and division operators have equal precedence, the division operation executes first due to the left-to-right associativity of both operators (see Figure 9-16).

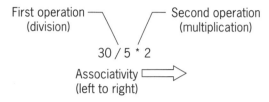

First operation
(division)

Second operation
(multiplication)

30 / 5 * 2

Associativity
(left to right)

Figure 9-16 Left-to-right associativity

If the multiplication operator had higher precedence than the division operator, the statement 30 / 5 * 2 would result in a value of 3 because the multiplication operation (5 * 2) would execute first. By contrast, the assignment operator and compound assignment operators—such as the compound multiplication assignment operator (*=)—have an associativity of right to left. Therefore, in the following code, the assignment operations take place from right to left. The variable x is incremented by 1 *before* it is assigned to the y variable using the compound multiplication assignment operator (*=). Then, the value of variable y is assigned to variable x. The result assigned to both the x and y variables is 8. Figure 9-17 illustrates the right to left associativity of the x = y *= ++x statement.

```
var x = 3;
var y = 2;
x = y *= ++x;
```

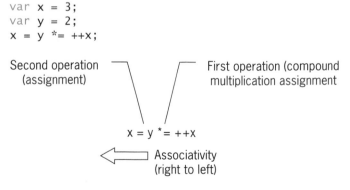

Second operation
(assignment)

First operation (compound
multiplication assignment

x = y *= ++x

Associativity
(right to left)

Figure 9-17 Right-to-left associativity

524

As you can see from the list in Table 9-12, parentheses have the highest precedence. Parentheses are used with expressions to change the associativity with which individual operations in an expression are evaluated. For example, the expression 5 + 2 ˙ 8, which evaluates to 21, can be rewritten as (5 + 2) ˙ 8, which evaluates to 56. The parentheses tell the JavaScript interpreter to add the numbers 5 and 2 before multiplying by 8. Using parentheses forces the statement to evaluate to 56 instead of 21.

Short Quiz 4

1. What is associativity and how does it affect operator precedence?

2. Which operator has the highest level of associativity?

3. Which operators have the lowest level of associativity?

Summing Up

- Functions refer to a related group of JavaScript statements that are executed as a single unit.

- The term *variable scope* refers to where in your program a declared variable can be used. A global variable is declared outside a function and is available to all parts of your program. A local variable is declared inside a function and is only available within that function.

- A data type is the specific category of information that a variable contains.

- JavaScript is a loosely typed programming language.

- An integer is a positive or negative number with no decimal places.

- A floating-point number contains decimal places or is written in exponential notation.

- A Boolean value is a logical value of true or false.

- An escape character tells the compiler or interpreter that the character after it has a special purpose.

- Operators are symbols used in expressions to manipulate operands, such as the addition operator (+) and multiplication operator (˙).

- A binary operator requires an operand before and after the operator.

- A unary operator requires a single operand either before or after the operator.

- Arithmetic operators are used in JavaScript to perform mathematical calculations such as addition, subtraction, multiplication, and division.

- Assignment operators are used for assigning a value to a variable.

- Comparison operators are used to compare two operands and determine if one numeric value is greater than another.

- The conditional operator executes one of two expressions based on the results of a conditional expression.

- Logical operators are used for comparing two Boolean operands for equality.

- Operator precedence is the order in which operations are evaluated in an expression.

Comprehension Check

1. A(n) _____ allows you to treat a related group of statements as a single unit.

   a. statement

   b. variable

   c. function

   d. event

2. Functions must contain parameters. True or False?

3. Explain how to return a value to a calling function.

4. A variable that is declared outside a function in a code declaration block is called a _____ variable.

   a. local

   b. class

   c. program

   d. global

5. When a program contains a global variable and a local variable with the same name, the local variable takes precedence when its function is called. True or False?

6. How can you declare a global variable? (Choose all that apply.)

   a. by declaring the variable outside of a function

   b. by declaring the variable anywhere in your script section with the `global` keyword

   c. by declaring the variable inside of a function without the `var` keyword

   d. by declaring the variable in a function named `global`

7. Explain the concept of data types.

8. JavaScript is a strongly typed programming language. True or False?

9. Explain the purpose of the `null` data type.

10. Which of the following values are integers? (Choose all that apply.)

    a. 1

    b. 1.1

    c. 4e12

    d. −10

11. Which of the following values are floating-point numbers? (Choose all that apply.)

    a. 3.0e5

    b. .78

    c. 1,385,456,200

    d. −976,345

12. Which of the following values can be assigned to a Boolean variable? (Choose all that apply.)

    a. 0

    b. 1

    c. true

    d. false

13. If you attempt to use a Boolean variable of false in a mathematical operation, JavaScript converts the variable to an integer value of 0. True or False?

14. The concatenation operator (+) is used for_____. (Choose all that apply.)

    a. adding numbers

    b. combining text strings

    c. combining variables

    d. incrementing numeric variables

15. Which of the following is the correct syntax for including double quotation and single quotation marks within a string that is already surrounded by double quotation marks?

    a. "Shaquille \"Shaq\" O\'Neal is a basketball player."

    b. "Shaquille "Shaq" O\'Neal is a basketball player."

    c. "Shaquille /"Shaq/" O/'Neal is a basketball player."

    d. "Shaquille ""Shaq"" O"Neal is a basketball player."

16. Explain the difference between unary and binary operators.

17. Explain how to use the conditional operator.

18. Which of the following characters separates expressions in the conditional expression used with a conditional operator?

    a. ?

    b. :

    c. ;

    d. &&

19. The Or (||) operator returns true if _____. (Choose all that apply.)

    a. the left operand and right operand both return a value of true

    b. the left operand returns a value of true

    c. the left operand and right operand both return a value of false

    d. the right operand returns a value of true

20. Which of the following expressions returns a value of 56?

   a. 7 ˙ (3 + 5)

   b. (7 ˙ 3) + 5

   c. (7 ˙ 3 + 5)

   d. 3 + 5 ˙ 7

Reinforcement Exercises

 Exercise 9-1

In this exercise, you will create a script that contains two functions.

1. Create a new HTML 5 document in your text editor and use "Two Functions" as the content of the `<title>` element.

2. Add a script section to the document head.

3. Add the first function to the script section as follows. This function writes a message to the screen using an argument that will ultimately be passed to it from the calling statement:

```
function printMessage(first_message) {
     document.write("<p>" + first_message + "</p>");
}
```

4. Add the second function, which displays a second message, to the end of the script section. In this case, the message ("This message was returned from a function.") is defined within the function itself. The only purpose of this function is to return the literal string "This message was returned from a function." to the calling statement.

```
function return_message() {
     return "<p>This message was returned from ↵
         a function.</p>";
}
```

5. Add a script section to the document body.

6. Type the following three statements, which call the functions in the document head. The first statement sends the text string "This message was printed by a function." This statement does not receive a return value. The second statement assigns the function call to a variable named `return_value`

but does not send any arguments to the function. The third statement writes the value of the return_value variable to the screen.

```
printMessage("This message was printed ⏎
    by a function.");
var return_value = return_message();
document.write(return_value);
```

7. Save the document as **TwoFunctions.html** in the Exercises folder for Chapter 9, and then validate the document with the W3C Markup Validation Service at **http://validator. w3.org/file-upload.html** to fix any errors. Once the document is valid, close it in your text editor.

8. Open the **TwoFunctions.html** document in your Web browser. Figure 9-18 shows how the document looks in a Web browser.

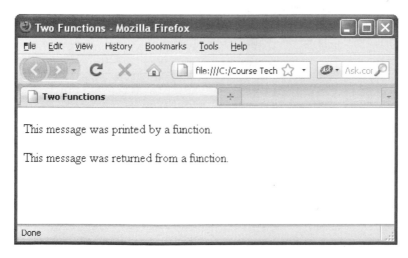

Figure 9-18   TwoFunctions.html in a Web browser

9. Close your Web browser window.

Exercise 9-2

In this exercise, you will create a script that uses assignment operators.

1. Create a new HTML 5 document in your text editor and use "Assignment Operators" as the content of the <title> element.

2. Add the following `<h1>` element to the document body:

   `<h1>Assignment Operators</h1>`

3. Add a script section to the document body.

4. Type the following statements in the script section. These statements perform several compound assignment operations on a variable named `dataVar`. After each assignment operation, the result is printed.

```
var dataVar = "Don ";
dataVar += "Gosselin";
document.writeln("<p>Variable after addition ↵
    assignment = " + dataVar + "<br />");
dataVar = 70;
dataVar += 30;
document.writeln("Variable after addition ↵
    assignment = " + dataVar + "<br />");
dataVar -= 50;
document.writeln("Variable after subtraction ↵
    assignment = " + dataVar + "<br />");
dataVar /= 10;
document.writeln("Variable after division ↵
    assignment = " + dataVar + "<br />");
dataVar *= 9;
document.writeln("Variable after multiplication ↵
    assignment = " + dataVar + "<br />");
dataVar %= 200;
document.writeln("Variable after modulus ↵
    assignment = " + dataVar + "</p>");
```

5. Save the document as **AssignmentOperators.html** in the Exercises folder for Chapter 9.

6. Use the W3C Markup Validation Service to validate the **AssignmentOperators.html** document and fix any errors. Once the document is valid, close it in your text editor, open it in your Web browser, and examine how the elements are rendered.

7. Close your Web browser window.

Exercise 9-3

In this exercise, you will create a script that uses comparison operators.

1. Create a new HTML 5 document in your text editor and use "Comparison Operators" as the content of the `<title>` element.

2. Add the following `<h1>` element to the document body:

   `<h1>Comparison Operators</h1>`

3. Add a script section to the document body.

4. Add the following statements to the script section that perform various comparison operations on two variables. Notice that the first comparison is performed using the conditional operator.

```
var conditionalValue;
var value1 = "Don";
var value2 = "Dave";
value1 == value2 ? document.write(
    "<p>value1 equal to value2: true<br />")
    : document.write(
    "<p>value1 equal to value2: false<br />");
value1 = 37;
value2 = 26;
conditionalValue = value1 == value2;
document.write("value1 equal to value2: "
    + conditionalValue + "<br />");
conditionalValue = value1 != value2;
document.write("value1 not equal to value2: "
    + conditionalValue + "<br />");
conditionalValue = value1 > value2;
document.write("value1 greater than value2: "
    + conditionalValue + "<br />");
conditionalValue = value1 < value2;
document.write("value1 less than value2: "
    + conditionalValue + "<br />");
conditionalValue = value1 >= value2;
document.write("value1 greater than or equal to ⏎
    value2: " + conditionalValue + "<br />");
conditionalValue = value1 <= value2;
document.write("value1 less than or equal to value2: "
    + conditionalValue + "<br />");
value1 = 21;
value2 = 21;
```

```
conditionalValue = value1 === value2;
document.write(
    "value1 equal to value2 AND the same data type: "
    + conditionalValue + "<br />");
conditionalValue = value1 !== value2;
document.write(
    "value1 not equal to value2 AND not the same ↵
    data type: " + conditionalValue
    + "</p>");
```

5. Save the document as **ComparisonOperators.html** in the Exercises folder for Chapter 9.

6. Use the W3C Markup Validation Service to validate the **ComparisonOperators.html** document and fix any errors. Once the document is valid, close it in your text editor, open it in your Web browser, and examine how the elements are rendered.

7. Close your Web browser window.

Exercise 9-4

In this exercise, you will create a script that uses logical operators.

1. Create a new HTML 5 document in your text editor and use "Order Fulfillment" as the content of the `<title>` element.

2. Add the following `<h1>` element to the document body:

    `<h1>Order Fulfillment</h1>`

3. Add a script section to the document body.

4. Add the following statements to the script section that use logical operators on two variables:

    ```
    var orderPlaced = true;
    var orderFilled = false;
    document.write("<p>Order has been placed: "
        + orderPlaced + "<br />");
    document.write("Order has been filled: "
        + orderFilled + "<br />");
    var orderComplete = orderPlaced && orderFilled;
    document.write("Order has been placed and filled: "
        + orderComplete + "</p>");
    ```

5. Save the document as **OrderFulfillment.html** in the Exercises folder for Chapter 9.

6. Use the W3C Markup Validation Service to validate the **OrderFulfillment.html** document and fix any errors. Once the document is valid, close it in your text editor, open it in your Web browser, and examine how the elements are rendered.

7. Close your Web browser window.

Exercise 9-5

In this exercise, you will create a script that displays a portion of a review for a production of the opera *Pagliacci*, performed by an opera company called Pine Knoll Productions. The review will be rendered using document.write() statements that combine text strings with escape characters. Note that you can create the same document more easily using only HTML elements. The purpose of this exercise is to demonstrate how text strings can be combined with escape characters.

1. Create a new HTML 5 document in your text editor and use "Pine Knoll Productions" as the content of the <title> element.

2. Add the following style section to the document head:

```
<style type="text/css">
body { font-family: 'Trebuchet MS', Arial,
Helvetica, sans-serif }
</style>
```

3. Add a script section to the document body.

4. Within the script section, add the following document.write() statements, which contain combinations of text, elements, and escape characters:

```
document.write("<p>Pine Knoll Productions ↵
    presents </p>");
document.write("<h1>Pagliacci</h1>");
document.write("<p><strong>by Ruggero ↵
    Leoncavallo</strong></p><hr />");
document.write("<p>The Pine Knoll Press calls ↵
    the company\'s production ");
document.write("of Leoncavallo\'s <em>Pagliacci</em> ↵
    a \"spectacular event\" ");
document.write("that will \"astound you\".");
```

5. Save the document as **Pagliacci.html** in the Exercises folder for Chapter 9.

6. Use the W3C Markup Validation Service to validate the **Pagliacci.html** document and fix any errors. Once the document is valid, close it in your text editor, open it in your Web browser, and examine how the elements are rendered.

7. Close your Web browser window.

Exercise 9-6

Next, you will create a script that assigns different data types to a variable and prints the variable's data type. You will use the `typeof` operator to determine the data type of each variable.

1. Create a new HTML 5 document in your text editor and use "Changing Data Types" as the content of the `<title>` element.

2. Add a script section to the document body.

3. Declare a variable in the script section named `changingType`:

   ```
   var changingType;
   ```

4. At the end of the script section, type the following line, which prints the data type contained in the `changingType` variable. The data type is currently "undefined" because `changingType` has not yet been assigned a value.

   ```
   document.write("<p>The changingType variable is "
         + typeof(changingType) + "<br />");
   ```

5. To the end of the script section, add the following two lines, which assign a string to the `changingType` variable and repeat the statement that prints the data type:

   ```
   changingType = "It's a jungle out there.";
   document.writeln("The changingType variable is "
         + typeof(changingType) + "<br />");
   ```

6. To the end of the script section, add the following lines, which change the `changingType` variable to the integer,

floating-point, Boolean, and null data types. The statement that prints each data type repeats each time the variable's data type changes.

```
changingType = 250;
document.writeln("The changingType variable is "
    + typeof(changingType) + "<br />");
changingType = 87.346;
document.writeln("The changingType variable is "
    + typeof(changingType) + "<br />");
changingType = true;
document.writeln("The changingType variable is "
    + typeof(changingType) + "<br />");
changingType = null;
document.writeln("The changingType variable is "
    + typeof(changingType) + "</p>");
```

7. Save the document as **ChangingTypes.html** in the Exercises folder for Chapter 9.

8. Use the W3C Markup Validation Service to validate the **ChangingTypes.html** document and fix any errors. Once the document is valid, close it in your text editor, open it in your Web browser, and examine how the elements are rendered.

9. Close your Web browser window.

Exercise 9-7

Next, you will create a script that contains the formula for converting Fahrenheit temperatures to Celsius. You will need to modify the formula so it uses the correct order of precedence to convert the temperature.

1. Create a new HTML 5 document in your text editor and use "Convert to Celsius" as the content of the <title> element.

2. Add a script section to the document body.

3. Within the script section, add the following declaration for a variable named fTemp that represents a Fahrenheit temperature. The variable is assigned a value of 86 degrees.

```
var fTemp = 86;
```

4. Add the following two statements to the end of the script section. The first statement declares a variable named cTemp that will store the converted temperature. The right operand includes the formula for converting from Fahrenheit to Celsius. (Remember that the formula as given below is incorrect; later in this exercise you will correct the order of precedence in the formula.) The last statement prints the value assigned to the cTemp variable.

```
var cTemp = fTemp - 32 * 5 / 9;
document.write("<p>" + fTemp
    + " Fahrenheit is equal to " + cTemp
    + " degrees Celsius.</p>");
```

5. Save the document as **ConvertToCelsius.html** in the Exercises folder for Chapter 9, and then open the document in your Web browser. A temperature of 86 degrees Fahrenheit is actually equivalent to 30 degrees Celsius. However, the formula incorrectly calculates that 86 degrees Fahrenheit is equivalent to 68.22222222222223 Celsius.

6. Close your Web browser window and return to the **ConvertToCelsius.html** document in your text editor.

7. Modify the order of precedence in the Fahrenheit-to-Celsius formula by adding parentheses as follows so that it correctly calculates a value of 30 degrees Celsius for 86 degrees Fahrenheit:

```
var cTemp = (fTemp - 32) * (5 / 9);
```

8. Save the **ConvertToCelsius.html** document, close it in your text editor, and then open it in your Web browser. The temperature should be calculated correctly as 30 degrees Celsius.

9. Close your Web browser window.

Discovery Projects

Save your Discovery Projects documents in the Projects folder for Chapter 9. Create the documents so they are well formed according to the HTML 5 DTD. Be sure to validate each document with the W3C Markup Validation Service.

Discovery Project 9-1

Create a Web page with five text boxes. Assign each text box's `value` attribute a value of zero. To each text box, add an `onchange` event handler that calls a function named `calcAvg()` and passes the function the value of that text box by referencing its document object, form name, and `name` and `value` attributes. Within the `calcAvg()` function, pass the five parameters to another function named `performCalc()`, assign the return value to a variable named `calcResult`, and then place the returned value to another text box with a `name` attribute of `result`. In the `performCalc()` function, calculate the average of the five numbers (by adding the five values and dividing by five), then return the result to the `calcAvg()` function. When you perform the calculation, use the `parseFloat()` function to ensure that the passed values are calculated as numbers. Save the document as **CalcAverage.html**.

Discovery Project 9-2

The formula for calculating body mass index (BMI) is *weight * 703 / height². For example, if you weigh 200 pounds and are 72 inches tall, you can calculate your body mass index with the expression (200 * 703) / (72 * 72).* Create a Web page that contains three text boxes: one for your weight in pounds, one for your height in inches, and one that will contain the BMI result. Create a script with a function named `calcBMI()` that performs the calculation using the values in the weight and height text boxes, and assign the result to the BMI text box. Convert the value to an integer by using the `parseInt()` function. Reference the text boxes from within the function by using the document object, form name, and `name` and `value` attributes of each text box (in other words, don't use function arguments). Perform the calculation by calling the function from an `onclick` event in a button element. Save the document as **BMI.html**.

Discovery Project 9-3

One built-in JavaScript function that you saw in this chapter is the eval() function, which evaluates expressions contained within strings. You can include a string literal or string variable as the argument for the eval() function. If the string literal or string variable you pass to the eval() function does not contain an expression that can be evaluated, you will receive an error. The statement var returnValue = eval("5 + 3"); returns the value 8 and assigns it to the returnValue variable. The statement var returnValue = eval("10"); also evaluates correctly and returns a value of 10, even though the string within the eval() function does not contain operators. The eval() function has one restriction: you cannot send it a text string that does not contain operators or numbers. If you do, an empty value is returned. For example, the statement var returnValue = eval("this is a text string"); assigns an empty value to the returnValue variable because it does not contain numbers or operators. However, the following statement evaluates correctly because the string sent to the eval() function contains the concatenation operator:

```
var returnValue = eval("'this is a text string' +
   ' and this is another text string'");
```

Use the eval() function to create a calculator program that includes push buttons and onclick event handlers. Use a variable named inputString to contain the operands and operators of a calculation. After a calculation is added to the inputString variable, perform the calculation using the eval() function. Use a single function named updateString() that accepts a single value representing a number or operator. Then, add the value to the inputString variable using the += assignment operator. After the inputString variable is updated, assign it as the value of a text box in a form. Save the document as **Calculator.html**.

CHAPTER 10

Building Arrays and Control Structures

In this chapter, you will:

◎ Store data in arrays

◎ Use `if` statements, `if...else` statements, and `switch` statements to make decisions

◎ Nest one `if` statement in another

◎ Use `while` statements, `do...while` statements, and `for` statements to repeatedly execute code

◎ Use `continue` statements to restart a looping statement

The code you have written so far has been linear in nature. In other words, your programs start at the beginning and end when the last statement in the program executes. Decision-making and flow-control statements allow you to determine the order in which statements execute in a program. Controlling the flow of code and making decisions during program execution are two of the most fundamental skills required in programming. In this chapter, you will learn about both skills. First, however, you will learn about a data type that is often used with flow-control and decision-making statements: arrays.

Storing Data in Arrays

An **array** contains a set of data represented by a single variable name. You can think of an array as a collection of variables contained within a single variable. You use arrays to store groups or lists of related information in a single, easily managed location. Lists of names, courses, test scores, and prices are typically stored in arrays. For example, Figure 10-1 shows that you can manage cell phone makes and models using a single array named `cellPhones`. Such an array is especially useful because it can refer to individual phones without requiring you to retype each make and model. You will learn how to refer to an individual item in an array later in this chapter.

The identifiers you use for an array name must follow the same rules as identifiers for variables. They must begin with an uppercase or lowercase ASCII letter, dollar sign ($), or underscore (_). Also, the names can include numbers (but not as the first character), cannot include spaces, and cannot be reserved words.

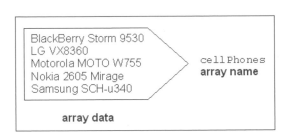

Figure 10-1   Example of an array

Declaring and Initializing Arrays

Arrays are represented in JavaScript by the `Array` object. The `Array` object contains a special constructor named `Array()` that is used for creating an array. A **constructor** is a special type of function that is the basis for creating reference variables (that is, variables whose data type is the reference data type). You create new arrays using the keyword `new`, the `Array()` constructor, and the following syntax:

```
var arrayName = new Array(number of elements);
```

Each piece of data contained in an array is called an **element**. Within the parentheses of the `Array()` construction, you include an integer that represents the number of elements to be contained in the array. The following code creates an array named cellPhones that has 10 elements:

```
var cellPhones = new Array(10);
```

An **index** is an element's numeric position within the array. The numbering of elements within an array starts with an index number of zero. (This numbering scheme can be very confusing for beginners.) You refer to a specific element by enclosing its index number in brackets at the end of the array name. For example, the first element in the cellPhones array is cellPhones[0], the second element is cellPhones[1], the third element is cellPhones[2], and so on. This also means that if you have an array of 10 elements, the tenth element in the array would be referred to using an index of 9. You assign values to individual array elements in the same fashion as you assign values to a standard variable, except that you include the index for an individual element of the array. The following code assigns values to the first three elements within the cellPhones array:

```
cellPhones[0] = "BlackBerry Storm 9530"; // first element
cellPhones[1] = "LG VX8360"; // second element
cellPhones[2] - "Motorola MOTO W755"; // third element
```

When you create a new array with the Array() constructor, declaring the number of array elements is optional. You can create the array without any elements and add new elements to the array as necessary. The size of an array can change dynamically. If you assign a value to an element that has not yet been created, the element is created automatically, along with any elements that might precede it. For example, the first statement in the following code creates the cellPhones array without any elements. The second statement then assigns "BlackBerry Storm 9530" to the third element, which also creates the first two elements (cellPhones[0] and cellPhones[1]) in the process. However, note that until you assign values to them, cellPhones[0] and cellPhones[1] will both contain undefined values.

```
cellPhones = new Array();
cellPhones[2] = "BlackBerry Storm 9530";
```

You can also assign values to array elements when you create the array. The following code assigns some values to the cellPhones array when it is created:

```
cellPhones = new Array("BlackBerry Storm 9530",
    "LG VX8360", "Motorola MOTO W755");
```

Should you declare the number of array elements when you first create a new array, or should you allow the size of the array to change dynamically? The basic rule of thumb is that you should only declare the size of the array if you know the exact number of elements that the array will store. Your program will perform faster if it does not need to continuously add new elements to an array at runtime.

However, if you don't know how many elements your array will require, you could receive a runtime error if your script attempts to access an array element that does not exist or has not been assigned a value. So, if you don't know how many elements your array will require, it's better to allow the script to size the array dynamically.

Most programming languages require all elements in an array to have the exact same data type. However, in JavaScript the values assigned to array elements can be of different data types. For example, the following code creates an array and stores values with different data types in the array elements:

```
var hotelReservation = new Array(4);
hotelReservation[0]
    = "Don Gosselin"; // guest name (string)
hotelReservation[1]
    = 5; // # of nights (integer)
hotelReservation[2]
    = 97.36; // price per night (floating point)
hotelReservation[3] = true; // nonsmoking room (Boolean)
```

Accessing Element Information

You access an element's value just as you access the value of any other variable, except that you include brackets and the element index. For example, the following code prints the values contained in the first three elements of the cellPhones array:

```
document.writeln(
    cellPhones[0]); // prints "BlackBerry Storm 9530"
document.writeln(
    cellPhones[1]); // prints "LG VX8360"
document.writeln(
    cellPhones[2]); // prints "Motorola MOTO W755"
```

Modifying Elements

You modify values in existing array elements in the same way you modify values in a standard variable, except that you include brackets and the element index. The following code assigns values to the first three elements in the cellPhones array:

```
cellPhones[0] = "BlackBerry Storm 9530"; // first element
cellPhones[1] = "LG VX8360"; // second element
cellPhones[2] = "Motorola MOTO W755"; // third element
```

After you have assigned a value to an array element, you can change it later, just as you can change other variables in a script. To change the first array element in the cellPhones array from "BlackBerry Storm 9530" to "BlackBerry 8830 World Edition", you use the following statement:

```
cellPhones[0] = "BlackBerry 8830 World Edition";
```

Determining the Number of Elements in an Array

The Array class contains a single property, the **length property**, which returns the number of elements in an array. You append the length property to the name of the array whose length you want to retrieve using the following syntax: *array_name*.length;. Remember that, unlike method names, property names are not followed by parentheses. The following statements illustrate how to use the length property to return the number of elements in the cellPhones[] array:

```
cellPhones = new Array();
cellPhones[0] = "BlackBerry Storm 9530"; // first element
cellPhones[1] = "LG VX8360"; // second element
cellPhones[2] = "Motorola MOTO W755"; // third element
document.write("<p>The cell phone array has "
    + cellPhones.length + " elements.</p>");
```

Short Quiz 1

1. How do you declare and initialize an array?

2. How do you access and modify the individual elements in an array?

3. How do you determine the number of elements in an array?

Making Decisions

When you write a computer program, regardless of the programming language, you often need to execute different sets of statements depending on predetermined criteria. For example, you might create a program that needs to execute one set of code in the morning and another set of code at night. Or, you might create a program that must execute one set of code when it runs in Internet Explorer and another when it runs in Firefox. Additionally, you might create a program that depends on user input to determine exactly what code to run. For instance, suppose you create a Web page through which users place online orders. If a user clicks the Add to Shopping Cart button, a set of statements that builds a list of items to be purchased must execute. However, if the user clicks the Checkout button to complete the transaction, an entirely different set of statements must execute. The process of determining the order in which program statements execute is called **decision making** or **flow control**.

The special types of JavaScript statements used for making decisions are called decision-making statements or decision-making structures. The most common type of decision-making statement is the if statement, which you will study first.

Using if Statements

The **if statement** is used to execute specific programming code if the evaluation of a conditional expression returns a value of true. The syntax for a simple if statement is as follows:

```
if (conditional expression)
    statement;
```

The if statement contains three parts: the keyword if, a conditional expression enclosed within parentheses, and executable statements. Note that the conditional expression must be enclosed within parentheses.

If the condition being evaluated returns a value of true, the statement immediately following the conditional expression executes. After the if statement executes, any subsequent code executes normally. Consider the following code. Here, the if statement uses the equal (==) comparison operator to determine whether the variable exampleVar is equal to 5. (You learned about operators in Chapter 9.) Because the condition returns a value of true, two alert dialog boxes appear. The first is generated by the if statement when the condition returns a value of true, and the second alert dialog box executes after the if statement is completed.

The statement immediately following the if statement can be written on the same line as the if statement itself. However, using a line break and indentation makes the code easier for the programmer to read.

```
var exampleVar = 5;
if (exampleVar == 5)      // CONDITION EVALUATES TO 'TRUE'
    window.alert("<p>The variable is equal to ↵
        '5'.</p>");
window.alert("<p>This dialog box is generated after ↵
    the if statement.</p>");
```

In contrast, the following code displays only the second alert dialog box. The condition evaluates to false because exampleVar is assigned the value 4 instead of 5.

```
var exampleVar = 4;
if (exampleVar == 5) // CONDITION EVALUATES TO 'FALSE'
    window.alert("<p>This dialog box will not ↵
        appear.</p>");
window.alert("<p>This is the only dialog box that ↵
    appears.</p>");
```

You can use a command block to construct a decision-making structure using multiple if statements. A **command block** is a set of statements contained within a set of braces, similar to the way function statements are contained within a set of braces. Each command block must have an opening brace ({) and a closing brace (}). If a command block is missing either brace, an error occurs. The following code shows a script that runs a command block if the conditional expression within the if statement evaluates to true:

```
var exampleVar = 5;
if (exampleVar == 5) { // CONDITION EVALUATES TO 'TRUE'
    document.write("<p>The condition evaluates to
        true.</p>");
    document.write("<p><code>exampleVar</code> is
        equal to 5.</p>");
    document.write("<p>Each of these lines will be
        printed.</p>");
}
document.write("<p>This statement always executes
    after the if statement.</p>");
```

When an if statement contains a command block, the statements in it execute when the if statement condition evaluates to true. After the command block executes, the code that follows it executes normally. When the condition evaluates to false, the command block is skipped, and the statements that follow it execute. If the conditional expression within the if statement in the preceding code evaluates to false, only the write() statement following the command block executes.

Next, you will start working on an astrology quiz for a company named Astrology by Promila. You can find the astrology quiz files in a folder named AstrologyQuiz in your Chapter folder for Chapter 10. The script will be set up so that users select answers using radio buttons created with the <input> tag within a form. In this first quiz, each question will be scored immediately. You will create the form containing the radio buttons and then use a series of if statements to score each question.

To create the astrology quiz program and its form section:

1. Open the **AstrologyQuiz.html** file in your text editor. The file is located in a folder named AstrologyQuiz in your Chapter folder for Chapter 10.

2. Locate the text <!-- Add quiz here --> and replace it with the following form and table:

```
<form action="" name="quiz">
<table style="width: 100%">
<tr>
</tr>
</form>
```

3. Add the following lines to the <tr> element for the first question. The four radio buttons represent the answers. Because each button within a radio button group requires the same

Name attribute, these four radio buttons have the same name of "question1". Each radio button is also assigned a value corresponding to its answer letter: a, b, c, or d. For each radio button group, the onclick event sends the button value to an individual function that scores the answer. Notice that the value for each button is sent to the function as a parameter.

```
<td><p><strong>1. Which zodiac sign looks like a ↵
    pair of fish?</strong></p><p>
<input type="radio" name="question1" value="a"
    onclick="scoreQuestion1('a')" />
    Pisces<br /><!-- correct answer -->
<input type="radio" name="question1" value="b"
    onclick="scoreQuestion1('b')" />Aquarius<br />
<input type="radio" name="question1" value="c"
    onclick="scoreQuestion1('c')" />Libra<br />
<input type="radio" name="question1" value="d"
    onclick="scoreQuestion1('d')" />Virgo</p></td>
```

You can build the program quickly by copying the input button code for the first question, pasting it into a new document, and then editing it to create questions 2 through 5. If you use this method to create the input buttons in the following steps, make sure that you change the question number for each input button name and the function it calls.

4. Add the lines for the second question. If you prefer, copy and paste the code you typed earlier, taking care to make the necessary edits.

```
<td><p><strong>2. Which of the following zodiac signs is
called "the bull"?</strong></p><p>
<input type="radio" name="question2" value="a"
    onclick="scoreQuestion2('a')" />Aries<br />
<input type="radio" name="question2" value="b"
    onclick="scoreQuestion2('b')" />Gemini<br />
<input type="radio" name="question2" value="c"
    onclick="scoreQuestion2('c')" />
    Leo<br /> <!-- correct answer -->
<input type="radio" name="question2" value="d"
    onclick="scoreQuestion2('d')" />Scorpio</p>
```

5. Add the lines for the third question, using copy and paste if you prefer.

```
<p><strong>3. How many signs are in the zodiac?
</strong></p><p>
<input type="radio" name="question3" value="a"
    onclick="scoreQuestion3('a')" />6<br />
<input type="radio" name="question3" value="b"
    onclick="scoreQuestion3('b')" />
    12<br /> <!-- correct answer -->
<input type="radio" name="question3" value="c"
    onclick="scoreQuestion3('c')" />14<br />
```

```
<input type="radio" name="question3" value="d"
    onclick="scoreQuestion3('d')" />24</p></td>
```

6. Add the following lines for the fourth question:

```
<td><br><p><strong>4. What is the last sign in the
astrological calendar?</strong></p><p>
<input type="radio" name="question4" value="a"
    onclick="scoreQuestion4('a')" />Aries<br />
<input type="radio" name="question4" value="b"
    onclick="scoreQuestion4('b')" />Sagittarius<br />
<input type="radio" name="question4" value="c"
    onclick="scoreQuestion4('c')" />
    Pisces<br /> <!-- correct answer -->
<input type="radio" name="question4" value="d"
    onclick="scoreQuestion4('d')" />Cancer</p>
```

7. Add the following lines for the fifth question:

```
<p><strong>5. Which of these is not an air
sign?</strong></p><p>
<input type="radio" name="question5" value="a"
    onclick="scoreQuestion5('a')" />Gemini<br />
<input type="radio" name="question5" value="b"
    onclick="scoreQuestion5('b')" />Libra<br />
<input type="radio" name="question5" value="c"
    onclick="scoreQuestion5('c')" />Aries<br />
<input type="radio" name="question5" value="d"
    onclick="scoreQuestion5('d')" />
    Virgo</p> <!-- correct answer --></td>
```

8. Save **AstrologyQuiz.html** in the Chapter folder for Chapter 10.

Next you will add the functions to score each of the questions. The functions contain if statements that evaluate each answer.

To add JavaScript code to score each of the questions:

1. Add the following script section to the document head:

```
<script type="text/javascript">
/* <![CDATA[ */
/* ]]> */
</script>
```

2. In the script section, add the following function, which scores the first question. A response of "Correct Answer" or "Incorrect Answer" appears depending on the user's answer.

```
function scoreQuestion1(answer) {
    if (answer == "a")
        window.alert("Correct Answer");
    if (answer == "b")
        window.alert("Incorrect Answer");
    if (answer == "c")
        window.alert("Incorrect Answer");
```

```
        if (answer == "d")
            window.alert("Incorrect Answer");
}
```

3. Add the following scoreQuestion2() function after the scoreQuestion1() function:

```
function scoreQuestion2(answer) {
        if (answer == "a")
            window.alert("Incorrect Answer");
        if (answer == "b")
            window.alert("Incorrect Answer");
        if (answer == "c")
            window.alert("Correct Answer");
        if (answer == "d")
            window.alert("Incorrect Answer");
}
```

4. Add the following scoreQuestion3() function after the scoreQuestion2() function:

```
function scoreQuestion3(answer) {
        if (answer == "a")
            window.alert("Incorrect Answer");
        if (answer == "b")
            window.alert("Correct Answer");
        if (answer == "c")
            window.alert("Incorrect Answer");
        if (answer == "d")
            window.alert("Incorrect Answer");
}
```

5. Add the following scoreQuestion4() function after the scoreQuestion3() function:

```
function scoreQuestion4(answer) {
        if (answer == "a")
            window.alert("Incorrect Answer");
        if (answer == "b")
            window.alert("Incorrect Answer");
        if (answer == "c")
            window.alert("Correct Answer");
        if (answer == "d")
            window.alert("Incorrect Answer");
}
```

6. Add the following scoreQuestion5() function after the scoreQuestion4() function:

```
function scoreQuestion5(answer) {
        if (answer == "a")
            window.alert("Incorrect Answer");
        if (answer == "b")
            window.alert("Incorrect Answer");
        if (answer == "c")
            window.alert("Incorrect Answer");
```

```
        if (answer == "d")
            window.alert("Correct Answer");
    }
```

7. Save the **AstrologyQuiz.html** document, validate it with the W3C Markup Validation Service at **http:// validator.w3.org/file-upload.html**, and fix any errors.

8. Open the **AstrologyQuiz.html** document in your Web browser. As you select a response for each question, you will immediately learn whether the answer is correct. Figure 10-2 shows the output if you select a wrong answer for Question 1.

Figure 10-2 AstrologyQuiz.html in a Web browser

9. Close your Web browser window.

Using `if...else` Statements

So far you've learned how to use an `if` statement to execute a statement (or statements) if a condition evaluates to true. In some situations, however, you may want to execute one set of statements when the condition evaluates to true and another set of statements when the condition evaluates to false. In that case, you need to add an else clause to your if statement. For instance, suppose you create a script that displays a confirmation dialog box asking users to indicate whether they invest in the stock market by clicking an OK or Cancel radio button. An if statement in the script might contain a conditional expression that evaluates the user's input. If the condition evaluates to true (that is, if the user clicked the OK button), then the if statement would display a Web page on recommended stocks. If the condition evaluates to false (that is, if the user clicked the Cancel button), then the statements in an else clause would display a Web page on other types of investment opportunities.

The **window.confirm() method** displays a confirm dialog box that contains an OK button and a Cancel button. The syntax for the window.confirm() method is window.confirm(*message*);. When a user clicks the OK button in the confirm dialog box, a value of true is returned. When a user clicks the Cancel button, a value of false is returned. For example, the following statement displays the dialog box shown in Figure 10-3:

```
window.confirm("Would you like a cup of coffee?");
```

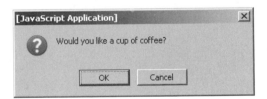

Figure 10-3   Confirm dialog box

An if statement that includes an else clause is called an **if...else statement**. You can think of an else clause as being a backup plan that is implemented when the condition returns a value of false. The syntax for an if...else statement is as follows:

```
if (conditional expression)
     statement;
else
     statement;
```

An if statement can be constructed without the else clause. However, the else clause can only be used with an if statement.

You can use command blocks to construct an if...else statement as follows:

```
if (conditional expression) {
     statements;
}
else {
     statements;
}
```

The following code shows an example of an `if...else` statement:

```
var today = "Tuesday"
if (today == "Monday")
    document.write("<p>Today is Monday</p>");
else
    document.write("<p>Today is not Monday</p>");
```

In the preceding code, the `today` variable is assigned a value of "Tuesday". If the condition (`today == "Monday"`) evaluates to false, control of the program passes to the `else` clause, and the statement `document.write("<p>Today is not Monday</p>");` executes, causing the string "Today is not Monday" to print. If the `today` variable had been assigned a value of "Monday", the condition (`today == "Monday"`) would have evaluated to true, and the statement `document.write("<p>Today is Monday</p>");` would have executed. Only one set of statements executes: either the statements following the `if` statement or the statements following the `else` clause. When either set of statements executes, any code following the `if...else` statements executes normally.

The JavaScript code for the AstrologyQuiz.html document you created earlier uses multiple `if` statements to evaluate the results of the quiz. Although the multiple `if` statements function properly, they can be simplified by using an `if...else` statement. Next, you will simplify the AstrologyQuiz.html program by replacing multiple `if` statements with one `if...else` statement.

To add `if...else` statements to AstrologyQuiz.html:

1. Return to the **AstrologyQuiz.html** document in your text editor and immediately save the document as **AstrologyQuiz2.html**.

2. Because you only need the `if` statement to test for the correct answer, you can group all the incorrect answers in the `else` clause. Modify each of the functions that scores a question so that the multiple `if` statements are replaced with an `if...else` statement. The following code shows how the statements should look for the `scoreQuestion1()` function:

Keep in mind that the correct answers for Questions 2 through 5 are *c*, *b*, *c*, and *d*, respectively. You'll need to modify the preceding code accordingly for each question. Copy and paste code and then edit it to save on typing time.

```
if (answer == 'a')
    window.alert("Correct Answer");
else
    window.alert("Incorrect Answer");
```

3. Save the **AstrologyQuiz2.html** document, validate it with the W3C Markup Validation Service at **http:// validator. w3.org/file-upload.html**, and fix any errors.

4. Open the **AstrologyQuiz2.html** document in your Web browser. The program should function the same as when it contained only `if` statements.

5. Close your Web browser window.

Using Nested `if` and `if...else` Statements

As you have seen, you can use a control structure such as an `if` or `if...else` statement to allow a program to decide which statements to execute. In some cases, however, you may want the statements executed by the control structure to make other decisions. For instance, you may have a program that uses an `if` statement to ask users if they like sports. If users answer *yes*, you may want to run another `if` statement that asks users whether they like team sports or individual sports. You can include any code you want within the code block for an `if` statement or an `if...else` statement, including other `if` or `if...else` statements.

When one decision-making statement is contained within another, they are referred to as **nested decision-making structures**. An `if` statement contained within an `if` statement or an `if...else` statement is called a nested `if` statement. Similarly, an `if...else` statement contained within an `if` or `if...else` statement is called a nested `if...else` statement. You use nested `if` and `if...else` statements to perform conditional evaluations that must be executed after the original conditional evaluation. For example, the following code evaluates two conditional expressions before the `write()` statement executes:

```
var salesTotal = window.prompt("What is the sales ↵
    total?", 0);
if (salesTotal > 50)
        if (salesTotal < 100)
            document.write("<p>The sales total is ↵
                between 50 and 100.</p>");
```

The `document.write()` statement in the preceding example only executes if the conditional expressions in both `if` statements evaluate to true.

The preceding code uses the **window.prompt() method**, which displays a prompt dialog box with a message, a text box, an OK button, and a Cancel button. Any text that a user enters into a prompt dialog box can be assigned to a variable. The syntax for the `window.prompt()` method is *variable* = window.prompt(*message*, *default text*);. For example, the following code displays the dialog box shown in Figure 10-4:

```
var yourAge = window.prompt("How old are you?",
    "Enter your age here.");
```

Figure 10-4   Prompt dialog box

The JavaScript code in the AstrologyQuiz2.html document is some-what inefficient because it contains multiple functions that perform essentially the same task of scoring the quiz. A more efficient method of scoring the quiz is to include nested decision-making structures within a single function.

Next, you will modify the JavaScript code in the AstrologyQuiz2.html document to contain a single function that checks the correct answer for all the questions using nested if . . . else statements.

To add nested if . . . else statements to the astrology quiz program:

1. Return to the **AstrologyQuiz2.html** document in your text editor and immediately save it as **AstrologyQuiz3.html**.

2. Delete the five functions that score each question.

3. In the script section, add the first line for the single function that will check all the answers. The function will receive two arguments: the number argument, which represents the question number, and the answer argument, which will score the answer selected by the user. Code within the body of the function uses the number argument to determine which question to store and the answer argument to determine the answer selected by the user.

```
function scoreQuestions(number, answer) {
```

4. Add the following code to score Question 1:

```
if (number == 1) {
    if (answer == "a")
        window.alert("Correct Answer");
    else
        window.alert("Incorrect Answer");
}
```

5. Add the following code to score Question 2:

```
else if (number == 2) {
    if (answer == "c")
        window.alert("Correct Answer");
    else
        window.alert("Incorrect Answer");
}
```

6. Add the following code to score Question 3:

```
else if (number == 3) {
    if (answer == "b")
        window.alert("Correct Answer");
    else
        window.alert("Incorrect Answer");
}
```

7. Add the following code to score Question 4:

```
else if (number == 4) {
    if (answer == "c")
        window.alert("Correct Answer");
    else
        window.alert("Incorrect Answer");
}
```

8. Add the following code to score Question 5:

```
else if (number == 5) {
    if (answer == "d")
        window.alert("Correct Answer");
    else
        window.alert("Incorrect Answer");
}
```

9. Add a closing brace (}) for the scoreQuestions() function. The completed function should appear in your document as follows:

```
function scoreQuestions(number, answer) {
    if (number == 1) {
        if (answer == "a")
            window.alert("Correct Answer");
        else
            window.alert("Incorrect Answer");
    }
    else if (number == 2) {
        if (answer == "c")
            window.alert("Correct Answer");
        else
            window.alert("Incorrect Answer");
    }
    else if (number == 3) {
        if (answer == "b")
            window.alert("Correct Answer");
        else
            window.alert("Incorrect Answer");
    }
    else if (number == 4) {
        if (answer == "c")
            window.alert("Correct Answer");
        else
            window.alert("Incorrect Answer");
    }
    else if (number == 5) {
        if (answer == "d")
            window.alert("Correct Answer");
        else
            window.alert("Incorrect Answer");
    }
}
```

10. Within each of the <input> elements, change the function called within the onclick event handler to

scoreQuestions(*number*, *answer*). Change the number argument to the appropriate question number and the answer argument to the appropriate answer. For example, the event handler for Question 1 should read scoreQuestions(1, 'a').

11. Save the **AstrologyQuiz3.html** document, validate it with the W3C Markup Validation Service at **http:// validator.w3.org/file-upload.html**, and fix any errors.

12. Open the **AstrologyQuiz3.html** document in your Web browser. The program should function just as it did with the multiple if statements and the multiple functions.

13. Close your Web browser window.

Using switch Statements

Another JavaScript statement that is used for controlling program flow is the switch statement. The **switch statement** controls program flow by executing a specific set of statements depending on the value of an expression. The switch statement compares the value of an expression to a value contained within a special statement called a case label. A **case label** in a switch statement represents a specific value and contains one or more statements that execute if the value of the case label matches the value of the switch statement's expression. For example, your script for an insurance company might include a variable named customerAge. A switch statement can evaluate the variable and compare it to a case label within the switch construct. The switch statement might contain several case labels for different age groups that calculate insurance rates based on a customer's age. If the customerAge variable is equal to 25, the statements that are part of the "25" case label execute and calculate insurance rates for customers who are 25 or older. Although you could accomplish the same task by using if or if . . . else statements, a switch statement makes it easier to organize the different branches of code that can be executed. The syntax for the switch statement is as follows:

```
switch (expression) {
    case label:
        statement(s);
    case label:
        statement(s);
    . . .
    default:
        statement(s);
}
```

A case label consists of the keyword case, followed by a literal value or variable name, followed by a colon. JavaScript compares the value

A single statement or multiple statements can follow a case label. However, unlike if statements, multiple statements for a case label do not need to be enclosed within a command block.

Other programming languages, such as Java and C++, require all case labels within a switch statement to be of the same data type.

556

returned from the switch statement expression to the literal value or variable name following the case keyword. If a match is found, the case label statements execute. For example, the case label case 3.17: represents a floating-point integer value of 3.17. If the value of a switch statement expression equals 3.17, then the case 3.17: label statements execute. You can use a variety of data types as case labels within the same switch statement. The following code shows examples of four case labels:

```
case exampleVar:     // variable name
    statement(s)
case "text string": // string literal
    statement(s)
case 75:             // integer literal
    statement(s)
case -273.4:         // floating-point literal
    statement(s)
```

Another type of label used within switch statements is the default label. The **default label** contains statements that execute when the value returned by the switch statement expression does not match a case label. A default label consists of the keyword default followed by a colon.

When a switch statement executes, the value returned by the expression is compared to each case label in the order in which it is encountered. Once a matching label is found, its statements execute. Unlike the if...else statement, execution of a switch statement does not automatically stop after particular case label statements execute. Instead, the switch statement continues evaluating the rest of the case labels in the list. Once a matching case label is found, evaluation of additional case labels is unnecessary. If you are working with a large switch statement with many case labels, evaluation of additional case labels can potentially slow down your program.

A break statement is also used to exit other types of control statements, such as the while, do...while, and for looping statements. You'll learn about these statements later in this chapter.

To avoid slow performance, you need to give some thought to how and when to end a switch statement. A switch statement ends automatically after the JavaScript interpreter encounters its closing brace (}). You can, however, use a special kind of statement, called a break statement, to end a switch statement once it has performed its required task. A **break statement** is used to exit control statements such as the switch, while, do...while, and for looping statements. To end a switch statement once it performs its required task, include a break statement within each case label.

The following code shows a switch statement contained within a function. When the function is called, it is passed an argument named americanCity. The switch statement compares the contents of the americanCity argument to the case labels. If a match is found, the city's state is returned and a break statement ends the switch statement. If a match is not found, the value "United States" is returned from the default label.

```
function city_location(americanCity) {
    switch (americanCity) {
        case "Boston":
            return "Massachusetts";
            break;
        case "Chicago":
            return "Illinois";
            break;
        case "Los Angeles":
            return "California";
            break;
        case "Miami":
            return "Florida";
            break;
        case "New York":
            return "New York";
            break;
        default:
            return "United States";
    }
}
document.write("<p>" + city_location("Boston")
    + "</p>");
```

Next, you will modify the astrology quiz program so that the scoreAnswers() function contains a switch statement instead of nested if...else statements. Each case statement in the modified program will check for the question number that is passed from the function number argument. The switch statement makes better programming sense than the nested if...else statements, because it eliminates the need to check the question number multiple times.

To add a switch statement to the astrology quiz program:

1. Return to the **AstrologyQuiz3.html** document, and immediately save it as **AstrologyQuiz4.html**.

2. Change the if...else statements within the scoreQuestions() function to the following switch statement:

```
switch (number) {
    case 1:
        if (answer == 'a')
            window.alert("Correct Answer");
        else
            window.alert("Incorrect Answer");
        break;
    case 2:
        if (answer == 'c')
            window.alert("Correct Answer");
        else
```

```
                              window.alert("Incorrect Answer");
                    break;
          case 3:
                    if (answer == 'b')
                              window.alert("Correct Answer");
                    else
                              window.alert("Incorrect Answer");
                    break;
          case 4:
                    if (answer == 'c')
                              window.alert("Correct Answer");
                    else
                              window.alert("Incorrect Answer");
                    break;
          case 5:
                    if (answer == 'd')
                              window.alert("Correct Answer");
                    else
                              window.alert("Incorrect Answer");
                    break;
     }
```

3. Save the **AstrologyQuiz4.html** document, validate it with the W3C Markup Validation Service at **http://validator.w3.org/file-upload.html**, and fix any errors.

4. Open the **AstrologyQuiz4.html** document in your Web browser. The program should function just as it did with the nested if...else statements.

5. Close your Web browser window.

Short Quiz 2

1. When will an if statement execute?

2. Why would you use a command block with a decision-making statement?

3. Why would you nest decision-making statements?

4. What type of label represents a specific value and contains one or more statements that execute if its value matches the value of the switch statement's expression?

5. Describe how the statements in a switch statement execute. When does a switch statement end?

Repeating Code

The statements you have worked with so far execute one after the other in a linear fashion. The `if`, `if...else`, and `switch` statements select only a single branch of code to execute, then continue to the statement that follows. But what if you want to repeat the same statement, function, or code section five times, 10 times, or 100 times? For example, you might want to perform the same calculation until a specific number is found. In that case, you need to use a **loop statement**, a control structure that repeatedly executes a statement or a series of statements while a specific condition is true or until a specific condition becomes true. In this chapter, you'll learn about three types of loop statements: `while` statements, `do...while` statements, and `for` statements.

Using `while` Statements

One of the simplest types of loop statements is the **`while` statement**, which repeats a statement or series of statements as long as a given conditional expression evaluates to true. The syntax for the `while` statement is as follows:

```
while (conditional expression) {
    statement(s);
}
```

The conditional expression in the `while` statement is enclosed within parentheses following the keyword `while`. As long as the conditional expression evaluates to true, the statement or command block that follows executes repeatedly. Each repetition of a looping statement is called an **iteration**. When the conditional expression evaluates to false, the loop ends and the next statement following the `while` statement executes.

A `while` statement keeps repeating until its conditional expression evaluates to false. To ensure that the `while` statement ends after the desired tasks have been performed, you must include code that tracks the progress of the loop and changes the value produced by the conditional expression. You track the progress of a `while` statement or any other loop with a counter. A **counter** is a variable that is incremented or decremented with each iteration of a loop statement.

The following code shows a simple script that includes a `while` statement. The script declares a variable named `count` and assigns it an initial value of 1. The `count` variable is then used in the `while` statement conditional expression (`count <= 5`). As long as the `count` variable is less than or equal to five, the `while` statement loops. Within

Many programmers often name counter variables `count`, `counter`, or something similar. The letters *i, j, k, l, x, y,* and *z* are also commonly used as counter names. Using a name such as `count`, or the letter *i* (for increment) or a higher letter, helps you remember (and lets other programmers know) that the variable is being used as a counter.

the body of the `while` statement, the `document.write()` statement prints the value of the `count` variable, then the `count` variable increments by a value of one. The `while` statement loops until the `count` variable increments to a value of 6.

```
var count = 1;
while (count <= 5) {
        document.write(count + "<br />");
        ++count;
}
document.write("<p>You have printed 5 numbers.</p>");
```

The preceding code prints the numbers 1 to 5, with each number representing one iteration of the loop. When the counter reaches 6, the message "You have printed 5 numbers." prints, demonstrating that the loop has ended. Figure 10-5 shows the output of this simple script.

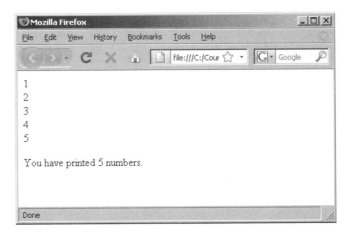

Figure 10-5   Output of a `while` statement using an increment operator

You can also control the repetitions in a `while` loop by decrementing (decreasing the value of) counter variables. Consider the following script:

```
var count = 10;
while (count > 0) {
        document.write(count + "<br />");
        --count;
}
document.write("<p>We have liftoff.</p>");
```

In this example, the initial value of the `count` variable is 10, and the decrement operator (`--`) is used to decrease `count` by one. When the `count` variable is greater than zero, the statement within the `while` loop prints the value of the `count` variable. When the value of `count` is equal to zero, the `while` loop ends and the statement immediately after it prints. Figure 10-6 shows the script output.

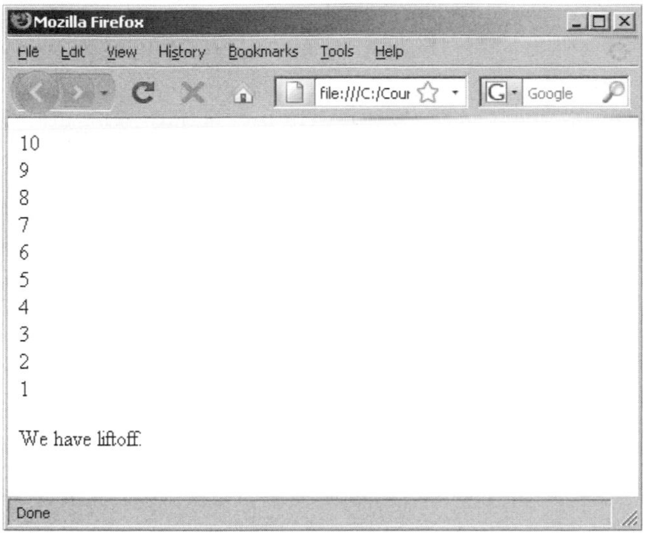

Figure 10-6 Output of a `while` statement using a decrement operator

There are many ways to change the value of a counter variable and to use a counter variable to control the repetitions of a `while` loop. The following example uses the `*=` assignment operator to multiply the value of the `count` variable by two. When the `count` variable reaches a value of 64, the `while` statement ends. Figure 10-7 shows the script output.

```
var count = 1;
while (count <= 100) {
     document.write(count + "<br />");
     count *= 2;
}
```

Figure 10-7 Output of a `while` statement using the `*=` assignment operator

To ensure that the `while` statement will eventually end, you must include code within the body of the `while` statement that changes the value of the conditional expression. For example, suppose that you have a `while` statement that prints odd numbers between 0 and 100. You need to include code within the body of the `while` statement that ends the loop after the last odd number (99) prints. If you do not include code that changes the value used by the conditional expression, your program will be caught in an infinite loop. In an **infinite loop**, a loop statement never ends because its conditional expression is never false. Consider the following `while` statement:

```
var count = 1;
while (count <= 10) {
    window.alert("The number is " + count + ".");
}
```

In most cases, you must force a Web browser to close if it is caught in an infinite loop. The method for forcing an application to close varies between operating systems.

Although the `while` statement in the preceding example includes a conditional expression that checks the value of a `count` variable, there is no code within the `while` statement body that changes the `count` variable value. The `count` variable will continue to have a value of 1 through each iteration of the loop. That means an alert dialog box containing the text string "The number is 1." will appear over and over again, no matter how many times the user clicks the OK button.

Next, you will create a new version of the astrology quiz program that is to be scored by a single `while` statement containing a nested `if` statement. Although this `while` statement is somewhat more complicated than the `if`, `if...else`, and `switch` statements you created previously, it requires many fewer lines of code. You will also include a Score button that grades the entire quiz after a user is finished. (Remember that the earlier version of the program graded the quiz answer by answer.)

To create a version of the astrology quiz program that is scored by a `while` statement:

1. Return to the **AstrologyQuiz4.html** document and immediately save it as **AstrologyQuiz5.html**.

2. Delete the entire `scoreQuestions()` function from the `<head>` section, and then add the following lines to create two arrays named `answers[]` and `correctAnswers[]`. The `answers[]` array will hold the answers selected each time the quiz runs, and the `correctAnswers[]` array will hold the correct response for each of the questions. The code also assigns the correct responses to each element of the `correctAnswers[]` array.

```
var answers = new Array(5);
var correctAnswers = new Array(5);
correctAnswers[0] = "a";
correctAnswers[1] = "c";
correctAnswers[2] = "b";
correctAnswers[3] = "c";
correctAnswers[4] = "d";
```

3. Add the following function, which assigns the response from each question to the appropriate element in the answers[] array. The program sends the actual question number (1–5) to the function by using the onclick event of each radio button. To assign question responses to the correct element, 1 must be subtracted from the question variable because the elements in an array start with 0.

```
function recordAnswer(question, answer) {
    answers[question-1] = answer;
}
```

4. Type the following definition for a function that will score the quiz. You will call this function from a new Score button.

```
function scoreQuiz() {
}
```

5. In the scoreQuiz() function, add the following statement, which declares a new variable and assigns it an initial value of 0. The totalCorrect variable holds the number of correct answers.

```
var totalCorrect = 0;
```

6. Add the following variable declaration and while statement at the end of the scoreQuiz() function. In this code, a counter named count is declared and initialized to a value of 0, because 0 is the starting index of an array. The conditional expression within the while statement checks to see if count is less than the length of the array, which is one number higher than the largest element in the answers[] array. With each iteration of the loop, the statement in the while loop increments the count variable by one.

```
var count = 0;
while (count < correctAnswers.length) {
    ++count;
}
```

7. Add the following if statement to the beginning of the while loop, above the statement that increments the count variable. This if statement compares each element within the

answers[] array to each corresponding element within the
correctAnswers[] array. If the elements match, then the
totalCorrect variable increments by one.

```
if (answers[count] == correctAnswers[count])
    ++totalCorrect;
```

8. Using alert dialog boxes too frequently is considered poor
Web design practice. For this reason, this version of the
astrology quiz will write the score to a text box named
score in the form named "quiz". After the while loop in the
scoreQuiz() function, add the following code that prints how
many questions were answered correctly in the score text
box. (You will create this text box shortly.)

```
document.quiz.score.value = "You scored "
    + totalCorrect + " out of 5 answers correctly!";
```

9. In the onclick event handlers for each radio button, change
the name of the called function from scoreQuestions() to
recordAnswer(), but use the same arguments that you used
for the scoreQuestions() function. For example, the onclick
event handlers for the Question 1 radio buttons should now
read onclick="recordAnswer(1, 'a')".

10. Finally, add the following <input> elements immediately
above the last </td> tag. The button <input> element creates
a command button whose onclick event handler calls the
scoreQuiz() function. The text <input> element will contain
the quiz score.

```
<p>
    <input type="button" value="Score"
        onclick="scoreQuiz();" />
    <input type="text" name="score" size="40"
        style="color: white; border-style: none; ↵
        border-color: inherit; border-width: medium; ↵
        background-color: Transparent" />
</p>
```

11. Save the **AstrologyQuiz5.html** document, validate it
with the W3C Markup Validation Service at
http:// validator.w3.org/file-upload.html, and fix any errors.

12. Open the **AstrologyQuiz5.html** document in your Web
browser. Test the program by answering all five questions and
clicking the **Score** button. Figure 10-8 shows how the program
appears in a Web browser.

13. Close your Web browser window.

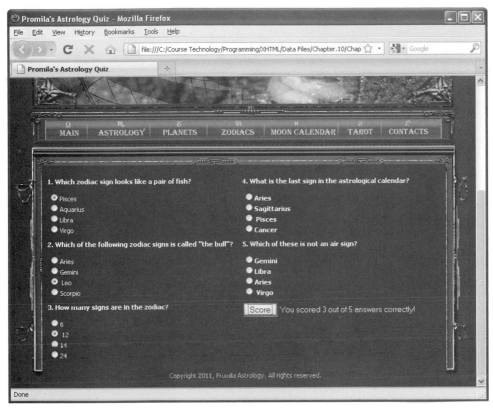

Figure 10-8   AstrologyQuiz5.html in a Web browser

Using do . . . while Statements

Another JavaScript looping statement, similar to the while statement, is the do . . . while statement. The **do . . . while statement** executes a statement or statements once, then repeats the execution as long as a given conditional expression evaluates to true. The syntax for the do . . . while statement is as follows:

```
do {
     statement(s);
} while (conditional expression);
```

As you can see in the syntax description, the statements execute before a conditional expression is evaluated. Unlike the simpler while statement, the statements in a do . . . while statement always execute once before a conditional expression is evaluated.

The following do . . . while statement executes once before the conditional expression evaluates the count variable. Therefore, a single line that reads "The count is equal to 2." prints. After the conditional expression (count < 2) executes, the count variable is equal to 2. This causes the conditional expression to return a value of false, and the do . . . while statement ends.

```
var count = 2;
do {
    document.write("<p>The count is equal to "
        + count + ".</p>");
    ++count;
} while (count < 2);
```

Note that this do . . . while example includes a counter within the body of the do . . . while statement. As with the while statement, you need to include code that changes the conditional expression in order to prevent an infinite loop.

In the following example, the while statement never executes because the count variable does not fall within the range of the conditional expression:

```
var count = 2;
while (count > 2) {
    document.write("<p>The count is equal to "
        + count + ".</p>");
    ++count;
}
```

The following script shows an example of a do . . . while statement that prints the days of the week using an array:

```
var daysOfWeek = new Array();
daysOfWeek[0] = "Monday"; daysOfWeek[1] = "Tuesday";
daysOfWeek[2] = "Wednesday"; daysOfWeek[3] = "Thursday";
daysOfWeek[4] = "Friday"; daysOfWeek[5] = "Saturday";
daysOfWeek[6] = "Sunday";
var count = 0;
do {
    document.write(daysOfWeek[count] + "<br />");
    ++count;
} while (count < daysOfWeek.length);
```

In the preceding example, an array is created containing the days of the week. A variable named count is declared and initialized to zero. (Remember, the first subscript or index in an array is zero.) Therefore, in the example, the statement daysOfWeek[0]; refers to Monday. The first iteration of the do . . . while statement prints "Monday" and then increments the count variable by one. The conditional expression in the while statement then checks to determine when the last element of the array has been printed. As long as the count is less than the length of the array (which is one number higher than the largest element in the daysOfWeek[] array), the loop continues. Figure 10-9 shows the output of the script in a Web browser.

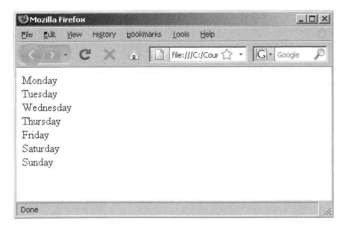

Figure 10-9 Days of Week script in a Web browser

Next, you will replace the `while` statement in the astrology quiz program with a `do...while` statement.

To replace the `while` statement in the astrology quiz program with a `do...while` statement:

1. Return to the **AstrologyQuiz5.html** document, and immediately save it as **AstrologyQuiz6.html**.

2. Change the `while` statement within the `scoreQuiz()` function to the following `do...while` statement:

```
do {
    if (answers[count] == correctAnswers[count])
            ++totalCorrect;
    ++count;
} while (count < 5);
```

3. Save the **AstrologyQuiz6.html** document, validate it with the W3C Markup Validation Service at **http:// validator.w3.org/file-upload.html**, and fix any errors.

4. Open the **AstrologyQuiz6.html** document in your Web browser. The program should function just as it did with the nested `while` statement.

5. Close your Web browser window.

Using `for` Statements

So far you have learned how to use the `while` and `do...while` statements to repeat, or loop through, code. You can also use the **for statement** to loop through code and repeat a statement or series of statements as long as a given conditional expression evaluates to true. The `for` statement performs essentially the same function as the `while` statement: If a conditional expression within the `for` statement evaluates to true, the `for` statement executes repeatedly until the conditional expression evaluates to false.

One of the primary differences between the `while` statement and the `for` statement is that, in addition to a conditional expression, the `for` statement can also include code that initializes a counter and changes its value with each iteration. This is useful because it provides a specific place for you to declare and initialize a counter and to update its value, which helps prevent infinite loops. The syntax of the `for` statement is as follows:

```
for (counter declaration and initialization; condition;
    update statement) {
    statement(s);
}
```

When the JavaScript interpreter encounters a `for` loop, the following steps occur:

1. The counter variable is declared and initialized. For example, if the initialization expression in a `for` loop is `var count = 1;`, a variable named `count` is declared and assigned an initial value of 1. The initialization expression is only started once, when the `for` loop is first encountered.

2. The `for` loop condition is evaluated.

3. If the condition evaluation in Step 2 returns a value of true, the `for` loop statements execute, Step 4 occurs, and the process starts over again with Step 2. If the condition evaluation in Step 2 returns a value of false, the `for` statement ends and the next statement following the `for` statement executes.

4. The update statement in the `for` statement is executed. For example, the `count` variable may be incremented by one.

 You can omit any of the three parts of the `for` statement, but you must include the semicolons that separate each section. If you omit a section, be sure to include code within the body that will end the `for` statement or your program may get caught in an infinite loop.

The following script shows a `for` statement that prints the contents of an array:

```
var brightestStars = new Array();
brightestStars[0] = "Sirius";
brightestStars[1] = "Canopus";
brightestStars[2] = "Arcturus";
brightestStars[3] = "Rigel";
brightestStars[4] = "Vega";
for (var count = 0; count < brightestStars.length;
    ++count) {
    document.write(brightestStars[count] + "<br />");
}
```

As you can see in this example, the counter is initialized, evaluated, and incremented within the parentheses. You do not need to include a declaration for the count variable before the for statement, nor do you need to increment the count variable within the body of the for statement. Figure 10-10 shows the output.

Figure 10-10 Output of brightest stars script

Using a for statement is more efficient than using a while statement because you do not need as many lines of code. Consider the following while statement:

```
var count = 1;
while (count < brightestStars.length) {
    document.write(count + "<br />");
    ++count;
}
```

You could achieve the same flow control more efficiently by using a for statement, as follows:

```
for (var count = 1; count < brightestStars.length;
    ++count) {
    document.write(count + "<br />");
}
```

Sometimes, however, using a while statement is preferable to using a for statement, especially for looping statements that do not need to declare, initialize, or update a counter variable. The following code relies on a Boolean value returned from a confirm dialog box, rather than a counter, for program control:

```
var i = true;
while (i == true)
    i = window.confirm("Do you want to redisplay ↵
        this dialog box?");
```

You could accomplish the same task in the preceding example by using a for statement, but in this case, the third part of the for statement, which updates the counter, would be unnecessary. This is because the counter is updated by the value returned from the `window.confirm()` method; a value of true would cause the loop to reiterate, while a value of false would cause the loop to exit. Therefore, this code is better written using a `while` statement. If you use a `for` statement instead of a `while` statement in the preceding example, you must not include the update section in the `for` statement. You must also remember to retain the semicolon that separates the conditional section from the update section. If you include the update section, you could create an infinite loop.

The following code shows an example of the Days of Week script you saw earlier. This time, however, the script includes a `for` statement instead of a `do...while` statement. Notice that the declaration of the `count` variable, the conditional expression, and the statement that increments the `count` variable are now all contained within the `for` statement. Using a `for` statement instead of a `do...while` statement simplifies the script because you do not need as many lines of code.

```
var daysOfWeek = new Array();
daysOfWeek[0] = "Monday"; daysOfWeek[1] = "Tuesday";
daysOfWeek[2] = "Wednesday"; daysOfWeek[3] = "Thursday";
daysOfWeek[4] = "Friday"; daysOfWeek[5] = "Saturday";
daysOfWeek[6] = "Sunday";
for (var count = 0; count < daysOfWeek.length; ++count) {
    document.write(daysOfWeek[count] + "<br />");
}
```

Next, you will create a final version of the astrology quiz program that is scored with a `for` statement instead of a `do...while` statement.

To replace the do...`while` statement in the astrology quiz program with a `for` statement:

1. Return to the **AstrologyQuiz6.html** document, and immediately save it as **AstrologyQuiz7.html**.

2. Delete the declaration for the `count` variable within the `scoreQuiz()` function.

3. Change the `do...while` statement within the `scoreQuiz()` function to the following `for` statement:

```
for (var count = 0;
    count < correctAnswers.length; ++count) {
    if (answers[count] == correctAnswers[count])
        ++totalCorrect;
}
```

4. Save the **AstrologyQuiz7.html** document, validate it with the W3C Markup Validation Service at **http:// validator.w3.org/file-upload.html**, and fix any errors.

5. Open the **AstrologyQuiz7.html** document in your Web browser. The program should function just as it did with the nested do . . . while statement.

6. Close your Web browser window and text editor.

Using continue Statements to Restart Execution

When you studied switch statements, you learned how to use a break statement to exit switch, while, do . . . while, and for statements. A similar statement, used only with looping statements, is the **continue statement**, which restarts a loop with a new iteration. For example, suppose you have a script that uses a for statement to loop through the elements of an array containing a list of stocks. For stocks worth more than $10 per share, the script prints information such as purchase price and number of shares on the screen. However, you use the continue statement to skip any stocks worth less than $10 per share and move on to a new iteration. For example, when the count variable equals 3 in the following code, the continue statement also stops the current iteration of the for loop, and the script skips printing the number 3. However, the loop continues to iterate until the conditional expression count <= 5 is false. Figure 10-11 shows the output in a Web browser.

```
for (var count = 1; count <= 5; ++count) {
    if (count == 3)
        continue;
        document.write("<p>" + count + "</p>");
}
```

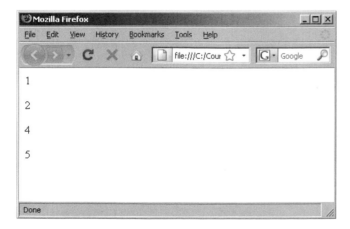

Figure 10-11   Output of a for loop with a continue statement

In comparison, consider the following code, which contains a break statement:

```
for (var count = 1; count <= 5; ++count) {
    if (count == 3)
        break;
    document.write("<p>" + count + "</p>");
}
```

The preceding code contains an if statement that checks whether the current value of the count variable equals 3. When the count variable equals 3, the break statement immediately ends the for loop and displays the output shown in Figure 10-12.

Figure 10-12   Output of a for loop with a break statement

Short Quiz 3

1. Why is a counter critical to repetition statements?

2. How do you break out of an infinite loop?

3. Which type of repetition statement always executes its statements once, even if the conditional expression returns a value of false?

4. What are the primary differences between the while statement and the for statement?

5. How do you restart a repetition statement?

Summing Up

- An array contains a set of data represented by a single variable name. You can think of an array as a collection of variables contained within a single variable.

- A constructor is a special type of function used as the basis for creating reference variables (that is, variables whose data type is the reference data type).

- Each piece of data contained in an array is called an element.

- An index is an element's numeric position within the array.

- The Array class contains a single property, the length property, which returns the number of elements in an array.

- The process of determining the order in which program statements execute is called decision making or flow control.

- The if statement is used to execute specific programming code if the evaluation of a conditional expression returns a value of true.

- A command block is a set of statements contained within a set of braces, similar to the way function statements are contained within a set of braces.

- An if statement that includes an else clause is called an if...else statement.

- When one decision-making statement is contained within another, they are called nested decision-making structures.

- The switch statement controls program flow by executing a specific set of statements depending on the value of an expression.

- A break statement is used to exit control statements such as the switch, while, do...while, and for looping statements.

- A loop statement is a control structure that repeatedly executes a statement or a series of statements while a specific condition is true or until a specific condition becomes true.

- The while statement is used for repeating a statement or series of statements as long as a given conditional expression evaluates to true.

- Each repetition of a looping statement is called an iteration.

- An infinite loop is a situation in which a loop statement never ends because its conditional expression is never false.

- The do . . . while statement executes a statement or statements once, then repeats the execution as long as a given conditional expression evaluates to true.

- The for statement is used for repeating a statement or series of statements as long as a given conditional expression evaluates to true. The for statement can also include code that initializes a counter and changes its value with each iteration.

- The continue statement halts a looping statement and restarts the loop with a new iteration.

Comprehension Check

1. The identifiers you use for an array name must follow the same rules as identifiers for variables. True or False?

2. What is the correct syntax for creating an array named taxRules that contains five elements?

   a. new Array(taxRules) = 5;

   b. Array(taxRules) + 5;

   c. var taxRules = Array(5);

   d. var taxRules = new Array(5);

3. An error occurs if you attempt to assign a value to an element that has not yet been created. True or False?

4. Which of the following properties returns the number of elements in an array?

   a. length

   b. size

   c. elements

   d. indexes

5. Which of the following characters are used to create a command block?

   a. ()

   b. []

   c. {}

   d. <>

6. Which of the following is the correct syntax for an `if` statement?

   a. `if (singleIncome > 326450),`

      ```
      window.alert("Your federal income tax (↵
         rate is 35%.");
      ```

   b. `if (singleIncome > 326450);`

      ```
      window.alert("Your federal income tax (↵
         rate is 35%.");
      ```

   c. `if (singleIncome > 326450)`

      ```
      window.alert("Your federal income tax (↵
         rate is 35%.");
      ```

   d. `if singleIncome > 326450`

      ```
      window.alert("Your federal income tax (↵
         rate is 35%.");
      ```

7. An `if` statement can include multiple statements provided that they _____.

   a. execute after the `if` statement's closing semicolon

   b. are not contained within a command block

   c. do not include other `if` statements

   d. are contained within a command block

8. Which is the correct syntax for an `else` clause?

   a. ```
      else "document.write('Your federal income (↵
         tax rate is 28%.')";
      ```

   b. ```
      else; document.write("Your federal income (↵
         tax rate is 28%.");
      ```

   c. ```
      else (document.write("Your federal income (↵
         tax rate is 28%."));
      ```

   d. ```
      else document.write("Your federal income (↵
         tax rate is 28%.");
      ```

9. Decision-making structures cannot be nested. True or False?

10. The `switch` statement controls program flow by executing a specific set of statements depending on _____.

 a. whether an `if` statement executes from within a function

 b. the version of JavaScript being executed

 c. the value returned by a conditional expression

 d. the result of an `if . . . else` statement

11. When the value returned by a `switch` statement expression does not match a `case` label, the statements within the _____ label execute.

 a. `error`

 b. `else`

 c. `exception`

 d. `default`

12. You can exit a `switch` statement using a(n) _____ statement.

 a. `complete`

 b. `end`

 c. `quit`

 d. `break`

13. Each repetition of a looping statement is called a(n) _____.

 a. recurrence

 b. iteration

 c. cycle

 d. synchronization

14. Counter variables _____. (Choose all that apply.)

 a. can only be incremented

 b. can only be decremented

 c. can be changed using any conditional expression

 d. do not change

15. Which of the following is the correct syntax for a `while` statement?

    a. ```
        while (i <= population.length) {
            document.write(population[i]);
            ++i;
        }
        ```

    b.  ```
        while (i <= population.length, ++i) {
            document.write(population[i]);
        }
        ```

    c. ```
        while (i <= population.length);
            document.write(population[i]);
            ++i;
        ```

    d.  ```
        while (i <= population.length; document.write(i)) {
            ++ population[i];
        }
        ```

16. Which of the following is the correct syntax for a `do...while` statement?

    a. ```
        do {
            document.write(counties[i]);
            while (i < counties.length)
        }
        ```

    b.  ```
        do { while (i < counties.length)
            document.write(counties[i]);
        }
        ```

    c. ```
        do {
            document.write(counties[i]);
        } while (i < counties.length);
        ```

    d.  ```
        do while (i < counties.length) {
            document.write(counties[i]);
        }
        ```

17. When is a `for` statement initialization expression executed?

    a. when the `for` statement begins executing

    b. with each repetition of the `for` statement

    c. when the counter variable is incremented

    d. when the `for` statement ends

18. Which of the following is the correct syntax for a `for` statement?

    a. ```
       for (var i = ; i < federalHoliday.length; ++i)
           document.write(federalHoliday[i]);
       ```

    b. ```
       for (var i = 0, i < holiday.length, ++i)
           document.write(federalHoliday[i]);
       ```

    c. ```
       for {
           document.write(federalHoliday[i]);
       } while (var i = 0; i < holiday.length; ++i)
       ```

    d. ```
       for (var i = 0; i < holiday.length);
           document.write(federalHoliday[i]);
       ++i;
       ```

19. Explain how an infinite loop is caused.

20. The _____ statement halts a looping statement and restarts the loop with a new iteration.

    a. `restart`

    b. `continue`

    c. `break`

    d. `halt`

Reinforcement Exercises

 Exercise 10-1

In this exercise, you will create a document that uses `if...else` statements and confirm dialog boxes to verify that a passenger meets the eligibility requirements to sit in an airplane's exit row.

1. Create a new document in your text editor.

2. Type the `<!DOCTYPE>` declaration, `<html>` element, document head, and `<body>` element. Use the Strict DTD and "Exit Row Requirements" as the content of the `<title>` element.

3. Create a script section in the document body:

   ```
   <script type="text/javascript">
   /* <![CDATA[ */
   /* ]]> */
   </script>
   ```

4. Add the following if . . . else statements to the script section. These statements use confirm dialog boxes in the conditional expressions to determine whether a passenger meets the eligibility requirements to sit in an airplane's exit row.

```
if (window.confirm("Are you under 15 years old?"))
    document.write("<p>By federal law, children ⏎
        under age 15 may not sit in emergency ⏎
        exit rows.</p>");
else if (!window.confirm("Are you capable of ⏎
    lifting 50 or more pounds?"))
    document.write("<p>You must be able to ⏎
        lift 50 or more pounds to sit in an exit ⏎
        row.</p>");
else if (!window.confirm("Are you willing ⏎
    to assist the crew in the event of an ⏎
    emergency?"))
    document.write("<p>To sit in an exit row, ⏎
        you must be willing to assist the crew ⏎
        in the event of an emergency.</p>");
else
    document.write("<p>You meet the criteria ⏎
        for sitting in an exit row.</p>");
```

5. Save the document as **ExitRows.html** in the Exercises folder for Chapter 10.

6. Use the W3C Markup Validation Service to validate the **ExitRows.html** document and fix any errors. Once the document is valid, close it in your text editor, open it in your Web browser, and examine how the elements are rendered.

7. Close your Web browser window.

 Exercise 10-2

In this exercise, you will write a while statement that prints all even numbers between 1 and 100 to the screen.

1. Create a new document in your text editor.

2. Type the <!DOCTYPE> declaration, <html> element, document head, and <body> element. Use the Strict DTD and "Even Numbers" as the content of the <title> element.

3. Create a script section with a while statement that prints all even numbers between 1 and 100 to the screen.

4. Save the document as **EvenNumbers.html** in the Exercises folder for Chapter 10.

5. Use the W3C Markup Validation Service to validate the **EvenNumbers.html** document and fix any errors. Once the document is valid, close it in your text editor, open it in your Web browser, and examine how the elements are rendered.

6. Close your Web browser window.

 ## Exercise 10-3

In this exercise, you will identify and fix the logic flaws in a while statement.

1. Create a new document in your text editor.

2. Type the <!DOCTYPE> declaration, <html> element, document head, and <body> element. Use the Strict DTD and "While Logic" as the content of the <title> element.

3. Create a script section in the document head that includes the following code:

```
<script type="text/javascript">
/* <![CDATA[ */
var count = 0;
var numbers = new Array(100);
while (count > 100) {
    numbers[count] = count;
    ++count;
}
while (count > 100) {
    document.write(numbers[count]);
    ++count;
}
/* ]]> */
</script>
```

4. The code you typed in the preceding step is intended to fill the array with the numbers 1 through 100 and then print them to the screen. However, the code contains several logic flaws that prevent it from running correctly. Identify and fix the logic flaws.

5. Save the document as **WhileLogic.html** in the Exercises folder for Chapter 10.

6. Use the W3C Markup Validation Service to validate the **WhileLogic.html** document and fix any errors. Once the document is valid, close it in your text editor, open it in your Web browser, and examine how the elements are rendered.

7. Close your Web browser window.

Exercise 10-4

Standard & Poor's issues a list of bond ratings that determines the investment quality of individual bonds. The bond ratings range from AAA to D, with AAA representing the highest-quality bonds. In this exercise, you will create a document with a simple form that displays the investment quality of each Standard & Poor's bond rating.

1. Create a new document in your text editor.

2. Type the <!DOCTYPE> declaration, <html> element, document head, and <body> element. Use the Transitional DTD and "Bond Ratings" as the content of the <title> element.

3. Create a script section in the document head that includes the following checkRating() function and switch statement:

```
<script type="text/javascript">
/* <![CDATA[ */
function checkRating(rating) {
    switch (rating) {
        case "AAA":
            window.alert("Highest Quality");
        case "AA":
            window.alert("High Quality");
        case "A":
            window.alert("Upper Medium");
        case "BBB":
            window.alert("Medium");
        case "BB":
            window.alert("Speculative");
        case "B":
            window.alert("Highly Speculative");
        case "CCC":
            window.alert("Extremely ⏎
                Speculative");
        case "CC":
            window.alert("Probable Default");
        case "D":
            window.alert("Default");
    }
}
/* ]]> */
</script>
```

4. Add code to the `switch` statement you created in the previous step so that after the statements in a `case` label execute, the `switch` statement ends.

5. Modify the `switch` statement so that a default value of "You did not enter a valid bond rating!" is displayed in an alert dialog box if none of the `case` labels match the `rating` variable.

6. Add the following form to the document body. The form includes an `onclick` event handler that calls the `checkRating()` function. The value of the single text box is passed to the `checkRating()` function.

```
<form name="bondRating" action="">
<input type="text" name="rating" />
<input type="button" value="Check Bond Rating"
onclick="checkRating(document.bondRating. ↵
    rating.value);" />
</form>
```

7. Save the document as **BondRatings.html** in the Exercises folder for Chapter 10.

8. Use the W3C Markup Validation Service to validate the **BondRatings.html** document and fix any errors. Once the document is valid, close it in your text editor, open it in your Web browser, and examine how the elements are rendered.

9. Close your Web browser window.

 ## Exercise 10-5

In this exercise, you will modify a nested `if` statement to create a single `if` statement that uses a compound conditional expression. Use logical operators such as || (OR) and && (AND) to execute a conditional or looping statement based on multiple criteria.

1. Create a new document in your text editor.

2. Type the `<!DOCTYPE>` declaration, `<html>` element, document head, and `<body>` element. Use the Strict DTD and "Oil Prices" as the content of the `<title>` element.

3. Create a script section in the document head that includes the following variable declaration and nested `if` statement:

```
<script type="text/javascript">
/* <![CDATA[ */
var oilPrice = 52.85;
if (oilPrice > 50) {
    if (oilPrice < 60)
        document.write("<p>Oil prices are between ↵
            $50.00 and $60.00 a barrel.</p>");
}
/* ]]> */
</script>
```

4. Modify the nested if statement you created in the previous step so that it uses a single if statement with a compound conditional expression to determine whether oil prices are between $50.00 and $60.00 a barrel. You will need to use the && (AND) logical operator.

5. Save the document as **OilPrices.html** in the Exercises folder for Chapter 10.

6. Use the W3C Markup Validation Service to validate the **OilPrices.html** document and fix any errors. Once the document is valid, close it in your text editor, open it in your Web browser, and examine how the elements are rendered.

7. Close your Web browser window.

Discovery Projects

Save your Discovery Projects documents in the Projects folder for Chapter 10. Create the documents so that they are well formed according to the strict DTD. Be sure to validate each document with the W3C Markup Validation Service.

 Discovery Project 10-1

Many companies normally charge a shipping and handling fee for purchases. Create a Web page that allows a user to enter a purchase price into a text box; include a JavaScript function that calculates shipping and handling. Add functionality to the script that adds a minimum shipping and handling fee of $1.50 for any purchase that is less than or equal to $25.00. For any orders over $25.00, add 10% to the total purchase price for shipping and handling, but do not include the $1.50 minimum shipping and handling fee. The formula for calculating a percentage is *price * percent* / 100. For example, the formula for calculating 10% of a $50.00 purchase price is 50 * 10 / 100, which results in a shipping and handling fee of $5.00. After you determine the total cost of the order (purchase plus shipping and handling), display it in an alert dialog box. Save the document as **CalcShipping.html**.

Discovery Project 10-2

The American Heart Association recommends that you stay within 50 to 85 percent of your maximum heart rate while exercising. This range is called your target heart rate. One common formula for calculating maximum heart rate is to subtract your age from 220. Create a Web page that you can use to calculate your target heart rate. Use a form that contains a text box in which users can enter their age, and a command button that uses an `onclick` event handler to call a function named `calcHeartRate()`. Within `calcHeartRate()`, include a statement that calculates the maximum heart rate and assigns the result to a variable. Use two other statements that calculate the minimum (50%) and maximum (85%) target heart rates. To calculate the minimum target heart rate, you use the formula *maximum_heart_rate* * .5; to calculate the maximum target heart rate, use the formula *maximum_heart_rate* * .85. After you calculate the minimum and maximum target heart rates, display the result in another text box in the form. For example, a 35-year-old person should have minimum and maximum target heart rates of 92 to 157 beats per minute. Save the document as **TargetHeartRate.html**.

Discovery Project 10-3

Create a Web page that you can use to calculate mileage per gallon for your car. Add a form to the Web page that contains four text `<input>` elements: starting mileage, ending mileage, gallons used, and miles per gallon. Assign initial starting values of 0 to the `value` attributes for each of the `<input>` elements. Add `onchange` event handlers to the starting mileage, ending mileage, and gallons used text boxes, each of which calls a JavaScript function named `calcMPG()`. Create the `calcMPG()` function in a script section in the document head. Within the `calcMPG()` function, declare three variables named `startMiles`, `endMiles`, and `gallons`, and initialize each variable with the value assigned to the starting mileage, ending mileage, and gallons. Create an `if...else` statement that uses the `isNaN()` function within a compound conditional expression to determine whether the `startMiles`, `endMiles`, and `gallons` variables contain numeric values. If the variables do not contain numeric values, display an alert dialog box informing the user that he or she must enter numeric values. If the variables do contain numeric values, the `else` clause should calculate the miles per gallon and assign the result to the Miles per Gallon text box in the form. The formula for calculating miles per gallon is (*ending_mileage* − *starting_mileage*) / *gallons*. The formula includes parentheses to force the order of precedence to calculate the subtraction operation before the division operation. (Recall from Chapter 9 that a division operation has higher precedence than a subtraction operation.) One problem with the calculation is that you will receive an error if you attempt to divide by zero. For this reason, you need to use a nested `if` statement within the `else` clause to verify that the `gallons` variable contains a numeric value greater than zero. Otherwise, the statements within the `if` statement should not execute. Save the document as **GasMileage.html**.

Discovery Project 10-4

In most cases, a year is a leap year if it is evenly divisible by 4. However, years that are also evenly divisible by 100 are not leap years, unless they are also divisible by 400. Write a script that allows a user to enter a year and then determines whether it is a leap year. Include a form with a single text box in which the user can enter a year. Display an alert dialog box to inform the user whether the year entered is a standard year or a leap year. Save the document as **LeapYear.html**.

Discovery Project 10-5

A prime number is a number that can only be divided by itself or by one. Examples of prime numbers include 1, 3, 5, 13, and 17. Write a script that prints the prime numbers between 1 and 999 in a table that consists of 10 columns. You will need to use several looping and conditional statements to test all division possibilities. Use `document.write()` statements to create the table elements and a counter variable to create the table so that it consists of 10 columns. The counter variable should start with an initial value of 0 and be incremented by one each time your code identifies a prime number and prints it in a table cell. Once the counter variable reaches a value of 10 (meaning that 10 cells have been added to the current row), print `</tr><tr>` to start a new row and reset the variable to 0. Save the document as **PrimeNumbers.html**.

Manipulating the Browser Object Model

In this chapter, you will:

◎ Study the browser object model

◎ Work with the `Window` object

◎ Study the `History`, `Location`, `Navigator`, and `Screen` objects

In some situations, you may need to use JavaScript to control the Web browser. For example, you might want to change the Web page being displayed or write information to the Web browser's status bar. Or, you may want to control elements of the Web page itself. To control the Web browser window or the Web page, you use the browser object model. This chapter discusses the components of the browser object model.

Understanding the Browser Object Model

The **browser object model (BOM)**, or **client-side object model**, is a hierarchy of objects, each of which provides program access to a different aspect of the Web browser window or the Web page. You can use the methods and properties of objects in the browser object model to manipulate the window and elements displayed in a Web browser. The most basic objects in the browser object model are illustrated in Figure 11-1.

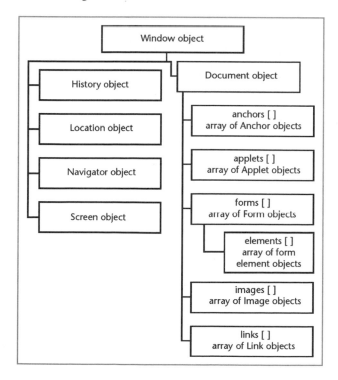

Figure 11-1 Browser object model

? The browser object model is also called the JavaScript object model or the Navigator object model. However, other scripting technologies, such as VBScript, can also control aspects of the Web browser window or Web page. Therefore, the term *browser object model* or *client-side object model* is more accurate.

i+ The concept of object models is fairly complex. You do not need to understand the details of working with object models to work with the browser object model in JavaScript. Instead, you should simply understand that object models define groups of interrelated objects.

587

You do not have to create any objects or arrays explicitly in the browser object model; they are created automatically when a Web browser opens a Web page. The top-level object in the browser object model is the **Window object**, which represents a Web browser window. The Web browser automatically creates the `Window` object for you. The `Window` object is called the **global object** because all other objects in the browser object model are contained within it. For example, the `Window` object contains the `Document` object, just as a Web browser window contains a Web page document. You use the methods and properties of the `Window` object to control the Web browser window, and you use the methods and properties of the `Document` object to control the Web page. Figure 11-2 illustrates the concepts of the `Window` object and the `Document` object.

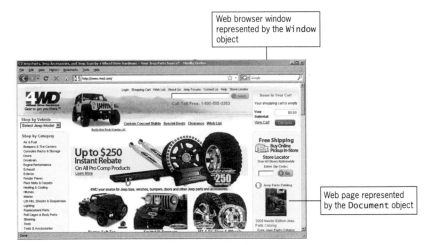

Figure 11-2   `Window` object and `Document` object

Using the Document Object

The `Document` object is arguably the most important object in the browser object model because it represents the Web page displayed in a browser. You are already familiar with the `write()` and `writeln()` methods, which refer to the `Document` object. The statement `document.write("Go Patriots!");` adds the text "Go Patriots!" to a Web page when it is rendered by a Web browser. All elements on a Web page are contained within the `Document` object, and each element is represented in JavaScript by its own object. This means that the `Document` object contains all of the elements you create on a Web page. For example, the `Form` object, which is used by JavaScript to represent forms created with the `<form>` element, is contained within the Document object, which is contained within the Window object. The Radio object, which is used by JavaScript to represent a radio button created with an `<input>` element, is contained within the Form object, which is contained within the Document object, which is contained within the Window object.

In this book, objects in the browser object model are referred to with an initial uppercase letter (Document object). However, when you use the object name in code, you must use a lowercase letter. For example, the following statement refers to the Document object: `document.write("Go Patriots!");`. Note the use of the lowercase *d* in document.

The Document object branch of the browser object model is represented by its own object model called the Document Object Model, or DOM. You will learn more about the DOM in Chapter 13.

589

Referencing JavaScript Objects

Some of the objects in the browser object model represent arrays. In Figure 11-1, objects that are arrays are followed by brackets, such as forms[] or images[]. The arrays contain objects created from the corresponding elements on a Web page. For example, the images[] array contains Image objects that represent all the `<img>` elements on a Web page. Image objects for each `<img>` element are assigned to the elements of the images[] array in the order that they appear on the Web page. The first Image object is represented by images[0], the second Image object is represented by images[1], and so on.

As you learned in Chapter 8, you can use JavaScript to reference any element on a Web page by using periods to append the element's name to the name of any elements in which it is nested, starting with the Document object. For elements that are represented by arrays, you can reference the object through the array instead of with the element name. Consider an Image object, which contains a src property that contains the URL assigned to an `<img>` element's src attribute. Assuming that the image is assigned a name of companyLogo, use the following code to display the image's URL in an alert dialog box:

```
<img src="company_logo.gif" name="companyLogo"
    height="100" width="200" onclick="window.alert(↵
    'This image is located at the following URL: '
    + document.companyLogo.src);"
    alt="Image of a company logo." />
```

Instead of referencing the image by name, you can access it through the images[] array. The following `<img>` element includes an onclick event handler that uses the Document object to display the image's URL in an alert dialog box. The code assumes that the image is the first one on the page by referencing the first element (0) in the images[] array.

```
<img src="company_logo.gif" height="100" width="200"
    onclick="window.alert( ↵
    'This image is located at the following URL:' ↵
    + document.images[0].src);"
    alt="Image of a company logo." />
```

Next, you start working on a simple Web site for an online bicycle retailer named DRG Cycles. You will find four prewritten Web pages in the DRGCycles folder within your Chapter folder for Chapter 11: index.html, cannondale.html, intense.html, and pinarello.html. The index.html document is the home page; the other pages display photos and information about different bicycles. You will modify these Web pages throughout the chapter.

In this exercise, you add an advertisement to the DRG Cycles home page. The ad changes when users click the image. You will change the image using the images[] array.

To add an advertisement that changes when users click the image:

1. Open your text editor, then open the **index.html** document from the DRGCycles folder in your Chapter folder for Chapter 11.

2. Locate the <img> element that displays the banner1.png image and add an onclick event handler, as follows. When the user clicks the image, an onclick event handler changes the image to another image named banner2.png. Note that the banner image is the 27th image on the page, so the images[] array references element 26.

```
<img src="images/banner1.png" width="234"
    height="60" alt="Banner ads"
    onclick="document.images[26].src ↵
    ='images/banner2.png';" />
```

3. Save the **index.html** document and open it in your Web browser. Figure 11-3 shows how the Web page appears. Click the image to make sure that it changes to banner2.png.

Figure 11-3 DRG Cycles Web page with an advertisement

4. Close your Web browser window.

The code you entered in the preceding exercise refers to the 27th element (26) in the images[] array. If other images are added to the Web page before the preceding statement, then referring to the 27th element in the images[] array would result in the wrong URL being displayed. When referring to the current object (in this case, the Image object for the preceding statement), you can simply use the this keyword instead of including the Document object and images[] array. The this keyword refers to the current object. The following code shows the example you saw before the last exercise, but this time it is written with the this keyword:

```
<img src="company_logo.gif" height="100" width="200"
    onclick="window.alert('This image is located ↵
    at the following URL: ' + this.src);"
    alt="Image of a company logo." />
```

Next, you will modify the onclick event handler in the index.html document so that it uses this references instead of referring to the Document object and images[] array.

To modify the event handler in the index.html document so that it uses this references instead of referring to the Document object and images[] array:

1. Return to the **index.html** file in your text editor.

2. Modify the onclick event handler in the banner image as follows:

    ```
    <img src="images/banner1.png" width="234"
        height="60" alt="Banner ads"
        onclick="this.src='images/banner2.png';" />
    ```

3. Save the **index.html** document and open it in your Web browser. Figure 11-4 shows how the Web page appears after clicking the banner image.

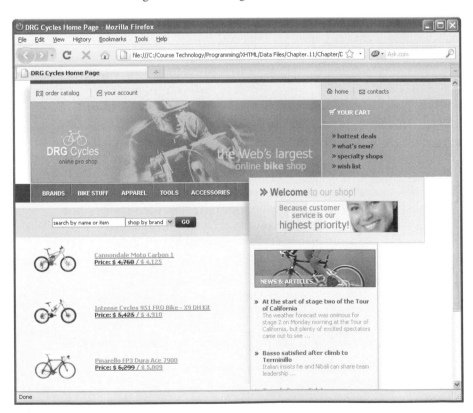

Figure 11-4   DRG Cycles Web page after adding a this reference

4. Close your Web browser window.

Short Quiz 1

1. Explain what the browser object model is and why it's important to JavaScript.

2. What is the top-level object in the browser object model?

3. Explain how to reference arrays that are part of the browser object model.

Manipulating the Browser with the Window Object

The Window object includes several properties that contain information about the Web browser window. For instance, the status property contains information displayed in a Web browser's status bar. Also contained in the Window object are various methods that allow you to manipulate the Web browser window itself. You have already used some methods of the Window object, including the window.alert(), window.confirm(), and window.prompt() methods, which all display dialog boxes. Table 11-1 lists the Window object properties, and Table 11-2 lists the Window object methods.

Property	Description
closed	Returns a Boolean value that indicates whether a window has been closed
defaultStatus	Sets the default text that is written to the status bar
document	Returns a reference to the Document object
history	Returns a reference to the History object
location	Returns a reference to the Location object
name	Returns the name of the window
opener	Refers to the window that opened the current window
self	Returns a self-reference to the Window object; identical to the window property
status	Specifies temporary text that is written to the status bar
window	Returns a self-reference to the Window object; identical to the self property

Table 11-1   Window object properties

Method	Description
alert()	Displays a simple message dialog box with an OK button
blur()	Removes focus from a window
clearInterval()	Cancels an interval that was set with setInterval()
clearTimeout()	Cancels a timeout that was set with setTimeout()
close()	Closes a Web browser window
confirm()	Displays a confirmation dialog box with OK and Cancel buttons
focus()	Makes a Window object the active window
moveBy()	Moves the window relative to the current position
moveTo()	Moves the window to an absolute position
open()	Opens a new Web browser window
print()	Prints the document displayed in the current window
prompt()	Displays a dialog box prompting a user to enter information
resizeBy()	Resizes a window by a specified amount
resizeTo()	Resizes a window to a specified size
scrollBy()	Scrolls the window by a specified amount
scrollTo()	Scrolls the window to a specified position
setInterval()	Repeatedly executes a function after a specified number of milliseconds have elapsed
setTimeout()	Executes a function once after a specified number of milliseconds have elapsed

Table 11-2   Window object methods

Some Web browsers, including Internet Explorer, have custom properties and methods for the Window object. This book describes only properties and methods that are common to browser objects in all current Web browsers.

Another way of referring to the Window object is by using the **self property**, which refers to the current Window object. Using the self property is identical to using the window property to refer to the Window object. For example, the following lines are identical:

```
window.alert("Your order has been received.");
self.alert("Your order has been received.");
```

Some JavaScript programmers prefer to use the window property; others prefer to use the self property. The choice is yours. However, when attempting to decipher JavaScript code created by other programmers, be aware that both properties refer to the current Window object.

Because a Web browser assumes that you are referring to the global object, you do not need to refer explicitly to the Window object when using one of its properties or methods. For example, the alert() method is a method of the Window object. Throughout this text, you have used the full syntax of `window.alert(text);`, although the syntax `alert(text);` without the Window object works equally well. However, it's good practice to use the `window` or `self` references when referring to a property or method of the Window object to clearly identify them as belonging to the Window object. If you do not use the `window` or `self` reference, then you or another programmer might confuse a property or method of the Window object with JavaScript variables or functions.

Understanding Windows and Events

In Chapter 8, you learned how to use events with your Web pages. Events are particularly important when it comes to working with the browser object model because they allow you to execute the methods and change the properties of objects in the browser object model. In this section, you learn more about mouse events.

The *click* and *dblclick* Events

You have already extensively used the `click` event with form controls, such as radio buttons, to execute JavaScript code. However, keep in mind that the `click` event can be used with other types of elements. Earlier in this chapter, you used the `click` event to change the image displayed on the DRG Cycles Web page. The `click` event is often used for the anchor element. In fact, the primary event associated with the anchor element is the `click` event. When a user clicks a link, the Web browser handles execution of the `onclick` event handler automatically, so you do not need to add an `onclick` event handler to your anchor elements.

Sometimes, however, you might want to override an anchor element's automatic `onclick` event handler with your own code. For instance, you may want to warn the user about the content of a Web page that a particular link will open. To override the automatic `click` event with your own code, you add an `onclick` event handler that executes custom code to the <a> element. When you override an internal event handler with your own code, your code must return a value of true or false using the return statement. With the <a> element, a value of true indicates that you want the Web browser to perform its default event handling operation of opening the URL referenced in the link. A value of false indicates that you do not want the <a> element to perform its default event handling operation. For example, the <a> element in the following code includes an `onclick` event handler. The `warnUser()` function that is called by the `onclick` event handler returns a value generated by the `window.confirm()` method. Recall that when a user clicks the OK button in a confirm dialog box, a value of true is returned. When a user clicks the Cancel button, a value of false is returned. Notice the two return statements in the following code. The return statement in the warnUser() function returns a value to the onclick event handler. The return statement in the onclick event handler returns the same value to the Web browser.

```
...
<script type="text/javascript">
/* <![CDATA[ */
function warnUser() {
    return window.confirm("This link is only for↵
        Red Sox fans. Are you sure you want to↵
        continue?");
}
/* ]]> */
</script>
</head>
<body>
<p><a href="redsox.html"
onclick="return warnUser();">
Red Sox Fan Club</a></p>
</body>
</html>
```

The dblclick event works the same as the click event, except that users need to double-click the mouse instead of single-clicking it. The dblclick event is rarely used, and it is not generally used with links because they are driven by single mouse clicks. From the user's point of view, single clicks are much easier than double-clicks.

The *mouseover* and *mouseout* Events

You use the mouseover and mouseout events to create **rollover** effects, which occur when your mouse moves over an element. The mouseover event occurs when the mouse passes over an element and the mouseout event occurs when the mouse moves off an element. These events are also commonly used to change an element's style, such as the formatting of a link when the mouse passes over it. To refer to a CSS style in JavaScript, you use the this reference and the style property in an event handler within the element itself. You use the **style property** to modify an element's CSS properties with JavaScript. To refer to a style with the this reference, you use a period to append the style property to it, followed by another period and a CSS property. CSS properties without hyphens are referred to in JavaScript with all lowercase letters. However, when you refer to a CSS property that contains a hyphen in JavaScript code, you remove the hyphen, convert the first word to lowercase, and convert the first letter of subsequent words to uppercase. For example, the text-decoration property is referred to as textDecoration, `font-family` is referred to as `fontFamily`, `font-size` is referred to as `fontSize`, and so on. In the following code, the `onmouseover` event handler underlines the link when the mouse passes over it, and the `onmouseout` event handler removes the link when the mouse passes off it:

```
<a href="redsox.html"
onmouseover="this.style.textDecoration='underline';"
onmouseout="this.style.textDecoration='none';">
Red Sox Fan Club</a>
```

The `mouseover` and `mouseout` events are also commonly used to display an alternate image or explanatory text when the mouse passes over an element. The following table cell shows a more complex example of the `mouseover` and `mouseout` events. The cell contains five links representing different types of homes that a real estate agent is selling. When the user passes the mouse over a link, the link changes from blue to red and an image of the house is displayed. Moving the mouse off the link changes the link back to blue and displays an empty image. Figure 11-5 shows the page with the mouse over the Townhouse link.

```
<td>
    <p>
        <a href="cottage.html"
            onmouseover="document.images[9].src↵
            ='cottage.jpg';this.style.color='Red'"
            onmouseout="document.images[9].src↵
            ='noselection.jpg';this.style.color↵
            ='Blue'">Cottage:<strong>
            $149,000</strong></a><br />
        <a href="ranch.html"
            onmouseover="document.images[9].src↵
            ='ranch.jpg';this.style.color='Red'"
            onmouseout="document.images[9].src↵
            ='noselection.jpg';this.style.color↵
            ='Blue'">Ranch:<strong>
            $189,000</strong></a><br />
        <a href="townhouse.html"
            onmouseover="document.images[9].src↵
            ='townhouse.jpg';this.style.color='Red'"
            onmouseout="document.images[9].src↵
            ='noselection.jpg';this.style.color↵
            ='Blue'">Townhouse:<strong>
            $319,000</strong></a><br />
        <a href="colonial.html"
            onmouseover="document.images[9].src↵
            ='colonial.jpg';this.style.color='Red'"
            onmouseout="document.images[9].src↵
            ='noselection.jpg';this.style.color↵
            ='Blue'">Colonial:<strong>
            $389,000</strong></a><br />
```

```
<a href="contemporary.html"
        onmouseover="document.images[9].src
        ='contemporary.jpg';this.style.color='Red'"
        onmouseout="document.images[9].src
        ='noselection.jpg';this.style.color
        ='Blue'">Contemporary:<strong>
        $474,000</strong></a></p>
    </td>
```

Figure 11-5 Real estate page with the mouse over the Townhouse link

 You can find a working copy of the real estate page in a folder named RealEstate in your Chapter folder for Chapter 11.

 By default, Firefox does not allow scripts to change status bar text. To allow scripts to change status bar text on Windows systems, select the Tools menu, select Options, and then select Content in the Options dialog box. Click the Advanced button next to the Enable JavaScript button, and then click the Change status bar text box in the Advanced JavaScript Settings dialog box. Click OK twice to close each dialog box. To make the same setting on Linux systems, select Preferences from the Edit menu; on Macintosh systems, select Preferences from the Firefox menu.

The `defaultStatus` property specifies the default text that appears in the status bar whenever the mouse is not positioned over a link. The syntax for the `defaultStatus` property is `window.defaultStatus = "status bar text here";`. You will now add the `defaultStatus` property to the DRG Cycles Web page so the text "Welcome to DRG Cycles!" is displayed in the status bar by default. You will also add `onmouseover` event handlers to each of the bike model links; these event handlers display messages in an `<input>` box about clicking the link for more information. Finally, you will add `onmouseout` event handlers that remove the value assigned to the `<input>` box by changing its value to an empty string.

To add the **defaultStatus** property and **onmouseover** and **onmouseout** event handlers to the DRG Cycles Web page:

1. Return to the **index.html** document in your text editor.

2. Add the following script section immediately above the closing `</head>` tag. The script contains a single statement that sets the Web page's default status bar text to "Welcome to DRG Cycles!"

```
<script type="text/javascript">
/* <![CDATA[ */
window.defaultStatus = "Welcome to DRG Cycles!";
/* ]]> */
</script>
```

3. Locate `<!--[Add form here]-->` in the document body and replace it with the following form, which contains a single text box that will display messages when the mouse passes over a bike model link:

```
<form action="" name="messageForm">
  <p><input type="text" name="bikeLink" size="40"
      style="color:Blue; font-weight:bold; ↵
      border-style:none; border-color: inherit; ↵
      border-width:medium; background-color: ↵
      Transparent" /></p>
</form>
```

4. Add `onmouseover` event handlers to the `<tr>` element containing the bicycle model links to modify the value assigned to the text box when the mouse pointer passes over the link. Also, add `onmouseout` event handlers that reset the text box to an empty string. For example, the `<tr>` element for the Cannondale bike should appear as follows:

```
<tr onmouseover ="document.messageForm.bikeLink. ↵
    value ='Click for more info on the CANNONDALE'"
    onmouseout ="document.messageForm.bikeLink. ↵
    value =''">
```

5. Save the **index.html** document and open it in your Web browser. Figure 11-6 shows how the Web page appears when you hold your mouse pointer over Intense Cycles 951 FRO Bike - X9 DH Kit.

Figure 11-6 DRG Cycles Web page after adding the `defaultStatus` property and `onmouseover` and `onmouseout` event handlers

6. Close your Web browser window.

One of the more common uses of rollovers is to replace (or swap) an image on a Web page with another image. Consider the following code. By default, the v500tec.gif file is displayed. The `onmouseover` event handler changes the image to showroom.gif, and the `onmouseout` event handler changes the image back to the v500tec.gif file. Figure 11-7 shows the Web page before the mouse is placed on the image. Once the mouse moves over the image, the image shown in Figure 11-8 is displayed.

```
<p><img src="v500tec.gif" height="90px" width="700px"
    alt="Banner images"
    onmouseover="this.src='showroom.gif'"
    onmouseout="this.src='v500tec.gif'" /></p>
```

Figure 11-7   Web page before the mouse passes over the image

Figure 11-8   Web page with the mouse placed over the image

The *mousedown* and *mouseup* Events

The mousedown event occurs when you point to an element and
hold the mouse button down; the mouseup event occurs when you
release the mouse button. The following code shows the <img>
element that displays the motorcycle and showroom images, this
time using mousedown and mouseup events:

```
<p><img src="v500tec.gif" height="90px" width="700px"
    alt="Banner images"
    onmousedown="this.src='showroom.gif'"
    onmouseup="this.src='v500tec.gif'" /></p>
```

Next, you will modify the <img> element that displays the banner
ads in the index.html document so the second image in the banner is
displayed when you hold the mouse button down over the image.

To modify the <img> element that displays the banner ads in the index.html document so that the second image in the banner is displayed when you hold the mouse over it:

1. Return to the **index.html** document in your text editor.

2. Replace the `onclick` event handler in the banner-ad `<img>` element with `onmousedown` and `onmouseup` event handlers that swap the images.

   ```
   <img src="images/banner1.png" width="234" height="60"
       alt="Banner ads"
       onmousedown="this.src='images/banner2.png';"
       onmouseup="this.src='images/banner1.png'" />
   ```

3. Save the **index.html** document and open it in your Web browser. Press and hold the mouse button over the banner image, then release it. You should see the images change when you press and release the mouse button.

4. Close your Web browser window.

Opening and Closing Windows

Most Web browsers allow you to open new browser windows in addition to the browser window(s) that may already be open. You may need to open a new browser window for several reasons. For example, you may want to launch a new Web page in a separate window, allowing users to continue viewing the current page in the current window. Or, you may want to use an additional window to display information such as a picture or an order form.

Whenever a new Web browser window is opened, a new `Window` object is created to represent the new window. You can have as many browser windows open as your system will support, each displaying a different Web page. For example, you can have one browser window display Microsoft's Web site, another browser window display Firefox's Web site, and so on.

You may be familiar with how to open a link in a new window by using the `<a>` element's `target` attribute. For example, the following link opens the Wikipedia home page in a new window named `wikiWindow`:

```
<p><a href="http://www.wikipedia.org/"
    target="wikiWindow">
    Wikipedia home page</a></p>
```

Whenever the user clicks the preceding link, the Web browser looks for another browser window named wikiWindow. If the window exists, the link is opened in it. If the window does not exist, a new window named wikiWindow is created where the link opens.

 Some Web browsers, including Firefox and Internet Explorer, can be configured to open new pages in either a new window or a tab in the current window. To configure Firefox to open pages in a new window, select the Tools menu, select Options, and then select Tabs in the Options dialog box. Select the check box that opens pages in a new window and then click OK. To configure Internet Explorer to open pages in a new window, select the Tools menu, select Internet Options, and then select the General tab in the Internet Options dialog box. In the Tabs section, click the Settings button. In the Tabbed Browsing Settings dialog box, select the radio button that opens links in a new window and then click OK twice to close each dialog box.

The links in the DRG Cycles Web page now open in the current window; they do not open in a new window. Next, you will modify the links so they use the <a> element's target attribute to open each URL in a separate window.

To modify the links in the DRG Cycles Web page so that they use the <a> element's target attribute to open each URL in a separate window:

1. Return to the **index.html** document in your text editor.

2. Add the following attribute before the closing bracket for each of the <a> elements that open the bike model pages. Note that there are two <a> elements for each bike: one for the bike's picture and another for its description.

   ```
   target="bikeInfo"
   ```

3. Save the **index.html** document and open it in your Web browser. Click one of the links to see if the Web page opens in a new browser window. If you click other links on the DRG Cycles Web page, you should notice that each Web page opens in the bikeInfo window (if it is currently open) instead of opening in a separate window. Figure 11-9 shows the bikeInfo window opened to the Pinarello Web page.

604

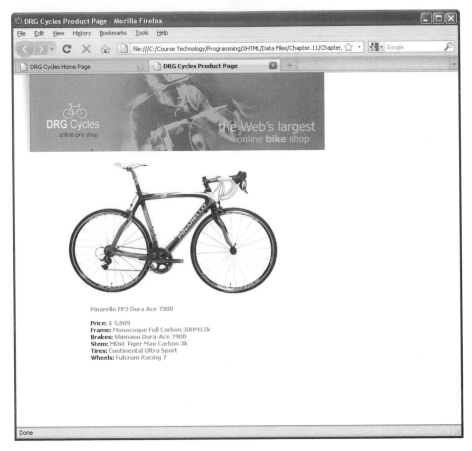

Figure 11-9   Pinarello Web page opened in the `bikeInfo` window

> **4.** Close your Web browser window.

Opening a Window

The problem with using the `target` attribute is that it is deprecated in HTML 5 and XHTML. To open new windows in HTML 5 and the strict DTD, you must use the **open() method** of the `Window` object. The syntax for the `open()` method is as follows:

```
window.open(url, name, options, replace);
```

Table 11-3 lists the arguments of the `window.open()` method.

Argument	Description
URL	Represents the Web address or filename to be opened
name	Assigns a value to the name property of the new Window object
options	Represents a string that allows you to customize the new Web browser window's appearance
replace	A Boolean value that determines whether the URL should create a new entry in the Web browser's history list or replace the entry

Table 11-3   Arguments of the Window object's open() method

You can include all or none of the window.open() method arguments. The statement window.open("http://www.wikipedia.org"); opens the Wikipedia home page in a new Web browser window, as shown in Figure 11-10. If you exclude the URL argument, a blank Web page opens. For example, the statement window.open(); opens the browser window displayed in Figure 11-11.

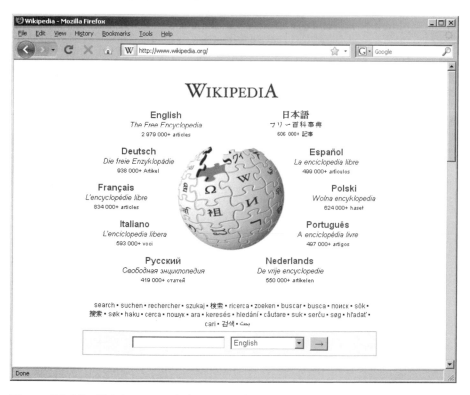

Figure 11-10   Web browser window opened with the URL argument of the open() method

606

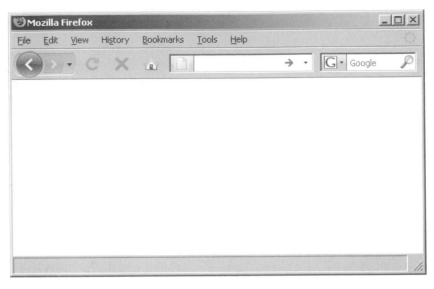

Figure 11-11 Blank Web browser window opened with the `window.open()` statement

If you are writing code that requires a user to click a link or a button, then you can use an event handler to call the `window.open()` method, and the window will open successfully. However, if you include JavaScript code that opens a new window without a request from the user, then the pop-up blocker feature that is available in most current Web browsers will prevent the window from opening.

When you open a new Web browser window, you can customize its appearance by using the `options` argument of the `window.open()` method. Table 11-4 lists some common options that you can use with the `window.open()` method.

Name	Description
`height`	Sets the window's height
`left`	Sets the horizontal coordinate of the left side of the window, in pixels
`location`	Includes the URL Location text box
`menubar`	Includes the menu bar
`resizable`	Determines if the new window can be resized
`scrollbars`	Includes scroll bars
`status`	Includes the status bar
`toolbar`	Includes the Standard toolbar
`top`	Sets the vertical coordinate of the top of the window, in pixels
`width`	Sets the window's width

Table 11-4 Common options of the `Window` object's `open()` method

All the options listed in Table 11-4, with the exception of the width and height options, are set using values of "yes" or "no", or 1 for yes and 0 for no. To include the status bar, for example, the options string should read "status=yes". You set the width and height options using integers representing pixels. For example, to create a new window that is 200 pixels high by 300 pixels wide, the string should read "height=200,width=300". When including multiple items in the options string, you must separate the items by commas. If you exclude the options string of the window.open() method, then all the standard options are included in the new Web browser window. However, if you include the options string, you must include all the components you want to create for the new window; that is, the new window is created with only the components you specify.

Figure 11-12 shows the Photo Gallery Web page from the Woodland Park Zoo in Seattle, Washington. If you select a link from one of the menus on the page, such as the Fennec fox link that is highlighted in Figure 11-12, the Photo Gallery Slideshow Web page shown in Figure 11-13 opens.

Figure 11-12 Woodland Park Zoo Photo Gallery Web page

Figure 11-13 Woodland Park Zoo Photo Gallery Slideshow
Web page displaying a fox

Notice that the Photo Gallery Slideshow Web page does not display
toolbars, the menu, the URL Location box, or the scroll bars. Also,
keep in mind that it is sized to specific dimensions. If you tried to
resize the window, you would find that it couldn't be resized. The
Photo Gallery Web page uses a JavaScript statement similar to the
following to open the Photo Gallery Slideshow Web page when a user
clicks the name of an animal:

```
var OpenWin = window.open(page, "CtrlWindow",
"toolbar=no,menubar=no,location=no,scrollbars=no, ⏎
resizable=no,width=380,height=405");
```

The `name` argument of the `window.open()` method is essentially the
same as the value assigned to the deprecated `target` attribute in that
it specifies the name of the window where the URL should open. If
the `name` argument is already in use by another Web browser window,

then JavaScript changes focus to the existing Web browser window instead of creating a new window. For instance, the Photo Gallery Web page opens the Photo Gallery Slideshow Web page and assigns it a name of "CtrlWindow". If the CtrlWindow Web page already exists when you select another menu item from the Photo Gallery Web page, then the CtrlWindow Web page is reused; another window does not open. This is especially important with a Web page such as the Photo Gallery Web page, which allows you to view dozens of different Web pages for each of the animals listed in the menu. Imagine how crowded a user's screen would be if the program kept opening a new Photo Gallery Slideshow Web page window for each selected animal.

Next, you will modify the DRG Cycles Web page so the links use the window.open() method instead of the target attribute to open the URLs in a separate page.

To modify the DRG Cycles Web page so the links use the window.open() method instead of the target attribute to open the URLs in a separate page:

1. Return to the **index.html** document in your text editor.

2. Add the following global variable declaration and function to the end of the script section. The function will be called by onclick event handlers in each of the links.

```
var bikeWindow;
function showBike(linkTarget) {
  bikeWindow = window.open(linkTarget, "bikeInfo",
    "toolbar=no,menubar=no,location=no, ↵
    scrollbars=no,resizable=no,width=620, ↵
    height=575");
}
```

3. Next, replace the target attribute in the six <a> elements with an onclick event handler that calls the showBike() function, passing to it the URL of the target Web page. The onclick event handler should also return a value of "false" to prevent the index.html Web page from being replaced with the target Web page that you are opening in a separate window.

4. Save the **index.html** document and open it in your Web browser. Click one of the links to see if the Web page opens in a new browser window. Figure 11-14 shows how the window appears with the cannondale.html Web page displayed.

Figure 11-14   Window opened with the open() method

5.   Close your Web browser windows.

A Window object's name property can be used only to specify a target window with a link and cannot be used in JavaScript code. If you want to control the new window by using JavaScript code located within the Web browser in which it was *created*, then you must assign the new Window object created with the window.open() method to a variable. The statement that opens the Photo Gallery Slideshow Web page assigns an object representing the new Web browser window to a variable named OpenWin. You can use any of the properties and methods of the Window object with a variable that represents a Window object.

One problem with Web pages such as the DRG Cycles Web page is that windows that open in response to the user clicking a link can get hidden or "lost" behind other windows on the user's screen. For example, suppose that the user clicks the Cannondale Moto Carbon 1 link on the DRG Cycles Web page, thereby opening a new window. Then suppose that the user returns to the DRG Cycles Web page (without closing the Cannondale Moto Carbon 1 window) and clicks a different link. The window that displays the bicycle pages is not automatically displayed as the active window on the screen. That is, it does not necessarily appear as the top window; it could instead be hidden behind other windows. The user may continually click links, thinking that nothing is happening in response to his or her clicks, when in fact the code is working. The problem might be that the windows are open but not visible. In order to make a window the active window, you use the **focus() method** of the Window object. You append the focus() method to the variable that represents the window, not to the name argument of the window.open() method. For example, to make the Photo Gallery Slideshow window the active window, you use the following statement:

OpenWin.focus();

Next, you add a focus() method to the showBike() function in the DRG Cycles Web page.

To add a focus() method to the showBike() function in the DRG Cycles Web page:

1. Return to the **index.html** document in your text editor.

2. Add the following statement to the end of the showBike() function:

   bikeWindow.focus();

3. Save the **index.html** document and open it in your Web browser. Click one of the links to open the window that displays the bicycle pages. Leave the Web page open, navigate back to the DRG Cycles Web page, and click a different link. The window that displays the bicycle pages should become the active window and display the URL for the Web page link you clicked.

4. Close your Web browser windows.

Closing a Window

The **close() method**, which closes a Web browser window, is the method you will probably use the most with variables representing other Window objects. To close the Web browser window represented by the OpenWin variable, you use the statement OpenWin.close();. To close the current window, you use the statement window.close() or self.close().

Next, you add links to each of the bicycle Web pages that call the close() method, which will close the window.

 It is not necessary to include the Window object or self property when using the open() and close() methods of the Window object. However, the Document object also contains methods named open() and close(), which are used for opening and closing Web pages. Therefore, the Window object is usually included with the open() and close() methods to distinguish between the Window object and the Document object.

To add links to each of the bicycle Web pages that call the close() method:

1. Return to your text editor and open the **cannondale.html** document from the DRGCycles folder in your Chapter folder for Chapter 11.

2. Locate the table cell that displays the image of the Cannondale bike along with its specifications. Add the following paragraph and anchor elements to the end of the table cell. The onclick event handler in the anchor element calls the close() method, which will close the window.

```
<p><a href="" onclick="self.close();">
    Close Window</a></p>
```

3. Save and close the **cannondale.html** document.

4. Repeat Steps 2 and 3 for the **intense.html** and **pinarello.html** documents.

5. Open the **index.html** document in your Web browser and click one of the links. Figure 11-15 shows the new link (which closes the window) in the Pinarello FP3 Dura Ace 7900 Web page.

Figure 11-15   Pinarello Web page after adding a link with a close() method

6. Click the **Close Window** link to close the window you opened.

7. Close the Web browser window containing the DRG Cycles Web page.

Working with Timeouts and Intervals

As you develop Web pages, you may need to have some JavaScript code execute repeatedly, without user intervention. Alternately, you may want to create animation or allow for some kind of repetitive task that executes automatically. For example, you may want to include an advertising image that changes automatically every few seconds. Or, you may want to use animation to change the ticking hands of an online analog clock (in which case each position of the clock hands would require a separate image).

You use the `Window` object's timeout and interval methods to create code that executes automatically. The **setTimeout() method** is used in JavaScript to execute code after a specific amount of time has elapsed. Code executed with the `setTimeout()` method executes only once. The syntax for the `setTimeout()` method is `var variable = setTimeout("code", milliseconds);`. This statement declares that the variable will refer to the `setTimeout()` method. The `code` argument must be enclosed in double or single quotation marks and can be a single JavaScript statement, a series of JavaScript statements, or a function call. The amount of time the Web browser should wait before executing the `code` argument of the `setTimeout()` method is expressed in milliseconds.

> A millisecond is one-thousandth of a second; there are 1,000 milliseconds in a second. For example, five seconds is equal to 5,000 milliseconds.

The **clearTimeout() method** is used to cancel a `setTimeout()` method before its code executes. The `clearTimeout()` method receives a single argument, which is the variable that represents a `setTimeout()` method call. The variable that represents a `setTimeout()` method call must be declared as a global variable. (Recall from Chapter 9 that a global variable is declared outside of a function and is available to all parts of a JavaScript program.)

The script section in the following code contains a `setTimeout()` method and a `clearTimeout()` method call. The `setTimeout()` method is set to execute after 10,000 milliseconds (10 seconds) have elapsed. If a user clicks the OK button, the `buttonPressed()` function calls the `clearTimeout()` method.

```
...
<script type="text/javascript">
/* <![CDATA[ */
var buttonNotPressed = setTimeout(
    "window.alert('You must press the OK button ↵
        to continue!')", 10000);
```

```
function buttonPressed() {
    clearTimeout(buttonNotPressed);
    window.alert("The setTimeout() method↵
        was cancelled!");
}
/* ]]> */
</script>
</head>
<body>
<form action="">
<input type="button" value=" OK "
    onclick="buttonPressed();" />
</form>
</body>
</html>
```

Two other JavaScript methods that create code and execute automatically are setInterval() and clearInterval(). The **setInterval() method** is similar to the setTimeout() method, except that it repeatedly executes the same code after being called only once. The **clearInterval() method** is used to clear a setInterval() method call in the same fashion that the clearTimeout() method clears a setTimeout() method call. The setInterval() and clearInterval() methods are most often used for starting animation code that executes repeatedly. The syntax for the setInterval() method is the same as the syntax for the setTimeout() method: var *variable* = setInterval("*code*", *milliseconds*);. As with the clearTimeout() method, the clearInterval() method receives a single argument, which is the global variable that represents a setInterval() method call.

By combining the src attribute of the Image object with the setTimeout() or setInterval() methods, you can create simple animation on a Web page. In this context, "animation" does not necessarily mean a complex cartoon character, but any situation in which a sequence of images changes automatically. However, Web animation can include the traditional type, involving cartoons and movement (like advertising with changing images or the ticking hands of the clock mentioned earlier). The following code uses the setInterval() method to automatically swap the motorcycle images you saw in Figures 11-7 and 11-8 every couple of seconds.

```
...
<script type="text/javascript">
/* <![CDATA[ */
var curBanner="cycle1";
function changeBanner() {
    if (curBanner == "cycle2") {
        document.images[0].src = "v500tec.gif";
        curBanner = "cycle1";
    }
    else {
```

```
        document.images[0].src = "showroom.gif";
        curBanner = "cycle2";
    }
}
/* ]]> */
</script>
</head>
<body onload="var begin=setInterval('changeBanner()', ↵
    2000);">
<p><img src="v500tec.gif" height="90px" width="700px"
alt="Banner images" /></p>
</body>
</html>
```

Next, you will modify the DRG Cycles Web page so that it uses the
setInterval() method to change the banner image automatically.

To modify the DRG Cycles Web page so that it uses the setInterval() method to change the banner image automatically:

1. Return to the **index.html** document in your text editor.

2. To the end of the script section, add the following global variable and bannerAd() function. The bannerAd() function will
   be called by a setInterval() method. As a result, the images
   will change automatically.

   ```
   var curImage="banner1";
   function bannerAd() {
       if (curImage == "banner2") {
           document.images[26].src = "images/banner1.png";
           curImage = "banner1";
       }
       else {
           document.images[26].src = "images/banner2.png";
           curImage = "banner2";
       }
   }
   ```

3. Modify the opening <body> tag so it includes an onload event
   handler that calls the setInterval() method and bannerAd()
   function, as follows:

   ```
   <body onload="var changeImages=setInterval ↵
       ('bannerAd()',2000);">
   ```

4. Finally, remove the onmousedown and onmouseup event
   handlers from the <img> banner element.

5. Save the **index.html** document and then open it in your Web
   browser. The image should begin alternating automatically.

6. Close your Web browser window.

Short Quiz 2

1. What are the different ways that you can refer to the `Window` object?

2. Explain how to override an internal event handler with your own code.

3. How do you open and close a window? How do you customize its appearance?

4. Explain how to use timeouts and intervals to execute JavaScript code repeatedly.

Working with the `History`, `Location`, `Navigator`, and `Screen` Objects

In this section, you will learn how to work with the `History`, `Location`, `Navigator`, and `Screen` objects.

Using the `History` Object

The **`History` object** maintains an internal list (known as a history list) of all the documents that have been opened during the current Web browser session. Each browser window contains its own internal `History` object. You cannot view the URLs contained in the history list, but you can write a script that uses the history list to navigate to Web pages that have been opened during a Web browser session.

Two important security features are associated with the `History` object. First, the `History` object will not actually display the URLs contained in the history list. This is important because individual user information in a Web browser, such as the types of Web sites a user likes to visit, is private information. Preventing others from viewing the URLs in a history list is an essential security feature because it keeps people's online interests confidential. This security feature is available in both Firefox and Internet Explorer.

A second important security feature of the `History` object is specific to Internet Explorer and the domain in which a Web page exists. As mentioned earlier, you can write a script that uses the history list to navigate to Web pages that have been opened during a Web browser session. In Internet Explorer, you can use JavaScript code to navigate through a history list. However, this is only possible if the currently displayed Web page exists within the same domain as the Web page containing the JavaScript code that is attempting to move through the list. For example, a user may open the home page for a company that sells office supplies. Suppose that the user then clicks a link on the company's home page that opens another Web page in the company's domain, such as an online ordering page. In this case, the office supply company's home page is added to the user's history list. JavaScript code on the online ordering page can use the History object to navigate back to the company's home page. If JavaScript code attempts to access the History object of a Web browser that contains a URL located in a different domain, the Web browser ignores the JavaScript code. This security feature helps prevent malicious programmers and unscrupulous Web sites from seizing control of your browser or even your computer. As a general rule, you should only use the History object to help visitors navigate through your particular Web site.

The History object includes the three methods listed in Table 11-5.

Method	Description
back()	Produces the same result as clicking a Web browser's Back button
forward()	Produces the same result as clicking a Web browser's Forward button
go()	Opens a specific document in the history list

Table 11-5   Methods of the History object

When you use a method or property of the History object, you must include a reference to the History object itself. For example, the back() and forward() methods allow a script to move backward or forward in a Web browser's history. To use the back() method, you must use the syntax history.back().

The go() method is used for navigating to a specific Web page that has been previously visited. The argument of the go() method is an integer that indicates how many pages you want to navigate forward or backward in the history list. For example, history.go(-2); opens the Web page that is two pages back in the history list; the statement history.go(3); opens the Web page that is three pages forward in the history list. The statement history.go(-1); is equivalent to using the back() method, and the statement history.go(1); is equivalent to using the forward() method.

The History object contains a single property, the length property, which contains the specific number of documents that have been opened during the current browser session. To use the `length` property, you use the syntax `history.length;`. The `length` property does not contain the URLs of the documents themselves, but only an integer representing how many documents have been opened. The following code uses an alert dialog box to display the number of Web pages that have been visited during a Web browser session:

```
window.alert("You have visited " + history.length
    + " Web pages.");
```

The `History` object is included in this chapter to introduce you to all of the major objects in the browser object model. However, you should avoid using the `History` object to navigate to Web pages that have been opened during a Web browser session. Instead, you should use the full URL with the `href` property of the `Location` object, as explained in the next section.

Using the `Location` Object

When you want to allow users to open one Web page from within another Web page, you usually create a hypertext link with the <a> element. You can also use JavaScript code and the `Location` object to open Web pages. The **Location object** allows you to change to a new Web page from within JavaScript code. One reason you may want to change Web pages with JavaScript code is to redirect your Web site visitors to a different or updated URL. The `Location` object contains several properties and methods for working with the URL of the document that is currently open in a Web browser window. When you use a method or property of the `Location` object, you must include a reference to the `Location` object itself. For example, to use the `href` property, you must write `location.href = ` *URL*`;`. Table 11-6 lists the `Location` object's properties, and Table 11-7 lists the `Location` object's methods.

Properties	Description
hash	A URL's anchor
host	The host and domain name (or IP address) of a network host
hostname	A combination of the URL's host name and port sections
href	The full URL address
pathname	The URL's path
port	The URL's port
protocol	The URL's protocol
search	A URL's search or query portion

Table 11-6   Properties of the `Location` object

Method	Description
assign()	Loads a new Web page
reload()	Causes the page that currently appears in the Web browser to open again
replace()	Replaces the currently loaded URL with a different one

Table 11-7 Methods of the Location object

The properties of the Location object allow you to modify individual portions of a URL. When you modify any properties of the Location object, you generate a new URL, and the Web browser automatically attempts to open that new URL. Instead of modifying individual portions of a URL, it is usually easier to change the href property, which represents the entire URL. For example, the statement location.href = "http://www.google.com"; opens the Google home page.

The assign() method of the Location object performs the same action as changing the href property: It loads a new Web page. The statement location.assign ("http://www.google.com"); is equivalent to the statement location.href = "http://www.google.com";.

The reload() method of the Location object is equivalent to the Reload button in Firefox or the Refresh button in Internet Explorer. It causes the page that currently appears in the Web browser to open again. You can use the reload() method without any arguments, as in location.reload();, or you can include a Boolean argument of true or false. Including an argument of true forces the current Web page to reload from the server where it is located, even if no changes have been made to it. For example, the statement location.reload(true); forces the current page to reload. If you include an argument of false, or do not include any argument at all, then the Web page reloads only if it has changed.

The replace() method of the Location object is used to replace the currently loaded URL with a different one. This method works somewhat differently from loading a new document by changing the href property. The replace() method actually overwrites one document with another and replaces the old URL entry in the Web browser's history list. In contrast, the href property opens a different document and adds it to the history list.

You can use this.location to retrieve the URL of the current Web page.

Using the Navigator Object

The **Navigator object** is used to obtain information about the current Web browser. It gets its name from Netscape Navigator, but it is also supported by Firefox, Internet Explorer, and other current browsers.

Some Web browsers, including Internet Explorer, contain unique methods and properties of the Navigator object that cannot be used with other browsers. Table 11-8 lists properties of the Navigator object that are supported by most current Web browsers, including Firefox and Internet Explorer.

Properties	Description
appCodeName	The Web browser code name
appName	The Web browser name
appVersion	The Web browser version
platform	The operating system in use on the client computer
userAgent	The string stored in the HTTP user-agent request header, which contains information about the browser, the platform name, and compatibility

Table 11-8 Properties of the Navigator object

The Navigator object is most commonly used to determine which type of Web browser is running. The statement browserType = navigator.appName; returns the name of the Web browser in which the code is running to the browserType variable. You can then use the browserType variable to determine which code to run for the specific type of browser. The **with statement** eliminates the need to retype the name of an object when properties of the same object are being referenced in a series. To use the with statement, you create a structure similar to an if statement and pass the name of the object as a conditional expression. You can then refer to all of the object properties without referring to the object itself. The following with statement prints the five properties of the Navigator object for Firefox 3.0. Figure 11-16 shows the output.

```
with (navigator) {
    document.write("<p>Browser code name: "
        + appCodeName + "<br />");
    document.write("Web browser name: "
        + appName + "<br />");
    document.write("Web browser version: "
        + appVersion + "<br />");
    document.write("Operating platform: "
        + platform + "<br />");
    document.write("User agent: " + userAgent
        + "</p>");
}
```

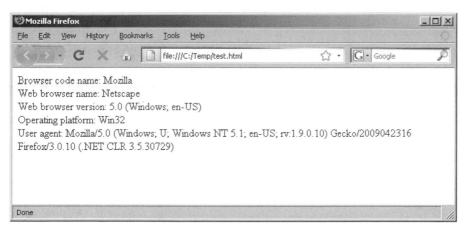

Figure 11-16 Navigator object properties in Firefox

Using the Screen Object

Computer displays can vary widely, depending on the type and size of the monitor, the type of installed graphics card, and the screen resolution and color depth selected by the user. For example, some notebook computers have small screens with limited resolution, while some desktop systems can have large monitors with very high resolution. The wide range of possible display settings makes it challenging to determine the size and positioning of windows generated by JavaScript. The **Screen object** is used to obtain information about the display screen's size, resolution, and color depth. Table 11-9 lists the properties of the Screen object that are supported by most current Web browsers, including Firefox and Internet Explorer.

Properties	Description
availHeight	Returns the height of the display screen, not including operating system features such as the Windows taskbar
availWidth	Returns the width of the display screen, not including operating system features such as the Windows taskbar
colorDepth	Returns the display screen's bit depth if a color palette is in use; if a color palette is not in use, returns the value of the pixelDepth property
height	Returns the height of the display screen
pixelDepth	Returns the display screen's color resolution in bits per pixel
width	Returns the width of the display screen

Table 11-9 Properties of the Screen object

The `colorDepth` and `pixelDepth` properties are most useful in determining the color resolution that the display supports. For example, if the `colorDepth` property returns a value of 32, which indicates high-color resolution, then you can use JavaScript to display a high-color image. However, if the `colorDepth` property returns a value of 16, which indicates medium-color resolution, then you may want to use JavaScript to display a lower-color image. The following code illustrates how to use the `colorDepth` property to determine which version of an image to display:

```
if (screen.colorDepth >= 32)
    document.write(
        "<img href='companyLogo_highres.jpg' />");
else if (screen.colorDepth >= 16)
    document.write(
        "<img href='companyLogo_mediumres.jpg' />");
else
    document.write(
        "<img href='companyLogo_lowres.jpg' />");
```

The remaining `Screen` object properties determine the size of the display area. For example, on a computer with a screen resolution of 1280 by 768, the following statements print "Your screen resolution is 1280 by 768."

```
var screenWidth = screen.width;
var screenHeight = screen.height;
document.write("<p>Your screen resolution is " +
    screenWidth + " by " + screenHeight + ".</p>");
```

One of the more common uses of the `Screen` object properties is to center a Web browser window in the display area. For windows generated with the `window.open()` method, you can center a window when it first opens by assigning values to the `left` and `top` options of the `options` argument. To center a window horizontally, subtract the width of the window from the screen width, divide the remainder by two, and assign the result to the `left` option. Similarly, to center a window vertically, subtract the height of the window from the screen height, divide the remainder by two, and assign the result to the `top` option. The following code demonstrates how to create a new window and center it in the display area:

> Remember that the statements for opening a new window must be called from an event handler; otherwise, a Web browser's pop-up blocker will prevent the window from opening.

```
var winWidth=300;
var winHeight=200;
var leftPosition = (screen.width-winWidth)/2;
var topPosition = (screen.height-winHeight)/2;
var optionString = "width=" + winWidth + ",height="
    + winHeight + ",left=" + leftPosition + ",top="
    + topPosition;
OpenWin = window.open("", "CtrlWindow",
    optionString);
```

Next, you will modify the DRG Cycles Web page so that the bicycle window is centered in the display area.

To modify the DRG Cycles Web page so that the bicycle window is centered in the display area:

1. Return to the **index.html** document in your text editor.

2. Modify the showBike() function as follows so that it uses the Screen object to calculate the left and top positions of the bicycle window:

```
function showBike(linkTarget) {
    var propertyWidth=620;
    var propertyHeight=575;
    var winLeft = (screen.width-propertyWidth)/2;
    var winTop = (screen.height-propertyHeight)/2;
    var winOptions = "toolbar=no,menubar=no, ↵
        location=no,scrollbars=no,resizable=no";
    winOptions += ",width=" + propertyWidth;
    winOptions += ",height=" + propertyHeight;
    winOptions += ",left=" + winLeft;
    winOptions += ",top=" + winTop;
    bikeWindow = window.open(linkTarget,
        "bikeInfo", winOptions);
    bikeWindow.focus();
}
```

3. Save the **index.html** document, and then validate it with the W3C Markup Validation Service. Once the document is valid, close it in your text editor and open it in your Web browser. Click one of the bike links. The bicycle window should open and be centered on your screen.

4. Close your Web browser windows.

Short Quiz 3

1. Explain the security features of the History object.

2. How do you use the History object to navigate backward or forward in a Web browser's history?

3. How do you use the Location object to change to a new Web page?

4. What is the Navigator object and how do you use it?

Summing Up

- The browser object model (BOM) or client-side object model is a hierarchy of objects, each of which provides program access to a different aspect of the Web browser window or the Web page.

- The top-level object in the browser object model is the `Window` object, which represents a Web browser window.

- The `Document` object is arguably the most important object in the browser object model because it represents the Web page displayed in a browser.

- For elements that are represented by arrays, you can reference the object through the array instead of with the element name.

- Because the `Window` object is the global object, you do not have to include it in your statements.

- When you override an internal event handler with your own code, your code must return a value of true or false using the return statement.

- A rollover is an effect that occurs when your mouse moves over an element.

- You use the `style` property to modify an element's CSS properties with JavaScript.

- Whenever a new Web browser window is opened, a new `Window` object is created to represent the new window.

- When you open a new Web browser window, you can customize its appearance by using the `options` argument of the `window.open()` method.

- A `Window` object's `name` property can be used only to specify a target window with a link and cannot be used in JavaScript code.

- To control a new window by using JavaScript code located within the Web browser in which it was created, you must assign the new `Window` object created with the `window.open()` method to a variable.

- The `setTimeout()` method is used in JavaScript to execute code after a specific amount of time has elapsed.

- The `clearTimeout()` method is used to cancel a `setTimeout()` method before its code executes.

- The `setInterval()` method repeatedly executes the same code after being called only once.

- The `clearInterval()` method is used to clear a `setInterval()` method call.

- The `History` object maintains an internal list (known as a history list) of all the documents that have been opened during the current Web browser session.

- The `Location` object allows you to change to a new Web page from within JavaScript code.

- The `Navigator` object is used to obtain information about the current Web browser.

- The `with` statement eliminates the need to retype the name of an object when properties of the same object are being referenced in a series.

- The `Screen` object is used to obtain information about the display screen's size, resolution, and color depth.

Comprehension Check

1. Which of the following objects is also referred to as the global object?

   a. `Document` object

   b. `Window` object

   c. `Browser` object

   d. `Screen` object

2. Which of the following elements in the browser object model are referenced with arrays? (Choose all that apply.)

   a. images

   b. paragraphs

   c. forms

   d. links

3. Which of the following terms does not refer to the browser object model?

    a. Firefox object model

    b. JavaScript object model

    c. client-side object model

    d. Navigator object model

4. You must use the `Window` object or `self` property when referencing a property or method of the `Window` object. True or False?

5. Explain how to override an event with an event handler function.

6. Which of the following events are used to create rollover effects? (Choose all that apply.)

    a. `onclick`

    b. `onload`

    c. `onmouseover`

    d. `onmouseout`

7. Explain how to open a blank window with the `window.open()` method.

8. You use the options string of the `window.open()` method to specify any elements that you do not want created for the new window. True or False?

9. Which of the following arguments of the options string of the `window.open()` method identifies the horizontal coordinate where the window will be positioned?

    a. `left`

    b. `leftPosition`

    c. `x-axis`

    d. `moveTo`

10. Explain why you should include the `Window` object or `self` property when using the `open()` and `close()` methods of the `Window` object.

11. How do you control a new window that you have created with JavaScript code?

    a. by using the appropriate element in the windows[] array of the Windows object

    b. by using the name argument of the window.open() method

    c. by assigning the new Window object created with the window.open() method to a variable

    d. You cannot control a new window with JavaScript code.

12. Explain the difference between the setTimeout() and setInterval() methods. Which method is most often used for starting animation code that executes repeatedly?

13. How do you use JavaScript to modify an element's CSS properties?

14. Which of the following arguments do you pass to the history.go() method to navigate three pages back in the history list?

    a. 3

    b. -3

    c. 2

    d. 4

15. You can use JavaScript code to navigate through a history list, but only if the currently displayed Web page exists within the same domain as the Web page containing the JavaScript code that is attempting to move through the list. True or False?

16. The full URL of a Web page is located in the _____ property of the Location object.

    a. href

    b. hash

    c. src

    d. url

17. Which property of the `Navigator` object returns the Web browser name?

    a. `browser`

    b. `browserName`

    c. `appName`

    d. `platform`

18. Explain how to use the `with` statement to reference an object's properties.

19. Which of the following properties of the `Screen` object returns the height of the display screen, not including operating system features such as the Windows taskbar?

    a. `displayHeight`

    b. `screenHeight`

    c. `availHeight`

    d. `height`

20. Explain how to center a window when it is created with the `window.open()` method.

Reinforcement Exercises

 Exercise 11-1

Most Windows applications include an About dialog box that displays copyright information and other details about the program. In this exercise, you will create a script that opens a new window that is similar to an About dialog box.

1. Create a new HTML 5 document in your text editor and use "About Dialog Box Example" as the content of the `<title>` element.

2. Add a form to the document body that includes a single command button that reads "About this JavaScript Program".

3. Add code to the Web page that opens a new browser window when a user clicks the command button. Make the new window 100 pixels high by 300 pixels wide, and center it in the screen. Do not use any other display options. The new browser window should display a document named About.html (which you will create later in this exercise).

4. Save the document as **AboutExample.html** in the Exercises folder for Chapter 11.

5. Use the W3C Markup Validation Service to validate the **AboutExample.html** document and fix any errors. Once the document is valid, close it in your text editor.

6. Create another Web page that displays a single paragraph with the following text. Be sure to use your name in the paragraph.

   ```
   <p>This program was created by your name.</p>
   ```

7. Add a button to the document body that closes the current window.

8. Save the document as **About.html** in the Exercises folder for Chapter 11.

9. Use the W3C Markup Validation Service to validate the **About.html** document and fix any errors. Once the document is valid, close it in your text editor.

10. Open **AboutExample.html** in your Web browser and test the script's functionality. The About window should appear centered in your screen.

11. Close your Web browser window.

Exercise 11-2

In this exercise, you create a script that repeatedly flashes advertising messages in a text box for a company named Central Valley Florist.

1. Create a new HTML 5 document in your text editor and use "Central Valley Florist" as the content of the `<title>` element.

2. Add a script section to the document head.

3. Next, add the following heading elements and form to the document body, which will display a message in a text box:

   ```
   <h1>Central Valley Florist</h1>
   <h2>Valentine's Day Specials</h2>
   <form name="advertising" action="">
   <p><input type="text" name="message" size="60"
   value="Place your Valentine's Day orders today!" /></p>
   </form>
   ```

4. In the script section, add the following code, which changes the message that is displayed in the text box:

```
var curMessage="message1";
var changeMessage;
function adMessage(){
  if (curMessage == "message2"){
    document.advertising.message.value
      = "Place your Valentine's Day orders today!";
    curMessage = "message1";
  }
  else {
    document.advertising.message.value
      = "All orders must be received by ↵
            February 12th!";
    curMessage = "message2";
  }
}
```

5. Finally, add the following onload event handler to the opening <body> tag:

```
<body onload="var changeQuote=setInterval ↵
    ('adMessage()',2000);">
```

6. Save the document as **ValentinesDayOrders.html** in the Exercises folder for Chapter 11.

7. Use the W3C Markup Validation Service to validate the **ValentinesDayOrders.html** document and fix any errors. Once the document is valid, close it in your text editor and then open it in your Web browser. The message should change every few seconds.

8. Close your Web browser window.

 Exercise 11-3

In this exercise, you will create a script that redirects users to a different Web page after 10 seconds, or allows them to click a hyperlink.

1. Create a new HTML 5 document in your text editor and use "New Web Address" as the content of the <title> element.

2. Add a script section to the document head.

3. In the script section, add the following global variable declaration and function to handle the task of redirecting the Web page:

```
var killRedirect;
function updatedURL() {
    location.href="UpdatedURL.html";
}
```

4. Add the following `onload` event handler to the opening `<body>` tag:

```
<body onload="killRedirect = ↵
setTimeout('updatedURL()', 10000);">
```

5. Add the following elements and text to the document body:

```
<h2>The URL for the Web page you are trying to
reach has changed!</h2>
<p><strong>You will be automatically redirected in
ten seconds. Click the link if JavaScript is
disabled in your browser.</strong></p>
<p>Be sure to update your bookmark!</p>
<p><a href="UpdatedURL.html">UpdatedURL.html</a></p>
```

6. Save the document as **Redirect.html** in the Exercises folder for Chapter 11.

7. Use the W3C Markup Validation Service to validate the **Redirect.html** document and fix any errors. Once the document is valid, close it in your text editor.

8. Create another Web page that displays a single paragraph with the following text:

```
<p>You have reached the updated Web page.</p>
```

9. Save the document as **UpdatedURL.html** in the Exercises folder for Chapter 11.

10. Use the W3C Markup Validation Service to validate the **UpdatedURL.html** document and fix any errors. Once the document is valid, close it in your text editor and then open the **Redirect.html** document in your Web browser. In 10 seconds, the UpdatedURL.html document should open automatically.

11. Close your Web browser window.

Exercise 11-4

In addition to specifying the size and position of a window when it first opens, you can also change the size and position of an open window by using methods of the `Window` object. The `resizeTo()` method resizes a window to a specified size, and the `moveTo()` method moves a window to an absolute position. Using these methods with properties of the `Screen` object, you will create a script that resizes and repositions an open window so that it fills the screen.

1. Create a new HTML 5 document in your text editor and use "Maximize Browser Window" as the content of the `<title>` element.

2. Add a form to the document body that includes two command buttons: one that reads "Create New Window" and another that reads "Maximize New Window".

3. Add a script section to the document head.

4. Add the following function for the Create New Window button. This function opens a document named MaxWindow.html (which you will create shortly) in a new browser window that is centered in the screen when a user clicks the command button.

```
var maxWindow;
function createWindow() {
    var winWidth=300;
    var winHeight=100;
    var winLeft = (screen.width-winWidth)/2;
    var winTop = (screen.height-winHeight)/2;
    var winOptions = ",width=" + winWidth;
    winOptions += ",height=" + winHeight;
    winOptions += ",left=" + winLeft;
    winOptions += ",top=" + winTop;
    maxWindow = window.open("MaxWindow.html",
        "newWindow", winOptions);
    maxWindow.focus();
}
```

5. Add the following function for the Maximize New Window button. The first statement in the function uses the `moveTo()` method of the `Window` object to move the window named maxWindow (which is created by the `createWindow()`

function) to position 0, 0, which represents the upper-left corner of the screen. The second statement uses the resizeTo() method of the Window object and the availWidth and availHeight properties of the Screen object to maximize the window. The final statement changes focus to the maximized window.

```
function maximizeWindow() {
    maxWindow.moveTo(0,0);
    maxWindow.resizeTo(screen.availWidth,
        screen.availHeight);
    maxWindow.focus();
}
```

6. Save the document as **MaximizeBrowser.html** in the Exercises folder for Chapter 11.

7. Use the W3C Markup Validation Service to validate the **MaximizeBrowser.html** document and fix any errors. Once the document is valid, close it in your text editor.

8. Create a Web page that conforms to the strict DTD, and add the following text and elements to the document body:

```
<p><strong>Resizing and Repositioning
Example</strong></p>
<form action="">
<p><input type="button" value="Close Window"
    onclick="window.close();" /></p>
</form>
```

9. Save the document as **MaxWindow.html** in the Exercises folder for Chapter 11.

10. Use the W3C Markup Validation Service to validate the **MaxWindow.html** document and fix any errors. Once the document is valid, close it in your text editor.

11. Open **MaximizeBrowser.html** in your Web browser, and click the **Create New Window** button. The new window should appear centered in the screen. Return to the **MaximizeBrowser.html** file in your Web browser, and click the Maximize New Window button. The new window should be resized and repositioned to fill the screen.

12. Close your Web browser windows.

Exercise 11-5

In this exercise, you will create a Web page for a greeting card company. The page will contain links that display images of greeting cards in a separate window. Your Exercises folder for Chapter 11 contains the following greeting card images that you can use for this project: birthday.jpg, halloween.jpg, mothersday.jpg, newyear.jpg, and valentine.jpg.

1. Create a new HTML 5 document in your text editor and use "Gosselin Greeting Cards" as the content of the `<title>` element.

2. Add the following text and elements to the document body. The `onclick` events in the links call a function named `showCard()` that handles the process of displaying each greeting card in a separate window. You create the `showCard()` function later in this exercise.

```
<h1>Gosselin Greeting Cards</h1>
<h2>All Occasions</h2>
<hr />
<p><a href="valentine.jpg"
onclick="showCard('valentine.jpg');return false">
Valentine's Day</a><br />
<a href="mothersday.jpg"
onclick="showCard('mothersday.jpg');return false">
Mother's Day</a><br />
<a href="halloween.jpg"
onclick="showCard('halloween.jpg');return false">
Halloween</a><br />
<a href="newyear.jpg"
onclick="showCard('newyear.jpg');return false">
New Year</a><br />
<a href="birthday.jpg"
onclick="showCard('birthday.jpg');return false">
Birthday</a></p>
```

3. Add a script section to the document head.

4. Add the following global variable to the script section. This variable will represent the window that displays the greeting card images.

```
var cardWindow;
```

5. Add the following function to the end of the script section. The function opens a new window, centered in the screen, that displays the selected greeting card image.

```
function showCard(linkTarget) {
    var propertyWidth=400;
    var propertyHeight=350;
    var winLeft = (screen.width-propertyWidth)/2;
    var winTop = (screen.height-propertyHeight)/2;
    var winOptions =
        "toolbar=no,menubar=no,location=no, ↵
        scrollbars=yes,resizable=no";
    winOptions += ",width=" + propertyWidth;
    winOptions += ",height=" + propertyHeight;
    winOptions += ",left=" + winLeft;
    winOptions += ",top=" + winTop;
    cardWindow = window.open(linkTarget,
        "cardInfo", winOptions);
    cardWindow.focus();
}
```

6. Save the document as **GreetingCards.html** in the Exercises folder for Chapter 11.

7. Use the W3C Markup Validation Service to validate the **GreetingCards.html** document and fix any errors. Once the document is valid, close it in your text editor, open it in your Web browser, and test the functionality.

8. Close your Web browser window.

 ## Exercise 11-6

You have probably seen Web sites that invite you to add them to your browser's favorites list. With Internet Explorer, you can create a link that automatically adds the Web page to the favorites list by assigning a value of `javascript:window.external.AddFavorite(url, site name)` to the link's `href` property. Firefox does not contain similar functionality, so you need to use the `Navigator` object to determine the browser type. In this exercise, you will create a script that contains functionality for adding Course Technology's Web site to a browser's favorites list.

1. Create a new HTML 5 document in your text editor and use "Add to Favorites" as the content of the `<title>` element.

2. Add a script section to the document body.

3. Add the following statements to the script section. The first two statements retrieve the browser's name and version from the `Navigator` object. The remaining statements create text variables that will be used to create the bookmark link.

```
var browserName = navigator.appName;
var browserVer = parseInt(navigator.appVersion);
var linkText = "Add Course Technology ↵
    to your favorites!";
var url = "http://www.course.com";
var pageName = "Course Technology";
var favLink = "";
```

4. Add the following `if` statement to the end of the script section. The conditional expression determines whether the browser name is equal to "Microsoft Internet Explorer" and whether the browser version is greater than or equal to 4. If so, statements within the `if` statement build a link that automatically adds the Course Technology Web site to the favorites list in Internet Explorer.

```
if (browserName == "Microsoft Internet Explorer"
    && browserVer >= 4) {
    favLink = "<p><a href=\"javascript:window. ↵
        external.AddFavorite(url, pageName)\"";
    favLink += " onmouseover=\"window.status='";
    favLink += linkText + "'; return true\"";
    favLink += " onmouseout=\"window.status=";
    favLink += "'''" + "; return true\"";
    favLink += ">" + linkText + "</a></p>";
    document.write(favLink);
}
```

5. Add the following `else` clause to the end of the script section to print "Add Course Technology to your favorites! (Ctrl+D)" for all other browsers:

```
else
    document.write("<p>Add Course Technology ↵
        to your favorites! (Ctrl+D)</p>");
```

6. Save the document as **AddToFavorites.html** in the Exercises folder for Chapter 11, and validate the document with the W3C Markup Validation Service. Once the document is valid, close it in your text editor and then open it in Internet Explorer and test the functionality.

7. Close your Web browser window.

Discovery Projects

For the following projects, save the files you create in your Projects folder for Chapter 11. Be sure to validate each Web page with the W3C Markup Validation Service.

 Discovery Project 11-1

Your Projects folder for Chapter 11 contains five advertising images for a concert series, concert1.gif through concert5.gif. Create a script that cycles through the images and displays each one for five seconds. Save the document as **ConcertAds.html**.

 Discovery Project 11-2

Create a Web page with a list of your favorite links. At the top of the page, include a check box with the text "Open link in a new window." If a user clicks the check box, the links on the page should open in a new window. Otherwise, the links should be loaded into the current window. Save the document as **LinkWindow.html**.

 Discovery Project 11-3

A common use of the onmouseover and onmouseout event handlers is to change the button image displayed for a navigational link on a Web page. For example, holding your mouse over an image of a Home button (that jumps to the Web site's home page) could replace the image with one that is more vivid in order to clearly identify the page that is the target of the link. Your Projects folder for Chapter 11 contains eight images: home1.gif, home2.gif, faq1.gif, faq2.gif, guestbook1.gif, guestbook2.gif, join1.gif, and join2.gif. These images represent typical navigational buttons you find on a Web site. The second version of each button is slightly more vivid than the first version. Create a Web page that displays the first version of each button as image links, using the <a> element. Holding your mouse over each image should display the more vivid version of the image, while moving your mouse off the image should display the less vivid version. Do not worry about actually creating a Web page as the target of each link; just assign an empty string to each <a> element's href attribute. Save the document as **Buttons.html**.

Discovery Project 11-4

You have probably come across Web sites that briefly display a sponsor's advertisement before redirecting you to the page you originally requested. Create such an ad for a real estate company named Central Valley Realtors. Start by creating a Web page named **CVR1.html**. In the document body, create a table with two columns. In the left column, display the cvb1.gif image, which is located in your Projects folder for Chapter 11. The cvb1.gif file is an animated GIF file that displays an advertisement for a company named Central Valley Builders. In the right column, display three paragraphs. In the first paragraph, display the word "Advertisement". In the second paragraph, display the text "The Central Valley Realtors home page will be displayed in *n* seconds." Use a text field for the number of seconds, which means you will need to create a form to contain the text field. Set the default value of the text field to 15 seconds. In the third paragraph, include a "Skip advertisement" link that opens a Web page named CVR2.html (which is the "real" home page for Central Valley Realtors). Within the CVR1.html page's opening <body> tag, add an onload event handler that calls a function named startAdPage(). Within the startAdPage() function, include two statements: one that uses a setInterval() method to call a function named changeAd() every five seconds, and another statement that uses a setInterval() method to call a function named startCountdown() every second. Create the changeAd() function so that, every five seconds, it alternates the image in the document body with the three images in your Projects folder for Chapter 11: cvb1.gif, cvb2,gif, and cvb3.gif. Create the startCountdown() function so that it changes the value assigned to the text field in the document body to the value of a variable named count, which is decreased by a value of 1 (from 15 to 1) each time the startCountdown() function executes. When the count reaches zero, clear both of the intervals and redirect the browser to the CVR2.html page. Create the **CVR2.html** page so it contains an <h1> element that reads "Central Valley Realtors" and a paragraph element that reads "Welcome to our home page."

Validating Form Data with JavaScript

In this chapter, you will:

◎ Use JavaScript to manipulate and validate form elements

◎ Learn how to manipulate input fields with JavaScript

◎ Learn how to manipulate selection lists with JavaScript

◎ Learn how to validate submitted data

In Chapter 6, you learned the basics of how to create forms that a user submits to a server. Forms are one of the most common Web page elements used with JavaScript. You use JavaScript to make sure that data was entered properly into the form fields and to perform other types of preprocessing before the data is sent to the server. Without JavaScript, the only action that a Web page can take on form data is to send it to a server for processing. In this chapter, you will learn how to use JavaScript to manipulate and validate submitted data.

Using JavaScript with Forms

JavaScript is often used to validate or process form data before the data is submitted to a server-side script. For example, customers may use an online form to order merchandise from your Web site. When customers click the form's Submit button, you need to make sure that their information, such as the shipping address and credit card number, is entered correctly. To use JavaScript to access form controls and verify form information, you use the **Form object**, which represents a form on a Web page. The Form object is part of the browser object model, which you studied in Chapter 11; the Form object contains properties, methods, and events that you can use to manipulate forms and form controls.

 If a form requires complex validation or processing, it is a good idea to have a server-side script do the work. Servers are usually much more powerful than a desktop computer or workstation.

You can use JavaScript to access form controls created with any of the primary form elements: <input>, <button>, <select>, and <textarea>. This chapter focuses on how to use JavaScript with the <input> and <select> elements. However, you can also use many of the JavaScript techniques you learn in this chapter with the <button> and <textarea> elements.

Referencing Forms and Form Elements

Recall from Chapter 11 that some of the objects in the browser object model are arrays of other objects. For instance, the Document object includes a forms[] array that contains all the forms on a Web page. If a window does not contain any forms, the forms[] array is empty. The first form in a document is referred to as document.forms[0], the second form is referred to as document.forms[1], and so on.

Prior to the development of XHTML, the most common way to refer to a form with JavaScript was to append the value assigned to the <form> element's name attribute to the Document object. For example, if you had a form with a name attribute that was assigned a value of "orderForm", you referred to the form in JavaScript as document.orderForm. However, the <form> element's name attribute is deprecated in XHTML. Although you can still use it with the transitional DTD, it is no longer available with the strict DTD. Therefore, if you want your Web pages to be well formed according to the strict DTD, you must avoid using the name attribute with your <form> elements. To make things even more confusing, the name attribute *is* available in HTML 5. As long as your goal is to write valid HTML 5 Web pages, you can usually refer to a form by its name attribute. In this chapter, you will work with the forms[] array to understand how it works.

Just as the Document object has a forms[] array, the Form object has an elements[] array. You can use it to reference each element on a form. The **elements[] array** contains objects representing each of the controls in a form. Each element on a form is assigned to the elements[] array in the order in which it is encountered by the JavaScript interpreter. To refer to an element on a form, you reference the form's index number in the forms[] array, followed by the appropriate element index number from the elements[] array. For example, if you want to refer to the first element in the first form on a Web page, use the statement document.forms[0].elements[0];. The third element in the second form is referenced using the statement document.forms[1].elements[2];. The following code shows an example of how each element on a form is assigned to the elements[] array:

```
<form action = "post">
// The following element is assigned to elements[0]
Customer name: <input type = "text"
name = "customer" /><br />
// The following element is assigned to elements[1]
E-mail address: <input type = "text"
name = "email" /><br />
// The following element is assigned to elements[2]
Telephone: <input type = "text" name = "phone" /><br />
// The following element is assigned to elements[3]
Fax: <input type = "text" name = "fax" /><br />
</form>
```

The name attribute is also available for form control elements. In fact, if you plan to have your script submit a form to a server-side script, you must include a name attribute for each form element. This gives the server-side script a way to identify each piece of form data. Naming an element also gives you an alternative to referencing the element by its position in the elements[] array, which can be tedious if you have many fields on a form. For example, if you have an element named quantity in the first form on a Web page, you can refer to it using the statement document.forms[0].quantity;.

Referencing a form by its position in the forms[] array is usually not difficult because most Web pages rarely include more than one form.

641

Working with the Form Object

Tables 12-1, 12-2, and 12-3 list the properties, events, and methods of the Form object.

Property	Description
acceptCharset	Returns a comma-separated list of possible character sets that the form supports
action	Returns the URL to which form data is submitted
elements[]	Returns an array of a form's elements
enctype	Sets or returns a string representing the MIME type of the data being submitted
length	Returns an integer representing the number of elements in the form
method	Sets or returns a string representing one of the two options for submitting form data: "get" or "post"
name	Sets or returns the value assigned to the form's name attribute
target	Sets or returns the target window where responses are displayed after submitting the form

Table 12-1   Form object properties

Event	Description
submit	Executes when a form's submit button is clicked

Table 12-2   Form object events

Method	Description
submit()	Submits a form without the use of a submit button

Table 12-3   Form object methods

In this chapter, you will work on a simple Web site for a company named DRG Technologies. Your goal is to submit a subscription form for the company's technology journal. Your Chapter folder for Chapter 12 contains a folder named DRGTechnologies that contains the files you will need for the project. Figure 12-1 shows the subscription page you will use.

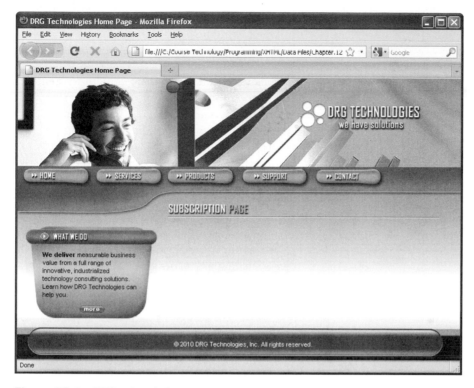

Figure 12-1 DRG subscription page

Because the focus of this book is client-side JavaScript, the scripts you write will submit the forms to a document named FormProcessor.html rather than to a Web server. The document FormProcessor.html, which is located in the DRGTechnologies folder in your Chapter folder for Chapter 12, uses JavaScript code to display the values submitted from a form. The only purpose of the FormProcessor.html document is to display form data and provide a simple simulation of the response you would normally receive from a server-side scripting program.

Next, you start creating the technology journal subscription page for DRG Technologies. The Web page will contain a subscription form that you will work on throughout this chapter.

To start creating the technology journal subscription page for DRG Technologies:

1. Open your text editor, and then open the **subscription.html** document, which is located in the DRGTechnologies folder in your Chapter folder for Chapter 12.

2. Locate <!--[Add form here]--> in the document body and replace it with the following heading element:

   ```
   <h2>Customer Information</h2>
   ```

3. Add the following elements after the <h2> element to create the form section. Throughout the rest of this chapter, you will add form elements between these tags. Notice that the form's action attribute submits the form data to the FormProcessor.html document, and the method attribute submits the data using the "get" option to append the data as one long string to the FormProcessor.html URL. This allows the JavaScript code in FormProcessor.html to display the data in the Web browser.

   ```
   <form action = "FormProcessor.html" method = "get"
   enctype = "application/x-www-form-urlencoded">
   <p><input type = "submit" value = "Subscribe" /></p>
   </form>
   ```

4. Save the document, but do not open it in a Web browser because it does not yet contain any form elements.

Short Quiz 1

1. Explain how to use the Form object so that JavaScript can access form controls and verify form information.

2. Explain the two ways in which you can reference forms with JavaScript.

3. How do you use the elements[] array to reference elements on a form?

Manipulating Input Fields

In this section, you will learn how to use JavaScript to manipulate the various form controls that you can create with the <input> element.

Input Field Objects

The elements[] array stores objects that represent each type of form control. Each type of control that can be created with an <input> element is represented by an object that is similar to the name of the control. A text box is represented by an Input object, a radio button list is represented by a Radio object, a check box is represented by a `Checkbox` object, and so on. Don't worry about the exact names of each type of input field object because you will never need to refer to them in your scripts. However, you do need to understand that each of these objects includes various properties and methods. The availability of each property or method depends on the type of form control. For example, the `Input` object includes a `checked` property that is only available to check boxes and radio buttons. Tables 12-4 and 12-5 list the properties and methods of the input field objects, along with the form controls for which they are available.

Property	Description	Form controls
accept	Sets or returns a comma-separated list of MIME types that can be uploaded	File boxes
accessKey	Sets or returns a keyboard shortcut that users can press to jump to a control, or to select and deselect a control	Check boxes, radio buttons, submit buttons, image submit buttons, text boxes, password boxes, file boxes, hidden text boxes
alt	Sets or returns alternate text for an image	Image submit buttons
checked	Sets or returns the checked status of a check box or radio button	Check boxes, radio buttons
defaultChecked	Determines the control that is checked by default in a check box group or radio button group	Check boxes, radio buttons
defaultValue	Sets or returns the default text that appears in a form control	Text boxes, password boxes, file boxes
disabled	Sets or returns a Boolean value that determines whether a control is disabled	Check boxes, radio buttons, submit buttons, image submit buttons, text boxes, password boxes, file boxes, hidden text boxes
form	Returns a reference to the form that contains the control	Check boxes, radio buttons, submit buttons, image submit buttons, text boxes, password boxes, file boxes, hidden text boxes
maxLength	Sets or returns the maximum number of characters that can be entered into a field	Text boxes, password boxes
name	Sets or returns the value assigned to the element's `name` attribute	Check boxes, radio buttons, submit buttons, image submit buttons, text boxes, password boxes, file boxes, hidden text boxes

Table 12-4   Input field object properties and their associated form controls *(continues)*

Property	Description	Form controls
readOnly	Sets or returns a Boolean value that determines whether a control is read only	Text boxes, password boxes
size	Sets or returns a field's width (in characters)	Text boxes, password boxes
src	Sets or returns the URL of an image	Image submit buttons
tabIndex	Sets or returns a control's position in the tab order	Check boxes, radio buttons, submit buttons, image submit buttons, text boxes, password boxes, file boxes, hidden text boxes
type	Returns the type of input element: button, check box, file, hidden, image, password, radio, submit, or text	Check boxes, radio buttons, submit buttons, image submit buttons, text boxes, password boxes, file boxes, hidden text boxes
useMap	Sets or returns the name of an image map	Image submit buttons
value	Sets or returns the value of form controls	Check boxes, radio buttons, submit buttons, image submit buttons, text boxes, password boxes, file boxes, hidden text boxes

Table 12-4   Input field object properties and their associated form controls

Method	Description	Form controls
blur()	Removes focus from a form control	Check boxes, radio buttons, submit buttons, text boxes, text areas, password boxes, file boxes
click()	Activates a form control's click event	Check boxes, radio buttons, submit buttons
focus()	Changes focus to a form control	Check boxes, radio buttons, submit buttons, text boxes, password boxes, file boxes
select()	Selects the text in a form control	Text boxes, password boxes, file boxes

Table 12-5   Input field object methods and their associated form controls

You will use several of the input field object properties and methods in this chapter. One property you have already used is the value property. Recall that in Chapter 10 you created a quiz using a form.

The Web page included a script with the following statement that displayed the number of questions that were answered correctly:

```
document.quiz.score.value = "You scored "
     + totalCorrect + " out of 5 answers correctly!";
```

The preceding statement uses the Document object to set the value property in a control named score located in a form named quiz. The following code shows the same statement, but this time it uses the forms[] and elements[] arrays to set the value in the text box:

```
document.forms[0].elements[0].value = "You scored "
     + totalCorrect + " out of 5 answers correctly!";
```

Text Boxes

Most form validation with JavaScript takes place when you submit the form. You will learn about this kind of validation later in this chapter. However, you can use a few tricks to ensure that users enter the correct information in the first place. For any fields that require numeric values, for instance, you can use JavaScript's built-in isNaN() function to determine whether the user actually entered a number. Recall from Chapter 9 that the isNaN() function determines whether a value is the special value NaN (not a number). The isNaN() function returns a value of true if it is passed a value that is not a number; if passed a value that is a number, the function returns a value of false. The following function shows a statement that passes the value of a text box named "subtotal" to the isNaN() function:

```
isNaN(document.forms[0].subtotal.value);
```

Next, you add text <input> elements to the Subscription form to collect basic customer data.

To add text <input> elements to the Subscription form:

1. Return to the **subscription.html** document in your text editor.

2. Above the paragraph element that contains the Submit button, add the following table to contain the billing and shipping information text boxes. The table will consist of a single row containing two cells.

```
<table>
</table>
```

3. Within the table, add the following text `<input>` elements. The left cell will contain the customer's billing information, and the right cell will contain the shipping information.

648

```
<tr style = "vertical-align: top">
    <td valign = "top">
        <h3>
            Billing Information</h3>
        <p>
            Name<br />
            <input type = "text"
                name = "name_billing"
                size = "56" /></p>
        <p>
            Address<br />
            <input type = "text"
                name = "address_billing"
                size = "56" /></p>
        <p>
            City, State, Zip<br />
            <input type = "text"
                name = "city_billing" size = "34" />
            <input type = "text"
                name = "state_billing" size = "2"
                maxlength = "2" />
            <input type = "text"
                name = "zip_billing" size = "10"
                maxlength = "10" /></p>
    </td>
    <td> </td>
    <td valign = "top">
        <h3>
            Shipping Information</h3>
        <p>
            Name<br />
            <input type = "text"
                name = "name_shipping"
                size = "56" /></p>
        <p>
            Address<br />
            <input type = "text"
                name = "address_shipping"
                size = "56" /></p>
        <p>
            City, State, Zip<br />
            <input type = "text"
                name = "city_shipping"
                size = "34" />
            <input type = "text"
                name = "state_shipping"
                size = "2" maxlength = "2" />
            <input type = "text"
                name = "zip_shipping"
                size = "10" maxlength = "5" /></p>
    </td>
</tr>
```

4. Above the closing `</table>` tag, add the following elements for the telephone number:

```
<tr><td><p>
    Telephone<br />
    (<input type = "text" name = "area"
        size = "3" maxlength = "3" />)
    <input type = "text" name = "exchange"
        size = "3" maxlength = "3" />
    <input type = "text" name = "phone"
        size = "4" maxlength = "4" /></p>
</td></tr>
```

5. Save the **subscription.html** document and then open it in your Web browser. The text `<input>` elements you entered should appear as shown in Figure 12-2.

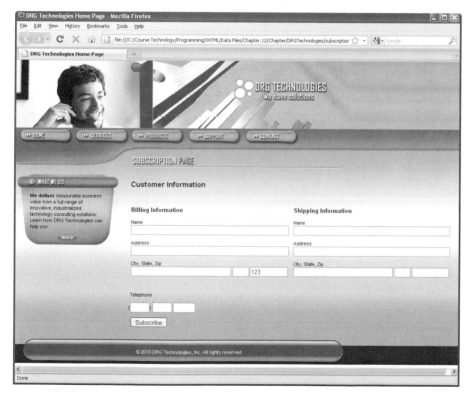

Figure 12-2 Subscription form after adding text `<input>` elements

6. Close your Web browser window.

Next, you will add an `isNaN()` function to the subscription.html document to check whether a value entered in the Zip code or telephone number fields is a number. The function will be called from the change event within each field. The change event is called when the value in a control changes. If the value entered is not a number, the function returns a value of false, forcing the user to enter a numeric value into the field.

To add a function to the subscription.html document that checks whether a value entered in the Zip code or telephone number fields is a number:

1. Return to the **subscription.html** document in your text editor.

2. Add the following script section to the end of the document head:

```
<script type = "text/javascript">
/* <![CDATA[ */
/* ]]> */
</script>
```

3. Add the following checkForNumber() function to the script section in the document head. The function checks whether the argument passed to it is a number. If it is not a number, an alert message is displayed and the function returns a value of false to prevent the blur event from occurring. Otherwise, the function returns a value of true, allowing the blur event to occur.

```
function checkForNumber(fieldValue) {
    var numberCheck = isNaN(fieldValue);
    if (numberCheck == true) {
        window.alert("You must enter a ↵
            numeric value!");
        return false;
    }
        else
                return true;
    }
```

4. Add the following onblur event handler to the <input> elements for the two Zip code fields and the three telephone number fields. Notice that the function is passed a value of this.value, which uses the this reference to refer to the value property of the current form element.

```
onblur = "return checkForNumber(this.value);"
```

5. Save the **subscription.html** document and then open it in your Web browser. Test the validation code by entering some nonnumeric values in the Zip code and telephone number fields.

6. Close your Web browser window.

Password Boxes

In JavaScript, you can check whether a user entered the same password twice by using an if statement to compare the values entered in the password and confirmation fields.

Next, you add a user name field, password field, and password confirmation field to the subscription.html document, along with code that determines whether the user entered the same password in the password fields.

To add a user name field, password fields, and validation code to the subscription.html document:

1. Return to the **subscription.html** document in your text editor.

2. After the paragraph containing the telephone number, add the following lines for the user name field and password fields:

```
<p>User name<br />
<input type = "text" name = "userName"
    size = "50" /></p>
<p>Password<br />
<input type = "password" name = "password"
    size = "50" /></p>
<p>Confirm password<br />
<input type = "password" name = "password_confirm"
    size = "50" onblur = "confirmPassword();" /></p>
```

3. Add the following confirmPassword() function to the end of the script section. The function compares the values entered in the password and password confirmation fields. If the values are not the same, the function uses the focus() method to move the cursor back into the password field.

```
function confirmPassword() {
    if (document.forms[0].password_confirm.value
        != document.forms[0].password.value) {
        window.alert("You did not enter ↵
            the same password!");
        document.forms[0].password.focus();
        }
}
```

4. Save the **subscription.html** document, and then open it in your Web browser. Test the password fields to ensure that they properly validate the entered passwords.

5. Close your Web browser window.

Push Buttons

With <input> elements of the "button" type you are required to use JavaScript code to handle the button's click event. For example, if you want to use a push button to navigate to another page, you must assign JavaScript code similar to location.href = "URL" to the button's onclick event handler. Unlike other types of <input> elements, you are not required to include the name and value attributes because a user cannot change the value of a push button. If you include the name and value attributes, the default value set with the value attribute is transmitted to a Web server along with the rest of the form data. The following code creates a push button that uses JavaScript code to display a simple dialog box:

```
<p><input type = "button" name = "push_button"
    value = "Click Here"
    onclick = "window.alert('You clicked a push button.');" />
<p>
```

The code for the <input> element creates a button with a value of "Click Here" and a name of push_button. Clicking the push button displays a dialog box that contains the text "You clicked a push button." (See Figure 12-3.)

Figure 12-3   A push button in a Web browser

Radio Buttons

When multiple form elements share the same name, JavaScript creates an array out of the elements using the shared name. Radio buttons, for instance, share the same name so that a single name=value pair can be submitted to a server-side script. For example, assume that you have a group of radio buttons named `maritalStatus`. You can use the following statement to access the value of the second radio button in the group:

```
document.forms[0].maritalStatus[1].value;
```

When an array is created from a group of buttons that share the same name, you can use the `checked` property to determine which element in the group is selected. The `checked` property returns a value of true if a check box or radio button is selected, and returns a value of false if it is not. If you have a group of radio buttons named `maritalStatus`, you can use a statement like the following to determine if the first radio button in the group is selected:

```
document.forms[0].maritalStatus[0].checked;
```

Next, you add radio buttons to the subscription.html document to allow users to select a delivery option. You will add the radio buttons within a table to make it easier to align them on the page.

To add radio buttons to the subscription.html document:

1. Return to the **subscription.html** document in your text editor.

2. Add the following `<h3>` element, opening `<table>` element, and table header information to the end of the form, but above the paragraph element that contains the submit buttons:

```
<h3>Delivery Rates</h3>
<table style="width: 50%">
    <tr style="text-align: center">
        <th>6 issues</th>
        <th>12 issues</th>
        <th>18 issues</th>
        <th>24 issues</th></tr>
```

3. Add the following table row elements that specify payment amounts by number of issues. Notice that each radio button's name attribute is assigned the name of "delivery" so that the radio buttons are part of the same group.

```
<tr style="text-align: center">
    <td><input type="radio" name="delivery"
        value="17.50" />$17.50</td>
    <td><input type="radio" name="delivery"
        value="26.95" />$26.95</td>
    <td><input type="radio" name="delivery"
        value="32.90" />$32.90</td>
    <td><input type="radio" name="delivery"
        value="46.00" />$46.00</td></tr>
```

4. Type the closing `</table>` tag. Keep the file open for the next steps.

Next, you will add another group of radio buttons to the Subscription form. The group contains two buttons, Monthly ($8.95) and Yearly ($19.95), which determine whether the customer wants to be billed automatically on a monthly or yearly basis rather than pay for a specific number of issues. When the user selects a button, any selected radio button in the group should be deselected. To deselect a radio button, you need to loop through the array that represents the group and assign a value of false to the checked button.

To add monthly and yearly subscription radio buttons to the subscription.html document:

1. Return to the **subscription.html** document in your text editor.

2. Add the following radio buttons for automatic renewal above the paragraphs that contain the submit buttons. The buttons call an `onclick` event handler named `billAutomatically()`, which you will create next.

```
<p>
    <strong>Automatic Renewal</strong>:
    <input type = "radio" name = "autoRenew"
    onclick = "billAutomatically();" />
    Monthly ($8.95)
    <input type = "radio" name = "autoRenew"
    onclick = "billAutomatically();" />
    Yearly ($19.95)
</p>
```

3. Add the following two functions to the end of the script section. The `billAutomatically()` function disables any selected radio button in the payment per number of issues group, and the `billByIssue()` function disables the selected radio button in the automatic renewal group.

```
function billAutomatically() {
    for (var i = 0; i < document.forms[0].delivery
        .length; ++i) {
        if (document.forms[0].delivery[i]
            .checked == true) {
            document.forms[0].delivery[i]
                .checked = false;
            break;
        }
    }
}
function billByIssue() {
    for (var i = 0; i < document.forms[0].autoRenew
        .length; ++i) {
        if (document.forms[0].autoRenew[i]
            .checked == true) {
            document.forms[0].autoRenew[i]
                .checked = false;
```

```
                break;
            }
        }
    }
```

4. Add `onclick` event handlers to the radio buttons in the
   delivery rates group that call the `billByIssue()` function,
   as follows:

```
<td>
    <input type = "radio" name = "delivery"
        value = "17.50"
        onclick = "billByIssue()" />$17.50</td>
<td>
    <input type = "radio" name = "delivery"
        value = "26.95"
        onclick = "billByIssue()" />$26.95</td>
<td>
    <input type = "radio" name = "delivery"
        value = "32.90"
        onclick = "billByIssue()" />$32.90</td>
<td>
    <input type = "radio" name = "delivery"
        value = "46.00"
        onclick = "billByIssue()" />$46.00</td>
```

5. Save the **subscription.html** document, and then open it in
   your Web browser. Test the radio buttons to ensure that you
   can only select one button from either group. Figure 12-4
   shows how the radio buttons appear in a Web browser.

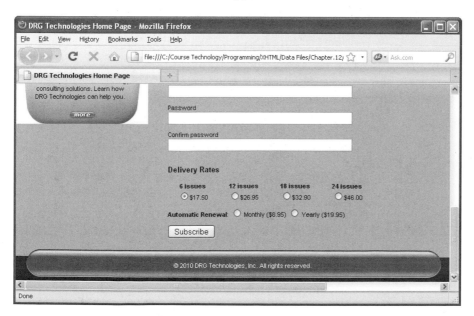

Figure 12-4   subscription.html file with radio buttons

6. Close your Web browser window.

Check Boxes

Check boxes are primarily used to allow the selection of certain items and the selection of multiple values from a list of items. However, you can also use check boxes with an `onclick` event handler to execute JavaScript code. For example, you can use a check box element in Billing Information and Shipping Information at the top of the form in the subscription.html document. Because it is common for a company to have the same billing and shipping address, you will add a check box element to the Subscription form that copies the values of the billing information fields to the shipping information fields.

To add a check box element to the Subscription form that copies the values of the billing information fields to the shipping information fields:

1. Return to the **subscription.html** document in your text editor.

2. Add the following `sameShippingInfo()` function to the end of the script section. The function uses an `if...else` statement to copy the values from the billing information fields to the shipping information fields when the check box is selected. When the check box is deselected, empty strings are assigned to the shipping information fields. Notice that the conditional expression in the `if` statement uses the `elements[]` array to refer to the check box control. You will not assign a name to the check box control because you do not want its value submitted to the Web server. Therefore, you must refer to it with the `elements[]` array.

```
function sameShippingInfo() {
    if (document.forms[0].elements[5].checked
            == true) {
        document.forms[0].name_shipping.value
            = document.forms[0].name_billing.value;
        document.forms[0].address_shipping.value
            = document.forms[0].address_billing
            .value;
        document.forms[0].city_shipping.value ⏎
            = document.forms[0].city_billing ⏎
            .value;
        document.forms[0].state_shipping.value
            = document.forms[0].state_billing
            .value;
        document.forms[0].zip_shipping.value
            = document.forms[0].zip_billing.value;
    }
    else {
        document.forms[0].name_shipping.value = "";
        document.forms[0].address_shipping
            .value = "";
```

```
            document.forms[0].city_shipping.value = "";
            document.forms[0].state_shipping
                .value = "";
            document.forms[0].zip_shipping.value = "";
        }
    }
```

3. Add the following check box element above the closing `</td>` tag for the table cell that contains the billing information fields:

```
<p><input type = "checkbox"
    onclick = "sameShippingInfo();" />
    Same shipping information</p>
```

4. Save the **subscription.html** document, and then open it in your Web browser. Enter values into the billing information fields and test the check box to see if it copies the values to the shipping information fields.

5. Close your Web browser window.

Next, you add check boxes to the subscription.html document to allow users to select the types of technology that interest them.

To add more check boxes to the subscription.html document:

1. Return to the **subscription.html** document in your text editor.

2. Above the paragraph that contains the submit button, add the following check box elements:

```
<p>
    What technologies are you interested in?</p>
<p>
    <input type = "checkbox" name = "technologies"
        value = "architecture" />Architecture <br />
    <input type = "checkbox" name = "technologies"
        value = "hardware" />Hardware <br />
    <input type = "checkbox" name = "technologies"
        value = "open_source" />Open source <br />
    <input type = "checkbox" name = "technologies"
        value = "data" />Data management <br />
    <input type = "checkbox" name = "technologies"
        value = "windows" />Windows<br />
    <input type = "checkbox" name = "technologies"
        value = "mac" />Macintosh<br />
    <input type = "checkbox" name = "technologies"
        value = "networking" />Networking
</p>
```

3. Save the **subscription.html** document, and then open it in your Web browser. Figure 12-5 shows how the check boxes appear.

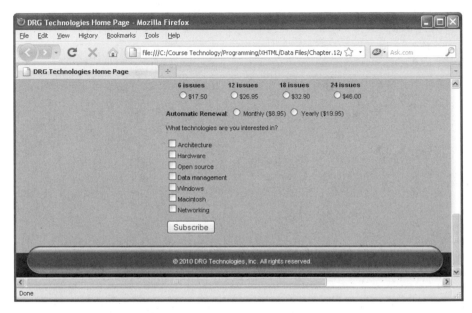

Figure 12-5   Subscription form after adding check boxes

4. Close your Web browser window.

Short Quiz 2

1. How do you use the `isNaN()` function to determine if an entered value is a number?

2. Why would you use the `name` and `value` attributes with a push button?

3. How do you manipulate a group of radio buttons with JavaScript?

Manipulating Selection Lists

The **Select object** represents a selection list in a form. The `Select` object includes an `options[]` array that contains an `Option` object for each `<option>` element in the selection list. The **Option object** represents an option in a selection list. You use the `Select` and `Option` objects with JavaScript to manipulate the options displayed in a selection list. The `Select` object contains the properties listed in Table 12-6 and the methods listed in Table 12-7.

Property	Description
`disabled`	Sets or returns a Boolean value that determines whether a control is disabled
`form`	Returns a reference to the form that contains the control
`length`	Returns the number of elements in the `options[]` array
`multiple`	Sets or returns a Boolean value that determines whether multiple options can be selected in a selection list
`name`	Sets or returns the value assigned to the element's name attribute
`options[]`	Returns an array of the options in a selection list
`selectedIndex`	Returns a number representing the element number in the `options[]` array of the first option selected in a selection list; returns 1 if no option is selected
`size`	Sets or returns the number of options to display
`type`	Returns the type of selection list; returns "select-one" if the `<select>` element does not include the `multiple` attribute, and returns "select-multiple" if the `<select>` element does include the `multiple` attribute

Table 12-6 Properties of the `Select` object

Method	Description
`add(element, before)`	Adds a new option to a selection list
`remove(index)`	Removes an option from a selection list

Table 12-7 Methods of the `Select` object

You append the properties in Table 12-6 to the name representing the `<select>` element. For example, you use the following statement to assign the number of elements in a selection list to a variable named `numItems`:

```
var numItems = document.forms[0].brand.length;
```

Similarly, the following statement assigns the currently selected option in the selection list to a variable named `curSelection`:

```
var curSelection = document.forms[0].brand.selectedIndex;
```

If the `size` attribute is excluded or set to 1, and the `<select>` element does not include the `multiple` attribute, then the selection list is a drop-down menu. For such menus, the first option element is automatically selected. However, for `<select>` elements that assign a value greater than 1 to the `size` attribute or that include the `multiple` attribute, you need to test whether the `selectedIndex` property contains a value of –1 to determine whether an option is selected in a selection list. If the property contains a value of –1, then no option is selected. For example, the following code tests whether an option is selected in the `brand` selection list:

```
if (document.forms[0].brand.selectedIndex == -1)
    window.alert("No option is selected.");
else
    window.alert("An option is selected.");
```

The `Option` object contains the properties listed in Table 12-8.

Property	Description
defaultSelected	Returns a Boolean value that determines whether the `<option>` element representing the currently selected item includes the selected attribute
disabled	Sets or returns a Boolean value that determines whether a control is disabled
form	Returns a reference to the form that contains the control
index	Returns a number representing the element number within the `options[]` array
label	Sets or returns alternate text to display for the option in the selection list
selected	Sets or returns a Boolean value that determines whether an option is selected
text	Sets or returns the text displayed for the option in the selection list
value	Sets or returns the text that is assigned to the `<option>` element's value attribute; this `value` is submitted to the server

Table 12-8   Properties of the `Option` object

You append the properties in Table 12-8 to the options[] array. For example, the following code tests whether the first element in the options[] array is selected for the brand selection list.

```
if (document.forms[0].brand.options[0].selected == true)
    window.alert("The first option is selected.");
else
    window.alert("The first option is not selected.");
```

The Option object does not contain any methods.

661

Next, you return to the subscription.html document and add a selection list that a subscriber uses to select his or her job title.

To add a selection list to the subscription.html document:

1. Return to the **subscription.html** document in your text editor.

2. Add the following selection list above the paragraph that contains the submit buttons:

   ```
   <p>What is your job title?</p>
   <p><select name = "jobTitle">
   <option value = "itStaff">IT staff</option>
   <option value = "consultant">Technical
       consultant</option>
   <option value = "integrator">Systems
       integrator</option>
   <option value = "manager">Manager</option>
   <option value = "director">Director</option>
   <option value = "vp">Vice President</option>
   <option value = "seniorManagement">CIO, CTO,
       CSO, CEO, COO, Chairman, President</option>
   <option value = "other">Other</option>
   </select></p>
   ```

3. Save the **subscription.html** document, and then open it in your Web browser. You should see the selection list at the bottom of the page. Because you did not include size and multiple attributes in the <select> element, the selection list appears as a drop-down menu.

4. Close your Web browser window.

Adding Options to a Selection List

Although the current ECMAScript recommendations suggest using the add() method of the Select object to add new options to a selection list, this method is not consistently implemented in current Web browsers. For instance, according to the ECMAScript recommendations, you should be able to add a new option to the end of a selection list by passing a value of null as the second parameter of the `add()` method. While this works in Firefox 2.0 and higher, it does not work in Internet Explorer 7.0 unless you eliminate the second parameter from the function call. Similarly, you should be able to pass an integer as the second parameter to indicate before which element the new element should be added. Conversely, this works in Internet Explorer 7.0, but it does not appear to work in Firefox 2.0. Until this method is consistently available, you should avoid using it to add an option to a selection list. Instead, to add an option to a selection list after a Web page renders it, you must create a new option with the `Option()` constructor, which is similar to creating an array with the `Array()` constructor. The syntax for the `Option()` constructor is as follows:

```
var variable_name = new Option(text, value,
    defaultSelected, selected);
```

Notice that the arguments passed to the `Option()` constructor match several of the properties of the `Option` object listed in Table 12-8. The arguments allow you to set the properties of the new option in a single statement. For example, the following statement declares a new option and assigns values to each of the properties of the `Option` object:

```
var gardeningItem = new Option("mulch", "mulch",
    false, false);
```

The preceding statement creates a new `Option` object represented by the `gardeningItem` variable and assigns values to the object's properties. You can also assign values to the properties after the new `Option` object is created. The following code performs the same tasks as the preceding statement:

 You do not have to assign values to all of the properties of a new `Option` object; you only need to assign values to the properties you need.

```
var gardeningItem = new Option();
gardeningItem.text = "mulch";
gardeningItem.value = "mulch";
```

After you create a new `Option` object and assign values to its properties, you assign the object to an empty element in an `options[]` array. For example, to assign the `Option` object created in the preceding code to the third element in an `options[]` array in a selection list named `gardeningList`, you use the following statement:

```
document.forms[0].gardeningList.options[2] = gardeningItem;
```

Next, you add code to the subscription.html document that allows subscribers to build a selection list of the technology journals to which they are currently subscribed.

To add code to the subscription.html document that allows subscribers to build a selection list of the technology journals to which they are currently subscribed:

1. Return to the **subscription.html** document in your text editor.

2. Add the following elements above the paragraph that contains the submit button. The first element is a text box where users can enter the name of a journal to which they subscribe. Note that the text box does not include a `name` argument; this prevents the field value from being submitted along with the rest of the form data. The Add Journal button includes an `onclick` event handler that calls a function named `addJournal()`, which you will add next. In order for the document to be well formed, the `<select>` element must include at least one `<option>` element. Therefore, you add a single `<option>` element that displays "Enter the technology journals you subscribe to" in the selection list. In the next section, you will add code to the `addJournal()` function that deletes this unnecessary element when the subscriber adds a journal to the selection list.

```
<p>Journal <input type = "text" size = "68" /></p>
<p><input type = "button" value = "Add Journal"
onclick = "addJournal();" style = "width: 120px"/></p>
<p><select name = "journals" multiple = "multiple"
      size = "10" style = "width: 500px">
<option value = "none">Enter the technology
journals you subscribe to</option>
</select></p>
```

3. Add the following `addJournal()` function to the end of the script section. Notice that the code uses the `elements[]` array to refer to the text box where users enter the names of journals to which they subscribe; this is necessary because the text box does not include a `name` argument. (Again, the lack of the `name` argument prevents the contents of the text box from being submitted with the other form data.) Also notice how the function determines where to add the new item in the `options[]` array. The number of items in the `options[]` array is retrieved using the `Select` object's `length` property and assigned to a variable named `nextItem`. The value assigned to the `nextItem` variable represents the number of elements in the array. As you'll recall, the length of the array is one more than the number of elements in the array (because the array begins with an element of 0). That means you can use the value to identify the next available element.

```
function addJournal() {
    if (document.forms[0].elements[31].value == "")
        window.alert("You must enter a ↵
            journal name.");
```

```
else {
    var journal = new Option();
    journal.text = document.forms[0]
        .elements[31].value;
    journal.value = document.forms[0]
        .elements[31].value;
    nextItem = document.forms[0].journals. ↵
        length;
    document.forms[0].journals.options[nextItem]
        = journal;
    document.forms[0].elements[31].value = "";
    }
}
```

4. Save the **subscription.html** document, and then open it in your Web browser. Scroll to the end of the Web page and try adding some journals to the journal list. One problem you may notice is that the "Enter the technology journals you subscribe to" option remains in the selection list after the user adds journals. You will fix this in the next section.

5. Close your Web browser window.

Removing Options from a Selection List

To remove a single option from a selection list, you pass the option's index number in the options[] array to the remove() method of the Select object. For example, use the following statement to remove the first element in the options[] array of the gardeningList selection list:

```
document.forms[0].gardeningList.remove(0);
```

When you remove an element from the array as in the preceding statement, the remaining elements are reordered. In other words, all of the element numbers following the deleted element are decreased by a value of 1.

You can remove all the options from an options[] array by appending the Select object's length property to the array without the brackets, and then by assigning the length property a value of 0. For example, to remove all the options in the options[] array of the gardeningList selection list, you use the following statement:

```
document.forms[0].gardeningList.options.length = 0;
```

Next, you add code to the subscription.html document that deletes journal names from the selection list.

To add code to the subscription.html document that deletes journal names from the selection list:

1. Return to the **subscription.html** document in your text editor.

2. Add the following elements to the end of the <p> element that contains the Add Journal button. The Delete Journal button includes an `onclick` event handler, which calls a function named `deleteJournal()`. You will add this function next. To the `onclick` event handler in the Clear List button, you will assign a statement that deletes all the items in the list.

   ```
   <input type = "button" value = "Delete Journal"
   onclick = "deleteJournal()" style = "width: 120px" />
   <input type = "button" value = "Clear_List"
   onclick = "document.forms[0].journals ↵
        .options.length = 0;"
   style = "width: 120px" />
   ```

3. Add the following `deleteJournal()` function to the end of the script section.

   ```
   function deleteJournal() {
       var selectedItem =
           document.forms[0].journals.selectedIndex;
       if (selectedItem == -1)
           window.alert("You must select a ↵
               journal name in the list.");
       else
           document.forms[0].journals
               .remove(selectedItem);
   }
   ```

4. Finally, add the following `if` statement to the beginning of the `else` statement in the `addJournal()` function. This statement deletes the "Enter the technology journals you subscribe to" option that is displayed by default in the selection list.

   ```
   if (document.forms[0].journals.options[0]
       && document.forms[0].journals
       .options[0].value == "none")
       document.forms[0].journals.options[0] = null;
   ```

5. Save the **subscription.html** document, and then open it in your Web browser. Scroll to the end of the Web page and try adding some journals to the journal list. After you add the first journal, "Enter the technology journals you subscribe to" should be removed from the list. Also, test the Delete Journal and Clear List buttons.

6. Close your Web browser window.

Changing Options in a Selection List

To change an option in a selection list, you simply assign new values to the option's `value` and `text` properties. For example, use the following statements to change the first option in the `gardeningList` selection list from "Pruners" to "Mulch":

```
document.forms[0].gardeningList.options[0].value = "Mulch";
document.forms[0].gardeningList.options[0].text = "Mulch";
```

The following code shows a completed example of a shopping list to which you can add new items. An Add Item button in the form calls a function named `addItem()`, which adds new items to the selection list. A new `Option` object named `gardeningItem` is created, and its `text` and `value` properties are assigned the value of the first text box in the form. A function named `deleteItem()`, which is called from the Delete Item button, handles deleting single items from the list. The `onclick` event handler in the Clear List button is assigned a statement that deletes all of the items in the list. A function named `changeItem()` changes the value of a selected item in the list to the value in the New Item text box. Figure 12-6 shows how the form appears in a Web browser.

```
...
<script type = "text/javascript">
/* <![CDATA[ */
function addItem() {
    if (document.forms[0].elements[0].value == "")
        window.alert("You must enter an item.");
    else {
        var gardeningItem = new Option();
        gardeningItem.text = document.forms[0]
            .elements[0].value;
        gardeningItem.value = document.forms[0]
            .elements[0].value;
        nextItem = document.forms[0].gardeningList
            .length;
        document.forms[0].gardeningList
            .options[nextItem] = gardeningItem;
        document.forms[0].elements[0].value = "";
    }
}
function deleteItem() {
    var selectedItem
        = document.forms[0].gardeningList.selectedIndex;
    if (selectedItem == -1)
        window.alert("You must select an item ↵
            in the list.");
```

```
        else
            document.forms[0].gardeningList
                .options[selectedItem] = null;
}
function changeItem() {
    var selectedItem = document.forms[0].gardeningList
        .selectedIndex;
    if (selectedItem == -1)
        window.alert("You must select an item in
            the list.");
    document.forms[0].gardeningList
        .options[selectedItem].value
        = document.forms[0].elements[0].value;
    document.forms[0].gardeningList
        .options[selectedItem].text
        = document.forms[0].elements[0].value;
}
/* ]]> */
</script>
</head>
<body>
<h1>Spring Planting</h1>
<h2>Gardening List</h2>
<form action = "">
<p>New Item <input type = "text" size = "68"
name = "elements[0]" /></p>
<p><input type = "button" value = "Add Item"
onclick = "addItem()"
style = "width: 120px" />
<input type = "button" value = "Delete Item"
onclick = "deleteItem()"
style = "width: 120px" />
<input type = "button" value = "Clear List"
onclick = "document.forms[0].gardeningList.options
    .length = 0;"
style = "width: 120px" />
<input type = "button" value = "Change Item"
onclick = "changeItem()"
style = "width: 120px" /></p>
<p><select name = "gardeningList" size = "10"
style = "width: 500px">
<option value = "pruners">Pruners</option>
<option value = "seeds">Seeds</option>
</select></p>
</form>
```

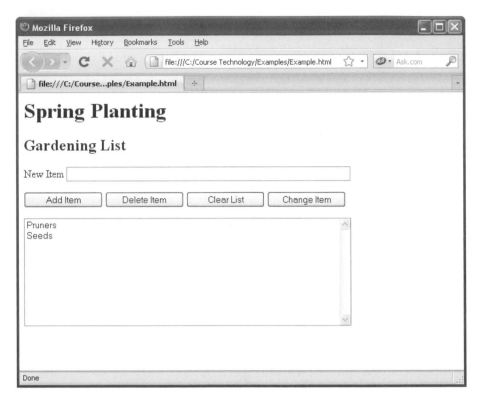

Figure 12-6   Shopping list form

Next, you add code to the subscription.html document that modifies journal names in the selection list.

To add code to the subscription.html document that modifies journal names in the selection list:

1. Return to the **subscription.html** document in your text editor.

2. Add the following elements to the end of the <p> element that contains the other buttons that build the list of journals. The Change Journal button includes an `onclick` event handler, which calls a function named `changeJournal()`. You will add this function next.

   ```
   <input type = "button" value = "Change Journal"
   onclick = "changeJournal()" style = "width: 120px" />
   ```

3. Add the following changeJournal() function to the end of the script section. The function is very similar to the changeItem() function you saw in the shopping list form.

```
function changeJournal() {
    var selectedItem =
        document.forms[0].journals.selectedIndex;
    if (selectedItem == -1)
        window.alert("You must select a journal ↵
            name in the list.");
    else {
        document.forms[0].journals
            .options[selectedItem].value
            = document.forms[0]
            .elements[31].value;
        document.forms[0].journals
            .options[selectedItem].text
            = document.forms[0].elements ↵
            [31].value;
    }
}
```

669

4. Save the **subscription.html** document, and then open it in your Web browser. Scroll to the end of the Web page, and try adding and changing some journals in the journal list.

Figure 12-7 shows how the document appears.

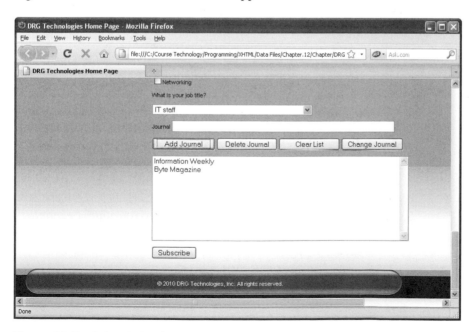

Figure 12-7 Subscription form with a selection list

5. Close your Web browser window.

Short Quiz 3

1. How do you use the `Select` object to manipulate selection lists with JavaScript?

2. How do you add options to a selection list with JavaScript?

3. How do you remove options from a selection list with JavaScript?

Validating Submitted Data

Earlier versions of HTML and XHTML supported an `onreset` event handler that allowed users to confirm that they wanted to reset a form's contents. However, the `onreset` event handler is not supported in HTML 5.

In Chapters 8 and 9, you learned about many of the event handlers that can be used in JavaScript. One event handler, `onsubmit`, is available for use with the `<form>` element. The **onsubmit event handler** executes when a form is submitted to a server-side script (in other words, when a submit button is selected on a form). The `onsubmit` event handler is often used to verify or validate a form's data before it is sent to a server. The `onsubmit` event handler is placed before the closing bracket of an opening `<form>` tag. The following code shows how to write a form tag with an `onsubmit` event handler:

```
<form action = "FormProcessor.html" method = "post"
    onsubmit = "JavaScript statements;" >
```

The `onsubmit` event handler must return a value of true or false, depending on whether the form should be submitted (true) or not (false). For example, the `onsubmit` event handlers in the following code return a value of true or false, depending on whether the user clicks the OK button or the Cancel button in the Confirm dialog box. If the user clicks OK, the Confirm dialog box returns a value of true, and the `submit` event executes. If the user clicks Cancel, the Confirm dialog box returns a value of false, and the `submit` event does not execute.

Remember that the Confirm dialog box returns a value of true if the user clicks OK and false if the user clicks Cancel.

```
<form action = "FormProcessor.html" method = "post"
    onsubmit = "return window.confirm('Are you sure↵
        you want to submit the form?');"
```

Next, you will add an `onsubmit` event handler to the subscription.html document to confirm that the user wants to submit the form.

**To add an onsubmit event handler to the
subscription.html document:**

1. Return to the **subscription.html** document in your text
   editor.

2. Add the following confirmSubmit() function to the end of the
   script section:

```
function confirmSubmit() {
    var submitForm = window.confirm(
        "Are you sure you want to submit the form?");
    if (submitForm == true)
        return true;
    return false;
}
```

3. Before the closing bracket of the opening <form> tag, add
   the following onsubmit event handler, which calls the
   confirmSubmit()function:

```
onsubmit = "return confirmSubmit()"
```

4. Save the **subscription.html** document, and then open it in
   your Web browser. Enter some data in the form's fields and
   click the **Subscribe** button to see if you receive the submit
   prompt. Click **OK** in the Confirm dialog box. The data you
   entered should appear in the FormProcessor.html document.

5. Close your Web browser window.

Although the onsubmit event handler is useful for confirming that
a user wants to submit a form, its most important purpose is to
validate form data. The validation of form data can mean many
things, ranging from ensuring that a field is not empty to performing
complex validation of credit card numbers. You have already seen
several examples of validation at the form level when you wrote code
that checked whether a value entered in a Zip code or telephone
number field was a number. You also wrote code that confirmed
that the user entered the same value in the password and password
confirmation boxes. In the next section, you'll learn how to perform
the final step in validating these types of fields: ensuring that they are
not empty when the form is submitted.

Validating Text and Password Boxes

To verify that text and password boxes are not empty, you can
use an if statement in the onsubmit event handler that checks
whether the field's value property contains a value. For example, the
following code uses an if statement to check whether two text fields
(firstName and lastName) contain text. This code could be called from

an onsubmit event handler. If the fields do contain text, a value of true is returned and the form is submitted. If the fields do not contain text, a value of false is returned and the form is not submitted. Notice that the conditional expression uses the || (Or) operator to confirm that both fields have been filled.

```
function submitForm() {
    if (document.forms[0].firstName.value == ""
        || document.forms[0].lastName.value == "") {
        window.alert("You must enter your first ↵
            and last names!");
        return false;
    }
    else
        return true;
}
```

Next, you add code to the confirmSubmit() function in the Subscription form to validate the text and password boxes.

To add code to the confirmSubmit() function in the Subscription form to validate the text and password boxes:

1. Return to the **subscription.html** document in your text editor.

2. Replace the statements within the confirmSubmit() function with the following statements, which validate the billing fields. The conditional statement uses multiple || (Or) operators to validate all of the billing fields in one expression.

```
if (document.forms[0].name_billing.value == ""
    || document.forms[0].address_billing.value == ""
    || document.forms[0].city_billing.value == ""
    || document.forms[0].state_billing.value == ""
    || document.forms[0].zip_billing.value == "") {
    window.alert("You must enter your ↵
        billing information.");
    return false;
}
```

3. Add the following statements to the end of the confirmSubmit() function to validate the shipping fields:

```
else if (document.forms[0].name_shipping.value == ""
    || document.forms[0].address_shipping.value == ""
    || document.forms[0].city_shipping.value == ""
    || document.forms[0].state_shipping.value == ""
    || document.forms[0].zip_shipping.value == "") {
    window.alert("You must enter your ↵
        shipping information.");
    return false;
}
```

4. Add the following statements to the end of the confirmSubmit() function to validate the telephone fields:

```
else if (document.forms[0].area.value == ""
    || document.forms[0].exchange.value == ""
    || document.forms[0].phone.value == "") {
    window.alert("You must enter your ↵
        telephone number.");
    return false;
}
```

5. Add the following statements to the end of the confirmSubmit() function to validate the user name:

```
else if (document.forms[0].userName.value == "") {
    window.alert("You must enter a user name.");
    return false;
}
```

6. Add the following statements to the end of the confirmSubmit() function to validate the password fields:

```
else if (document.forms[0].password.value == ""
    || document.forms[0].password_confirm.
    value == "") {
    window.alert("You must enter a password.");
    return false;
}
```

7. Finally, add the following return statement to the end of the confirmSubmit() function:

```
return true;
```

8. Save the **subscription.html** document, and then open it in your Web browser. Enter some data in the form's billing, shipping, telephone, and password fields, but leave some fields blank. Click the **Subscribe** button. Depending on which fields you left blank, you should see an alert message that tells you which fields need to be filled in.

9. Click the **OK** button, fill in the fields you left blank, and then click the **Subscribe** button. The data you entered should appear in the FormProcessor.html document.

10. Close your Web browser window.

Validating Radio Buttons

Recall that when multiple form elements share the same name, JavaScript creates an array out of the elements using the shared name. Radio buttons, for instance, share the same name so that a single name=value pair can be submitted to a server-side script. When you have an array that is created from a group of radio buttons that share the same name, you can use the checked property to determine which element in the group is selected. The checked property returns a value of true if a check box or radio button is selected, and returns a value of false if it is not. For example, if you have a group of radio buttons named maritalStatus, you can use an onsubmit event handler similar to the following to determine if one of the radio buttons is selected:

```
function submitForm() {
    var maritalStatusSelected = false;
    for (var i = 0; i < 5; ++i) {
        if (document.forms[0].maritalStatus[i].checked
            == true) {
            maritalStatusSelected = true;
            break;
        }
    }
    if (maritalStatusSelected == false) {
        window.alert("You must select your
            marital status.");
        return false;
    }
    else
        return true;
}
```

Next, you return to the Subscription form and add code to the confirmSubmit() function that validates the Delivery Rates radio buttons.

To add code to the confirmSubmit() function that validates the Delivery Rates radio buttons:

1. Return to the **subscription.html** document in your text editor.

2. The Delivery Rates radio buttons are contained within two groups: delivery and autoRenew. You need to ensure that a button is selected in one of the groups. First, add the following variable declaration and for statement above the return true; statement at the end of the confirmSubmit() function. The for statement checks whether a button is selected in the delivery group.

```
var deliverySelected = false;
for (var i = 0; i < 4; ++i) {
    if (document.forms[0].delivery[i].checked
        == true) {
        deliverySelected = true;
        break;
    }
}
```

3. Add the following `for` statement above the `return true;` statement at the end of the `confirmSubmit()` function to check whether a button is selected in the `autoRenew` group:

```
for (var j = 0; j < 2; ++j) {
    if (document.forms[0].autoRenew[j].checked
        == true) {
        deliverySelected = true;
        break;
    }
}
```

4. Add the following code above the `return true;` statement at the end of the `confirmSubmit()` function to cancel the form submission if one of the Delivery Rates radio buttons is not selected:

```
if (deliverySelected ! = true) {
    window.alert("You must select a delivery ↵
        rate option.");
    return false;
}
```

5. Save the **subscription.html** document, and then open it in your Web browser. Enter some data in all of the form's fields, but do not select a delivery option. When you click the **Subscribe** button, you should see an alert message that instructs you to select a delivery option. Click the **OK** button, select a delivery option, and then click **Subscribe**. The data you entered should appear in the FormProcessor.html document.

6. Close your Web browser window.

Validating Check Boxes

You can use the `checked` property to determine whether an individual check box has been selected. If check boxes are part of a group, you can validate them using the same functionality as the validation code for radio buttons because JavaScript creates an array out of elements with the same name. The following `onsubmit` event handler determines whether at least one check box is selected in a group of check boxes named `committees`:

```
function submitForm() {
    var committeesSelected = false;
    for (var i = 0; i < 4; ++i) {
        if (document.forms[0].committees[i].checked
            == true) {
            committeesSelected = true;
            break;
```

```
                    }
                }
                if (committeesSelected == false) {
                    window.alert("You must select at least↵
                        one committee.");
                    return committeesSelected;
                }
                else
                    return committeesSelected;
            }
```

Remember that if the `size` attribute is excluded or set to 1, and the `<select>` element does not include the `multiple` attribute, then the selection list is a drop-down menu. For such menus, the first option element is automatically selected.

Because the subscription check boxes are optional in the Subscription form, you can skip adding validation code for them.

Validating Selection Lists

Validating selection lists is a little easier than validating radio buttons and check boxes because you only need to test whether the selection list's `selectedIndex` property contains a value of −1. If it does, then no option is selected.

The following `onsubmit` event handler determines whether at least one option is selected in a selection list named `brand`:

```
function submitForm() {
    if (document.forms[0].brand.selectedIndex == -1) {
        window.alert("You must select at least↵
            one brand.");
        return false;
    }
    else
        return true;
}
```

The selection list in the Subscription form allows subscribers to build a list of journals to which they subscribe. However, depending on whether the `<select>` element includes the `multiple` attribute, one or more options must be chosen in the selection list before it can be submitted to a Web server with the rest of the form data. Because you cannot count on subscribers to select all of the journals they entered in the selection list before clicking the Subscribe button, you need to add code to the Subscription form that selects all of the journals when the form is submitted. You will do this by adding a looping statement to the `confirmSubmit()` event handler function that selects each option in the journal selection list, using the `selected` property of the `Option` object.

To add a looping statement to the `confirmSubmit()` event handler function that selects each option in the journal selection list:

1. Return to the **subscription.html** document in your text editor.

2. Above the `return true;` statement at the end of the `confirmSubmit()` function, add the following code to select all of the journals in the selection list when the form is submitted:

```
for (var k = 0; k < document.forms[0].journals.length;
    ++k) {
    document.forms[0].journals.options[k].selected
        = true;
}
```

3. Save the **subscription.html** document, then validate it with the W3C Markup Validation Service and fix any errors. Once the document is valid, open it in your Web browser. Enter data in all of the form's fields, and be sure to enter some journal names. Click the **Subscribe** button. The data you entered, including the journal names, should appear in the FormProcessor.html document.

4. Close your Web browser window and text editor.

Short Quiz 4

1. How do you validate text and password boxes?

2. How do you validate radio buttons?

3. How do you validate selection lists?

Summing Up

- To use JavaScript to access form controls and verify form information, you use the Form object, which represents a form on a Web page.

- The elements[] array contains objects that represent each of the controls in a form.

- For any fields that require numeric values, you can use JavaScript's built-in isNaN() function to determine whether the user actually entered a number.

- In JavaScript, you can check whether a user entered the same password twice by using an if statement to compare the values entered in the password and confirmation fields.

- With <input> elements of the "button" type, you are required to use JavaScript code to handle the button's click event.

- When multiple form elements share the same name, JavaScript creates an array out of the elements using the shared name.

- When an array is created from a group of buttons that share the same name, you can use the checked property to determine which element in the group is selected.

- You can use check boxes with an onclick event handler to execute JavaScript code.

- The Select object represents a selection list in a form.

- The Option object represents an option in a selection list.

- To add an option to a selection list after a Web page renders it, you must create a new option with the Option() constructor.

- To remove a single option from a selection list, you pass the option's index number in the options[] array to the remove() method of the Select object.

- You can remove all the options from an options[] array by appending the Select object's length property to the array without the brackets, and then by assigning the length property a value of 0.

- The onsubmit event handler executes when a form is submitted to a server-side script.

- To verify that text and password boxes are not empty, you can use an `if` statement in the `onsubmit` event handler that checks whether the field's `value` property contains a value.

- You can use the `checked` property to determine whether an individual check box has been selected.

- To validate selection lists, you need to test whether the selection list's `selectedIndex` property contains a value of −1. If it does, then no option is selected.

Comprehension Check

1. You can only validate form controls created with `<input>` elements. True or False?

2. Objects representing each of the controls in a form are stored in the _____ array.

   a. `forms[]`

   b. `controls[]`

   c. `inputs[]`

   d. `elements[]`

3. You can refer to a form control object with which of the following methods? (Choose all that apply.)

   a. the control's `name` attribute

   b. the `elements[]` array

   c. the `controls[]` array

   d. the `fields[]` array

4. Explain how to ensure that users enter a number into a text field.

5. How do you validate the contents of two password boxes?

6. When multiple form elements share the same name, JavaScript creates an array out of the elements using the shared name. True or False?

7. Which of the following attributes determines whether a check box or radio button is selected?

    a. `checked`

    b. `defaultChecked`

    c. `selected`

    d. `false`

8. What value does the `selectedIndex` property of the `Select` object return if no option is selected?

    a. −1

    b. 0

    c. 1

    d. false

9. How do you use the `Option()` constructor to add a new option after a Web page renders a selection list?

10. Which of the following attributes returns the number of elements in an `options[]` array?

    a. `size`

    b. `index`

    c. `length`

    d. `range`

11. What is the correct syntax for removing the first element from an `options[]` array in a selection list named `customers`?

    a. `document.forms[0].customers.options[0] = null;`

    b. `document.forms[0].customers.remove(0);`

    c. `document.forms[0].customers.options[0] = 0;`

    d. `document.forms[0].customers.options[0] = -1;`

12. How do you change options in a selection list with JavaScript?

13. Why would you use the `onsubmit` event handler?

14. How do you create an `onsubmit` event handler?

15. Where do you place the onsubmit event handler?

    a. in a submit <input> element

    b. in the closing </form> tag

    c. in the form control that calls the submit event

    d. in the opening <form> tag

16. What must the onsubmit event handler return?

17. Explain how to verify that text and password boxes are not empty.

18. How do you validate radio buttons?

19. How do you validate check boxes?

20. Explain how to validate selection lists.

Reinforcement Exercises

 Exercise 12-1

In this exercise, you will create a script that automatically moves a user's cursor to the next field after a specified number of characters have been entered into the current field. The exercise uses a simple form that allows users to enter their 10-digit telephone number. The form will contain three text boxes for the area code, exchange, and number portions of the telephone number.

1. Create a new HTML 5 document in your text editor and use "Auto Next Field" as the content of the <title> element.

2. In the document body, add the following form that contains three text boxes. The first two text boxes, for the area code and exchange, use the onkeyup event to call an event handler function named nextField(). Two arguments are passed to the nextField() function: a this reference, which passes the name of the current control, and the name of the destination control. Notice that each of the text boxes includes maxlength attributes.

```
<form action = "FormProcessor.html" method = "get"
enctype = "application/x-www-form-urlencoded">
<p><strong>Enter your 10-digit telephone number: ↵
   </strong>
```

```
<input type = "text" name = "area_code" size = "4"
    onkeyup = "nextField(this, document.forms[0] ↵
        .exchange)"
    maxlength = "3" />
<input type = "text" name = "exchange" size = "4"
    onkeyup = "nextField(this, document.forms[0] ↵
        .number)"
    maxlength = "3" />
<input type = "text" name = "number" size = "5"
maxlength = "4" /></p>
</form>
```

3. Add a script section to the document head.

4. In the script section, add the following `nextField()` function, which is called from the `onkeyup` events in the `<input>` elements. Notice how the conditional expression compares the length of the field to the `maxLength` property. The current value assigned to the field is retrieved with the `value` property. Then, a property named `length` is appended to the `value` property. The `length` property is a property of the `String` class, and it returns the number of characters in a string. If the length of the field is equal to the value assigned to the `maxLength` property, the `focus()` statement moves the focus to the field identified by the `destField` parameter.

```
function nextField(startField, destField) {
    if (startField.value.length
        ==startField.maxLength)
    destField.focus();
}
```

5. Save the document as **AutoNextField.html** in the Exercises folder for Chapter 12.

6. Use the W3C Markup Validation Service to validate the **AutoNextField.html** document and fix any errors. Once the document is valid, close it in your text editor and then open it in your Web browser.

7. Enter an area code into the first text box. When you finish, focus transfers to the second text box. Enter an exchange into the second text box. When you finish, the focus is transferred to the third text box.

8. Close your Web browser window.

Exercise 12-2

When you first open a Web page with a form in a browser, none of the form controls have the focus. In this exercise, you create a Web page that sets the focus when the Web page first opens. The Web page you create will contain a simple inquiry form that might be sent to a real estate agent.

1. Create a new HTML 5 document in your text editor and use "Realtor Inquiry" as the content of the `<title>` element.

2. Add the following heading element and form to the document body. The form contains several text boxes that gather customer and property details, and a selection list that allows customers to select a specific type of property.

```
<h1>Real Estate Inquiry</h1>
<form action = "FormProcessor.html" method = "get"
enctype = "application/x-www-form-urlencoded">
<p>Name<br />
<input type = "text" name = "visitor_name"
size = "50" /></p>
<p>E-mail address<br />
<input type = "text" name = "e-mail" size = "50" /></p>
<p>Phone<br />
<input type = "text" name = "phone" size = "50" /></p>
<p>Area of town<br />
<input type = "text" name = "area" size = "50" /></p>
<p>Property <select name = "property_type">
<option value = "unselected">Select a Property Type
</option>
<option value = "condo">Condos</option>
<option value = "single">Single Family Homes</option>
<option value = "multi">Multifamily Homes</option>
<option value = "mobile">Mobile Homes</option>
<option value = "land">Land</option>
</select>Sq. feet <input type = "text"
     name = "feet" size = "5" /></p>
<p>Bedrooms <input type = "text" name = "bedrooms"
size = "5" />
Maximum price <input type = "text" name = "price"
size = "12" /></p>
<p>How should we contact you? <input type = "radio"
name = "contactHow" value = "call_me" /> Call me
<input type = "radio" name = "contactHow"
value = "e-mail_me" /> E-mail me</p>
<p><input type = "submit" /></p>
</form>
```

3. Add a script section to the document head.

4. In the script section, add the following `setFormFocus()` function, which uses the `focus()` method of the `Input` object to set the focus on the first control in the form. The form is named `visitor_name`:

```
function setFormFocus() {
    document.forms[0].visitor_name.focus();
}
```

5. In the opening `<body>` tag, add the following `onload` event handler, which calls the `setFormFocus()` method when the page first loads:

```
onload = "setFormFocus();"
```

6. Save the document as **RealEstateInquiry.html** in the Exercises folder for Chapter 12, and then open the document in your Web browser. The first control on the form should receive the focus as soon as the form is rendered.

7. Close your Web browser window.

 Exercise 12-3

In this exercise, you will add default values to the text boxes you created in the last exercise. You will also add `onfocus` event handlers to each text box to remove the default values when the text box receives the focus.

1. Return to the **RealEstateInquiry.html** document you created in the last exercise.

2. Add `value` attributes to each of the text `<input>` elements to create default values, as follows:

```
<form action = "FormProcessor.html" method = "get"
enctype = "application/x-www-form-urlencoded">
<p>Name<br />
<input type = "text" name = "visitor_name" size = "50"
    value = "Enter your name" /></p>
<p>E-mail address<br />
<input type = "text" name = "e-mail" size = "50"
    value = "Enter your e-mail address" /></p>
<p>Phone<br />
<input type = "text" name = "phone" size = "50"
    value = "Enter your phone number" /></p>
<p>Area of town<br />
```

```
<input type = "text" name = "area" size = "50"
    value = "What area of town are you ↵
        interested in?"/></p>
<p>Property <select name = "property_type">
<option value = "unselected">Select a Property
    Type</option>
<option value = "condo">Condos</option>
<option value = "single">Single Family Homes</option>
<option value = "multi">Multifamily Homes</option>
<option value = "mobile">Mobile Homes</option>
<option value = "land">Land</option>
</select> Sq. feet <input type = "text"
    name = "feet" size = "5" value = "???" /></p>
<p>Bedrooms <input type = "text"
    name = "bedrooms" size = "5" value = "???" />
Maximum price <input type = "text" name = "price"
    size = "12" value = "$$$" /></p>
<p>How should we contact you? <input type = "radio"
    name = "contactHow" value = "call_me" /> Call me
<input type = "radio" name = "contactHow" value =
"e-mail_me" /> E-mail me</p>
<p><input type = "submit" /></p>
</form>
```

3. Add onclick event handlers to each <input> element to check whether the value of the control is equal to its default value. If so, change the value to an empty string (" "). For example, the onclick event handler for the visitor_name <input> element is as follows:

```
onclick = "if (this.value == 'Enter your name') ↵
    this.value = '';")
```

4. Add validation code to the RealEstateInquiry.html document that verifies the text boxes are not empty and do not contain the default values when the form is submitted. For the square feet, number of bedrooms, and maximum price fields, include validation code that verifies the user entered a numeric value. Also, add validation code that verifies whether users have selected values from the selection list and the radio button group.

5. Save the **RealEstateInquiry.html** document, validate it with the W3C Markup Validation Service, and fix any errors. Once the document is valid, close it in your text editor and then open it in your Web browser. Selecting each control should remove the default values.

6. Close your Web browser window.

Exercise 12-4

In this exercise, you will create a Web page that allows you to search the Web using several popular search engines displayed in a selection list. The code you write will perform a search by appending the search item to the URL for the selected search engines. The URLs for different search engines such as Yahoo! and Google require slightly different syntax for submitting a search. For example, with Yahoo! you append the search item to the URL http://search.yahoo.com/search?p=; for Google you append the search item to the URL http://www.google.com/search?q=. The required search syntax for each URL will be assigned to the value attribute of the option that represents the search engine in the selection list.

1. Create a new HTML 5 document in your text editor and use "Multiple Search Engines" as the content of the <title> element.

2. Add the following form to the document body. Notice that the value attribute of each option in the selection list is assigned the correct URL syntax for each search engine.

```
<form action = "" name = "searchForm">
<p>Search for <input type = "text"
     name = "searchTerm" />
     from <select name = "engines">
     <option value = "http://www.altavista.com/ ↵
          cgi-bin/query?kl=XX&amp;pgx=q&amp;
          Translate=on&amp;q=">
          Alta Vista</option>
     <option value = "http://search.aol.com/ ↵
          dirsearch.adp?query = ">AOL</option>
      <option value = "http://www.google.com/ ↵
          search?q = ">Google</option>
     <option value = "http://search.lycos.com/ ↵
          default.asp? lpv=1&amp;loc=searchhp&amp; ↵
          tab = web&amp;query=">Lycos</option>
     <option value = "http://search.yahoo.com/ ↵
          search?p = "selected = "selected">
          Yahoo!</option>
</select>
<input type = "button" value = "Search"
     onclick = "doSearch()" /></p>
</form>
```

3. Add a script section to the document head.

4. Add the following function to the script section. The first statement retrieves the selected index. The if statement first checks to see if a search engine is selected. If one is, the else statement appends the search term to the search engine's URL and assigns the combined value to the href attribute of the Location object.

687

```
function doSearch() {
    var selectedItem = document.searchForm.engines
        .selectedIndex;
    if (selectedItem == -1)
        window.alert("You must select a ↵
            search engine.");
    else
        location.href = document.searchForm.engines
            .options[selectedItem].value
            + document.searchForm.searchTerm.value;
}
```

5. Save the document as **MultiSearchEngines.html** in the Exercises folder for Chapter 12, validate the document with the W3C Markup Validation Service, and fix any errors. Once the document is valid, close it in your text editor and then open it in your Web browser. Test the form to ensure that you can search with each of the search engines in the selection list.

6. Close your Web browser window.

Discovery Projects

For the following projects, save the documents you create in your Projects folder for Chapter 12. Be sure to validate each Web page with the W3C Markup Validation Service.

Discovery Project 12-1

Pick your favorite sport and search the Internet for current player rosters of five teams. Create a Web page that contains two selection lists: one displays a drop-down menu of team names, and the other is a multi-line selection list that displays player names. Write JavaScript code that changes the list of players in the second selection list after you select a new team name from the first selection list. Save each team roster in its own variable, and use the techniques you learned in this chapter to dynamically add the player names to the selection list. Save the page as **TeamRosters.html**.

Discovery Project 12-2

Create a Web page for a takeout pizza restaurant. Use radio buttons to allow customers to select the type of pizza, such as vegetarian or meat lover's. Include check boxes for selecting additional toppings such as extra cheese, mushrooms, or anchovies. Include a price for each pizza and each additional item, and keep a running total in a text box. Save the page as **PizzaToGo.html**.

Discovery Project 12-3

Create a script that requires Web page visitors to accept your terms and conditions by selecting a check box before proceeding. Save the page as **AcceptTerms.html**. Include two links: an Accept link and a Decline link. The Accept link should open a page named **AcceptPage.html** that displays the text "Thank you for accepting our terms." The Decline link should open a page named **DeclinePage.html** that displays the text "You did not accept our terms." In the AcceptTerms.html document, create a single event handler function named confirmTerms() that determines whether the check box is selected, then returns a value of true if it is or false if it isn't. Call the confirmTerms() function from the Accept link. If the check box is selected, open the AcceptPage.html document. If the check box is not selected, display an alert dialog box informing the user that he or she must accept the terms. If the user clicks the Decline link, open the DeclinePage.html document.

Discovery Project 12-4

Create a Web page that contains a table with three columns. In the left and right columns, create two selection lists. Fill both selection lists with unique items, such as product names. In the middle column, add two buttons: one button should contain the characters ">>" and the other button should contain the characters "<<". Write a script that moves the selection list items between the two columns. For example, if the left column contains the name "iPod Nano", clicking the >> button should move the name to the right column. Save the script as **MoveMenuItems.html**.

Discovery Project 12-5

Create a registration form similar to one you might encounter when registering for an online Web site. Include three sections named Personal Information, Security Information, and Preferences. In the Personal Information section, add text boxes for users to enter their name and e-mail address. Include default text in both text boxes, but write code that removes the default text from each text box when a user clicks it. In the Security Information section, add password and password confirmation fields. Write code that ensures that the same value is entered into both fields. Also, add a selection list of security challenge questions and an answer text box to help identify users who lose their password. The selection list should contain questions such as "What is your mother's maiden name?", "What is the name of your pet?", and "What is your favorite color?" In the Preferences section, add radio buttons that confirm whether a user wants special offers sent to his or her e-mail address. Also, include check boxes for users to specify their special interests, such as entertainment, business, and shopping. Add a Submit button that calls a `submit()` event handler function when the button is clicked. The `submit()` event handler function should ensure that the user has entered values into each text box, and that the values submitted are not the same as the default text. The `submit()` event handler function should also ensure that the user selects a security challenge question, a radio button to confirm whether special offers should be sent to his or her e-mail address, and at least one special interest check box. Submit the form to the FormProcessor.html script; a copy is stored in your Projects folder for Chapter 12. Save the document as **Registration.html**.

CHAPTER 13

Introduction to the Document Object Model (DOM)

In this chapter, you will:

◎ Study the HTML Document Object Model (DOM)

◎ Work with the `Image` object

◎ Learn how to access document elements

Today, more and more businesses want their Web sites to include formatting and images that can be updated without requiring the user to reload a Web page from the server. They also want to use animation and interactive Web pages in innovative ways to attract and retain visitors and to make their Web sites effective and easy to navigate. You cannot create these kinds of effects with standard Extensible Hypertext Markup Language (XHTML); instead, you need to use Dynamic HTML (DHTML). One of the most important aspects of DHTML is the Document Object Model (DOM). In this chapter, you will learn about the DOM and how it fits in with DHTML.

Understanding the HTML Document Object Model

As you have probably realized by now, Web pages are much more useful when they are dynamic. In Internet terminology, the word **dynamic** means several things. Primarily, it refers to Web pages that respond to user requests through buttons or other kinds of controls. Among other things, a dynamic Web page can allow a user to change the document background color, submit a form, process a query, and participate in an online game or quiz. The term *dynamic* also refers to various effects, such as animation, that appear automatically in a Web browser. To make Web pages truly dynamic, you need more than just XHTML. **Dynamic HTML (DHTML)** refers to a combination of technologies that make Web pages dynamic. DHTML is actually a combination of JavaScript, XHTML, CSS, and the Document Object Model. You should already be familiar with JavaScript, XHTML, and CSS, but to be successful with JavaScript, you also need to learn about the Document Object Model.

 Remember that DHTML does not refer to a single technology but to several combined technologies.

At the core of DHTML is the **Document Object Model**, or **DOM**, which represents the HTML or XML of a Web page that is displayed in a browser. The Document Object Model that represents HTML content is referred to as the HTML DOM, and the Document Object Model that represents XML content is referred to as the XML DOM. Throughout this book, you have created Web pages that conform to XHTML. Because XHTML documents are just another type of XML document, you can manipulate them with both the HTML DOM and the XML DOM. But which is preferable? The W3C formally recommends using the XML DOM instead of the HTML DOM. Nonetheless, it's easier to use the HTML DOM with basic types of

DHTML techniques, such as those discussed in this chapter and the next. Keep in mind, however, that you must use the XML DOM when using some advanced JavaScript techniques, such as AJAX, which is discussed in Appendix E.

Each element on a Web page is represented in the HTML DOM by its own object. The fact that each element is an object makes it possible for a JavaScript program to access individual elements on a Web page and change them individually, without having to reload the page from the server. Although the individual technologies that make up DHTML have been accepted standards for some time, the implementation of DHTML has evolved slowly. One of the main delays in implementation has to do with the DOM. Earlier versions of Internet Explorer and Navigator included DOMs that were almost completely incompatible with each other. This meant that you needed to write different JavaScript code sections for different browsers. At the time of this writing, several competing browsers are compatible with a standardized version of the DOM, Level 3, that is recommended by the World Wide Web Consortium (W3C). These browsers include Internet Explorer 5.0 and higher, as well as Firefox and other Mozilla-based Web browsers.

When it comes to Web page authoring, the most important part of the HTML DOM is the Document object. Through this object, you can access other objects that represent elements on a Web page. Throughout this book, you have used the HTML DOM to access and manipulate form elements. Similarly, you can use JavaScript to manipulate the images on a Web page through the Image object. The value you assign to an <img> element's name attribute becomes the name of an associated Image object. To access an Image object named companyLogo, you must append the image name to the Document object as follows: document.companyLogo. (You will learn how to work with the Image object in the next section.)

For a complete listing of objects in the HTML DOM, see the W3Schools' HTML DOM reference at *http://w3schools.com/ jsref/default.asp.*

Next, you will study several of the Document object's properties and methods.

HTML DOM Document Object Methods

The Document object contains several methods used for dynamically generating Web pages and manipulating elements. Table 13-1 lists the methods of the Document object that are specified in the W3C DOM.

Method	Description
close()	Closes a new document that was created with the open() method
getElementsByName(*name*)	Returns a collection of elements represented by *name*
getElementsByTagName(*tag name*)	Returns a collection of elements represented by *tag name*
getElementById(*ID*)	Returns the element represented by *ID*
open()	Opens a new document in a window
write(*text*)	Writes new text to a document
writeln(*text*)	Writes new text to a document, followed by a line break

Table 13-1   HTML DOM Document object methods

HTML DOM Document Object Properties

The HTML DOM Document object contains various properties used for manipulating Web page objects. Table 13-2 lists the properties of the Document object that are specified in the W3C DOM.

Property	Description
anchors[]	Returns an array of the document's anchor elements
body	Returns the document's <body> element
cookie	Returns the current document's cookie string, which contains small pieces of information about a user that are stored by a Web server in text files on the user's computer
domain	Returns the domain name of the server where the current document is located
forms[]	Returns an array of the document's forms
images[]	Returns an array of the document's images
links[]	Returns an array of a document's links
referrer	Returns the Uniform Resource Locator (URL) of the document that provided a link to the current document
title	Returns or sets the title of the document as specified by the <title> element in the document <head> section
URL	Returns the URL of the current document

Table 13-2   HTML DOM Document object properties

The only property you can dynamically change after a Web page is rendered is the title property, which allows you to change the document title that is specified by the <title> element in the document <head> section. For example, the following statement can be used to change the text displayed in the title bar after the Web page is rendered:

```
document.title = "Pete's Pizzeria Home Page";
```

Opening and Closing the Document Object

Although the Document object's write() and writeln() methods
are part of the DOM, they cannot be used to change content after a
Web page has been rendered. You can write code that executes the
write() and writeln() methods in the current document after it is
rendered, but they replace the content that is currently displayed in
the Web browser window.

You can, however, use the **open() method** to create a new document
in a window and then use the write() and writeln() methods to
add content to the new document. The **close() method** notifies the
Web browser that you are finished writing to the window and that the
document should be displayed. Although later versions of Internet
Explorer and Netscape do not require you to use the open() and
close() methods with the write() and writeln() methods, some
older browsers do not display any content in the window until you
execute the close() method. In addition, some browsers, including
Firefox, do not stop the spinning icon in the browser's upper-right
corner that indicates a document is loading until the close() method
executes. Because Firefox is the most widely used browser, you should
always use the open() and close() methods when dynamically
creating document content.

You should always use the open() and close() methods when you
want to use the write() and writeln() methods to update the text
displayed in an existing window. Specifically, if you do not use the
close() method to notify the Web browser that you are finished
writing to the window, any new calls to the write() and writeln()
methods are appended to the existing text that is currently displayed
in the window.

Next, you start working on a Web site for a flight-training school
called DRG Aviation. You will find three prewritten Web pages
named index.html, flighttraining.html, and instruments.html in
the DRGAviation folder in your Chapter folder for Chapter 13. The
index.html file is the home page, the flighttraining.html file contains
information on private pilot training, and the instruments.html file
contains information on flight instrument training. You will modify
these Web pages throughout the chapter.

The DRG Aviation Web pages do not contain <h1> elements. You will
write code that uses the title property of each DRG Aviation Web
page as its <h1> element.

To write code that uses the `title` property of each DRG Aviation Web page as its `<h1>` element:

1. Start your text editor and open the home page for DRG Aviation, **index.html**, from the DRGAviation folder in your Chapter folder for Chapter 13.

2. Locate the table with an ID of "content" and add the following script section above it. The script section contains statements that add the value of the Document object's `title` property to the Web page as an `<h1>` element.

```
<script type="text/javascript">
/* <![CDATA[ */
document.open();
document.write("<h1>" + document.title
    + "</h1>");
document.close();
/* ]]> */
</script>
```

3. Save the **index.html** file, but leave the document open in your text editor.

4. Open the **flighttraining.html** file. Above the `<div>` element with an ID of "content", add the script section shown in Step 2.

5. Save the **flighttraining.html** file, but leave the document open in your text editor.

6. Open the **instruments.html** file. Above the `<div>` element with an ID of "content", add the script section shown in Step 2.

7. Save the **instruments.html** file, but leave the document open in your text editor.

8. Return to the **index.html** file in your Web browser. As you can see in Figure 13-1, the first heading on the page, DRG Aviation Home, is created by using the value assigned to the `title` property of the Web page's Document object.

Figure 13-1   DRG Aviation home page

9.   Close your Web browser window.

Short Quiz 1

1.   How can you make Web pages dynamic?

2.   What is the most important aspect of DHTML and why?

3.   Explain why you would use the open() and close() methods of the DOM.

Using the Image Object

This chapter cannot possibly explain all the objects in the HTML DOM, but you should be familiar with the Image object. An **Image object** represents an image created using the <img> element. You need to use an Image object if you want to dynamically change an image that is displayed on a Web page. As you learned in Chapter 11, the `images[]` array contains `Image` objects that represent all the `<img>` elements on a Web page. `Image` objects for each `<img>` element are assigned to the elements of the `images[]` array in the order that they appear on the Web page. The first `Image` object is represented by `images[0]`, the second `Image` object is represented by `images[1]`, and so on.

The `Image` object contains various properties that you can use to manipulate your objects. Table 13-3 lists these properties.

Property	Description
align	Returns or sets the alignment of an image in relation to the surrounding text; you can assign one of the following values to this property: left, right, top, middle, or bottom
alt	Returns or sets the image's alternate text
border	Returns or sets the border width, in pixels
height	Returns or sets the image height, in pixels
isMap	Returns a Boolean value that indicates whether the image is a server-side image map
longDesc	Returns or sets an image's long description
name	Returns or sets the image name
src	Returns or sets the URL of the displayed image
useMap	Returns or sets the image to be used as a client-side image map
vspace	Returns or sets the amount of vertical space, in pixels, above and below the image
width	Returns or sets the image width, in pixels

Table 13-3   `Image` object properties

You have already used one of the most important parts of the `Image` object, the **src property**, which allows JavaScript to dynamically change an image. Changing the value assigned to the `src` property changes the `src` attribute associated with an `<img>` element, which dynamically changes an image displayed on a Web page. For instance, you can change the displayed image for an image named `companyLogo` by using a statement such as `document.companyLogo.src = "new_image.jpg";`.

Next, you will add an image to the DRG Aviation home page that asks visitors if they have ever dreamed of flying. Clicking the image displays another image that advertises a "discovery flight" from DRG Aviation. The DRGAviation/images folder in your Chapter folder for Chapter 13 contains two images named dream.gif and discover.gif that you can use for the exercise.

To add an image to the DRG Aviation home page:

1. Return to the **index.html** file in your text editor.

2. Within the table that has an ID of "content", locate the <div> element with an ID of "special" and add the following image element immediately above it. The onclick event handler uses the this reference to change the value assigned to the src property to "discover.gif". Recall that the this reference simply refers to the current element.

    ```
    <img src="images/dream.gif" width="288" height="204"
    alt="Visual formatting element"
    onclick="this.src='images/discover.gif'" />
    ```

3. Save the **index.html** file and open it in your Web browser. When the file first opens, it displays the image shown in Figure 13-2.

Figure 13-2   Default image displayed on the DRG Aviation home page

4. Click the image. The current image is replaced with the image shown in Figure 13-3.

Figure 13-3 DRG Aviation home page after clicking the banner image

    5.   Close your Web browser window.

Animation with the **Image** Object

As you learned in Chapter 11, you can create simple animation on a
Web page by combining the src attribute of the Image object with the
setTimeout() or setInterval() method. The following code uses
the setInterval() method to automatically swap two advertising
images every couple of seconds. Figure 13-4 shows the two images
displayed in a browser.

```
...
<script type="text/javascript">
/* <![CDATA[ */
var curBanner="soccer1";
function changeBanner() {
    if (curBanner == "soccer2") {
        document.images[0].src
            = "soccer1.gif";
        curBanner = "soccer1";
    }
```

```
            else {
                document.images[0].src
                    = "soccer2.gif";
                curBanner = "soccer2";
            }
        }
        /* ]]> */
        </script>
        </head>
        <body onload="var
            begin=setInterval('changeBanner()',2000);">
        <p><img src="soccer1.gif" name="banner"
            alt="Changing image for Central Valley
            Sporting Goods" /></p>
        </body>
        </html>
```

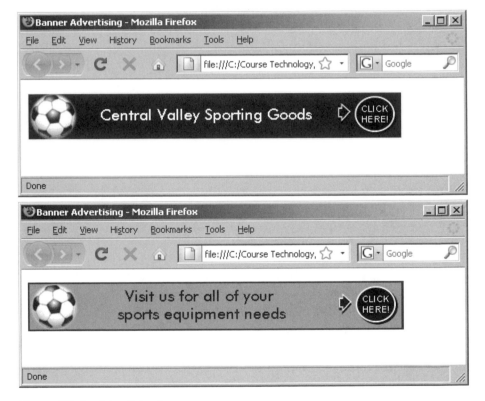

Figure 13-4   Advertising images

 The Central Valley Sporting Goods Web page is provided as a file named SportingGoods.html in the Chapter folder for Chapter 13 on your Data Disk.

While the advertising images can be loosely termed "animation," true animation requires a different image, or frame, for each movement that a character or object makes. While swapping two images is simple enough, you need to understand more about working with the Image object when you want animation to include multiple images.

As an example of a more complex animation sequence, Figure 13-5 shows 16 frames; each frame shows a unicycle in a slightly different position.

This book does not teach the artistic skills necessary for creating frames in an animation sequence. Instead, the goal is to show how to use JavaScript and the **Image** object to perform simple animation by swapping frames displayed by an <img> element.

Figure 13-5 Unicycle animation frames

You create an animated sequence with JavaScript by using the setInterval() or setTimeout() method to cycle through the frames in an animation series. Each iteration of a setInterval() or setTimeout() method changes the frame displayed by an <img> element. The speed of the animation depends on how many milliseconds are passed as an argument to the setInterval() or setTimeout() method.

The following code animates the frames in Figure 13-5. The code assigns the frames to a unicycle[] array. Once the Turn button is clicked, a setInterval() method calls the turn() function, which executes an if...else statement that changes the displayed frame based on the curUnicycle variable. Once the curUnicycle variable reaches 15 (the highest element in an array with 16 elements), it resets to zero (the first element in the array), and the animation sequence starts over from the beginning. The name of each image for the frames corresponds to an element number in the unicycle[] array. The Stop button uses the clearInterval() method to stop the setInterval() method. Figure 13-6 shows an example of the script in a Web browser.

```
<!DOCTYPE html PUBLIC "-//W3C//DTD XHTML 1.0 Strict//EN"
"http://www.w3.org/TR/xhtml1/DTD/xhtml1-strict.dtd">
<html xmlns="http://www.w3.org/1999/xhtml">
<head>
<title>Unicycle</title>
<meta http-equiv="content-type"
    content="text/html;charset=iso-8859-1" />
<script type="text/javascript">
/* <![CDATA[ */
var turnUnicycle;
var unicycle = new Array(16);
var curUnicycle = 0;
unicycle[0] = "unicycle0.gif";
unicycle[1] = "unicycle1.gif";
unicycle[2] = "unicycle2.gif";
unicycle[3] = "unicycle3.gif";
unicycle[4] = "unicycle4.gif";
unicycle[5] = "unicycle5.gif";
unicycle[6] = "unicycle6.gif";
unicycle[7] = "unicycle7.gif";
unicycle[8] = "unicycle8.gif";
unicycle[9] = "unicycle9.gif";
unicycle[10] = "unicycle10.gif";
unicycle[11] = "unicycle11.gif";
unicycle[12] = "unicycle12.gif";
unicycle[13] = "unicycle13.gif";
unicycle[14] = "unicycle14.gif";
unicycle[15] = "unicycle15.gif";
function turn() {
    if (curUnicycle == 15)
        curUnicycle = 0;
    else
        ++curUnicycle;
    document.images[0].src
        = unicycle[curUnicycle];
}
function startTurning() {
    if (turnUnicycle != null)
        clearInterval(turnUnicycle);
    turnUnicycle = setInterval("turn()", 100);
}
/* ]]> */
</script>
</head>
<body>
<p><img src="unicycle0.gif" height="75"
width="75" /></p>
<form action="">
<p><input type="button" value=" Turn "
onclick="startTurning();" />
<input type="button" value=" Stop "
onclick="clearInterval(turnUnicycle);" /></p>
</form>
</body>
</html>
```

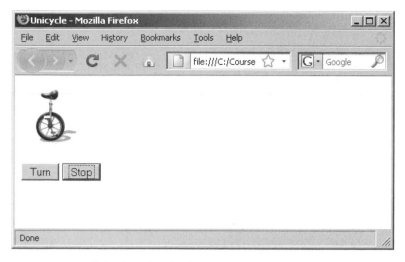

You can find a copy of the preceding Unicycle animation page, named Unicycle.html, along with the required image files in the Chapter folder for Chapter 13 on your Data Disk.

703

Figure 13-6   Unicycle animation in a Web browser

Notice that the preceding code includes a function named `startTurning()`, which is called from the Turn button in the document body. The `if` statement determines whether the animation is already running by checking to see if the `turnUnicycle` variable is equal to null. This technique enables you to quickly check whether an object exists or if a variable has been initialized. If the `setInterval()` method has been called and assigned to the `turnUnicycle` variable, then the conditional expression returns a value of true, which causes the `if` statement to execute the `clearInterval()` method and cancel the animation. If you do not include the `if` statement, then the user could click the Turn button several times, which would cause multiple instances of the `setInterval()` method to occur. Multiple instances of the same `setInterval()` method cause your computer to execute as many animation sequences as there are instances of the `setInterval()` method, which could make the animation appear to run faster than desired or function erratically.

Next, you will modify the Private Pilot Training page so that it includes an animated image of an airplane. The DRGAviation/images folder in your Chapter folder for Chapter 13 contains 24 images, airplane0.gif through airplane23.gif, that you can use for this exercise.

To modify the Private Pilot Training page so that it includes an animated image of an airplane:

1. Return to the **flighttraining.html** file in your text editor.

2. Add the following script section to the document head, just above the closing </head> tag:

```
<script type="text/javascript">
/* <![CDATA[ */
/* ]]> */
</script>
```

3. In the script section, add the following variable definitions and function, which change the displayed image. The code is very similar to the unicycle animation code you saw earlier in this section.

```
var plane = new Array(24);
var curPlane = 0;
plane[0] = "airplane0.gif";
plane[1] = "airplane1.gif";
plane[2] = "airplane2.gif";
plane[3] = "airplane3.gif";
plane[4] = "airplane4.gif";
plane[5] = "airplane5.gif";
plane[6] = "airplane6.gif";
plane[7] = "airplane7.gif";
plane[8] = "airplane8.gif";
plane[9] = "airplane9.gif";
plane[10] = "airplane10.gif";
plane[11] = "airplane11.gif";
plane[12] = "airplane12.gif";
plane[13] = "airplane13.gif";
plane[14] = "airplane14.gif";
plane[15] = "airplane15.gif";
plane[16] = "airplane16.gif";
plane[17] = "airplane17.gif";
plane[18] = "airplane18.gif";
plane[19] = "airplane19.gif";
plane[20] = "airplane20.gif";
plane[21] = "airplane21.gif";
plane[22] = "airplane22.gif";
plane[23] = "airplane23.gif";
function fly() {
    if (curPlane == 23)
        curPlane = 0;
    else
        ++curPlane;
    document.images[8].src = "images/"
        + plane[curPlane];
}
```

4. Add an onload event handler to the opening <body> element as follows. The setInterval() method is used to start the animation:

```
<body onload="setInterval('fly()', 150)">
```

5. Locate the `<td>` element that displays the Photo2.jpg file as a background image. Add the following image element to the `<td>` element to display the first file in the airplane animation, airplane0.gif:

```
<img src="images/airplane0.gif"
    width="263" height="175"
    alt="Image of an airplane." />
```

6. Save the **flighttraining.html** file, and then open it in your Web browser. An image of an airplane appears to fly on your screen, as shown in Figure 13-7.

Figure 13-7 flighttraining.html after adding an animated image of an airplane

7. Close your Web browser window.

Image Caching

In the airplane program, you may have noticed that the loading of each image was jerky, erratic, or slow, and that the URL for each image flickered in the status bar each time the image changed. This happened because JavaScript does not save a copy of the image in memory that can be used whenever necessary. Instead, each time a different image is loaded by an `<img>` element, JavaScript must open or reopen the image from its source. You probably accessed the airplane image files directly from the Data Disk on your local computer, and if you have a particularly fast computer, you may not have noticed a loading problem. If you did notice erratic loading of the images, then you can imagine how erratic and slow the animation would appear if you had to download the images from the Web server each time they are loaded. A technique for eliminating multiple downloads of the same file is called **image caching**. Image caching temporarily stores image files in memory on a local computer. This technique allows JavaScript to store and retrieve an image from memory rather than download the image each time it is needed.

Images are cached using the `Image()` constructor of the `Image` object. The `Image()` constructor creates a new `Image` object. Caching an image in JavaScript requires three steps:

1. Create a new object using the `Image()` constructor.

2. Assign a graphic file to the `src` property of the new `Image` object.

3. Assign the `src` property of the new `Image` object to the `src` property of an `<img>` element.

In the following code, the `src` attribute of the `<img>` element is initially set to an empty string `""`. In the script section, a new `Image` object named `newImage` is created. The `newImage` object is used to save and access the memory cache containing the image file. A file named graphic.jpg is assigned to the `src` property of the `newImage` object. The `src` property of the `newImage` object is then assigned to the `src` property of the `<img>` element.

```
<body>
<img src="" height="100" width="100" alt="Description" />
<script type="text/javascript">
/* <![CDATA[ */
var newImage = new Image();
newImage.src = "graphic.jpg";
document.images[0].src = newImage.src;
/* ]]> */
</script>
</body>
```

Be sure to understand that, in the preceding code, the graphic.jpg file is not assigned directly to the `src` property of the `<img>` element. Instead, the `newImage` object is assigned to the `src` property of the `<img>` element. If you assigned the graphic.jpg file directly to the `src` property of the `<img>` element using the statement `document.myImage.src = "graphic.jpg";`, then the file would reload from its source each time it was needed. The `newImage` object opens the file once and saves it to a memory cache.

The following code shows a version of the unicycle animation code modified to use image caching. The lines that add each image file to the `unicycle[]` array have been replaced by a `for` loop, which assigns a new object to each element of the `unicycle[]` array until the `imagesLoaded` variable is greater than the length of the array. In the `for` loop, each object in the `unicycle[]` array is assigned an image file using the `src` property. In the `turn()` function, the `unicycle[curUnicycle]` operator in the statement `document.images[0].src = unicycle[curUnicycle];` now includes the `src` property so that the statement reads `document.images[0].src = unicycle[curUnicycle].src;`.

```
<!DOCTYPE html
PUBLIC "-//W3C//DTD XHTML 1.0 Strict//EN"
"http://www.w3.org/TR/xhtml1/DTD/↵
    xhtml1-strict.dtd">
<html xmlns="http://www.w3.org/1999/xhtml">
<head>
<title>Unicycle</title>
<meta http-equiv="content-type"
    content="text/html;charset=iso-8859-1" />
<script type="text/javascript">
/* <![CDATA[ */
var turnUnicycle;
var unicycle = new Array(16);
var curUnicycle = 0;
for (var imagesLoaded=0; imagesLoaded < 16;
    ++imagesLoaded) {
    unicycle[imagesLoaded] = new Image();
    unicycle[imagesLoaded].src = "unicycle"
        + imagesLoaded + ".gif";
}
function turn() {
    if (curUnicycle == 15)
        curUnicycle = 0;
    else
        ++curUnicycle;
    document.images[0].src
        = unicycle[curUnicycle].src;
}
function startTurning() {
    if (turnUnicycle != null)
        clearInterval(turnUnicycle);
    turnUnicycle = setInterval("turn()",
        100);
}
/* ]]> */
</script>
</head>
<body>
<p><img src="unicycle0.gif" height="75"
    width="75" /></p>
```

You can find a copy of the preceding Unicycle Web page, named UnicycleCache1.html, along with the required image files in the Chapter folder for Chapter 13 on your Data Disk.

```
<form action="">
<p><input type="button" value=" Turn "
onclick="startTurning();" />
<input type="button" value=" Stop "
onclick="clearInterval(turnUnicycle);" /></p>
</form>
</body>
</html>
```

Next, you will modify the airplane animation in the flighttraining.html document to include image caching.

To modify the airplane animation in the flighttraining.html document to include image caching:

1. Return to the **flighttraining.html** file in your text editor.

2. Replace the 24 statements that assign each airplane frame to the plane[] array with the following for loop. The imagesLoaded variable keeps track of the number of cached images, and the for loop creates a new Image object within each element of the plane[] array. Each object in the plane[] array is then assigned an image file using the src property.

   ```
   for (var imagesLoaded=0; imagesLoaded < 24;
        ++imagesLoaded) {
   plane[imagesLoaded] = new Image();
   plane[imagesLoaded].src
        = "images/airplane"
        + imagesLoaded + ".gif";
   }
   ```

3. Delete the "images/ +" string from the document.images[8].src = "images/" + plane[curPlane]; statement in the fly() function. In place of the string, add the src property so that the statement reads as follows:

   ```
   document.images[8].src = plane[curPlane].src;
   ```

4. Save the **flighttraining.html** document, and open it in your Web browser. If the animation was erratic before, the new animation should appear smoother.

5. Close your Web browser window.

Even when you use image caching, the images must all be loaded into an Image object before the animation will function correctly. Often, you will want the animation to start as soon as a page finishes loading, as is the case with the airplane animation. However, even though a page has finished loading, all the images may not have finished downloading and may not be stored in image caches. If you run the airplane animation across an Internet connection, the onload

event handler of the <body> element may execute the animation
sequence before all the frames are transferred and assigned to Image
objects (depending on Internet connection speed). The animation
will still function, but it will be erratic until all the images have been
successfully stored in Image objects. To be certain that all images are
downloaded into a cache before commencing an animation sequence,
you use the onload event handler of the Image object.

The following code shows another modified version of the unicycle
script. This time, the program does not include a Turn or Stop button.
Instead, the for loop now contains an if statement that checks
whether the imagesLoaded variable is equal to 15, which indicates
that all the images have been downloaded. Once the imagesLoaded
variable equals 15, the turn() function executes using the same
setInterval() statement that was originally located in the onclick
event for the Turn button. Notice that the code no longer includes
the startTurning() function. Once all the images are cached in the
unicycle[] array, the turn() function executes automatically.

```
<!DOCTYPE html
PUBLIC "-//W3C//DTD XHTML 1.0 Strict//EN"
"http://www.w3.org/TR/xhtml1/DTD/↵
    xhtml1-strict.dtd">
<html xmlns="http://www.w3.org/1999/xhtml">
<head>
<title>Unicycle</title>
<meta http-equiv="content-type"
    content="text/html;charset=iso-8859-1" />
<script type="text/javascript">
/* <![CDATA[ */
var turnUnicycle;
var unicycle = new Array(16);
var curUnicycle = 0;
for (var imagesLoaded=0; imagesLoaded < 16;
    ++imagesLoaded) {
    unicycle[imagesLoaded] = new Image();
    unicycle[imagesLoaded].src = "unicycle"
        + imagesLoaded + ".gif";
    if (imagesLoaded == 15)
        turnUnicycle
            = setInterval("turn()", 100);
}
function turn() {
    if (curUnicycle == 15)
        curUnicycle = 0;
    else
        ++curUnicycle;
    document.images[0].src
        = unicycle[curUnicycle].src;
}
/* ]]> */
</script>
```

You can find a copy of the preceding Unicycle Web page, named UnicycleCache2.html, along with the required image files in the Chapter folder for Chapter 13 on your Data Disk.

710

```
</head>
<body>
<p><img src="unicycle0.gif" height="75"
    width="75" /></p>
</body>
</html>
```

Next, you add an if statement that executes the animation after all the images load.

To add an if statement to the airplane animation that executes the animation after all the images load:

1. Return to the **flighttraining.html** file in your text editor.

2. Add the following if statement to the end of the for loop. After all the images are loaded, the if statement uses the setInterval() method to call the fly() function.

   ```
   if (imagesLoaded == 23)
       setInterval("fly()", 150);
   ```

3. Delete the onload event handler from the opening <body> tag. You no longer need it because the animation is started by the image onload event handler.

4. Save the **flighttraining.html** file and open it in your Web browser. The animation should begin as soon as all the images load.

5. Close your Web browser window.

Short Quiz 2

1. Why do you need to use the Image object?

2. How do you create basic animation with the Image object?

3. Why and how do you need to ensure that all images are downloaded into a cache before commencing an animation sequence?

Accessing Document Elements

Up to this point in the book, you have accessed HTML elements as properties of the Document object. For example, the statement document.forms[0].email.value returns the value in a text box named email from the first form in a document. Although this method works well, it has its limitations because you can only access anchor, form, image, and link elements. But what if you want to access a paragraph (`<p>`) or table (`<table>`) element? To access any element in a document with JavaScript—and modify it dynamically—you must use one of the following methods of the Document object: `getElementsByName()`, `getElementsByTagName()`, or `getElementById()`. The use of these methods is required for many types of DHTML and AJAX techniques, so you will use them for the remainder of this book.

Accessing Elements by Name

The **getElementsByName() method** returns an array of elements with a name attribute that matches a specified value. You append the getElementsByName() method to the Document object and pass it a single argument representing the name attribute of the elements you want to retrieve. For example, consider the following form, which creates four check boxes. The name attribute of each check box is assigned a value of committees.

```
<form action="FormProcessor.html" method="get"
enctype="application/x-www-form-urlencoded"
onsubmit="return submitForm()">
<p>Which committees would you like to serve on?</p>
<p><input type="checkbox" name="committees"
value="program_dev" />Program Development
<br />
<input type="checkbox" name="committees"
value="fundraising" />Fundraising<br />
<input type="checkbox" name="committees"
value="pub_relations" />Public Relations
<br />
<input type="checkbox" name="committees"
value="education" />Education</p>
<p><input type="submit" /></p>
</form>
```

In Chapter 12, you saw the following event handler function, which executes when the form is submitted. This function uses the forms[] array to access the array of elements that represent the check boxes with the name attribute of committees and determine whether at least one check box in the group is selected.

```
function submitForm() {
    var committeesSelected = false;
    for (var i = 0; i < 4; ++i) {
        if (document.forms[0].committees[i]
            .checked == true) {
            committeesSelected = true;
            break;
        }
    }
}
```

```
        if (committeesSelected == false) {
            window.alert("You must select at ⏎
                least one committee.");
                return committeesSelected;
        }
        else
            return committeesSelected;
}
```

Now consider the following modified version of the event handler function. In this version, the function uses the getElementsByName() method to return an array of elements that represent the check boxes with the name attribute of committees.

```
function submitForm() {
    var committeesSelected = false;
    var selectedCommittees = document
        .getElementsByName("committees");
    for (var i=0; i<selectedCommittees.length;
        ++i) {
        if (selectedCommittees[i].checked
            == true) {
            committeesSelected = true;
            break;
        }
    }
    if (committeesSelected == false) {
        window.alert("You must select at ⏎
            least one committee.");
            return committeesSelected;
    }
    else
        return committeesSelected;
}
```

Keep in mind that the getElementsByName() method always returns an array, even if there is only one element in the document with a matching name attribute. If a document only contains a single element with the specified name, you must refer to it in your JavaScript code by using the first index (0) of the returned array. For example, suppose that you have a form with a text box whose name attribute is assigned a value of "email", and it is the only element in the document with that value assigned to its name attribute. The following statement demonstrates how to create an array consisting of a single element with a value of "email" assigned to its name attribute, and then display its value in an alert dialog box:

```
var email = document.getElementsByName(
    "email");
window.alert(email[0].value);
```

With methods like getElementsByName(), which always return an array, you can also append the index number of the element you want to access to the statement containing the method, as follows:

```
window.alert(document.getElementsByName(
    "email")[0].value);
```

Next, you will modify the flighttraining.html document so that it uses the getElementsByName() method to refer to the element containing the airplane image.

To modify the flighttraining.html document so that it uses the getElementsByName() method to refer to the element containing the airplane image:

1. Return to the **flighttraining.html** file in your text editor.

2. Locate the following statement in the fly() function:

   ```
   document.images[8].src = plane[curPlane].src;
   ```

3. Modify the statement you located in the previous step so that it uses the getElementsByName() method to refer to the element containing the airplane image:

   ```
   document.getElementsByName(
       "airplaneImage")[0].src
       = plane[curPlane].src;
   ```

4. Add the following bolded name attribute (with a value of "airplaneImage") to the element containing the airplane image:

   ```
   <td><img src="airplane0.gif"
   name="airplaneImage" height="300" width="200"
   alt="Image of an airplane." /></td>
   ```

5. Save the **flighttraining.html** file, and open it in your Web browser. The animation should begin as soon as all the images load.

6. Close your Web browser window.

Accessing Elements by Tag Name

The **getElementsByTagName() method** is similar to the getElementsByName() method, with an important exception: Instead of returning an array of elements with a name attribute that matches a specified value, it returns an array of elements that matches a specified tag name. You append the getElementsByTagName() method to the Document object and pass it a single argument representing the name of the elements you want to retrieve. As an example, the following statement returns an array of all the paragraph (<p>) tags in a document:

```
var docParagraphs = document
    .getElementsByTagName("p");
```

714

 Be sure not to include the tag name's brackets (such as "<p>") in the argument you pass to the getElementsByTagName() method.

Consider the following modified version of the form that contains the committee check boxes. This version contains radio buttons that allow users to select "Yes" if they want to serve on a committee or "No" if they don't. Clicking one of the radio buttons calls a function named enableCommittees() and passes it a Boolean value of true (to disable the committee check boxes) or false (to enable them).

```
<form action="FormProcessor.html" method="get"
enctype="application/x-www-form-urlencoded"
onsubmit="return submitForm()">
<p>Would you like to serve on a committee?</p>
<p><input type="radio" name="committeeInvolvement"
checked="checked" onclick="enableCommittees(false)" /> Yes
<input type="radio" name="committeeInvolvement"
onclick="enableCommittees(true)" /> No</p>
<p>Which committees would you like to serve on? </p>
<p><input type="checkbox" name="committees"
value="program_dev" />Program Development
<br />
<input type="checkbox" name="committees"
value="fundraising" />Fundraising<br />
<input type="checkbox" name="committees"
value="pub_relations" />Public Relations
<br />
<input type="checkbox" name="committees"
value="education" />Education</p>
<p><input type="submit" /></p>
</form>
```

The following enableCommittees() function demonstrates how to use the getElementsByTagName() method. The function's first statement uses the getElementsByTagName() method to return an array of all the <input> elements in the document, which is then assigned to a variable named committeeBoxes[]. Then, the for loop iterates through each of the elements in the committeeBoxes[] array and checks the value of each Input object's type property. If the type property is equal to "checkbox", then the element is enabled or disabled by assigning the value of the boolValue variable to the disabled property of the Input object.

```
function enableCommittees(boolValue) {
    var committeeBoxes = document
        .getElementsByTagName("input");
    for (var i-0; i<committeeBoxes.length;
    ++i) {
        if (committeeBoxes[i].type
            == "checkbox")
            committeeBoxes[i].disabled
            = boolValue;
    }
}
```

The getElementsByTagName() method works the same way as the getElementsByName() method in that it always returns an array, even if only one element in the document matches the specified tag name. For example, with a document that contains a single form submitted with the POST method, the following document.write() statement refers to the first element in the array returned from a getElementsByTagName() method that is passed a value of "form". The statement prints, "The form will be submitted with the post method."

```
document.write(
    "<p>The form will be submitted with the "
    + document.getElementsByTagName(
    "form")[0].method + " method.</p>");
```

Next, you will modify the flighttraining.html document to use the getElementsByTagName() method instead of the getElementsByName() method to refer to the element containing the airplane image.

To modify the flighttraining.html document to use the getElementsByTagName() method to refer to the element containing the airplane image:

1. Return to the **flighttraining.html** file in your text editor.

2. Modify the last statement in the fly() function so that it uses the getElementsByTagName() method and the <img> tag name to refer to the element containing the airplane image, as follows:

    ```
    document.getElementsByTagName("img")[8].src
        = plane[curPlane].src;
    ```

3. Save the **flighttraining.html** file, and open it in your Web browser. The animation should begin as soon as all the images load.

4. Close your Web browser window.

Accessing Elements by ID

The getElementsByName() and getElementsByTagName() methods are extremely useful if you need to work with collections of elements that have the same name attribute or are of the same type. However, if you are only interested in accessing a single element, you should use the **getElementById() method**, which returns the first element in a document with a matching id attribute. You append the getElementById() method to the Document object and pass it a single argument representing the ID of the element you want to retrieve. For example, consider again a document that contains a single form submitted with the POST method and that has a value of customerInfo assigned to its ID attribute. The following document.write() statement uses the getElementById() method to access the form and its method attribute:

```
document.write(
    "<p>The form will be submitted with the "
    + document.getElementById(
    "customerInfo").method + " method.</p>");
```

As another example, the following statement uses the getElementById() method to retrieve a value entered into a text box that is assigned an id attribute of email:

```
window.alert(
    "You entered the following e-mail address: "
    + document.getElementById("email").value);
```

Be sure to notice that the getElementById() method does not refer to an array because it only returns a single element, unlike the getElementsByName() and getElementsByTagName() methods, which return arrays. If your document contains multiple elements with the same id attribute, then the getElementById() method only returns the first matching element.

 A common mistake when using the getElementById() method is to capitalize the last "d," as in getElementByID(), which causes an error because JavaScript is case sensitive.

Next, you will modify the flighttraining.html document so that it uses the getElementById() method instead of the getElementsByTagName() method to refer to the element containing the airplane image.

To modify the flighttraining.html document so that it uses the getElementById() method instead of the getElementsByTagName() method to refer to the element containing the airplane image:

1. Return to the **flighttraining.html** file in your text editor.

2. Modify the name="airplaneImage" attribute in the <img> element to **id="airplaneImage"**.

3. Modify the last statement in the fly() function so that it uses the getElementById() method and the airplaneImage ID to refer to the element containing the airplane image, as follows:

    ```
    document.getElementById("airplaneImage").src
        = plane[curPlane].src;
    ```

4. Save the **flighttraining.html** file, and open it in your Web browser. The animation should begin as soon as all the images load.

5. Close your Web browser window.

Modifying Elements with the innerHTML Property

Another element used for accessing elements is the **innerHTML property**, which sets and retrieves the contents of a specified element. The innerHTML property was originally introduced by Microsoft into Internet Explorer browsers, but it has been adopted by most current Web browsers. The W3C has not officially approved the innerHTML property as part of the DOM, but it probably will at some point because of the method's growing popularity and versatility. In comparison to the document.write() and document.writeln() methods, which cannot be used to change content after a Web page has been rendered, the innerHTML property allows you to retrieve and modify the contents of almost any element without having to reload the entire Web page. In fact, many JavaScript programmers view the innerHTML property as a replacement for the document.write() and document.writeln() methods.

Although the innerHTML property is popular with many JavaScript programmers, it also has detractors. To learn about the arguments against using the innerHTML property, along with some alternative solutions, search the Web for "alternatives to innerHTML." These alternative solutions primarily use fairly complex techniques involving the XML DOM. It's important to point out that one of the greatest benefits of JavaScript is its simplicity and ease of use, but using the XML DOM to manipulate Web pages is anything but simple. In this author's opinion, any techniques that continue to make JavaScript easier to understand and use, such as the innerHTML property, should be embraced over more complex solutions.

To use the innerHTML property, you append it to an object representing the element whose value you want to retrieve or modify. As an example, the following paragraph element contains an anchor element that displays the text "How's this for a deal?". An onmouseover event uses the innerHTML property and a this reference to change the contents of the anchor element to "Order now and receive 20% off!". Then, an onmouseout event uses the innerHTML property and a this reference to change the contents of the anchor element back to "How's this for a deal?".

```
<p><a href="sales.html" id="salesLink"
onmouseover="this.innerHTML='Order now ↵
    and receive 20% off!'"
onmouseout="this.innerHTML='How\'s this for ↵
    a deal?'">How's this for a deal?</a></p>
```

You can also append the innerHTML property to an element that is returned from the getElementById(), getElementsByName(), or getElementsByTagName() method. The following example shows the same code that uses the innerHTML property to change the link text, but this version uses the getElementById() method instead of a this reference:

```
<p><a href="sales.html" id="salesLink"
onmouseover="document.getElementById( ↵
    'salesLink').innerHTML='Order now and ↵
    receive 20% off!'"
onmouseout="document.getElementById( ↵
    'salesLink').innerHTML='How\'s this for ↵
    a deal?'">How's this for a deal?</a></p>
```

Next, you will modify the DRG Aviation pages so that they use the innerHTML property to set the value assigned to the <h1> element.

To modify the DRG Aviation pages so that they use the innerHTML property to set the value assigned to the <h1> element:

1. Return to the **flighttraining.html** file in your text editor.

2. Replace the document.open(), document.write(), and document.close() statements in the second script section with the following statements, which use the getElementById() method, getElementsByTagName()

method, and `innerHTML` property to set the value assigned to the <h1> element:

```
document.write("<h1 id='mainHeading'></h1>");
document.getElementById("mainHeading")
    .innerHTML = document
    .getElementsByTagName("title")[0]
    .innerHTML;
```

3. Save the **flighttraining.html** file, and validate it with the W3C Markup Validation Service. Once the file is valid, close it in your text editor.

4. Return to the **index.html** file in your text editor, and modify the script section with the same changes you made in Step 2.

5. Save the **index.html** file, and validate it with the W3C Markup Validation Service. Once the file is valid, close it in your text editor.

6. Return to the **instruments.html** file in your text editor, and modify the script section with the same changes you made in Step 2.

7. Save the **instruments.html** file, and validate it with the W3C Markup Validation Service. Once the file is valid, close it in your text editor.

8. Open the **index.html** file in your Web browser. The first heading on the page, DRG Aviation, uses the `innerHTML` property to access the value assigned to the `title` property of the Web page's `document` object. Test the links for the Flight Training and Instrument Training Web pages. The headings should display the value assigned to the `title` property of each Web page's `document` object.

9. Close your Web browser and text editor.

Short Quiz 3

1. Explain how to access elements by name.

2. Explain how to access elements by tag name.

3. Explain how to access elements by ID.

4. Explain how to modify elements with the `innerHTML` property.

Summing Up

- Dynamic HTML (DHTML) refers to a combination of technologies that make Web pages dynamic.

- DHTML is a combination of JavaScript, XHTML, CSS, and the Document Object Model.

- At the core of DHTML is the Document Object Model, or DOM, which represents the Web page displayed in a browser.

- The Document Object Model that represents HTML content is referred to as the HTML DOM, and the Document Object Model that represents XML content is referred to as the XML DOM.

- Through the Document object, you can access other objects that represent elements on a Web page.

- The open() method creates a new document in a window.

- The close() method notifies the Web browser that you are finished writing to the window and that the document should be displayed.

- You should always use the open() and close() methods when you want to use the document.write()and document.writeln() methods to update the text displayed in an existing window.

- An Image object represents an image created using the <img> element.

- One of the most important properties of the Image object is the src property, which allows JavaScript to change an image dynamically.

- By combining the src attribute of the Image object with the setTimeout() or setInterval() method, you can create simple animation on a Web page.

- Image caching is a technique for eliminating multiple downloads of the same file. Image caching temporarily stores image files in memory, which allows JavaScript to retrieve an image from memory rather than downloading the image each time it is needed.

- You use the onload event handler of the Image object to be certain that all images are downloaded into a cache before commencing an animation sequence.

- The `getElementsByName()` method returns an array of elements with a `name` attribute that matches a specified value.

- The `getElementsByTagName()` method returns an array of elements that matches a specified tag name.

- The `getElementById()` method returns the first element in a document with a matching `id` attribute.

- The `innerHTML` property sets and retrieves the content of a specified element.

Comprehension Check

1. Explain what the word *dynamic* means in Internet terminology.

2. DHTML refers to a combination of which of the following technologies? (Choose all that apply.)

   a. JavaScript

   b. XHTML

   c. CSS

   d. DOM

3. Which of the following Document Object Models can you use to manipulate an XHTML document? (Choose all that apply.)

   a. HTML DOM

   b. XHTML DOM

   c. JSCRIPT DOM

   d. XML DOM

4. Several current browsers, including Firefox and other Mozilla-based Web browsers, Internet Explorer 5.0 and higher, and Netscape 6 and higher, are not compatible with a standardized version of the DOM. In other words, you must write different JavaScript code sections for each type of browser. True or False?

5. The `Document` object is the only element on a Web page that is represented in the DOM by its own object. True or False?

6. Which of the following `Document` object methods should you always use when you want to use the `write()` and `writeln()` methods to update the text displayed in an existing window? (Choose all that apply.)

   a. `close()`

   b. `open()`

   c. `getElementById()`

   d. `getElementsByName()`

7. Which of the following `Document` object properties can be dynamically changed after a Web page is rendered?

   a. `referrer`

   b. `title`

   c. `URL`

   d. `domain`

8. The `close()` method of the `Document` object closes the current window. True or False?

9. Which of the following `Document` object properties returns an array? (Choose all that apply.)

   a. `anchors`

   b. `cookies`

   c. `images`

   d. `forms`

10. Which of the following can be used to refer to an image with JavaScript code? (Choose all that apply.)

    a. `name` attribute

    b. `src` attribute

    c. `value` attribute

    d. `images[]`

11. Which property of the Image object allows JavaScript to change an image dynamically?

    a. URL

    b. value

    c. href

    d. src

12. Why should you use image caching, and what are the procedures for adding image caching to your Web pages?

13. To be certain that all images are downloaded into a cache before commencing an animation sequence, you use the _____ of the Image object.

    a. images[] array

    b. animation property

    c. loadImages() method

    d. onload event handler

14. Why do you use the getElementsByName(), getElementsByTagName(), and getElementById() methods?

15. What value must you pass to the getElementsByName() method?

    a. the id attribute of the element you want to retrieve

    b. the tag name of the elements you want to retrieve

    c. the index of the element in the elements[] array

    d. the name attribute of the elements you want to retrieve

16. The getElementsByName() method only returns an array if it locates multiple elements that match the passed argument; a single variable is returned if only one array element is returned. True or False?

17. Which of the following is the correct syntax for executing the `getElementsByTagName()` method and returning all of a document's <p> tags?

   a. `document.getElementsByTagName("<p>")`

   b. `document.getElementsByTagName("p")`

   c. `document.getElementsByTagName(<p>)`

   d. `document.getElementsByTagName() = "<p>"`

18. The `getElementById()` method always returns an array even if only one element is returned. True or False?

19. Which of the following can be used to access the `innerHTML` property? (Choose all that apply.)

   a. the `this` reference

   b. the `getElementsByName()` method

   c. the `getElementsByTagName()` method

   d. the `getElementById()` method

20. The W3C has not officially approved the `innerHTML` property as part of the DOM. True or False?

Reinforcement Exercises

 Exercise 13-1

The DOM `Anchor` object represents a link on a Web page that is created with an <a> element. Attributes of the <a> element, such as the `href` attribute, are also available as properties of the `Anchor` object. This exercise demonstrates how to use the `href` property of the `Anchor` object, along with the `innerHTML` property, to dynamically change the URL and text of an anchor element. The exercise is an investment information page that provides a link to a recommended investment on Yahoo! Finance according to a particular sector, such as consumer goods or healthcare.

1. Create a new document in your text editor.

2. Type the <!DOCTYPE> declaration, <html> element, header information, and the <body> element. Use the strict DTD and "Investment Picks" as the content of the <title> element.

3. Add the following heading to the document body:

    `<h1>Investment Picks</h1>`

4. Add the following elements and text to the end of the
    document body. The form contains buttons for stock
    recommendations in the nine major sectors (according to
    Yahoo! Finance). Each radio button contains an `onclick` event
    that calls an event handler named `updateInvestmentLink()`,
    which you will add next. Two arguments are passed to
    the `updateInvestmentLink()` function: the name of the
    investment (which will be used as link text) and a URL
    (which will be used as the link's URL).

```
<form action=""
enctype="application/x-www-form-urlencoded">
<p><input type="radio" name="industry"
onclick="updateInvestmentLink('Gold', ↵
'http://finance.yahoo.com/q?s=^YHOh714')" /> Basic
   Materials<br />
<input type="radio" name="industry"
onclick="updateInvestmentLink('General Electric ↵
Industries Ltd.', 'http://finance.yahoo.com/ ↵
q/pr?s=ge')" /> Conglomerates<br />
<input type="radio" name="industry"
onclick="updateInvestmentLink('Tyson Foods ↵
Inc.', 'http://finance.yahoo.com/ ↵
q/pr?s=tsn')" /> Consumer Goods<br />
<input type="radio" name="industry"
onclick="updateInvestmentLink( ↵
'Catalyst Health Solutions', ↵
'http://finance.yahoo.com/q/pr?s=chsi')" />
Financial<br />
<input type="radio" name="industry"
onclick="updateInvestmentLink('Genentech ↵
Inc.', 'http://finance.yahoo.com/ ↵
q/pr?s=dna')" /> Healthcare<br />
<input type="radio" name="industry"
onclick="updateInvestmentLink( ↵
'Toll Brothers', ↵
'http://finance.yahoo.com/q/pr?s=tol')" />
Industrial Goods<br />
<input type="radio" name="industry"
onclick="updateInvestmentLink( ↵
'Sinclair Broadcast Group Inc.', ↵
'http://finance.yahoo.com/q/pr?s=sbgi')" />
Services<br />
<input type="radio" name="industry"
onclick="updateInvestmentLink( ↵
'Verizon Communications Inc.', ↵
'http://finance.yahoo.com/q/pr?s=vz')" />
Technology<br />
<input type="radio" name="industry"
```

```
onclick="updateInvestmentLink(↵
'Northwest Natural Gas Co.',↵
'http://finance.yahoo.com/q/pr?s=nwn')" />
Utilities</p>
</form>
<p><a href="http://finance.yahoo.com/"
id="recommendedInvestment">Yahoo! Finance</a></p>
```

5. Add the following script section to the document head:

```
<script type="text/javascript">
/* <![CDATA[ */
/* ]]> */
</script>
```

6. Add the following updateInvestmentLink() function to the script section. The first statement uses the innerHTML property and the urlText parameter (which is passed as the first argument from the radio buttons) to change the text of the anchor element. The second statement uses the href property of the Anchor object and the urlValue parameter (which is passed as the second argument from the radio buttons) to change the value of the href attribute.

```
function updateInvestmentLink(urlText,
    urlValue) {
    document.getElementById(
        'recommendedInvestment').innerHTML
        = urlText + " (Yahoo! Finance)";
    document.getElementById(
        'recommendedInvestment').href
        = urlValue;
}
```

7. Save the document as **InvestmentPicks.html** in your Exercises folder for Chapter 13, and then validate the document with the W3C Markup Validation Service. Once the document is valid, close it in your text editor.

8. Open the **InvestmentPicks.html** document in your Web browser and test the radio buttons. Clicking each radio button should change the text and URL of the link at the bottom of the page. Be sure to test the link to ensure that it opens the correct URL.

9. Close your Web browser window.

Exercise 13-2

In this exercise, you will create a Web page with an animation of a man using a jackhammer. Your Exercises folder for Chapter 13 contains 11 images that are required for this program: jackhammer0.gif through jackhammer10.gif.

1. Create a new document in your text editor.

2. Type the `<!DOCTYPE>` declaration, `<html>` element, header information, and the `<body>` element. Use the strict DTD and "Jackhammer" as the content of the `<title>` element.

3. Add the following script section to the document head:

```
<script type="text/javascript">
/* <![CDATA[ */
/* ]]> */
</script>
```

4. Add the following text and elements to the document body. The text and elements include an `<img>` element to display the image, and a form with buttons that controls the animation.

```
<h1>Jackhammer Man</h1>
<p><img src="jackhammer1.gif" height="113" width="100"
alt="Image of a man with a jackhammer." /></p>
<form action="" enctype="text/plain"><p>
<input type="button"
value="Start Bouncing"
onclick="startBouncing();" />
<input type="button" value="Stop Bouncing"
onclick="clearInterval(begin);" /></p>
</form>
```

5. Add the following variable declarations to the script section:

```
var jackhammers = new Array(11);
var curJackhammer = 0;
var direction;
var begin;
jackhammers[0] = "jackhammer0.gif";
jackhammers[1] = "jackhammer1.gif";
jackhammers[2] = "jackhammer2.gif";
jackhammers[3] = "jackhammer3.gif";
jackhammers[4] = "jackhammer4.gif";
jackhammers[5] = "jackhammer5.gif";
jackhammers[6] = "jackhammer6.gif";
jackhammers[7] = "jackhammer7.gif";
```

```
jackhammers[8] = "jackhammer8.gif";
jackhammers[9] = "jackhammer9.gif";
jackhammers[10] = "jackhammer10.gif";
```

6. Add the following functions to the script section. These functions control the animation.

```
function bounce() {
    if (curJackhammer == 10)
        curJackhammer = 0;
    else
        ++curJackhammer;
    document.getElementsByTagName(
        "img")[0].src
        = jackhammers[curJackhammer].src;
    if (curJackhammer == 0)
        direction = "up";
    else if (curJackhammer == 10)
        direction = "down";
    document.getElementsByTagName(
        "img")[0].src
        = jackhammers[curJackhammer];
}
function startBouncing() {
    if (begin)
        clearInterval(begin);
    begin = setInterval("bounce()",90);
}
```

7. Save the document as **Jackhammer.html** in your Exercises folder for Chapter 13, and validate it with the W3C Markup Validation Service. Once the document is valid, open it in your Web browser and test the animation buttons.

8. Close your Web browser window.

 Exercise 13-3

In this exercise, you will add image caching to the jackhammer animation.

1. Return to the **Jackhammer.html** document in your text editor, and immediately save it as **JackhammerCache.html**.

2. Delete the following statements from the script section. These statements assign the image filenames to the jackhammers[] array:

```
jackhammers[0] = "jackhammer0.gif";
jackhammers[1] = "jackhammer1.gif";
jackhammers[2] = "jackhammer2.gif";
```

```
jackhammers[3] = "jackhammer3.gif";
jackhammers[4] = "jackhammer4.gif";
jackhammers[5] = "jackhammer5.gif";
jackhammers[6] = "jackhammer6.gif";
jackhammers[7] = "jackhammer7.gif";
jackhammers[8] = "jackhammer8.gif";
jackhammers[9] = "jackhammer9.gif";
jackhammers[10] = "jackhammer10.gif";
```

3. Above the bounce() function, add the following for loop to handle the image caching.

```
for(var i = 0; i < 11; ++i) {
    jackhammers[i] = new Image();
    jackhammers[i].src = "jackhammer"
        + i + ".gif";
    if (i == 10)
        begin = setInterval("bounce()", 90);
}
```

4. Replace the last statement in the bounce() function with the following statement, which assigns the cached image to the <img> element:

```
document.getElementsByTagName("img")[0].src
    = jackhammers[curJackhammer].src;
```

5. Delete the startBouncing() function from the end of the script section. You no longer need the function because the animation starts automatically after the images finish loading.

6. Delete the form from the document body. You no longer need the animation buttons because the animation starts automatically after the images finish loading.

7. Save the **JackhammerCache.html** document, and validate it with the W3C Markup Validation Service. Once the document is valid, close it in your text editor and open it in your Web browser. The animation should begin as soon as the images finish loading.

8. Close your Web browser window.

Exercise 13-4

The DOM includes Table, TableRow, and TableCell objects that contain various methods and properties for dynamically manipulating tables on a Web page. For example, the Table object contains insertRow() and deleteRow() methods that allow you to add and delete rows in a table, while the TableRow object contains the insertCell() and deleteCell() methods, which allow you to add and delete cells in a table. To refer to a table, you use the getElementById() method to access the table through its id attribute. The Table object also contains a row[] array that stores all the rows in the selected table. Similarly, the TableRow object contains a cells[] array that stores all the cells in the selected row. To access an array containing all of the cells in the first row of a table with an id attribute of myTable, you use a statement similar to document.getElementById("myTable").rows[selectedItem].cells.

Next, you will create a Web page for Central Valley Chocolates that allows users to add and remove chocolate orders from a "shopping cart" table.

1. Create a new document in your text editor.

2. Type the <!DOCTYPE> declaration, <html> element, header information, and the <body> element. Use the strict DTD and "Central Valley Chocolates" as the content of the <title> element.

3. Add the following text and heading elements to the document body:

    ```
    <h1>Central Valley Chocolates</h1>
    <h2>Gourmet Chocolates</h2>
    ```

4. Add the following table to the end of the document body. Each row in the table contains three cells: the first cell describes the type of chocolate, the second cell lists the price, and the third cell contains an Add button that will call a function named addItem(). The argument passed to the addItem() function uses the getElementById() method to access the current row through its id attribute. The rowIndex property is a property of the TableRow object and returns the current row's index number in the Table object's rows[] array.

    ```
    <table border="1" id="chocolateTable">
    <tr id="ch1">
    <td>Chocolate Truffles</td><td>$34.99</td><td>
    <input type="button" value="Add"
    onclick="addItem(document.getElementById(
    'ch1').rowIndex)" /></td></tr>
    <tr id="ch2">
    <td>Pecan Caramel Duets</td><td>$14.99</td><td>
    <input type="button" value="Add"
    ```

For more information on the Table, TableRow, and TableCell objects, see the W3School's HTML DOM Reference at *http://w3schools.com/jsref/default.asp*.

```
onclick="addItem(document.getElementById(
'ch2').rowIndex)" /></td></tr>
<tr id="ch3">
<td>Chocolate Covered Cherries</td><td>$28.99</td> <td>
<input type="button" value="Add"
onclick="addItem(document.getElementById(↵
'ch3').rowIndex)" /></td></tr>
<tr id="ch4">
<td>White Chocolate Ganaches</td><td>$22.99</td><td>
<input type="button" value="Add"
onclick="addItem(document.getElementById(↵
'ch4').rowIndex)" /></td></tr>
<tr id="ch5">
<td>Chocolate Mints</td><td>$17.99</td><td>
<input type="button" value="Add"
onclick="addItem(document.getElementById(↵
'ch5').rowIndex)" /></td></tr>
<tr id="ch6">
<td>Chocolate Caramels</td><td>$14.99</td><td>
<input type="button" value="Add"
onclick="addItem(document.getElementById(↵
'ch6').rowIndex)" /></td></tr>
<tr id="ch7">
<td>Chocolate Toffee Bark</td><td>$9.99</td><td>
<input type="button" value="Add"
onclick="addItem(document.getElementById(↵
'ch7').rowIndex)" /></td></tr>
</table>
```

5. Add the following text and elements to the end of the document body. The table will store the shopping cart items selected by the user, and the paragraph element will display the sales total.

```
<h2>Your Shopping Cart</h2>
<table id="shoppingCart" border="1">
<tr><td>Your shopping cart is empty</td></tr>
</table>
<p id="total"> </p>
```

6. Add the following script section to the document head:

```
<script type="text/javascript">
/* <![CDATA[ */
/* ]]> */
</script>
```

7. Add the following global variables and function definition to the script section. The emptyCart variable will determine whether the shopping cart is empty, and the salesTotal variable will store the current sales total. The curRow variable will be incremented to create unique IDs for each table row. The

function is passed a single parameter representing the current row's index number in the Table object's rows[] array.

```
var emptyCart = true;
var salesTotal = 0;
var curRow = 1;
function addItem(selectedItem) {
}
```

8. Add the following if statement to the addItem() function. This code determines whether the shopping cart is empty; if so, it uses the deleteRow() method of the Table object to delete the single row in the table that displays the text "Your shopping cart is empty".

```
if (emptyCart == true) {
    document.getElementById('shoppingCart')
        .deleteRow(0);
    emptyCart = false;
}
```

9. Add the following statements to the end of the addItem() function. These statements assign the description and price to the selectedItem and itemPrice variables. Notice that the statements use the cells[] array of the TableRows object to access the cell values through the innerHTML property.

```
var curItem = document.getElementById(
    "chocolateTable")
.rows[selectedItem].cells;
var selectedItem = curItem[0].innerHTML;
var itemPrice = curItem[1].innerHTML;
```

10. Add the following statements to the end of the addItem() function. These statements use the insertRow() and insertCell() methods and the innerHTML property to create a new row and cell in the shopping cart table. The second-to-last statement uses the innerHTML property to create a button element that calls a function named removeItem(), and the last statement increments the curRow variable, which assigns unique IDs to each table row. The function is passed a single argument: the rowIndex property of the TableRow object.

```
var lastItem = document.getElementById(
    "shoppingCart").rows.length;
var cartTable = document.getElementById(
    "shoppingCart");
var newRow = cartTable.insertRow(lastItem);
document.getElementById("chocolateTable")
    .rows[lastItem].id = "R" + curRow;
```

```
var itemCell = newRow.insertCell(0);
itemCell.innerHTML = selectedItem;
var priceCell = newRow.insertCell(1);
priceCell.innerHTML = itemPrice;
var actionCell = newRow.insertCell(2);
actionCell.innerHTML
    = "<input type='button' value='Remove' "
    + "onclick=\"removeItem('R" + curRow
    + "')\" />";
++curRow;
```

11. Add the following statements to the end of the addItem()
    function. These statements update the sales total and assign
    the new value to the paragraph element with the id attribute
    of total.

```
salesTotal += parseFloat(
    itemPrice.substring(1));
document.getElementById('total').innerHTML
    = "<strong>Sales total</strong>: $"
    + salesTotal.toFixed(2);
```

12. Finally, add the following removeItem() function to the end
    of the script section. This function removes items from the
    shopping cart table when the user clicks the item's Remove
    button.

```
function removeItem(rowNum) {
    if (document.getElementById(
        "shoppingCart").rows.length == 1) {
        document.getElementById(
            "shoppingCart").rows[0].cells[0]
            .innerHTML = "<td>Your shopping ↵
            cart is empty</td>";
        document.getElementById(
            "shoppingCart").rows[0].cells[1]
            .innerHTML = "<td>$0.00</td>";
        salesTotal = 0;
        document.getElementById(
            'total').innerHTML = "$"
            + salesTotal.toFixed(2);
        emptyCart = true;
    }
    else {
        var selectedRow = document
            .getElementById(rowNum).rowIndex;
        document.getElementById(
            "shoppingCart").deleteRow(
            selectedRow);
        var itemPrice = document
            .getElementById("shoppingCart")
            .rows[0].cells[1].innerHTML;
```

```
                            salesTotal = salesTotal - parseFloat(
                                itemPrice.substring(1));
                            document.getElementById('total')
                                .innerHTML = "$"
                                + salesTotal.toFixed(2);
                    }
                }
```

734

13. Save the document as **ChocolateOrder.html** in your
     Exercises folder for Chapter 13, and validate the document
     with the W3C Markup Validation Service. Once the
     document is valid, open it in your Web browser and test the
     program's functionality.

14. Close your Web browser window.

Discovery Projects

For the following projects, save the documents you create in your
Projects folder for Chapter 13. Be sure to validate the files you create
with the W3C Markup Validation Service.

Discovery Project 13-1

Create a Web page that generates addition tables and multiplication
tables for the values zero through ten. The document should include
buttons that open a new window to display each table. Generate each
table using `document.write()` methods. Both tables should use the
same window. Save the document as **MathTables.html**.

Discovery Project 13-2

You have probably seen many sites that use thumbnail images to display
smaller versions of an image file. If visitors want to see a larger image,
they can click the thumbnail version. The link will then display the
larger image or another Web page that displays the larger image along
with more information. The important thing to understand is that the
thumbnail version is not the original image reduced by using the `height`
and `width` attributes of the `<img>` element. Rather, the thumbnail
images are separate images that have been resized using image-editing
software. Real estate agents commonly use thumbnails on their Web
sites to display pictures of homes and other types of property.

Create a Web page for a real estate company that allows visitors to
toggle between small and large photos of a property. Your Projects

folder for Chapter 13 includes two photos named cottage_small.jpg and cottage_large.jpg that you can use for this exercise. Start by displaying the small version of the image on the Web page, and include a link that reads "View larger image". Clicking the link should replace the image file on the Web page with the larger version, and should change the link text to read "View smaller version". Clicking the "View smaller version" link should change the picture back to the smaller version. Use the `getElementById()` method to access the image element on the Web page, and be sure to change the height and width of the image each time you replace it. Save the document as **PineKnollProperties.html**.

Discovery Project 13-3

Create a Web page that allows you to dynamically build a table containing a team roster for a bowling league. Use the same techniques that you learned in Reinforcement Exercise 13-4 for dynamically manipulating tables on a Web page, including the `Table`, `TableRow`, and `TableCell` objects. The Web page should include two forms: one in which users can enter the names of team members and click an Add Bowler button, and another form that contains the dynamic table and lists the names of the bowling team members in individual rows. Each row should also contain a Remove Bowler button that removes a bowler's name from the list. The second form should be submitted to the **FormProcessor.html** document (a copy is in your Projects folder for Chapter 13). To submit bowler names that are added dynamically to the table, you must dynamically add `<input>` elements for each bowler. Use two functions named `addBowler()` and `removeBowler()` that add and remove bowlers' names from the list, respectively. Also include the text "Your team roster is empty." if no bowlers have been entered or if all bowler names have been removed. Save the document as **BowlingTeam.html**.

Discovery Project 13-4

Your Projects folder for Chapter 13 contains an animated GIF file of a running puppy, along with six individual images (puppy0.gif through puppy5.gif) that are used in the animation. Create a JavaScript program that animates the six images in the same way as the animated GIF file. Use image caching to start the animation as soon as the images finish loading, and be sure to use the `getElementsByName()`, `getElementsByTagName()`, or `getElementById()` method to dynamically update the image element. Save the document as **RunningPuppy.html**.

Discovery Project 13-5

Your Projects folder for Chapter 13 contains an animated GIF file of a pushpin that is bouncing back and forth, along with 10 individual images (pin0.gif through pin9.gif) that are used in the animation. Create a JavaScript program that animates the 10 images in the same way as the animated GIF file. You will need to write code that displays pin0.gif through pin9.gif, and then displays pin9.gif to pin0.gif. Use image caching to start the animation as soon as the images finish loading, and be sure to use the `getElementsByName()`, `getElementsByTagName()`, or `getElementById()` method to dynamically update the image element. Save the document as **BouncingPushPin.html**.

CHAPTER 14

Creating Dynamic HTML (DHTML)

In this chapter, you will:

- ◎ Use JavaScript to modify CSS styles
- ◎ Work with CSS positioning
- ◎ Create DHTML menus

In the last chapter, you learned about the DOM and how it works with Dynamic HTML (DHTML). In this chapter, you will become acquainted with some basic DHTML techniques. As you work through this chapter, keep in mind that DHTML is an expansive subject that could fill an entire book. Also, DHTML has a steep learning curve, mainly because it requires a strong knowledge of XHTML, Cascading Style Sheets (CSS), and JavaScript. Therefore, this chapter only touches on the most basic aspects of DHTML. Specifically, you will learn how to use JavaScript to dynamically modify CSS styles and dynamically position elements. You will also learn how to create DHTML menus and check for browser compatibility.

738

You need a solid understanding of CSS to work through the examples in this chapter.

Manipulating CSS with JavaScript

Although the primary purpose of CSS is to format the display of a Web page, you can use JavaScript to modify CSS styles and make the document dynamic after a Web browser renders it. As mentioned in Chapter 13, before the W3C's standardized version of the DOM was released, no DHTML standard worked with both Internet Explorer and Mozilla-based browsers such as Firefox. This incompatibility was particularly evident to programmers who needed to use JavaScript to manipulate CSS styles. Earlier versions of Internet Explorer and Mozilla-based browsers supported incompatible Document object properties and methods. Because JavaScript uses Document object properties and methods to access CSS styles, you had three options if you wanted to use JavaScript code to manipulate CSS in older browsers:

- Write code that functioned only in Mozilla-based browsers.

- Write code that functioned only in Internet Explorer.

- Write two sets of code and design the script so that the correct set would execute depending on which browser rendered the page.

This chapter primarily discusses DOM techniques that are compatible with the W3C's standardized version of DHTML. That approach makes sense because, at the time of this writing, more than 90 percent of Internet users access the Web with a W3C-compliant browser. If you anticipate that your DHTML code will run in older browsers, you need to learn the DHTML techniques for each type of browser.

Modifying Styles with the this Reference

In Chapter 11, you learned how to manipulate CSS styles in JavaScript with the this reference and the style property in an event handler within the element itself. Recall that to refer to a style with the this reference, you use a period to append the style property to it, followed by another period and a CSS property. CSS properties without hyphens are referred to with all lowercase letters in JavaScript. However, when you refer to a CSS property that contains a hyphen in JavaScript code, you remove the hyphen, convert the first word to lowercase, and convert the first letter of subsequent words to uppercase. For example, the text-decoration property is referred to as textDecoration, font-family is referred to as fontFamily, font-size is referred to as fontSize, and so on. To use the onclick event handler to modify the font size of the current element, you use the following statement:

```
onclick="this.style.fontSize='2em';"
```

The following example shows how to use onmouseover and onmouseout event handlers to give users the option of changing text to make it easier to read. Specifically, the example allows users to change the text color and weight of a line simply by passing the mouse pointer over it. Moving the mouse pointer away from the line returns it to the original text color and weight. Figure 14-1 shows the document in a Web browser when the mouse pointer passes over the third line.

```
<h1>World's Largest Cities by Population</h1>
<p><strong>Place your mouse over any line to change its
color and weight.</strong></p><hr />
<p onmouseover="this.style.color = 'blue'; ↵
    this.style.fontWeight = 'bold'"
    onmouseout="this.style.color = 'black'; ↵
    this.style.fontWeight = 'normal'">
    Mumbai, India / 13,922,120</p>
<p onmouseover="this.style.color = 'blue'; ↵
    this.style.fontWeight = 'bold'"
    onmouseout="this.style.color = 'black'; ↵
    this.style.fontWeight = 'normal'">
    Shanghai, China / 13,831,900</p>
<p onmouseover="this.style.color = 'blue'; ↵
    this.style.fontWeight = 'bold'"
    onmouseout="this.style.color = 'black'; ↵
    this.style.fontWeight = 'normal'">
    Karachi, Pakistan / 12,991,000</p>
<p onmouseover="this.style.color = 'blue'; ↵
    this.style.fontWeight = 'bold'"
    onmouseout="this.style.color = 'black'; ↵
    this.style.fontWeight = 'normal'">
    Delhi, India / 12,259,230</p>
<p onmouseover="this.style.color = 'blue'; ↵
    this.style.fontWeight = 'bold'"
    onmouseout="this.style.color = 'black'; ↵
    this.style.fontWeight = 'normal'">
    Istanbul, Turkey / 11,372,613</p>
```

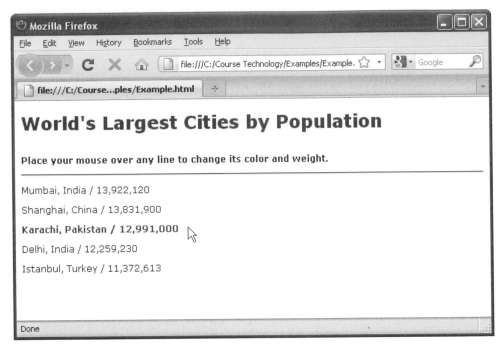

Figure 14-1   Web page with `onmouseover` and `onmouseout` event handlers that change text display

In this chapter, you work on the same DRG Aviation Web pages you used in Chapter 13. You will start by modifying the menu buttons so that when the mouse passes over each image, `onmouseover` and `onmouseout` events swap the displayed image with a more vivid one and then change back to the original image when the mouse pointer is removed.

Be sure to work with a copy of the folder so you don't overwrite the original source files.

To modify the menus in the DRG Aviation Web pages:

1. Copy the DRGAviation folder from your Chapter folder for Chapter 13 to your Chapter folder for Chapter 14.

2. Start your text editor and open the home page for DRG Aviation, **index.html**.

3. Locate the Home, Training, and Instruments links and add `onmouseover` and `onmouseout` event handlers for each link. These event handlers will swap the default images with the index2.jpg, training2.jpg, and instruments2.jpg images, which are in the images folder within the DRGAviation folder. A swapped image will then change back to the original image when the mouse pointer is removed. The modified statements should appear as follows:

```
<td><a href="index.html">
    <img src="images/index.jpg" width="110" height="36"
```

```
        alt="Visual formatting element"
        onmouseover="this.src='images/index2.jpg'"
        onmouseout="this.src='images/index.jpg'" /></a>
</td>
<td><a href="flighttraining.html">
    <img src="images/training.jpg" width="110"
        height="36" alt="Visual formatting element"
        onmouseover="this.src='images/training2.jpg'"
        onmouseout="this.src='images/training.jpg'" /></a>
</td>
<td><a href="instruments.html">
    <img src="images/instruments.jpg" width="110"
        height="36" alt="Visual formatting element"
        onmouseover="this.src='images/instruments2.jpg'"
        onmouseout="this.src='images/instruments.jpg'" />
</a></td>
```

4. Save the **index.html** document and then open it in your Web browser. Test the onmouseover and onmouseout event handlers in the links. Figure 14-2 shows how the Training link appears when the mouse pointer passes over it.

Figure 14-2   Training link when the mouse pointer passes over it

5. Close your Web browser window.

You can also pass the `this` reference as an argument to a function. The `onclick` event handler in the following paragraph element calls a function named `changeColor()` and passes it the `this` reference. When the `this` reference is passed to the function, it becomes the `curElement` variable, which is defined within the function definition's parentheses. The single statement within the function then uses the `curElement` variable to change the element to red.

```
function changeColor(curElement) {
    curElement.style.color = "red";
}
<p onclick="changeColor(this)">
Red paragraph.</p>
```

The following code shows a modified version of the world's largest cities Web page. This time, `this` references are passed to functions that change the display of each line.

```
. . .
<script type="text/javascript">
/* <![CDATA[ */
function changeDisplay(curLine) {
    curLine.style.color = "blue";
    curLine.style.fontWeight = "bold";
}
function restoreDisplay(curLine) {
    curLine.style.color = "black";
    curLine.style.fontWeight = "normal";
}
/* ]]> */
</script>
</head>
<body>
<h1>World's Largest Cities by Population</h1>
<p><strong>Place your mouse over any line to change its
color and weight.</strong></p><hr />
<p onmouseover="changeDisplay(this)"
    onmouseout="restoreDisplay(this)">
    Mumbai, India / 13,922,120</p>
<p onmouseover="changeDisplay(this)"
    onmouseout="restoreDisplay(this)">
    Shanghai, China / 13,831,900</p>
<p onmouseover="changeDisplay(this)"
    onmouseout="restoreDisplay(this)">
    Karachi, Pakistan / 12,991,000</p>
<p onmouseover="changeDisplay(this)"
    onmouseout="restoreDisplay(this)">
    Delhi, India / 12,259,230</p>
<p onmouseover="changeDisplay(this)"
    onmouseout="restoreDisplay(this)">
    Istanbul, Turkey / 11,372,613</p>
</body>
</html>
```

Modifying Styles with Methods of the Document Object

To modify CSS properties without using the this reference, you must first gain access to the styles by using
the getElementById(), getElementsByName(), or
getElementsByTagName() methods of the Document object.
The statements in the following function show how to use the
getElementById() method to access the element with an ID attribute
of ff1 and modify its color and font-size properties. Notice that
the ID attribute is passed to the changeStyle() function by passing
this.id as the argument.

```
function changeStyle(curID) {
    var curElement = document
        .getElementById(curID);
    curElement.style.color = "red";
    curElement.style.fontSize = "18pt";
}
<h1 id="ff1" onclick="changeStyle(this.id)">
Sunshine Deli</h1>
```

The following code is from the world's largest cities Web page you
saw earlier. This time, however, the styles for each line are accessed by
using getElementById() methods.

```
...
<script type="text/javascript">
/* <![CDATA[ */
function changeDisplay(curLine) {
    var changeElement = document
        .getElementById(curLine);
    changeElement.style.color = "blue";
    changeElement.style.fontWeight = "bold";
}
function restoreDisplay(curLine) {
    var changeElement = document
        .getElementById(curLine);
    changeElement.style.color = "black";
    changeElement.style.fontWeight = "normal";
}
/* ]]> */
</script>
</head>
<body>
<h1>World's Largest Cities by Population</h1>
<p><strong>Place your mouse over any line to change its
color and weight.</strong></p><hr />
<p id="p1" onmouseover="changeDisplay(this.id)"
    onmouseout="restoreDisplay(this.id)">
    Mumbai, India / 13,922,120</p>
<p id="p2" onmouseover="changeDisplay(this.id)"
    onmouseout="restoreDisplay(this.id)">
    Shanghai, China / 13,831,900</p>
```

```
<p id="p3" onmouseover="changeDisplay(this.id)"
    onmouseout="restoreDisplay(this.id)">
    Karachi, Pakistan / 12,991,000</p>
<p id="p4" onmouseover="changeDisplay(this.id)"
    onmouseout="restoreDisplay(this.id)">
    Delhi, India / 12,259,230</p>
<p id="p5" onmouseover="changeDisplay(this.id)"
    onmouseout="restoreDisplay(this.id)">
    Istanbul, Turkey / 11,372,613</p>
</body>
</html>
```

Next, you modify the functions in the DRG Aviation home page so that they modify the style of the anchor elements by using the getElementById() method instead of the this reference.

To modify the functions in the DRG Aviation home page so that they use the getElementById() method instead of the this reference:

1. Return to the **index.html** document in your text editor.

2. Modify the images so that they include id attributes. Also, modify the onmouseover and onmouseout event handler functions in the menu links so that they use the getElementById() function. Your modified anchor elements should appear as follows:

```
<td><a href="index.html">
    <img id="home" src="images/index.jpg"
        width="110" height="36"
        alt="Visual formatting element"
        onmouseover="document.getElementById ↵
            (this.id).src ='images/index2.jpg'"
        onmouseout="document.getElementById ↵
            (this.id).src ='images/index.jpg'" /></a>
</td>
<td><a href="flighttraining.html">
    <img id="training" src="images/training.jpg"
        width="110" height="36"
        alt="Visual formatting element"
        onmouseover="document.getElementById ↵
            (this.id).src ='images/training2.jpg'"
        onmouseout="document.getElementById(this. ↵
            id).src ='images/training.jpg'" /></a>
</td>
<td><a href="instruments.html">
    <img id="instruments" src="images/instruments.jpg"
        width="110" height="36"
        alt="Visual formatting element"
        onmouseover="document.getElementById ↵
            (this.id).src ='images/instruments2.jpg'"
        onmouseout="document.getElementById ↵
            (this.id).src ='images/instruments.jpg'" />
        </a></td>
```

3. Save the **index.html** document, and then validate it with the W3C Markup Validation Service. Once the document is valid, close it in your text editor, and then open it in your Web browser. Test the `onmouseover` and `onmouseout` event handlers in the links. The Web pages should work and look the same as they did before you added the `getElementById()` methods.

4. Close your Web browser window.

Checking Browser Compatibility

If you anticipate that your script may run in a browser that is not compatible with the W3C's standardized version of DHTML, you should write code that checks whether the browser is compliant with the W3C DOM. If the browser is not compliant, your script should open an alternate Web page that does not include DHTML, or your script should display a message advising the user to upgrade his or her browser.

A JavaScript program that checks which type of browser is running is commonly called a **browser sniffer**. Although there are several ways to write a browser sniffer, including using properties of the `Navigator` object, the easiest way to test whether a Web browser is compatible with the W3C DOM is to check whether the browser includes the `getElementById()` method. You can perform this check by using a statement similar to `if (document.getElementById)`. If the method is available in the browser, a value of true is returned, meaning that the browser is compatible with the W3C DOM.

The browser sniffer script in the following code opens a DHTML version of a butterfly animation script only if the browser is compatible with the W3C DOM. If the browser is not compatible, a non-DHTML version of the Web page opens.

```
. . .
<script type="text/javascript">
/* <![CDATA[ */
function checkBrowser() {
    if (document.getElementById)
        document.location.href
            = "ButterflyDHTML.html";
    else
        document.location.href
            = "ButterflyNoDHTML.html";
}
/* ]]> */
</script>
</head>
<body onload="checkBrowser();">
</body>
</html>
```

Short Quiz 1

1. How do you modify styles with methods of the Document object?

2. Why doesn't this book use code that checks whether the browser is compliant with the W3C DOM?

3. Explain how to use a browser sniffer.

Understanding CSS Positioning

Although you have used the <img> element to create simple animations with JavaScript, you can only use it to create stationary animations. That is, an animation created with the <img> element does not travel across the screen. Actually, there is no way to reposition an image on a Web page unless you use **CSS positioning** to lay out Web elements. Table 14-1 lists common CSS positioning properties.

Property	Description
clip	Determines the region of an element that is displayed
display	Specifies whether to display an element
height, width	Determines an image's height and width
top, left	Determines the position of an element's upper-left corner in relation to the upper-left corner of the document window
overflow	Determines how to handle an image that is bigger than its assigned space
position	Specifies the type of CSS positioning
bottom, right	Determines the position of an element's lower-right corner in relation to the upper-left corner of the document window
visibility	Specifies whether an element is visible
z-index	Determines the order in which dynamically positioned elements are layered

Table 14-1   CSS positioning properties

CSS positioning is a lengthy topic; this chapter touches only on the basics.

The most critical CSS positioning property is the position property, which determines the type of positioning applied to an element. Table 14-2 lists the values that can be assigned to the position property.

A value of "static" essentially means that you cannot use CSS positioning with an element. To use CSS positioning, you must use one of the other three values listed in Table 14-2.

Positioning Type	Description
absolute	Positions an element in a specific location on a Web page
fixed	Positions an element in relation to the browser window
relative	Positions an element in relation to other elements on a Web page
static	Positions an element according to the normal flow of other elements and text on a Web page; elements that include this positioning type cannot be moved with CSS positioning

Table 14-2 CSS positioning values

Dynamic Positioning

The easiest way to dynamically position an element with CSS is to use the left and top properties. The left property specifies an element's horizontal distance from the upper-left corner of the window, and the top property specifies an element's vertical distance from the upper-left corner of the window. Both property values are assigned in pixels. For example, the following code dynamically positions three images of a bird on a Web page. Figure 14-3 shows how the images appear in a Web browser.

```
<p>
    <img src="up.gif"
    style="position: absolute; left: 40px; ↵
        top: 200px" alt="Image of a bird"
        height="218" width="200" />
</p>
<p>
    <img src="down.gif"
    style="position: absolute; left: 250px; ↵
        top: 80px" alt="Image of a bird"
        height="218" width="200" />
</p>
<p>
    <img src="up.gif"
    style="position: absolute; left: 480px;
        top: 10px" alt="Image of a bird"
        height="218" width="200" />
</p>
```

748

You can find a copy of the ThreeBirds.html document and the images it displays in your Chapter folder for Chapter 14.

Figure 14-3   Dynamically positioned images

Next, you dynamically position an image on the Instruments page of the DRG Aviation site. The images folder in the DRGAviation folder contains a GIF image named airplane.gif that you can use for this exercise.

To dynamically position an image on the Instruments page of the DRG Aviation site:

1. In your text editor, open the **instruments.html** document, which is in the DRGAviation folder in your Chapter folder for Chapter 14.

2. Add the following <div> element with CSS-positioned <img> elements immediately after the opening <body> tag. The CSS properties position the same image in different locations on the screen.

```
<div><img src="images/airplane.gif"
    style="position: absolute; left: 220px; ↵
    top: 100px" alt="Image of an airplane"
    height="38" width="128" />
<img src="images/airplane.gif"
    style="position: absolute; left: 300px; ↵
    top: 50px" alt="Image of an airplane"
    height="38" width="128" />
```

```
<img src="images/airplane.gif"
    style="position: absolute; left: 380px; ↵
    top: 100px" alt="Image of an airplane"
    height="38" width="128" /></div>
```

3. Save the **instruments.html** document, and then open it in your Web browser. Figure 14-4 shows how the images appear.

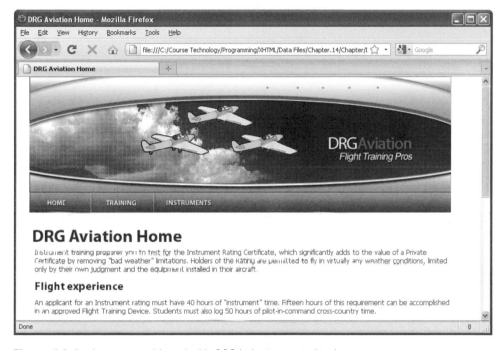

Figure 14-4   Images positioned with CSS in instruments.html

4. Close your Web browser window.

Traveling Animation

The simple stationary animations you have seen so far were created by swapping the image files assigned to an <img> element's src attribute. With DHTML, you can use dynamic positioning to create traveling animation—that is, images that appear to travel across the screen. The following code demonstrates how to create traveling animation with an animated GIF image of a butterfly. The butterfly travels from the lower-left side of the screen, over the paragraph, to the upper-right corner. The global topPosition and leftPosition variables define the initial starting position of the image. An onload event handler in the opening <body> tag uses the setInterval()

function to execute the flyButterfly() function, which handles the animation. The first statement in the function gets the element ID of the butterfly image, while the second and third statements assign values to the element's left and top properties. By default, the style attribute in the image element uses the visibility style to hide the image, so the fourth statement in the flyButterfly() function displays the image. The remaining statements modify the values assigned to the topPosition and leftPosition variables, which the function uses to dynamically position the butterfly image. Figure 14-5 shows how the Web page appears in a browser.

```
...
    <script type="text/javascript">
    /* <![CDATA[ */
        var topPosition = 250;
        var leftPosition = -100;
        function flyButterfly() {
            var butterfly = document.getElementById(
                "butterfly");
            butterfly.style.left = leftPosition
                + "px";
            butterfly.style.top = topPosition
                + "px";
            butterfly.style.visibility = "visible";
            topPosition -= 2;
            leftPosition += 10;
            if (leftPosition >= screen.availWidth
                - 300) {
                topPosition = 250;
                leftPosition = -100;
            }
        }
    /* ]]> */
    </script>
</head>
<body onload="setInterval('flyButterfly()', 100);">
    <p>
        <img src="butterfly.gif" id="butterfly"
            style="position: absolute; ↵
            left: -100px; top: 250px; ↵
            visibility: hidden"
            alt="Image of a butterfly" height="120"
            width="150" />
    </p>
...
```

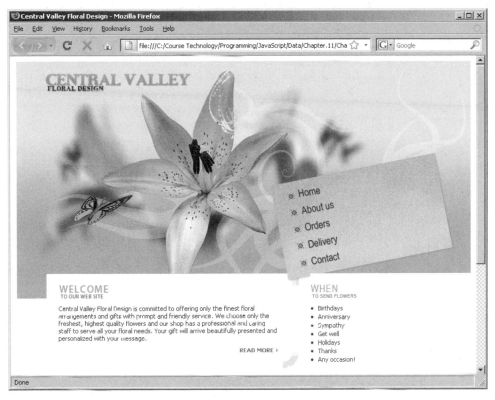

Figure 14-5 Butterfly animation Web page

Next, you will animate the airplane image you added to the DRG Aviation site so that the plane appears to fly across the screen from left to right. The starting horizontal position of the airplane will be −122 pixels, so that it appears to fly from off the screen into the document area. You will use the `Math.random()` function to randomly generate the vertical position, in pixels, where the airplane will begin each time it flies across the screen. To ensure that the starting position is within the top and bottom boundaries of the document area, you need to set the minimum and maximum values that the `Math.random()` function will generate by using the following formula:

You can find a copy of the butterfly animation document in the FloralDesign folder, which is in your Chapter folder for Chapter 14.

```
var randomNumber = Math.floor(Math.random()
    * (maximum - minimum + 1)) + minimum);
```

The value you assign to the *minimum* variable will be 70 (pixels), while the value you assign to the *maximum* variable will be the available screen height minus 200 (again, in pixels). To determine the available screen height, you will use the `availHeight` property of the `Screen` object.

To animate the airplane image you added to the Instruments page of the DRG Aviation site so that it appears to fly across the screen:

1. Return to the **instruments.html** document in your text editor, and add a script section to the document head. Then, add the following global variables to the script section. The `leftPosition` variable sets the initial left position at −122 pixels, the `minVertical` variable sets the minimum vertical position to 70 pixels, and the `maxVertical` variables use the `screen.availHeight` property to set the maximum vertical position to the available screen height, minus 200. The statement that initializes the `topPosition` variable uses the formula for generating random values to dynamically return a vertical starting position between the values assigned to the `minVertical` and `maxVertical` variables. The randomly generated value is also assigned to the `topCeiling` variable, which determines the top and bottom positions of the airplane in its flight path. The last variable, `verticalDirection`, determines whether the plane is ascending or descending in its flight path.

```
var leftPosition = -122;
var minVertical = 70;
var maxVertical = screen.availHeight - 200;
var topPosition = Math.floor(Math.random()
       * (maxVertical - (minVertical + 1))
       + minVertical);
var topCeiling = topPosition;
var verticalDirection = "up";
```

2. Add the following `flightCoordinates()` function, which handles the dynamic positioning of the airplane image. The first statement in the function gets the image element's ID, while the second and third statements assign values to the element's `left` and `top` properties. The `if...else` statements then change the values assigned to the global variables in order to set the position of the plane when the `flightCoordinates()` function is called next. The horizontal position of the plane cycles between −122 pixels (the starting point) and the available screen width, minus 200 pixels. The `verticalDirection` variable determines whether to increment or decrement the value of the `topPosition` variable. The `flightCoordinates()` function is called using a `setInterval()` method from the `onload` event handler of the `<body>` element.

```
function flightCoordinates() {
    var flight = document.getElementById(
        "airplane");
    flight.style.left = leftPosition + "px";
    flight.style.top = topPosition + "px";
    if (verticalDirection == "up")
        --topPosition;
    else if (verticalDirection == "down")
        ++topPosition;
    if (topPosition == topCeiling - 60)
        verticalDirection = "down";
    else if (topPosition == topCeiling + 60)
        verticalDirection = "up";
    ++leftPosition;
    if (leftPosition == screen.availWidth - 200) {
        leftPosition = -122;
        topPosition = Math.floor(Math.random()
            * (maxVertical - (minVertical + 1))
            + minVertical);
        topCeiling = topPosition;
        verticalDirection = "up";
    }
}
```

3. Within the <div> element you added in the last exercise, replace the three <img> elements with the following single <img> element. Be sure that the element includes an id attribute that is assigned a value of "airplane".

```
<img src="images/airplane.gif" id="airplane"
style="position: absolute; left: -122px; top: 200px"
alt="Image of an airplane" height="38"
width="128" />
```

4. Add an onload event handler to the opening <body> tag that calls the setInterval() function, as follows:

```
<body onload="setInterval( ↵
    'flightCoordinates()', 25);">
```

5. Save the **instruments.html** document, and open it in your Web browser. The airplane image should appear to fly across the screen from random starting vertical positions, as shown in the composite screen in Figure 14-6.

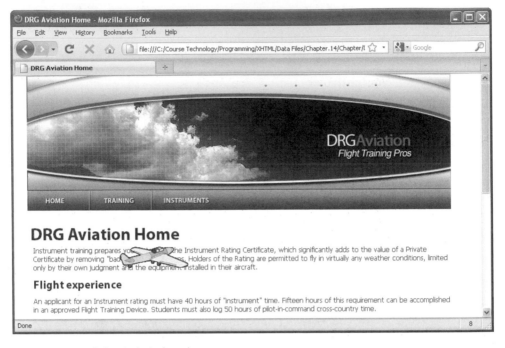

Figure 14-6   Animated airplane image

6. Close your Web browser window.

Short Quiz 2

1. What is the most critical CSS positioning property, and what values can you assign to it?

2. What is the easiest way to dynamically position Web page elements?

3. How do you create traveling animation?

Creating DHTML Menus

Creating menus is one of the more popular uses of DHTML. Three types of menus are discussed in this section: expandable menus, navigation menus, and sliding menus. DHTML menus are most often used for organizing navigational links to other Web pages, although they are also useful for displaying and hiding information. As you work through this section, keep in mind that these techniques are only for browsers that are compatible with the W3C DOM. Older browsers that do not support the W3C DOM require different DHTML techniques to achieve the menu effects described in this section.

Using Expandable Menus

The **display property** specifies whether to display an element on a Web page. You can use the display property to simulate expandable and collapsible menus on a Web page. You typically use the display property with a **block-level element**, which gives a Web page its structure. Most Web browsers render block-level elements so that they appear on their own line. Block-level elements can contain other block-level elements or inline elements. The <p> and heading elements (<h1>, <h2>, and so on) are examples of common block-level elements that you have used. **Inline elements**, or **text-level elements**, describe the text that appears on a Web page. Unlike block-level elements, inline elements do not appear on their own lines; instead, they appear within the line of the block-level element that contains them. Examples of inline elements include the <b> (bold) and <hr/> (line break) elements. One block-level element you may already know is the **<div> element**, which formats a group of block-level and inline elements with styles. By placing elements and text within a <div> element, you can use the display property to simulate expandable and collapsible menus.

If you assign a block-level element's display property a value of "none", the associated element is not displayed. In fact, the Web page does not even allocate space for the element on the page. However, if you use JavaScript to assign a value of "block" to a block-level element's display property, the Web page is reformatted to allocate sufficient space for the element and its contents, which are then displayed.

The following code shows a Web page that displays Hall of Fame players for the National Football League. The style section defines a class selector named collapsed for the <div> element. You should already be familiar with the concept, but if not, recall that a class selector defines different groups of styles for the same element. You create a class selector within a <style> element by using a period to append a name for the class to a selector. You then assign the class name to the class attribute of elements in the document that you want to format with the class's style definitions. The collapsed class selector includes the display property, which turns off the display of each <div> element when the Web page is first rendered. Anchor elements within the document body then use onmouseover and onmouseout event handlers to show and hide the `<div>` elements. Figure 14-7 shows the document in a Web browser when the mouse pointer passes over the Cleveland Browns link.

```
...
<style type="text/css">
    div.collapsed
    {
        display: none;
    }
</style>
</head>
<body>
    <h1>
        National Football League</h1>
    <h2>
        Hall of Fame Players</h2>
    <p>
        <a href="" onmouseover="document↵
            .getElementById('bills')↵
            .style.display='block';"
            onmouseout="document↵
            .getElementById('bills')↵
            .style.display='none';">
            Buffalo Bills</a></p>
    <div id="bills" class="collapsed">
        <p>
            Joe DeLamielleure '03, Jim Kelly '02,
            Marv Levy '01 (coach), James Lofton '03,
            Billy Shaw '99, Thurman Thomas '07</p>
    </div>
    <p>
        <a href="" onmouseover="document↵
            .getElementById('browns')↵
            .style.display='block';"
            onmouseout="document↵
            .getElementById('browns')↵
            .style.display='none';">
            Cleveland Browns</a></p>
    <div id="browns" class="collapsed">
        <p>
            Doug Atkins '82, Jim Brown '71,
            Paul Brown '67 (coach/owner),
            Willie Davis '81, Len Dawson '87,
            Joe DeLamielleure '03, Len Ford '76,
            Frank Gatski '85, Otto Graham '65,
            Lou Groza '74, Gene Hickerson '07,
            Henry Jordan '95, Leroy Kelly '94,
            Dante Lavelli '75, Mike McCormack '84,
            Tommy McDonald '98, Bobby Mitchell '83,
            Marion Motley '68, Ozzie Newsome '99,
            Paul Warfield '83, Bill Willis '77</p>
    </div>
    ...
```

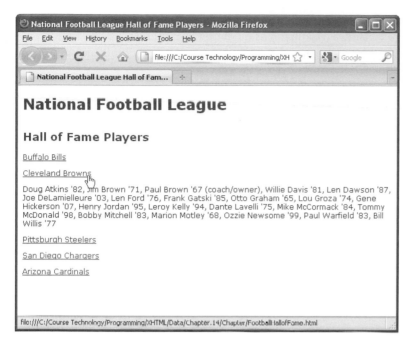

Figure 14-7 Web page with expandable menus

 You can find a copy of the FootballHallofFame.html file in your Chapter folder for Chapter 14.

Next, you modify the right frame of the Instrument Training Web page so that the content beneath each heading is contained within expandable menus.

To add expandable menus to the Instrument Training Web page:

1. Return to the **instruments.html** document in your text editor.

2. Add the following style section above the closing `</head>` tag. The style section contains a single class selector that hides the content of any `<div>` elements to which it is applied when the Web page first opens.

```
<style type="text/css">
div.collapseInfo { display: none }
</style>
```

3. Place the elements and text beneath the Flight Experience heading within a `<div>` element, as follows. The `<div>` element has an `id` attribute of "experience" and is assigned the `collapseInfo` class selector.

```
<div id="experience" class="collapseInfo">
<p>An applicant for an Instrument rating must have 40 hours
of &quot;instrument&quot; time. Fifteen hours of this
requirement can be accomplished in an approved Flight
Training Device. Students must also log 50 hours of pilot-
in-command cross-country time.</p>
<p>The FAA Approved Instrument course at DRG Aviation is
taught in Cessna 172&#39;s and in Flight Simulators. The
aircraft are all equipped with intercoms and headsets to
assist you in communications with Air Traffic Control
(ATC).</p>
</div>
```

4. Modify the Flight Experience heading so that the text is contained within an anchor element. Also, add a `style` attribute as well as `onclick`, `onmouseover`, and `onmouseout` event handlers to the anchor element. The `style` attribute turns off the underline beneath the link. The `onclick` event handler calls a function named `showInfo()`, which displays and hides the information in the `<div>` element. You add the `showInfo()` function next. The `onmouseover` and `onmouseout` event handlers show and hide the underline beneath the anchor element.

```
<h2>
    <a href="" style="text-decoration: none"
        onclick="return showInfo('experience');"
        onmouseover="this.style.textDecoration ↵
            ='underline'"
        onmouseout="this.style.textDecoration ↵
            ='none'">
        Flight Experience</a>
</h2>
```

5. Add the following `showInfo()` function to the end of the script section in the document head. The `showInfo()` function displays and hides the content of the `<div>` element.

```
function showInfo(heading) {
    var curHeading = document
        .getElementById(heading);
        if (curHeading.style.display == "block")
            curHeading.style.display = "none";
        else
            curHeading.style.display = "block";
    return false;
}
```

6. Add similar elements and event handlers to the remaining headings and information on the page.

7. Save the **instruments.html** document, and then validate it with the W3C Markup Validation Service. Once the document is valid, close it in your text editor, and then open it in your Web browser. Click each of the headings to see if they expand and collapse. Figure 14-8 shows how the Web page appears after a user clicks the Syllabus heading.

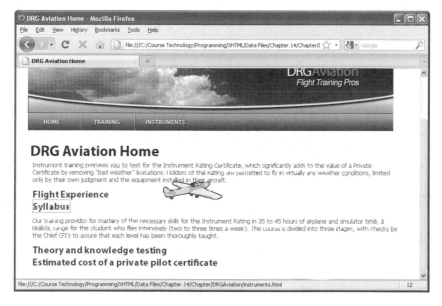

Figure 14-8   Instrument Training Web page after adding expandable menus

8. Close your Web browser window.

Using Navigation Menus

You are probably already familiar with drop-down menus, or pull-down menus, which are similar to the menus you find in a Windows application. Menus can greatly improve the design of your Web page, and they help visitors navigate through your Web site. In Chapter 11, you saw some Web pages from the Woodland Park Zoo. The Photo Gallery Web page, shown in Figure 14-9, contains a navigation menu that helps users find the Web page for a particular animal.

Figure 14-9 Navigation menu for the Woodland Park Zoo Photo Gallery Web page

Although you can create a navigation menu in several ways, the easiest way is to use a table to contain your menu items. First, you create a master table whose purpose is to contain nested tables for each individual menu. The following code shows the beginnings of a table that will create a navigation menu for an electronics store. Figure 14-10 shows the document in a Web browser.

```
<table>
    <tr align="left">
        <td onmouseover="document
            .getElementById('b1').src
            ='button1over.png'"
            onmouseout="document
            .getElementById('b1').src
            ='button1up.png'"><a href="">
            <img src="button1up.png" id="b1"
                border="0" vspace="1"
                hspace="1" />
            </a></td>
        <td onmouseover="document
            .getElementById('b2').src
            ='button2over.png'"
            onmouseout="document
            .getElementById('b2').src
```

```
                   ='button2up.png'"><a href="">
                   <img src="button2up.png" id="b2"
                       border="0" vspace="1"
                       hspace="1" /></a>
           </td>
           <td onmouseover="document
               .getElementById('b3').src
               ='button3over.png'"
               onmouseout="document
               .getElementById('b3').src
               ='button3up.png'"><a href="">
                   <img src="button3up.png" id="b3"
                       border="0" vspace="1"
                       hspace="1" /></a>
           </td>
           <td onmouseover="document
               .getElementById('b4').src
               ='button4over.png'"
               onmouseout="document
               .getElementById('b4').src
               ='button4up.png'"><a href="">
                   <img src="button4up.png" id="b4"
                       border="0" vspace="1"
                       hspace="1" /></a>
           </td>
       </tr>
</table>
<h1>
    DRG Electronics</h1>
<p>
    Use the menu to help find what you
    are looking for.</p>
```

Figure 14-10   Document with a top navigation menu

You nest the contents of a navigation menu within the same cell as the top navigation menu heading. The following code shows a `<div>` element in which the Audio menu items are nested within the same cell as the Audio menu:

```
<td>
    onmouseover="document.getElementById(↵
    'b1').src='button1over.png'"
    onmouseout="document.getElementById(↵
    'b1').src='button1up.png'"><a href=""><br />
    <img src="button1up.png" id="b1" border="0"
        vspace="1" hspace="1" /></a>
    <div class="dropmenu">
        <ul>
            <li><a href="audiosys.html">
                Audio Systems</a></li>
            <li><a href="audioplayers.html">
                iPods and MP3 Players</a></li>
            <li><a href="headphones.html">
                Headphones</a></li>
        </ul>
    </div>
</td>
```

To show and hide each menu, you use the **`visibility` property**, which determines whether an element is visible. The `visibility` property differs from the `display` property in that it allocates space for an element on a Web page. Recall that a Web browser does not allocate space for an element with a value of "none" assigned to its `display` property. If you assign a value of "hidden" to an element's `visibility` property, space is allocated for the element, but it is not displayed. You display a hidden element by assigning a value of "visible" to the `visibility` property.

The following code shows another version of the table elements for the Audio menu. This time, the `<div>` element containing the menu includes a `style` property that hides the element and sets its position to absolute. In the following code, the `onmouseover` and `onmouseout` event handlers for the table cells include statements that use the `visibility` property to show and hide the menu. Figure 14-11 shows the Web page in a browser with the mouse pointer over the Audio menu.

```
<td>
    onmouseover="document.getElementById(↵
    'b1').src='button1over.png';↵
    document.getElementById(↵
    'audio').style.visibility='visible'"
    onmouseout="document.getElementById(↵
    'b1').src='button1up.png';↵
    document.getElementById(↵
    'audio').style.visibility='hidden'"><a href="">
```

```
    <img src="button1up.png" id="b1" border="0"
        vspace="1" hspace="1" /></a><br />
    <div id="audio" class="dropmenu"
        style="visibility:hidden; ↵
           position:absolute">
        <ul>
            <li><a href="audiosys.html">
            Audio Systems</a></li>
            <li><a href="audioplayers.html">
            iPods and MP3 Players</a></li>
            <li><a href="headphones.html">
            Headphones</a></li>
        </ul>
    </div>
</td>
```

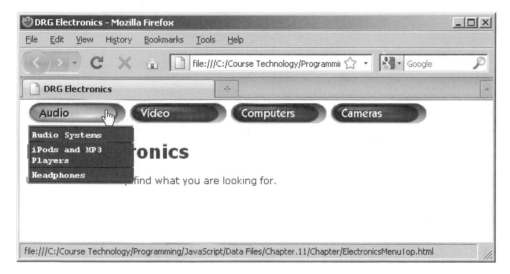

Figure 14-11   Audio menu in the top navigation menu

 You can find a copy of the ElectronicsMenuTop.html document in your Chapter folder for Chapter 14.

Next, you will add a navigation menu to the flighttraining.html document.

To add a navigation menu to the flighttraining.html document:

1. Open the **flighttraining.html** document in your text editor.

2. Locate the table containing the three <a> elements that provide links to each of the DRG Aviation Web pages. The single row within the table includes three cells that contain the links.

The row also contains a cell that displays a visual formatting image named filler.jpg. Replace everything within the `<tr>` element with the following `<td>` element, which displays a single button named Navigation. This creates a single menu that contains the three links for each of the DRG Aviation Web pages.

```
<td id="navmenu" onmouseover="document.getElementById(
    'navimage').src='images/navigation2.jpg';
    document.getElementById('navigation').style
    .visibility='visible'"
    onmouseout="document.getElementById(
    'navimage').src='images/navigation.jpg';
    document.getElementById('navigation').style
    .visibility='hidden'">
    <a href=""><br /><img id="navimage"
    src="images/navigation.jpg"
    width="110" height="36"
    alt="Visual formatting element" /></a></td>
```

3. Above the closing `</td>` tag that you added in the last step, add the following nested `<div>` element, which contains the links to the DRG Aviation Web pages:

```
<div id="navigation" class="dropmenu"
style="visibility: hidden; position: absolute">
    <ul>
        <li><a href="index.html">Home</a></li>
        <li><a href="flighttraining.html">
        Flight Training</a></li>
        <li><a href="instruments.html">Instrument
        Training</a></li>
    </ul>
</div>
```

4. Immediately after the closing `</td>` tag that contains the navigation element, add the following cell, which displays a visual formatting element:

```
<td>
    <img id="menu" src="images/fillerbig.jpg" width="640"
    height="36" alt="Visual formatting element" />
</td>
```

5. Save the **flighttraining.html** document, and then open it in your Web browser. Figure 14-12 shows how the document appears with the navigation menu open and the mouse held over the Flight Training link.

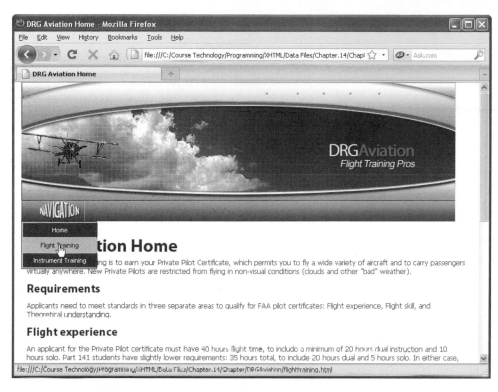

Figure 14-12 DRG Aviation home page with a navigation menu

6. Close your Web browser window.

The following code shows a modified version of the Audio menu for the electronics store Web page. This time, the table is formatted so the menus appear on the left side of the screen. The code also uses the `display` property instead of the `visibility` property to allow the nested tables to expand and contract beneath each menu heading. Notice that the `position` property in the `<div>` elements is assigned a value of "relative" instead of "absolute". This forces the `<div>` elements to expand and contract to display the nested tables. Figure 14-13 shows the Web page in a browser with the Audio menu expanded.

```
<tr align="left">
    <td onmouseover="document.getElementById(
        'b1').src='button1over.png';
        document.getElementById('audio')
        .style.display='block'"
        onmouseout="document.getElementById(
        'b1').src='button1up.png';
        document.getElementById('audio')
        .style.display='none'">
        <a href="">
```

766

```
        <img src="button1up.png" id="b1"
            border="0" vspace="1"
            hspace="1" /></a>
    <div id="audio" class="dropmenu"
        style="display: none; ↵
            position: relative">
        <ul>
            <li><a href="audiosys.html">
                Audio Systems</a></li>
            <li><a href="audioplayers.html">
                iPods and MP3 Players</a></li>
            <li><a href="headphones.html">
                Headphones</a></li>
        </ul>
    </div>
</td>
</tr>
```

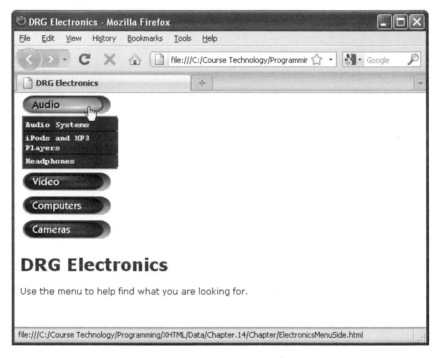

Figure 14-13   Left navigation menu

 You can find a copy of the ElectronicsMenuSide.html document in your Chapter folder for Chapter 14.

Using Sliding Menus

As their name implies, **sliding menus** are menus that appear to slide open and closed. Although the visibility and display properties are useful for showing and hiding menus, they display their associated elements without any sort of effect. To simulate a sliding effect, you must use simple animation techniques along with the left and top properties, depending on whether you are creating a horizontal or vertical menu. To "hide" the contents of a horizontal navigation menu, you must assign a negative value to the table's left property. To hide the contents of a vertical navigation menu, you must assign a negative value to the table's top property.

For example, consider the following Audio menu from the vertical menu version of the script that you saw earlier. Notice the values assigned to the style attribute of the <div> element. The position property is set to "absolute", and the value assigned to the top property is −76px. These settings hide the menu at the top of the screen. The z-index property is assigned a value of −1, which forces the <div> element to render behind the Audio menu button.

```
<td valign="top"
    onmouseover="document.getElementById('b1').src↵
    ='button1over.png'; showAudio()"
    onmouseout="document.getElementById('b1').src↵
    ='button1up.png'; hideAudio()"><a href="">
    <img src="button1up.png" id="b1" border="0"
        vspace="1" hspace="1" /></a><br />
    <div id="audio" class="dropmenu"
        style="position: absolute; top: -76px;↵
            z-index: -1">
        <ul>
            <li><a href="audiosys.html">
            Audio Systems</a></li>
            <li><a href="audioplayers.html">
            iPods and MP3 Players</a></li>
            <li><a href="headphones.html">
            Headphones</a></li>
        </ul>
    </div>
</td>
```

The onmouseover event handler for the <td> element calls a function named showAudio(), which uses a setInterval() method to call a function named showAudioMenu(), which in turn makes each menu visible. The showAudioMenu() function continuously changes the top property of the <div> element until it is equal to 36px, which aligns the top of the menu just below the Audio button. The onmouseout event handlers in each <table> element call a function named hideAudio(). This function uses a setInterval() method to call a function named hideAudioMenu(), which hides the Audio menu. The code in the hideAudio() function is very similar to that in the showAudio() function, except that it continuously decreases the top property of the <div> element until it is equal to −75px, which hides the menu at the top of the document window.

The following code displays the showAudio(), showAudioMenu(), hideAudio(), and hideAudioMenu() functions. The first statement declares a variable named audioPosition, which tracks the position of the Audio menu as it slides up and down. Note that the variable is assigned an initial value of −76px, which hides the menu at the top of the document window. The second statement declares a variable named audioSlider, which is the variable that represents the setInterval() method called by the Audio menu.

```
var audioPosition = -76;
var audioSlider;
function showAudio() {
    clearInterval(audioSlider);
    audioSlider = setInterval("showAudioMenu()",
        10);
}
function showAudioMenu() {
    if (audioPosition <= 36) {
        audioPosition = audioPosition + 2;
        document.getElementById("audio").style.top
            = audioPosition + "px";
    }
    else
        document.getElementById("audio").style
            .zIndex = 1;
}
function hideAudio() {
    clearInterval(audioSlider);
    audioSlider = setInterval("hideAudioMenu()",
        10);
}
function hideAudioMenu() {
    if (audioPosition > -75) {
        audioPosition = audioPosition - 2;
        document.getElementById("audio").style.top
            = audioPosition + "px";
    }
    document.getElementById("audio").style
        .zIndex = -1;
}
```

The Video, Computers, and Cameras menus use similar functions to handle their sliding functionality. You can find a completed version of the electronics store sliding menus, named ElectronicsMenuSlide.html, in your Chapter folder for Chapter 14. Open the file and hold your mouse over the menus to test their sliding functionality.

Next, you will modify the navigation menu for the flighttraining.html page of the DRG Aviation Web site so that it includes sliding functionality.

To add sliding functionality to the Navigation menu of the DRG Aviation home page:

1. Return to the **flighttraining.html** document in your text editor.

2. Locate the `style` attribute for the `<div>` element that displays the Navigation menu. Remove the `visibility` property, and then set the `top` property to 156px and the `z-index` property to −1. These settings hide the menu behind the table cell that contains the Navigation menu button.

3. Replace the second statement assigned to the `onmouseover` event handler for the table cell that displays the Navigation button so that it calls a function named `showNavigation()`. Also, replace the second statement assigned to the `onmouseout` event handler for the table cell that displays the Navigation button so that it calls a function named `hideNavigation()`. The modified `<td>` tag should appear as follows:

```
<td id="navmenu"
    onmouseover="document.getElementById(
        'navimage').src='images/navigation2.jpg';
        showNavigation()"
    onmouseout="document
        .getElementById('navimage').src
        ='images/navigation.jpg';
        hideNavigation()">
```

4. Add the following code to the end of the script section to give the sliding menu its functionality. These statements are virtually identical to those for the sliding Electronics menu.

```
var navigationPosition = 156;
var navigationSlider;
function showNavigation() {
    clearInterval(navigationSlider);
    navigationSlider
        = setInterval("showNavigationMenu()", 10);
}
function showNavigationMenu() {
    if (navigationPosition <= 235) {
        navigationPosition = navigationPosition + 2;
        document.getElementById("navigation").style
            .top = navigationPosition + "px";
}
```

```
        else
            document.getElementById("navigation").style
                .zIndex = 1;
    }
    function hideNavigation() {
        clearInterval(navigationSlider);
        navigationSlider = setInterval(
            "hideNavigationMenu()", 10);
    }
    function hideNavigationMenu() {
        if (navigationPosition > 156) {
            navigationPosition = navigationPosition - 2;
            document.getElementById("navigation").style
                .top = navigationPosition + "px";
    }
        document.getElementById("navigation").style
            .zIndex = -1;
    }
```

5. Save the **flighttraining.html** document, and then validate it with the W3C Markup Validation Service. Once the document is valid, close it in your text editor and then open it in your Web browser. Test the sliding functionality of the Navigation menu.

6. Close your Web browser window and text editor.

Short Quiz 3

1. Explain how to create expandable menus.

2. Explain how to create navigation menus.

3. Explain how to create sliding menus.

Summing Up

- The easiest way to refer to a CSS style in JavaScript is to use the `this` reference and the `style` property in an event handler within the element itself.

- You use the `style` property to modify an element's CSS properties with JavaScript.

- A JavaScript program that checks which type of browser is running is commonly called a browser sniffer.

- CSS positioning is used to lay out elements on a Web page.

- The most critical CSS positioning property is the `position` property, which determines the type of positioning applied to an element.

- The easiest way to dynamically position an element with CSS is to use the `left` and `top` properties.

- With DHTML, you can use dynamic positioning to create animations that "travel" across the screen by modifying the global `topPosition` and `leftPosition` variables that define an image's position.

- DHTML menus are most often used for organizing navigational links to other Web pages, although they are also useful for displaying and hiding information.

- The `display` property specifies whether to display an element on a Web page. You can use the `display` property to simulate expandable and collapsible menus on a Web page. You typically use the `display` property with a block-level element, which gives a Web page its structure.

- Inline, or text-level, elements describe the text that appears on a Web page.

- One block-level element you may already know is the `<div>` element, which formats a group of block-level and inline elements with styles. By placing elements and text within a `<div>` element, you can use the `display` property to simulate expandable and collapsible menus.

- A class selector defines different groups of styles for the same element.

- To show and hide each menu, you use the `visibility` property, which determines whether an element is visible.

- Sliding menus are menus that appear to slide open and closed.

- To simulate a sliding effect, you must use simple animation techniques along with the `left` and `top` properties, depending on whether you are creating a horizontal or vertical menu.

Comprehension Check

1. Before the W3C's standardized version of the DOM was released, no DHTML standard worked with both Internet Explorer and Mozilla-based browsers. If you want to use JavaScript code to manipulate CSS in older browsers, what options do you have?

2. What is the correct syntax for using the `style` property with an `onmouseover` event handler to display an underline beneath a link?

   a. `onmouseover.this="style.textDecoration=underline"`

   b. `onmouseover(this.style.textDecoration="underline")`

   c. `onmouseover="this.style: textDecoration; underline"`

   d. `onmouseover="this.style.textDecoration= 'underline'"`

3. If you pass the `this` reference to a function as a parameter named `linkTarget`, which of the following statements changes the element's text color to blue?

   a. `linkTarget.style.color = "blue";`

   b. `linkTarget.style.textColor = "blue";`

   c. `this.style.color = "blue";`

   d. `this.style = "textColor: blue";`

4. Which of the following statements changes the value of the `font-family` style to Arial for an element with an `id` value of `salesTotal`?

   a. `document.getElementById("salesTotal").style.`
      `font-family = "Arial";`

   b. `document.getElementById("salesTotal").style.`
      `FontFamily = "Arial";`

   c. `document.getElementById("salesTotal").`
      `style(font-family) = "Arial";`

   d. `document.getElementById("salesTotal").style.`
      `fontFamily = "Arial";`

5. How do you use DHTML to show and hide an underline beneath an `<a>` element when the user places the mouse pointer over a link?

6. To determine whether a Web browser is compatible with the W3C DOM, you check whether the browser includes the _____.

   a. `display` property

   b. `position` property

   c. `setInterval()` or `setTimeout()` methods

   d. `getElementById()` method

7. Which of the following CSS properties can you use to dynamically position an element? (Choose all that apply.)

   a. `right`

   b. `left`

   c. `bottom`

   d. `top`

8. Which of the following values can be applied to the `position` property and prevent you from using CSS positioning with an element?

   a. relative

   b. absolute

   c. fixed

   d. static

9. Explain the difference between the `display` and `visibility` properties.

10. What value do you assign to the `display` property to prevent an element from being displayed?

    a. false

    b. hidden

    c. hide

    d. none

11. What value do you assign to the `visibility` property to prevent an element from being visible?

    a. hidden

    b. none

    c. false

    d. hide

12. Which of the following `style` attributes prevents an element from being moved with CSS positioning?

    a. `style="position: absolute; left: 100px; top: 120px"`

    b. `style="position: relative; left: 100px; top: 120px"`

    c. `style="position: static; left: 100px; top: 120px"`

    d. `style="position: fixed; left: 100px; top: 120px"`

13. The `bottom` and `right` properties determine the position of an element's lower-right corner in relation to the _____.

    a. lower-right corner of the document window

    b. upper-left corner of the document window

    c. lower-right corner of the visible screen area

    d. upper-left corner of the browser window

14. The _____ property determines the order in which dynamically positioned elements are layered.

    a. `ordering`

    b. `z-index`

    c. `visibility`

    d. `layer`

15. Explain how to create traveling animation with DHTML.

16. What determines an element's starting position when creating traveling animation with DHTML?

    a. the values assigned to the global `topPosition` and `leftPosition` variables

    b. the values assigned to the `left` and `top` style properties in the opening `<body>` tag

    c. the values assigned to an element's `left` and `top` style properties

    d. You cannot determine an element's starting position when creating traveling animation with DHTML; the element's position is randomly generated for each animation sequence.

17. You can use the _____ property to simulate expandable and collapsible menus on a Web page.

    a. display

    b. slide

    c. static

    d. z-order

18. To allocate sufficient space for a sliding menu, you must use the _____ along with simple animation techniques.

    a. slide property

    b. top and bottom properties

    c. left and top properties

    d. z-order property

19. If you assign a value of "hidden" to an element's visibility property, space is allocated for the element, but it is not displayed. True or False?

20. Explain how to use tables to create a navigation menu.

Reinforcement Exercises

 Exercise 14-1

In this chapter, you learned how to use CSS positioning to set and return the position of elements on a Web page. However, this approach only works with elements that include properties such as position, left, and top. To find the position of an element that does not include CSS positioning properties, you can use the offsetLeft and offsetTop properties. Similarly, you can use the offsetWidth and offsetHeight properties to return the size of an element on a Web page. All four of these offset properties are available to most current Web browsers. In this exercise, you will create a document that uses the offsetTop and offsetWidth properties to display context-sensitive help for the fields on a form. The exercise will also use the CSS cursor property to dynamically change the cursor to a help cursor when the mouse pointer passes over a form element that contains context-sensitive help.

1. Create a new document in your text editor.

2. Type the `<!DOCTYPE>` declaration, `<html>` element, document head, and `<body>` element. Use the strict DTD and "Form Help" as the content of the `<title>` element.

3. Add the following elements and text to the document body. The form contains four text boxes for a user name, password, password confirmation, and challenge question. Each text box contains an `onmouseover` event that changes the cursor to a help cursor and an `onclick` event that passes the element's `id` attribute to a function named `showHelp()`, which you will create shortly. The `<div>` element will be used to display the context-sensitive help information for each field. Note that the `<div>` element is initially hidden by assigning a value of "hidden" to the `visibility` property.

```
<h1>Form Help</h1>
<form action="" method="get"
enctype="application/x-www-form-urlencoded">
<p><strong>User name</strong><br />
<input type="text" id="username" size="50"
onmouseover="this.style.cursor='help'"
    onclick="showHelp(this.id)" /></p>
<p><strong>Password</strong><br />
<input type="password" id="password" size="50"
onmouseover="this.style.cursor='help'"
    onclick="showHelp(this.id)" /></p>
<p><strong>Confirm password</strong><br />
<input type="password" id="password_confirm" size="50"
onmouseover="this.style.cursor='help'"
    onclick="showHelp(this.id)" /></p>
<p><strong>What is your mother's maiden name?
</strong><br />
<input type="password" id="challenge" size="50"
onmouseover="this.style.cursor='help'"
    onclick="showHelp(this.id)" /></p>
</form>
<div id="box" style="position: absolute; ↵
    visibility: hidden; width: 250px; ↵
    background-color:#FFFFC0; font: Comic Sans MS; ↵
    color: #A00000;border:1px dashed #D00000"></div>
```

4. Add a script section to the document head.

5. Create the following `showHelp()` function in the script section. The first two statements use the `getElementById()` methods to retrieve the form element represented by the `elementId` parameter and the `<div>` element that is assigned an `id` attribute value of "box".

```
function showHelp(elementId) {
    var curElement = document.getElementById(
        elementId);
    var helpElement = document.getElementById(
        "box");
}
```

6. Add the following `switch` statement to the end of the `showHelp()` function. The statement evaluates the `elementId` parameter and then uses the `innerHTML` property to assign the appropriate help text to the `<div>` element. Be sure to enter each text string on a single line.

```
switch (elementId) {
    case "username":
        helpElement.innerHTML = "Enter a ↵
            unique user name that is between ↵
            5 and 12 characters.";
        break;
    case "password":
        helpElement.innerHTML = "Enter a ↵
            password between 6 and 10 ↵
            characters that contains both ↵
            upper and lowercase letters and ↵
            at least one numeric character. ";
        break;
    case "password_confirm":
        helpElement.innerHTML
            = "Confirm your selected password. ";
        break;
    case "challenge":
        helpElement.innerHTML
            = "Enter your mother's maiden ↵
            name. This value will be used ↵
            to confirm your identity in ↵
            the event that you forget ↵
            your password. ";
        break;
}
```

7. Finally, add the following statements to the end of the `showHelp()` function. The first statement adds an anchor element to the `innerHTML` property of the `<div>` element that users can click to hide the context-sensitive help box. The second statement displays the `<div>` element by assigning a value of "visible" to the visibility property. The third statement obtains the width of the current form field using the `offsetWidth` property, adds 20 pixels to better position the help box, and then assigns the result to the `left` property of the `<div>` element. The fourth statement obtains the top position of the current form field by using the `offsetTop` property and assigns the result to the `top` property of the `<div>` element.

```
helpElement.innerHTML += "<a href=''↵
    onclick=\"document.getElementById('box')↵
    .style.visibility='hidden'; return false;\">
    Close</a>";
document.getElementById("box").style.visibility
    = "visible";
document.getElementById("box").style.left
    = curElement.offsetWidth + 20 + "px";
document.getElementById("box").style.top
    = curElement.offsetTop + "px";
```

8. Save the document as **FormHelp.html** in your Exercises folder for Chapter 14, and validate the document with the W3C Markup Validation Service. Once the document is valid, open it in your Web browser and test the context-sensitive help functionality.

9. Close your Web browser window.

 ## Exercise 14-2

In this exercise, you will create a document with a link that appears to shake when you move your cursor over it.

1. Create a new document in your text editor.

2. Type the <!DOCTYPE> declaration, <html> element, document head, and <body> element. Use the strict DTD and "Shaking Link" as the content of the <title> element.

3. Add a script section to the document head.

4. Add the following link to the document body. The link includes an onmouseover event handler that uses the setInterval() method to call a function named shakeLink(), which you will add next. The onmouseout event handler clears the setInterval() method.

```
<p><a id="earthquake" style="position: relative"
    href="http://www.earthquake.com"
    onmouseover="shakeVar=setInterval(↵
        'shakeLink()', 10);"
    onmouseout="clearTimeout(shakeVar);">
    Global Earthquake Response Center</a></p>
```

5. Add the following code to the script section. The shakeLink() function, which is called by the onmouseover event handler in the link, gives the script its functionality.

```
var shakeVar;
var direction = "left";
function shakeLink() {
    if (direction == "left") {
        document.getElementById("earthquake")
            .style.left="3px";
        direction = "right";
    }
    else {
        document.getElementById("earthquake")
            .style.left="0px";
        direction = "left";
    }
}
```

6. Save the document as **ShakingLink.html** in your Exercises folder for Chapter 14, and validate the document with the W3C Markup Validation Service. Once the document is valid, open it in your Web browser. Place your mouse pointer over the link and verify that the link starts to shake. Move your mouse pointer off the link and verify that it stops shaking.

7. Close your Web browser window.

Exercise 14-3

In your Web travels, you have probably encountered "mouse trails"— that is, some sort of image or stylistic element that follows the cursor as it moves around a Web page. You create mouse trails by using DHTML along with the onmousemove event and the screenX and screenY properties of the Event object of the HTML DOM. The screenX property returns the horizontal coordinate of the cursor when an event occurs, and the screenY property returns the vertical coordinate of the cursor when an event occurs. In this exercise, you will create a Web page that contains a definition and image of a comet. When the mouse is moved over a <div> element that contains the page's text and elements, a mouse trail will appear that resembles a comet's tail. Your Exercises folder for Chapter 14 contains an image named comet.jpg that you can use for this exercise.

1. Create a new document in your text editor.

2. Type the <!DOCTYPE> declaration, <html> element, header information, and the <body> element. Use the strict DTD and "Mouse Trail" as the content of the <title> element.

3. Add the following style section to the document head:

```
<style type="text/css">
h1 { font-family: arial; color: navy; }
p, td { font-family: arial; font-size: 12px;
color: black; }
</style>
```

4. Create the following <div> element in the document body. The element's onmousemove event calls an event handler named moveMouse(). The event handler function is passed an argument named event, which is an object that contains information about the event that occurred. You will use the event argument to access the screenX and screenY properties.

```
<div onmousemove="moveMouse(event)">
</div>
```

5. Add the following text and elements as the content of the <div> element. The content contains a heading element, a description of the comet from Wikipedia, and an image of a comet.

```
<h1>Comet</h1>
<p><a href="http://en.wikipedia.org/wiki/Comet">
Wikipedia</a>
defines a comet as follows:</p>
<table border="1" cellpadding="5">
<colgroup span="1" width="275" />
<colgroup span="1" width="200" />
<tr><td valign="top">A comet is a small body in the solar
system that orbits the Sun and (at least occasionally)
exhibits a coma (or atmosphere) and/or a tail – both
primarily from the effects of solar radiation upon the
comet's nucleus, which itself is a minor body composed of
rock, dust, and ice. Comets' orbits are constantly
changing: Their origins are in the outer solar system, and
they have a propensity to be highly affected (or
perturbed) by relatively close approaches to the major
planets. Some are moved into sun-grazing orbits that
destroy the comets when they near the Sun, while others
are thrown out of the solar system forever.</td>
<td><img src="comet.jpg" alt="Image of a comet"
height="200" width="250" /></td>
</tr></table>
```

6. Add the following script section and global variables to the document head. The trailInterval variable determines the length of the "trail" that follows the mouse. The xPosition and yPosition variables will store the horizontal and vertical mouse coordinates. The animationStarted

variable determines whether the animation that controls the mouse trail has been started. Note that the xPosition and yPosition variables are assigned an initial value of −10. Each portion of the trail will be created with an empty <div> element that is assigned a background color of blue, which will make the trail appear as a series of blue squares. This allows you to create a mouse trail without any image files. The initial values assigned to the xPosition and yPosition variables hide the blue squares that appear when the Web page first loads.

```
<script type="text/javascript">
/* <![CDATA[ */
var trailInterval = 12;
var xPosition = -10;
var yPosition = -10;
var animationStarted = false;
/* ]]> */
</script>
```

7. Add the following for loop to the end of the script section. The loop contains a single document.write() statement that creates the number of <div> elements that will make up the mouse trail according to the value assigned to the trailInterval variable. Each <div> element is assigned a unique id value of "trail" + i (the i represents the current counter). Because the trailInterval variable is assigned a value of 12, the for loop creates 12 <div> elements with id values of "trail0" through "trail11". You will use each id value to control the display of the mouse trail. Each <div> element's position property is assigned a value of "absolute" so that it can be dynamically positioned; the background-color property is assigned a value of "blue". The top and left properties are assigned the values of the xPosition and yPosition variables, respectively. (Recall that an initial value of −10 is assigned to these variables, which hides the <div> elements when the Web page first loads.) Notice the values assigned to the width, height, and font-size properties. Each of these properties is assigned a value of i (the for loop counter variable) divided by 2. This code creates 12 <div> elements; the first will have a width, height, and font size of 0.5, and the final element will have a width, height, and font size of 6. These elements will appear as a series of gradually diminishing blue squares that make up the mouse trail.

```
for (i = 1; i <= trailInterval; i++) {
    document.write("<div id='trail" + i
        + "' style='position: absolute; ⏎
        background-color: blue; top: "
```

```
                        + yPosition + "px; left:" + xPosition
                        + "px; width: " + i/2 + "px; height: " + i/2
                        + "px; font-size: " + i/2 + "px'></div>");
    }
```

8. Add the following `mouseMove()` function to the end of the script section. The function assigns the horizontal and vertical mouse coordinates to the `xPosition` and `yPosition` variables using the `screenX` and `screenY` properties of the `Event` object. Because Firefox and Internet Explorer use different mappings for the vertical mouse coordinates, the `if...else` statement uses the `appName` property of the `Navigator` object to determine the name of the browser and assign the appropriate value to the `yPosition` variable. The last `if` statement checks the value of the `animationStarted` variable to determine whether the animation that controls the mouse trail has started. If the variable contains a value of false, it is assigned a value of true and the `animate()` function is called. The `animate()` function will contain the code that causes the `<div>` elements to "follow" the cursor to create the mouse trail. You will create the `animate()` function in Step 9.

```
function moveMouse(e) {
    xPosition = e.screenX + 10;
    if (navigator.appName
        == "Microsoft Internet Explorer") {
        yPosition = e.screenY - 122;
    }
    else if (navigator.appName == "Mozilla") {
        yPosition = e.screenY - 65;
    }
    if (!animationStarted) {
        animationStarted = true;
        animate();
    }
}
```

9. To the end of the script section, add the following `animate()` function. The function declares two local variables, `div1` and `div2`. The `for` loop iterates through each `<div>` element and changes its value to the value of the previous `<div>` element. This causes each `<div>` element to replace the previous one, which creates the mouse trail. The last statement in the function uses the `setTimeout()` method to execute the function every 40 milliseconds.

```
function animate(){
    var div1, div2;
    for (i = 1; i <= trailInterval; i++){
        div1 = document.getElementById(
```

```
        "trail"+i);
    if (i < trailInterval){
        div2 = document.getElementById(
            "trail"+(i+1));
        div1.style.top = div2.style.top;
        div1.style.left = div2.style.left;
    }
    else {
        div1.style.top = yPosition + "px";
        div1.style.left = xPosition
            + "px";
    }
    }
    setTimeout("animate()",40);
}
```

10. Save the document as **MouseTrail.html** in your Exercises folder for Chapter 14, and then validate the document with the W3C Markup Validation Service. Once the document is valid, close it in your text editor.

11. Open the **MouseTrail.html** document in your Web browser. Move your mouse over the text and elements to test the mouse trail.

12. Close your Web browser window.

Exercise 14-4

In this exercise, you will create a Web page with a ball that bounces randomly within the document area of the Web browser. To create the calculation that causes the ball to bounce randomly, you need to determine the width and height of the browser window's document portion. With the exception of Internet Explorer, the Window object for most current Web browsers includes innerWidth and innerHeight properties. These properties return the width and height, respectively, of the document displayed in a Web browser. To return the width and height of the document displayed in Internet Explorer, you must use the clientWidth and clientHeight properties of the document.documentElement object. Your Exercises folder for Chapter 14 contains an image named ball.gif that you can use for this exercise.

1. Create a new document in your text editor.

2. Type the <!DOCTYPE> declaration, <html> element, document head, and <body> element. Use the strict DTD and "Bounce" as the content of the <title> element.

3. Add the following `<div>` element to the document body to dynamically position the ball.gif image:

```
<div id="ballElement"
style="position:absolute; left:0px;top:0px">
<img id="ballImage" src="ball.gif"
alt="Image of a ball"
height="48" width="48" /></div>
```

4. Add a script section to the document head.

5. In the script section, add the following global variables, which will store information about the speed, position, and direction of the bouncing ball. The last variable will represent a `setTimeout()` method.

```
var bounceSpeed = 5;
var widthMax = 0;
var heightMax = 0;
var xPosition = 0;
var yPosition = 0;
var xDirection = "right";
var yDirection = "down";
var ballBounce;
```

6. At the end of the script section, add the following `setBall()` function, which contains an `if...else` statement to determine the width of the window's document portion according to the browser type. The last statement uses the `setTimeout()` method to call a function named `bounceBall()`, which dynamically moves the ball image. Notice that the `clearTimeout()` statement clears the current `setTimeout()` statement before calling the `bounceBall()` function. You will create the `bounceBall()` function next.

```
function setBall() {
    if (navigator.appName
        == "Microsoft Internet Explorer") {
        widthMax = document.documentElement
            .clientWidth;
        heightMax = document.documentElement
            .clientHeight;
    }
    else {
        widthMax = window.innerWidth-14;
        heightMax = window.innerHeight;
    }
    clearTimeout(ballBounce);
    bounceBall();
}
```

7. Create the following `bounceBall()` function at the end of the script section:

```
function bounceBall() {
}
```

8. Add the following statements to the `bounceBall()` function. These statements calculate the path and direction of the bouncing ball.

```
if (xDirection == "right" && xPosition > (widthMax
    - document.getElementById("ballImage").width
    - bounceSpeed))
    xDirection = "left";
else if (xDirection == "left" && xPosition < (0
    + bounceSpeed))
    xDirection = "right";
if (yDirection == "down" && yPosition > (heightMax
    - document.getElementById("ballImage").height
    - bounceSpeed))
    yDirection = "up";
else if (yDirection == "up" && yPosition < (0
    + bounceSpeed))
    yDirection = "down";
if (xDirection == "right")
    xPosition = xPosition + bounceSpeed;
else if (xDirection == "left")
    xPosition = xPosition - bounceSpeed;
else
    xPosition = xPosition;
if (yDirection == "down")
    yPosition = yPosition + bounceSpeed;
else if (yDirection == "up")
    yPosition = yPosition - bounceSpeed;
else
    yPosition = yPosition;
```

9. Add the following statements to the end of the `bounceBall()` function. These statements use the values that were assigned to the `xPosition` and `yPosition` variables in the preceding `if...else` statements to dynamically position the ball. The last statement uses a `setTimeout()` method to call the function again in 30 milliseconds.

```
document.getElementById("ballElement").style
    .left = xPosition + "px";
document.getElementById("ballElement").style
    .top = yPosition + "px";
clearTimeout(ballBounce);
setTimeout('bounceBall()',30);
```

10. Add the following statement to the end of the script section. If the window is resized, this statement restarts the animation by calling the setBall() method, which retrieves the new dimensions of the document and restarts the bounceBall() function.

```
window.onresize = setBall;
```

11. Finally, add the following onload event handler to the opening <body> tag to call the setBall() function when the document first loads:

```
<body onload="setBall()">
```

12. Save the document as **Bounce.html** in your Exercises folder for Chapter 14, and then validate the document with the W3C Markup Validation Service. Once the document is valid, close it in your text editor.

13. Open the **Bounce.html** document in your Web browser. The ball should start bouncing as soon as the page finishes loading. Try resizing the window to see if the animation adjusts to the new document size.

14. Close your Web browser window.

 ## Exercise 14-5

The clip CSS position property determines the region of an element that is displayed. To determine which portions of an element are displayed, you assign the clip property a value of "rect(*top right bottom left*)". The *top*, *right*, *bottom*, and *left* parameters specify values, in pixels, of the amount of space to clip around the element. Be sure not to separate the parameters in the rect() value with commas, as you would with the arguments you pass to a method or function. For example, to clip 10 pixels from all sides of an element, you assign a value of "rect(10px 10px 10px 10px)" to the clip property. In this exercise, you will use the clip property to create a screen transition effect of a shrinking box; the box covers an entire Web page when it first loads, then shrinks and disappears.

1. Create a new document in your text editor.

2. Type the <!DOCTYPE> declaration, <html> element, document head, and <body> element. Use the strict DTD and "Boxed In" as the content of the <title> element.

3. In the document body, add the following <div> element, which will be used to create the shrinking box:

```
<div id="il" style="position: absolute; ↵
    background-color: blue"></div>
```

4. Add a script section to the document body.

5. In the script section, add the following global variables, which will store information about the shrinking box:

```
var clipSpeed=5;
var clipRight = 0;
var clipLeft = 0;
var clipTop = 0;
var boxSize;
var stopShrinking;
var clipBottom = 0;
var clipBox=document.getElementById("il").style;
```

6. At the end of the script section, add the following startShrinking() function, which contains an if...else statement to determine the width of the window's document portion according to the browser type. The last statement uses the setInterval() method to call a function named shrinkBox(), which dynamically shrinks the box. You will create the shrinkBox() function next.

```
function startShrinking() {
    if (navigator.appName
        == "Microsoft Internet Explorer") {
        boxSize = document.documentElement
            .clientWidth / document.documentElement
            .clientHeight;
        clipRight = document.documentElement
            .clientWidth;
        clipBox.width = clipRight + "px";
            clipBottom=document.documentElement
            .clientHeight;
        clipBox.height=clipBottom + "px";
    }
    else {
            boxSize = window.innerWidth/
            window.innerHeight;
            clipRight=window.innerWidth;
            clipBox.width = clipRight + "px";
            clipBottom=window.innerHeight;
            clipBox.height=clipBottom + "px";
    }
    stopShrinking=setInterval("shrinkBox()",100);
}
```

7. Add the following `shrinkBox()` function to the end of the script section. The statements in this function dynamically shrink the box until it disappears.

```
function shrinkBox() {
    if (navigator.appName
        == "Microsoft Internet Explorer")
        minBoxSize = document.documentElement
            .clientWidth/2;
    else
        minBoxSize = window.innerWidth/2;
        if (clipLeft > minBoxSize) {
            clearInterval(stopShrinking);
            clipBox.display = "none";
        }
        clipBox.clip = "rect(" + clipTop + "px "
            + clipRight + "px "
            + clipBottom + "px " + clipLeft + "px)"
        clipLeft += boxSize * clipSpeed;
        clipTop += clipSpeed;
        clipRight -= boxSize * clipSpeed;
        clipBottom -= clipSpeed;
}
```

8. Add an `onload` event handler to the opening `<body>` tag that calls the `startShrinking()` function, as follows:

```
<body onload="startShrinking()">
```

9. Save the document as **BoxedIn.html** in your Exercises folder for Chapter 14, and then validate the document with the W3C Markup Validation Service. Once the document is valid, close it in your text editor.

10. Open the **BoxedIn.html** document in your Web browser. As soon as the page finishes loading, the document portion of the window should be filled with a blue rectangle that gradually shrinks until it disappears.

11. Close your Web browser window.

Discovery Projects

For the following projects, save the documents you create in your Projects folder for Chapter 14. Be sure to validate the documents you create with the W3C Markup Validation Service.

Discovery Project 14-1

Your Projects folder for Chapter 14 contains six images of leaves: leaf1.gif through leaf6.gif. Use each image as many times as you like to create a Web page with falling leaves. Use image caching to ensure that all the images are loaded before the animation begins. Include code that randomly selects which leaf image to display. The formula for randomly selecting a leaf is `Math.floor(Math.random() * numImages)`. Because there are six leaf images, the *numImages* argument should be 6. Also, use the `Math.random()` method to randomly select how fast each leaf falls and the position where it begins falling. Determine the height and width of the document area by using the `document.documentElement.clientHeight` and `document.documentElement.clientWidth` properties in Internet Explorer, or the `window.innerWidth` and `window.innerHeight` for all other browsers. Save the document as **Autumn.html**.

Discovery Project 14-2

Your Projects folder for Chapter 14 contains an image file of a mosquito named bug.gif. Use the same bounce techniques from Reinforcement Exercise 14-4 to dynamically animate the image so the mosquito appears to fly randomly around the page and bounce off the boundaries of the window's document portion. However, instead of animating a single image, create at least five animated images that move along different paths in the window. To ensure that each image moves along a different path, you only need to set a unique vertical position for each image's starting point. Use a separate `<div>` element for each image. All images should appear to "fly in" from the left side of the screen, so the starting horizontal value for each `<div>` element must be negative. Make sure that some images begin traveling in an upward direction and that some images begin traveling in a downward direction. You will need to store information about the speed, position, and direction of each image in arrays. Use a separate `setInterval()` or `setTimeout()` method to begin animating each image. Save the document as **Buzz.html**.

Discovery Project 14-3

In Reinforcement Exercise 14-5, you used the `clip` property to create a screen transition effect of a box that covers an entire Web page when it first loads, then shrinks and disappears. Use the same technique to create a box that covers an entire Web page, then gradually opens from right to left like a curtain. Remember that you must determine the height and width of the document area by using the `document.documentElement.clientHeight` and `document.documentElement.clientWidth` properties in Internet Explorer, or the `window.innerWidth` and `window.innerHeight` for all other browsers. Save the document as **Curtain.html**.

Discovery Project 14-4

Create a Web page that contains a drop-down menu with items for five types of sports, such as football and baseball. Each menu should display at least three links to Web sites that contain information about each sport. For example, the Football menu may contain links to NFL.com (*http://www.nfl.com*), ESPN's NFL page (*http://sports.espn.go.com/nfl/index*), and Yahoo! Sports NFL page (*http://sports.yahoo.com/nfl;_ylt=AsRakGSbKIS7qaEoSsk90ls5nYcB*). Save the document as **SportsNews.html**.

Discovery Project 14-5

You have probably seen the "warp" or "starfield" animation effect that simulates flying through space. With the warp animation, stars usually begin as small points of light in the middle of the computer screen, and then gradually grow larger and eventually fly off the screen. Use the DHTML techniques that you learned in this chapter to simulate this type of warp animation. This advanced project requires a strong understanding of JavaScript's mathematical functions to properly calculate the trajectory of each star and gradually increase its size as it approaches the edge of the screen. If you do not have a strong math background, do your best to create a simple warp animation with a few stars that begin in the middle of the screen and eventually fly off the edge of the screen. Save the document as **Warp.html**.

Numeric Character References and Character Entities

A numeric character reference inserts a special character using its numeric position in the Unicode character set. To display a character using a numeric character reference, you place an ampersand (&) and the number sign (#) before the character's Unicode number and a semicolon after the Unicode number. A character entity reference, or character entity, uses a descriptive name for a special character instead of its Unicode number. To display a character using a character entity, you place an ampersand (&) before the character entity's descriptive name and a semicolon after the name. Note that you do not include the number sign (#) after the ampersand as you do with numeric character references.

The following tables list the available numeric character references and character entities.

Latin 1 character set

Character	Description	Numeric Character Reference	Character Entity
	Space	&#32;	
!	Exclamation mark	&#33;	
"	Quotation mark	&#34;	&quot;
#	Number sign	&#35;	
$	Dollar sign	&#36;	
%	Percent sign	&#37;	
&	Ampersand	&#38;	&amp;
'	Apostrophe	&#39;	
(	Left parenthesis	&#40;	
)	Right parenthesis	&#41;	
*	Asterisk	&#42;	
+	Plus sign	&#43;	
,	Comma	&#44;	
-	Hyphen	&#45;	
.	Period	&#46;	
/	Forward slash	&#47;	
0	Numeral 0	&#48;	
1	Numeral 1	&#49;	
2	Numeral 2	&#50;	
3	Numeral 3	&#51;	
4	Numeral 4	&#52;	
5	Numeral 5	&#53;	
6	Numeral 6	&#54;	
7	Numeral 7	&#55;	
8	Numeral 8	&#56;	
9	Numeral 9	&#57;	
:	Colon	&#58;	
;	Semicolon	&#59;	
<	Less than	&#60;	&lt;
=	Equals sign	&#61;	
>	Greater than	&#62;	&gt;
?	Question mark	&#63;	
@	At symbol	&#64;	
A	Capital A	&#65;	

(continues)

(continued)

Latin 1 character set

Character	Description	Numeric Character Reference	Character Entity
B	Capital B	&#66;	
C	Capital C	&#67;	
D	Capital D	&#68;	
E	Capital E	&#69;	
F	Capital F	&#70;	
G	Capital G	&#71;	
H	Capital H	&#72;	
I	Capital I	&#73;	
J	Capital J	&#74;	
K	Capital K	&#75;	
L	Capital L	&#76;	
M	Capital M	&#77;	
N	Capital N	&#78;	
O	Capital O	&#79;	
P	Capital P	&#80;	
Q	Capital Q	&#81;	
R	Capital R	&#82;	
S	Capital S	&#83;	
T	Capital T	&#84;	
U	Capital U	&#85;	
V	Capital V	&#86;	
W	Capital W	&#87;	
X	Capital X	&#88;	
Y	Capital Y	&#89;	
Z	Capital Z	&#90;	
[	Left square bracket	&#91;	
\	Backslash	&#92;	
]	Right square bracket	&#93;	
^	Caret	&#94;	
_	Underscore	&#95;	
`	Acute accent	&#96;	
a	Small a	&#97;	

(continues)

(continued)

Latin 1 character set

Character	Description	Numeric Character Reference	Character Entity
b	Small b	&#98;	
c	Small c	&#99;	
d	Small d	&#100;	
e	Small e	&#101;	
f	Small f	&#102;	
g	Small g	&#103;	
h	Small h	&#104;	
i	Small i	&#105;	
j	Small j	&#106;	
k	Small k	&#107;	
l	Small l	&#108;	
m	Small m	&#109;	
n	Small n	&#110;	
o	Small o	&#111;	
p	Small p	&#112;	
q	Small q	&#113;	
r	Small r	&#114;	
s	Small s	&#115;	
t	Small t	&#116;	
u	Small u	&#117;	
v	Small v	&#118;	
w	Small w	&#119;	
x	Small x	&#120;	
y	Small y	&#121;	
z	Small z	&#122;	
{	Left brace	&#123;	
|	Vertical bar	|	
}	Right brace	&#125;	
~	Tilde	&#126;	
	Nonbreaking space		
¡	Inverted exclamation mark	&#161;	&iexcl;
¢	Cent sign	&#162;	&cent;

(continues)

(continued)

Latin 1 character set

Character	Description	Numeric Character Reference	Character Entity
£	Pound sterling	&#163;	&pound;
¤	General currency sign	&#164;	&curren;
¥	Yen sign	&#165;	&yen;
¦	Broken vertical bar	&#166;	¦ or &brkbar;
§	Section sign	&#167;	&sect;
¨	Diaeresis / umlaut	&#168;	¨ or ¨
©	Copyright	&#169;	&copy;
ª	Feminine ordinal	&#170;	&ordf;
«	Left angle quote	&#171;	&laquo;
¬	Not sign	&#172;	&not;
	Soft hyphen	&#173;	&shy;
®	Registered trademark	&#174;	&reg;
¯	Macron accent	&#175;	¯ or &hibar;
°	Degree sign	&#176;	&deg;
±	Plus or minus	&#177;	&plusmn;
²	Superscript two	&#178;	&sup2;
³	Superscript three	&#179;	&sup3;
´	Acute accent	&#180;	&acute;
µ	Micro sign	&#181;	&micro;
¶	Paragraph sign	&#182;	&para;
·	Middle dot	&#183;	&middot;
¸	Cedilla	&#184;	&cedil;
¹	Superscript one	&#185;	&sup1;
º	Masculine ordinal	&#186;	&ordm;
»	Right angle quote	&#187;	&raquo;
¼	Fraction one-fourth	&#188;	&frac14;
½	Fraction one-half	&#189;	&frac12;
¾	Fraction three-fourths	&#190;	&frac34;
¿	Inverted question mark	&#191;	&iquest;

(continues)

(continued)

Latin 1 character set

Character	Description	Numeric Character Reference	Character Entity
À	Capital A, grave accent	&#192;	&Agrave;
Á	Capital A, acute accent	&#193;	&Aacute;
Â	Capital A, circumflex	&#194;	&Acirc;
Ã	Capital A, tilde	&#195;	&Atilde;
Ä	Capital A, diaeresis / umlaut	&#196;	&Auml;
Å	Capital A, ring	&#197;	&Aring;
Æ	Capital AE ligature	&#198;	&AElig;
Ç	Capital C, cedilla	&#199;	&Ccedil;
È	Capital E, grave accent	&#200;	&Egrave;
É	Capital E, acute accent	&#201;	&Eacute;
Ê	Capital E, circumflex	&#202;	&Ecirc;
Ë	Capital E, diaeresis / umlaut	&#203;	&Euml;
Ì	Capital I, grave accent	&#204;	&Igrave;
Í	Capital I, acute accent	&#205;	&Iacute;
Î	Capital I, circumflex	&#206;	&Icirc;
Ï	Capital I, diaeresis / umlaut	&#207;	&Iuml;
Ð	Capital Eth, Icelandic	&#208;	&ETH;
Ñ	Capital N, tilde	&#209;	&Ntilde;
Ò	Capital O, grave accent	&#210;	&Ograve;
Ó	Capital O, acute accent	&#211;	&Oacute;

(continues)

(continued)

Latin 1 character set

Character	Description	Numeric Character Reference	Character Entity
Ô	Capital O, circumflex	&#212;	&Ocirc;
Õ	Capital O, tilde	&#213;	&Otilde;
Ö	Capital O, diaeresis / umlaut	&#214;	&Ouml;
×	Multiply sign	&#215;	&times;
Ø	Capital O, slash	&#216;	&Oslash;
Ù	Capital U, grave accent	&#217;	&Ugrave;
Ú	Capital U, acute accent	&#218;	&Uacute;
Û	Capital U, circumflex	&#219;	&Ucirc;
Ü	Capital U, diaeresis / umlaut	&#220;	&Uuml;
Ý	Capital Y, acute accent	&#221;	&Yacute;
Þ	Capital Thorn, Icelandic	&#222;	&THORN;
ß	Small sharp s, German sz	&#223;	&szlig;
à	Small a, grave accent	&#224;	&agrave;
á	Small a, acute accent	&#225;	&aacute;
â	Small a, circumflex	&#226;	&acirc;
ã	Small a, tilde	&#227;	&atilde;
ä	Small a, diaeresis / umlaut	&#228;	&auml;
å	Small a, ring	&#229;	&aring;
æ	Small ae ligature	&#230;	&aelig;
ç	Small c, cedilla	&#231;	&ccedil;
è	Small e, grave accent	&#232;	&egrave;
é	Small e, acute accent	&#233;	&eacute;

(continues)

(continued)

Latin 1 character set

Character	Description	Numeric Character Reference	Character Entity
ê	Small e, circumflex	&#234;	&ecirc;
ë	Small e, diaeresis / umlaut	&#235;	&euml;
ì	Small i, grave accent	&#236;	&igrave;
í	Small i, acute accent	&#237;	&iacute;
î	Small i, circumflex	&#238;	&icirc;
ï	Small i, diaeresis / umlaut	&#239;	&iuml;
ð	Small eth, Icelandic	&#240;	&eth;
ñ	Small n, tilde	&#241;	&ntilde;
ò	Small o, grave accent	&#242;	&ograve;
ó	Small o, acute accent	&#243;	&oacute;
ô	Small o, circumflex	&#244;	&ocirc;
õ	Small o, tilde	&#245;	&otilde;
ö	Small o, diaeresis / umlaut	&#246;	&ouml;
÷	Division sign	&#247;	&divide;
ø	Small o, slash	&#248;	&oslash;
ù	Small u, grave accent	&#249;	&ugrave;
ú	Small u, acute accent	&#250;	&uacute;
û	Small u, circumflex	&#251;	&ucirc;
ü	Small u, diaeresis / umlaut	&#252;	&uuml;
ý	Small y, acute accent	&#253;	&yacute;
þ	Small thorn, Icelandic	&#254;	&thorn;
ÿ	Small y, diaeresis / umlaut	&#255;	&yuml;

Latin extended-A and Latin extended-B character set

Character	Description	Numeric Character Reference	Character Entity
Œ	Latin capital ligature oe	&#338;	&OElig;
œ	Latin small ligature oe	&#339;	&oelig;
Š	Latin capital letter S with caron	&#352;	&Scaron;
š	Latin small letter s with caron	&#353;	&scaron;
Ÿ	Latin capital letter Y with diaeresis	&#376;	&Yuml;
ƒ	Latin small f with hook	&#402;	&fnof;

Greek character set

Character	Description	Character Entity	Numeric Character Reference
A	Greek capital letter alpha	&Alpha;	&#913;
B	Greek capital letter beta	&Beta;	&#914;
Γ	Greek capital letter gamma	&Gamma;	&#915;
Δ	Greek capital letter delta	&Delta;	&#916;
E	Greek capital letter epsilon	&Epsilon;	&#917;
Z	Greek capital letter zeta	&Zeta;	&#918;
H	Greek capital letter eta	&Eta;	&#919;
Θ	Greek capital letter theta	&Theta;	&#920;
I	Greek capital letter iota	&Iota;	&#921;
K	Greek capital letter kappa	&Kappa;	&#922;
Λ	Greek capital letter lambda	&Lambda;	&#923;
M	Greek capital letter mu	&Mu;	&#924;
N	Greek capital letter nu	&Nu;	&#925;
ϑ	Greek capital letter xi	&Xi;	&#926;
O	Greek capital letter omicron	&Omicron;	&#927;
Π	Greek capital letter pi	&Pi;	&#928;
P	Greek capital letter rho	&Rho;	&#929;
Σ	Greek capital letter sigma	&Sigma;	&#931;
T	Greek capital letter tau	&Tau;	&#932;
Ψ	Greek capital letter upsilon	&Upsilon;	&#933;
Φ	Greek capital letter phi	&Phi;	&#934;
Ξ	Greek capital letter chi	&Chi;	&#935;

(continues)

(continued)

Greek character set

Character	Description	Character Entity	Numeric Character Reference
Χ	Greek capital letter psi	&Psi;	&#936;
ς	Greek capital letter omega	&Omega;	&#937;
α	Greek small letter alpha	&alpha;	&#945;
β	Greek small letter beta	&beta;	&#946;
γ	Greek small letter gamma	&gamma;	&#947;
δ	Greek small letter delta	&delta;	&#948;
×	Greek small letter epsilon	&epsilon;	&#949;
ζ	Greek small letter zeta	&zeta;	&#950;
η	Greek small letter eta	&eta;	&#951;
υ	Greek small letter theta	&theta;	&#952;
ι	Greek small letter iota	&iota;	&#953;
κ	Greek small letter kappa	&kappa;	&#954;
λ	Greek small letter lambda	&lambda;	&#955;
μ	Greek small letter mu	&mu;	&#956;
ν	Greek small letter nu	&nu;	&#957;
φ	Greek small letter xi	&xi;	&#958;
o	Greek small letter omicron	&omicron;	&#959;
Π	Greek small letter pi	&pi;	&#960;
ρ	Greek small letter rho	&rho;	&#961;
ς	Greek small letter final sigma	&sigmaf;	&#962;
σ	Greek small letter sigma	&sigma;	&#963;
τ	Greek small letter tau	&tau;	&#964;
ψ	Greek small letter upsilon	&upsilon;	&#965;
ω	Greek small letter phi	&phi;	&#966;
ξ	Greek small letter chi	&chi;	&#967;
χ	Greek small letter psi	&psi;	&#968;
ϖ	Greek small letter omega	&omega;	&#969;
ϑ	Greek small letter theta symbol	&thetasym;	&#977;
Υ	Greek upsilon with hook symbol	&upsih;	&#978;
ϖ	Greek pi symbol	&piv;	&#982;

General punctuation

Character	Description	Character Entity	Numeric Character Reference
•	Bullet	&bull;	&#8226;
…	Horizontal ellipsis	&hellip;	&#8230;
′	Prime, minutes, feet	&prime;	&#8242;
″	Double prime, seconds, inches	&Prime;	&#8243;
‾	Overline, spacing overscore	&oline;	&#8254;
/	Fraction slash	&frasl;	&#8260;
"	Quotation mark	&quot;	&#34;
&	Ampersand	&amp;	&#38;
<	Less-than sign	&lt;	&#60;
>	Greater-than sign	&gt;	&#62;
ˆ	Modifier letter circumflex accent	&circ;	&#710;
˜	Small tilde	&tilde;	&#732;
	En space		
	Em space		
	Thin space		
	Left-to-right mark	&lrm;	&#8206;
	Right-to-left mark	&rlm;	&#8207;
–	En dash	&ndash;	&#8211;
—	Em dash	&mdash;	&#151;
'	Left single quotation mark	&lsquo;	&#8216;
'	Right single quotation mark	&rsquo;	&#8217;
‚	Single low-9 quotation mark	&sbquo;	&#8218;
"	Left double quotation mark	&ldquo;	&#8220;
"	Right double quotation mark	&rdquo;	&#8221;
„	Double low-9 quotation mark	&bdquo;	&#8222;
†	Dagger	&dagger;	&#8224;
‡	Double dagger	&Dagger;	&#8225;

Currency symbols

Character	Description	Character Entity	Numeric Character Reference
€	Euro	&euro;	&#8364;

Letter-like symbols

Character	Description	Character Entity	Numeric Character Reference
℘	Script capital, power set, Weierstrass p	&weierp;	&#8472;
ℑ	Blackletter capital I, imaginary part	&image;	&#8465;
ℜ	Blackletter capital R, real part symbol	&real;	&#8476;
™	Trademark sign	&trade;	&#8482;
ℵ	Alef symbol, first transfinite cardinal	&alefsym;	&#8501;

Arrows

Character	Description	Character Entity	Numeric Character Reference
←	Leftward arrow	&larr;	&#8592;
↑	Upward arrow	&uarr;	&#8593;
→	Rightward arrow	&rarr;	&#8594;
↓	Downward arrow	&darr;	&#8595;
↔	Left-right arrow	&harr;	&#8596;
↵	Downward arrow with corner leftward, carriage return	&crarr;	&#8629;
⇐	Leftward double arrow	&lArr;	&#8656;
⇑	Upward double arrow	&uArr;	&#8657;
⇒	Rightward double arrow	&rArr;	&#8658;
⇓	Downward double arrow	&dArr;	&#8659;
⇔	Left-right double arrow	&hArr;	&#8660;

Mathematical operators

Character	Description	Character Entity	Numeric Character Reference
∀	For all	&forall;	&#8704;
∂	Partial differential	&part;	&#8706;
∃	There exists	&exist;	&#8707;
∅	Empty set, null set, diameter	&empty;	&#8709;
∇	Nabla, backward difference	&nabla;	&#8711;
⊂	Element of	&isin;	&#8712;

(continues)

(continued)

Mathematical operators

Character	Description	Character Entity	Numeric Character Reference
∉	Not an element of	&notin;	&#8713;
∋	Contains as member	&ni;	&#8715;
∏	N-ary product, product sign	&prod;	&#8719;
∑	N-ary summation	&sum;	&#8721;
−	Minus sign	&minus;	&#8722;
∗	Asterisk operator	&lowast;	&#8727;
√	Square root, radical sign	&radic;	&#8730;
∝	Proportional to	&prop;	&#8733;
∞	Infinity	&infin;	&#8734;
∠	Angle	&ang;	&#8736;
∧	Logical and, wedge	&and;	&#8743;
∨	Logical or, vee	&or;	&#8744;
∩	Intersection, cap	&cap;	&#8745;
∪	Union, cup	&cup;	&#8746;
∫	Integral	&int;	&#8747;
∴	Therefore	&there4;	&#8756;
~	Tilde operator, varies with, similar to	&sim;	&#8764;
≅	Approximately equal to	&cong;	&#8773;
≈	Almost equal to, asymptotic to	&asymp;	&#8776;
≠	Not equal to	&ne;	&#8800;
≡	Identical to	&equiv;	&#8801;
≤	Less than or equal to	&le;	&#8804;
≥	Greater than or equal to	&ge;	&#8805;
⊂	Subset of	&sub;	&#8834;
⊃	Superset of	&sup;	&#8835;
⊄	Not a subset of	&nsub;	&#8836;
⊆	Subset of or equal to	&sube;	&#8838;
⊇	Superset of or equal to	&supe;	&#8839;
⊕	Circled plus, direct sum	&oplus;	&#8853;
⊗	Circled times, vector product	&otimes;	&#8855;
⊥	Up tack, orthogonal to, perpendicular	&perp;	&#8869;
·	Dot operator	&sdot;	&#8901;

Technical and geometric symbols

Character	Description	Character Entity	Numeric Character Reference
⌈	Left ceiling, apl upstile	&lceil;	&#8968;
⌉	Right ceiling	&rceil;	&#8969;
⌊	Left floor, apl downstile	&lfloor;	&#8970;
⌋	Right floor	&rfloor;	&#8971;
⟨	Left-pointing angle bracket	&lang;	&#9001;
⟩	Right-pointing angle bracket	&rang;	&#9002;
◊	Lozenge	&loz;	&#9674;

Miscellaneous symbols

Character	Description	Character Entity	Numeric Character Reference
♠	Black spade suit	&spades;	&#9824;
♣	Black club suit	&clubs;	&#9827;
♥	Black heart suit	&hearts;	&#9829;
♦	Black diamond suit	&diams;	&#9830;

CSS Levels 1 and 2 Reference

This appendix lists the properties available for CSS recommendation Level 1 (CSS1) and CSS recommendation Level 2 (CSS2). You can find the latest information on CSS at the W3C's Web site at *www.w3.org/Style/CSS/*.

Background Properties

Property	Description	Values
background	Sets all the background properties in one declaration	*background-color* | *background-image* | *background-repeat* | *background-attachment* | *background-position*
background-attachment	Determines whether an image specified with background-image will scroll with a Web page's content or be in a fixed position	scroll | fixed
background-color	Sets the background color of an element	*color_name* | *hex_number* | *rgb_number* | transparent
background-image	Sets the background image of an element	none | url('*url*')
background-position	Specifies the initial position of an image specified with background-image	left top | left center | left bottom | right top | right center | right bottom | center top | center center | center bottom | x% l% | *xpos ypos*
background-repeat	Determines how an image specified with background-image is repeated on the page	repeat | repeat-x | repeat-y | no-repeat

Border and Outline Properties

Property	Description	Values
border	Sets all of the border properties in one declaration	*border-width* │ *border-style* │ *border-color*
border-bottom	Sets all of the width, style, and color properties for an element's bottom border in one declaration	*border-bottom-width* │ *border-bottom-style* │ *border-bottom-color*
border-bottom-color	Sets the bottom border color of an element	*color_name* │ *hex_number* │ *rgb_number* │ transparent
border-bottom-style	Sets the bottom border style of an element	none │ hidden │ dotted │ dashed │ solid │ double │ groove │ ridge │ inset │ outset
border-bottom-width	Sets the bottom border width of an element	thin │ medium │ thick │ *length*
border-color	Sets the color of an element's four borders	*color_name* │ *hex_number* │ *rgb_number* │ transparent
border-left	Sets all of the width, style, and color properties for an element's left border in one declaration	*border-left-width* │ *border-left-style* │ *border-left-color*
border-left-color	Sets the left border color of an element	*color_name* │ *hex_number* │ *rgb_number* │ transparent
border-left-style	Sets the left border style of an element	none │ hidden │ dotted │ dashed │ solid │ double │ groove │ ridge │ inset │ outset
border-left-width	Sets the left border width of an element	thin │ medium │ thick │ *length*
border-right	Sets all of the width, style, and color properties for an element's right border in one declaration	*border-right-width* │ *border-right-style* │ *border-right-color*
border-right-color	Sets the right border color of an element	*color_name* │ *hex_number* │ *rgb_number* │ transparent
border-right-style	Sets the right border style of an element	none │ hidden │ dotted │ dashed │ solid │ double │ groove │ ridge │ inset │ outset
border-right-width	Sets the right border width of an element	thin │ medium │ thick │ *length*
border-style	Sets the style of an element's borders	none │ hidden │ dotted │ dashed │ solid │ double │ groove │ ridge │ inset │ outset

(continues)

(continued)

Property	Description	Values
border-top	Sets all of the width, style, and color properties for an element's top border in one declaration	*border-top-width* | *border-top-style* | *border-top-color*
border-top-color	Sets the top border color of an element	*color_name* | *hex_number* | *rgb_number* | transparent
border-top-style	Sets the top border style of an element	none | hidden | dotted | dashed | solid | double | groove | ridge | inset | outset
border-top-width	Sets the top border width of an element	thin | medium | thick | *length*
border-width	Sets all of the border properties in one declaration	thin | medium | thick | *length*
outline	Sets all of the outline properties in one declaration	*outline-color* | *outline-style* | *outline-width*
outline-color	Sets the outline color of an element or a group of elements	*color name* | *hex_number* | *rgb_number* | invert
outline-style	Sets the outline style of an element or a group of elements	none | hidden | dotted | dashed | solid | double | groove | ridge | inset | outset
outline-width	Sets the outline width of an element or a group of elements	thin | medium | thick | *length*

Dimension Properties

Property	Description	Values
height	Determines the height of an element	auto | *length* | %
max-height	Determines the maximum height of an element	none | *length* | %
max-width	Determines the maximum width of an element	none | *length* | %
min-height	Determines the minimum height of an element	*length* | %
min-width	Determines the minimum width of an element	*length* | %
width	Determines the width of an element	auto | *length* | %

Font Properties

Property	Description	Values
font	Sets all the font properties in one declaration	*font-style* | *font-variant* | *font-weight* | *font-size/ line-height* | *font-family* | caption | icon | menu | message-box | small-caption | status-bar
font-family	Specifies a list of font names or generic font names	*family-name* | *generic-family*
font-size	Specifies the size of a font	xx-small | x-small | small | medium | large | x-large | xx-large | smaller | larger | *length* | %
font-style	Sets the style of a font	normal | italic | oblique
font-variant	Specifies whether the font should appear in small caps	normal | small-caps
font-weight	Sets the weight of a font	normal | bold | bolder | lighter | 100 | 200 | 300 | 400 | 500 | 600 | 700 | 800 | 900

List Properties

Property	Description	Values
list-style	Sets all of the list-style-type, list-style-image, and list-style-position properties in one declaration	*list-style-type* | *list-style-position* | *list-style-image*
list-style-image	Defines an image that will be used as a bullet in an unordered list	none | url
list-style-position	Determines the indentation for the bullet or number in an unordered or ordered list	inside | outside
list-style-type	Specifies the bullet or numbering style for an unordered or ordered list	none | circle | disc | square | armenian | decimal | decimal-leading-zero | georgian | lower-alpha | lower-greek | lower-latin | lower-roman | upper-alpha | upper-latin | upper-roman

Margin Properties

Property	Description	Values
margin	Sets all of the margin properties in one declaration	auto | *length* | %
margin-bottom	Sets the bottom margin of an element	auto | *length* | %
margin-left	Sets the left margin of an element	auto | *length* | %
margin-right	Sets the right margin of an element	auto | *length* | %
margin-top	Sets the top margin of an element	auto | *length* | %

Padding Properties

Property	Description	Values
padding	Sets all of the padding properties in one declaration	*padding-top* | *padding-right* | *padding-bottom* | *padding-left*
padding-bottom	Sets the bottom padding of an element	*length unit* | *percentage unit*
padding-left	Sets the left padding of an element	*length unit* | *percentage unit*
padding-right	Sets the right padding of an element	*length unit* | *percentage unit*
padding-top	Sets the top padding of an element	*length unit* | *percentage unit*

Positioning Properties

Property	Description	Values
bottom	Determines the position of an element's bottom margin in relation to the document window	auto | *length* | %
clip	Determines the region of an element that is displayed	rect (*top, right, bottom, left*) | auto
display	Specifies whether to display an element	none | block | inline | inline-block | inline-table | list-item | run-in | table | table-caption | table-cell | table-column | table-column-group | table-footer-group | table-header-group | table-row | table-row-group
left	Determines the position of an element's left margin in relation to the document window	auto|*length*|%

(continues)

(continued)

Property	Description	Values
overflow	Determines how to handle an image that is bigger than its assigned space	visible | hidden | scroll | auto
position	Specifies the type of CSS positioning	absolute | fixed | relative | static
right	Determines the position of an element's right margin in relation to the document window	auto | *length* | %
top	Determines the position of an element's top margin in relation to the document window	auto | *length* | %
visibility	Specifies whether an element is visible	visible | hidden | collapse
z-index	Determines the order in which dynamically positioned elements are layered	auto | *number*

Print Properties

Property	Description	Values
orphans	Specifies the minimum number of lines in a block element that must be left at the bottom of a page	*integer*
page-break-after	Determines how the page will break after an element	auto | always | avoid | left | right
page-break-before	Determines how the page will break before an element	auto | always | avoid | left | right
page-break-inside	Determines how the page will break inside an element	auto | avoid
widows	Specifies the minimum number of lines in a block element that must be left at the top of a page	*integer*

Text Properties

Property	Description	Values
color	Specifies the text color	*color_name* | *hex_number* | *rgb_number*
direction	Determines the text direction of the writing system	ltr | rtl
letter-spacing	Adjusts spacing between letters	normal | *length*
line-height	Determines the line height of an element's text	normal | *number* | *length* | %
text-align	Determines the horizontal alignment of an element's text	left | right | center | justify
text-decoration	Adds decorations to an element's text	none | underline | overline | line-through | blink
text-indent	Specifies the indentation of an element's text	*length* | %
text-transform	Determines the capitalization of an element's text	none | capitalize | uppercase | lowercase
vertical-align	Determines the vertical positioning of an element	*length* | % | baseline | sub | super | top | text-top | middle | bottom | text-bottom
white space	Determines how to handle an element's white space	normal | nowrap | pre | pre-line | pre-wrap
word-spacing	Adjusts spacing between words	normal | *length*

Table Properties

Property	Description	Values
border-collapse	Determines whether to collapse a table's borders	collapse | separate
border-spacing	Controls the spacing between the borders of a table's adjacent cells	length | *length*
caption-side	Specifies where to place a table's caption	top | bottom
empty-cells	Determines whether to display the borders and backgrounds of empty cells	hide | show
table-layout	Forces the browser to lay out the table based on the width of the table and its columns, not on the contents of its cells	auto | fixed

JavaScript Reference

Comment Types

Line Comments

```
<script type="text/javascript">
// Line comments are preceded by two slashes.
</script>
```

Block Comments

```
<script type="text/javascript">
/*
This line is part of the block comment.
This line is also part of the block comment.
*/
/* This is another way of creating a block comment. */
</script>
```

JavaScript Reserved Words

abstract	else	instanceof	switch
boolean	enum	int	synchronized
break	export	interface	this
byte	extends	long	throw
case	false	native	throws
catch	final	new	transient
char	finally	null	true
class	float	package	try
const	for	private	typeof
continue	function	protected	var
debugger	goto	public	void
default	if	return	volatile
delete	implements	short	while
do	import	static	with
double	in	super	

Events

JavaScript Events

Event	Triggered When
abort	The loading of an image is interrupted.
blur	An element, such as a radio button, becomes inactive.
change	The value of an element, such as a text box, changes.
click	The user clicks an element once.
error	An error occurs when a document or image is being loaded.
focus	An element, such as a command button, becomes active.
load	A document or image loads.
mouseout	The mouse moves off an element.
mouseover	The mouse moves over an element.
reset	A form's fields are reset to its default values.
select	A user selects a field in a form.
submit	A user submits a form.
unload	A document unloads.

Elements and Associated Events

Element	Description	Event
`<a>`	Anchor	`onfocus, onblur, onclick, ondblclick, onmousedown, onmouseup, onmouseover, onmousemove, onmouseout, onkeypress, onkeydown, onkeyup`
`<img>`	Image	`onclick, ondblclick, onmousedown, onmouseup, onmouseover, onmousemove, onmouseout, onkeypress, onkeydown, onkeyup`
`<body>`	Document body	`onload, onunload, onclick, ondblclick, onmousedown, onmouseup, onmouseover, onmousemove, onmouseout, onkeypress, onkeydown, onkeyup`
`<form>`	Form	`onsubmit, onreset, onclick, ondblclick, onmousedown, onmouseup, onmouseover, onmousemove, onmouseout, onkeypress, onkeydown, onkeyup`
`<input>`	Form control	`tabindex, accesskey, onfocus, onblur, onselect, onchange, onclick, ondblclick, onmousedown, onmouseup, onmouseover, onmousemove, onmouseout, onkeypress, onkeydown, onkeyup`
`<textarea>`	Text area	`onfocus, onblur, onselect, onchange, onclick, ondblclick, onmousedown, onmouseup, onmouseover, onmousemove, onmouseout, onkeypress, onkeydown, onkeyup`
`<select>`	Selection	`onfocus, onblur, onchange`

Primitive Data Types

Data Type	Description
Integer numbers	Positive or negative numbers with no decimal places
Floating-point numbers	Positive or negative numbers with decimal places or numbers written using exponential notation
Boolean	A logical value of true or false
String	Text such as "Hello World"
Undefined	A variable that has never had a value assigned to it, has not been declared, or does not exist
Null	An empty value

JavaScript Escape Sequences

Escape Sequence	Character
\\	Backslash
\b	Backspace
\r	Carriage return
\"	Double quotation mark
\f	Form feed
\t	Horizontal tab
\n	New line
\0	Null character
\'	Single quotation mark
\v	Vertical tab
\x *XX*	Latin-1 character specified by the *XX* characters, which represent two hexadecimal digits
\x *XXXX*	Unicode character specified by the *XXXX* characters, which represent four hexadecimal digits

Operators

JavaScript Operator Types

Operator Type	Description
Arithmetic	Used for performing mathematical calculations
Assignment	Assigns values to variables
Comparison	Compares operands and returns a Boolean value
Logical	Used for performing Boolean operations on Boolean operands
String	Performs operations on strings
Special	Special operators are used for various purposes and do not fit within other operator categories

Arithmetic Binary Operators

Operator	Name	Description
+	Addition	Adds two operands
–	Subtraction	Subtracts one operand from another operand
*	Multiplication	Multiplies one operand by another operand
/	Division	Divides one operand by another operand
%	Modulus	Divides one operand by another operand and returns the remainder

Arithmetic Unary Operators

Operator	Name	Description
++	Increment	Increases an operand by a value of 1
– –	Decrement	Decreases an operand by a value of 1
–	Negation	Returns the opposite value (negative or positive) of an operand

Assignment Operators

Operator	Name	Description
=	Assignment	Assigns the value of the right operand to the left operand
+=	Compound addition assignment	Combines or adds the values of the right and left operands and assigns the new value to the left operand
–=	Compound subtraction assignment	Subtracts the value of the right operand from the value of the left operand and assigns the new value to the left operand
*=	Compound multiplication assignment	Multiplies the value of the right operand by the value of the left operand and assigns the new value to the left operand
/=	Compound division assignment	Divides the value of the left operand by the value of the right operand and assigns the new value to the left operand
%=	Compound modulus assignment	Divides the value of the left operand by the value of the right operand and assigns the remainder to the left operand (modulus)

Comparison Operators

Operator	Name	Description
==	Equal	Returns true if the operands are equal
===	Strict equal	Returns true if the operands are equal and of the same type
!=	Not equal	Returns true if the operands are not equal
!==	Strict not equal	Returns true if the operands are not equal or not of the same type
>	Greater than	Returns true if the left operand is greater than the right operand
<	Less than	Returns true if the left operand is less than the right operand
>=	Greater than or equal	Returns true if the left operand is greater than or equal to the right operand
<=	Less than or equal	Returns true if the left operand is less than or equal to the right operand

Logical Operators

Operator	Name	Description
&&	And	Returns true if both the left operand and right operand return a value of true; otherwise, it returns a value of false
||	Or	Returns true if either the left operand or right operand returns a value of true; if neither operand returns a value of true, then the expression containing the || operator returns a value of false
!	Not	Returns true if an expression is false and returns false if an expression is true

Operator Precedence

Operators	Description	Associativity
.	Objects—highest precedence	Left to right
[]	Array elements—highest precedence	Left to right
()	Functions/evaluation—highest precedence	Left to right
new	New object—highest precedence	Right to left
!	Not	Right to left
-	Unary negation	Right to left
++	Increment	Right to left
--	Decrement	Right to left
typeof	Data type	Right to left
void	Void	Right to left
delete	Delete object	Right to left
* / %	Multiplication/division/modulus	Left to right
+ -	Addition/subtraction/concatenation	Left to right
< <= > >=	Comparison	Left to right
instanceof	Object type	Left to right
in	Object property	Left to right
== != === !==	Equality	Left to right
&&	Logical and	Left to right
||	Logical or	Left to right
?:	Conditional	Right to left
= += -= *= /= %=	Compound assignment	Right to left
,	Comma—lowest precedence	Left to right

Control Structures and Statements

if Statements

```
if (conditional expression) {
     statement(s);
}
```

if...else Statements

```
if (conditional expression) {
     statement(s);
}
else {
     statement(s);
}
```

switch Statements

```
switch (expression) {
    case label:
        statement(s);
        break;
    case label:
        statement(s);
        break;
    ...
    default:
        statement(s);
}
```

while Statements

```
while (conditional expression) {
    statement(s);
}
```

do...while Statements

```
do {
    statement(s);
} while (conditional expression);
```

for Statements

```
for (initialization expression; condition; update statement) {
    statement(s);
}
```

for...in Statements

```
for (variable in object) {
    statement(s);
}
```

with Statements

```
with (object) {
    statement(s);
}
```

break Statements

A break statement is used to exit switch statements and other program control statements such as the while, do...while, for, and for...in looping statements. To end a switch statement once it performs its required task, you should include a break statement within each case label.

continue Statements

The continue statement halts a looping statement and restarts the loop with a new iteration. You use the continue statement when you want to stop the loop for the current iteration, but want the loop to continue with a new iteration.

Built-In JavaScript Functions

Function	Description
eval()	Evaluates expressions contained within strings
isFinite()	Determines whether a number is finite
isNaN()	Determines whether a value is the special value NaN (Not a Number)
parseInt()	Converts string literals to integers
parseFloat()	Converts string literals to floating-point numbers
encodeURI()	Encodes a text string so that it becomes a valid URI
encodeURIComponent()	Encodes a text string so that it becomes a valid URI component
decodeURI()	Decodes text strings encoded with encodeURI()
decodeURIComponent()	Decodes text strings encoded with encodeURIComponent()

Built-In JavaScript Classes
Array Class
Methods

Method	Description
Array()	Array object constructor
concat()	Combines two arrays into a single array
join()	Combines all elements of an array into a string
pop()	Removes and returns the last element from an array
push()	Adds and returns a new array element

(continues)

(continued)

Method	Description
reverse()	Transposes elements of an array
shift()	Removes and returns the first element from an array
slice()	Creates a new array from a section of an existing array
splice()	Adds or removes array elements
sort()	Sorts elements of an array
unshift()	Adds new elements to the start of an array and returns the new array length

Properties

Property	Description
length	Returns the number of elements in an array

Date Class

Methods

Method	Description
Date()	Date object constructor
getDate()	Returns the date of a Date object
getDay()	Returns the day of a Date object
getFullYear()	Returns the year of a Date object in four-digit format
getHours()	Returns the hour of a Date object
getMilliseconds()	Returns the milliseconds of a Date object
getMinutes()	Returns the minutes of a Date object
getMonth()	Returns the month of a Date object
getSeconds()	Returns the seconds of a Date object
getTime()	Returns the time of a Date object
getTimezoneOffset()	Returns the time difference between the user's computer and GMT
getUTCDate()	Returns the date of a Date object in universal time
getUTCDay()	Returns the day of a Date object in universal time
getUTCFullYear()	Returns the four-digit year of a Date object in universal time
getUTCHours()	Returns the hours of a Date object in universal time
getUTCMilliseconds()	Returns the milliseconds of a Date object in universal time
getUTCMinutes()	Returns the minutes of a Date object in universal time
getUTCMonth()	Returns the month of a Date object in universal time

(continues)

(continued)

Method	Description
getUTCSeconds()	Returns the seconds of a Date object in universal time
getYear()	Returns the year of a Date object
parse()	Returns a string containing the number of milliseconds since January 1, 1970
setDate()	Sets the date of a Date object
setFullYear()	Sets the four-digit year of a Date object
setHours()	Sets the hours of a Date object
setMilliseconds()	Sets the milliseconds of a Date object
setMinutes()	Sets the minutes of a Date object
setMonth()	Sets the month of a Date object
setSeconds()	Sets the seconds of a Date object
setTime()	Sets the time of a Date object
setUTCDate()	Sets the date of a Date object in universal time
setUTCDay()	Sets the day of a Date object in universal time
setUTCFullYear()	Sets the four-digit year of a Date object in universal time
setUTCHours()	Sets the hours of a Date object in universal time
setUTCMilliseconds()	Sets the milliseconds of a Date object in universal time
setUTCMinutes()	Sets the minutes of a Date object in universal time
setUTCMonth()	Sets the month of a Date object in universal time
setUTCSeconds()	Sets the seconds of a Date object in universal time
setYear()	Sets the two-digit year of a Date object
toGMTString()	Converts a Date object to a string in GMT time zone format
toLocaleString()	Converts a Date object to a string, set to the current time zone
toString()	Converts a Date object to a string

Math Class

Methods

Method	Description
abs(x)	Returns the absolute value of x
acos(x)	Returns the arc cosine of x
asin(x)	Returns the arc sine of x
atan(x)	Returns the arc tangent of x
atan2(x, y)	Returns the angle from the x-axis

(continues)

(continued)

Method	Description
ceil(x)	Returns the value of x rounded to the next highest integer
cos(x)	Returns the cosine of x
exp(x)	Returns the exponent of x
floor(x)	Returns the value of x rounded to the next lowest integer
log(x)	Returns the natural logarithm of x
max(x,y)	Returns the larger of two numbers
min(x,y)	Returns the smaller of two numbers
pow(x,y)	Returns the value of x raised to the y power
random()	Returns a random number
round(x)	Returns the value of x rounded to the nearest integer
sin(x)	Returns the sine of x
sqrt(x)	Returns the square root of x
tan(x)	Returns the tangent of x

Properties

Property	Description
E	Euler's constant e, which is the base of a natural logarithm; this value is approximately 2.7182818284590452354
LN10	The natural logarithm of 10, which is approximately 2.302585092994046
LN2	The natural logarithm of 2, which is approximately 0.6931471805599453
LOG10E	The base-10 logarithm of e, the base of the natural logarithms; this value is approximately 0.4342944819032518
LOG2E	The base-2 logarithm of e, the base of the natural logarithms; this value is approximately 1.4426950408889634
PI	A constant representing the ratio of the circumference of a circle to its diameter, which is approximately 3.1415926535897932
SQRT1_2	The square root of 1/2, which is approximately 0.7071067811865476
SQRT2	The square root of 2, which is approximately 1.4142135623730951

Number Class

Methods

Method	Description
Number()	Number object constructor
toExponential()	Converts a number to a string in exponential notation using a specified number of decimal places
toFixed()	Converts a number to a string with a specified number of decimal places
toLocaleString()	Converts a number to a string that is formatted with local numeric formatting conventions
toPrecision()	Converts a number to a string with a specific number of decimal places, either in exponential notation or in fixed notation
toString()	Converts a number to a string using a specified radix

Properties

Property	Description
MAX_VALUE	The largest positive number that can be used in JavaScript
MIN_VALUE	The smallest positive number that can be used in JavaScript
NaN	The value NaN, which stands for "Not a Number"
NEGATIVE_INFINITY	The value of negative infinity
POSITIVE_INFINITY	The value of positive infinity

String Class

Methods

Method	Description
charAt(*index*)	Returns the character at the specified position in a text string; returns an empty string if the specified position is greater than the length of the string
charCodeAt(*index*)	Returns the Unicode character at the specified position in a text string; returns NaN if the specified position is greater than the length of the string
concat(*value1*, *value2*, ...)	Creates a new string by combining the *value* arguments

(continues)

(continued)

Method	Description
indexOf(*text*, *index*)	Returns the position number in a string of the first character in the *text* argument. If the *index* argument is included, then the indexOf() method starts searching at that position within the string. Returns –1 if the text is not found.
lastIndexOf(*text*, *index*)	Returns the position number in a string of the last instance of the first character in the *text* argument. If the *index* argument is included, then the lastIndexOf() method starts searching at that position within the string. Returns –1 if the character or string is not found.
match()	Returns an array containing the results that match the *pattern* argument
replace(*text*, *pattern*)	Creates a new string with all instances of the *text* argument replaced with the value of the *pattern* argument
search(*pattern*)	Returns the position number in a string of the first instance of the first character in the *text* argument
slice(*starting index*, *ending index*)	Extracts text from a string starting with the position number in the string of the *starting index* argument and ending with the position number of the *ending index* argument; allows negative argument values
split(*text*, *limit*)	Separates a string into an array at the character or characters specified by the *text* argument; the *limit* argument determines the maximum length of the array
substring(*starting index*, *ending index*)	Extracts text from a string starting with the position number in the string of the *starting index* argument and ending with the position number of the *ending index* argument; does not allow negative argument values
toLowerCase()	Converts a text string to lowercase
toString()	Returns the primitive value of a string
toUpperCase()	Converts a text string to uppercase
valueOf()	Returns the primitive value of a string

Properties

Property	Description
length	Returns the number of characters in a string

Objects of the Browser Object Model

Document Object

Methods

Method	Description
close()	Closes a new document that was created with the open() method
getElementById(*ID*)	Returns the element represented by *ID*
getElementsByName(*name*)	Returns a collection of elements represented by *name*
open()	Opens a new document in a window or frame
write(*text*)	Writes new text to a document
writeln(*text*)	Writes new text to a document, followed by a line break

Properties

Property	Description
anchors	Returns a collection of the document's anchor elements
applets	Returns a collection of the document's applets, which are Java programs that run within a Web page
body	Returns the document's <body> or <frameset> element
cookie	Returns the current document's cookie string, which contains small pieces of information about a user that are stored by a Web server in text files on the user's computer
domain	Returns the domain name of the server where the current document is located
forms	Returns a collection of the document's forms
images	Returns a collection of the document's images
links	Returns a collection of the document's links
referrer	Returns the Uniform Resource Locator (URL) of the document that provided a link to the current document
title	Returns or sets the title of the document as specified by the <title> element in the document <head> section
URL	Returns the URL of the current document

History Object

Methods

Method	Description
back()	Produces the same result as clicking a Web browser's Back button
forward()	Produces the same result as clicking a Web browser's Forward button
go()	Opens a specific document in the history list

Properties

Property	Description
length	Contains the specific number of documents that have been opened during the current browser session

Location Object

Methods

Method	Description
assign()	Loads a new Web page
reload()	Causes the page that currently appears in the Web browser to open again
replace()	Replaces the currently loaded URL with a different one

Properties

Property	Description
assign()	Loads a new Web page
hash	A URL's anchor
host	The host and domain name (or IP address) of a network host
hostname	A combination of the URL's host name and port sections
href	The full URL address
pathname	The URL's path
port	The URL's port
protocol	The URL's protocol
search	A URL's search or query portion

Navigator Object

Properties

Property	Description
appCodeName	The Web browser code name
appName	The Web browser name
appVersion	The Web browser version
platform	The operating system in use on the client computer
userAgent	The string stored in the HTTP user-agent request header, which contains information about the browser, the platform name, and compatibility

Screen Object

Properties

Property	Description
availHeight	Returns the available height, in pixels, of the screen that displays the Web browser
availWidth	Returns the available width, in pixels, of the screen that displays the Web browser
colorDepth	Returns the number of bits that are used for color on the screen
height	Returns the total height, in pixels, of the screen that displays the Web browser
width	Returns the total width, in pixels, of the screen that displays the Web browser

Window Object

Methods

Method	Description
alert()	Displays a simple message dialog box with an OK button
blur()	Removes focus from a window
clearInterval()	Cancels an interval that was set with setInterval()
clearTimeout()	Cancels a timeout that was set with setTimeout()
close()	Closes a Web browser window

(continues)

(continued)

Method	Description
confirm()	Displays a confirmation dialog box with OK and Cancel buttons
focus()	Makes a Window object the active window
moveBy()	Moves the window relative to the current position
moveTo()	Moves the window to an absolute position
open()	Opens a new Web browser window
print()	Prints the document displayed in the window or frame
prompt()	Displays a dialog box prompting a user to enter information
resizeBy()	Resizes a window by a specified amount
resizeTo()	Resizes a window to a specified size
scrollBy()	Scrolls the window by a specified amount
scrollTo()	Scrolls the window to a specified position
setInterval()	Repeatedly executes a function after a specified number of milliseconds have elapsed
setTimeout()	Executes a function once after a specified number of milliseconds have elapsed

Properties

Property	Description
closed	Returns a Boolean value that indicates whether a window has been closed
defaultStatus	Sets the default text that is written to the status bar
document	Returns a reference to the Document object
frames[]	Returns an array listing the Frame objects in a window
history	Returns a reference to the History object
location	Returns a reference to the Location object
name	Returns the name of the window
navigator	Returns a reference to the Navigator object
opener	Refers to the window that opened the current window
parent	Returns the parent frame that contains the current frame
self	Returns a self-reference to the Window object; identical to the window property

(continues)

(continued)

Property	Description
status	Specifies temporary text that is written to the status bar
top	Returns the topmost `Window` object that contains the current frame
window	Returns a self-reference to the `Window` object; identical to the `self` property

Objects of the Document Object Model

`Form` Object

Methods

Method	Description
reset()	Resets a form without the use of a reset button
submit()	Submits a form without the use of a submit button

Properties

Property	Description
action	Returns the URL to which form data will be submitted
encoding	Sets and returns a string representing the MIME type of the data being submitted
length	Returns an integer representing the number of elements in the form
method	Sets and returns a string representing one of the two options for submitting form data: "get" or "post"

Events

Event	Description
reset	Executes when a form's reset button is clicked
submit	Executes when a form's submit button is clicked

Image Object

Properties

Property	Description
border	A read-only property containing the border width, in pixels, as specified by the border attribute of the <img> element
complete	A Boolean value that returns true when an image is completely loaded
height	A read-only property containing the height of the image as specified by the height attribute of the <img> element
hspace	A read-only property containing the amount of horizontal space, in pixels, to the left and right of the image, as specified by the hspace attribute of the <img> element
lowsrc	The URL of an alternate, low-resolution image
name	A name assigned to the element
src	The URL of the displayed image
vspace	A read-only property containing the amount of vertical space, in pixels, above and below the image, as specified by the vspace attribute of the <img> element
width	A read-only property containing the width of the image as specified by the width attribute of the <img> element

Events

Property	Description
onabort	Executes when the user cancels the loading of an image, usually by clicking the Stop button
onerror	Executes when an error occurs while an image is loading
onload	Executes after an image is loaded

Input Object

Methods and Their Associated Form Controls

Method	Description	Form Controls
blur()	Removes focus from a form control	Buttons, check boxes, radio buttons, reset buttons, submit buttons, text boxes, text areas, password boxes, file boxes, selection lists
click()	Activates a form control's click event	Buttons, check boxes, radio buttons, reset buttons, submit buttons, selection lists

(continues)

(continued)

Method	Description	Form Controls
focus()	Changes focus to a form control	Buttons, check boxes, radio buttons, reset buttons, submit buttons, text boxes, text areas, password boxes, file boxes, selection lists
select()	Selects the text in a form control	Text boxes, text areas, password boxes, file boxes

Properties and Their Associated Form Controls

Property	Description	Form Controls
checked	Sets and returns the checked status of a check box or radio button	Check boxes, radio buttons
defaultChecked	Determines the control that is checked by default in a check box group or radio button group	Check boxes, radio buttons
defaultValue	Specifies the default text that will appear in a form control	Text boxes, text areas, password boxes, file boxes
form	Returns a reference to the form that contains the control	Buttons, check boxes, radio buttons, reset buttons, submit buttons, text boxes, text areas, password boxes, file boxes, selection lists, hidden text boxes
length	Returns the number of items within a selection list's options[] array	Selection lists
name	Returns the value assigned to the element's name attribute	Buttons, check boxes, radio buttons, reset buttons, submit buttons, text boxes, text areas, password boxes, file boxes, selection lists, hidden text boxes
selectedIndex	Returns an integer that represents the element displayed in a selection list, according to its position	Selection lists
type	Returns the type of form element: button, check box, file, hidden, password, radio, reset, select-one, select-multiple, submit, text, or text area	Buttons, check boxes, radio buttons, reset buttons, submit buttons, text boxes, text areas, password boxes, file boxes, selection lists, hidden text boxes
value	Sets and returns the value of form controls	Buttons, check boxes, radio buttons, reset buttons, submit buttons, text boxes, text areas, password boxes, file boxes, hidden text boxes

Events and Their Associated Form Controls

Event	Description	Form Controls
blur	An element, such as a radio button, becomes inactive.	Buttons, check boxes, radio buttons, reset buttons, submit buttons, text boxes, text areas, password boxes, file boxes, selection lists
change	The value of an element, such as a text box, changes.	Text boxes, text areas, password boxes, file boxes, selection lists
click	The user clicks an element once.	Buttons, check boxes, radio buttons, reset buttons, submit buttons
focus	An element, such as a command button, becomes active.	Buttons, check boxes, radio buttons, reset buttons, submit buttons, text boxes, text areas, password boxes, file boxes, selection lists

Managing State Information and Security

The Web was not originally designed to store information about a user's visit to a Web site. However, the ability to store user information, including preferences, passwords, and other data, is very important because it allows you to improve the usability of a Web page. The three most common tools for maintaining state information are hidden form fields, query strings, and cookies, which you will study in this appendix. Given the sensitive nature of user information, it's also essential that you understand the JavaScript security issues described in this appendix.

Understanding State Information

Hypertext Transfer Protocol (HTTP) manages the hypertext links used to navigate the Web and ensures that Web browsers correctly process and display the various types of information contained in Web pages. Information about individual visits to a Web site is called **state information**. HTTP was originally designed to be **stateless**, which means that Web browsers stored no persistent data about a visit to a Web site. This stateless design allowed early Web servers to quickly process requests for Web pages because they did not need to "remember" any unique requirements for different clients. Similarly, Web browsers did not require any special information to load a particular Web page from a server. Although this stateless design was efficient, it was also limiting; because a Web server could not store and access individual user information, the browser was forced to treat every visit to a Web page as an entirely new session, even if the browser had just opened a different Web page on the same server. This design hampered interactivity and limited the amount of personal attention a Web site could provide for users. Today, state information is maintained for a variety of reasons. Among other things, maintaining state information allows a server to:

- Customize individual Web pages based on user preferences.

- Temporarily store information for a user as a browser navigates within a multipart form.

- Allow a user to create bookmarks for returning to specific locations within a Web site.

- Provide shopping carts that store order information.

- Store user IDs and passwords.

- Use counters to track the number of times a user has visited a site.

Saving State Information with Query Strings

One way to preserve information after a user's visit to a Web page is to append a query string to the end of a URL. A **query string** is a set of name=value pairs appended to a target URL. It consists of a single text string that contains one or more pieces of information. You can use a query string to pass information, such as search criteria, from one Web page to another.

Passing Data with a Query String

To pass data from one Web page to another using a query string, add a question mark (?) immediately after a URL, followed by the query string (in name=value pairs) for the information you want to preserve. In this manner, you can pass information to another Web page, similar to passing arguments to a function or method. You separate individual name=value pairs within the query string by using ampersands (&). The following code provides an example of an <a> element that contains a query string consisting of three name=value pairs:

```
<a href="http://www.URL.com/TargetPage.html?↵
firstName=Don&lastName=Gosselin&occupation=writer">
Link Text</a>
```

 The search property of the Location object is so named because many Internet search engines use its query string to store search criteria.

The passed query string is then assigned to the search property of the target Web page Location object. This search property contains a URL's query or search parameters. For the preceding example, after the TargetPage.html document opens, the query string "?firstName=Don&lastName=Gosselin&occupation=writer" is available as the value of the search property of the Location object.

Parsing Data from a Query String

For a Web page to use the information in a query string, your JavaScript program must first parse the string, using a combination of several methods and the length property of the String object. (This is also true when you want to use data contained in a cookie, as you'll learn later in this appendix.) The first parsing task is to remove the question mark at the start of the query string, using the substring() method combined with the length property. The substring() method takes two arguments: a starting index number and an ending index number. The first character in a string has an index number of 0, similar to the first element in an array. Because you want to exclude the first character of the string (the question mark), which has an index of 0, you use a starting index of 1. For the ending index number, you use the length property, which tells the substring() method to include the remainder, or length, of the string. The following code assigns the search property of the Location object to a variable named queryData and uses the substring() method and length property to remove the starting question mark:

```
// Assigns the query string to the queryData variable
var queryData = location.search;
// Removes the opening question mark from the string
queryData = queryData.substring(1,
    queryData.length);
```

The next step is to convert the individual pieces of information in the queryData variable into array elements, using the split() method. You pass to the split() method the character that separates each individual piece of information in a string. In this case, you will pass the ampersand character because it separates the name=value pairs in the query string. However, keep in mind that you can split a string at any character. The following code converts the information in the queryData variable into an array named queryArray[]:

```
// splits queryData into an array
var queryArray = queryData.split("&");
```

The following code shows a completed version of the parsing script that uses a for loop to print the values in queryArray[]:

```
// Assigns the query string to queryData
var queryData = location.search;
// Removes the opening question mark from the string
queryData - queryData.substring(1, queryData.length);
// Splits queryData into an array
var queryArray = queryData.split("&");
for (var i=0; i<queryArray.length; ++i) {
    document.write(queryArray[i] + "<br />");
}
```

Figure D-1 shows the output in a Web browser when the location.search property in the preceding code contains the following string value:

?firstName=Don&lastName=Gosselin&occupation=writer

Figure D-1   Output of a parsing script in a Web browser

Saving State Information with Cookies

Query strings do not permanently maintain state information; it is available only during the current session of a Web page. Once a Web page that reads a query string closes, the query string is lost. Hidden form fields maintain state information between Web pages, but their data is also lost once the Web page that reads the hidden fields closes. You can save the contents of a query string or hidden form fields by submitting the form data using a server-side scripting language, but that method requires a separate, server-based application. To enable the storage of state information beyond the current Web page session, Netscape created cookies. **Cookies** are small pieces of information about a user that are stored by a Web server in text files on the user's computer. The W3C DOM defines cookie specifications.

Each time the Web client visits a Web server, saved cookies for the requested Web page are sent from the client to the server. The server then uses the cookies to customize the Web page for the client. Cookies were originally created for use with CGI scripts, but they are now commonly used by JavaScript and other scripting languages.

You have probably seen cookies in action if you have ever visited a Web site where you entered a user name in a prompt dialog box or text field and then were greeted by that user name the next time you visited the Web site. This could occur with each subsequent visit to the same Web site, whether it is during the same browser session or a different session days or weeks later. The Web page remembers this information by storing it locally on your computer in a cookie. Another example of a cookie is a counter that keeps track of how many times an individual user has visited a Web site.

Cookies can be temporary or persistent. **Temporary cookies** remain available only for the current browser session. **Persistent cookies** remain available beyond the current browser session, and are stored in a text file on a client computer. In this section, you will create both persistent and temporary cookies.

Web browsers enforce a number of limitations on the use of cookies. Each individual server or domain can store a maximum of 20 cookies on a user's computer. In addition, the total cookies per browser cannot exceed 300, and the largest cookie size is 4 KB. If these limits are exceeded, a Web browser may start discarding older cookies.

Creating and Modifying Cookies

You use the `cookie` property of the `Document` object to create cookies in name=value pairs, the same way you use name=value pairs with a query string. The syntax for the `cookie` property is as follows:

```
document.cookie = name + "=" + value;
```

The `cookie` property is created with a required `name` attribute and four optional attributes: `expires`, `path`, `domain`, and `secure`.

The *name* Attribute

The only required parameter of the `cookie` property is the `name` attribute, which specifies the cookie's name=value pair. Cookies created with only the `name` attribute are temporary because they are available only for the current browser session. The following code creates a cookie with a name=value pair of "firstName=Don":

```
document.cookie = "firstName=" + "Don";
```

838

? To modify an existing cookie, you simply assign a new name=value pair to the `document.cookie` property. If the name=value pair already exists, it will be overwritten.

The cookie property of the Document object can be confusing. For other JavaScript properties, assigning a new value to the property *replaces* the old value. In contrast, assigning a new value to the cookie property adds another entry to a list of cookies, rather than simply replacing the last value. The following example builds a list of cookies:

```
document.cookie = "firstName=" + "Don";
document.cookie = "lastName=" + "Gosselin";
document.cookie = "occupation=" + "writer";
```

A Web browser automatically separates each name=value pair in the cookie property with a semicolon and a space. Therefore, the value assigned to the cookie property for the preceding cookies contains the following value:

```
firstName=Don; lastName=Gosselin; occupation=writer
```

By default, cookies themselves cannot include semicolons or other special characters, such as commas or spaces. Cookies have this limitation because they are transmitted between Web browsers and Web servers using HTTP, which does not allow certain nonalphanumeric characters to be transmitted in their native format. However, you can use special characters in your cookies if you use **encoding**, which involves converting special characters in a text string to their corresponding hexadecimal ASCII value, preceded by a percent sign. For example, 20 is the hexadecimal ASCII equivalent of a space character, and 25 is the hexadecimal ASCII equivalent of a percent sign (%). In URL-encoded format, each space character is represented by %20, and each percent sign is represented by %25. After encoding, the contents of the string "tip=A standard tip is 15%" would read as follows:

```
tip=A%20standard%20tip%20is%20%15%25
```

The built-in **encodeURIComponent() function** is used in JavaScript for encoding the individual parts of a URI. More specifically, the encodeURIComponent() function converts special characters in the individual parts of a URI to their corresponding hexadecimal ASCII value, preceded by a percent sign. The syntax for the function is encodeURIComponent(*text*);. The encodeURIComponent() function does not encode standard alphanumeric characters such as A, B, C or 1, 2, 3, or any of the following special characters: - _ . ! ~ * ' ( ). It also does not encode the following characters, which have a special meaning in a URI: ; / ? : @ & = + $,. For example, the / character is not encoded because it is used for designating a path on a file system. When you read a cookie or other text string encoded with the encodeURIComponent() function, you must first decode it with the **decodeURIComponent() function**. The syntax for this function is decodeURIComponent(*text*);. The following code encodes several cookies with the `encodeURIComponent()` function and assigns them to the `cookie` property of the `Document` object:

```
document.cookie = "firstName="
    + encodeURIComponent("Don");
document.cookie = "lastName="
    + encodeURIComponent("Gosselin");
document.cookie = "occupation="
    + encodeURIComponent("writer");
```

JavaScript also includes the `encodeURI()` and `decodeURI()` functions, which can be used to encode and decode entire URIs. Be sure to distinguish these functions from `encodeURIComponent()` and `decodeURIComponent()`, which encode and decode the individual parts of a URI.

If you transmit a URI that contains spaces from current Web browsers (including Firefox and Internet Explorer), the browser automatically encodes the spaces for you before transmitting the cookie. However, special characters such as the percent sign are not automatically encoded. This can cause problems with older browsers and Web servers that do not recognize certain special characters unless they are encoded. Additionally, older Web browsers do not automatically encode spaces in URIs. For these reasons, you should manually encode and decode cookies using the `encodeURIComponent()` and `decodeURIComponent()` functions if you anticipate that your scripts will run in older Web browsers.

Older versions of JavaScript use the deprecated `escape()` and `unescape()` methods for encoding and decoding text strings.

Setting Cookie Expiration Dates

For a cookie to persist beyond the current browser session, you must use the `expires` attribute of the `cookie` property. The **expires attribute** determines how long a cookie can remain on a client system before it is deleted. Cookies created without an `expires` attribute are available only for the current browser session. The syntax for assigning the `expires` attribute to the `cookie` property, along with an associated name=value pair, is `expires=date`. The name=value pair and the `expires=date` pair are separated by a semicolon. The date portion of the `expires` attribute must be a text string in Coordinated Universal Time (usually abbreviated as UTC) format, which looks like this:

Coordinated Universal Time is also known as Greenwich Mean Time (GMT), Zulu time, and world time.

```
Weekday Mon DD HH:MM:SS Time Zone YYYY
```

The following is an example of Coordinated Universal Time:

```
Mon Dec 27 14:15:18 PST 2011
```

Take care not to encode the `expires` attribute using the `encodeURIComponent()` method. JavaScript does not recognize a UTC date when it is in URI-encoded format. If you use the `encodeURIComponent()` method with the `expires` attribute, JavaScript cannot set the cookie expiration date.

You can manually type a string in UTC format, or you can create the string with the Date object, which automatically creates the string in UTC format. To use a Date object with the expires attribute, you specify the amount of time you want a cookie to be valid by using a combination of the Date object's set and get methods. The following statement declares a Date object named cookieDate, and then changes the date portion of the new object by using the setDate() and getDate() methods. Notice that you can nest Date object methods inside other Date object methods. In the following example, the setDate() method sets the date portion of cookieDate by using the getDate() method to retrieve the date, and adds seven to increase the date by one week. You might use a cookie that expires after one week (or less) to store data that needs to be maintained for a limited amount of time. For example, a travel agency may store data in a cookie to temporarily hold a travel reservation that expires after a week.

```
cookieDate.setDate(myDate.getDate() + 7);
```

After you create a Date object and specify the date you want the cookie to expire, you must use the toUTCString() method to convert the Date object to a string, formatting it in Coordinated Universal Time. The following code creates a new cookie and assigns an expiration date one year from now. Before the expires attribute is assigned to the cookie property, the Date object uses the toUTCString() method to convert the date to a string in Coordinated Universal Time.

```
var expiresDate = new Date();
expiresDate.setFullYear(expiresDate.getFullYear() + 1);
document.cookie = "firstName="
    + encodeURIComponent("Don")
    + "; expires=" + expiresDate.toUTCString();
```

Deleting Cookies from Your Browser

When developing a JavaScript program, you may accidentally create, but not delete, persistent cookies that your program does not need. Unused persistent cookies can sometimes interfere with the execution of a JavaScript cookie program. For this reason, it's a good idea to delete your browser cookies periodically, especially while developing a JavaScript program that uses cookies. To delete cookies in Firefox, select the Tools menu and then select Clear Recent History. In the Clear Recent History dialog box, select Everything in the Time range to clear box (if necessary), click the Details button (if necessary), and then click the Cookies button. Be sure to deselect any items in the Details section that you do not want to clear, and then click the Clear Now button. To delete cookies in Internet Explorer, select Internet Options from the Tools menu, click the General tab of the Internet Options dialog box, and then click the Delete button. In the Delete

Browsing History dialog box, select Cookies, along with any other items you want to delete, and then click Delete.

Configuring Availability of Cookies to Other Web Pages on the Server

The **path attribute** determines the availability of a cookie to other Web pages on a server. The `path` attribute is assigned to the `cookie` property, along with an associated name=value pair, using the syntax `path=path name`. By default, a cookie is available to all Web pages in the same directory. However, if you specify a path, the cookie is available to all Web pages in the specified path and to all Web pages in all subdirectories in the path. For example, the following statement makes the cookie named `firstName` available to all Web pages located in the /marketing directory or any of its subdirectories:

```
document.cookie = "firstName="
    + encodeURIComponent("Don"
    + ";path=/marketing");
```

To make a cookie available to all directories on a server, use a slash to indicate the root directory, as in the following example:

```
document.cookie = "firstName="
    + encodeURIComponent("Don" + ";path=/");
```

When you are developing JavaScript programs that create cookies, the programs may not function correctly if the directory containing your Web page contains other programs that create cookies. Cookies from other programs that are stored in the same directory with unused cookies you created during development can make your JavaScript cookie program run erratically. Therefore, you should always place JavaScript cookie programs in their own directory and use the `path` attribute to specify any subdirectories your program requires.

Sharing Cookies Across a Domain

Using the `path` attribute allows cookies to be shared across a server. Some Web sites, however, are very large and use a number of servers. The **domain attribute** is used for sharing cookies across multiple servers in the same domain. (You cannot share cookies outside of a domain.) The `domain` attribute is assigned to the `cookie` property, along with an associated name=value pair, using the syntax `domain=domain name`. For example, if the Web server `programming.gosselin.com` needs to share cookies with the Web server `writing.gosselin.com`, the `domain` attribute for cookies set by `programming.gosselin.com` should be set to `.gosselin.com`, as shown in the following code. That way, cookies created by

programming.gosselin.com are available to writing.gosselin.com
and to all other servers in the domain gosselin.com.

```
document.cookie = "firstName="
    + encodeURIComponent("Don"
    + ";domain=.gosselin.com");
```

Securing Cookie Transmissions

Internet connections are not always considered safe for transmitting sensitive information. Unscrupulous people can steal personal
information online, such as credit card numbers, passwords, and
Social Security numbers. To protect private data transferred across
the Internet, Netscape developed Secure Sockets Layer, or SSL,
to encrypt data and transfer it across a secure connection. The
URLs for Web sites that support SSL usually start with the HTTPS
protocol instead of HTTP. The **secure attribute** indicates that a
cookie can only be transmitted across a secure Internet connection
using HTTPS or another security protocol. Generally, when working
with client-side JavaScript, the secure attribute should be omitted.
However, if you want to use this attribute, you assign it to the
cookie property with a Boolean value of true or false, along with an
associated name–value pair, using the syntax secure=*boolean value*.
For example, to activate the secure attribute for a cookie, you use a
statement similar to the following:

```
document.cookie = "firstName="
    + encodeURIComponent("Don"
    + ";secure=true");
```

Reading Cookies with JavaScript

So far, you have stored both temporary and persistent cookies. Next,
you need to learn how to retrieve stored cookie values—in other
words, how to read cookies. The cookies for a particular Web page
are available in the cookie property of the Document object. Cookies
consist of one continuous string that must be parsed before their data
can be used. To parse a cookie, you must:

1. Decode it using the decodeURIComponent() function.

2. Use the methods of the String object to extract individual
   name=value pairs.

Parsing cookie data is very similar to parsing query strings, except
that you do not need to remove the question mark at the beginning of
the string. Also, the individual cookies are separated by a semicolon
and a space instead of ampersands. To give you an idea of how data
is extracted from cookies, the following code creates three encoded

cookies, then reads them from the `cookie` property and decodes them. The `split()` method is then used to copy each name=value pair into the elements of an array named `cookieArray[]`.

```
document.cookie = "city="
    + encodeURIComponent("Boston");
document.cookie = "team="
    + encodeURIComponent("Red Sox");
document.cookie = "sport="
    + encodeURIComponent("baseball");
var cookieString = decodeURIComponent(
    document.cookie);
var cookieArray = cookieString.split("; ");
```

Notice that the `split()` method in the preceding code splits the cookies by using two characters: a semicolon and a space. If you do not include the space in the `split()` method, the name portion of each name=value pair in the new array has an extra space before it. Once you split the cookies into separate array elements, you still need to determine which cookie holds the value you need. The following `for` loop cycles through each element in the array, using an `if` statement and several string methods to check whether the name portion of each name=value pair is equal to *team*. The conditional expression in the `if` statement uses the `substring()` method to return the name portion of the name=value pair in the variable named `yourTeam`. The first argument in the `substring()` method specifies the starting point of the substring as the first character (0). The second argument in the `substring()` method is the `indexOf()` method appended to the `yourTeam` variable, which returns the index number of the equal sign. If the substring is equal to *team*, then the `for` loop ends using a `break` statement, and the text *Your team is the* is written to the browser along with the value portion of the name=value pair. The statements that return the value portion of the name=value pair also use the `substring()` method along with the `indexOf()` method. However, this time the first argument starts the substring at the index number of the equal sign plus 1, which is the character following the equal sign. The second argument in the `substring()` method specifies that the ending point of the `substring` is the length of the data variable.

```
var yourTeam;
for (var count = 0; count < 3; ++count) {
    yourTeam = cookieArray[count];
    if (yourTeam.substring(0,
        yourTeam.indexOf("=")) == "team") {
            document.writeln("Your team is the "
                + yourTeam.substring(
                yourTeam.indexOf("=") + 1,
                yourTeam.length));
            break;
    }
}
```

The preceding code is a little difficult to understand at first. If you are having trouble understanding how to manipulate strings, try experimenting with different string methods.

Deleting Cookies with JavaScript

You can delete cookies, although the process is not intuitive. To delete a cookie, you must set its expiration to a date in the past. The following code deletes the firstName cookie by setting its expires attribute to one week ago:

```
var expiresDate = new Date();
expiresDate.setDate(expiresDate.getDate() - 7);
document.cookie = "firstName=don" + "; expires="
    + expiresDate.toUTCString();
```

 Using string methods to parse a cookie is the only way to extract individual pieces of information from a long cookie string, so it is important that you understand how they work.

Understanding Security Issues

Viruses, worms, data theft by hackers, and other types of security threats are now a fact of life when it comes to Web-based applications. If you put an application into a production environment without considering security issues, you are asking for trouble. To combat security violations, you need to consider both Web server security issues and secure coding issues. Web server security involves technologies such as firewalls, which combine software and hardware to prevent access to private networks connected to the Internet. Another important technology is the Secure Sockets Layer (SSL) protocol, which encrypts data and transfers it across a secure connection. These types of security technologies work well in the realm of the Internet. However, JavaScript programs are downloaded and execute locally within the Web browser of a client computer, and are not governed by technologies such as firewalls and Secure Sockets Layer.

Although Web server security is critical, it is properly covered in other books on Apache, Internet Information Services, and other types of Web servers. Be sure to research security issues for your Web server and operating system before activating a production Web site.

This section discusses security issues that relate to Web browsers and JavaScript.

Secure Coding with JavaScript

To provide even stronger software security, many technology companies, including Microsoft and Oracle, now require their developers and other technical staff to adhere to secure coding practices and principles. **Secure coding**, or **defensive coding**, refers to writing code in a way that minimizes any intentional or accidental security issues. Secure coding has become a major goal for many information technology companies, primarily because of the exorbitant cost of fixing security flaws in commercial software. According to one study, it is 100 times more expensive to fix security flaws in released software than it is to apply secure coding techniques during the development phase. The National Institute of Standards & Technology estimates the annual cost of identifying and correcting software errors to be $60 billion. In addition, government officials have expressed considerable interest in regulating software security. Tom Ridge, former Secretary of the U.S. Department of Homeland Security, said, "A few lines of code can wreak more havoc than a bomb." Intense government scrutiny gives information technology companies a strong incentive to voluntarily improve the security of software products before state and federal governments pass legislation that requires security certification of commercial software.

Basically, all code is insecure unless proven otherwise. Unfortunately, there is no magic formula for writing secure code, although you can use various techniques to minimize security threats in your scripts. Your first line of defense in securing your JavaScript programs is to validate all user input. You have studied various input validation techniques in this book, including validating data with regular expressions and using exceptions to handle errors as they occur in your scripts. Be sure to use these techniques in your scripts, especially those that run on commercial Web sites. The remainder of this section discusses security issues that relate to Web browsers and JavaScript.

JavaScript Security Concerns

The Web was originally designed to be read-only, meaning that its primary purpose was to locate and display documents that existed on other areas of the Web. With the development of programming languages such as JavaScript, Web pages can now contain programs in addition to static content. This ability to execute programs within a Web page raises several security concerns for JavaScript programmers:

- Protection of a Web page and JavaScript program against malicious tampering

- Privacy of individual client information

- Protection of the client or Web site's local file system from theft or tampering

Another security concern is the privacy of individual client information in the Web browser window. Your e-mail address, bookmarks, and history list are valuable information that many direct marketers would love to have, in order to bombard you with advertising geared toward your likes and dislikes. Without security restrictions, a JavaScript program could read this information from your Web browser. One of the most important JavaScript security features is its *lack* of certain functionality. For example, many programming languages include objects and methods that enable a program to read, write, and delete files. To prevent mischievous scripts from stealing information or causing damage by changing or deleting files, JavaScript does not allow any file manipulation. Similarly, JavaScript does not include a mechanism for creating a network connection. This limitation prevents JavaScript programs from infiltrating a private network or intranet from which information may be stolen or damaged. Another helpful limitation is that JavaScript cannot run system commands or execute programs on a client. The ability to read and write cookies is JavaScript's only type of access to a client. Web browsers, however, strictly govern cookies and do not allow access to them outside the originating domain.

The Same-Origin Policy

Another JavaScript security feature involves the **same-origin policy**, which restricts how JavaScript code in one window or frame accesses a Web page in another window or frame on a client computer. For windows and frames to view and modify the elements and properties of documents displayed in other windows and frames, they must have the same protocol (such as HTTP) and exist on the same Web server. For example, documents from the following two domains cannot access each other's elements and properties because they use different protocols. The first domain's protocol is HTTP and the second domain's protocol is HTTPS. As mentioned earlier, HTTPS is used on secure networks (that is, networks that run SSL).

```
http://www.gosselin.com
https://www.gosselin.com
```

The same-origin policy applies not only to the domain name but to the server on which a document is located. Therefore, documents from the following two domains cannot access each other's elements and properties because they are located on different servers, even though they exist in the same domain of gosselin.com:

```
http://www.programming.gosselin.com
http://www.writing.gosselin.com
```

The same-origin policy prevents malicious scripts from modifying the content of other windows and frames, and prevents the theft of private browser information and information displayed on secure Web pages. How crucial is the same-origin policy? Consider the src attribute of the Document object, which determines the URL displayed in a window or frame. If a client has multiple windows or frames open on its system, and the same-origin policy did not exist, a Web page in one window or frame could change the Web pages displayed in other windows or frames. Unscrupulous or malicious advertisers could then try to force you to view only their Web pages. The security of private networks and intranets would also be at risk without the same-origin policy. Consider a user who has one Web browser open to a page on the Internet and another Web browser open to a secure page from his private network or intranet. Without the same-origin policy, the Internet Web page would have access to the information displayed on the private Web page.

The same-origin policy also protects the integrity of your Web page design. For example, without the same-origin policy, a frame in one window could modify the elements and properties of JavaScript objects and XHTML code in other windows and frames.

In some circumstances, you will want two documents from related Web sites on different servers to be able to access each other's elements and properties. Consider a situation in which a document in the `programming.gosselin.com` domain needs to access content, such as form data, from a document in the `writing.gosselin.com` domain. To allow documents from different origins in the same domain to access each other's elements and properties, you use the `domain` property of the `Document` object. The **domain property** changes the origin of a document to its root domain name by using the statement `document.domain = "`*domain*`";`. For example, adding the statement `document.domain = "gosselin.com";` to documents from both `programming.gosselin.com` and `writing.gosselin.com` allows the documents to access each other's elements and properties, even though they are located on different servers.

Updating Web Pages with AJAX

The most recent version of the JavaScript language is ECMAScript Edition 3, which was first released in December 1999. The next major edition of the JavaScript language will be ECMAScript Edition 4, although the developers have not made significant progress on the new version at the time of this writing, and the release date is unknown. While Web browsers have undergone numerous enhancements since Edition 3 was released, the core JavaScript language has remained essentially unchanged for almost a decade. This is unusual for software development technologies, because Web developers are constantly looking for new and better tools to write their programs. Unwilling to simply await the arrival of Edition 4, JavaScript programmers have managed to accommodate their own demand for increased functionality by combining JavaScript with other technologies.

One such technology is DHTML, which makes Web pages dynamic by combining JavaScript, XHTML, CSS, and the Document Object Model (DOM). DHTML does a great job of making Web pages more dynamic and will continue to be a vital technique in Web page development. The fact that DHTML runs entirely within a user's Web browser was once considered an advantage because it made server data and other external resources unnecessary. However, as the Internet matured and broadband access became commonplace, developers began demanding a way to make their Web pages interact more dynamically with a Web server. For example, consider a browser's request for a Web page. In response, the Web server returns the requested page. If the user wants to refresh the Web page, the Web

The term *AJAX* was first used in an article written in 2005 by Jesse James Garrett, entitled *Ajax: A New Approach to Web Applications* (http://adaptivepath.com/publications/essays/archives/000385.php). The article discussed how Garrett's company, Adaptive Path, was using a combination of technologies, which they collectively referred to as AJAX, to add richness and responsiveness to Web pages. Since then, AJAX has become very popular among JavaScript developers.

server returns the entire page again—not just the changed portions of the page. For Web page data that must always be up to date, such as stock prices, continuously reloading the entire page is too slow, even at broadband speeds. As you will learn in this appendix, the solution is to use AJAX.

Introduction to AJAX

Asynchronous JavaScript and XML (AJAX) refers to a combination of technologies that allows Web pages displayed on a client computer to quickly interact and exchange data with a Web server without reloading the entire page. Although its name implies a combination of JavaScript and XML, AJAX primarily relies on JavaScript and HTTP requests to exchange data between a client computer and a Web server. AJAX gets its name from the fact that XML is often the format used for exchanging data between a client computer and a Web server (although it can also exchange data using standard text strings). Other technologies that compose AJAX include XHTML, CSS, and the Document Object Model. However, these technologies primarily handle the display and presentation of data within the Web browser (the same as with DHTML), while HTTP and XML are responsible for data exchange. JavaScript ties everything together.

It's important to note that Garrett and Adaptive Path did not invent anything new. Rather, they improved Web page interactivity by combining JavaScript, XML, XHTML, CSS, and the DOM with the key component of AJAX, the XMLHttpRequest object, which is available in modern Web browsers. The **XMLHttpRequest object** uses HTTP to exchange data between a client computer and a Web server. Unlike standard HTTP requests, which usually replace the entire page in a Web browser, the XMLHttpRequest object can be used to request and receive data without reloading a Web page. By combining the XMLHttpRequest object with DHTML techniques, you can update and modify individual portions of your Web page with data received from a Web server. The XMLHttpRequest object has been available in most modern Web browsers since around 2001. However, Garrett's article was the first to clearly document the techniques for combining the XMLHttpRequest object with other techniques to exchange data between a client computer and a Web server.

Another factor in AJAX's popularity was the release in 2005 of Google Suggest search functionality, making Google one of the first commercial Web sites to implement an AJAX application. As you type a search item in the Google Web site, Google Suggest lists additional search suggestions based on the text you type. For example, if you type "javascript", the search suggestions shown in Figure E-1 appear. The important thing to understand is that as you type each letter, JavaScript code uses the XMLHttpRequest object to send the string in the text box to the Google server, which attempts to match the typed characters with a list of suggestions. The Google server then returns the suggestions to the client computer (without reloading the Web page), and JavaScript code populates the suggestion list with the response text.

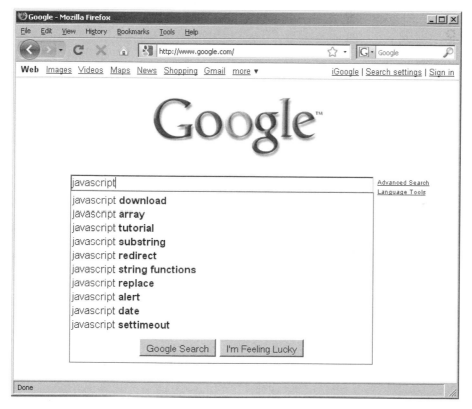

Figure E-1   Google Suggest list box

Figures E-2 and E-3 illustrate the difference between a standard HTTP request and an HTTP request with the XMLHttpRequest object. In Figure E-2, the client makes a standard HTTP request for *http://www.google.com*, which is returned from the server and displayed in the client's Web browser. Figure E-3 illustrates the request process with Google when a user types "kona hawaii vacation" into the text box. Instead of requesting an entire Web page, the XMLHttpRequest object only requests recommended search terms for the "Kona Hawaii vacation" string. The server returns the recommended search terms to the client, which in turn uses JavaScript to display the terms in the suggestion list.

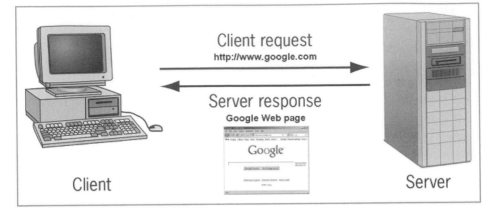

Figure E-2   Standard HTTP request

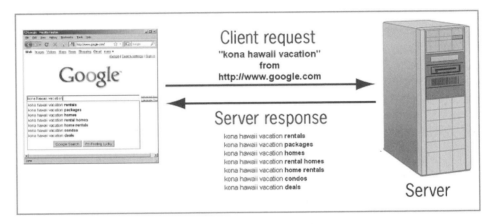

Figure E-3   HTTP request with the `XMLHttpRequest` object

Understanding AJAX's Limitations

The same-origin policy, which was described in Appendix D, restricts how JavaScript code in one window accesses a Web page in another window on a client computer. For windows to view and modify the elements and properties of documents displayed in other windows, they must have the same protocol (such as HTTP) and exist on the same Web server. Because JavaScript is the basis of AJAX programming, you cannot use the `XMLHttpRequest` object to directly access content on another domain's server; the data you request with the `XMLHttpRequest` object must be located on the Web server where your JavaScript program is running. In other words, you cannot directly bypass your own Web server and grab data off someone else's Web server. However, the same-origin policy only applies to

JavaScript, and not to other programs running on your Web server. This means that you can use a server-side script as a proxy to access data from another domain. In computer terms, a **proxy** refers to a server that acts or performs requests for other clients and servers. The server-side proxy script can return the data to the client computer as it is requested with the XMLHttpRequest object.

Accessing Content on a Separate Domain

The purpose of the same-origin policy is to prevent malicious scripts from modifying the content of other windows and frames, and to prevent the theft of private browser information and information displayed on secure Web pages. However, the ability of one Web server to access Web pages and data on another Web server is the foundation of the World Wide Web. Although you should never attempt to pass off content from another Web site as your own, there are legitimate reasons why you would use a server-side script to access data from another domain, particularly when it comes to accessing Web services and RSS feeds. A **Web service**, or **XML Web service**, is a software component that resides on a Web server. Web services do not contain a graphical user interface or even a command-line interface. Instead, they simply provide services and data in the form of methods and properties; it is up to the client accessing a Web service to provide an implementation for a program that calls the Web service. **RSS** (for **RDF Site Summary** or **Rich Site Summary**) is an XML format that allows Web sites to publish content that can be read by other Web sites. Typical types of data published with RSS feeds include news listings, blogs, and digital content such as podcasts. For example, much of the content on MSNBC's Web site at *www.msnbc. msn.com* is delivered through RSS feeds.

 To find the available methods and properties for a particular Web service, visit the site of the Web service provider.

 Countless RSS feeds are available on the Internet; you can find them by searching for "RSS feeds" in any search engine.

As an example of a Web service, consider a Web page that displays the prices of commodities you might want to track, such as crude oil, natural gas, gold, or silver. The Web page may periodically call methods of a Web service that return the most recent trading price for each commodity. The developer of a server-side script only needs to know which method of the Web service to call for each type of commodity, such as a getSilverPrice() method that returns the current price of silver. The Web service itself does not care what you do with the received data; it is up to you to display the data on a Web page, store it in a database, and use it in your application. In the case of AJAX, you might pass the data to a JavaScript program running on a client.

This appendix includes an example of using AJAX to display streaming stock quote information from Yahoo! Finance. When you enter a stock quote into Yahoo! Finance, the returned results include a

Although the download data link from Yahoo! Finance returns particular stock data by default, you can compose your own URL that downloads additional data for the specific ticker symbols. See *www.dividendgrowth.org/ FundamentalAnalysis/ YahooData.htm* for a complete list of data format symbols that you can use when downloading a CSV file from Yahoo! Finance.

link that allows you to download a CSV (comma-separated values) file containing the basic stock quote information, such as opening price and average volume. The default URL format of this CSV file is as follows:

```
http://finance.yahoo.com/d/quotes.csv?
    s={ticker symbols separated by+}
    &f={data format tags}&e=.csv
```

By default, the CSV file is named quotes.csv, and it is assigned three name=value pairs: *s* for ticker symbols, *f* for data formats, and *e* for file extension (.csv). You use plus signs (+) to separate the ticker symbols assigned to the name=value pair. The data that is downloaded from Yahoo! Finance to the CSV file is determined by the special tags assigned to the data formats name=value pair. By default, the values sl1d1t1c1ohgv are assigned to the data formats name=value pair; these values represent the ticker symbol (s), last price (l1), date (d1), time (t1), change (c1), open price (o), daily high (h), daily low (g), and volume (v). Notice that the data format symbols are not separated by spaces or any other symbols. For example, the following URL is for a CSV file downloaded from Yahoo! Finance for Oracle Corp. (ORCL):

```
http://finance.yahoo.com/d/quotes.csv?
    s=ORCL&f=sl1d1t1c1ohgv&e=.csv
```

Because the returned CSV file from Yahoo! Finance is a simple text file, with each entry separated by commas, you can use a script to parse the file and use the values in your Web pages. You will study the stock quote Web page throughout this appendix. For now, you need to understand that the Web page relies on a server-side PHP script to retrieve and parse stock information from Yahoo! Finance. The PHP script executes when it is passed a stock ticker with the `XMLHttpRequest` object. After the PHP script retrieves the information for the specified stock, it returns the data to the JavaScript code that called it. When you first open the stock quote Web page, it defaults to the quote data for the NASDAQ Composite Index (^IXIC), as shown in Figure E-4.

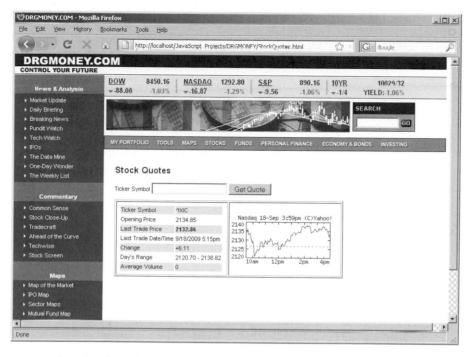

Figure E-4 Stock quote page displaying the default NASDAQ Composite Index quote data

Entering a new ticker symbol and clicking the Get Quote button automatically retrieves quote data for the specified stock from the Yahoo! Finance page. Figure E-5 displays the updated stock quote page after entering the ticker symbol for Oracle Corporation, ORCL.

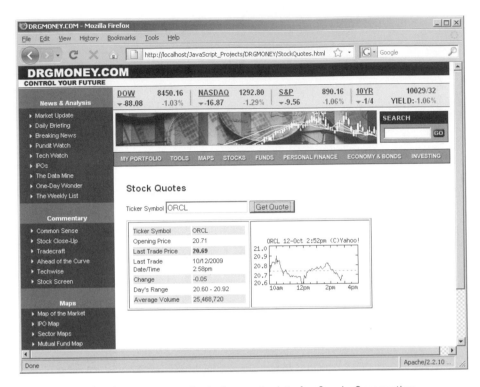

Figure E-5   Stock quote page displaying quote data for Oracle Corporation

The stock quote page relies on the following PHP script to retrieve data from the Yahoo! Finance page. The script downloads a CSV file from the Yahoo! Finance page that displays the quote data. Then, the script builds an XML tree from the CSV file and returns the result to the client with an echo statement, which is similar to JavaScript's document.write() statement. The focus of this book is JavaScript programming, not PHP programming, so you will not analyze the following code any further. However, PHP shares many similarities with JavaScript, so you can probably figure out most statements in the following code on your own.

```php
<?php
header("Content-Type: text/xml");
$QuoteXML = "<?xml version='1.0' ↵
    encoding='iso-8859-1' standalone='yes' ?>\n";
$TickerSymbol = $_GET["checkQuote"];
$Quote = fopen("http://finance.yahoo.com/d/quotes.csv?s ↵
    =$TickerSymbol&f=sl1d1t1c1p2ohgv&e=.csv", "r");
$QuoteString = fread($Quote, 2000);
fclose($Quote);
$QuoteString = str_replace("\"", "", $QuoteString);
$QuoteArray = explode(",", $QuoteString);
$QuoteXML .= "<quote>\n";
$QuoteXML .= "<ticker>{$QuoteArray[0]}</ticker>\n";
```

```
$QuoteXML .= "<lastTrade>{$QuoteArray[1]}</lastTrade>\n";
$QuoteXML .= "<lastTradeDate>{$QuoteArray[2]} ↵
    </lastTradeDate>\n";
$QuoteXML .= "<lastTradeTime>{$QuoteArray[3]} ↵
    </lastTradeTime>\n";
$QuoteXML .= "<change>{$QuoteArray[4]}</change>\n";
$QuoteXML .= "<changePercent>{$QuoteArray[5]} ↵
    </changePercent>\n";
$QuoteXML .= "<open>{$QuoteArray[6]}</open>\n";
$QuoteXML .= "<rangeHigh>{$QuoteArray[7]}</rangeHigh>\n";
$QuoteXML .= "<rangeLow>{$QuoteArray[8]}</rangeLow>\n";
$QuoteXML .= "<volume>{$QuoteArray[9]}</volume>\n";
$QuoteXML .= "<chart>http://ichart.yahoo.com/t?s ↵
    =$TickerSymbol</chart>\n";
$QuoteXML .= "</quote>";
header("Content-Length: " . strlen($QuoteXML));
header("Cache-Control: no-cache");
echo $QuoteXML;
?>
```

When you run the preceding PHP script, it builds an XML tree containing the data for the stock ticker symbol passed to it. Then, the AJAX code in your JavaScript program uses node manipulation techniques to parse the data. (You will learn how to do this as you progress through this appendix.) The following code is an example of the XML tree that the PHP script generates when you pass it the ticker symbol ORCL (for Oracle Corporation):

```
<quote>
    <ticker>ORCL</ticker>
    <lastTrade>21.81</lastTrade>
    <lastTradeDate>10/16/2009</lastTradeDate>
    <lastTradeTime>4:00pm</lastTradeTime>
    <change>+0.49</change>
    <changePercent>+2.30%</changePercent>
    <open>21.23</open>
    <rangeHigh>22.03</rangeHigh>
    <rangeLow>21.18</rangeLow>
    <volume>65051668</volume>
    <chart>http://ichart.yahoo.com/t?s=</chart>
</quote>
```

One point you should understand from the code is that PHP, like JavaScript, is not rocket science. Given the JavaScript skills you have learned in this book, and with a little additional study, you can easily learn PHP or any other server-side language. For now, keep in mind that any PHP scripts you see in this appendix are server-side scripting programs; they serve as a counterpoint to JavaScript programs, which are client-side scripting programs. In fact, client-side and server-side scripting languages share much of the same syntax and functionality, although server-side scripting languages can usually do quite a bit more than JavaScript.

Running AJAX from a Web Server

Throughout this book, you have opened Web pages directly from your local computer or network with your Web browser. However, in this appendix, you will open files from a Web server. Opening a local file in a Web browser requires the use of the file:/// protocol. Because AJAX relies on the XMLHttpRequest object to retrieve data, you must open your AJAX files from a Web server with the HTTP (http://) or HTTPS (https://) protocol. You can turn a computer into a Web server by installing Web server software on it. The most popular Web server software on the Internet is Apache HTTP Server (typically referred to as Apache), which is used by more than half of today's Web sites. The second most popular Web server is Microsoft Internet Information Services (IIS) for Windows operating systems, which is used on about one-third of current Web sites.

Overview of Creating an AJAX Script

After you have installed and configured your Web server, you perform the following steps to create an AJAX script:

- Instantiate an XMLHttpRequest object for the Web browser where the script will run.

- Use the XMLHttpRequest object to send a request to the server.

- Read and process the data returned from the server.

Before you can write an AJAX script, you need to know a little more about HTTP to understand how AJAX exchanges data between client computers and Web servers.

Working with HTTP

When discussing HTTP, it's helpful to start by reviewing basic terminology. As you know, when a user attempts to access a Web page, either by entering its URL in a browser's Address box or clicking a link, the user's browser asks a Web server for the Web page. This process is known as a **request**. The Web server's reply (which might consist of the requested Web page or a message about it) is known as the **response**. Every Web page is identified by a unique address called the Uniform Resource Locator, or **URL**. A URL consists of two basic parts: a protocol (usually HTTP) and either the domain name for a Web server or a Web server's Internet Protocol address. **Hypertext Transfer Protocol (HTTP)** is a set of rules that defines how requests are made by an HTTP client to an HTTP server, and how responses are returned from the server to the client. The term **HTTP**

client refers to the application, usually a Web browser, that makes the request. **HTTP server** is another name for a Web server, and refers to a computer that receives HTTP requests and returns responses to HTTP clients. A colon, two forward slashes, and a domain name follow the protocol portion of a URL. The term **host** refers to a computer system that is being accessed by a remote computer. In a URL, a specific filename, or a combination of directories and a file-name, can follow the domain name or IP address. If the URL does not specify a filename, the requesting Web server looks for a default Web page in the root or specified directory. Default Web pages usu-ally have names similar to index.html or default.html. For instance, if you enter *http://www.oracle.com/technology/documentation/* in your browser's Address box, the Web server automatically opens a file named index.html.

The W3C and the Internet Engineering Task Force (IETF) jointly develop HTTP. The IETF is a volunteer organization devoted to the development and promotion of Internet standards, most notably TCP/IP. Recall that the W3C does not actually release a version of a particular technology. Instead, it issues a formal recommenda-tion, which essentially means that the technology is (or will be) a recognized industry standard. The most recent version of HTTP that is commonly used today is 1.1, which is defined by RFC 2616 and recommendations. You can find the HTTP recommendations on the W3C Web site at *http://www.w3.org/Protocols*.

Understanding HTTP Messages

Most people who use the Web don't realize what is going on behind the scenes when it comes to requesting a Web page and receiv-ing a response from a Web server. HTTP client requests and server responses are both known as **HTTP messages**. When you submit a request for a Web page, the HTTP client opens a connection to the server and submits a request message. The Web server then returns a response message that is appropriate to the type of request. The request and response messages are in the following format:

```
Start line containing the request method for
requests or status line for responses
Header lines (zero or more)
Blank line
Message body (optional)
```

The specific contents of each line depend on whether it is part of a request or response message. The first line either identifies the method (such as "get" or "post") for requests or the status returned from a response. Following the first line, each message can include

An Internet Protocol, or IP address, is another way to uniquely identify com-puters or devices con-nected to the Internet. An IP address consists of four groups of numbers separated by periods. Each Internet domain name is associated with a unique IP address.

Although HTTP is probably the most widely used protocol on the Internet, it is not the only one. HTTP is a component of Transmission Control Protocol/Internet Protocol (TCP/IP), a large collec-tion of communication protocols used on the Internet. Other common protocols include Hypertext Transfer Protocol Secure (HTTPS), which provides secure Internet connections that are used in Web-based financial transactions and other types of communi-cation that require secu-rity and privacy; and File Transfer Protocol (FTP), which is used for transfer-ring files across the Internet.

859

zero or more lines containing **headers**, which define information about the request or response message and the contents of the message body. The RFC2616 recommendation defines 46 HTTP 1.1 headers, which are categorized by generic headers that can be used in request or response messages and headers that are specific to a request, a response, or the message body. The format for using a header is *header: value.*

For example, the following lines define two generic headers that can be used in either request or response messages: `Connection` and `Date`. The `Connection` header specifies that the HTTP connection should close after the Web client receives a response from the Web server. The `Date` header identifies the message's origination date and time in Greenwich Mean Time format.

```
Connection: close
Date: Fri, 27 June 2008 18:32:07 GMT
```

One generic header that requires special mention for AJAX applications is the `Cache-Control` header, which specifies how a Web browser should cache any server content it receives. Most Web browsers try to reduce the amount of data that needs to be retrieved from a server by caching retrieved data on a local computer. **Caching** refers to the temporary storage of data for faster access. If caching is enabled in a Web browser, the browser will attempt to locate any necessary data in its cache before making a request from a Web server. For example, assume that caching is turned on when you open the stock quote Web page. If you enter the same stock symbol more than once and click the Get Quotes button, the browser will retrieve the stock data stored in its cache, not the most recent data from the server. While this technique improves Web browser performance, it goes against the reason for using AJAX, which is to dynamically update portions of a Web page with the most recent data from a server. For this reason, you should always include the `Cache-Control` header in your AJAX programs and assign it a value of "no-cache", as follows:

```
Cache-Control: no-cache
```

A blank line always follows the last header line. Optionally, a message body can follow the blank line in the messages. In most cases, the message body contains form data for "post" requests or some type of document (such as a Web page or XML page) or other type of content (such as an image file) that is returned with a server response. However, message bodies are not required for either request or response messages. For example, with a "get" request, no message

See RFC 2616 for complete listings and descriptions of the available HTTP 1.1 headers.

The HTTP headers are case insensitive.

body is necessary because any form data that is part of the request is appended to the URL. Response messages are also not required to include a message body. This may seem strange—if a server doesn't return a Web page, then what is returned? What's the point in sending a request to a Web server if it doesn't return anything? Although "get" and "post" requests are by far the two most common types of HTTP requests, five other methods can be used with an HTTP request: HEAD, DELETE, OPTIONS, PUT, and TRACE. Most of these methods are rarely used. However, the HEAD method is commonly used for returning information about a document, but not the document itself. For example, you may use the HEAD method to determine the last modification date of a Web page before requesting it from the Web server.

Later in this appendix, you will learn more about managing the response messages returned from a server. First, however, you will learn about sending a request message.

Sending HTTP Requests

Without a scripting language such as JavaScript, most Web browsers are usually limited to using the "get" and "post" methods with an HTTP request. The "get" method is used for standard Web page requests, but can have a query string or form data appended to the URL. For example, if you enter the address for the U.S. Postal Service Web site (*http://www.usps.com*) in your Web browser, the browser creates a request message that begins with the following start line:

```
GET / HTTP/1.1
```

The preceding line identifies the method as "get" and 1.1 as the HTTP version. Also, notice the forward slash after "get", which identifies the root directory on the Web server as the location of the requested file. Because no HTML document was specified in the URL, the request looks in the Web server's root directory for a default Web page such as index.htm. However, if the URL contains a specific directory or filename, it is included in the start line. For example, a URL request that contains a directory and filename, such as *http://www.usps.com/business/welcome.htm*, generates the following start line in a request message:

```
GET /business/welcome.htm HTTP/1.1
```

When requesting a URL, most Web browsers include the headers listed in Table E-1 in generated request messages.

Header	Description
Host	Identifies the host portion of a requested URL
Accept-Encoding	Defines the encoding formats that the HTTP client accepts
Accept	Defines the MIME types that the HTTP client accepts
Accept-Language	Lists the languages that the HTTP client accepts in a response
Accept-Charset	Defines the character sets that the HTTP client accepts
User-Agent	Identifies the user agent, such as a Web browser, that submitted the request
Referer	Identifies the referring URL from which the request was made

Table E-1   Common request headers

The following code shows an example of a request header. When you search for "ebay" on Google and click the eBay link (*www.ebay.com/*) that is returned in the search results, the following request message is generated in Firefox:

```
GET /12/!!e!75i!!(U~$(KGrHgoOKiYEjlLmep38BKss!
RMNOw~~_0.JPG HTTP/1.1
Host: i.ebayimg.com
User-Agent: Mozilla/5.0 (Windows; U; Windows NT 5.1;
en-US; rv:1.9.0.14) Gecko/2009082707 Firefox/3.0.14
(.NET CLR 3.5.30729)
Accept: text/html,application/xhtml+xml,application/
xml;q=0.9,*/*;q=0.8
Accept-Language: en-us,en;q=0.5
Accept-Encoding: gzip,deflate
Accept-Charset: ISO-8859-1,utf-8;q=0.7,*;q=0.7
Keep-Alive: 300
Connection: keep-alive
Referer: http://www.ebay.com/
blank line
```

A "post" request is similar to a "get" request, except that any submitted data is included in the message body immediately following the blank line after the last header. To provide more information about the message body, requests made with the "post" method usually include some of the headers listed in Table E-2.

Header	Description
Content-Encoding	Defines the encoding format of the message body
Content-Language	Identifies the language of the message body
Content-Length	Identifies the size of the message body
Content-Location	Specifies the location of the message body contents
Content-Type	Identifies the MIME type of the message body
Expires	Defines the expiration date of the message body contents
Last-Modified	Identifies the last modification date of the message body contents

Table E-2   Common message body headers

Next, you will learn about the HTTP responses that the user's browser receives from a Web server.

The message body headers listed in Table E-2 are used for response messages as well as request messages.

Receiving HTTP Responses

HTTP response messages take the same format as request messages, except for the contents of the start line and headers. Instead of containing a request method, the start line (also known as the status line) returns the protocol and version of the HTTP server (such as HTTP/1.1) along with a status code and descriptive text. The status codes returned from an HTTP server consist of three digits. The codes that begin with 1 (101, 102, etc.) are purely informational, indicating that the request was received, for example. Codes that begin with 2 indicate a successful request. The following list summarizes the types of messages provided by the three-digit codes that begin with 1 through 5. Table E-3 lists the most common response codes.

- 1xx: (informational)—Request was received
- 2xx: (success)—Request was successful
- 3xx: (redirection)—Request cannot be completed without further action
- 4xx: (client error)—Request cannot be fulfilled due to a client error
- 5xx: (server error)—Request cannot be fulfilled due to a server error

Code	Text	Description
200	OK	The request was successful.
301	Moved Permanently	The requested URL has been permanently moved.
302	Moved Temporarily	The requested URL has been temporarily moved.
404	Not Found	The requested URL was not found.
500	Internal Server Error	The request could not be completed due to an internal server error.

Table E-3   Common response codes

For successful requests with HTTP 1.1, the start line in the response message consists of the following status line:

HTTP/1.1 200 OK

Zero or more response headers follow the status line. Table E-4 lists the most common response headers.

Header	Description
Vary	Determines whether the server can respond to subsequent requests with the same response
Server	Returns information about the server software that processed the request
Location	Redirects clients to a different URI

Table E-4 Common response headers

Because responses return documents (such as an XHTML document) or other types of files (such as image files), response messages usually include one or more of the message body headers listed in Table E-4.

The response returned from a server can be much more involved than the original request that generated it. The initial request from an HTTP client for a Web page often results in the server issuing multiple additional requests for resources required by the requested URL, such as style sheets, images, and so on. As a simplified example, the following statements represent the basic response returned for a request for the United States Postal Service Web site, although keep in mind that additional requests may be issued for resources required by the URL:

```
HTTP/1.x 200 OK
Server: Netscape-Enterprise/6.0
Content-Type: text/html
Content-Encoding: gzip
Cache-Control: no-cache, must-revalidate
Date: Sun, 20 Sep 2009 23:00:05 GMT
Content-Length: 15174
Connection: keep-alive
Vary: Accept-Encoding
blank line
<!DOCTYPE HTML>
<html><head>
<title>USPS - The United States Postal Service (U.S. Postal
Service)</title>
...
```

Requesting Server Data

The XMLHttpRequest object is the key to turning your JavaScript script into an AJAX program because it allows you to use JavaScript and HTTP to exchange data between a Web browser and a Web server. More specifically, you use the methods and properties of an instantiated XMLHttpRequest object with JavaScript to build and send request messages, and to receive and process response messages. The XMLHttpRequest object contains the methods listed in Table E-5 and the properties listed in Table E-6.

Method	Description
abort()	Cancels the current HTTP request
getAllResponseHeaders()	Returns a text string containing all of the headers that were returned with a response in *header: value* format, separated by line breaks
getResponseHeader(header_name)	Returns a text string containing the value assigned to the specified header
open(method,URL[,async,user,password])	Specifies the method and URL for an HTTP request; assigning a value of true to the *async* argument performs the request asynchronously, while a value of false performs the request synchronously; the default is true
send([content])	Submits an HTTP request using the information assigned with the open() method; the optional content argument contains the message body
setRequestHeader(header_name,value)	Creates an HTTP header using the *header_name* and *value* arguments

Table E-5 XMLHttpRequest object methods

Property	Description
onreadystatechange	Specifies the name of the event handler function that executes whenever the readyState property value changes
readyState	Contains one of the following values, which represent the state of the HTTP request: 0 (uninitialized), 1 (open), 2 (sent), 3 (receiving), or 4 (loaded)
responseText	Contains the HTTP response as a text string
responseXML	Contains the HTTP response as an XML document
status	Contains the HTTP status code (such as 200 for "OK" or 404 for "Not Found") that was returned with the response
statusText	Contains the HTTP status text (such as "OK" or "Not Found") that was returned with the response

Table E-6 XMLHttpRequest object properties

Before you can use any of the methods and properties listed in Tables E-5 and E-6, you must learn how to instantiate an XMLHttpRequest object.

Instantiating an XMLHttpRequest Object

The first step for using AJAX to exchange data between an HTTP client and a Web server is to instantiate an XMLHttpRequest object. For Mozilla-based browsers such as Firefox, and for Internet Explorer 7 and higher, you instantiate an XMLHttpRequest object with the XMLHttpRequest constructor, as follows:

```
var httpRequest = new XMLHttpRequest();
```

Although the XMLHttpRequest object is available in most modern Web browsers, it is not standardized by the W3C or any other standards organization. Fortunately, Internet Explorer 7 and higher versions now use the same syntax for instantiating an XMLHttpRequest object as Mozilla-based browsers. However, to instantiate an XMLHttpRequest object in older versions of Internet Explorer, you must instantiate the object as an ActiveX object. **ActiveX** is a technology that allows programming objects to be easily reused with any programming language that supports Microsoft's **Component Object Model (COM)**. COM is an architecture for cross-platform development of client/server applications. For Internet Explorer 6, you use the following syntax to instantiate an XMLHttpRequest object by passing a value of "Msxml2.XMLHTTP" to the ActiveX object constructor:

```
var httpRequest = new ActiveXObject(
    "Msxml2.XMLHTTP");
```

To make things even more confusing, Internet Explorer 5.5 requires slightly different syntax to instantiate an XMLHttpRequest object by passing a value of "Microsoft.XMLHTTP" instead of "Msxml2.XMLHTTP" to the ActiveX object constructor:

```
var httpRequest = new ActiveXObject(
    "Microsoft.XMLHTTP");
```

As of October 2010, Internet Explorer 6 and 5.5 are still used by a small percentage of the browser market. Therefore, you should include the appropriate syntax for each browser to test for and instantiate an XMLHttpRequest object according to the following rules:

1. For Mozilla-based browsers or Internet Explorer 7 and higher, use the XMLHttpRequest constructor.

2. For Internet Explorer 6, pass a value of "Msxml2.XMLHTTP" to the ActiveX object constructor.

3. For Internet Explorer 5.5, pass a value of "Microsoft. XMLHTTP" to the ActiveX object constructor.

4. For all other browsers, inform the user that his or her browser does not support AJAX.

Most JavaScript programmers use a series of nested `try...catch` statements to instantiate an `XMLHttpRequest` object according to the Web browser that is running the script. For example, the following code declares a variable named `httpRequest` and then attempts to use the `XMLHttpRequest` constructor in the `try` statement to declare an `XMLHttpRequest` object. If the Web browser running the code does not contain an `XMLHttpRequest` constructor, then it is not a Mozilla-based browser or a current version of Internet Explorer (7 or higher). If this is the case, the `try` statement throws an exception to the `catch` statement, which contains a nested `try...catch` statement. The nested `try` statement attempts to declare an `XMLHttpRequest` object by passing a value of "Msxml2.XMLHTTP" to the ActiveX object constructor. If the Web browser running the code does not support this value with the ActiveX object constructor, the browser is not Internet Explorer, and the `try` statement throws an exception to the nested `catch` statement. Finally, if the nested `try` statement cannot instantiate an `XMLHttpRequest` object with the ActiveX object constructor, the nested `catch` statement prints "Your browser does not support AJAX!".

```
var httpRequest;
// instantiate an object for Mozilla-based browsers
// and Internet Explorer 7 and higher
try {
    httpRequest = new XMLHttpRequest();
}
// instantiate an ActiveX object for
// Internet Explorer 6
catch (requestError) {
    try {
        httpRequest = new ActiveXObject(
            "Msxml2.XMLHTTP");
    }
    catch (requestError) {
        document.write("<p>Your browser does ↵
            not support AJAX!</p>");
        return false;
    }
}
```

If you only need to support Internet Explorer 6 and higher, then the preceding code is sufficient. However, to support Internet Explorer 5.5, you must include another `try...catch` statement within the nested `catch` statement. This statement attempts to pass a value of "Microsoft.XMLHTTP" to the ActiveX object constructor. The following code demonstrates how to use two nested `try...catch` statements within a main `try...catch` statement to instantiate an `XMLHttpRequest` object for the appropriate Web browser. If none of the three `try` statements can instantiate an XMLHttpRequest object, the final catch statement prints "Your browser does not support AJAX!".

```
var httpRequest;
// instantiate an object for Mozilla-based browsers
// and Internet Explorer 7 and higher
try {
    httpRequest = new XMLHttpRequest();
}
catch (requestError) {
    // instantiate an ActiveX object for
    // Internet Explorer 6
    try {
        httpRequest = new ActiveXObject(
            "Msxml2.XMLHTTP");
    }
    catch (requestError) {
        // instantiate an ActiveX object for
        // Internet Explorer 5.5
        try {
            httpRequest = new ActiveXObject(
                "Microsoft.XMLHTTP");
        }
        catch (requestError) {
            document.write(
                "<p>Your browser does not ↵
                support AJAX!</p>");
            return false;
        }
    }
}
```

Opening and closing HTTP connections requires significant computer memory and processing time. To improve performance between client requests and server responses, HTTP/1.1 automatically keeps the client-server connection open until the client or server explicitly closes it by assigning a value of "close" to the Connection header. This means that you can make your AJAX programs faster by reusing an instantiated XMLHttpRequest object instead of re-creating it each time you send a server request. The following code demonstrates how to create a global variable named curRequest, which is assigned an instantiated XMLHttpRequest object in a function named getRequestObject(). This function is only called once, when the Web page first loads. After the getRequestObject() function creates the appropriate XMLHttpRequest object, the last statement in the function returns the curRequest variable to a calling statement. Notice the if statement that follows the getRequestObject() function. If the curRequest variable is equal to false, then it has not been instantiated with the XMLHttpRequest object and the getRequestObject() function is called. The return statement in the getRequestObject() function returns the httpRequest variable, which represents the XMLHttpRequest object. The statement that called the getRequestObject() function then assigns the XMLHttpRequest object to the curRequest variable. However, if the curRequest variable is *not* equal to false (meaning that the Web page has already been loaded), then the getRequestObject() function is bypassed because the XMLHttpRequest object already exists.

```
var curRequest = false;
function getRequestObject() {
    try {
        httpRequest = new XMLHttpRequest();
    }
    catch (requestError) {
        try {
            httpRequest = new ActiveXObject(
                "Msxml2.XMLHTTP");
        }
        catch (requestError) {
            try {
                httpRequest = new
                    ActiveXObject(
                    "Microsoft.XMLHTTP");
            }
            catch (requestError) {
                window.alert("Your browser
                does not support AJAX!");
                return false;
            }
        }
    }
    return httpRequest;
}
if (!curRequest)
    curRequest = getRequestObject();
```

Opening and Sending a Request

After you instantiate an XMLHttpRequest object, you use the open() method with the instantiated object to specify the request method (such as "get" or "post") and URL. The following statement is the open() method used by the stock quote Web page. The statement specifies the "get" method and a URL named StockCheck.php, which is the PHP script that retrieves the stock information from Yahoo! Finance. The requested stock is appended to the URL as a query string in the format checkQuote=tickerSymbol. The value assigned to the tickerSymbol variable is passed with the Get Quote button's onclick event to a function containing the XMLHttpRequest code.

```
stockRequest.open("get","StockCheck.php?"
    + "checkQuote=" + tickerSymbol);
```

The open() method also accepts three optional arguments. The third argument, *async*, can be assigned a value of true or false to determine whether the request will be handled synchronously or asynchronously. The fourth and fifth optional arguments—a user name and password—are only necessary if the Web server requires authentication. If you omit the *async* argument, it defaults to a value of true, which performs the request asynchronously. The following statement demonstrates how to handle the request synchronously and pass a user name ("dongosselin") and password ("rosebud") to the open() method:

```
stockRequest.open("get", "StockCheck.php?"
    + "checkQuote=" + tickerSymbol, false,
    "dongosselin", "rosebud");
```

In the last section, you learned how to reuse an instantiated XMLHttpRequest object instead of re-creating it each time you send a server request. When you reuse an existing XMLHttpRequest object, it may already be in the process of sending a request to the server. To improve performance, you should call the abort() method of the XMLHttpRequest object to cancel any existing HTTP requests before beginning a new one. Append the abort() method to an instantiated XMLHttpRequest object and call the method before calling the open() method, as follows:

```
stockRequest.abort();
stockRequest.open("get","StockCheck.php?"
    + "checkQuote=" + tickerSymbol, false,
    "dongosselin", "rosebud");
```

After you have defined the basic request criteria with the open() method, you use the send() method with the instantiated XMLHttpRequest object to submit the request to the server. The send() method accepts a single argument containing the message body. If "get" is specified with the open() method, you must pass a value of null to the send() method, as follows:

```
stockRequest.send(null);
```

Recall that when a Web browser submits an HTTP request, it usually includes various response and message body headers. When running basic "get" requests with the XMLHttpRequest object, you do not usually need to specify additional HTTP headers. For example, the following statements are all you need to open and send a request with the stock quote Web page:

```
stockRequest.abort();
stockRequest.open("get","StockCheck.php?"
    + "checkQuote=" + tickerSymbol);
stockRequest.send(null);
```

"Post" requests are a little more involved. With form data, a Web browser automatically handles the task of creating name=value pairs from form element name attributes and field values. When submitting form data as the message body with the XMLHttpRequest object, you must manually build the name=value pairs that will be submitted to the server. The first statement in the following code creates a variable named requestBody that is assigned the value "checkQuote="; the URI-encoded value is assigned to the tickerSymbol variable. The last statement then passes the requestBody variable as an argument to the send() method.

```
var requestBody = "checkQuote="
    + encodeURIComponent(tickerSymbol);
stockRequest.send(requestBody);
```

With "post" requests, you must at least submit the Content-Type header before executing the send() method to identify the MIME type of the message body. You should also submit the Content-Length header to specify the size of the message body, and submit the Connection header to specify that the connection with the server should be closed after the response is received. Use the setRequestHeader() method to specify HTTP headers and values to submit with the HTTP request. You pass two arguments to the method: the name of the header and its value. For example, the following code uses the setRequestHeader() method to define the Content-Type, Content-Length, and Connection headers before submitting the request for the stock quote Web page:

```
stockRequest.abort();
stockRequest.open("post","StockCheck.php");
var requestBody = "checkQuote="
    + encodeURIComponent(tickerSymbol);
stockRequest.setRequestHeader("Content-Type",
    "application/x-www-form-urlencoded");
stockRequest.setRequestHeader("Content-Length",
    requestBody.length);
stockRequest.setRequestHeader("Connection",
    "close");
stockRequest.send(requestBody);
```

Receiving Server Data

After you submit a request with the XMLHttpRequest object, the message body in the server response is assigned to the object's responseXML or responseText properties. These properties contain the HTTP response as an XML document and as a text string, respectively. Note that the message body is only assigned to the `responseXML` property if the server response includes the `Content-Type` header assigned a MIME type value of "text/xml". You can process the contents of the `responseXML` property by using the same node-manipulating techniques that you learned in Chapter 13. For example, the following statements demonstrate how to manipulate the value assigned to the `responseXML` property for the stock quote Web page. The first statement assigns the value of the returned `responseXML` property to a variable named `stockValues`. The remaining statements then use the `innerHTML()` method and node properties to assign the values of the XML document stored in the `stockValues` variable to the appropriate element.

```
var stockValues = stockRequest.responseXML;
document.getElementById("ticker").innerHTML
    = stockValues.getElementsByTagName("ticker")[0]
    .childNodes[0].nodeValue;
document.getElementById("openingPrice")
    .innerHTML = stockValues.getElementsByTagName(
    "open")[0].childNodes[0].nodeValue;
document.getElementById("lastTrade").innerHTML
    = "<strong>" + stockValues.getElementsByTagName(
    "lastTrade")[0].childNodes[0].nodeValue
    + "</strong>";
document.getElementById("lastTradeDT").innerHTML
    = stockValues.getElementsByTagName(
    "lastTradeDate")[0].childNodes[0].nodeValue
    + " " + stockValues.getElementsByTagName(
    "lastTradeTime")[0].childNodes[0].nodeValue;
document.getElementById("change").innerHTML
    = stockValues.getElementsByTagName(
    "change")[0].childNodes[0].nodeValue;
document.getElementById("range").innerHTML
    = stockValues.getElementsByTagName(
    "rangeLow")[0].childNodes[0]
    .nodeValue + " - "
    + stockValues.getElementsByTagName(
    "rangeHigh")[0].childNodes[0].nodeValue;
var volume = parseInt(stockValues
    .getElementsByTagName(
    "volume")[0].childNodes[0].nodeValue);
document.getElementById("volume").innerHTML
    = volume.toLocaleString();
document.getElementById("chart").innerHTML
    = "<img src=" + stockValues
    .getElementsByTagName("chart")[0]
    .childNodes[0].nodeValue
    + " alt='Stock line chart from Yahoo.com.' />";
```

To use the `responseText` property, consider the following simplified version of the PHP script you saw earlier, which retrieves data from the Yahoo! Finance page:

```php
<?php
header("Content-Type: text/html");
$TickerSymbol = $_GET["checkQuote"];
$Quote = fopen("http://finance.yahoo.com/d/ ↵
    quotes.csv?s=$TickerSymbol&f=s1l1d1t1c1p2ohgv ↵
    &e=.csv", "r");
$QuoteString = fread($Quote, 2000);
fclose($Quote);
echo $QuoteString;
?>
```

873

Don't worry about under-standing the PHP script. The only thing you need to know is that this version returns a text string instead of an XML document.

The second statement in the preceding code assigns a value of "text/html" to the Content-Type header. Instead of building an XML tree, the code simply returns a text string similar to the following text that is returned for the NASDAQ Composite Index (^IXIC):

```
"^IXIC",2421.64,"3/30/2009","5:16pm",
+3.76,2419.91,2432.20,2403.01,0
```

The following statements demonstrate how to use the returned response string with JavaScript. The first statement uses the split() method of the String object to split the string at each of the commas into an array named responseArray. The remaining statements then use the innerHTML() method to assign the values in responseArray to the appropriate elements.

```javascript
var responseArray
    = stockRequest.responseText.split(",");
document.getElementById('ticker').innerHTML
    = responseArray[0].slice(1,
    responseArray[0].length-1);
document.getElementById('openingPrice').innerHTML
    = responseArray[5];
document.getElementById('lastTradeDT').innerHTML
    = responseArray[2].slice(1,
    responseArray[2].length-1) + " "
    + responseArray[3].slice(1,
    responseArray[3].length-1);
document.getElementById('lastTrade').innerHTML
    = "<strong>" + responseArray[1] + "</strong>";
document.getElementById('change').innerHTML
    = responseArray[4];
document.getElementById('range').innerHTML
    = responseArray[7]
    + " - " + responseArray[6];
var volume = parseInt(responseArray[8]);
document.getElementById('volume').innerHTML
    = volume.toLocaleString();
document.getElementById('chart').innerHTML
    = "<img src=http://ichart.yahoo.com/t?s="
    + tickerSymbol
    + " alt='Stock line chart from Yahoo.com.' />";
```

The specific procedures for accessing the values of the responseText and responseXML properties with JavaScript depend on whether you submitted a synchronous or asynchronous request.

Sending and Receiving Synchronous Requests and Responses

The value of the open() method's third argument determines whether the HTTP request is performed synchronously or asynchronously. A **synchronous request** stops processing the JavaScript code until a response is returned from the server. To create a synchronous request, you should check the value of the XMLHttpRequest object's status property, which contains the HTTP status code (such as 200 for "OK" or 404 for "Not Found") returned with the response, to ensure that the response was received successfully.

The following statements demonstrate how to use the returned status code and response string. The second statement passes a value of false as the third argument of the open() method to create a synchronous request. The if statement then determines whether the value assigned to the status property is 200. If so, the response was successful and the statements within the if statement execute. The statements within the if statement are the same ones you saw previously for manipulating the value assigned to the responseXML property for the stock quote Web page. If any other status code is returned, the else statement prints a message with the status code and text.

```
stockRequest.abort();
stockRequest.open("get", "StockCheck.php?"
    + "checkQuote=" + tickerSymbol, false);
if (stockRequest.status == 200) {
    stockRequest.send(null);
    var stockValues = stockRequest.responseXML;
    document.getElementById("ticker").innerHTML
        = stockValues.getElementsByTagName(
        "ticker")[0].childNodes[0].nodeValue;
...
}
else {
    document.write("<p>HTTP response error "
        + stockRequest.status + ": "
        + stockRequest.statusText + "</p>");
}
```

Although synchronous responses are easier to handle than asynchronous responses, one major drawback is that a script will not continue processing until a synchronous response is received.

Therefore, if the server doesn't respond for some reason (perhaps because it is running slowly due to high traffic or maintenance requirements), your Web page will appear to be dead in the water. Users can stop the script by clicking the browser's Stop button. However, a synchronous request with the `send()` method does not contain any mechanism for specifying the length of time allowed for receiving a response. To ensure that your script continues running if a server problem occurs, you should use asynchronous requests with the `send()` method.

Sending and Receiving Asynchronous Requests and Responses

An **asynchronous request** allows JavaScript to continue processing while it waits for a server response. To create an asynchronous request, you pass a value of true as the third argument of the `open()` method or omit the argument altogether. To receive a response for an asynchronous request, you must use the `XMLHttpRequest` object's `readyState` property and `onreadystatechange` event. The `readyState` property contains one of the following values, which represents the state of the HTTP request: 0 (uninitialized), 1 (open), 2 (sent), 3 (receiving), or 4 (loaded). The `onreadystatechange` event is triggered whenever the value assigned to the `readyState` property changes. You assign this event the name of a function that will execute whenever the `readyState` property changes. For example, the `open()` method in the following code defines an asynchronous request because it includes a value of true as the method's third argument. (Recall that you can also omit this argument to define an asynchronous request.) The fourth statement assigns a function named `fillStockInfo()` as the event handler function for the `onreadystatechange` event.

```
stockRequest.abort();
stockRequest.open("get","StockCheck.php?"
     + "checkQuote=" + tickerSymbol);
stockRequest.send(null);
stockRequest.onreadystatechange=fillStockInfo;
```

The value assigned to the `readyState` property is updated automatically according to the current statement of the HTTP request. However, you cannot process the response until the `readyState` property is assigned a value of 4, meaning that the response is finished loading. For this reason, you include an `if` statement in the `fillStockInfo()` function that checks the value assigned to the `readyState` property. As shown in the following example, once the readyState property is assigned a value of 4 and the status property is assigned a value of 200, the if statement processes the response:

```
function fillStockInfo() {
    if (stockRequest.readyState == 4
        && stockRequest.status == 200) {
        var stockValues = stockRequest.responseXML;
        document.getElementById("ticker").innerHTML
            = stockValues.getElementsByTagName(
            "ticker")[0].childNodes[0].nodeValue;
    ...
    }
}
```

Refreshing Server Data Automatically

To automatically refresh data obtained from an HTTP server, you use JavaScript's setTimeout() or setInterval() methods to send a request to the server, and to read and process the data returned from the server. As an example, the following code contains a completed version of the JavaScript section that gives the stock quote Web page its functionality. A global variable named tickerSymbol is declared at the beginning of the script section and assigned a default value of ^IXIC, which is the ticker symbol for the NASDAQ Composite Index. The getStockQuote() function, which calls the getRequestObject() function and then opens and submits the HTTP request, is initially called from an onload event in the <body> tag, and is subsequently called each time a user clicks the Get Quote button. The last statement in the getStockQuote() function uses a setTimeout() method to call the function every 10,000 milliseconds (or every 10 seconds). The setTimeout() method reinitializes each time the getStockQuote() function executes.

```
<script type="text/javascript">
/* <![CDATA[ */
var stockRequest = false;
var tickerSymbol = "^IXIC";
function getRequestObject() {
    try {
        httpRequest = new XMLHttpRequest();
    }
    catch (requestError) {
        try {
            httpRequest = new ActiveXObject(
            "Msxml2.XMLHTTP");
        }
        catch (requestError) {
            try {
                httpRequest = new ActiveXObject(
```

876

```
                    "Microsoft.XMLHTTP");
            }
            catch (requestError) {
                window.alert("Your browser ↵
                    does not support AJAX!");
                return false;
            }
        }
    }
    return httpRequest;
}
function getStockQuote(newTicker) {
    if (!stockRequest)
        stockRequest = getRequestObject();
    if (newTicker)
        tickerSymbol = newTicker;
    stockRequest.abort();
    stockRequest.open("get","StockCheck.php?"
        + "checkQuote=" + tickerSymbol, true);
    stockRequest.send(null);
    stockRequest.onreadystatechange=fillStockInfo;
    clearTimeout(updateQuote);
    var updateQuote = setTimeout(
        'getStockQuote()', 10000);
}
function fillStockInfo() {
    if (stockRequest.readyState==4
        && stockRequest.status == 200) {
        var stockValues = stockRequest.responseXML;
    document.getElementById("ticker").innerHTML
        = stockValues.getElementsByTagName(
        "ticker")[0].childNodes[0].nodeValue;
    document.getElementById("openingPrice")
        .innerHTML = stockValues
        .getElementsByTagName("open")[0]
        .childNodes[0].nodeValue;
    document.getElementById("lastTrade").innerHTML
        = "<strong>" + stockValues
        .getElementsByTagName(
        "lastTrade")[0].childNodes[0].nodeValue
        + "</strong>";
    document.getElementById("lastTradeDT")
        .innerHTML = stockValues
        .getElementsByTagName("lastTradeDate")[0]
        .childNodes[0].nodeValue + " "
        + stockValues.getElementsByTagName(
        "lastTradeTime")[0].childNodes[0]
        .nodeValue;
    document.getElementById("change").innerHTML
        = stockValues.getElementsByTagName(
        "change")[0].childNodes[0].nodeValue;
```

```
            document.getElementById("range").innerHTML
                = stockValues.getElementsByTagName(
                "rangeLow")[0].childNodes[0].nodeValue
                + " - " + stockValues
                .getElementsByTagName("rangeHigh")[0]
                .childNodes[0].nodeValue;
            var volume = parseInt(stockValues
                .getElementsByTagName(
                "volume")[0].childNodes[0].nodeValue);
            document.getElementById("volume").innerHTML
                = volume.toLocaleString();
            document.getElementById("chart").innerHTML
                = "<img src=" + stockValues
                .getElementsByTagName("chart")[0]
                .childNodes[0].nodeValue
                + " alt='Stock line chart from ↵
                Yahoo.com.' />";
        }
    }
    /* ]]> */
    </script>
```

Index